TRAINING & REFERENCE

murach's SQL Server 2016 for developers

Bryan Syverson
Joel Murach

MIKE MURACH & ASSOCIATES, INC.

4340 N. Knoll Ave. • Fresno, CA 93722
www.murach.com • murachbooks@murach.com

Authors:	Bryan Syverson
	Joel Murach
Editor:	Ray Halliday
Production:	Maria Spera

Books for database developers

Murach's SQL Server 2016 for Developers

Murach's Oracle SQL and PL/SQL for Developers (2nd Edition)

Murach's MySQL (2nd Edition)

Books for .NET developers

Murach's C# 2015

Murach's ASP.NET 4.6 Web Programming with C# 2015

Murach's Visual Basic 2015

Murach's ASP.NET 4.5 Web Programming with VB 2012

Books for developers

Murach's Python Programming

Murach's Beginning Java with Eclipse

Murach's Java Programming (4th Edition)

Murach's Android Programming (2nd Edition)

Books for web developers

Murach's HTML5 and CSS3 (3rd Edition)

Murach's JavaScript and jQuery (3rd Edition)

Murach's Java Servlets and JSP (3rd Edition)

Murach's PHP and MySQL (2nd Edition)

For more on Murach books, please visit us at www.murach.com

10 9 8 7 6 5 4 3 2
ISBN-13: 978-1-890774-96-7

Content

Expanded contents

Section 2   The essential SQL skills

Chapter 3   How to retrieve data from a single table

Chapter 4   How to retrieve data from two or more tables

Chapter 5   **How to code summary queries**

Chapter 6   **How to code subqueries**

Section 3 Database design and implementation

Chapter 10 How to design a database

Chapter 11 How to create a database and its tables with SQL Statements

Section 4   Advanced SQL skills

Introduction

If you want to learn SQL, you've picked the right book. And if you want to learn the specifics of SQL for SQL Server 2016, you've made an especially good choice. Along the way, you'll learn a lot about relational database management systems in general and about SQL Server in particular.

Why learn SQL? First, because most programmers would be better at database programming if they knew more about SQL. Second, because SQL programming is a valuable specialty in itself. And third, because knowing SQL is the first step toward becoming a database administrator. In short, knowing SQL makes you more valuable on the job.

Who this book is for

This book is the ideal book for application developers who need to work with a SQL Server database. It shows you how to code the SQL statements that you need for your applications. It shows you how to code these statements so they run efficiently. And it shows you how to take advantage of the most useful advanced features that SQL Server has to offer.

This book is also a good choice for anyone who wants to learn standard SQL. Since SQL is a standard language for accessing database data, most of the SQL code in this book will work with any database management system. As a result, once you use this book to learn how to use SQL to work with a SQL Server database, you can transfer most of what you have learned to another database management system such as Oracle, DB2, or MySQL.

This book is also the right *first* book for anyone who wants to become a database administrator. Although this book doesn't present all of the advanced skills that are needed by a top DBA, it will get you started. Then, when you have finished this book, you'll be prepared for more advanced books on the subject.

4 reasons why you'll learn faster with this book

- Unlike most SQL books, this one starts by showing you how to query an existing database rather than how to create a new database. Why? Because that's what you're most likely to need to do first on the job. Once you master those skills, you can learn how to design and implement a database, whenever you need to do that. Or, you can learn how to work with other database features like views and stored procedures, whenever you need to do that.

- Like all our books, this one includes hundreds of examples that range from the simple to the complex. That way, you can quickly get the idea of how a feature works from the simple examples, but you'll also see how the feature is used in the real world from the complex examples.

- Like most of our books, this one has exercises at the end of each chapter that give you hands-on experience by letting you practice what you've learned. These exercises also encourage you to experiment and to apply what you've learned in new ways.

- If you page through this book, you'll see that all of the information is presented in "paired pages," with the essential syntax, guidelines, and examples on the right page and the perspective and extra explanation on the left page. This helps you learn more with less reading, and it is the ideal reference format when you need to refresh your memory about how to do something.

What you'll learn in this book

- In section 1, you'll learn the concepts and terms you need for working with any database. You'll also learn how to use Microsoft SQL Server 2016 and the Management Studio to run SQL statements on your own PC.

- In section 2, you'll learn all the skills for retrieving data from a database and for adding, updating, and deleting that data. These chapters move from the simple to the complex so you won't have any trouble if you're a SQL novice. And they present skills like using outer joins, summary queries, and subqueries that will raise your SQL expertise if you already have SQL experience.

- In section 3, you'll learn how to design a database and how to implement that design by using either SQL statements or the Management Studio. When you're done, you'll be able to design and implement your own databases. But even if you're never called upon to do that, this section will give you perspective that will make you a better SQL programmer.

- In section 4, you'll learn the skills for working with database features like views, scripts, stored procedures, functions, triggers, and transactions. In addition, you'll learn the skills for working with database security, XML, BLOBs, and CLR integration. These are the features that give a database much of its power. So once you master them, you'll have a powerful set of SQL skills.

Prerequisites

Although you will progress through this book more quickly if you have some development experience, everything you need to know about databases and SQL is presented in this book. As a result, you don't need to have any programming background to use this book to learn SQL.

However, if you want to use C# or Visual Basic to work with a SQL Server database as described in chapter 19, you need to have some experience using C# or Visual Basic to write ADO.NET code. For example, this chapter assumes you can understand the code that's presented in chapter 20 of *Murach's C# 2015* or chapter 16 of *Murach's Visual Basic 2012*.

What software you need for this book

All of the software you need for this book is available from Microsoft's website for free. That includes:

- SQL Server 2016 Express (only runs on Windows 8 and later)
- SQL Server Management Studio
- Visual Studio Express (only necessary for chapter 19)

In appendix A, you'll find complete instructions for installing these items on your PC.

However, SQL Server 2016 only runs on Windows 8 and later. As a result, if you have an earlier version of Windows, such as Windows 7, you'll need to upgrade your operating system to a newer one, such as Windows 10.

What you can download from our website

You can download all the source code for this book from our website. That includes:

- Scripts that create the databases used by this book
- The source code for all examples in this book
- The solutions for all exercises in this book

In appendix A, you'll find complete instructions for installing these items on your PC.

Support materials for trainers and instructors

If you're a corporate trainer or a college instructor who would like to use this book for a course, we offer these supporting materials: (1) a complete set of PowerPoint slides that you can use to review and reinforce the content of this book; (2) instructional objectives that describe the skills a student should have upon completion of each chapter; (3) test banks that measure mastery of those skills; (4) additional exercises for each chapter that aren't in this book; and (5) solutions to those exercises.

To learn more about these materials, please go to our website at www.murachforinstructors.com if you're an instructor. If you're a trainer, please go to www.murach.com and click on the *Courseware for Trainers* link, or contact Kelly at 1-800-221-5528 or kelly@murach.com.

Please let us know how this book works for you

When we started working on this book, our goal was (1) to provide a SQL Server book for application developers that will help them work more effectively; (2) to cover the database design and implementation skills that application developers are most likely to use; and (3) to do both in a way that helps you learn faster and better than you can with any other SQL Server book.

Now, if you have any comments about this book, we would appreciate hearing from you. If you like this book, please tell a friend. And good luck with your SQL Server projects!

Joel Murach

Joel Murach
Author
joel@murach.com

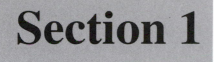

Section 1

An introduction to SQL

Before you begin to learn the fundamentals of programming in SQL, you need to understand the concepts and terms related to SQL and relational databases. That's what you'll learn in chapter 1. Then, in chapter 2, you'll learn about some of the tools you can use to work with a SQL Server database. That will prepare you for using the skills you'll learn in the rest of this book.

1

An introduction to relational databases and SQL

Before you can use SQL to work with a SQL Server database, you need to be familiar with the concepts and terms that apply to database systems. In particular, you need to understand what a relational database is. That's what you'll learn in the first part of this chapter. Then, you'll learn about some of the basic SQL statements and features provided by SQL Server.

An introduction
to client/server systems

In case you aren't familiar with client/server systems, the first two topics that follow introduce you to their essential hardware and software components. These are the types of systems that you're most likely to use SQL with. Then, the last topic gives you an idea of how complex client/server systems can be.

The hardware components
of a client/server system

Figure 1-1 presents the three hardware components of a client/server system: the clients, the network, and the server. The *clients* are usually the PCs that are already available on the desktops throughout a company. And the *network* is the cabling, communication lines, network interface cards, hubs, routers, and other components that connect the clients and the server.

The *server*, commonly referred to as a *database server*, is a computer that has enough processor speed, internal memory (RAM), and disk storage to store the files and databases of the system and provide services to the clients of the system. This computer is usually a high-powered PC, but it can also be a midrange system like an IBM System x or Unix system, or even a mainframe system. When a system consists of networks, midrange systems, and mainframe systems, often spread throughout the country or world, it is commonly referred to as an *enterprise system*.

To back up the files of a client/server system, a server usually has a tape drive or some other form of offline storage. It often has one or more printers or specialized devices that can be shared by the users of the system. And it can provide programs or services like e-mail that can be accessed by all the users of the system.

In a simple client/server system, the clients and the server are part of a *local area network (LAN)*. However, two or more LANs that reside at separate geographical locations can be connected as part of a larger network such as a *wide area network (WAN)*. In addition, individual systems or networks can be connected over the Internet.

A simple client/server system

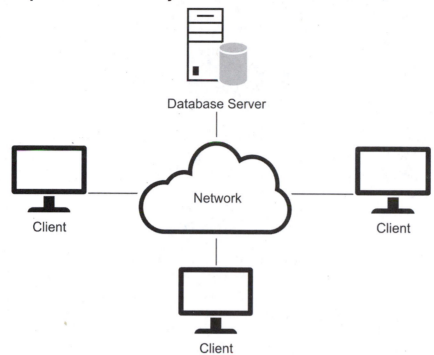

The three hardware components of a client/server system

- The *clients* are the PCs, Macs, or workstations of the system.
- The *server* is a computer that stores the files and databases of the system and provides services to the clients. When it stores databases, it's often referred to as a *database server*.
- The *network* consists of the cabling, communication lines, and other components that connect the clients and the servers of the system.

Client/server system implementations

- In a simple *client/server system* like the one shown above, the server is typically a high-powered PC that communicates with the clients over a *local area network* (*LAN*).
- The server can also be a midrange system, like an IBM System x or a Unix system, or it can be a mainframe system. Then, special hardware and software components are required to make it possible for the clients to communicate with the midrange and mainframe systems.
- A client/server system can also consist of one or more PC-based systems, one or more midrange systems, and a mainframe system in dispersed geographical locations. This type of system is commonly referred to as an *enterprise system*.
- Individual systems and LANs can be connected and share data over larger private networks, such as a *wide area network* (*WAN*), or a public network like the Internet.

Figure 1-1   The hardware components of a client/server system

The software components
of a client/server system

Figure 1-2 presents the software components of a typical client/server system. In addition to a *network operating system* that manages the functions of the network, the server requires a *database management system (DBMS)* like Microsoft SQL Server or Oracle. This DBMS manages the databases that are stored on the server.

In contrast to a server, each client requires *application software* to perform useful work. This can be a purchased software package like a financial accounting package, or it can be custom software that's developed for a specific application.

Although the application software is run on the client, it uses data that's stored on the server. To do that, it uses a *data access API (application programming interface)* such as ADO.NET. Since the technique you use to work with an API depends on the programming language and API you're using, you won't learn those techniques in this book. Instead, you'll learn about a standard language called *SQL*, or *Structured Query Language*, that lets any application communicate with any DBMS. (In conversation, SQL is pronounced as either *S-Q-L* or *sequel*.)

Once the software for both client and server is installed, the client communicates with the server via *SQL queries* (or just *queries*) that are passed to the DBMS through the API. After the client sends a query to the DBMS, the DBMS interprets the query and sends the results back to the client.

As you can see in this figure, the processing done by a client/server system is divided between the clients and the server. In this case, the DBMS on the server is processing requests made by the application running on the client. Theoretically, at least, this balances the workload between the clients and the server so the system works more efficiently. In contrast, in a file-handling system, the clients do all of the work because the server is used only to store the files that are used by the clients.

Client software, server software, and the SQL interface

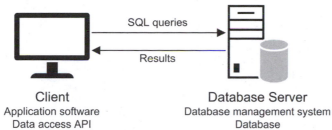

Client
Application software
Data access API

Database Server
Database management system
Database

Server software

- To store and manage the databases of the client/server system, each server requires a *database management system* (*DBMS*) like Microsoft SQL Server.
- The processing that's done by the DBMS is typically referred to as *back-end processing*, and the database server is referred to as the *back end*.

Client software

- The *application software* does the work that the user wants to do. This type of software can be purchased or developed.
- The *data access API* (*application programming interface*) provides the interface between the application program and the DBMS. The newest Microsoft API is ADO.NET, which can communicate directly with SQL Server. Older APIs required a data access model, such as ADO or DAO, plus a driver, such as OLE DB or ODBC.
- The processing that's done by the client software is typically referred to as *front-end processing*, and the client is typically referred to as the *front end*.

The SQL interface

- The application software communicates with the DBMS by sending *SQL queries* through the data access API. When the DBMS receives a query, it provides a service like returning the requested data (the *query results*) to the client.
- *SQL* stands for *Structured Query Language*, which is the standard language for working with a relational database.

Client/server versus file-handling systems

- In a client/server system, the processing done by an application is typically divided between the client and the server.
- In a file-handling system, all of the processing is done on the clients. Although the clients may access data that's stored in files on the server, none of the processing is done by the server. As a result, a file-handling system isn't a client/server system.

Figure 1-2   The software components of a client/server system

Other client/server system architectures

In its simplest form, a client/server system consists of a single database server and one or more clients. Many client/server systems today, though, include additional servers. In figure 1-3, for example, you can see two client/server systems that include an additional server between the clients and the database server.

The first illustration is for a simple Windows-based system. With this system, only the user interface for an application runs on the client. The rest of the processing that's done by the application is stored in one or more *business components* on the *application server*. Then, the client sends requests to the application server for processing. If the request involves accessing data in a database, the application server formulates the appropriate query and passes it on to the database server. The results of the query are then sent back to the application server, which processes the results and sends the appropriate response back to the client.

Similar processing is done by a web-based system, as illustrated by the second example in this figure. In this case, though, a *web browser* running on the client is used to send requests to a *web application* running on a *web server* somewhere on the Internet. The web application, in turn, can use *web services* to perform some of its processing. Then, the web application or web service can pass requests for data on to the database server.

Although this figure should give you an idea of how client/server systems can be configured, you should realize that they can be much more complicated than what's shown here. In a Windows-based system, for example, business components can be distributed over any number of application servers, and those components can communicate with databases on any number of database servers. Similarly, the web applications and services in a web-based system can be distributed over numerous web servers that access numerous database servers. In most cases, though, it's not necessary for you to know how a system is configured to use SQL.

Before I go on, you should know that client/server systems aren't the only systems that support SQL. For example, traditional mainframe systems and newer *thin client* systems also use SQL. Unlike client/server systems, though, most of the processing for these types of systems is done by a mainframe or another high-powered machine. The terminals or PCs that are connected to the system do little or no work.

A Windows-based system that uses an application server

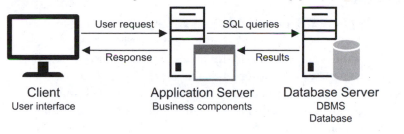

A simple web-based system

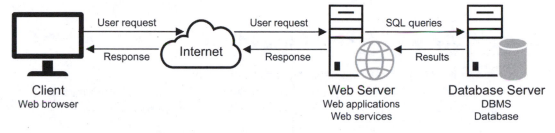

Description

- In addition to a database server and clients, a client/server system can include additional servers, such as *application servers* and *web servers*.

- Application servers are typically used to store *business components* that do part of the processing of the application. In particular, these components are used to process database requests from the user interface running on the client.

- Web servers are typically used to store *web applications* and *web services*. Web applications are applications that are designed to run on a web server. Web services are like business components, except that, like web applications, they are designed to run on a web server.

- In a web-based system, a *web browser* running on a client sends a request to a web server over the Internet. Then, the web server processes the request and passes any requests for data on to the database server.

- More complex system architectures can include two or more application servers, web servers, and database servers.

Figure 1-3   Other client/server system architectures

An introduction to the relational database model

In 1970, Dr. E. F. Codd developed a model for a new type of database called a *relational database*. This type of database eliminated some of the problems that were associated with standard files and other database designs. By using the relational model, you can reduce data redundancy, which saves disk storage and leads to efficient data retrieval. You can also view and manipulate data in a way that is both intuitive and efficient. Today, relational databases are the de facto standard for database applications.

How a database table is organized

The model for a relational database states that data is stored in one or more *tables*. It also states that each table can be viewed as a two-dimensional matrix consisting of *rows* and *columns*. This is illustrated by the relational table in figure 1-4. Each row in this table contains information about a single vendor.

In practice, the rows and columns of a relational database table are often referred to by the more traditional terms, *records* and *fields*. In fact, some software packages use one set of terms, some use the other, and some use a combination. In this book, I use the terms *rows* and *columns* because those are the terms used by SQL Server.

In general, each table is modeled after a real-world entity such as a vendor or an invoice. Then, the columns of the table represent the attributes of the entity such as name, address, and phone number. And each row of the table represents one instance of the entity. A value is stored at the intersection of each row and column, sometimes called a *cell*.

If a table contains one or more columns that uniquely identify each row in the table, you can define these columns as the *primary key* of the table. For instance, the primary key of the Vendors table in this figure is the VendorID column. In this example, the primary key consists of a single column. However, a primary key can also consist of two or more columns, in which case it's called a *composite primary key*.

In addition to primary keys, some database management systems let you define additional keys that uniquely identify each row in a table. If, for example, the VendorName column in the Vendors table contains unique data, it can be defined as a *non-primary key*. In SQL Server, this is called a *unique key*.

Indexes provide an efficient way of accessing the rows in a table based on the values in one or more columns. Because applications typically access the rows in a table by referring to their key values, an index is automatically created for each key you define. However, you can define indexes for other columns as well. If, for example, you frequently need to sort the Vendor rows by zip code, you can set up an index for that column. Like a key, an index can include one or more columns.

The Vendors table in an Accounts Payable database

Primary key   **Columns**

	VendorID	VendorName	VendorAddress1	VendorAddress2	VendorCity
1	1	US Postal Service	Attn: Supt. Window Services	PO Box 7005	Madison
2	2	National Information Data Ctr	PO Box 96621	NULL	Washington
3	3	Register of Copyrights	Library Of Congress	NULL	Washington
4	4	Jobtrak	1990 Westwood Blvd Ste 260	NULL	Los Angeles
5	5	Newbrige Book Clubs	3000 Cindel Drive	NULL	Washington
6	6	California Chamber Of Commerce	3255 Ramos Cir	NULL	Sacramento
7	7	Towne Advertiser's Mailing Svcs	Kevin Minder	3441 W Macarthur Blvd	Santa Ana
8	8	BFI Industries	PO Box 9369	NULL	Fresno
9	9	Pacific Gas & Electric	Box 52001	NULL	San Francisc
10	10	Robbins Mobile Lock And Key	4669 N Fresno	NULL	Fresno
11	11	Bill Marvin Electric Inc	4583 E Home	NULL	Fresno
12	12	City Of Fresno	PO Box 2069	NULL	Fresno
13	13	Golden Eagle Insurance Co	PO Box 85826	NULL	San Diego
14	14	Expedata Inc	4420 N. First Street, Suite 108	NULL	Fresno
15	15	ASC Signs	1528 N Sierra Vista	NULL	Fresno
16	16	Internal Revenue Service	NULL	NULL	Fresno

Rows

Concepts

- A *relational database* consists of *tables*. Tables consist of *rows* and *columns*, which can also be referred to as *records* and *fields*.

- A table is typically modeled after a real-world entity, such as an invoice or a vendor.

- A column represents some attribute of the entity, such as the amount of an invoice or a vendor's address.

- A row contains a set of values for a single instance of the entity, such as one invoice or one vendor.

- The intersection of a row and a column is sometimes called a *cell*. A cell stores a single value.

- Most tables have a *primary key* that uniquely identifies each row in the table. The primary key is usually a single column, but it can also consist of two or more columns. If a primary key uses two or more columns, it's called a *composite primary key*.

- In addition to primary keys, some database management systems let you define one or more *non-primary keys*. In SQL Server, these keys are called *unique keys*. Like a primary key, a non-primary key uniquely identifies each row in the table.

- A table can also be defined with one or more *indexes*. An index provides an efficient way to access data from a table based on the values in specific columns. An index is automatically created for a table's primary and non-primary keys.

Figure 1-4   How a database table is organized

How the tables in a relational database are related

The tables in a relational database can be related to other tables by values in specific columns. The two tables shown in figure 1-5 illustrate this concept. Here, each row in the Vendors table is related to one or more rows in the Invoices table. This is called a *one-to-many relationship*.

Typically, relationships exist between the primary key in one table and the *foreign key* in another table. The foreign key is simply one or more columns in a table that refer to a primary key in another table. In SQL Server, relationships can also exist between a unique key in one table and a foreign key in another table.

Although one-to-many relationships are the most common, two tables can also have a one-to-one or many-to-many relationship. If a table has a *one-to-one relationship* with another table, the data in the two tables could be stored in a single table. However, it's often useful to store large objects such as images, sound, and videos in a separate table. Then, you can join the two tables with the one-to-one relationship only when the large objects are needed.

In contrast, a *many-to-many relationship* is usually implemented by using an intermediate table that has a one-to-many relationship with the two tables in the many-to-many relationship. In other words, a many-to-many relationship can usually be broken down into two one-to-many relationships.

The relationship between the Vendors and Invoices tables in the database

Primary key

	VendorID	VendorName	VendorAddress1	VendorAddress2	VendorCity
113	114	Postmaster	Postage Due Technician	1900 E Street	Fresno
114	115	Roadway Package System, Inc	Dept La 21095	NULL	Pasadena
115	116	State of California	Employment Development D...	PO Box 826276	Sacramento
116	117	Suburban Propane	2874 S Cherry Ave	NULL	Fresno
117	118	Unocal	P.O. Box 860070	NULL	Pasadena
118	119	Yesmed, Inc	PO Box 2061	NULL	Fresno
119	120	Dataforms/West	1617 W. Shaw Avenue	Suite F	Fresno
120	121	Zylka Design	3467 W Shaw Ave #103	NULL	Fresno
121	122	United Parcel Service	P.O. Box 505820	NULL	Reno
122	123	Federal Express Corporation	P.O. Box 1140	Dept A	Memphis

	InvoiceID	VendorID	InvoiceNumber	InvoiceDate	InvoiceTotal	PaymentTotal
29	29	108	121897	2016-01-19 00:00:00	450.00	450.00
30	30	123	1-200-5164	2016-01-20 00:00:00	63.40	63.40
31	31	104	P02-3772	2016-01-21 00:00:00	7125.34	7125.34
32	32	121	97/486	2016-01-21 00:00:00	953.10	953.10
33	33	105	94007005	2016-01-23 00:00:00	220.00	220.00
34	34	123	963253232	2016-01-23 00:00:00	127.75	127.75
35	35	107	RTR-72-366...	2016-01-25 00:00:00	1600.00	1600.00
36	36	121	97/465	2016-01-25 00:00:00	565.15	565.15
37	37	123	963253260	2016-01-25 00:00:00	36.00	36.00
38	38	123	963253272	2016-01-26 00:00:00	61.50	61.50
39	39	110	0-2058	2016-01-28 00:00:00	37966.19	37966.19

Foreign key

Concepts

- The tables in a relational database are related to each other through their key columns. For example, the VendorID column is used to relate the Vendors and Invoices tables above. The VendorID column in the Invoices table is called a *foreign key* because it identifies a related row in the Vendors table. A table may contain one or more foreign keys.

- When you define a foreign key for a table in SQL Server, you can't add rows to the table with the foreign key unless there's a matching primary key in the related table.

- The relationships between the tables in a database correspond to the relationships between the entities they represent. The most common type of relationship is a *one-to-many relationship* as illustrated by the Vendors and Invoices tables. A table can also have a *one-to-one relationship* or a *many-to-many relationship* with another table.

Figure 1-5   How the tables in a relational database are related

How the columns in a table are defined

When you define a column in a table, you assign properties to it as indicated by the design of the Invoices table in figure 1-6. The most critical property for a column is its data type, which determines the type of information that can be stored in the column. With SQL Server 2016, you typically use one of the *data types* listed in this figure. As you define each column in a table, you generally try to assign the data type that will minimize the use of disk storage because that will improve the performance of the queries later.

In addition to a data type, you must identify whether the column can store a *null value*. A null represents a value that's unknown, unavailable, or not applicable. If you don't allow null values, then you must provide a value for the column or you can't store the row in the table.

You can also assign a *default value* to each column. Then, that value is assigned to the column if another value isn't provided. You'll learn more about how to work with nulls and default values later in this book.

Each table can also contain a numeric column whose value is generated automatically by the DBMS. In SQL Server, a column like this is called an *identity column*, and you establish it using the Is Identity, Identity Seed, and Identity Increment properties. You'll learn more about these properties in chapter 11. For now, just note that the primary key of both the Vendors and the Invoices tables—VendorID and InvoiceID—are identity columns.

The columns of the Invoices table

Common SQL Server data types

Type	Description
bit	A value of 1 or 0 that represents a True or False value.
int, bigint, smallint, tinyint	Integer values of various sizes.
money, smallmoney	Monetary values that are accurate to four decimal places.
decimal, numeric	Decimal values that are accurate to the least significant digit. The values can contain an integer portion and a decimal portion.
float, real	Floating-point values that contain an approximation of a decimal value.
datetime, smalldatetime	Dates and times.
char, varchar	A string of letters, symbols, and numbers in the ASCII character set.
nchar, nvarchar	A string of letters, symbols, and numbers in the Unicode character set.

Description

- The *data type* that's assigned to a column determines the type and size of the information that can be stored in the column.

- Each column definition also indicates whether or not it can contain *null values*. A null value indicates that the value of the column is unknown.

- A column can also be defined with a *default value*. Then, that value is used if another value isn't provided when a row is added to the table.

- A column can also be defined as an *identity column*. An identity column is a numeric column whose value is generated automatically when a row is added to the table.

Figure 1-6   How the columns in a table are defined

How relational databases compare to other data models

Now that you understand how a relational database is organized, you're ready to learn how relational databases differ from other data models. Specifically, you should know how relational databases compare to conventional file systems, *hierarchical databases*, and *network databases*. Figure 1-7 presents the most important differences.

To start, you should realize that because the physical structure of a relational database is defined and managed by the DBMS, it's not necessary to define that structure within the programs that use the database. Instead, you can simply refer to the tables and columns you want to use by name and the DBMS will take care of the rest. In contrast, when you use a conventional file system, you have to define and control the files of the system within each application that uses them. That's because a conventional file system is just a collection of files that contain the data of the system. In addition, if you modify the structure of a file, you have to modify every program that uses it. That's not necessary with a relational database.

The hierarchical and network database models were predecessors to the relational database model. The hierarchical database model is limited in that it can only represent one-to-many relationships, also called *parent/child relationships*. The network database model is an extension of the hierarchical model that provides for all types of relationships.

Although hierarchical and network databases don't have the same drawbacks as conventional file systems, they still aren't as easy to use as relational databases. In particular, each program that uses a hierarchical or network database must navigate through the physical layout of the tables they use. In contrast, this navigation is automatically provided by the DBMS in a relational database system. In addition, programs can define ad hoc relationships between the tables of a relational database. In other words, they can use relationships that aren't defined by the DBMS. That's not possible with hierarchical and network databases.

Another type of database that's not mentioned in this figure is the *object database*. This type of database is designed to store and retrieve the objects that are used by applications written in an object-oriented programming language such as C#, C++, or Java. Although object databases have some advantages over relational databases, they also have some disadvantages. In general, object databases have not yet become widely used. However, they have acquired a niche in some areas such as engineering, telecommunications, financial services, high energy physics, and molecular biology.

A comparison of relational databases and conventional file systems

Feature	Conventional file system	Relational database
Definition	Each program that uses the file must define the file and the layout of the records within the file	Tables, rows, and columns are defined within the database and can be accessed by name
Maintenance	If the definition of a file changes, each program that uses the file must be modified	Programs can be used without modification when the definition of a table changes
Validity checking	Each program that updates a file must include code to check for valid data	Can include checks for valid data
Relationships	Each program must provide for and enforce relationships between files	Can enforce relationships between tables using foreign keys; ad hoc relationships can also be used
Data access	Each I/O operation targets a specific record in a file based on its relative position in the file or its key value	A program can use SQL to access selected data in one or more tables of a database

A comparison of relational databases and other database systems

Feature	Hierarchical database	Network database	Relational database
Supported relationships	One-to-many only	One-to-many, one-to-one, and many-to-many	One-to-many, one-to-one, and many-to-many; ad hoc relationships can also be used
Data access	Programs must include code to navigate through the physical structure of the database	Programs must include code to navigate through the physical structure of the database	Programs can access data without knowing its physical structure
Maintenance	New and modified relationships can be difficult to implement in application programs	New and modified relationships can be difficult to implement in application programs	Programs can be used without modification when the definition of a table changes

Description

- To work with any of the data models other than the relational database model, you must know the physical structure of the data and the relationships between the files or tables.

- Because relationships are difficult to implement in a conventional file system, redundant data is often stored in these types of files.

- The *hierarchical database* model provides only for one-to-many relationships, called *parent/child relationships*.

- The *network database* model can accommodate any type of relationship.

- Conventional files, hierarchical databases, and network databases are all more efficient than relational databases because they require fewer system resources. However, the flexibility and ease of use of relational databases typically outweigh this inefficiency.

Figure 1-7   How relational databases compare to other data models

An introduction to SQL and SQL-based systems

In the topics that follow, you'll learn how SQL and SQL-based database management systems evolved. In addition, you'll learn how some of the most popular SQL-based systems compare.

A brief history of SQL

Prior to the release of the first *relational database management system (RDBMS)*, each database had a unique physical structure and a unique programming language that the programmer had to understand. That all changed with the advent of SQL and the relational database management system.

Figure 1-8 lists the important events in the history of SQL. In 1970, Dr. E. F. Codd published an article that described the relational database model he had been working on with a research team at IBM. By 1978, the IBM team had developed a database system based on this model, called System/R, along with a query language called *SEQUEL* (*Structured English Query Language*). Although the database and query language were never officially released, IBM remained committed to the relational model.

The following year, Relational Software, Inc. released the first relational database management system, called *Oracle*. This RDBMS ran on a minicomputer and used SQL as its query language. This product was widely successful, and the company later changed its name to Oracle to reflect that success.

In 1982, IBM released its first commercial SQL-based RDBMS, called *SQL/DS* (*SQL/Data System*). This was followed in 1985 by *DB2* (*Database 2*). Both systems ran only on IBM mainframe computers. Later, DB2 was ported to other systems, including those that ran the Unix and Windows operating systems. Today, it continues to be IBM's premier database system.

During the 1980s, other SQL-based database systems, including SQL Server, were developed. Although each of these systems used SQL as its query language, each implementation was unique. That began to change in 1989, when the *American National Standards Institute* (*ANSI*) published its first set of standards for a database query language. These standards have been revised a few times since then, most recently in 2011. As each database manufacturer has attempted to comply with these standards, their implementations of SQL have become more similar. However, each still has its own *dialect* of SQL that includes additions, or *extensions*, to the standards.

Although you should be aware of the SQL standards, they will have little effect on your job as a SQL programmer. The main benefit of the standards is that the basic SQL statements are the same in each dialect. As a result, once you've learned one dialect, it's relatively easy to learn another. On the other hand, porting applications that use SQL from one database to another isn't as easy as it should be. In fact, any non-trivial application will require at least modest modifications.

Important events in the history of SQL

Year	Event
1970	Dr. E. F. Codd developed the relational database model.
1978	IBM developed the predecessor to SQL, called Structured English Query Language (SEQUEL). This language was used on a database system called System/R, but neither the system nor the query language was ever released.
1979	Relational Software, Inc. (later renamed Oracle) released the first relational DBMS, Oracle.
1982	IBM released their first relational database system, SQL/DS (SQL/Data System).
1985	IBM released DB2 (Database 2).
1987	Microsoft released SQL Server.
1989	The American National Standards Institute (ANSI) published the first set of standards for a database query language, called ANSI/ISO SQL-89, or SQL1. Because they were not stringent standards, most commercial products could claim adherence.
1992	ANSI published revised standards (ANSI/ISO SQL-92, or SQL2) that were more stringent than SQL1 and incorporated many new features. These standards introduced levels of compliance that indicated the extent to which a dialect met the standards.
1999	ANSI published SQL3 (ANSI/ISO SQL:1999). These standards incorporated new features, including support for objects. Levels of compliance were dropped and were replaced by a core specification along with specifications for nine additional packages.
2003	ANSI published SQL:2003. These standards introduced XML-related features, standardized sequences, and identity columns.
2006	ANSI published SQL:2006, which defined how SQL can be used with XML. The standards also allowed applications to integrate XQuery into their SQL code.
2008	ANSI published SQL:2008. These standards introduced INSTEAD OF triggers and the TRUNCATE statement.
2011	ANSI published SQL:2011. These standards include improved support for temporal databases.

Description

- SQL-92 initially provided for three *levels of compliance*, or *levels of conformance*: entry, intermediate, and full. A transitional level was later added between the entry and intermediate levels because the jump between those levels was too great.

- SQL:1999 includes a *core specification* that defines the essential elements for compliance, plus nine *packages*. Each package is designed to serve a specific market niche.

- Although SQL is a standard language, each vendor has its own *SQL dialect*, or *variant*, that may include extensions to the standards. SQL Server's SQL dialect is called *Transact-SQL*.

How knowing "standard SQL" helps you

- The most basic SQL statements are the same for all SQL dialects.
- Once you have learned one SQL dialect, you can easily learn other dialects.

How knowing "standard SQL" does not help you

- Any non-trivial application will require modification when moved from one SQL database to another.

Figure 1-8   A brief history of SQL

A comparison of Oracle, DB2, MySQL, and SQL Server

Although this book is about SQL Server, you may want to know about some of the other SQL-based relational database management systems. Figure 1-9 compares SQL Server with three of the most popular: Oracle, DB2, and MySQL.

Oracle has a huge installed base of customers and continues to dominate the marketplace, especially for servers running the Unix or Linux operating system. Oracle works well for large systems and has a reputation for being extremely reliable, but also has a reputation for being expensive and difficult to use.

DB2 was originally designed to run on IBM mainframe systems and continues to be the premier database for those systems. It also dominates in hybrid environments where IBM mainframes and newer servers must coexist. Although it has a reputation for being expensive, it also has a reputation for being reliable and easy to use.

MySQL runs on all major operating systems and is widely used for web applications. MySQL is an *open-source database*, which means that any developer can view and improve its source code. In addition, the MySQL Community Server is free for most users, although Oracle also sells other editions of MySQL that include customer support and advanced features.

SQL Server was designed by Microsoft to run on Windows and is widely used for small- to medium-sized departmental systems. It has a reputation for being inexpensive and easy to use.

Until 2016, SQL Server ran only under the Windows operating system. In contrast, Oracle and MySQL ran under most modern operating systems. As a result, if a company used Linux as the operating system for its database servers, it couldn't use SQL Server and had to use Oracle or MySQL. However, in 2016, Microsoft released a preview version of SQL Server that runs under Linux, and it plans to release a final version in 2017. This should allow SQL Server to compete with Oracle and MySQL when a company prefers to use Linux, not Windows, for its database servers.

If you search the Internet, you'll find that dozens of other relational database products are also available. These include proprietary databases like Informix, Sybase, and Teradata. And they include open-source databases like PostgreSQL.

A comparison of Oracle, DB2, MySQL, and SQL Server

	Oracle	DB2	MySQL	SQL Server
Released	1979	1985	2000	1987
Platforms	Unix/Linux	OS/390, z/OS, and AIX	Unix/Linux	Windows
	z/OS	Unix/Linux	Windows	Linux
	Windows	Windows	Mac OS	
	Mac OS	Mac OS		

Description

- Oracle is typically used for large, mission-critical systems that run on one or more Unix servers.

- DB2 is typically used for large, mission-critical systems that run on legacy IBM mainframe systems using the z/OS or OS/390 operating system.

- MySQL is a popular *open-source database* that runs on all major operating systems and is commonly used for web applications.

- SQL Server is typically used for small- to medium-sized systems that run on one or more Windows servers. However, Microsoft plans to release a version of SQL Server that runs on Linux in 2017.

Figure 1-9   A comparison of Oracle, DB2, MySQL, and SQL Server

The Transact-SQL statements

In the topics that follow, you'll learn about some of the SQL statements provided by SQL Server. As you'll see, you can use some of these statements to manipulate the data in a database, and you can use others to work with database objects. Although you may not be able to code these statements after reading these topics, you should have a good idea of how they work. Then, you'll be better prepared to learn the details of coding these statements when they're presented in sections 2 and 3 of this book.

An introduction to the SQL statements

Figure 1-10 summarizes some of the most common SQL statements. As you can see, these statements can be divided into two categories. The statements that work with the data in a database are called the *data manipulation language* (*DML*). These four statements are the ones that application programmers use the most. You'll see how these statements work later in this chapter, and you'll learn the details of using them in section 2 of this book.

The statements that work with the objects in a database are called *the data definition language* (*DDL*). On large systems, these statements are used exclusively by *database administrators*, or *DBAs*. It's the DBA's job to maintain existing databases, tune them for faster performance, and create new databases. On smaller systems, though, the SQL programmer may also be the DBA. You'll see examples of some of these statements in the next figure, and you'll learn how to use them in chapter 11.

SQL statements used to work with data (DML)

Statement	Description
SELECT	Retrieves data from one or more tables.
INSERT	Adds one or more new rows to a table.
UPDATE	Changes one or more existing rows in a table.
DELETE	Deletes one or more existing rows from a table.

SQL statements used to work with database objects (DDL)

Statement	Description
CREATE DATABASE	Creates a new database.
CREATE TABLE	Creates a new table in a database.
CREATE INDEX	Creates a new index for a table.
ALTER TABLE	Changes the structure of an existing table.
ALTER INDEX	Changes the structure of an existing index.
DROP DATABASE	Deletes an existing database.
DROP TABLE	Deletes an existing table.
DROP INDEX	Deletes an existing index.

Description

- The SQL statements can be divided into two categories: the *data manipulation language* (*DML*) that lets you work with the data in the database and the *data definition language* (*DDL*) that lets you work with the objects in the database.

- SQL programmers typically work with the DML statements, while *database administrators* (*DBAs*) use the DDL statements.

Figure 1-10   An introduction to the SQL statements

Typical statements
for working with database objects

To give you an idea of how you use the DDL statements you saw in the previous figure, figure 1-11 presents five examples. The first statement creates an accounts payable database named AP. This is the database that's used in many of the examples throughout this book.

The second statement creates the Invoices table you saw earlier in this chapter. If you don't understand all of this code right now, don't worry. You'll learn how to code statements like this later in this book. For now, just realize that this statement defines each column in the table, including its data type, whether or not it allows null values, and its default value if it has one. In addition, it identifies identity columns, primary key columns, and foreign key columns.

The third statement in this figure changes the Invoices table by adding a column to it. Like the statement that created the table, this statement specifies all the attributes of the new column. Then, the fourth statement deletes the column that was just added.

The last statement creates an index on the Invoices table. In this case, the index is for the VendorID column, which is used frequently to access the table. Notice the name that's given to this index. This follows the standard naming conventions for indexes, which you'll learn about in chapter 11.

A statement that creates a new database

```
CREATE DATABASE AP;
```

A statement that creates a new table

```
CREATE TABLE Invoices
(
    InvoiceID        INT            NOT NULL IDENTITY PRIMARY KEY,
    VendorID         INT            NOT NULL REFERENCES Vendors(VendorID),
    InvoiceNumber    VARCHAR(50)    NOT NULL,
    InvoiceDate      SMALLDATETIME  NOT NULL,
    InvoiceTotal     MONEY          NOT NULL,
    PaymentTotal     MONEY          NOT NULL DEFAULT 0,
    CreditTotal      MONEY          NOT NULL DEFAULT 0,
    TermsID          INT            NOT NULL REFERENCES Terms(TermsID),
    InvoiceDueDate   SMALLDATETIME  NOT NULL,
    PaymentDate      SMALLDATETIME  NULL
);
```

A statement that adds a new column to the table

```
ALTER TABLE Invoices
ADD BalanceDue MONEY NOT NULL;
```

A statement that deletes the new column

```
ALTER TABLE Invoices
DROP COLUMN BalanceDue;
```

A statement that creates an index on the table

```
CREATE INDEX IX_Invoices_VendorID
    ON Invoices (VendorID);
```

Description

- The REFERENCES clause for a column indicates that the column contains a foreign key, and it names the table and column that contains the primary key. Because the Invoices table includes foreign keys to the Vendors and Terms tables, these tables must be created before the Invoices table.

- Because default values are specified for the PaymentTotal and CreditTotal columns, these values don't need to be specified when a row is added to the table.

- Because the PaymentDate column accepts nulls, a null value is assumed if a value isn't specified for this column when a row is added to the table.

Figure 1-11   Typical statements for working with database objects

How to query a single table

Figure 1-12 shows how to use a SELECT statement to query a single table in a database. At the top of this figure, you can see some of the columns and rows of the Invoices table. Then, in the SELECT statement that follows, the SELECT clause names the columns to be retrieved, and the FROM clause names the table that contains the columns, called the *base table*. In this case, six columns will be retrieved from the Invoices table.

Notice that the last column, BalanceDue, is calculated from three other columns in the table. In other words, a column by the name of BalanceDue doesn't actually exist in the database. This type of column is called a *calculated value*, and it exists only in the results of the query.

In addition to the SELECT and FROM clauses, this SELECT statement includes a WHERE clause and an ORDER BY clause. The WHERE clause gives the criteria for the rows to be selected. In this case, a row is selected only if it has a balance due that's greater than zero. And the returned rows are sorted by the InvoiceDate column.

This figure also shows the *result table*, or *result set*, that's returned by the SELECT statement. A result set is a logical table that's created temporarily within the database. When an application requests data from a database, it receives a result set.

The Invoices base table

	InvoiceID	VendorID	InvoiceNumber	InvoiceDate	InvoiceTotal	PaymentTotal	CreditTotal	TermsID
1	1	122	989319-457	2015-12-08 00:00:00	3813.33	3813.33	0.00	3
2	2	123	263253241	2015-12-10 00:00:00	40.20	40.20	0.00	3
3	3	123	963253234	2015-12-13 00:00:00	138.75	138.75	0.00	3
4	4	123	2-000-2993	2015-12-16 00:00:00	144.70	144.70	0.00	3
5	5	123	963253251	2015-12-16 00:00:00	15.50	15.50	0.00	3
6	6	123	963253261	2015-12-16 00:00:00	42.75	42.75	0.00	3
7	7	123	963253237	2015-12-21 00:00:00	172.50	172.50	0.00	3
8	8	89	125520-1	2015-12-24 00:00:00	95.00	95.00	0.00	1
9	9	121	97/488	2015-12-24 00:00:00	601.95	601.95	0.00	3
10	10	123	263253250	2015-12-24 00:00:00	42.67	42.67	0.00	3
11	11	123	963253262	2015-12-25 00:00:00	42.50	42.50	0.00	3
12	12	96	I77271-O01	2015-12-26 00:00:00	662.00	662.00	0.00	2
13	13	95	111-92R-10096	2015-12-30 00:00:00	16.33	16.33	0.00	2
14	14	115	25022117	2016-01-01 00:00:00	6.00	6.00	0.00	4
15	15	48	P02-88D77S7	2016-01-03 00:00:00	856.92	856.92	0.00	3

A SELECT statement that retrieves and sorts selected columns and rows from the Invoices table

```
SELECT InvoiceNumber, InvoiceDate, InvoiceTotal,
    PaymentTotal, CreditTotal,
    InvoiceTotal - PaymentTotal - CreditTotal AS BalanceDue
FROM Invoices
WHERE InvoiceTotal - PaymentTotal - CreditTotal > 0
ORDER BY InvoiceDate;
```

The result set defined by the SELECT statement

	InvoiceNumber	InvoiceDate	InvoiceTotal	PaymentTotal	CreditTotal	BalanceDue
1	39104	2016-03-10 00:00:00	85.31	0.00	0.00	85.31
2	963253264	2016-03-18 00:00:00	52.25	0.00	0.00	52.25
3	31361833	2016-03-21 00:00:00	579.42	0.00	0.00	579.42
4	263253268	2016-03-21 00:00:00	59.97	0.00	0.00	59.97
5	263253270	2016-03-22 00:00:00	67.92	0.00	0.00	67.92
6	263253273	2016-03-22 00:00:00	30.75	0.00	0.00	30.75

Concepts

- You use the SELECT statement to retrieve selected columns and rows from a *base table*. The result of a SELECT statement is a *result table*, or *result set*, like the one shown above.

- A result set can include *calculated values* that are calculated from columns in the table.

- The execution of a SELECT statement is commonly referred to as a *query*.

Figure 1-12   How to query a single table

How to join data from two or more tables

Figure 1-13 presents a SELECT statement that retrieves data from two tables. This type of operation is called a *join* because the data from the two tables is joined together into a single result set. For example, the SELECT statement in this figure joins data from the Invoices and Vendors tables.

An *inner join* is the most common type of join. When you use an inner join, rows from the two tables in the join are included in the result table only if their related columns match. These matching columns are specified in the FROM clause of the SELECT statement. In the SELECT statement in this figure, for example, rows from the Invoices and Vendors tables are included only if the value of the VendorID column in the Vendors table matches the value of the VendorID column in one or more rows in the Invoices table. If there aren't any invoices for a particular vendor, that vendor won't be included in the result set.

Although this figure shows only how to join data from two tables, you should know that you can extend this idea to join data from three or more tables. If, for example, you want to include line item data from a table named InvoiceLineItems in the results shown in this figure, you can code the FROM clause of the SELECT statement like this:

```
FROM Vendors
    INNER JOIN Invoices
        ON Vendors.VendorID = Invoices.VendorID
    INNER JOIN InvoiceLineItems
        ON Invoices.InvoiceID = InvoiceLineItems.InvoiceID
```

Then, in the SELECT clause, you can include any of the columns in the InvoiceLineItems table.

In addition to inner joins, SQL Server supports *outer joins* and *cross joins*. You'll learn more about the different types of joins in chapter 4.

A SELECT statement that joins data from the Vendors and Invoices tables

```
SELECT VendorName, InvoiceNumber, InvoiceDate, InvoiceTotal
FROM Vendors INNER JOIN Invoices
    ON Vendors.VendorID = Invoices.VendorID
WHERE InvoiceTotal >= 500
ORDER BY VendorName, InvoiceTotal DESC;
```

The result set defined by the SELECT statement

	VendorName	InvoiceNumber	InvoiceDate	InvoiceTotal
1	Bertelsmann Industry Svcs. Inc	509786	2016-02-18 00:00:00	6940.25
2	Cahners Publishing Company	587056	2016-02-28 00:00:00	2184.50
3	Computerworld	367447	2016-02-11 00:00:00	2433.00
4	Data Reproductions Corp	40318	2016-02-01 00:00:00	21842.00
5	Dean Witter Reynolds	75C-90227	2016-02-11 00:00:00	1367.50
6	Digital Dreamworks	P02-3772	2016-01-21 00:00:00	7125.34
7	Federal Express Corporation	963253230	2016-03-07 00:00:00	739.20
8	Ford Motor Credit Company	9982771	2016-03-24 00:00:00	503.20
9	Franchise Tax Board	RTR-72-366...	2016-01-25 00:00:00	1600.00
10	Fresno County Tax Collector	P02-88D77S7	2016-01-03 00:00:00	856.92
11	IBM	Q545443	2016-02-09 00:00:00	1083.58
12	Ingram	31359783	2016-02-03 00:00:00	1575.00
13	Ingram	31361833	2016-03-21 00:00:00	579.42
14	Malloy Lithographing Inc	0-2058	2016-01-28 00:00:00	37966.19
15	Malloy Lithographing Inc	P-0259	2016-03-19 00:00:00	26881.40
16	Malloy Lithographing Inc	0-2060	2016-03-24 00:00:00	23517.58
17	Malloy Lithographing Inc	P-0608	2016-03-23 00:00:00	20551.18

Concepts

- A *join* lets you combine data from two or more tables into a single result set.

- The most common type of join is an *inner join*. This type of join returns rows from both tables only if their related columns match.

- An *outer join* returns rows from one table in the join even if the other table doesn't contain a matching row.

Figure 1-13   How to join data from two or more tables

How to add, update, and delete data in a table

Figure 1-14 shows how you can use the INSERT, UPDATE, and DELETE statements to modify the data in a table. The first statement in this figure, for example, uses the INSERT statement to add a row to the Invoices table. To do that, the INSERT clause names the columns whose values are supplied in the VALUES clause. You'll learn more about specifying column names and values in chapter 7. For now, just realize that you have to specify a value for a column unless it's an identity column, a column that allows null values, or a column that's defined with a default value.

The two UPDATE statements in this figure illustrate how you can change the data in one or more rows of a table. The first statement, for example, assigns a value of 35.89 to the CreditTotal column of the invoice in the Invoices table with invoice number 367447. The second statement adds 30 days to the invoice due date for each row in the Invoices table whose TermsID column has a value of 4.

To delete rows from a table, you use the DELETE statement. The first DELETE statement in this figure, for example, deletes the invoice with invoice number 4-342-8069 from the Invoices table. The second DELETE statement deletes all invoices with a balance due of zero.

Before I go on, you should know that INSERT, UPDATE, and DELETE statements are often referred to as *action queries* because they perform an action on the database. In contrast, SELECT statements are referred to as *queries* since they simply query the database. When I use the term *query* in this book, then, I'm usually referring to a SELECT statement.

A statement that adds a row to the Invoices table

```
INSERT INTO Invoices (VendorID, InvoiceNumber, InvoiceDate,
    InvoiceTotal, TermsID, InvoiceDueDate)
VALUES (12, '3289175', '4/18/2016', 165, 3, '5/18/2016');
```

A statement that changes the value of the CreditTotal column for a selected row in the Invoices table

```
UPDATE Invoices
SET CreditTotal = 35.89
WHERE InvoiceNumber = '367447';
```

A statement that changes the values in the InvoiceDueDate column for all invoices with the specified TermsID

```
UPDATE Invoices
SET InvoiceDueDate = InvoiceDueDate + 30
WHERE TermsID = 4;
```

A statement that deletes a selected invoice from the Invoices table

```
DELETE FROM Invoices
WHERE InvoiceNumber = '4-342-8069';
```

A statement that deletes all paid invoices from the Invoices table

```
DELETE FROM Invoices
WHERE InvoiceTotal - PaymentTotal - CreditTotal = 0;
```

Concepts

- You use the INSERT statement to add rows to a table.
- You use the UPDATE statement to change the values in one or more rows of a table based on the condition you specify.
- You use the DELETE statement to delete one or more rows from a table based on the condition you specify.
- The execution of an INSERT, UPDATE, or DELETE statement is often referred to as an *action query*.

Warning

- Until you read chapter 7 and understand the effect that these statements can have on the database, do not execute the statements shown above.

Figure 1-14   How to add, update, and delete data in a table

SQL coding guidelines

SQL is a freeform language. That means that you can include line breaks, spaces, and indentation without affecting the way the database interprets the code. In addition, SQL is not case-sensitive like some languages. That means that you can use uppercase or lowercase letters or a combination of the two without affecting the way the database interprets the code.

Although you can code SQL statements with a freeform style, we suggest that you follow the coding recommendations presented in figure 1-15. First, you should start each clause of a statement on a new line. In addition, you should continue long clauses onto multiple lines and you should indent the continued lines. You should also capitalize the first letter of each keyword in a statement to make them easier to identify, you should capitalize the first letter of each word in table and column names, and you should end each statement with a semicolon. Although the semicolon isn't currently required in most cases, it will be in a future version of SQL Server. So you should get used to coding it now. Finally, you should use *comments* to document code that's difficult to understand.

The examples at the top of this figure illustrate these coding recommendations. The first example presents an unformatted SELECT statement. As you can see, this statement is difficult to read. In contrast, this statement is much easier to read after our coding recommendations are applied, as you can see in the second example.

The third example illustrates how to code a *block comment*. This type of comment is typically coded at the beginning of a statement and is used to document the entire statement. Block comments can also be used within a statement to describe blocks of code, but that's not common.

The fourth example in this figure includes a *single-line comment*. This type of comment is typically used to document a single line of code. A single-line comment can be coded on a separate line as shown in this example, or it can be coded at the end of a line of code. In either case, the comment is delimited by the end of the line.

Although many programmers sprinkle their code with comments, that shouldn't be necessary if you write your code so it's easy to read and understand. Instead, you should use comments only to clarify portions of code that are hard to understand. Then, if you change the code, you should be sure to change the comments too. That way, the comments will always accurately represent what the code does.

A SELECT statement that's difficult to read

```
select invoicenumber, invoicedate, invoicetotal,
invoicetotal - paymenttotal - credittotal as balancedue
from invoices where invoicetotal - paymenttotal -
credittotal > 0 order by invoicedate
```

A SELECT statement that's coded with a readable style

```
Select InvoiceNumber, InvoiceDate, InvoiceTotal,
    InvoiceTotal - PaymentTotal - CreditTotal As BalanceDue
From Invoices
Where InvoiceTotal - PaymentTotal - CreditTotal > 0
Order By InvoiceDate;
```

A SELECT statement with a block comment

```
/*
Author: Bryan Syverson
Date: 1/22/2016
*/
SELECT InvoiceNumber, InvoiceDate, InvoiceTotal,
    InvoiceTotal - PaymentTotal - CreditTotal AS BalanceDue
FROM Invoices;
```

A SELECT statement with a single-line comment

```
SELECT InvoiceNumber, InvoiceDate, InvoiceTotal,
    InvoiceTotal - PaymentTotal - CreditTotal AS BalanceDue
    -- The fourth column calculates the balance due for each invoice
FROM Invoices;
```

Coding recommendations

- Start each new clause on a new line.
- Break long clauses into multiple lines and indent continued lines.
- Capitalize the first letter of each keyword and each word in column and table names.
- End each statement with a semicolon (;).
- Use *comments* only for portions of code that are difficult to understand.

How to code a comment

- To code a *block comment*, type /* at the start of the block and */ at the end.
- To code a *single-line comment*, type -- followed by the comment.

Description

- Line breaks, white space, indentation, and capitalization have no effect on the operation of a statement.
- Comments can be used to document what a statement does or what specific parts of a statement do. They are not executed by the system.

Note

- Throughout this book, SQL keywords are capitalized so they're easier to identify. However, it's not necessary or customary to capitalize SQL keywords in your own code.

Figure 1-15   SQL coding guidelines

How to work with other database objects

In addition to the tables you've already learned about, relational databases can contain other objects. In the two topics that follow, you'll be introduced to four of those objects: views, stored procedures, triggers, and user-defined functions. Then, in section 4, you'll learn more about how to code and use these objects.

How to work with views

A *view* is a predefined query that's stored in a database. To create a view, you use the CREATE VIEW statement as shown in figure 1-16. This statement causes the SELECT statement you specify to be stored with the database. In this case, the CREATE VIEW statement creates a view named VendorsMin that retrieves three columns from the Vendors table.

Once you've created the view, you can refer to it instead of a table in most SQL statements. For this reason, a view is sometimes referred to as a *viewed table*. For example, the SELECT statement in this figure refers to the VendorsMin view rather than to the Vendors table. Notice that this SELECT statement makes use of the * operator, which causes all three of the columns defined by the view to be returned.

If you choose to, you can let a user query certain views but not query the tables on which the views are based. In this way, views can be used to restrict the columns and rows of a table that the user can see. In addition, you can simplify a user's access to one or more tables by coding complex SELECT queries as views.

A CREATE VIEW statement for a view named VendorsMin

```
CREATE VIEW VendorsMin AS
    SELECT VendorName, VendorState, VendorPhone
    FROM Vendors;
```

The virtual table that's represented by the view

	VendorName	VendorState	VendorPhone
1	US Postal Service	WI	(800) 555-1205
2	National Information Data Ctr	DC	(301) 555-8950
3	Register of Copyrights	DC	NULL
4	Jobtrak	CA	(800) 555-8725
5	Newbrige Book Clubs	NJ	(800) 555-9980
6	California Chamber Of Commerce	CA	(916) 555-6670
7	Towne Advertiser's Mailing Svcs	CA	NULL
8	BFI Industries	CA	(559) 555-1551
9	Pacific Gas & Electric	CA	(800) 555-6081
10	Robbins Mobile Lock And Key	CA	(559) 555-9375

A SELECT statement that uses the VendorsMin view

```
SELECT * FROM VendorsMin
WHERE VendorState = 'CA'
ORDER BY VendorName;
```

The result set that's returned by the SELECT statement

	VendorName	VendorState	VendorPhone
1	Abbey Office Furnishings	CA	(559) 555-8300
2	American Express	CA	(800) 555-3344
3	ASC Signs	CA	NULL
4	Aztek Label	CA	(714) 555-9000
5	Bertelsmann Industry Svcs. Inc	CA	(805) 555-0584
6	BFI Industries	CA	(559) 555-1551
7	Bill Jones	CA	NULL
8	Bill Marvin Electric Inc	CA	(559) 555-5106
9	Blanchard & Johnson Associates	CA	(214) 555-3647

Description

- A *view* consists of a SELECT statement that's stored with the database. Because views are stored as part of the database, they can be managed independently of the applications that use them.

- A view behaves like a virtual table. Since you can code a view name anywhere you'd code a table name, a view is sometimes called a *viewed table*.

- Views can be used to restrict the data that a user is allowed to access or to present data in a form that's easy for the user to understand. In some databases, users may be allowed to access data only through views.

Figure 1-16   How to work with views

How to work with stored procedures, triggers, and user-defined functions

A *stored procedure* is a set of one or more SQL statements that are stored together in a database. To create a stored procedure, you use the CREATE PROCEDURE statement as shown in figure 1-17. Here, the stored procedure contains a single SELECT statement. To use the stored procedure, you send a request for it to be executed. One way to do that is to use the Transact-SQL EXEC statement as shown in this figure. You can also execute a stored procedure from an application program by issuing the appropriate statement. How you do that depends on the programming language and the API you're using to access the database.

When the server receives the request, it executes the stored procedure. If the stored procedure contains a SELECT statement like the one in this figure, the result set is sent back to the calling program. If the stored procedure contains INSERT, UPDATE, or DELETE statements, the appropriate processing is performed.

Notice that the stored procedure in this figure accepts an *input parameter* named @State from the calling program. The value of this parameter is then substituted for the parameter in the WHERE clause so that only vendors in the specified state are included in the result set. When it's done with its processing, a stored procedure can also pass *output parameters* back to the calling program. In addition, stored procedures can include *control-of-flow language* that determines the processing that's done based on specific conditions. You'll learn more about how to code stored procedures in chapter 15.

A *trigger* is a special type of stored procedure that's executed automatically when an insert, update, or delete operation is executed on a table or when a DDL statement is executed on a database. Triggers are used most often to validate data before a row is added or updated, but they can also be used to maintain the relationships between tables or to provide information about changes to the definition of a database.

A *user-defined function*, or *UDF*, is also a special type of procedure. After it performs its processing, a UDF can return a single value or an entire table to the calling program. You'll learn how to code and use user-defined functions and triggers in chapter 15.

A CREATE PROCEDURE statement
for a procedure named spVendorsByState

```
CREATE PROCEDURE spVendorsByState @StateVar char(2) AS
    SELECT VendorName, VendorState, VendorPhone
    FROM Vendors
    WHERE VendorState = @StateVar
    ORDER BY VendorName;
```

A statement that executes the spVendorsByState stored procedure

```
EXEC spVendorsByState 'CA';
```

The result set that's created when the stored procedure is executed

	VendorName	VendorState	VendorPhone
1	Abbey Office Furnishings	CA	(559) 555-8300
2	American Express	CA	(800) 555-3344
3	ASC Signs	CA	NULL
4	Aztek Label	CA	(714) 555-9000
5	Bertelsmann Industry Svcs. Inc	CA	(805) 555-0584
6	BFI Industries	CA	(559) 555-1551
7	Bill Jones	CA	NULL
8	Bill Marvin Electric Inc	CA	(559) 555-5106

Concepts

- A *stored procedure* is one or more SQL statements that have been compiled and stored with the database. A stored procedure can be started by application code on the client.

- Stored procedures can improve database performance because the SQL statements in each procedure are only compiled and optimized the first time they're executed. In contrast, SQL statements that are sent from a client to the server have to be compiled and optimized every time they're executed.

- In addition to SELECT statements, a stored procedure can contain other SQL statements such as INSERT, UPDATE, and DELETE. It can also contain *control-of-flow language*, which lets you perform conditional processing within the stored procedure.

- A *trigger* is a special type of procedure that's executed when rows are inserted, updated, or deleted from a table or when the definition of a database is changed. Triggers are typically used to check the validity of the data in a row that's being updated or added to a table.

- A *user-defined function* (*UDF*) is a special type of procedure that can return a value or a table.

Figure 1-17   How to use stored procedures, triggers, and user-defined functions

How to use SQL from an application program

This book teaches you how to use SQL from within the SQL Server environment. However, SQL is commonly used from application programs too. So in the topics that follow, you'll get a general idea of how that works. And you'll see that it's easy to recognize the SQL statements in an application program because they're coded just as they would be if they were running on their own.

Common data access models

Figure 1-18 shows two common ways for an application to access a SQL Server database. First, you can access a SQL Server database from a .NET application written using a .NET language such as C# or Visual Basic. To do that, you can use *ADO.NET*. This is a *data access model* developed by Microsoft, and it can communicate directly with SQL Server.

Because ADO.NET uses a *disconnected data architecture*, its use has become widespread, particularly for web-based applications. That's because web-based applications by necessity work with *disconnected data*. That means that once an application has sent a response to the client, it doesn't maintain its connection to the database.

The second data access model in this figure is JDBC, which is used by Java applications. Unlike ADO.NET, JDBC requires additional software, called a *driver*, to communicate with SQL Server.

Two common options for accessing SQL Server data

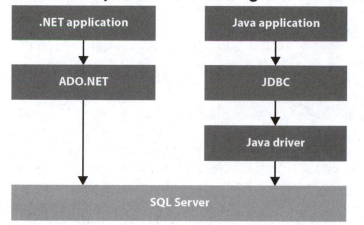

Description

- To work with the data in a SQL Server database, an application uses a *data access model*. For an application written in a .NET language such as C# or Visual Basic that model is typically *ADO.NET*. For an application written in Java, that model is typically *JDBC* (*Java Database Connectivity*).

- Each data access model defines a set of objects you can use to connect to and work with a SQL Server database. For example, both of the models shown above include a connection object that you can use to specify the information for connecting to a database.

- Some of the data access models require additional software, called *drivers*, to communicate with SQL Server. For example, JDBC requires a Java driver.

- ADO.NET, a data access model developed by Microsoft, includes its own driver so it can communicate directly with SQL Server.

Figure 1-18   Common data access models

How to use ADO.NET from a .NET application

To illustrate how you use a data access model, figure 1-19 introduces you to the basic ADO.NET objects that you use in a .NET application. Then, in the next two figures, you'll see some actual code that creates and uses these objects. Keep in mind, though, that there's a lot more you need to know about ADO.NET than what's presented here.

When you develop a .NET application, you can choose from several languages, but the most popular are Visual Basic and C#. The language you choose is largely a matter of personal preference. To learn more about using ADO.NET with Visual Basic or C#, I recommend our current books on the subject. For more information, please see our website at www.murach.com.

To access a database using the objects shown here, you execute *command* objects. Then, a *connection* object is used to connect to the database, perform the requested operation, and return the result. If you execute a command that contains a SELECT statement, the result is a result set that contains the rows you requested. Then, you can read the rows in the result set using a *data reader* object. If you execute a command that contains an INSERT, UPDATE, or DELETE statement, the result is a value that indicates if the operation was successful.

Although this is a common technique for working with ADO.NET, you should realize that there are other techniques. For example, a quick way to create a database application is to use the *data sources* feature of Visual Studio. When you use this feature, Visual Studio generates the ADO.NET code for working with the database. This is a quick and easy way to develop simple applications or to prototype larger applications.

Basic ADO.NET objects in a .NET application

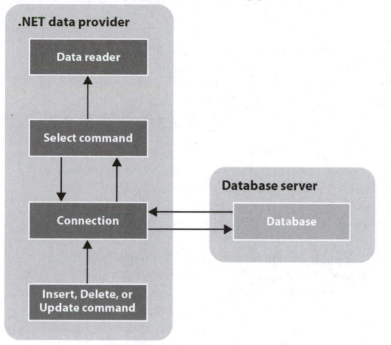

Description

- To work with the data in a SQL Server database from a .NET application, you can use ADO.NET objects like the ones shown above.

- A *.NET data provider* provides the classes that let you create the objects that you use to retrieve data from a database and to store data in a database.

- To retrieve data from a database, you execute a *command* object that contains a SELECT statement. Then, the command object uses a *connection* object to connect to the database and retrieve the data. You can then read the results one row at a time using a *data reader* object.

- To insert, update, or delete data in a database, you execute a command object that contains an INSERT, UPDATE, or DELETE statement. Then, the command object uses a connection to connect to the database and update the data. You can then check the value that's returned to determine if the operation was successful.

- After data is retrieved from a database or updated in a database, the connection is closed and the resources used by the connection are released. This is referred to as a *disconnected data architecture*.

Figure 1-19   How to use ADO.NET from a .NET application

Visual Basic code that retrieves data from a SQL Server database

Figure 1-20 presents a Visual Basic function that uses the ADO.NET objects shown in the previous figure. This function is from a simple application that accepts a vendor ID from the user, retrieves the information for the vendor with that ID from the Vendors table, and then displays that information. Although I don't expect you to understand this code, I hope it will give you a feel for how you use SQL from an application program.

This function starts by creating a new Vendor object. Although it's not shown here, this object contains properties that correspond to the columns in the Vendors table. Then, this function creates the connection object that will be used to connect to the database and sets the connection string for that object. The connection string provides ADO.NET with the information it needs to connect to the database.

Once the connection string is set, the next group of statements defines the Command object that will be executed to retrieve the data from the database. The first statement in this group creates the command object. Then, the next statement assigns the connection object to the command object. That means that when the statement that this object will contain is executed, it will use the connection string in the connection object to connect to the database.

The next statement in this group specifies the SELECT statement to be executed. If you review this statement, you'll see that the WHERE clause includes a parameter named @VendorID that will contain the value of the vendor ID. This value is set by the last statement in this group.

The next statement opens the connection to the database. Then, the next group of statements retrieves the vendor row and stores it in a Vendor object. To do that, it starts by executing the command to create a data reader. Then, if the vendor is found, it assigns the values of the columns in the row to the properties of the Vendor object. Otherwise, the Vendor object is set to Nothing.

After all of the rows are processed, the data reader and connection are closed. Then, the Vendor object is returned to the calling procedure.

Now that you've reviewed this code, you can see that there's a lot involved in accessing a SQL Server database from an application program. However, you can also see that only one statement in this figure actually involves using SQL. That's the statement that specifies the SELECT statement to be executed. Of course, if the program also provided for updating the data in the Vendors table, it would include INSERT, UPDATE, and DELETE statements. With the skills that you'll learn in this book, though, you won't have any trouble coding the SQL statements you need for your applications.

A Visual Basic function that uses ADO.NET objects to retrieve data from a SQL Server database

```vb
Public Shared Function GetVendor(vendorID As Integer) As Vendor
    Dim vendor As New Vendor

    ' Create the connection object
    Dim connection As New SqlConnection()
    connection.ConnectionString = "Data Source=localhost\SqlExpress;" & _
        "Initial Catalog=AP;Integrated Security=True"

    ' Create the command object and set the connection,
    ' SELECT statement, and parameter value
    Dim selectCommand As New SqlCommand
    selectCommand.Connection = connection
    selectCommand.CommandText = "SELECT VendorID, " & _
        "VendorName, VendorAddress1, VendorAddress2, " & _
        "VendorCity, VendorState, VendorZipCode " & _
        "FROM Vendors WHERE VendorID = @VendorID"
    selectCommand.Parameters.AddWithValue("@VendorID", vendorID)

    ' Open the connection to the database
    connection.Open()

    ' Retrieve the row specified by the SELECT statement
    ' and load it into the Vendor object
    Dim reader As SqlDataReader = selectCommand.ExecuteReader
    If reader.Read Then
        vendor.VendorID = CInt(reader("VendorID"))
        vendor.VendorName = reader("VendorName").ToString
        vendor.VendorAddress1 = reader("VendorAddress1").ToString
        vendor.VendorAddress2 = reader("VendorAddress2").ToString
        vendor.VendorCity = reader("VendorCity").ToString
        vendor.VendorState = reader("VendorState").ToString
        vendor.VendorZipCode = reader("VendorZipCode").ToString
    Else
        vendor = Nothing
    End If
    reader.Close()

    ' Close the connection to the database
    connection.Close()

    Return vendor
End Function
```

Description

- To issue a SQL statement from a Visual Basic program, you can create ADO.NET objects like the ones shown above.

- After you create the ADO.NET objects, you have to set the properties of those objects that define how they work. For example, the ConnectionString property of a connection object contains the information ADO.NET needs to connect to a database.

Figure 1-20   Visual Basic code that retrieves data from a SQL Server database

C# code that retrieves data from a SQL Server database

Figure 1-21 presents C# code that uses the ADO.NET objects to retrieve data from a SQL Server database. This code provides the same functionality as the Visual Basic code presented in figure 1-20. If you compare the code presented in these two figures, you'll see that both Visual Basic and C# use the same ADO.NET objects that are provided as part of the .NET Framework.

The main difference is that the C# language uses a different syntax than Visual Basic. This syntax is similar to the syntax that's used by C++ and Java. As a result, if you already know C++ or Java, it should be relatively easy for you to learn C#. Conversely, once you learn C#, it's easier to learn C++ or Java.

A C# method that uses ADO.NET objects
to retrieve data from a SQL Server database

```csharp
public static Vendor GetVendor(int vendorID)
{
    Vendor vendor = new Vendor();

    // Create the connection object
    SqlConnection connection = new SqlConnection();
    connection.ConnectionString = "Data Source=localhost\\SqlExpress;" +
        "Initial Catalog=AP;Integrated Security=True";

    // Create the command object and set the connection,
    // SELECT statement, and parameter value
    SqlCommand selectCommand = new SqlCommand();
    selectCommand.Connection = connection;
    selectCommand.CommandText = "SELECT VendorID, " +
        "VendorName, VendorAddress1, VendorAddress2, " +
        "VendorCity, VendorState, VendorZipCode " +
        "FROM Vendors WHERE VendorID = @VendorID";
    selectCommand.Parameters.AddWithValue("@VendorID", vendorID);

    // Open the connection to the database
    connection.Open();

    // Retrieve the row specified by the SELECT statement
    // and load it into the Vendor object
    SqlDataReader reader = selectCommand.ExecuteReader();
    if (reader.Read())
    {
        vendor.VendorID = (int)reader["VendorID"];
        vendor.VendorName = reader["VendorName"].ToString();
        vendor.VendorAddress1 = reader["VendorAddress1"].ToString();
        vendor.VendorAddress2 = reader["VendorAddress2"].ToString();
        vendor.VendorCity = reader["VendorCity"].ToString();
        vendor.VendorState = reader["VendorState"].ToString();
        vendor.VendorZipCode = reader["VendorZipCode"].ToString();
    }
    else
    {
        vendor = null;
    }
    reader.Close();

    // Close the connection to the database
    connection.Close();

    return vendor;
}
```

Description

- To issue a SQL statement from a C# application, you can use ADO.NET objects like the ones shown above.

Figure 1-21   C# code that retrieves data from a SQL Server database

Perspective

To help you understand how SQL is used from an application program, this chapter has introduced you to the hardware and software components of a client/server system. It has also described how relational databases are organized and how you use some of the basic SQL statements to work with the data in a relational database. With that as background, you're ready to start using SQL Server. In the next chapter, then, you'll learn how to use some of the tools provided by SQL Server.

Terms

client
server
database server
network
client/server system
local area network (LAN)
enterprise system
wide area network (WAN)
network operating system
database management system
    (DBMS)
back end
application software
data access API (application
    programming interface)
front end
SQL (Structured Query Language)
SQL query
query results
application server
web server
business component
web application
web service
web browser
thin client
relational database
table
row
column
record
field
cell

primary key
composite primary key
non-primary key
unique key
index
foreign key
one-to-many relationship
one-to-one relationship
many-to-many relationship
data type
null value
default value
identity column
hierarchical database
parent/child relationship
network database
object database
relational database management
    system (RDBMS)
Oracle
DB2 (Database 2)
ANSI (American National Standards
    Institute)
levels of compliance
levels of conformance
core specification
package
SQL dialect
extension
SQL variant
Transact-SQL
open-source database
data manipulation language (DML)

data definition language (DDL)
database administrator (DBA)
base table
result table
result set
calculated value
join
inner join
outer join
cross join
action query
comment
block comment
single-line comment
view

viewed table
stored procedure
input parameter
output parameter
control-of-flow language
user-defined function (UDF)
trigger
data access model
ADO.NET
JDBC (Java Database Connectivity)
disconnected data architecture
driver
command
connection
data source

2

How to use the Management Studio

In the last chapter, you learned about some of the SQL statements you can use to work with the data in a relational database. Before you learn the details of coding these statements, however, you need to become familiar with a tool that you can use to execute these statements against a relational database. Since this book is about SQL Server 2016, this chapter will teach you about the primary tool for working with SQL Server 2016, the SQL Server Management Studio.

An introduction to SQL Server 2016

The current version of Microsoft SQL Server, SQL Server 2016, is a complete database management system. It consists of a *database server* that provides the services for managing SQL Server databases and *client tools* that provide an interface for working with the databases. Of these client tools, the Management Studio is the primary tool for working with a database server.

Before I go on, you should know that you can follow along with the skills presented in this chapter if you have access to SQL Server 2016. If that's not the case, you can refer to appendix A of this book to learn how to download and install it. In addition, you can refer to appendix A to download all of the database and source code files used in this book. Once you do that, you can work along with the book examples.

If you install SQL Server as described in appendix A of this book, a free version of SQL Server, called the SQL Server 2016 Express Edition, will be installed on your machine. Although the Express Edition restricts the number of processors, the amount of memory, and the amount of data that SQL Server can manage, it provides a realistic testing environment that is 100% compatible with the other versions of SQL Server 2016. In fact, SQL Server Express is adequate for many small and medium sized applications. And since it's free and easy to use, it's perfect for learning about SQL Server. For example, I used SQL Server Express to create and test all of the statements presented in this book.

Note, however, that SQL Server Express is strictly a database server, or *database engine*. In other words, it doesn't provide some of the client tools that you'll learn about in this chapter. In particular, it doesn't include the Management Studio. That's why appendix A recommends that you install an edition of SQL Server called SQL Server 2016 Express Edition with Tools. This edition includes the Management Studio, and it's also available for free.

A summary of the SQL Server 2016 tools

Figure 2-1 summarizes the SQL Server 2016 client tools that you'll learn how to use in this book: the Management Studio and the Configuration Manager. Although other tools exist for working with a SQL Server 2016 database, they are commonly used by database administrators and other specialists, not application developers. That's why they aren't presented in this book.

A summary of the SQL Server 2016 tools

Tool	Description
SQL Server Management Studio	The primary graphical tool that a developer uses to work with a SQL Server 2016 database. You can use this tool to work directly with database objects and to develop and test SQL statements.
SQL Server Configuration Manager	A graphical tool that you can use to start and stop the database server.

Description

- To work with a SQL Server database and the data it contains, you can use the SQL Server 2016 tools described above.

- After you install SQL Server 2016, you can access the Management Studio and the Configuration Manager from the Start→All Programs→Microsoft SQL Server 2016 program group. To start one of these tools, just select it from that program group.

Figure 2-1   The SQL Server 2016 tools

How to start and stop the database engine

If you've installed SQL Server Express on your own system, you can use the SQL Server Configuration Manager to start and stop the database engine as described in figure 2-2. By default, the database engine starts automatically when the operating system starts, which is usually what you want. However, you may occasionally need to stop and then restart the engine. For example, some changes you make to the database server won't go into effect until you restart the engine.

By the way, if you simply want to find out if the database engine is running, you can do that by selecting SQL Server 2016 Services in the left pane. Then, you can look at the State column in the right pane. In this figure, for example, the Configuration Manager shows that the SQL Server Express database engine is running.

How to enable remote connections

When you install SQL Server 2016, remote connections are disabled by default. This is a security precaution that prevents other computers from connecting to this instance of SQL Server before it has been properly secured. As a result, if you have installed SQL Server 2016 and you want to allow other computers to be able to access this instance of SQL Server, you must enable remote connections. To do that, you can use the SQL Server Configuration Manager tool as described in figure 2-2. Of course, if databases that contain sensitive data are running under this instance of SQL Server, you'll want to secure the database properly before you enable remote connections.

The SQL Server Configuration Manager (Services)

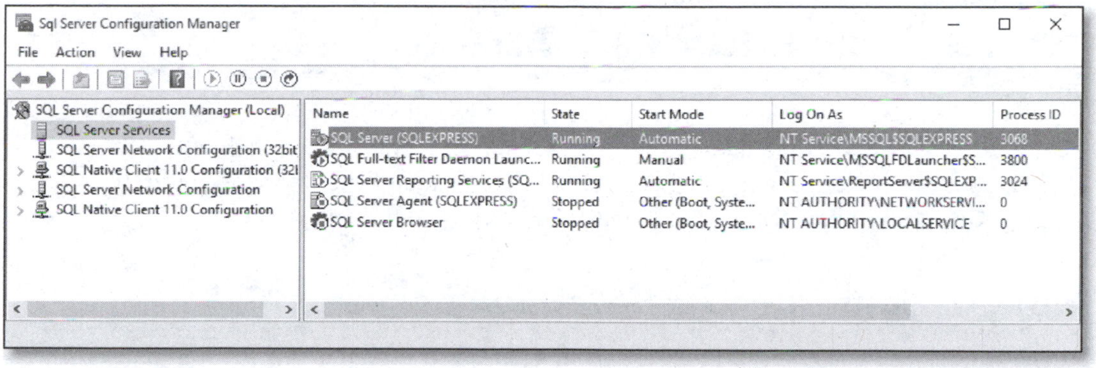

The SQL Server Configuration Manager (Network Configuration)

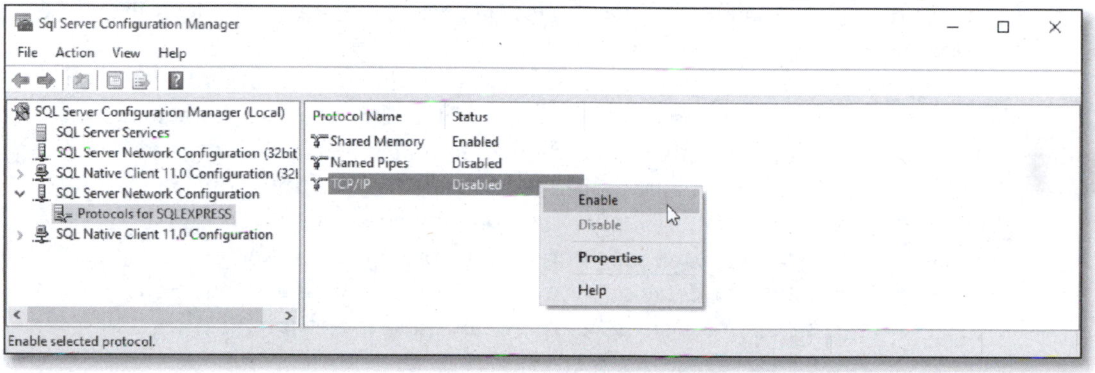

Description

- After you install SQL Server Express, the database server will start automatically each time you start your PC by default.

- To display the Configuration Manager, select Start→All Apps→Microsoft SQL Server 2016→Configuration Tools→SQL Server Configuration Manager.

- To start or stop a service, select the service in the right pane, and use the buttons in the toolbar to start or stop the service.

- To change the start mode for a service, right-click on the service in the right pane, select the Properties command to display the properties for the service, select the Service tab, and select the start mode you want from the Start Mode combo box.

- By default, remote connections are disabled for SQL Server 2016. To enable them, expand the SQL Server Network Configuration node and select the Protocols node for the server. Then, right-click on the protocol you want to enable and select the Enable command.

Figure 2-2   How to work with the database server

An introduction to the Management Studio

Once the SQL Server database engine is installed, configured, and running, you can use the Management Studio to connect to an instance of the SQL Server database engine. Then, you can use the Management Studio to work with the SQL Server database engine as described throughout this chapter.

How to connect to a database server

When you start the Management Studio, a dialog box like the one in figure 2-3 is displayed. This dialog box lets you select the instance of SQL Server you want to connect to, and it lets you enter the required connection information.

As you can see in this figure, you can use one of two types of authentication to connect to a server. In most cases, you can select the Windows Authentication option to let Windows supply the appropriate login name and password for you.

However, if you aren't able to use Windows Authentication, you can use SQL Server authentication. For example, you may need to use SQL Server authentication if you're accessing your school's or company's server. In that case, you can contact the database administrator to get an appropriate SQL Server login name and password. For more information about both types of authentication, please refer to chapter 17.

How to connect using Windows authentication

How to connect using SQL Server authentication

Description

- When you start the Management Studio, it displays a dialog box that allows you to specify the information that's needed to connect to the appropriate database server.

- To connect to a database server, you use the Server Name combo box to enter or select a path that specifies the database server. You begin by entering the name of the computer, followed by a backslash, followed by the name of the SQL Server database server.

- To connect to the SQL Server Express database engine when it's running on your PC, you can use the localhost keyword to specify your computer as the host machine, and you can use "SqlExpress" to specify SQL Server Express as the database engine.

- If you select Windows authentication, SQL Server will use the login name and password that you use for your computer to verify that you are authorized to connect to the database server.

- If you select SQL Server authentication, you'll need to enter an appropriate login name and password. This type of authentication is typically used only with non-Windows clients.

Figure 2-3   How to connect to a database server

How to navigate through the database objects

Figure 2-4 shows how to use the Management Studio to navigate through the database objects that are available from the current database server. By default, the Object Explorer window is displayed on the left side of the Management Studio window. If it isn't displayed, you can use the View menu to display it.

This window displays the instance of SQL Server that the Management Studio is connected to, all of the databases that are attached to this instance of SQL Server, and all objects within each database. These objects include tables, columns, keys, constraints, triggers, indexes, views, stored procedures, functions, and so on.

To navigate through the database objects displayed in the Object Explorer, you can click on the plus (+) and minus (-) signs to the left of each node to expand or collapse the node. In this figure, for example, I expanded the Databases node. That way, all databases on the server are shown. Then, I expanded the node for the database named AP to browse through all of the objects for this database, and I expanded the Tables node for the AP database to view all of the tables for this database. Finally, I expanded the Vendors table node to show the types of database objects that are available for a table.

To work with a specific object, you can right-click on it to display a shortcut menu. To view or modify the design of a table, for example, you can right-click on the table and select the Design command. You'll learn how to use this command later in this chapter.

When you're working with the Management Studio, you may occasionally want to free up more space for the pane that's displayed to the right of the Object Explorer. To do that, you can click on the AutoHide button that's displayed in the top right of the Object Explorer. This button looks like a pushpin, and it automatically hides the Object Explorer when you click on it. Then, a tab for the Object Explorer is displayed on the left side of the Management Studio, and you can display the window by pointing to this tab. You can turn off the AutoHide feature by displaying the window and clicking on the AutoHide button again.

Before I go on, I want to point out the qualifier that's used on all of the table names in this figure: dbo. This qualifier indicates the schema that the tables belong to. In SQL Server, a *schema* is a container that holds objects. If you don't specify a schema when you create an object, it's stored in the default schema, dbo. As you'll learn in chapter 17, you can use schemas to make it easier to implement the security for a database. For now, you can assume that all the objects you work with are stored in the dbo schema.

The SQL Server Management Studio

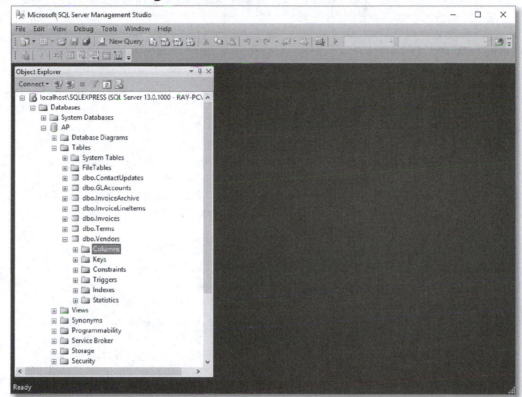

Description

- The Management Studio is a graphical tool that you can use to work with the objects in a SQL Server database.

- If the Object Explorer isn't displayed, you can use the View menu to display it. You can close this window by clicking the Close button at the top of the window.

- To navigate through the database objects displayed in the Object Explorer, click on the plus (+) and minus (-) signs to the left of each node to expand or collapse the node.

- To display a menu of commands for working with an object, right-click on the object.

- If you want to automatically hide the Object Explorer, you can click on the AutoHide button at the top of the Object Explorer. Then, you can display the window by pointing to the Object Explorer tab that's displayed along the left side of the Management Studio window.

Figure 2-4   How to navigate through the database objects

How to manage the database files

Before you can work with the objects that are stored within a database, you need to create the database and its objects. If you have the files for an existing SQL Server database, the easiest way to create the database is to *attach* those files to the database server.

How to attach a database

Figure 2-5 shows how to use the Management Studio to *attach* the database files for a SQL Server database to an instance of the server. A SQL Server database consists of two types of files. The first file is the main data file, and it has an extension of mdf. The second file is the log file, and it has an extension of ldf.

If you have the data file for a database, the easiest way to attach the database is to use the existing data file. To do that, you right-click on the Databases folder and select the Attach Database command to display the Attach Databases dialog box. Then, you can click on the Add button and use the resulting dialog box to select the mdf file for the database. This should add both the data file and the log file for the database to the Database Details pane at the bottom of the dialog box. In this figure, for example, the Attach Databases dialog box shows both the mdf and ldf files for the database named AP. Finally, click OK to attach the database.

If you want to attach a database that doesn't have a log file, or if you want to create a new log file for a database, you can remove the log file for the database before you click the OK button. To do that, select the log file in the Database Details pane and click the Remove button. Then, when you click the OK button, the Management Studio will create a new log file for the database.

Before you attach database files, you need to decide where you'd like to store them. In most cases, you'll store them in the default directory shown in this figure. This is the directory where SQL Server 2016 stores the database files for databases you create from scratch. For example, when you run the script that creates the databases for this book as described in appendix A, SQL Server will store the database files in this directory. If you want to store the files for a database in a different location, though, you can do that too. You just need to remember where you store them.

How to detach a database

After you attach a database file, you will sometimes need to *detach* it. If, for example, you try to move a database file that's attached to a server, you'll get an error message that indicates that the file is in use. To get around this, you can detach the database file as described in figure 2-5. Then, you can move the database file and reattach it to the server later.

The Attach Databases dialog box

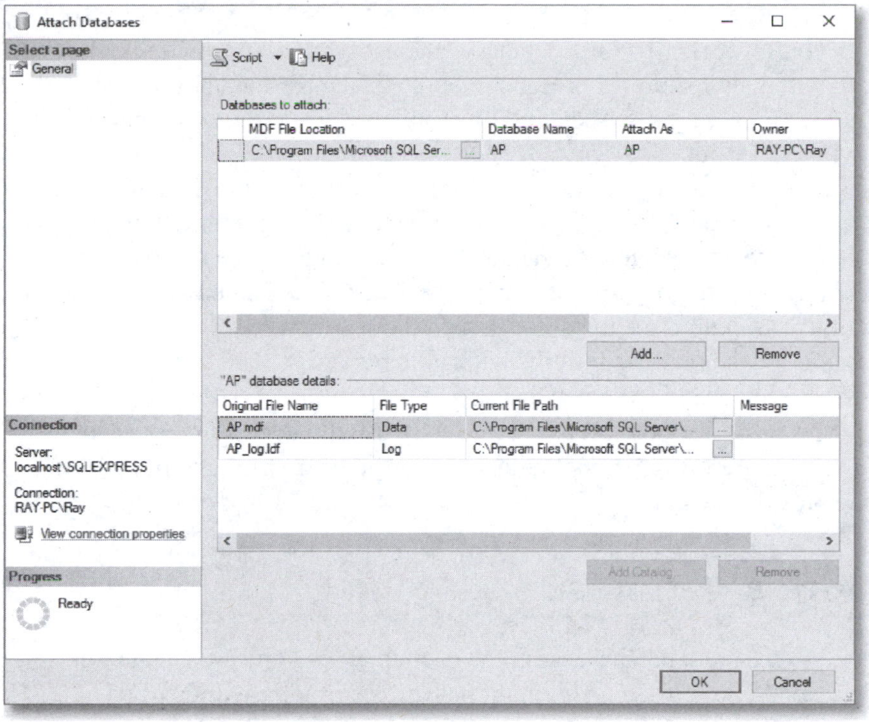

The default directory for SQL Server 2016 databases

```
C:\Program Files\Microsoft SQL Server 2016\MSSQL13.SQLEXPRESS\MSSQL\DATA
```

Description

- To attach a database, right-click on the Databases folder and select the Attach command to display the Attach Databases dialog box shown above. Then, click on the Add button and use the resulting dialog box to select the mdf file for the database. This should add both the data file and the log file for the database to the Database Details pane at the bottom of the dialog box. Finally, click OK to attach the database.

- If you want to attach a database that doesn't have a log file, or if you want to create a new log file for a database, you can remove the log file for the database before you click the OK button. To do that, select the log file in the Database Details pane and click the Remove button.

- To detach a database, right-click on its icon and select the Tasks→Detach command to display the Detach Database dialog box. Then, click on the OK button.

Figure 2-5   How to attach or detach a database

How to back up a database

Whenever you're working with a database, and especially before you begin experimenting with new features, it's a good idea to back up the database as shown in figure 2-6. Then, if you accidentally modify or delete data, you can easily restore it.

By default, the Management Studio creates a full backup of the database and it stores the file for this database in the Backup directory shown in this figure. The file for the backup is the name of the database with an extension of bak. In this figure, for example, the backup file for the AP database is named AP.bak.

By default, the backup is set to expire in zero days, which means that the backup file will be saved on disk until the backup is run again. Then, the old backup file will be replaced by the new backup.

For the purposes of this book, those settings are usually adequate. However, if they aren't, you can use an incremental backup, or you can set the number of expiration days for the backup.

How to restore a database

If you need to *restore* a database from the backup copy, you can use the procedure described in figure 2-6. Although the Restore Database dialog box isn't shown in this figure, you shouldn't have any trouble using it.

By default, the Restore Database dialog box restores the current database to the most recent backup of the database, which is usually what you want. However, if you want to restore the database to a specific point in time, you can use the Restore Database dialog box to specify a date and time. Then, when you click OK, SQL Server will use the log files to restore the database to the specific point in time.

The Back Up Database dialog box

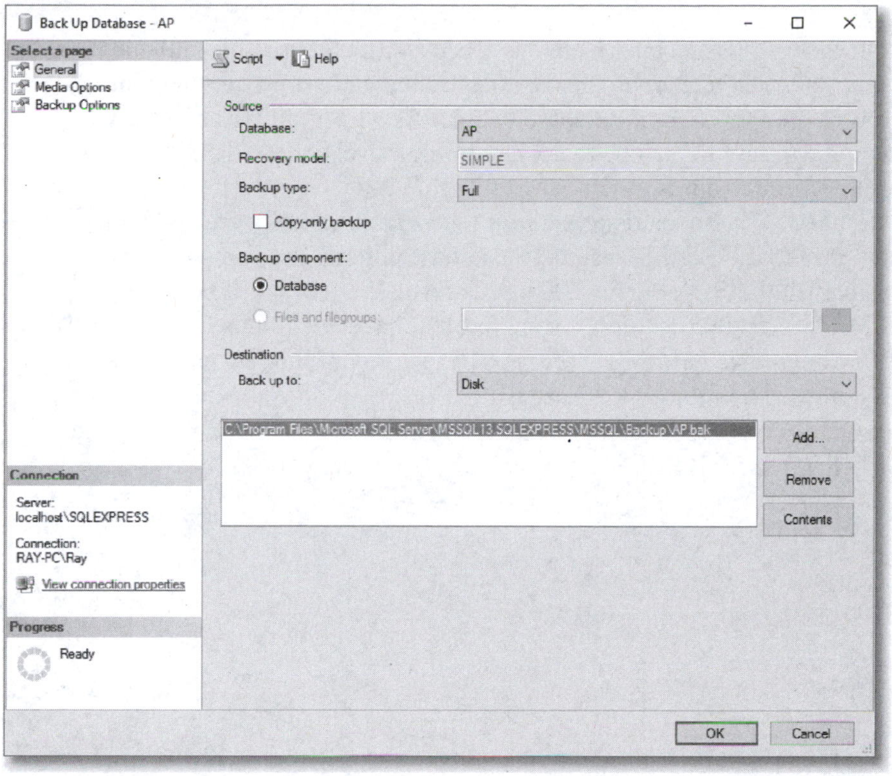

The default directory for SQL Server 2016 database backups

```
C:\Program Files\Microsoft SQL Server\MSSQL13.SQLEXPRESS\MSSQL\Backup
```

Description

- To back up a database, right-click on the database and select the Tasks→Back Up command to display the Back Up Database dialog box. For the purposes of this book, the default settings are usually adequate for backing up the database. As a result, you can usually click OK to back up the database.

- To restore a database, right-click on the database and select the Tasks→Restore→Database command to display the Restore Database dialog box. Then, click OK to restore the database. This replaces the current database with the most recent backup of the database.

Figure 2-6   How to back up and restore a database

How to set the compatibility level for a database

The SQL Server 2016 database engine is backwards compatible and can run older versions of SQL Server databases as if they were running under an older version of the SQL Server database engine. As a result, after you attach a database, you may want to change the compatibility level for the database so it's appropriate for your purposes as described in figure 2-7.

For example, if you attach database files that were originally created under SQL Server 2008 to the SQL Server 2016 database engine, the compatibility level will remain set to SQL Server 2008. As a result, you will still be able to use most SQL Server 2008 features, even ones that have been deprecated, and you won't be able to use new SQL Server 2016 features. If that's what you want, you can leave the compatibility level set as it is. However, if you want to try using new SQL Server 2016 features with this database, you need to change the compatibility level to SQL Server 2016.

The Database Properties dialog box with the compatibility level options

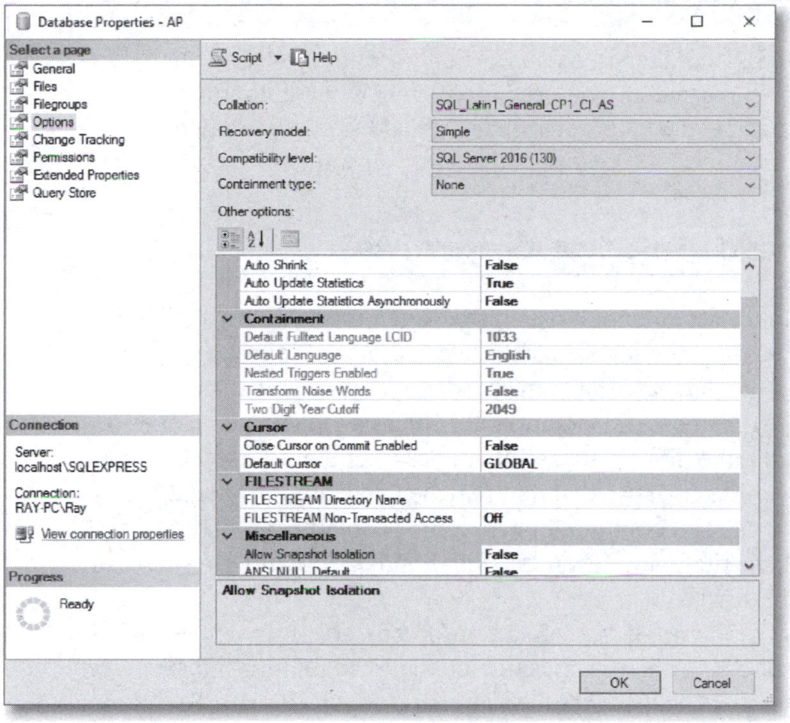

Description

- The SQL Server 2016 database engine is backwards compatible and can run older versions of SQL Server databases just as if they were running under an older version of the SQL Server database engine.

- To set the compatibility level for a database to SQL Server 2016 , right-click the database, select the Properties command, click on the Options item, and select SQL Server 2016 from the Compatibility Level drop-down list.

Figure 2-7   How to set the compatibility level for a database

How to view and modify the database

Before you use SQL to query a database, you need to know how the database is defined. In particular, you need to know how the columns in each table are defined and how the tables are related. In addition, you may need to modify the database definition so it works the way you want.

How to view the database diagrams

The easiest way to view the relationships between the tables in a database is to display a *database diagram* for the database as described in figure 2-8. In this figure, for example, the database diagram shows the relationships between five of the tables in the AP database. In addition, this diagram shows the names of each column in each table. For a database that doesn't contain many tables, like the AP database, a single database diagram may be adequate for the database. However, for a database that contains a large number of tables, it may be helpful to use several database diagrams. Then, each diagram can focus on a subset of related tables within the database.

When you first display a database diagram for a database, the tables may be placed in an illogical order, and the lines that indicate the relationships between the tables may be tangled. This makes the diagram difficult to read. To fix this, you can use standard Windows techniques to move and size the tables in the diagram. For example, you can drag the title bar of a table to move it, you can drag the edge of a table to resize it, and you can right-click anywhere in the diagram to get a context-sensitive shortcut menu. You can use these menus to add or remove tables from the diagram, or to automatically size a table. With a bit of fiddling around, you should be able to organize your diagram so it's easy to see the relationships between the tables.

When you display a database diagram, the relationships between tables are displayed as links as shown in this figure. You can tell what type of relationship exists between two tables by looking at the endpoints of the link. The "one" side is represented by a key, and the "many" side is represented by an infinity symbol. In this diagram, all of the relationships are one-to-many. For example, one row in the Vendors table can be related to many rows in the Invoices table.

As you review this diagram, notice that you can't tell which columns in each table form the relationship. However, you can see which columns are defined as primary key columns. As you may remember from chapter 1, these are the columns that are typically used on the "one" side of the relationships. From that information, you should be able to figure out which columns identify the foreign keys by reading the names of the columns. For example, it's fairly obvious that the DefaultAccountNo column in the Vendors table is related to the AccountNo column in the GLAccounts table. If you can't determine the relationships just by reading the column names, you can review the primary and foreign keys for each table by using the Object Explorer as described in the next figure.

The relationships between the tables in the AP database

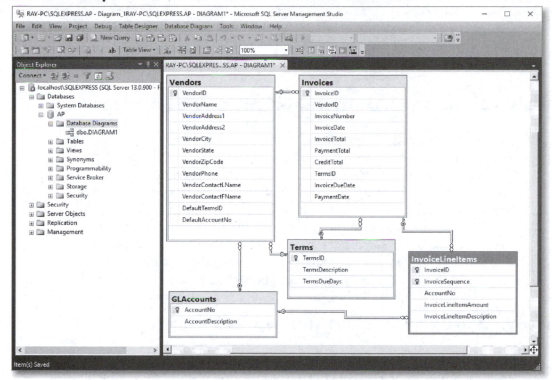

Description

- *Database diagrams* can be used to illustrate the relationships between the tables in a database.

- To view a database diagram, expand the Database Diagrams node for the database, and double-click on the diagram you want to display. If you get a dialog box that says that the database doesn't have one or more of the required support objects for database diagramming, you can select Yes to create the support objects.

- The relationships between the tables in the diagram appear as links, where the endpoints of the links indicate the type of relationship. A key indicates the "one" side of a relationship, and the infinity symbol (∞) indicates the "many" side of a relationship.

- The primary key for a table appears as a key icon that's displayed to the left of the column or columns that define the primary key.

- You can use standard Windows techniques to move and size the tables in a database diagram to make the diagram easier to understand.

Figure 2-8   How to view the relationships between tables

If necessary, you can use a database diagram to add columns, to remove columns, or to change the names of existing columns. However, these changes actually modify the definition of the database. As a result, you'll only want to use them if the database is under development and you're sure that existing code doesn't depend on any existing columns that you delete or modify.

How to view the column definitions of a table

To view the column definitions of a table, you can use the Object Explorer to expand the Columns node for a table as shown in figure 2-9. In this figure, for example, the Object Explorer shows the columns for the Vendors table. This shows the name and data type for each column, along with an indication of whether or not it can contain null values.

In addition, the columns that define keys are marked with a key icon. Here, the first key icon indicates that the VendorID column is the primary key (PK), and the next two key icons indicate that the DefaultTermsID and DefaultAccountNo columns are foreign keys (FK).

How to modify the column definitions

If you want to modify the columns in a table, or if you want to view more detailed information about a column, you can display the table in a Table Designer tab. To do that, right-click on the table and select the Design command. In this figure, for example, you can see that the Table Designer tab for the Vendors table is displayed on the right side of the Management Studio.

The Table Designer tab is divided into two parts. The top of the tab shows three columns that display the name and data type for the column as well as whether the column allows null values. If you want, you can use these columns to modify these values. For example, if you don't want to allow null values for a column, you can remove the appropriate check mark from the Allow Nulls column.

If you want to display additional information about a column, you can select the column by clicking on its row selector. Then, additional properties are displayed in the Column Properties tab that's displayed at the bottom of the window. In this figure, for example, the properties for the DefaultTermsID column are displayed. As you can see, these properties indicate that this column has a default value of 3. Note that the properties that are available change depending on the data type of the column. For a column with the varchar data type, for example, the properties also indicate the length of the column. You'll learn more about that in chapter 8.

The columns in the Vendors table

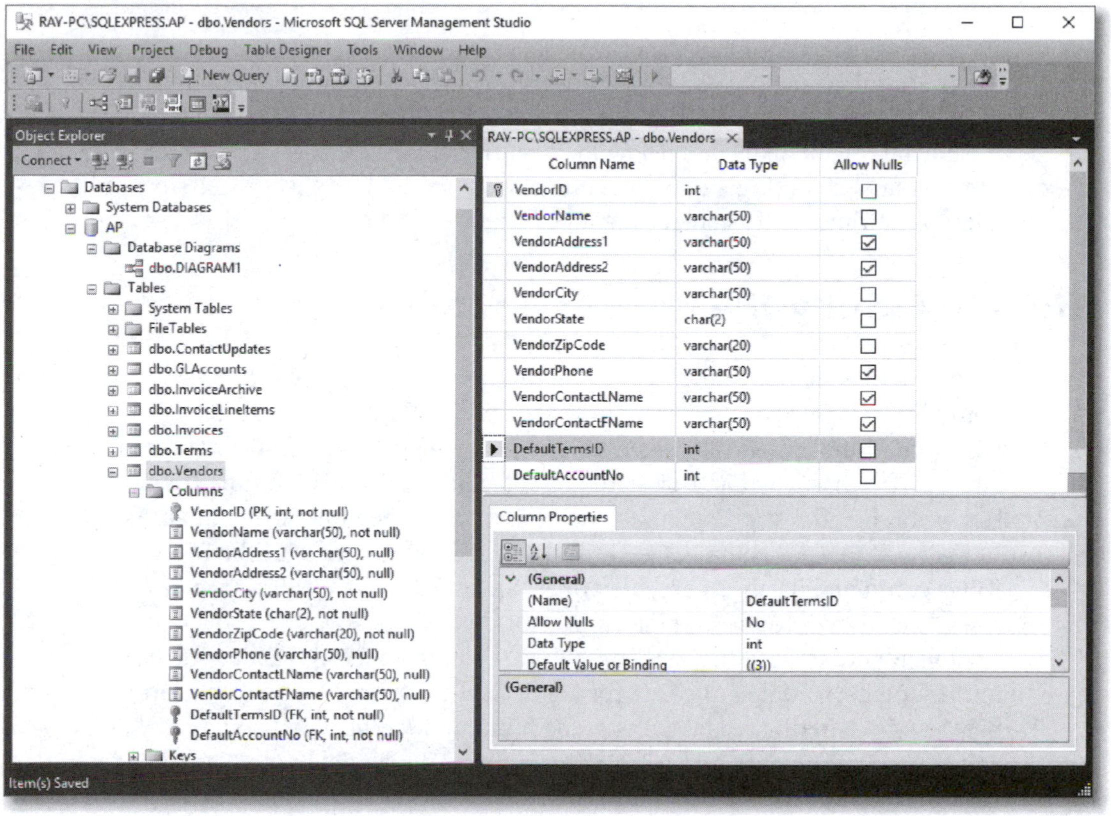

Description

- To view the columns for a table, expand the Tables node, expand the node for the table, and expand the Columns node. This displays the columns in the Object Explorer.

- To modify the columns for a table, expand the Tables node, right-click on the table, and select the Design command to display the table in a Table Designer tab. Then, you can click on the row selector to the left of the column name to display the properties for the column in the Column Properties tab at the bottom of the window. If necessary, you can use the Table Designer tab or the Column Properties tab to modify the properties for a column.

Figure 2-9   How to view or modify the column definitions of a table

How to view the data of a table

If you want to quickly view some data for a table, you can right-click on the table and select the Select Top 1000 Rows command. This automatically generates and executes a query that displays the top 1000 rows of the table in a Results tab that's displayed below the generated query. This works similarly to entering and executing a query as shown in figure 2-11, but it's faster since the query is automatically generated and executed.

How to modify the data of a table

For tables that have more than 200 rows, you'll need to use SQL statements to modify the data for the table. However, for smaller tables such as the Terms table, the Management Studio provides an easy way to modify the data for the table. To do that, you can right-click on the table and select the Edit Top 200 Rows command. This displays the top 200 rows of the table in an editable grid. In figure 2-10, for example, the Terms table is shown after the Edit Top 200 Rows command has been executed on it. Since this table has fewer than 200 rows, this allows you to edit the entire table.

Once you execute the Edit Top 200 Rows command on a table, you can insert, update, or delete the data for the table. For example, you can insert a new row by entering it in the row at the bottom of the grid that contains NULL values. You can update existing data by clicking on the data you want to update and editing the data. And you can delete an existing row by right-clicking on the row selector to the left of the row and selecting the Delete command.

When you update the data for an existing row, the changes aren't committed to the database until you move the cursor to a different row. In this figure, for example, I have changed the number of days for the fifth row from 90 to 80. However, the changes haven't been committed to the database yet. That's why a red warning icon is displayed after the data for the second and third columns in this row. As a result, you can press the Esc key to roll back these changes. Or, you can move the cursor to another row to commit the changes to the database.

The data in the Terms table with a row being modified

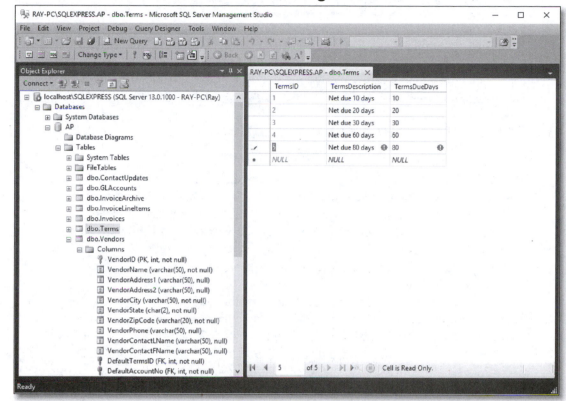

Description

- To view the data for a table, expand the Tables node, right-click on the table, and select the Select Top 1000 Rows command. This automatically generates and executes a query that displays the top 1000 rows of the table.

- To modify the data for a table, expand the Tables node, right-click on the table, and select the Edit Top 200 Rows command. This displays the top 200 rows of the table in an editable grid. Then, you can use the grid to insert, update, or delete data from the table.

Figure 2-10   How to view or modify the data of a table

How to work with queries

Now that you know how to use the Management Studio to attach a database and view the definition for that database, you're ready to learn how to use this tool to enter and execute queries. You can use this tool to test the queries that are presented throughout this book. As you will see, the Management Studio is a powerful tool that makes it easy to work with queries.

How to enter and execute a query

To enter and edit queries, the Management Studio provides a Query Editor window like the one in figure 2-11. The Query Editor is specifically designed for writing Transact-SQL statements, but it works like most text editors. To begin, you can open a new Query Editor window by clicking on the New Query button in the toolbar. Or, you can open an existing query in a Query Editor window by clicking on the Open button in the toolbar as described in figure 2-13. Once the Query Editor is open, you can use standard techniques to enter or edit the statement in this window.

As you enter statements, you'll notice that the Query Editor automatically applies colors to various elements. For example, keywords are displayed in blue by default, and literal values are displayed in red. This makes your statements easier to read and understand and can help you identify coding errors.

In addition, you'll notice that the Query Editor uses the *IntelliSense feature* to automatically display *completion lists* that you can use to enter parts of the SQL statement. In this figure, for example, one of these lists is being used to enter the InvoiceDate column. As you gain experience with the Management Studio, you'll find that IntelliSense can help you enter most types of SQL statements, even complex ones.

When using IntelliSense, you'll want to be sure that you identify the database the query uses before you start entering the query. That way, IntelliSense can include the names of the tables the database contains in the completion lists. To identify the database, you can select it from the Available Databases combo box in the toolbar. In addition, it's often helpful to enter the table name before you enter the columns. That way, IntelliSense can include the column names for the table in the completion lists.

By default, the IntelliSense feature is on. Since this feature can save you a lot of typing and reduce errors in your code, that's usually what you want. However, it's possible to turn some or all parts of this feature off. In addition, the IntelliSense feature isn't able to work correctly if you aren't connected to the correct SQL Server database engine or if your SQL statement contains some types of errors. As a result, if IntelliSense isn't working properly on your system, you should make sure that it's turned on, that you're connected to the database, and that your statement doesn't contain errors.

To execute a query, you can press F5 or click the Execute button in the toolbar. If the statement returns data, that data is displayed in the Results tab at the bottom of the Query Editor. In this figure, for example, the result set that's returned by the execution of a SELECT statement is displayed in the Results

A SELECT statement with a completion list

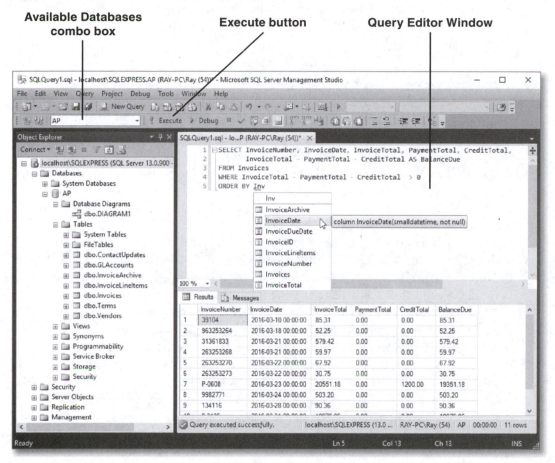

Available Databases combo box

Execute button

Query Editor Window

Description

- To open a new Query Editor window, click on the New Query button in the toolbar. To open a saved query in a Query Editor window, click on the Open button in the toolbar as described in figure 2-13.

- To select the database that you want to work with, use the Available Databases combo box in the toolbar.

- To enter a SQL statement, type it into the Query Editor window.

- As you enter a SQL statement, the *IntelliSense feature* automatically displays *completion lists* that help you complete the statement. To select an item from a list, use the Up or Down arrow key to select the item and press the Tab key. To hide a list, press the Esc key. To manually display a list, press Alt+Right-arrow or Ctrl+J.

- To execute a SQL statement, press the F5 key or click the Execute button in the toolbar. If the statement retrieves data, the data is displayed in the Results tab that's displayed at the bottom of the Query Editor. Otherwise, a message is displayed in the Messages tab that's displayed at the bottom of the Query Editor.

Figure 2-11   How to enter and execute a query

tab. If you execute an action query, the Messages tab is displayed instead of the Results tab. This tab will contain an indication of the number of rows that were affected by the query. The Messages tab is also used to provide error information, as you'll see in figure 2-12.

How to handle syntax errors

When you are entering a SQL statement, the IntelliSense feature will display wavy red underlining beneath any parts of the SQL statement that contain errors. In figure 2-12, for example, wavy red underlining is displayed beneath the first column in the SELECT statement, the InvoiceNum column. The reason for this error is that there isn't a column with this name in the Invoices table of the AP database, which is the selected database. As a result, you can correct this error by entering a valid column name, such as InvoiceNumber.

If an error occurs during the execution of a SQL statement, an error message is displayed in the Messages tab of the Query Editor. In this figure, for example, the error message indicates that InvoiceNum column is invalid. This, of course, is the same error that was detected by the IntelliSense feature.

One common error when working with SQL statements is to forget to select the correct database from the Available Databases combo box. In this figure, the AP database is selected, which is the correct database for the statement that's entered. However, if the ProductOrders database was selected, this statement would contain many errors since the Invoices table and its columns don't exist in that database. To correct this mistake, you can simply select the appropriate database for the statement.

This figure also lists some other common causes of errors. As you can see, these errors are caused by incorrect syntax. When an error is caused by invalid syntax, you can usually identify and correct the problem without much trouble. In some cases, though, you won't be able to figure out the cause of an error by the information that's provided by IntelliSense or the Messages tab. Then, you can get additional information about the error by searching the Internet to see if someone else has encountered a similar error and posted the solution for it.

How the Management Studio displays an error message

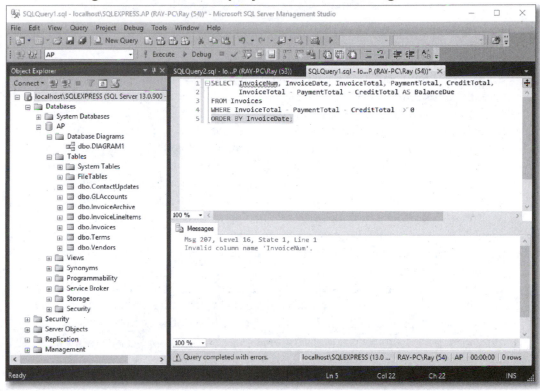

Common causes of errors

- Forgetting to select the correct database from the Available Databases combo box
- Misspelling the name of a table or column
- Misspelling a keyword
- Omitting the closing quotation mark for a character string

Description

- Before you execute a statement, IntelliSense may display wavy red underlining beneath the parts of a SQL statement that contain errors.
- If an error occurs during the execution of a SQL statement, the Management Studio displays an error message in the Messages tab of the Query Editor.
- Most errors are caused by incorrect syntax and can be detected and corrected without any additional assistance. If not, you can get more information about an error by looking it up in the documentation for SQL Server.

Figure 2-12   How to handle syntax errors

How to open and save queries

After you get a query working the way you want it to work, you may want to save it. Then, you can open it and run it again later or use it as the basis for a new query. To do that, you use the techniques in figure 2-13.

If you've used other Windows programs, you shouldn't have any trouble opening and saving query files. To save a new query, for example, or to save a modified query in the original file, you use the standard Save command. To save a modified query in a new file, you use the standard Save As command. And to open a query, you use the standard Open command. Note that when you save a query, it's saved with a file extension of sql.

As you work with queries, you may find it helpful to open two or more queries at the same time. To do that, you can open additional Query Editor windows by starting a new query or by opening an existing query. After you open two or more windows, you can switch between the queries by clicking on the appropriate tab. Then, if necessary, you can cut, copy, and paste code from one query to another.

If you open many queries and not all tabs are visible, you can use the Active Files list to switch between queries. To display this list, click on the drop-down arrow that's displayed to the right of the Query Editor tabs. Then, select the query you want from the list of active files.

The Open File dialog box

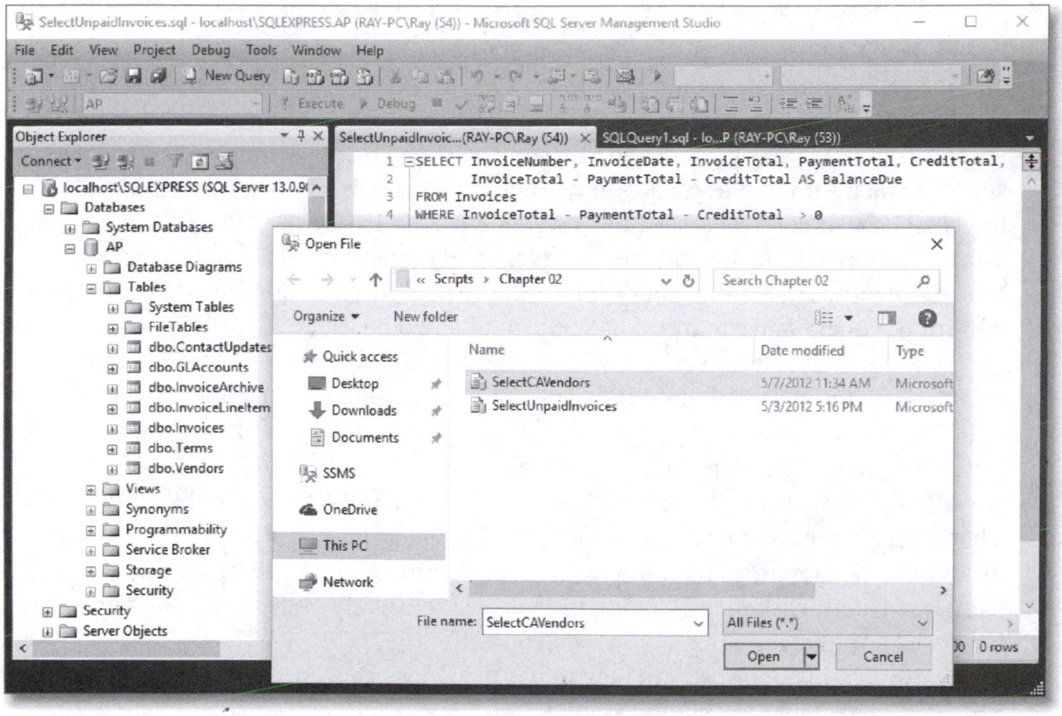

Description

- To save a query, click the Save button in the toolbar or press Ctrl+S. Then, if necessary, use the Save File As dialog box to specify a file name for the query.

- To open a query, click the Open button in the toolbar or press Ctrl+O. Then, use the Open File dialog box shown above to locate and open the query.

- To save all open queries, click the Save All button in the toolbar. Then, if necessary, use the Save File As dialog box to specify a file name for any queries that haven't already been named.

- To switch between open queries, click on the tab for the query you want to display. If you can't see the tab, click on the drop-down arrow that's displayed to the right of the Query Editor tabs, and select the query from the list of active files.

- To cut, copy, and paste code from one query to another, use the standard Windows techniques.

Figure 2-13   How to open and save queries

An introduction to the Query Designer

Figure 2-14 presents the Query Designer, a tool that can help you create queries using a graphical interface. In the Diagram pane, you select the tables and columns that you want to use in the query. Then, the columns you select are listed in the Criteria pane, and you can use this pane to set the criteria and sort sequence for the query. As you work in the Diagram and Criteria panes, the Query Designer generates a SQL statement and displays it in the SQL pane. When you have the statement the way you want it, you can click the OK button to insert the query into the Query Editor. From the Query Editor, you can edit the text for the query and run it just as you would any other query.

When you first start working with a database, the Query Designer can help you become familiar with the tables and columns it contains. In addition, it can help you build simple queries quickly and easily. If you analyze the SQL statements that it generates, it can also help you learn SQL.

Keep in mind, though, that the best way to learn SQL is to code it yourself. That's why this book emphasizes the use of the Query Editor. Plus, it can be difficult, and sometimes impossible, to create certain types of complex queries using the Query Designer. Because of that, you're usually better off using the Query Editor to enter complex queries yourself.

Although this figure shows how to use the Query Designer to create a SELECT statement, you should know that you can also use it to create INSERT, UPDATE, and DELETE statements. To start one of these queries, you can right-click anywhere in the Query Designer window, select the Change To submenu, and select the type of query that you want to create.

The Query Designer window

The three panes in the Query Designer window

Pane	Description
Diagram pane	Displays the tables used by the query and lets you select the columns you want to include in the query.
Criteria pane	Displays the columns selected in the Diagram pane and lets you specify the sort order and the criteria you want to use to select the rows for the result set. You can also use this pane to select or deselect the columns that are included in the output and to create calculated values.
SQL pane	Displays the SQL statement built by the Query Designer based on the information in the Diagram and Criteria panes.

Description

- You can use the Query Designer to build simple queries quickly and easily. However, you may not be able to create more complex queries this way.

- To display the Query Designer, right-click on a blank Query Editor window and select the Design Query in Editor command. Then, you can use the Query Designer window to create the query. When you click the OK button, the query will be inserted into the Query Editor where you can edit and run it just as you would any other query.

- To modify a query with the Query Designer, select the query, right-click on the selection, and select the Design Query in Editor command.

Figure 2-14   An introduction to the Query Designer

How to view the documentation for SQL Server

Sometimes, you need to look up information about SQL statements, or you need to get more information about an error message that's returned by SQL Server. To do that, you can use your browser to search the Internet. Often, this is the quickest and easiest way to find the information you're looking for.

However, there are also times when you need to view the official documentation for SQL Server. To do that, you can start a browser and navigate to the website for the Microsoft Developer Network (MSDN) as shown in figure 2-15.

How to display the MSDN website

The MSDN website has information about many Microsoft products. To display the part of the MSDN website that has information about SQL Server, you can begin by searching the Internet for "SQL Server documentation". Then, you can click on the search result that leads to the MSDN website.

How to look up information on the MSDN website

Once you've displayed the MSDN website, you can use the table of contents that are available from the left column to locate and display the information you need. To display the topic on the SELECT statement shown in this figure, for example, I clicked several links in the table of contents until I found the topic I wanted.

However, it's often faster to use the full-text search feature. For example, I could also have located this topic by entering "select statement" in the Search text box, pressing the Enter key to display a list of topics on that statement, and clicking the appropriate topic.

The documentation for the SELECT statement

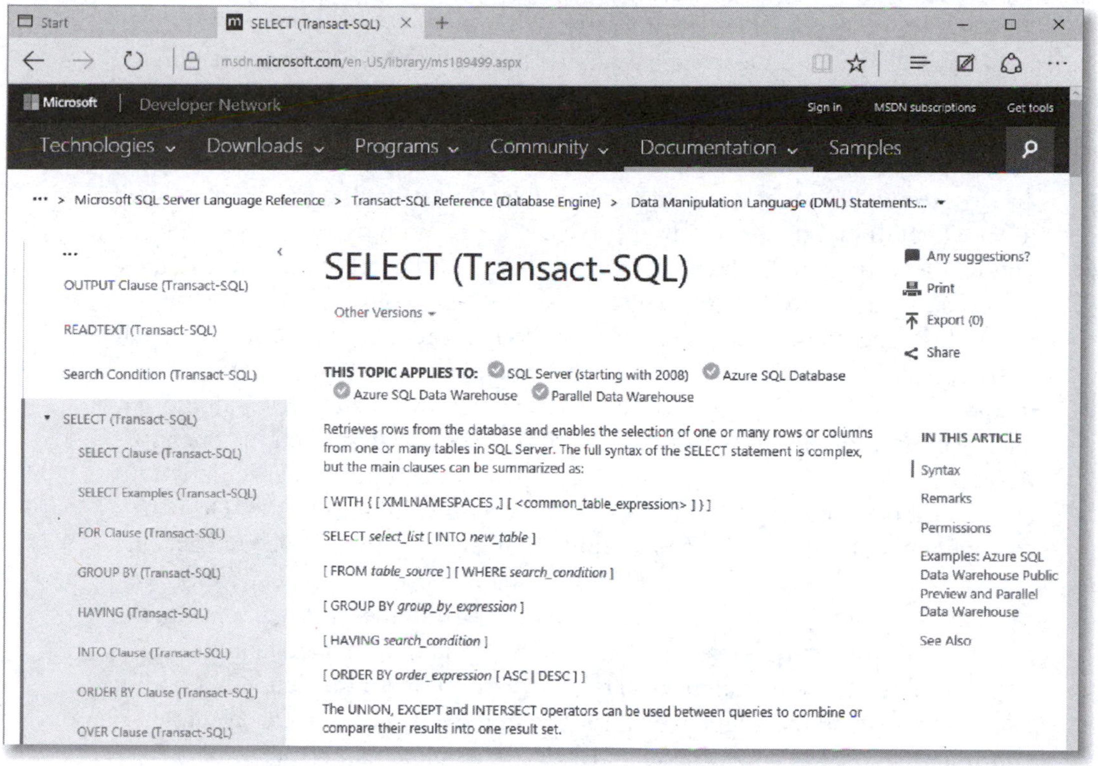

Description

- To view the official documentation for SQL Server 2016, you can start a web browser and navigate to the Microsoft Developer Network (MSDN) website. You can usually find that site by searching for "SQL Server documentation".

- The left column of the website displays the table of contents.

- To use the table of contents, click on a topic to display it in the middle pane.

- To use full-text search, click the search icon that looks like a magnifying glass, enter the text into the Search text box, and press the Enter key. Then, select the topic that you want from the resulting list of topics.

Figure 2-15   How to view the documentation for SQL Server

Perspective

In this chapter, you learned how to use the tools that you need to begin learning about SQL. To begin, you learned how to start and stop the database server. Then, you learned how to use the Management Studio to connect to the database server, to attach a database, to view the definition of a database, and to execute SQL statements against that database. Finally, you learned how to view the official documentation for SQL Server. With that as background, you're ready to go on to the next chapter where you'll start learning the details of coding your own SQL statements.

Before you go on to the next chapter, though, I recommend that you install SQL Server Express and the Management Studio on your system as described in appendix A. In addition, I recommend that you download and install the databases and sample code that come with this book as described in appendix A. That way, you can begin experimenting with these tools. In particular, you can enter and execute queries like the ones described in this chapter. Or, you can open any of the queries shown in this chapter, view their code, and execute them.

For now, though, focus on the mechanics of using the Management Studio to enter and execute queries, and don't worry if you don't understand the details of how the SQL statements are coded. You'll learn the details for coding SQL statements in the chapters that follow. In the next chapter, for example, you'll learn the details for coding a SELECT statement that retrieves data from a single table.

Terms

database server	schema
client tools	attach a database
database engine	detach a database
SQL Server 2016 Express Edition	restore a database
SQL Server Express	database diagram
SQL Server Management Studio	Query Editor
SQL Server Configuration Manager	IntelliSense feature
SQL Server Surface Area	completion list
Configuration	Query Designer
Microsoft Developer Network	
(MSDN)	

Before you do the exercises for this chapter

If you're working on your own PC, you'll need to set up your system as described in appendix A before you can do these exercises.

Exercises

1. Use the Management Studio to view all of the databases that are available from the server. If the AP database isn't available, follow the procedure in appendix A to create it. Then, view the tables that are available from the AP database. Finally, view the columns that are available from the Invoices table. Note the primary and foreign keys of this table and the definition for each column.

2. Right-click on the Vendors table and select the Design command to display the Vendors table in a Table Designer tab. Review the properties for each column in this table. In particular, note that the VendorID column is defined as an identity column.

3. Use the Management Studio to view the diagram for the AP database. Then, organize the tables and connecting lines in the diagram so they are easy to read. (Hint: You can use the Autosize Selected Tables button and the Arrange Tables button in the toolbar to help you do this.) Finally, review the information that's contained in each table, note the primary key of each table, and try to identify the relationships between the tables.

4. Open a new Query Editor window and then enter this SELECT statement:

    ```
    SELECT VendorName, VendorState
    FROM Vendors
    WHERE VendorState = 'CA'
    ```

    Press F5 to execute the query and display the results. If an error is displayed, correct the problem before you continue. (Hint: If you get an error message that indicates that 'Vendors' isn't a valid object, the AP database isn't the current database. To fix this error, select the AP database from the Available Databases combo box.) Then, save the query with a name of VendorsInCA and close it.

5. Open the query named VendorsInCA that you saved in exercise 4. Then, click the Execute Query toolbar button to execute it. (Hint: You may need to select the AP database from the Available Databases combo box.)

6. Look up information about the Query Editor on the MSDN website. The easiest way to do this is to display the part of the MSDN website and use the full-text search to look up "query editor". Continue experimenting with the MSDN website until you feel comfortable with it.

Section 2

The essential SQL skills

This section teaches you the essential SQL coding skills for working with the data in a SQL Server database. The first four chapters in this section show you how to retrieve data from a database using the SELECT statement. In chapter 3, you'll learn how to code the basic clauses of the SELECT statement to retrieve data from a single table. In chapter 4, you'll learn how to get data from two or more tables. In chapter 5, you'll learn how to summarize the data that you retrieve. And in chapter 6, you'll learn how to code subqueries, which are SELECT statements coded within other statements.

Next, chapter 7 shows you how to use the INSERT, UPDATE, and DELETE statements to add, update, and delete rows in a table. Chapter 8 shows you how to work with the various types of data that SQL Server supports. And finally, chapter 9 shows you how to use some of the SQL Server functions for working with data in your SQL statements. When you complete these chapters, you'll have the skills you need to code most any SELECT, INSERT, UPDATE, or DELETE statement.

3

How to retrieve data from a single table

In this chapter, you'll learn how to code SELECT statements that retrieve data from a single table. You should realize, though, that the skills covered here are the essential ones that apply to any SELECT statement you code…no matter how many tables it operates on, no matter how complex the retrieval. So you'll want to be sure you have a good understanding of the material in this chapter before you go on to the chapters that follow.

An introduction to the SELECT statement

To help you learn to code SELECT statements, this chapter starts by presenting its basic syntax. Next, it presents several examples that will give you an idea of what you can do with this statement. Then, the rest of this chapter will teach you the details of coding this statement.

The basic syntax of the SELECT statement

Figure 3-1 presents the basic syntax of the SELECT statement. The syntax summary at the top of this figure uses conventions that are similar to those used in other programming manuals. Capitalized words are *keywords* that you have to type exactly as shown. In contrast, you have to provide replacements for the lowercase words. For example, you can enter a list of columns in place of *select_list*, and you can enter a table name in place of *table_source*.

Beyond that, you can choose between the items in a syntax summary that are separated by pipes (|) and enclosed in braces ({}) or brackets ([]). And you can omit items enclosed in brackets. If you have a choice between two or more optional items, the default item is underlined. And if an element can be coded multiple times in a statement, it's followed by an ellipsis (…). You'll see examples of pipes, braces, default values, and ellipses in syntax summaries later in this chapter. For now, if you compare the syntax in this figure with the coding examples in the next figure, you should easily see how the two are related.

The syntax summary in this figure has been simplified so that you can focus on the four main clauses of the SELECT statement: SELECT, FROM, WHERE, and ORDER BY. Most of the SELECT statements you code will contain all four of these clauses. However, only the SELECT clause is required.

The SELECT clause is always the first clause in a SELECT statement. It identifies the columns that will be included in the result set. These columns are retrieved from the base tables named in the FROM clause. Since this chapter focuses on retrieving data from a single table, the FROM clauses in all of the statements shown in this chapter name a single base table. In the next chapter, though, you'll learn how to retrieve data from two or more tables.

The WHERE and ORDER BY clauses are optional. The ORDER BY clause determines how the rows in the result set are sorted, and the WHERE clause determines which rows in the base table are included in the result set. The WHERE clause specifies a search condition that's used to *filter* the rows in the base table. This search condition can consist of one or more *Boolean expressions*, or *predicates*. A Boolean expression is an expression that evaluates to True or False. When the search condition evaluates to True, the row is included in the result set.

In this book, I won't use the terms "Boolean expression" or "predicate" because I don't think they clearly describe the content of the WHERE clause. Instead, I'll just use the term "search condition" to refer to an expression that evaluates to True or False.

The simplified syntax of the SELECT statement

```
SELECT select_list
[FROM table_source]
[WHERE search_condition]
[ORDER BY order_by_list]
```

The four clauses of the SELECT statement

	Clause	Description
1	SELECT	Describes the columns that will be included in the result set.
2	FROM	Names the table from which the query will retrieve the data.
3	WHERE	Specifies the conditions that must be met for a row to be included in the result set. This clause is optional.
4	ORDER BY	Specifies how the rows in the result set will be sorted. This clause is optional.

Description

- You use the basic SELECT statement shown above to retrieve the columns specified in the SELECT clause from the base table specified in the FROM clause and store them in a result set.

- The WHERE clause is used to *filter* the rows in the base table so that only those rows that match the search condition are included in the result set. If you omit the WHERE clause, all of the rows in the base table are included.

- The search condition of a WHERE clause consists of one or more *Boolean expressions*, or *predicates*, that result in a value of True, False, or Unknown. If the combination of all the expressions is True, the row being tested is included in the result set. Otherwise, it's not.

- If you include the ORDER BY clause, the rows in the result set are sorted in the specified sequence. Otherwise, the rows are returned in the same order as they appear in the base table. In most cases, that means that they're returned in primary key sequence.

Note

- The syntax shown above does not include all of the clauses of the SELECT statement. You'll learn about the other clauses later in this book.

Figure 3-1   The basic syntax of the SELECT statement

SELECT statement examples

Figure 3-2 presents five SELECT statement examples. All of these statements retrieve data from the Invoices table. If you aren't already familiar with this table, you should use the Management Studio as described in the last chapter to review its definition.

The first statement in this figure retrieves all of the rows and columns from the Invoices table. Here, an asterisk (*) is used as a shorthand to indicate that all of the columns should be retrieved, and the WHERE clause is omitted so that there are no conditions on the rows that are retrieved. Notice that this statement doesn't include an ORDER BY clause, so the rows are in primary key sequence. You can see the results following this statement as they're displayed by the Management Studio. Notice that both horizontal and vertical scroll bars are displayed, indicating that the result set contains more rows and columns than can be displayed on the screen at one time.

The second statement retrieves selected columns from the Invoices table. As you can see, the columns to be retrieved are listed in the SELECT clause. Like the first statement, this statement doesn't include a WHERE clause, so all the rows are retrieved. Then, the ORDER BY clause causes the rows to be sorted by the InvoiceTotal column in ascending sequence.

The third statement also lists the columns to be retrieved. In this case, though, the last column is calculated from two columns in the base table, CreditTotal and PaymentTotal, and the resulting column is given the name TotalCredits. In addition, the WHERE clause specifies that only the invoice whose InvoiceID column has a value of 17 should be retrieved.

The fourth SELECT statement includes a WHERE clause whose condition specifies a range of values. In this case, only invoices with invoice dates between 01/01/2016 and 05/31/2016 are retrieved. In addition, the rows in the result set are sorted by invoice date.

The last statement in this figure shows another variation of the WHERE clause. In this case, only those rows with invoice totals greater than 50,000 are retrieved. Since none of the rows in the Invoices table satisfy this condition, the result set is empty.

A SELECT statement that retrieves all the data from the Invoices table

```
SELECT *
FROM Invoices;
```

	InvoiceID	VendorID	InvoiceNumber	InvoiceDate	InvoiceTotal	PaymentTotal	CreditTotal
1	1	122	989319-457	2015-12-08 00:00:00	3813.33	3813.33	0.00
2	2	123	263253241	2015-12-10 00:00:00	40.20	40.20	0.00
3	3	123	963253234	2015-12-13 00:00:00	138.75	138.75	0.00
4	4	123	2-000-2993	2015-12-16 00:00:00	144.70	144.70	0.00

(114 rows)

A SELECT statement that retrieves three columns from each row, sorted in ascending sequence by invoice total

```
SELECT InvoiceNumber, InvoiceDate, InvoiceTotal
FROM Invoices
ORDER BY InvoiceTotal;
```

	InvoiceNumber	InvoiceDate	InvoiceTotal
1	25022117	2016-01-01 00:00:00	6.00
2	24863706	2016-01-10 00:00:00	6.00
3	24780512	2016-02-22 00:00:00	6.00
4	21-4923721	2016-01-13 00:00:00	9.95

(114 rows)

A SELECT statement that retrieves two columns and a calculated value for a specific invoice

```
SELECT InvoiceID, InvoiceTotal, CreditTotal + PaymentTotal AS TotalCredits
FROM Invoices
WHERE InvoiceID = 17;
```

	InvoiceID	InvoiceTotal	TotalCredits
1	17	10.00	10.00

A SELECT statement that retrieves all invoices between given dates

```
SELECT InvoiceNumber, InvoiceDate, InvoiceTotal
FROM Invoices
WHERE InvoiceDate BETWEEN '2016-01-01' AND '2016-05-31'
ORDER BY InvoiceDate;
```

	InvoiceNumber	InvoiceDate	InvoiceTotal
1	25022117	2016-01-01 00:00:00	6.00
2	P02-88D77S7	2016-01-03 00:00:00	856.92
3	21-4748363	2016-01-03 00:00:00	9.95
4	4-321-2596	2016-01-05 00:00:00	10.00

(101 rows)

A SELECT statement that returns an empty result set

```
SELECT InvoiceNumber, InvoiceDate, InvoiceTotal
FROM Invoices
WHERE InvoiceTotal > 50000;
```

	InvoiceNumber	InvoiceDate	InvoiceTotal

Figure 3-2   SELECT statement examples

How to code the SELECT clause

Figure 3-3 presents an expanded syntax for the SELECT clause. The keywords shown in the first line allow you to restrict the rows that are returned by a query. You'll learn how to code them in a few minutes. First, though, you'll learn various techniques for identifying which columns are to be included in a result set.

How to code column specifications

Figure 3-3 summarizes the techniques you can use to code column specifications. You saw how to use some of these techniques in the previous figure. For example, you can code an asterisk in the SELECT clause to retrieve all of the columns in the base table, and you can code a list of column names separated by commas. Note that when you code an asterisk, the columns are returned in the order that they occur in the base table.

You can also code a column specification as an *expression*. For example, you can use an arithmetic expression to perform a calculation on two or more columns in the base table, and you can use a string expression to combine two or more string values. An expression can also include one or more functions. You'll learn more about each of these techniques in the topics that follow.

But first, you should know that when you code the SELECT clause, you should include only the columns you need. For example, you shouldn't code an asterisk to retrieve all the columns unless you need all the columns. That's because the amount of data that's retrieved can affect system performance. This is particularly important if you're developing SQL statements that will be used by application programs.

The expanded syntax of the SELECT clause

```
SELECT [ALL|DISTINCT] [TOP n [PERCENT] [WITH TIES]]
    column_specification [[AS] result_column]
    [, column_specification [[AS] result_column]] ...
```

Five ways to code column specifications

Source	Option	Syntax
Base table value	All columns	*
	Column name	column_name
Calculated value	Result of a calculation	Arithmetic expression (see figure 3-6)
	Result of a concatenation	String expression (see figure 3-5)
	Result of a function	Function (see figure 3-7)

Column specifications that use base table values

The * is used to retrieve all columns
```
SELECT *
```

Column names are used to retrieve specific columns
```
SELECT VendorName, VendorCity, VendorState
```

Column specifications that use calculated values

An arithmetic expression is used to calculate BalanceDue
```
SELECT InvoiceNumber,
    InvoiceTotal - PaymentTotal - CreditTotal AS BalanceDue
```

A string expression is used to calculate FullName
```
SELECT VendorContactFName + ' ' + VendorContactLName AS FullName
```

A function is used to calculate CurrentDate
```
SELECT InvoiceNumber, InvoiceDate,
    GETDATE() AS CurrentDate
```

Description

- Use SELECT * only when you need to retrieve all of the columns from a table. Otherwise, list the names of the columns you need.

- An *expression* is a combination of column names and operators that evaluate to a single value. In the SELECT clause, you can code arithmetic expressions, string expressions, and expressions that include one or more functions.

- After each column specification, you can code an AS clause to specify the name for the column in the result set. See figure 3-4 for details.

Note

- The ALL and DISTINCT keywords and the TOP clause let you control the number of rows that are returned by a query. See figures 3-8 and 3-9 for details.

Figure 3-3   How to code column specifications

How to name the columns in a result set

By default, a column in a result set is given the same name as the column in the base table. However, you can specify a different name if you need to. You can also name a column that contains a calculated value. When you do that, the new column name is called a *column alias*. Figure 3-4 presents two techniques for creating column aliases.

The first technique is to code the column specification followed by the AS keyword and the column alias. This is the ANSI-standard coding technique, and it's illustrated by the first example in this figure. Here, a space is added between the two words in the name of the InvoiceNumber column, the InvoiceDate column is changed to just Date, and the InvoiceTotal column is changed to Total. Notice that because a space is included in the name of the first column, it's enclosed in brackets ([]). As you'll learn in chapter 10, any name that doesn't follow SQL Server's rules for naming objects must be enclosed in either brackets or double quotes. Column aliases can also be enclosed in single quotes.

The second example in this figure illustrates another technique for creating a column alias. Here, the column is assigned to an alias using an equal sign. This technique is only available with SQL Server, not with other types of databases, and is included for compatibility with earlier versions of SQL Server. So although you may see this technique used in older code, I don't recommend it for new statements you write.

The third example in this figure illustrates what happens when you don't assign an alias to a calculated column. Here, no name is assigned to the column, which usually isn't what you want. That's why you usually assign a name to any column that's calculated from other columns in the base table.

Two SELECT statements that name the columns in the result set

A SELECT statement that uses the AS keyword (the preferred technique)

```
SELECT InvoiceNumber AS [Invoice Number], InvoiceDate AS Date,
    InvoiceTotal AS Total
FROM Invoices;
```

notice brackets

A SELECT statement that uses the equal operator (an older technique)

```
SELECT [Invoice Number] = InvoiceNumber, Date = InvoiceDate,
    Total = InvoiceTotal
FROM Invoices;
```

The result set for both SELECT statements

	Invoice Number	Date	Total	
1	989319-457	2015-12-08 00:00:00	3813.33	
2	263253241	2015-12-10 00:00:00	40.20	
3	963253234	2015-12-13 00:00:00	138.75	
4	2-000-2993	2015-12-16 00:00:00	144.70	
5	963253251	2015-12-16 00:00:00	15.50	

A SELECT statement that doesn't provide a name for a calculated column

```
SELECT InvoiceNumber, InvoiceDate, InvoiceTotal,
    InvoiceTotal - PaymentTotal - CreditTotal
FROM Invoices;
```

	InvoiceNumber	InvoiceDate	InvoiceTotal	(No column name)	
1	989319-457	2015-12-08 00:00:00	3813.33	0.00	
2	263253241	2015-12-10 00:00:00	40.20	0.00	
3	963253234	2015-12-13 00:00:00	138.75	0.00	
4	2-000-2993	2015-12-16 00:00:00	144.70	0.00	
5	963253251	2015-12-16 00:00:00	15.50	0.00	

Description

- By default, a column in the result set is given the same name as the column in the base table. If that's not what you want, you can specify a *column alias* or *substitute name* for the column.

- One way to name a column is to use the AS phrase as shown in the first example above. Although the AS keyword is optional, I recommend you code it for readability.

- Another way to name a column is to code the name followed by an equal sign and the column specification as shown in the second example above. This syntax is unique to Transact-SQL.

- It's generally considered a good practice to specify an alias for a column that contains a calculated value. If you don't, no name is assigned to it as shown in the third example above.

- If an alias includes spaces or special characters, you must enclose it in double quotes or brackets ([]). That's true of all names you use in Transact-SQL. SQL Server also lets you enclose column aliases in single quotes for compatibility with earlier releases.

Figure 3-4   How to name the columns in a result set

How to code string expressions

A *string expression* consists of a combination of one or more character columns and *literal values*. To combine, or *concatenate*, the columns and values, you use the *concatenation operator* (+). This is illustrated by the examples in figure 3-5.

The first example shows how to concatenate the VendorCity and VendorState columns in the Vendors table. Notice that because no alias is assigned to this column, it doesn't have a name in the result set. Also notice that the data in the VendorState column appears immediately after the data in the VendorCity column in the results. That's because of the way VendorCity is defined in the database. Because it's defined as a variable-length column (the varchar data type), only the actual data in the column is included in the result. In contrast, if the column had been defined with a fixed length, any spaces following the name would have been included in the result. You'll learn about data types and how they affect the data in your result set in chapter 8.

The second example shows how to format a string expression by adding spaces and punctuation. Here, the VendorCity column is concatenated with a *string literal*, or *string constant*, that contains a comma and a space. Then, the VendorState column is concatenated with that result, followed by a string literal that contains a single space and the VendorZipCode column.

Occasionally, you may need to include a single quotation mark or an apostrophe within a literal string. If you simply type a single quote, however, the system will misinterpret it as the end of the literal string. As a result, you must code two quotation marks in a row. This is illustrated by the third example in this figure.

How to concatenate string data

```
SELECT VendorCity, VendorState, VendorCity + VendorState
FROM Vendors;
```

	VendorCity	VendorState	(No column name)
1	Madison	WI	MadisonWI
2	Washington	DC	WashingtonDC
3	Washington	DC	WashingtonDC

How to format string data using literal values

```
SELECT VendorName,
    VendorCity + ', ' + VendorState + ' ' + VendorZipCode AS Address
FROM Vendors;
```

	VendorName	Address
1	US Postal Service	Madison, WI 53707
2	National Information Data Ctr	Washington, DC 20090
3	Register of Copyrights	Washington, DC 20559
4	Jobtrak	Los Angeles, CA 90025

How to include apostrophes in literal values

```
SELECT VendorName + '''s Address: ',
    VendorCity + ', ' + VendorState + ' ' + VendorZipCode
FROM Vendors;
```

	(No column name)	(No column name)
1	US Postal Service's Address:	Madison, WI 53707
2	National Information Data Ctr's Address:	Washington, DC 20090
3	Register of Copyrights's Address:	Washington, DC 20559
4	Jobtrak's Address:	Los Angeles, CA 90025
5	Newbrige Book Clubs's Address:	Washington, NJ 07882
6	California Chamber Of Commerce's Ad...	Sacramento, CA 95827

Description

- A *string expression* can consist of one or more character columns, one or more *literal values*, or a combination of character columns and literal values.

- The columns specified in a string expression must contain string data (that means they're defined with the char or varchar data type).

- The literal values in a string expression also contain string data, so they can be called *string literals* or *string constants*. To create a literal value, enclose one or more characters within single quotation marks (').

- You can use the *concatenation operator* (+) to combine columns and literals in a string expression.

- You can include a single quote within a literal value by coding two single quotation marks as shown in the third example above.

Figure 3-5   How to code string expressions

How to code arithmetic expressions

Figure 3-6 shows how to code *arithmetic expressions*. To start, it summarizes the five *arithmetic operators* you can use in this type of expression. Then, it presents three examples that illustrate how you use these operators.

The SELECT statement in the first example includes an arithmetic expression that calculates the balance due for an invoice. This expression subtracts the PaymentTotal and CreditTotal columns from the InvoiceTotal column. The resulting column is given the name BalanceDue.

When SQL Server evaluates an arithmetic expression, it performs the operations from left to right based on the *order of precedence*. This order says that multiplication, division, and modulo operations are done first, followed by addition and subtraction. If that's not what you want, you can use parentheses to specify how you want an expression evaluated. Then, the expressions in the innermost sets of parentheses are evaluated first, followed by the expressions in outer sets of parentheses. Within each set of parentheses, the expression is evaluated from left to right in the order of precedence. Of course, you can also use parentheses to clarify an expression even if they're not needed for the expression to be evaluated properly.

To illustrate how parentheses and the order of precedence affect the evaluation of an expression, consider the second example in this figure. Here, the expressions in the second and third columns both use the same operators. When SQL Server evaluates the expression in the second column, it performs the multiplication operation before the addition operation because multiplication comes before addition in the order of precedence. When SQL Server evaluates the expression in the third column, however, it performs the addition operation first because it's enclosed in parentheses. As you can see in the result set shown here, these two expressions result in different values.

Although you're probably familiar with the addition, subtraction, multiplication, and division operators, you may not be familiar with the modulo operator. This operator returns the remainder of a division of two integers. This is illustrated in the third example in this figure. Here, the second column contains an expression that returns the quotient of a division operation. Note that the result of the division of two integers is always an integer. You'll learn more about that in chapter 8. The third column contains an expression that returns the remainder of the division operation. If you study this example for a minute, you should quickly see how this works.

The arithmetic operators in order of precedence

*	Multiplication
/	Division
%	Modulo (Remainder)
+	Addition
–	Subtraction

A SELECT statement that calculates the balance due

```
SELECT InvoiceTotal, PaymentTotal, CreditTotal,
    InvoiceTotal - PaymentTotal - CreditTotal AS BalanceDue
FROM Invoices;
```

	Invoice Total	Payment Total	Credit Total	Balance Due
1	3813.33	3813.33	0.00	0.00
2	40.20	40.20	0.00	0.00
3	138.75	138.75	0.00	0.00

A SELECT statement that uses parentheses to control the sequence of operations

```
SELECT InvoiceID,
    InvoiceID + 7 * 3 AS OrderOfPrecedence,
    (InvoiceID + 7) * 3 AS AddFirst
FROM Invoices
ORDER BY InvoiceID;
```

	InvoiceID	OrderOfPrecedence	AddFirst
1	1	22	24
2	2	23	27
3	3	24	30

A SELECT statement that uses the modulo operator

```
SELECT InvoiceID,
    InvoiceID / 10 AS Quotient,
    InvoiceID % 10 AS Remainder
FROM Invoices
ORDER BY InvoiceID;
```

	InvoiceID	Quotient	Remainder
9	9	0	9
10	10	1	0
11	11	1	1

Description

- Unless parentheses are used, the operations in an expression take place from left to right in the *order of precedence*. For arithmetic expressions, multiplication, division, and modulo operations are done first, followed by addition and subtraction.

- Whenever necessary, you can use parentheses to clarify or override the sequence of operations. Then, the operations in the innermost sets of parentheses are done first, followed by the operations in the next sets, and so on.

Figure 3-6   How to code arithmetic expressions

How to use functions

Figure 3-7 introduces you to *functions* and illustrates how you use them in column specifications. A function performs an operation and returns a value. For now, don't worry about the details of how the functions shown here work. You'll learn more about all of these functions in chapter 9. Instead, just focus on how they're used in column specifications.

To code a function, you begin by entering its name followed by a set of parentheses. If the function requires one or more *parameters*, you enter them within the parentheses and separate them with commas. When you enter a parameter, you need to be sure it has the correct data type. You'll learn more about that in chapter 9.

The first example in this figure shows how to use the LEFT function to extract the first character of the VendorContactFName and VendorContactLName columns. The first parameter of this function specifies the string value, and the second parameter specifies the number of characters to return. The results of the two functions are then concatenated to form initials as shown in the result set for this statement.

The second example shows how to use the CONVERT function to change the data type of a value. This function requires two parameters. The first parameter specifies the new data type, and the second parameter specifies the value to convert. In addition, this function accepts an optional third parameter that specifies the format of the returned value. The first CONVERT function shown here, for example, converts the PaymentDate column to a character value with the format mm/dd/yy. And the second CONVERT function converts the PaymentTotal column to a variable-length character value that's formatted with commas. These functions are included in a string expression that concatenates their return values with the InvoiceNumber column and three literal values.

The third example uses two functions that work with dates. The first one, GETDATE, returns the current date. Notice that although this function doesn't accept any parameters, the parentheses are still included. The second function, DATEDIFF, gets the difference between two date values. This function requires three parameters. The first one specifies the units in which the result will be expressed. In this example, the function will return the number of days between the two dates. The second and third parameters specify the start date and the end date. Here, the second parameter is the invoice date and the third parameter is the current date, which is obtained using the GETDATE function.

A SELECT statement that uses the LEFT function

```
SELECT VendorContactFName, VendorContactLName,
    LEFT(VendorContactFName, 1) +
    LEFT(VendorContactLName, 1) AS Initials
FROM Vendors;
```

	VendorContactFName	VendorContactLName	Initials	
1	Francesco	Alberto	FA	
2	Ania	Irvin	AI	
3	Lukas	Liana	LL	

A SELECT statement that uses the CONVERT function

```
SELECT 'Invoice: #' + InvoiceNumber
    + ', dated ' + CONVERT(char(8), PaymentDate, 1)
    + ' for $' + CONVERT(varchar(9), PaymentTotal, 1)
FROM Invoices;
```

	(No column name)	
1	Invoice: #989319-457, dated 01/07/16 for $3,813.33	
2	Invoice: #263253241, dated 01/14/16 for $40.20	

A SELECT statement that computes the age of an invoice

```
SELECT InvoiceDate,
    GETDATE() AS 'Today''s Date',
    DATEDIFF(day, InvoiceDate, GETDATE()) AS Age
FROM Invoices;
```

	InvoiceDate	Today's Date	Age	
1	2016-04-02 00:00:00	2016-05-01	29	
2	2016-04-01 00:00:00	2016-05-01	30	
3	2016-03-31 00:00:00	2016-05-01	31	

Description

- An expression can include any of the *functions* that are supported by SQL Server. A function performs an operation and returns a value.

- A function consists of the function name, followed by a set of parentheses that contains any *parameters*, or *arguments*, required by the function. If a function requires two or more arguments, you separate them with commas.

- For more information on using functions, see chapter 9.

Figure 3-7   How to use functions

How to use the DISTINCT keyword to eliminate duplicate rows

By default, all of the rows in the base table that satisfy the search condition you specify in the WHERE clause are included in the result set. In some cases, though, that means that the result set will contain duplicate rows, or rows whose column values are identical. If that's not what you want, you can include the DISTINCT keyword in the SELECT clause to eliminate the duplicate rows.

Figure 3-8 illustrates how this works. Here, both SELECT statements retrieve the VendorCity and VendorState columns from the Vendors table. The first statement, however, doesn't include the DISTINCT keyword. Because of that, the same city and state can appear in the result set multiple times. In the results shown in this figure, for example, you can see that Anaheim CA occurs twice and Boston MA occurs three times. In contrast, the second statement includes the DISTINCT keyword, so each city/state combination is included only once.

Notice that, in addition to including the DISTINCT keyword, the second statement doesn't include the ORDER BY clause. That's because when you include the DISTINCT keyword, the result set is automatically sorted by its first column. In this case, that's the same column that was used to sort the result set returned by the first statement.

A SELECT statement that returns all rows

```
SELECT VendorCity, VendorState
FROM Vendors
ORDER BY VendorCity;
```

	VendorCity	VendorState
1	Anaheim	CA
2	Anaheim	CA
3	Ann Arbor	MI
4	Auburn Hills	MI
5	Boston	MA
6	Boston	MA
7	Boston	MA
8	Brea	CA

(122 rows)

A SELECT statement that eliminates duplicate rows

```
SELECT DISTINCT VendorCity, VendorState
FROM Vendors;
```

	VendorCity	VendorState
1	Anaheim	CA
2	Ann Arbor	MI
3	Auburn Hills	MI
4	Boston	MA
5	Brea	CA
6	Carol Stream	IL
7	Charlotte	NC
8	Chicago	IL

(53 rows)

Description

- The DISTINCT keyword prevents duplicate (identical) rows from being included in the result set. It also causes the result set to be sorted by its first column.

- The ALL keyword causes all rows matching the search condition to be included in the result set, regardless of whether rows are duplicated. Since this is the default, it's a common practice to omit the ALL keyword.

- To use the DISTINCT or ALL keyword, code it immediately after the SELECT keyword as shown above.

Figure 3-8   How to use the DISTINCT keyword to eliminate duplicate rows

How to use the TOP clause
to return a subset of selected rows

In addition to eliminating duplicate rows, you can limit the number of rows that are retrieved by a SELECT statement. To do that, you use the TOP clause. Figure 3-9 shows you how.

You can use the TOP clause in one of two ways. First, you can use it to retrieve a specific number of rows from the beginning, or top, of the result set. To do that, you code the TOP keyword followed by an integer value that specifies the number of rows to be returned. This is illustrated in the first example in this figure. Here, only five rows are returned. Notice that this statement also includes an ORDER BY clause that sorts the rows by the InvoiceTotal column in descending sequence. That way, the invoices with the highest invoice totals will be returned.

You can also use the TOP clause to retrieve a specific percent of the rows in the result set. To do that, you include the PERCENT keyword as shown in the second example. In this case, the result set includes six rows, which is five percent of the total of 114 rows.

By default, the TOP clause causes the exact number or percent of rows you specify to be retrieved. However, if additional rows match the values in the last row, you can include those additional rows by including WITH TIES in the TOP clause. This is illustrated in the third example in this figure. Here, the SELECT statement says to retrieve the top five rows from a result set that includes the VendorID and InvoiceDate columns sorted by the InvoiceDate column. As you can see, however, the result set includes six rows instead of five. That's because WITH TIES is included in the TOP clause, and the columns in the sixth row have the same values as the columns in the fifth row.

A SELECT statement with a TOP clause

```
SELECT TOP 5 VendorID, InvoiceTotal
FROM Invoices
ORDER BY InvoiceTotal DESC;
```

	VendorID	InvoiceTotal
1	110	37966.19
2	110	26881.40
3	110	23517.58
4	72	21842.00
5	110	20551.18

A SELECT statement with a TOP clause and the PERCENT keyword

```
SELECT TOP 5 PERCENT VendorID, InvoiceTotal
FROM Invoices
ORDER BY InvoiceTotal DESC;
```

	VendorID	InvoiceTotal
1	110	37966.19
2	110	26881.40
3	110	23517.58
4	72	21842.00
5	110	20551.18
6	110	10976.06

A SELECT statement with a TOP clause and the WITH TIES keyword

```
SELECT TOP 5 WITH TIES VendorID, InvoiceDate
FROM Invoices
ORDER BY InvoiceDate ASC;
```

	VendorID	InvoiceDate
1	122	2015-12-08 00:00:00
2	123	2015-12-10 00:00:00
3	123	2015-12-13 00:00:00
4	123	2015-12-16 00:00:00
5	123	2015-12-16 00:00:00
6	123	2015-12-16 00:00:00

Description

- You can use the TOP clause within a SELECT clause to limit the number of rows included in the result set. When you use this clause, the first *n* rows that meet the search condition are included, where *n* is an integer.

- If you include PERCENT, the first *n* percent of the selected rows are included in the result set.

- If you include WITH TIES, additional rows will be included if their values match, or *tie,* the values of the last row.

- You should include an ORDER BY clause whenever you use the TOP keyword. Otherwise, the rows in the result set will be in no particular sequence.

Figure 3-9   How to use the TOP clause to return a subset of selected rows

How to code the WHERE clause

Earlier in this chapter, I mentioned that to improve performance, you should code your SELECT statements so they retrieve only the columns you need. That goes for retrieving rows too: The fewer rows you retrieve, the more efficient the statement will be. Because of that, you'll almost always include a WHERE clause on your SELECT statements with a search condition that filters the rows in the base table so that only the rows you need are retrieved. In the topics that follow, you'll learn a variety of ways to code this clause.

How to use comparison operators

Figure 3-10 shows you how to use the *comparison operators* in the search condition of a WHERE clause. As you can see in the syntax summary at the top of this figure, you use a comparison operator to compare two expressions. If the result of the comparison is True, the row being tested is included in the query results.

The examples in this figure show how to use some of the comparison operators. The first WHERE clause, for example, uses the equal operator (=) to retrieve only those rows whose VendorState column have a value of IA. Since the state code is a string literal, it must be included in single quotes. In contrast, the numeric literal used in the second WHERE clause is not enclosed in quotes. This clause uses the greater than (>) operator to retrieve only those rows that have a balance due greater than zero.

The third WHERE clause illustrates another way to retrieve all the invoices with a balance due. Like the second clause, it uses the greater than operator. Instead of comparing the balance due to a value of zero, however, it compares the invoice total to the total of the payments and credits that have been applied to the invoice.

The fourth WHERE clause illustrates how you can use comparison operators other than the equal operator with string data. In this example, the less than operator (<) is used to compare the value of the VendorName column to a literal string that contains the letter M. That will cause the query to return all vendors with names that begin with the letters A through L.

You can also use the comparison operators with date literals, as illustrated by the fifth and sixth WHERE clauses. The fifth clause will retrieve rows with invoice dates on or before May 31, 2016, and the sixth clause will retrieve rows with invoice dates on or after May 1, 2016. Like string literals, date literals must be enclosed in single quotes. In addition, you can use different formats to specify dates as shown by the two date literals shown in this figure. You'll learn more about the acceptable date formats in chapter 8.

The last WHERE clause shows how you can test for a not equal condition. To do that, you code a less than sign followed by a greater than sign. In this case, only rows with a credit total that's not equal to zero will be retrieved.

Whenever possible, you should compare expressions that have similar data types. If you attempt to compare expressions that have different data types, SQL Server may implicitly convert the data type for you. Often, this implicit

The syntax of the WHERE clause with comparison operators

```
WHERE expression_1 operator expression_2
```

The comparison operators

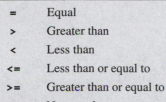

=	Equal
>	Greater than
<	Less than
<=	Less than or equal to
>=	Greater than or equal to
<>	Not equal

Examples of WHERE clauses that retrieve...

Vendors located in Iowa
```
WHERE VendorState = 'IA'
```

Invoices with a balance due (two variations)
```
WHERE InvoiceTotal - PaymentTotal - CreditTotal > 0
WHERE InvoiceTotal > PaymentTotal + CreditTotal
```

Vendors with names from A to L
```
WHERE VendorName < 'M'
```

Invoices on or before a specified date
```
WHERE InvoiceDate <= '2016-05-31'
```

Invoices on or after a specified date
```
WHERE InvoiceDate >= '5/1/16'
```

Invoices with credits that don't equal zero
```
WHERE CreditTotal <> 0
```

Description

- You can use a comparison operator to compare any two expressions that result in like data types. Although unlike data types may be converted to data types that can be compared, the comparison may produce unexpected results.

- If a comparison results in a True value, the row being tested is included in the result set. If it's False or Unknown, the row isn't included.

- To use a string literal or a *date literal* in a comparison, enclose it in quotes. To use a numeric literal, enter the number without quotes.

- Character comparisons performed on SQL Server databases are not case-sensitive. So, for example, 'CA' and 'Ca' are considered equivalent.

Figure 3-10   How to use the comparison operators

conversion is acceptable. However, implicit conversions will occasionally yield unexpected results. In that case, you can use the CONVERT function you saw earlier in this chapter or the CAST function you'll learn about in chapter 8 to explicitly convert data types so the comparison yields the results you want.

How to use the AND, OR, and NOT logical operators

Figure 3-11 shows how to use *logical operators* in a WHERE clause. You can use the AND and OR operators to combine two or more search conditions into a *compound condition*. And you can use the NOT operator to negate a search condition. The examples in this figure illustrate how these operators work.

The first two examples illustrate the difference between the AND and OR operators. When you use the AND operator, both conditions must be true. So, in the first example, only those vendors in New Jersey whose year-to-date purchases are greater than 200 are retrieved from the Vendors table. When you use the OR operator, though, only one of the conditions must be true. So, in the second example, all the vendors from New Jersey and all the vendors whose year-to-date purchases are greater than 200 are retrieved.

The third example shows a compound condition that uses two NOT operators. As you can see, this expression is somewhat difficult to understand. Because of that, and because using the NOT operator can reduce system performance, you should avoid using this operator whenever possible. The fourth example in this figure, for instance, shows how the search condition in the third example can be rephrased to eliminate the NOT operator. Notice that the condition in the fourth example is much easier to understand.

The last two examples in this figure show how the order of precedence for the logical operators and the use of parentheses affect the result of a search condition. By default, the NOT operator is evaluated first, followed by AND and then OR. However, you can use parentheses to override the order of precedence or to clarify a logical expression, just as you can with arithmetic expressions. In the next to last example, for instance, no parentheses are used, so the two conditions connected by the AND operator are evaluated first. In the last example, though, parentheses are used so that the two conditions connected by the OR operator are evaluated first. If you take a minute to review the results shown in this figure, you should be able to see how these two conditions differ.

The syntax of the WHERE clause with logical operators

```
WHERE [NOT] search_condition_1 {AND|OR} [NOT] search_condition_2 ...
```

Examples of queries using logical operators

A search condition that uses the AND operator

```
WHERE VendorState = 'NJ' AND YTDPurchases > 200
```

A search condition that uses the OR operator

```
WHERE VendorState = 'NJ' OR YTDPurchases > 200
```

A search condition that uses the NOT operator

```
WHERE NOT (InvoiceTotal >= 5000 OR NOT InvoiceDate <= '2016-07-01')
```

The same condition rephrased to eliminate the NOT operator

```
WHERE InvoiceTotal < 5000 AND InvoiceDate <= '2016-07-01'
```

A compound condition without parentheses

```
WHERE InvoiceDate > '01/01/2016'
    OR InvoiceTotal > 500
    AND InvoiceTotal - PaymentTotal - CreditTotal > 0
```

	InvoiceNumber	InvoiceDate	InvoiceTotal	BalanceDue
1	P02-88D77S7	2016-01-03 00:00:00	856.92	0.00
2	21-4748363	2016-01-03 00:00:00	9.95	0.00
3	4-321-2596	2016-01-05 00:00:00	10.00	0.00
4	963253242	2016-01-06 00:00:00	104.00	0.00

```
(100 rows)
```

The same compound condition with parentheses

```
WHERE (InvoiceDate > '01/01/2016'
    OR InvoiceTotal > 500)
    AND InvoiceTotal - PaymentTotal - CreditTotal > 0
```

	InvoiceNumber	InvoiceDate	InvoiceTotal	BalanceDue
1	39104	2016-03-10 00:00:00	85.31	85.31
2	963253264	2016-03-18 00:00:00	52.25	52.25
3	31361833	2016-03-21 00:00:00	579.42	579.42
4	263253268	2016-03-21 00:00:00	59.97	59.97

```
(11 rows)
```

Description

- You can use the AND and OR *logical operators* to create *compound conditions* that consist of two or more conditions. You use the AND operator to specify that the search must satisfy both of the conditions, and you use the OR operator to specify that the search must satisfy at least one of the conditions.

- You can use the NOT operator to negate a condition. Because this operator can make the search condition difficult to read, you should rephrase the condition if possible so it doesn't use NOT.

- When SQL Server evaluates a compound condition, it evaluates the operators in this sequence: (1) NOT, (2) AND, and (3) OR. You can use parentheses to override this order of precedence or to clarify the sequence in which the operations will be evaluated.

Figure 3-11   How to use the AND, OR, and NOT logical operators

How to use the IN operator

Figure 3-12 shows how to code a WHERE clause that uses the IN operator. When you use this operator, the value of the test expression is compared with the list of expressions in the IN phrase. If the test expression is equal to one of the expressions in the list, the row is included in the query results. This is illustrated by the first example in this figure, which will return all rows whose TermsID column is equal to 1, 3, or 4.

You can also use the NOT operator with the IN phrase to test for a value that's not in a list of expressions. This is illustrated by the second example in this figure. In this case, only those vendors who are not in California, Nevada, or Oregon are retrieved.

If you look at the syntax of the IN phrase shown at the top of this figure, you'll see that you can code a *subquery* in place of a list of expressions. Subqueries are a powerful tool that you'll learn about in detail in chapter 6. For now, though, you should know that a subquery is simply a SELECT statement within another statement. In the third example in this figure, for instance, a subquery is used to return a list of VendorID values for vendors who have invoices dated May 1, 2016. Then, the WHERE clause retrieves a vendor row only if the vendor is in that list. Note that for this to work, the subquery must return a single column, in this case, VendorID.

The syntax of the WHERE clause with an IN phrase

```
WHERE test_expression [NOT] IN ({subquery|expression_1 [, expression_2]...})
```

Examples of the IN phrase

An IN phrase with a list of numeric literals

```
WHERE TermsID IN (1, 3, 4)
```

An IN phrase preceded by NOT

```
WHERE VendorState NOT IN ('CA', 'NV', 'OR')
```

An IN phrase with a subquery

```
WHERE VendorID IN
    (SELECT VendorID
     FROM Invoices
     WHERE InvoiceDate = '2016-05-01')
```

Description

- You can use the IN phrase to test whether an expression is equal to a value in a list of expressions. Each of the expressions in the list must evaluate to the same type of data as the test expression.

- The list of expressions can be coded in any order without affecting the order of the rows in the result set.

- You can use the NOT operator to test for an expression that's not in the list of expressions.

- You can also compare the test expression to the items in a list returned by a *subquery* as illustrated by the third example above. You'll learn more about coding subqueries in chapter 6.

Figure 3-12   How to use the IN operator

How to use the BETWEEN operator

Figure 3-13 shows how to use the BETWEEN operator in a WHERE clause. When you use this operator, the value of a test expression is compared to the range of values specified in the BETWEEN phrase. If the value falls within this range, the row is included in the query results.

The first example in this figure shows a simple WHERE clause that uses the BETWEEN operator. It retrieves invoices with invoice dates between May 1, 2016 and May 31, 2016. Note that the range is inclusive, so invoices with invoice dates of May 1 and May 31 are included in the results.

The second example shows how to use the NOT operator to select rows that are not within a given range. In this case, vendors with zip codes that aren't between 93600 and 93799 are included in the results.

The third example shows how you can use a calculated value in the test expression. Here, the PaymentTotal and CreditTotal columns are subtracted from the InvoiceTotal column to give the balance due. Then, this value is compared to the range specified in the BETWEEN phrase.

The last example shows how you can use calculated values in the BETWEEN phrase. Here, the first value is the result of the GETDATE function, and the second value is the result of the GETDATE function plus 30 days. So the query results will include all those invoices that are due between the current date and 30 days from the current date.

The syntax of the WHERE clause with a BETWEEN phrase

```
WHERE test_expression [NOT] BETWEEN begin_expression AND end_expression
```

Examples of the BETWEEN phrase

A BETWEEN phrase with literal values

```
WHERE InvoiceDate BETWEEN '2016-05-01' AND '2016-05-31'
```

A BETWEEN phrase preceded by NOT

```
WHERE VendorZipCode NOT BETWEEN 93600 AND 93799
```

A BETWEEN phrase with a test expression coded as a calculated value

```
WHERE InvoiceTotal - PaymentTotal - CreditTotal BETWEEN 200 AND 500
```

A BETWEEN phrase with the upper and lower limits coded as calculated values

```
WHERE InvoiceDueDate BETWEEN GetDate() AND GetDate() + 30
```

Description

- You can use the BETWEEN phrase to test whether an expression falls within a range of values. The lower limit must be coded as the first expression, and the upper limit must be coded as the second expression. Otherwise, the result set will be empty.

- The two expressions used in the BETWEEN phrase for the range of values are inclusive. That is, the result set will include values that are equal to the upper or lower limit.

- You can use the NOT operator to test for an expression that's not within the given range.

Warning about date comparisons

- All columns that have the datetime data type include both a date and time, and so does the value returned by the GetDate function. But when you code a date literal like '2016-05-01', the time defaults to 00:00:00 on a 24-hour clock, or 12:00 AM (midnight). As a result, a date comparison may not yield the results you expect. For instance, May 31, 2016 at 2:00 PM isn't between '2016-05-01' and '2016-05-31'.

- To learn more about date comparisons, please see chapter 9.

Figure 3-13   How to use the BETWEEN operator

How to use the LIKE operator

One final operator you can use in a search condition is the LIKE operator shown in figure 3-14. You use this operator along with the *wildcards* shown at the top of this figure to specify a *string pattern*, or *mask*, you want to match. The examples shown in this figure illustrate how this works.

In the first example, the LIKE phrase specifies that all vendors in cities that start with the letters SAN should be included in the query results. Here, the percent sign (%) indicates that any characters can follow these three letters. So San Diego and Santa Ana are both included in the results.

The second example selects all vendors whose vendor name starts with the letters COMPU, followed by any one character, the letters ER, and any characters after that. Two vendor names that match that pattern are Compuserve and Computerworld.

The third example searches the values in the VendorContactLName column for a name that can be spelled two different ways: Damien or Damion. To do that, the mask specifies the two possible characters in the fifth position, E and O, within brackets.

The fourth example uses brackets to specify a range of values. In this case, the VendorState column is searched for values that start with the letter N and end with any letter from A to J. That excludes states like Nevada (NV) and New York (NY).

The fifth example shows how to use the caret (^) to exclude one or more characters from the pattern. Here, the pattern says that the value in the VendorState column must start with the letter N, but must not end with the letters K through Y. This produces the same result as the previous statement.

The last example in this figure shows how to use the NOT operator with a LIKE phrase. The condition in this example tests the VendorZipCode column for values that don't start with the numbers 1 through 9. The result is all zip codes that start with the number 0.

The LIKE operator provides a powerful technique for finding information in a database that can't be found using any other technique. Keep in mind, however, that this technique requires a lot of overhead, so it can reduce system performance. For this reason, you should avoid using the LIKE operator in production SQL code whenever possible.

If you need to search the text that's stored in your database, a better option is to use the *Full-Text Search* feature that's provided by SQL Server. This feature provides more powerful and flexible ways to search for text, and it performs more efficiently than the LIKE operator. However, Full-Text Search is an advanced feature that requires some setup and administration and is too complex to explain here. For more information, you can look up "full-text search" in the SQL Server documentation.

The syntax of the WHERE clause with a LIKE phrase

```
WHERE match_expression [NOT] LIKE pattern
```

Wildcard symbols

Symbol	Description
%	Matches any string of zero or more characters.
_	Matches any single character.
[ ]	Matches a single character listed within the brackets.
[-]	Matches a single character within the given range.
[^]	Matches a single character not listed after the caret.

WHERE clauses that use the LIKE operator

Example	Results that match the mask
WHERE VendorCity LIKE 'SAN%'	"San Diego" and "Santa Ana"
WHERE VendorName LIKE 'COMPU_ER%'	"Compuserve" and "Computerworld"
WHERE VendorContactLName LIKE 'DAMI[EO]N'	"Damien" and "Damion"
WHERE VendorState LIKE 'N[A-J]'	"NC" and "NJ" but not "NV" or "NY"
WHERE VendorState LIKE 'N[^K-Y]'	"NC" and "NJ" but not "NV" or "NY"
WHERE VendorZipCode NOT LIKE '[1-9]%'	"02107" and "08816"

Description

- You use the LIKE operator to retrieve rows that match a *string pattern*, called a *mask*. Within the mask, you can use special characters, called *wildcards*, that determine which values in the column satisfy the condition.

- You can use the NOT keyword before the LIKE keyword. Then, only those rows with values that don't match the string pattern will be included in the result set.

- Most LIKE phrases will significantly degrade performance compared to other types of searches, so use them only when necessary.

Figure 3-14   How to use the LIKE operator

How to use the IS NULL clause

In chapter 1, you learned that a column can contain a *null value*. A null isn't the same as zero, a blank string that contains one or more spaces (' '), or an empty string (''). Instead, a null value indicates that the data is not applicable, not available, or unknown. When you allow null values in one or more columns, you need to know how to test for them in search conditions. To do that, you can use the IS NULL clause as shown in figure 3-15.

This figure uses a table named NullSample to illustrate how to search for null values. This table contains two columns. The first column, InvoiceID, is an identity column. The second column, InvoiceTotal, contains the total for the invoice, which can be a null value. As you can see in the first example, the invoice with InvoiceID 3 contains a null value.

The second example in this figure shows what happens when you retrieve all the invoices with invoice totals equal to zero. Notice that the row that has a null invoice total isn't included in the result set. Likewise, it isn't included in the result set that contains all the invoices with invoices totals that aren't equal to zero, as illustrated by the third example. Instead, you have to use the IS NULL clause to retrieve rows with null values, as shown in the fourth example.

You can also use the NOT operator with the IS NULL clause as illustrated in the last example in this figure. When you use this operator, all of the rows that don't contain null values are included in the query results.

The syntax of the WHERE clause with the IS NULL clause

```
WHERE expression IS [NOT] NULL
```

The contents of the NullSample table

```
SELECT *
FROM NullSample;
```

	InvoiceID	InvoiceTotal
1	1	125.00
2	2	0.00
3	3	NULL
4	4	2199.99
5	5	0.00

A SELECT statement that retrieves rows with zero values

```
SELECT *
FROM NullSample
WHERE InvoiceTotal = 0;
```

	InvoiceID	InvoiceTotal
1	2	0.00
2	5	0.00

A SELECT statement that retrieves rows with non-zero values

```
SELECT *
FROM NullSample
WHERE InvoiceTotal <> 0;
```

	InvoiceID	InvoiceTotal
1	1	125.00
2	4	2199.99

A SELECT statement that retrieves rows with null values

```
SELECT *
FROM NullSample
WHERE InvoiceTotal IS NULL;
```

	InvoiceID	InvoiceTotal
1	3	NULL

A SELECT statement that retrieves rows without null values

```
SELECT *
FROM NullSample
WHERE InvoiceTotal IS NOT NULL;
```

	InvoiceID	InvoiceTotal
1	1	125.00
2	2	0.00
3	4	2199.99
4	5	0.00

Description

- A *null value* represents a value that's unknown, unavailable, or not applicable. It isn't the same as a zero, a blank space (' '), or an empty string ('').

- To test for a null value, you can use the IS NULL clause. You can also use the NOT keyword with this clause to test for values that aren't null.

- The definition of each column in a table indicates whether or not it can store null values. Before you work with a table, you should identify those columns that allow null values so you can accommodate them in your queries.

Figure 3-15   How to use the IS NULL clause

How to code the ORDER BY clause

The ORDER BY clause specifies the sort order for the rows in a result set. In most cases, you can use column names from the base table to specify the sort order as you saw in some of the examples earlier in this chapter. However, you can also use other techniques to sort the rows in a result set. In addition, you can use the new OFFSET and FETCH clauses of the ORDER BY clause to retrieve a range of rows from the sorted result set.

How to sort a result set by a column name

Figure 3-16 presents the expanded syntax of the ORDER BY clause. As you can see, you can sort by one or more expressions in either ascending or descending sequence. This is illustrated by the three examples in this figure.

The first two examples show how to sort the rows in a result set by a single column. In the first example, the rows in the Vendors table are sorted in ascending sequence by the VendorName column. Since ascending is the default sequence, the ASC keyword is omitted. In the second example, the rows are sorted by the VendorName column in descending sequence.

To sort by more than one column, you simply list the names in the ORDER BY clause separated by commas as shown in the third example. Here, the rows in the Vendors table are first sorted by the VendorState column in ascending sequence. Then, within each state, the rows are sorted by the VendorCity column in ascending sequence. Finally, within each city, the rows are sorted by the VendorName column in ascending sequence. This can be referred to as a *nested sort* because one sort is nested within another.

Although all of the columns in this example are sorted in ascending sequence, you should know that doesn't have to be the case. For example, I could have sorted by the VendorName column in descending sequence like this:

```
ORDER BY VendorState, VendorCity, VendorName DESC
```

Note that the DESC keyword in this example applies only to the VendorName column. The VendorState and VendorCity columns are still sorted in ascending sequence.

The expanded syntax of the ORDER BY clause

```
ORDER BY expression [ASC|DESC] [, expression [ASC|DESC]] ...
```

An ORDER BY clause that sorts by one column in ascending sequence

```
SELECT VendorName,
    VendorCity + ', ' + VendorState + ' ' + VendorZipCode AS Address
FROM Vendors
ORDER BY VendorName;
```

	VendorName	Address
1	Abbey Office Furnishings	Fresno, CA 93722
2	American Booksellers Assoc	Tarrytown, NY 10591
3	American Express	Los Angeles, CA 90096

An ORDER BY clause that sorts by one column in descending sequence

```
SELECT VendorName,
    VendorCity + ', ' + VendorState + ' ' + VendorZipCode AS Address
FROM Vendors
ORDER BY VendorName DESC;
```

	VendorName	Address
1	Zylka Design	Fresno, CA 93711
2	Zip Print & Copy Center	Fresno, CA 93777
3	Zee Medical Service Co	Washington, IA 52353

An ORDER BY clause that sorts by three columns

```
SELECT VendorName,
    VendorCity + ', ' + VendorState + ' ' + VendorZipCode AS Address
FROM Vendors
ORDER BY VendorState, VendorCity, VendorName;
```

	VendorName	Address
1	AT&T	Phoenix, AZ 85062
2	Computer Library	Phoenix, AZ 85023
3	Wells Fargo Bank	Phoenix, AZ 85038
4	Aztek Label	Anaheim, CA 928...
5	Blue Shield of C...	Anaheim, CA 928...
6	Diversified Printi...	Brea, CA 92621
7	Abbey Office Fu...	Fresno, CA 93722
8	ASC Signs	Fresno, CA 93703
9	BFI Industries	Fresno, CA 93792

Description

- The ORDER BY clause specifies how you want the rows in the result set sorted. You can sort by one or more columns, and you can sort each column in either ascending (ASC) or descending (DESC) sequence. ASC is the default.

- By default, in an ascending sort, nulls appear first in the sort sequence, followed by special characters, then numbers, then letters. Although you can change this sequence, that's beyond the scope of this book.

- You can sort by any column in the base table regardless of whether it's included in the SELECT clause. The exception is if the query includes the DISTINCT keyword. Then, you can only sort by columns included in the SELECT clause.

Figure 3-16   How to sort a result set by a column name

How to sort a result set by an alias, an expression, or a column number

Figure 3-17 presents three more techniques you can use to specify sort columns. First, you can use a column alias that's defined in the SELECT clause. The first SELECT statement in this figure, for example, sorts by a column named Address, which is an alias for the concatenation of the VendorCity, VendorState, and VendorZipCode columns. Within the Address column, the result set is also sorted by the VendorName column.

You can also use an arithmetic or string expression in the ORDER BY clause, as illustrated by the second example in this figure. Here, the expression consists of the VendorContactLName column concatenated with the VendorContactFName column. Here, neither of these columns is included in the SELECT clause. Although SQL Server allows this seldom-used coding technique, many other database systems do not.

The last example in this figure shows how you can use column numbers to specify a sort order. To use this technique, you code the number that corresponds to the column of the result set, where 1 is the first column, 2 is the second column, and so on. In this example, the ORDER BY clause sorts the result set by the second column, which contains the concatenated address, then by the first column, which contains the vendor name. The result set returned by this statement is the same as the result set returned by the first statement. Notice, however, that the statement that uses column numbers is more difficult to read because you have to look at the SELECT clause to see what columns the numbers refer to. In addition, if you add or remove columns from the SELECT clause, you may also have to change the ORDER BY clause to reflect the new column positions. As a result, you should avoid using this technique.

An ORDER BY clause that uses an alias

```
SELECT VendorName,
    VendorCity + ', ' + VendorState + ' ' + VendorZipCode AS Address
FROM Vendors
ORDER BY Address, VendorName;
```

	VendorName	Address
1	Aztek Label	Anaheim, CA 92807
2	Blue Shield of California	Anaheim, CA 92850
3	Malloy Lithographing Inc	Ann Arbor, MI 48106

An ORDER BY clause that uses an expression

```
SELECT VendorName,
    VendorCity + ', ' + VendorState + ' ' + VendorZipCode AS Address
FROM Vendors
ORDER BY VendorContactLName + VendorContactFName;
```

	VendorName	Address
1	Dristas Groom & McCormick	Fresno, CA 93720
2	Internal Revenue Service	Fresno, CA 93888
3	US Postal Service	Madison, WI 53707

An ORDER BY clause that uses column positions

```
SELECT VendorName,
    VendorCity + ', ' + VendorState + ' ' + VendorZipCode AS Address
FROM Vendors
ORDER BY 2, 1;
```

	VendorName	Address
1	Aztek Label	Anaheim, CA 92807
2	Blue Shield of California	Anaheim, CA 92850
3	Malloy Lithographing Inc	Ann Arbor, MI 48106

Description

- The ORDER BY clause can include a column alias that's specified in the SELECT clause.

- The ORDER BY clause can include any valid expression. The expression can refer to any column in the base table, even if it isn't included in the result set.

- The ORDER BY clause can use numbers to specify the columns to use for sorting. In that case, 1 represents the first column in the result set, 2 represents the second column, and so on.

Figure 3-17   How to sort a result set by an alias, an expression, or a column number

How to retrieve a range of selected rows

Earlier in this chapter, you saw how to use the TOP clause to return a subset of the rows selected by a query. When you use this clause, the rows are always returned from the beginning of the result set. In contrast, the new OFFSET and FETCH clauses let you return a subset of rows starting anywhere in a sorted result set. Figure 3-18 illustrates how these clauses work.

The first example in this figure shows how to use the OFFSET and FETCH clauses to retrieve rows from the beginning of a result set. In this case, the first five rows are retrieved. In contrast, the second example retrieves ten rows from the result set starting with the eleventh row. Notice that the FETCH clause in the first example uses the FIRST keyword, and the FETCH clause in the second example uses the NEXT keyword. Although these keywords are interchangeable, they're typically used as shown here.

You can also return all of the rows to the end of a result set after skipping the specified number of rows. To do that, you just omit the FETCH clause. For instance, if you omitted this clause from the second example in this figure, rows 11 through the end of the result set would be retrieved.

The OFFSET and FETCH clauses are most useful when a client application needs to retrieve and process one page of data at a time. For example, suppose an application can work with up to 20 rows of a result set at a time. Then, the first query would retrieve rows 1 through 20, the second query would retrieve rows 21 through 40, and so on.

Because a new result set is created each time a query is executed, the client application must make sure that the result set doesn't change between queries. For example, if after retrieving the first 20 rows of a result set as described above one of those rows is deleted, the row that would have been the 21st row now becomes the 20th row. Because of that, this row isn't included when the next 20 rows are retrieved. To prevent this problem, an application can execute all of the queries within a transaction whose isolation level is set to either SNAPSHOT or SERIALIZABLE. For information on how transactions and isolation levels work within SQL Server, see chapter 16.

The syntax of the ORDER BY clause for retrieving a range of rows

```
ORDER BY order_by_list
    OFFSET offset_row_count {ROW|ROWS}
    [FETCH {FIRST|NEXT} fetch_row_count {ROW|ROWS} ONLY]
```

An ORDER BY clause that retrieves the first five rows

```
SELECT VendorID, InvoiceTotal
FROM Invoices
ORDER BY InvoiceTotal DESC
    OFFSET 0 ROWS
    FETCH FIRST 5 ROWS ONLY;
```

	VendorID	InvoiceTotal
1	110	37966.19
2	110	26881.40
3	110	23517.58
4	72	21842.00
5	110	20551.18

An ORDER BY clause that retrieves rows 11 through 20

```
SELECT VendorName, VendorCity, VendorState, VendorZipCode
FROM Vendors
WHERE VendorState = 'CA'
ORDER BY VendorCity
    OFFSET 10 ROWS
    FETCH NEXT 10 ROWS ONLY;
```

	VendorName	VendorCity	VendorState	VendorZipCode
1	Robbins Mobile Lock And Key	Fresno	CA	93726
2	BFI Industries	Fresno	CA	93792
3	California Data Marketing	Fresno	CA	93721
4	Yale Industrial Trucks-Fresno	Fresno	CA	93706
5	Costco	Fresno	CA	93711
6	Graylift	Fresno	CA	93745
7	Shields Design	Fresno	CA	93728
8	Fresno County Tax Collector	Fresno	CA	93715
9	Gary McKeighan Insurance	Fresno	CA	93711
10	Ph Photographic Services .	Fresno	CA	93726

Description

- The OFFSET clause specifies the number of rows that should be skipped before rows are returned from the result set.

- The FETCH clause specifies the number of rows that should be retrieved after skipping the specified number of rows. If you omit the FETCH clause, all of the rows to the end of the result set are retrieved.

- The number of rows to be skipped and retrieved can be specified as an integer or an expression that results in an integer that is greater than or equal to zero.

- The OFFSET and FETCH clauses are most useful when a client application needs to retrieve one page of data at a time.

Figure 3-18   How to retrieve a range of selected rows

Perspective

The goal of this chapter has been to teach you the basic skills for coding SELECT statements. You'll use these skills in almost every SELECT statement you code. As you'll see in the chapters that follow, however, there's a lot more to coding SELECT statements than what's presented here. In the next three chapters, then, you'll learn additional skills for coding SELECT statements. When you complete those chapters, you'll know everything you need to know about retrieving data from a SQL Server database.

Terms

keyword	order of precedence
filter	function
Boolean expression	parameter
predicate	argument
expression	date literal
column alias	comparison operator
substitute name	logical operator
string expression	compound condition
concatenate	subquery
concatenation operator	string pattern
literal value	mask
string literal	wildcard
string constant	Full-Text Search
arithmetic expression	null value
arithmetic operator	nested sort

Exercises

1. Write a SELECT statement that returns three columns from the Vendors table: VendorContactFName, VendorContactLName, and VendorName. Sort the result set by last name, then by first name.

2. Write a SELECT statement that returns four columns from the Invoices table, named Number, Total, Credits, and Balance:

Number	Column alias for the InvoiceNumber column
Total	Column alias for the InvoiceTotal column
Credits	Sum of the PaymentTotal and CreditTotal columns
Balance	InvoiceTotal minus the sum of PaymentTotal and CreditTotal

    Use the AS keyword to assign column aliases.

3. Write a SELECT statement that returns one column from the Vendors table named Full Name. Create this column from the VendorContactFName and VendorContactLName columns. Format it as follows: last name, comma, first name (for example, "Doe, John"). Sort the result set by last name, then by first name.

4. Write a SELECT statement that returns three columns:

InvoiceTotal	From the Invoices table
10%	10% of the value of InvoiceTotal
Plus 10%	The value of InvoiceTotal plus 10%

    (For example, if InvoiceTotal is 100.0000, 10% is 10.0000, and Plus 10% is 110.0000.) Only return those rows with a balance due greater than 1000. Sort the result set by InvoiceTotal, with the largest invoice first.

5. Modify the solution to exercise 2 to filter for invoices with an InvoiceTotal that's greater than or equal to $500 but less than or equal to $10,000.

6. Modify the solution to exercise 3 to filter for contacts whose last name begins with the letter A, B, C, or E.

7. Write a SELECT statement that determines whether the PaymentDate column of the Invoices table has any invalid values. To be valid, PaymentDate must be a null value if there's a balance due and a non-null value if there's no balance due. Code a compound condition in the WHERE clause that tests for these conditions.

4

How to retrieve data from two or more tables

In the last chapter, you learned how to create result sets that contain data from a single table. Now, this chapter will show you how to create result sets that contain data from two or more tables. To do that, you can use either a join or a union.

How to work with inner joins

A *join* lets you combine columns from two or more tables into a single result set. In the topics that follow, you'll learn how to use the most common type of join, an *inner join*. You'll learn how to use other types of joins later in this chapter.

How to code an inner join

Figure 4-1 presents the *explicit syntax* for coding an inner join. As you'll see later in this chapter, SQL Server also provides an implicit syntax that you can use to code inner joins. However, the syntax shown in this figure is the one you'll use most often.

To join data from two tables, you code the names of the two tables in the FROM clause along with the JOIN keyword and an ON phrase that specifies the *join condition*. The join condition indicates how the two tables should be compared. In most cases, they're compared based on the relationship between the primary key of the first table and a foreign key of the second table. The SELECT statement in this figure, for example, joins data from the Vendors and Invoices tables based on the VendorID column in each table. Notice that because the equal operator is used in this condition, the value of the VendorID column in a row in the Vendors table must match the VendorID in a row in the Invoices table for that row to be included in the result set. In other words, only vendors with one or more invoices will be included. Although you'll code most inner joins using the equal operator, you should know that you can compare two tables based on other conditions, too.

In this example, the Vendors table is joined with the Invoices table using a column that has the same name in both tables: VendorID. Because of that, the columns must be qualified to indicate which table they come from. As you can see, you code a *qualified column name* by entering the table name and a period in front of the column name. Although this example uses qualified column names only in the join condition, you must qualify a column name anywhere it appears in the statement if the same name occurs in both tables. If you don't, SQL Server will return an error indicating that the column name is ambiguous. Of course, you can also qualify column names that aren't ambiguous. However, I recommend you do that only if it clarifies your code.

The explicit syntax for an inner join

```
SELECT select_list
FROM table_1
    [INNER] JOIN table_2
        ON join_condition_1
    [[INNER] JOIN table_3
        ON join_condition_2]...
```

A SELECT statement that joins the Vendors and Invoices tables

```
SELECT InvoiceNumber, VendorName
FROM Vendors JOIN Invoices
    ON Vendors.VendorID = Invoices.VendorID;
```

The result set

	InvoiceNumber	VendorName
1	QP58872	IBM
2	Q545443	IBM
3	547481328	Blue Cross
4	547479217	Blue Cross
5	547480102	Blue Cross
6	P02-88D77S7	Fresno County Tax Collector
7	40318	Data Reproductions Corp

`(114 rows)`

Description

- A *join* is used to combine columns from two or more tables into a result set based on the *join conditions* you specify. For an *inner join*, only those rows that satisfy the join condition are included in the result set.

- A join condition names a column in each of the two tables involved in the join and indicates how the two columns should be compared. In most cases, you use the equal operator to retrieve rows with matching columns. However, you can also use any of the other comparison operators in a join condition.

- In most cases, you'll join two tables based on the relationship between the primary key in one table and a foreign key in the other table. However, you can also join tables based on relationships not defined in the database. These are called *ad hoc relationships*.

- If the two columns in a join condition have the same name, you have to qualify them with the table name so that SQL Server can distinguish between them. To code a *qualified column name*, type the table name, followed by a period, followed by the column name.

Notes

- The INNER keyword is optional and is seldom used.

- This syntax for coding an inner join can be referred to as the *explicit syntax*. It is also called the *SQL-92 syntax* because it was introduced by the SQL-92 standards.

- You can also code an inner join using the *implicit syntax*. See figure 4-7 for more information.

Figure 4-1   How to code an inner join

When and how to use correlation names

When you name the tables to be joined in the FROM clause, you can assign temporary names to the tables called *correlation names* or *table aliases*. To do that, you use the AS phrase just as you do when you assign a column alias. After you assign a correlation name, you must use that name in place of the original table name throughout the query. This is illustrated in figure 4-2.

The first SELECT statement in this figure joins data from the Vendors and Invoices table. Here, both tables have been assigned correlation names that consist of a single letter. Although short correlation names like this can reduce typing, they can also make a query more difficult to read and maintain. As a result, you should only use correlation names when they simplify or clarify the query.

The correlation name used in the second SELECT statement in this figure, for example, simplifies the name of the InvoiceLineItems table to just LineItems. That way, the shorter name can be used to refer to the InvoiceID column of the table in the join condition. Although this doesn't improve the query in this example much, it can have a dramatic effect on a query that refers to the InvoiceLineItems table several times.

The syntax for an inner join that uses correlation names

```
SELECT select_list
FROM table_1 [AS] n1
    [INNER] JOIN table_2 [AS] n2
        ON n1.column_name operator n2.column_name
    [[INNER] JOIN table_3 [AS] n3
        ON n2.column_name operator n3.column_name]...
```

An inner join with correlation names that make the query more difficult to read

```
SELECT InvoiceNumber, VendorName, InvoiceDueDate,
    InvoiceTotal - PaymentTotal - CreditTotal AS BalanceDue
FROM Vendors AS v JOIN Invoices AS i
    ON v.VendorID = i.VendorID
WHERE InvoiceTotal - PaymentTotal - CreditTotal > 0
ORDER BY InvoiceDueDate DESC;
```

	InvoiceNumber	VendorName	InvoiceDueDate	BalanceDue	
1	0-2436	Malloy Lithographing Inc	2016-04-30 00:00:00	10976.06	
2	547480102	Blue Cross	2016-04-30 00:00:00	224.00	
3	9982771	Ford Motor Credit Company	2016-04-23 00:00:00	503.20	

`(11 rows)`

An inner join with a correlation name that simplifies the query

```
SELECT InvoiceNumber, InvoiceLineItemAmount, InvoiceLineItemDescription
FROM Invoices JOIN InvoiceLineItems AS LineItems
    ON Invoices.InvoiceID = LineItems.InvoiceID
WHERE AccountNo = 540
ORDER BY InvoiceDate;
```

	InvoiceNumber	InvoiceLineItemAmount	InvoiceLineItemDescription	
1	I77271-O01	478.00	Publishers Marketing	
2	972110	207.78	Prospect list	
3	133560	175.00	Card deck advertising	

`(6 rows)`

Description

- *Correlation names* are temporary table names assigned in the FROM clause. You can use correlation names when long table names make qualified column names long or confusing. A correlation name can also be called a *table alias*.

- If you assign a correlation name to a table, you must use that name to refer to the table within your query. You can't use the original table name.

- Although the AS keyword is optional, I recommend you use it because it makes the FROM clause easier to read.

- You can use a correlation name for any table in a join without using correlation names for all of the other tables.

- Use correlation names whenever they simplify or clarify the query. Avoid using correlation names when they make a query more confusing or difficult to read.

Figure 4-2   When and how to use correlation names

How to work with tables from different databases

Although it's not common, you may occasionally need to join data from tables that reside in different databases. To do that, you have to qualify one or more of the table names. Figure 4-3 shows you how.

To start, this figure presents the syntax of a *fully-qualified object name*. As you can see, a fully-qualified name consists of four parts: a server name, a database name, a schema name, and the name of the object itself. In this chapter, you'll learn how to qualify table names. However, you should realize that you can use this syntax with other objects as well.

The first SELECT statement in this figure illustrates the use of fully-qualified object names. This statement joins data from two tables (Vendors and Customers) in two different databases (AP and ProductOrders). Both databases are on the same server (DBServer) and are stored in the same schema (dbo). Here, correlation names are assigned to both of these tables to make them easier to refer to in the join condition.

Although you can qualify all table names this way, you typically specify only the parts that are different from the current settings. When you start the Management Studio, for example, you connect to a specific server. As long as you work with databases in that server, then, you don't need to include the server name. Similarly, before you execute a statement, you typically select the database it uses. So as long as you work with tables in that database, you don't need to include the database name. You can also omit the schema name as long as you work with tables in the user's default schema (see chapter 17) or in the dbo schema. That's why all of the statements you've seen up to this point have included only the table name.

When you omit one or more parts from a fully-qualified object name, you create a *partially-qualified object name*. The second SELECT statement in this figure, for example, shows how the first statement can be rewritten using partially-qualified object names. Here, the server name, database name, and schema name are all omitted from the Vendors table since it resides in the default schema (dbo) within the current database (AP) on the current server. The Customers table, however, must be qualified with the database name because it's not in the AP database. Notice that because the schema name falls between the database name and the table name, two periods were coded to indicate that this part of the name was omitted.

Before you can specify a server name as shown in this figure, you must add a *linked server* to the current instance of the server. A linked server is a virtual server that specifies all the information necessary to be able to connect to a local or remote server. To add a linked server, you can use the stored procedure named sp_addlinkedserver. In this figure, for example, the stored procedure adds a linked server named DBServer to the master database for the current instance of SQL Server. This server has all the information necessary to connect to an instance of SQL Server Express that's running on the local machine. However, a similar syntax could be used to connect to an instance of SQL Server running on a remote server.

The syntax of a fully-qualified object name

```
linked_server.database.schema.object
```

A join with fully-qualified table names

```
SELECT VendorName, CustLastName, CustFirstName,
    VendorState AS State, VendorCity AS City
FROM DBServer.AP.dbo.Vendors AS Vendors
    JOIN DBServer.ProductOrders.dbo.Customers AS Customers
    ON Vendors.VendorZipCode = Customers.CustZip
ORDER BY State, City;
```

The same join with partially-qualified table names

```
SELECT VendorName, CustLastName, CustFirstName,
    VendorState AS State, VendorCity AS City
FROM Vendors
    JOIN ProductOrders..Customers AS Customers
    ON Vendors.VendorZipCode = Customers.CustZip
ORDER BY State, City;
```

The result set

	VendorName	CustLastName	CustFirstName	State	City
1	Wells Fargo Bank	Marissa	Kyle	AZ	Phoenix
2	Aztek Label	Irvin	Ania	CA	Anaheim
3	Gary McKeighan Insurance	Neftaly	Thalia	CA	Fresno
4	Gary McKeighan Insurance	Holbrooke	Rashad	CA	Fresno
5	Shields Design	Damien	Deborah	CA	Fresno

```
(37 rows)
```

A stored procedure that adds a linked server

```
USE master;
EXEC sp_addlinkedserver
    @server='DBServer',
    @srvproduct='',
    @provider='SQLNCLI',
    @datasrc='localhost\SqlExpress';
```

Description

- A *fully-qualified object name* is made up of four parts: the server name, the database name, the schema name (typically dbo), and the name of the object (typically a table). This syntax can be used when joining tables from different databases or databases on different servers.

- If the server or database name is the same as the current server or database name, or if the schema name is dbo or the name of the user's default schema, you can omit that part of the name to create a *partially-qualified object name*. If the omitted name falls between two other parts of the name, code two periods to indicate that the name is omitted.

- Before you can specify a server name, you must add a *linked server* to the current instance of the server. To do that, you can use the stored procedure named sp_addlinkedserver. Then, you can specify the name of the linked server. To remove a linked server, you can use the stored procedure named sp_dropserver.

Figure 4-3   How to work with tables from different databases

To remove a linked server, you can use the stored procedure named sp_dropserver. For more information about working with linked servers, look up "Linked Servers (Database Engine)" in the documentation for SQL Server.

How to use compound join conditions

Although a join condition typically consists of a single comparison, you can include two or more comparisons in a join condition using the AND and OR operators. Figure 4-4 illustrates how this works.

In the first SELECT statement in this figure, you can see that the Invoices and InvoiceLineItems tables are joined based on two comparisons. First, the primary key of the Invoices table, InvoiceID, is compared with the foreign key of the InvoiceLineItems table, also named InvoiceID. As in previous examples, this comparison uses an equal condition. Then, the InvoiceTotal column in the Invoices table is tested for a value greater than the value of the InvoiceLineItemAmount column in the InvoiceLineItems table. That means that only those invoices that have two or more line items will be included in the result set. You can see part the result set in this figure.

Another way to code these conditions is to code the primary join condition in the FROM clause and the other condition in the WHERE clause. This is illustrated by the second SELECT statement in this figure.

When you code separate compound join conditions like this, the join condition in the ON expression is performed before the tables are joined, and the search condition in the WHERE clause is performed after the tables are joined. Because of that, you might expect a SELECT statement to execute more efficiently if you code the search condition in the ON expression. However, SQL Server examines the join and search conditions as it optimizes the query. So you don't need to worry about which technique is most efficient. Instead, you should code the conditions so they're easy to understand.

An inner join with two conditions

```
SELECT InvoiceNumber, InvoiceDate,
    InvoiceTotal, InvoiceLineItemAmount
FROM Invoices JOIN InvoiceLineItems AS LineItems
    ON (Invoices.InvoiceID = LineItems.InvoiceID) AND
        (Invoices.InvoiceTotal > LineItems.InvoiceLineItemAmount)
ORDER BY InvoiceNumber;
```

The same join with the second condition coded in a WHERE clause

```
SELECT InvoiceNumber, InvoiceDate,
    InvoiceTotal, InvoiceLineItemAmount
FROM Invoices JOIN InvoiceLineItems AS LineItems
    ON Invoices.InvoiceID = LineItems.InvoiceID
WHERE Invoices.InvoiceTotal > LineItems.InvoiceLineItemAmount
ORDER BY InvoiceNumber;
```

The result set

	InvoiceNumber	InvoiceDate	InvoiceTotal	InvoiceLineItemAmount
1	97/522	2016-02-28 00:00:00	1962.13	1197.00
2	97/522	2016-02-28 00:00:00	1962.13	765.13
3	I77271-O01	2015-12-26 00:00:00	662.00	50.00
4	I77271-O01	2015-12-26 00:00:00	662.00	75.60
5	I77271-O01	2015-12-26 00:00:00	662.00	58.40
6	I77271-O01	2015-12-26 00:00:00	662.00	478.00

Description

- A join condition can include two or more conditions connected by AND or OR operators.

- In most cases, your code will be easier to read if you code the join condition in the ON expression and search conditions in the WHERE clause.

Figure 4-4   How to use compound join conditions

How to use a self-join

A *self-join* is a join where a table is joined with itself. Although self-joins are rare, there are some unique queries that are best solved using self-joins.

Figure 4-5 presents an example of a self-join that uses the Vendors table. Notice that since the same table is used twice, correlation names are used to distinguish between the two occurrences of the table. In addition, each column name used in the query is qualified by the correlation name since the columns occur in both tables.

The join condition in this example uses three comparisons. The first two match the VendorCity and VendorState columns in the two tables. As a result, the query will return rows for vendors that reside in the same city and state as another vendor. Because a vendor resides in the same city and state as itself, however, a third comparison is included to exclude rows that match a vendor with itself. To do that, this condition uses the not equal operator to compare the VendorID columns in the two tables.

Notice that the DISTINCT keyword is also included in this SELECT statement. That way, a vendor appears only once in the result set. Otherwise, it would appear once for each row with a matching city and state.

This example also shows how you can use columns other than key columns in a join condition. Keep in mind, however, that this is an unusual situation and you're not likely to code joins like this often.

A self-join that returns vendors from cities in common with other vendors

```
SELECT DISTINCT Vendors1.VendorName, Vendors1.VendorCity,
    Vendors1.VendorState
FROM Vendors AS Vendors1 JOIN Vendors AS Vendors2
    ON (Vendors1.VendorCity = Vendors2.VendorCity) AND
        (Vendors1.VendorState = Vendors2.VendorState) AND
        (Vendors1.VendorID <> Vendors2.VendorID)
ORDER BY Vendors1.VendorState, Vendors1.VendorCity;
```

The result set

	VendorName	VendorCity	VendorState
1	AT&T	Phoenix	AZ
2	Computer Library	Phoenix	AZ
3	Wells Fargo Bank	Phoenix	AZ
4	Aztek Label	Anaheim	CA
5	Blue Shield of California	Anaheim	CA
6	Abbey Office Furnishings	Fresno	CA
7	ASC Signs	Fresno	CA
8	BFI Industries	Fresno	CA

(84 rows)

Description

- A *self-join* is a join that joins a table with itself.

- When you code a self-join, you must use correlation names for the tables, and you must qualify each column name with the correlation name.

- Self-joins frequently include the DISTINCT keyword to eliminate duplicate rows.

Figure 4-5   How to use a self-join

Inner joins that join more than two tables

So far in this chapter, you've seen how to join data from two tables. However, SQL Server lets you join data from up to 256 tables. Of course, it's not likely that you'll ever need to join data from more than a few tables. In addition, each join requires additional system resources, so you should limit the number of joined tables whenever possible.

The SELECT statement in figure 4-6 joins data from four tables: Vendors, Invoices, InvoiceLineItems, and GLAccounts. Each of the joins is based on the relationship between the primary key of one table and a foreign key of the other table. For example, the AccountNo column is the primary key of the GLAccounts table and a foreign key of the InvoiceLineItems table.

Below the SELECT statement, you can see three tables. The first one presents the result of the join between the Vendors and Invoices tables. This table can be referred to as an *interim table* because it contains interim results. Similarly, the second table shows the result of the join between the first interim table and the InvoiceLineItems table. And the third table shows the result of the join between the second interim table and the GLAccounts table after the ORDER BY sequence is applied.

As you review the three tables in this figure, keep in mind that SQL Server may not actually process the joins as illustrated here. However, the idea of interim tables should help you understand how multi-table joins work.

A SELECT statement that joins four tables

```
SELECT VendorName, InvoiceNumber, InvoiceDate,
    InvoiceLineItemAmount AS LineItemAmount, AccountDescription
FROM Vendors
    JOIN Invoices ON Vendors.VendorID = Invoices.VendorID
    JOIN InvoiceLineItems
        ON Invoices.InvoiceID = InvoiceLineItems.InvoiceID
    JOIN GLAccounts ON InvoiceLineItems.AccountNo = GLAccounts.AccountNo
WHERE InvoiceTotal - PaymentTotal - CreditTotal > 0
ORDER BY VendorName, LineItemAmount DESC;
```

The first interim table

	VendorName	InvoiceNumber	InvoiceDate
1	Blue Cross	547480102	2016-04-01 00:00:00
2	Cardinal Business Media, Inc.	134116	2016-03-28 00:00:00
3	Data Reproductions Corp	39104	2016-03-10 00:00:00
4	Federal Express Corporation	963253264	2016-03-18 00:00:00
5	Federal Express Corporation	263253268	2016-03-21 00:00:00
6	Federal Express Corporation	263253270	2016-03-22 00:00:00
7	Federal Express Corporation	263253273	2016-03-22 00:00:00

(11 rows)

The second interim table

	VendorName	InvoiceNumber	InvoiceDate	LineItemAmount
1	Blue Cross	547480102	2016-04-01 00:00:00	224.00
2	Cardinal Business Media, Inc.	134116	2016-03-28 00:00:00	90.36
3	Data Reproductions Corp	39104	2016-03-10 00:00:00	85.31
4	Federal Express Corporation	263253270	2016-03-22 00:00:00	67.92
5	Federal Express Corporation	263253268	2016-03-21 00:00:00	59.97
6	Federal Express Corporation	963253264	2016-03-18 00:00:00	52.25
7	Federal Express Corporation	263253273	2016-03-22 00:00:00	30.75

(11 rows)

The final result set

	VendorName	InvoiceNumber	InvoiceDate	LineItemAmount	AccountDescription
1	Blue Cross	547480102	2016-04-01 00:00:00	224.00	Group Insurance
2	Cardinal Business Media, Inc.	134116	2016-03-28 00:00:00	90.36	Direct Mail Advertising
3	Data Reproductions Corp	39104	2016-03-10 00:00:00	85.31	Book Printing Costs
4	Federal Express Corporation	263253270	2016-03-22 00:00:00	67.92	Freight
5	Federal Express Corporation	263253268	2016-03-21 00:00:00	59.97	Freight
6	Federal Express Corporation	963253264	2016-03-18 00:00:00	52.25	Freight
7	Federal Express Corporation	263253273	2016-03-22 00:00:00	30.75	Freight

(11 rows)

Description

- You can think of a multi-table join as a series of two-table joins proceeding from left to right. The first two tables are joined to produce an *interim result set* or *interim table*. Then, the interim table is joined with the next table, and so on.

Figure 4-6 Inner joins that join more than two tables

How to use the implicit inner join syntax

Earlier in this chapter, I mentioned that SQL Server provides an *implicit syntax* for joining tables. This syntax was used prior to the SQL-92 standards. Although I recommend you use the explicit syntax, you should be familiar with the implicit syntax in case you ever need to maintain SQL statements that use it.

Figure 4-7 presents the implicit syntax for an inner join along with two statements that use it. As you can see, the tables to be joined are simply listed in the FROM clause. Then, the join conditions are included in the WHERE clause.

The first SELECT statement, for example, joins data from the Vendors and Invoices table. Like the SELECT statement you saw back in figure 4-1, these tables are joined based on an equal comparison between the VendorID columns in the two tables. In this case, though, the comparison is coded as the search condition of the WHERE clause. If you compare the result set shown in this figure with the one in figure 4-1, you'll see that they're identical.

The second SELECT statement uses the implicit syntax to join data from four tables. This is the same join you saw in figure 4-6. Notice in this example that the three join conditions are combined in the WHERE clause using the AND operator. In addition, an AND operator is used to combine the join conditions with the search condition.

Because the explicit syntax for joins lets you separate join conditions from search conditions, statements that use the explicit syntax are typically easier to read than those that use the implicit syntax. In addition, the explicit syntax helps you avoid a common coding mistake with the implicit syntax: omitting the join condition. As you'll learn later in this chapter, an implicit join without a join condition results in a cross join, which can return a large number of rows. For these reasons, I recommend you use the explicit syntax in all your new SQL code.

The implicit syntax for an inner join

```
SELECT select_list
FROM table_1, table_2 [, table_3]...
WHERE table_1.column_name operator table_2.column_name
    [AND table_2.column_name operator table_3.column_name]...
```

A SELECT statement that joins the Vendors and Invoices tables

```
SELECT InvoiceNumber, VendorName
FROM Vendors, Invoices
WHERE Vendors.VendorID = Invoices.VendorID;
```

The result set

	InvoiceNumber	VendorName
1	QP58872	IBM
2	Q545443	IBM
3	547481328	Blue Cross
4	547479217	Blue Cross
5	547480102	Blue Cross
6	P02-88D77S7	Fresno County Tax Collector
7	40318	Data Reproductions Corp

A statement that joins four tables

```
SELECT VendorName, InvoiceNumber, InvoiceDate,
    InvoiceLineItemAmount AS LineItemAmount, AccountDescription
FROM Vendors, Invoices, InvoiceLineItems, GLAccounts
WHERE Vendors.VendorID = Invoices.VendorID
  AND Invoices.InvoiceID = InvoiceLineItems.InvoiceID
  AND InvoiceLineItems.AccountNo = GLAccounts.AccountNo
  AND InvoiceTotal - PaymentTotal - CreditTotal > 0
ORDER BY VendorName, LineItemAmount DESC;
```

The result set

	VendorName	InvoiceNumber	InvoiceDate	LineItemAmount	AccountDescription
1	Blue Cross	547480102	2016-04-01 00:00:00	224.00	Group Insurance
2	Cardinal Business Media, Inc.	134116	2016-03-28 00:00:00	90.36	Direct Mail Advertising
3	Data Reproductions Corp	39104	2016-03-10 00:00:00	85.31	Book Printing Costs
4	Federal Express Corporation	263253270	2016-03-22 00:00:00	67.92	Freight
5	Federal Express Corporation	263253268	2016-03-21 00:00:00	59.97	Freight
6	Federal Express Corporation	963253264	2016-03-18 00:00:00	52.25	Freight
7	Federal Express Corporation	263253273	2016-03-22 00:00:00	30.75	Freight

Description

- Instead of coding a join condition in the FROM clause, you can code it in the WHERE clause along with any search conditions. Then, you simply list the tables you want to join in the FROM clause separated by commas.

- This syntax for coding joins is referred to as the *implicit syntax*, or the *theta syntax*. It was used prior to the SQL-92 standards, which introduced the explicit syntax.

- If you omit the join condition from the WHERE clause, a cross join is performed. You'll learn about cross joins later in this chapter.

Figure 4-7   How to use the implicit inner join syntax

How to work with outer joins

Although inner joins are the type of join you'll use most often, SQL Server also supports *outer joins*. Unlike an inner join, an outer join returns all of the rows from one or both tables involved in the join, regardless of whether the join condition is true. You'll see how this works in the topics that follow.

How to code an outer join

Figure 4-8 presents the explicit syntax for coding an outer join. Because this syntax is similar to the explicit syntax for inner joins, you shouldn't have any trouble understanding how it works. The main difference is that you include the LEFT, RIGHT, or FULL keyword to specify the type of outer join you want to perform. As you can see in the syntax, you can also include the OUTER keyword, but it's optional and is usually omitted.

The table in this figure summarizes the differences between left, right, and full outer joins. When you use a *left outer join*, the result set includes all the rows from the first, or left, table. Similarly, when you use a *right outer join*, the result set includes all the rows from the second, or right, table. And when you use a *full outer join*, the result set includes all the rows from both tables.

The example in this figure illustrates a left outer join. Here, the Vendors table is joined with the Invoices table. Notice that the result set includes vendor rows even if no matching invoices are found. In that case, null values are returned for the columns in the Invoices table.

When coding outer joins, it's a common practice to avoid using right joins. To do that, you can substitute a left outer join for a right outer join by reversing the order of the tables in the FROM clause and using the LEFT keyword instead of RIGHT. This often makes it easier to read statements that join more than two tables.

In addition to the explicit syntax for coding outer joins, earlier versions of SQL Server provided for an implicit syntax. This worked much the same as the implicit syntax for coding inner joins. For outer joins, however, you used the *= operator in the WHERE clause to identify a left outer join, and you used the =* operator to identify a right outer join. Although you can't use these operators in SQL Server 2005 and later, you should at least be aware of them in case you come across them in older queries.

The explicit syntax for an outer join

```
SELECT select_list
FROM table_1
    {LEFT|RIGHT|FULL} [OUTER] JOIN table_2
        ON join_condition_1
    [{LEFT|RIGHT|FULL} [OUTER] JOIN table_3
        ON join_condition_2]...
```

What outer joins do

Joins of this type	Keep unmatched rows from
Left outer join	The first (left) table
Right outer join	The second (right) table
Full outer join	Both tables

A SELECT statement that uses a left outer join

```
SELECT VendorName, InvoiceNumber, InvoiceTotal
FROM Vendors LEFT JOIN Invoices
    ON Vendors.VendorID = Invoices.VendorID
ORDER BY VendorName;
```

	VendorName	InvoiceNumber	InvoiceTotal
1	Abbey Office Furnishings	203339-13	17.50
2	American Booksellers Assoc	NULL	NULL
3	American Express	NULL	NULL
4	ASC Signs	NULL	NULL
5	Ascom Hasler Mailing Systems	NULL	NULL
6	AT&T	NULL	NULL

`(202 rows)`

Description

- An *outer join* retrieves all rows that satisfy the join condition, plus unmatched rows in one or both tables.

- In most cases, you use the equal operator to retrieve rows with matching columns. However, you can also use any of the other comparison operators.

- When a row with unmatched columns is retrieved, any columns from the other table that are included in the result set are given null values.

Notes

- The OUTER keyword is optional and typically omitted.

- Prior to SQL Server 2005, you could also use the implicit syntax to code left outer and right outer joins. To do that, you listed the tables to be joined in the FROM clause, and you used the *= (left) and =* (right) operators in the WHERE clause to specify the join condition.

Figure 4-8   How to code an outer join

Outer join examples

To give you a better understanding of how outer joins work, figure 4-9 presents three more examples. These examples use the Departments and Employees tables shown at the top of this figure. In each case, the join condition joins the tables based on the values in their DeptNo columns.

The first SELECT statement performs a left outer join on these two tables. In the result set produced by this statement, you can see that department number 3 is included in the result set even though none of the employees in the Employees table work in that department. Because of that, a null value is assigned to the LastName column from that table.

The second SELECT statement uses a right outer join. In this case, all of the rows from the Employees table are included in the result set. Notice, however, that two of the employees, Watson and Locario, are assigned to a department that doesn't exist in the Departments table. Of course, if the DeptNo column in this table had been defined as a foreign key to the Departments table, this would not have been allowed. In this case, though, a foreign key wasn't defined, so null values are returned for the DeptName column in these two rows.

The third SELECT statement in this figure illustrates a full outer join. If you compare the results of this query with the results of the queries that use a left and right outer join, you'll see that this is a combination of the two joins. In other words, each row in the Departments table is included in the result set, along with each row in the Employees table. Because the DeptNo column from both tables is included in this example, you can clearly identify the row in the Departments table that doesn't have a matching row in the Employees table and the two rows in the Employees table that don't have matching rows in the Departments table.

The Departments table

	DeptName	DeptNo
1	Accounting	1
2	Payroll	2
3	Operations	3
4	Personnel	4
5	Maintenance	5

The Employees table

	EmployeeID	LastName	FirstName	DeptNo
1	1	Smith	Cindy	2
2	2	Jones	Elmer	4
3	3	Simonian	Ralph	2
4	4	Hernandez	Olivia	1
5	5	Aaronsen	Robert	2
6	6	Watson	Denise	6
7	7	Hardy	Thomas	5
8	8	O'Leary	Rhea	4
9	9	Locario	Paulo	6

A left outer join

```
SELECT DeptName, Departments.DeptNo,
    LastName
FROM Departments LEFT JOIN Employees
    ON Departments.DeptNo =
        Employees.DeptNo;
```

	DeptName	DeptNo	LastName
1	Accounting	1	Hernandez
2	Payroll	2	Smith
3	Payroll	2	Simonian
4	Payroll	2	Aaronsen
5	Operations	3	NULL
6	Personnel	4	Jones
7	Personnel	4	O'Leary
8	Maintenance	5	Hardy

A right outer join

```
SELECT DeptName, Employees.DeptNo,
    LastName
FROM Departments RIGHT JOIN Employees
    ON Departments.DeptNo =
        Employees.DeptNo;
```

	DeptName	DeptNo	LastName
1	Payroll	2	Smith
2	Personnel	4	Jones
3	Payroll	2	Simonian
4	Accounting	1	Hernandez
5	Payroll	2	Aaronsen
6	NULL	6	Watson
7	Maintenance	5	Hardy
8	Personnel	4	O'Leary
9	NULL	6	Locario

A full outer join

```
SELECT DeptName, Departments.DeptNo,
    Employees.DeptNo, LastName
FROM Departments FULL JOIN Employees
    ON Departments.DeptNo =
        Employees.DeptNo;
```

	DeptName	DeptNo	DeptNo	LastName
1	Accounting	1	1	Hernandez
2	Payroll	2	2	Smith
3	Payroll	2	2	Simonian
4	Payroll	2	2	Aaronsen
5	Operations	3	NULL	NULL
6	Personnel	4	4	Jones
7	Personnel	4	4	O'Leary
8	Maintenance	5	5	Hardy
9	NULL	NULL	6	Watson
10	NULL	NULL	6	Locario

Description

- From these examples, you can see that none of the employees in the Employees table work in the Operations department, and two of the employees (Watson and Locario) work in a department that doesn't exist in the Departments table.

Figure 4-9   Outer join examples

Outer joins that join more than two tables

Like inner joins, you can use outer joins to join data from more than two tables. The two examples in figure 4-10 illustrate how this works. These examples use the Departments and Employees tables you saw in the previous figure, along with a Projects table. All three of these tables are shown at the top of this figure.

The first example in this figure uses left outer joins to join the data in the three tables. Here, you can see once again that none of the employees in the Employees table are assigned to the Operations department. Because of that, null values are returned for the columns in both the Employees and Projects tables. In addition, you can see that two employees, Hardy and Jones, aren't assigned to a project.

The second example in this figure uses full outer joins to join the three tables. This result set includes unmatched rows from the Departments and Employees table just like the result set you saw in figure 4-9 that was created using a full outer join. In addition, the result set in this example includes an unmatched row from the Projects table: the one for project number P1014. In other words, none of the employees are assigned to this project.

The Departments table

	DeptName	DeptNo
1	Accounting	1
2	Payroll	2
3	Operations	3
4	Personnel	4
5	Maintenance	5

The Employees table

	EmployeeID	LastName	FirstName	DeptNo
1	1	Smith	Cindy	2
2	2	Jones	Elmer	4
3	3	Simonian	Ralph	2
4	4	Hernandez	Olivia	1
5	5	Aaronsen	Robert	2
6	6	Watson	Denise	6
7	7	Hardy	Thomas	5
8	8	O'Leary	Rhea	4
9	9	Locario	Paulo	6

The Projects table

	ProjectNo	EmployeeID
1	P1011	8
2	P1011	4
3	P1012	3
4	P1012	1
5	P1012	5
6	P1013	6
7	P1013	9
8	P1014	10

A SELECT statement that joins the three tables using left outer joins

```
SELECT DeptName, LastName, ProjectNo
FROM Departments
    LEFT JOIN Employees
        ON Departments.DeptNo = Employees.DeptNo
    LEFT JOIN Projects
        ON Employees.EmployeeID = Projects.EmployeeID
ORDER BY DeptName, LastName, ProjectNo;
```

	DeptName	LastName	ProjectNo
1	Accounting	Hernandez	P1011
2	Maintenance	Hardy	NULL
3	Operations	NULL	NULL
4	Payroll	Aaronsen	P1012
5	Payroll	Simonian	P1012
6	Payroll	Smith	P1012
7	Personnel	Jones	NULL
8	Personnel	O'Leary	P1011

A SELECT statement that joins the three tables using full outer joins

```
SELECT DeptName, LastName, ProjectNo
FROM Departments
    FULL JOIN Employees
        ON Departments.DeptNo = Employees.DeptNo
    FULL JOIN Projects
        ON Employees.EmployeeID = Projects.EmployeeID
ORDER BY DeptName;
```

	DeptName	LastName	ProjectNo
1	NULL	Watson	P1013
2	NULL	Locario	P1013
3	NULL	NULL	P1014
4	Accounting	Hernandez	P1011
5	Maintenance	Hardy	NULL
6	Operations	NULL	NULL
7	Payroll	Smith	P1012
8	Payroll	Simonian	P1012
9	Payroll	Aaronsen	P1012
10	Personnel	Jones	NULL
11	Personnel	O'Leary	P1011

Figure 4-10   Outer joins that join more than two tables

Other skills for working with joins

The two topics that follow present two additional skills for working with joins. In the first topic, you'll learn how to use inner and outer joins in the same statement. Then, in the second topic, you'll learn how to use another type of join, called a cross join.

How to combine inner and outer joins

Figure 4-11 shows how you can combine inner and outer joins. In this example, the Departments table is joined with the Employees table using an inner join. The result is an interim table that includes departments with one or more employees. Notice that the EmployeeID column is shown in this table even though it's not included in the final result set. That's because it's used by the join that follows.

After the Departments and Employees tables are joined, the interim table is joined with the Projects table using a left outer join. The result is a table that includes all of the departments that have employees assigned to them, all of the employees assigned to those departments, and the projects those employees are assigned. Here, you can clearly see that two employees, Hardy and Jones, haven't been assigned projects.

The Departments table

	DeptName	DeptNo
1	Accounting	1
2	Payroll	2
3	Operations	3
4	Personnel	4
5	Maintenance	5

The Employees table

	EmployeeID	LastName	FirstName	DeptNo
1	1	Smith	Cindy	2
2	2	Jones	Elmer	4
3	3	Simonian	Ralph	2
4	4	Hernandez	Olivia	1
5	5	Aaronsen	Robert	2
6	6	Watson	Denise	6
7	7	Hardy	Thomas	5
8	8	O'Leary	Rhea	4
9	9	Locario	Paulo	6

The Projects table

	ProjectNo	EmployeeID
1	P1011	8
2	P1011	4
3	P1012	3
4	P1012	1
5	P1012	5
6	P1013	6
7	P1013	9
8	P1014	10

A SELECT statement that combines an outer and an inner join

```
SELECT DeptName, LastName, ProjectNo
FROM Departments
    JOIN Employees
        ON Departments.DeptNo = Employees.DeptNo
    LEFT JOIN Projects
        ON Employees.EmployeeID = Projects.EmployeeID
ORDER BY DeptName;
```

The interim table

	DeptName	LastName	EmployeeID
1	Payroll	Smith	1
2	Personnel	Jones	2
3	Payroll	Simonian	3
4	Accounting	Hernandez	4
5	Payroll	Aaronsen	5
6	Maintenance	Hardy	7
7	Personnel	O'Leary	8

The result set

	DeptName	LastName	ProjectNo
1	Accounting	Hernandez	P1011
2	Maintenance	Hardy	NULL
3	Payroll	Smith	P1012
4	Payroll	Simonian	P1012
5	Payroll	Aaronsen	P1012
6	Personnel	Jones	NULL
7	Personnel	O'Leary	P1011

Description

- You can combine inner and outer joins within a single SELECT statement using the explicit join syntax. You can't combine inner and outer joins using the implicit syntax.

Figure 4-11 How to combine inner and outer joins

How to use cross joins

A *cross join* produces a result set that includes each row from the first table joined with each row from the second table. The result set is known as the *Cartesian product* of the tables. Figure 4-12 shows how to code a cross join using either the explicit or implicit syntax.

To use the explicit syntax, you include the CROSS JOIN keywords between the two tables in the FROM clause. Notice that because of the way a cross join works, you don't include a join condition. The same is true when you use the implicit syntax. In that case, you simply list the tables in the FROM clause and omit the join condition from the WHERE clause.

The two SELECT statements in this figure illustrate how cross joins work. Both of these statements combine data from the Departments and Employees tables. As you can see, the result is a table that includes 45 rows. That's each of the five rows in the Departments table combined with each of the nine rows in the Employees table. Although this result set is relatively small, you can imagine how large it would be if the tables included hundreds or thousands of rows.

As you study these examples, you should realize that cross joins have few practical uses. As a result, you'll rarely, if ever, need to use one.

How to code a cross join using the explicit syntax

The explicit syntax for a cross join
```
SELECT select_list
FROM table_1 CROSS JOIN table_2
```

A cross join that uses the explicit syntax
```
SELECT Departments.DeptNo, DeptName, EmployeeID, LastName
FROM Departments CROSS JOIN Employees
ORDER BY Departments.DeptNo;
```

How to code a cross join using the implicit syntax

The implicit syntax for a cross join
```
SELECT select_list
FROM table_1, table_2
```

A cross join that uses the implicit syntax
```
SELECT Departments.DeptNo, DeptName, EmployeeID, LastName
FROM Departments, Employees
ORDER BY Departments.DeptNo;
```

The result set created by the statements above

	DeptNo	DeptName	EmployeeID	LastName
1	1	Accounting	1	Smith
2	1	Accounting	2	Jones
3	1	Accounting	3	Simonian
4	1	Accounting	4	Hemandez
5	1	Accounting	5	Aaronsen
6	1	Accounting	6	Watson
7	1	Accounting	7	Hardy

(45 rows)

Description

- A *cross join* joins each row from the first table with each row from the second table. The result set returned by a cross join is known as a *Cartesian product*.

- To code a cross join using the explicit syntax, use the CROSS JOIN keywords in the FROM clause.

- To code a cross join using the implicit syntax, list the tables in the FROM clause and omit the join condition from the WHERE clause.

Figure 4-12   How to use cross joins

How to work with unions

Like a join, a *union* combines data from two or more tables. Instead of combining columns from base tables, however, a union combines rows from two or more result sets. You'll see how that works in the topics that follow.

The syntax of a union

Figure 4-13 shows how to code a union. As the syntax shows, you create a union by connecting two or more SELECT statements with the UNION keyword. For this to work, the result of each SELECT statement must have the same number of columns, and the data types of the corresponding columns in each table must be compatible.

In this syntax, I have indented all of the SELECT statements that are connected by the UNION operator to make it easier to see how this statement works. However, in a production environment, it's common to see the SELECT statements and the UNION operator coded at the same level of indentation.

If you want to sort the result of a union operation, you can code an ORDER BY clause after the last SELECT statement. Note that the column names you use in this clause must be the same as those used in the first SELECT statement. That's because the column names you use in the first SELECT statement are the ones that are used in the result set.

By default, a union operation removes duplicate rows from the result set. If that's not what you want, you can include the ALL keyword. In most cases, though, you'll omit this keyword.

Unions that combine data from different tables

The example in this figure shows how to use a union to combine data from two different tables. In this case, the ActiveInvoices table contains invoices with outstanding balances, and the PaidInvoices table contains invoices that have been paid in full. Both of these tables have the same structure as the Invoices table you've seen in previous figures.

This union operation combines the rows in both tables that have an invoice date on or after 2/1/2016. Notice that the first SELECT statement includes a column named Source that contains the literal value "Active." The second SELECT statement includes a column by the same name, but it contains the literal value "Paid." This column is used to indicate which table each row in the result set came from.

Although this column is assigned the same name in both SELECT statements, you should realize that doesn't have to be the case. In fact, none of the columns have to have the same names. Corresponding columns do have to have compatible data types. But the corresponding relationships are determined by the order in which the columns are coded in the SELECT clauses, not by their names. When you use column aliases, though, you'll typically assign the same name to corresponding columns so that the statement is easier to understand.

The syntax for a union operation

```
    SELECT_statement_1
UNION [ALL]
    SELECT_statement_2
[UNION [ALL]
    SELECT_statement_3]...
[ORDER BY order_by_list]
```

A union that combines invoice data from two different tables

```
    SELECT 'Active' AS Source, InvoiceNumber, InvoiceDate, InvoiceTotal
    FROM ActiveInvoices
    WHERE InvoiceDate >= '02/01/2016'
UNION
    SELECT 'Paid' AS Source, InvoiceNumber, InvoiceDate, InvoiceTotal
    FROM PaidInvoices
    WHERE InvoiceDate >= '02/01/2016'
ORDER BY InvoiceTotal DESC;
```

The result set

	Source	InvoiceNumber	InvoiceDate	InvoiceTotal
1	Paid	P-0259	2016-03-19 00:00:00	26881.40
2	Paid	0-2060	2016-03-24 00:00:00	23517.58
3	Paid	40318	2016-02-01 00:00:00	21842.00
4	Active	P-0608	2016-03-23 00:00:00	20551.18
5	Active	0-2436	2016-03-31 00:00:00	10976.06
6	Paid	509786	2016-02-18 00:00:00	6940.25
7	Paid	989319-447	2016-03-24 00:00:00	3689.99
8	Paid	989319-437	2016-02-01 00:00:00	2765.36
9	Paid	367447	2016-02-11 00:00:00	2433.00

```
(72 rows)
```

Description

- A *union* combines the result sets of two or more SELECT statements into one result set.

- Each result set must return the same number of columns, and the corresponding columns in each result set must have compatible data types.

- By default, a union eliminates duplicate rows. If you want to include duplicate rows, code the ALL keyword.

- The column names in the final result set are taken from the first SELECT clause. Column aliases assigned by the other SELECT clauses have no effect on the final result set.

- To sort the rows in the final result set, code an ORDER BY clause after the last SELECT statement. This clause must refer to the column names assigned in the first SELECT clause.

Figure 4-13   How to combine data from different tables

Unions that combine data from the same table

Figure 4-14 shows how to use unions to combine data from a single table. In the first example, rows from the Invoices table that have a balance due are combined with rows from the same table that are paid in full. As in the example in the previous figure, a column named Source is added at the beginning of each interim table. That way, the final result set indicates whether each invoice is active or paid.

The second example in this figure shows how you can use a union with data that's joined from two tables. Here, each SELECT statement joins data from the Invoices and Vendors tables. The first SELECT statement retrieves invoices with totals greater than $10,000. Then, it calculates a payment of 33% of the invoice total. The two other SELECT statements are similar. The second one retrieves invoices with totals between $500 and $10,000 and calculates a 50% payment. And the third one retrieves invoices with totals less than $500 and sets the payment amount at 100% of the total. Although this is somewhat unrealistic, it helps illustrate the flexibility of union operations.

Notice in this example that the same column aliases are assigned in each SELECT statement. Although the aliases in the second and third SELECT statements have no effect on the query, I think they make the query easier to read. In particular, it makes it easy to see that the three SELECT statements have the same number and types of columns.

A union that combines information from the Invoices table

```
SELECT 'Active' AS Source, InvoiceNumber, InvoiceDate, InvoiceTotal
FROM Invoices
WHERE InvoiceTotal - PaymentTotal - CreditTotal > 0
UNION
SELECT 'Paid' AS Source, InvoiceNumber, InvoiceDate, InvoiceTotal
FROM Invoices
WHERE InvoiceTotal - PaymentTotal - CreditTotal <= 0
ORDER BY InvoiceTotal DESC;
```

The result set

	Source	InvoiceNumber	InvoiceDate	InvoiceTotal
1	Paid	0-2058	2016-01-28 00:00:00	37966.19
2	Paid	P-0259	2016-03-19 00:00:00	26881.40
3	Paid	0-2060	2016-03-24 00:00:00	23517.58
4	Paid	40318	2016-02-01 00:00:00	21842.00
5	Active	P-0608	2016-03-23 00:00:00	20551.18

(114 rows)

A union that combines payment data from the same joined tables

```
SELECT InvoiceNumber, VendorName, '33% Payment' AS PaymentType,
    InvoiceTotal AS Total, (InvoiceTotal * 0.333) AS Payment
FROM Invoices JOIN Vendors
    ON Invoices.VendorID = Vendors.VendorID
WHERE InvoiceTotal > 10000
UNION
SELECT InvoiceNumber, VendorName, '50% Payment' AS PaymentType,
    InvoiceTotal AS Total, (InvoiceTotal * 0.5) AS Payment
FROM Invoices JOIN Vendors
    ON Invoices.VendorID = Vendors.VendorID
WHERE InvoiceTotal BETWEEN 500 AND 10000
UNION
SELECT InvoiceNumber, VendorName, 'Full amount' AS PaymentType,
    InvoiceTotal AS Total, InvoiceTotal AS Payment
FROM Invoices JOIN Vendors
    ON Invoices.VendorID = Vendors.VendorID
WHERE InvoiceTotal < 500
ORDER BY PaymentType, VendorName, InvoiceNumber;
```

The result set

	InvoiceNumber	VendorName	PaymentType	Total	Payment
6	P-0608	Malloy Lithographing Inc	33% Payment	20551.18	6843.5429400
7	509786	Bertelsmann Industry S...	50% Payment	6940.25	3470.1250000
8	587056	Cahners Publishing Co...	50% Payment	2184.50	1092.2500000
9	367447	Computerworld	50% Payment	2433.00	1216.5000000

(114 rows)

Figure 4-14   Unions that combine data from the same table

How to use the EXCEPT and INTERSECT operators

The EXCEPT and INTERSECT operators were introduced with SQL Server 2005. Like the UNION operator, the EXCEPT and INTERSECT operators work with two or more result sets as shown in figure 4-15. Because of that, all three of these operators can be referred to as *set operators*. In addition, the EXCEPT and INTERSECT operators follow many of the same rules as the UNION operator.

The first query shown in this figure uses the EXCEPT operator to return the first and last names of all customers in the Customers table except any customers whose first and last names also exist in the Employees table. Since Thomas Hardy is the only name that's the same in both tables, this is the only row that's excluded from the result set for the query that comes before the EXCEPT operator.

The second query shown in this figure uses the INTERSECT operator to return the first and last names of all customers in the Customers table whose first and last names also exist in the Employees table. Since Thomas Hardy is the only name that exists in both tables, this is the only row that's returned for the result set for this query.

When you use the EXCEPT and INTERSECT operators, you must follow many of the same rules that you must follow when working with the UNION operator. To start, both of the statements that are connected by these operators must return the same number of columns. In addition, the data types for these columns must be compatible. Finally, when two queries are joined by an EXCEPT or INTERSECT operator, the column names in the final result set are taken from the first query. That's why the ORDER BY clause uses the CustomerLast column specified by the first query instead of the LastName column specified by the second query. If you understand how the UNION operator works, you shouldn't have any trouble understanding these rules.

Although it's often possible to get the same result sets by using an inner join or a subquery instead of the EXCEPT and INTERSECT operators, these operators are a helpful feature of SQL Server that can make it easier to compare two result sets.

The syntax for the EXCEPT and INTERSECT operations

```
    SELECT_statement_1
{EXCEPT|INTERSECT}
    SELECT_statement_2
[ORDER BY order_by_list]
```

The Customers table

	CustomerFirst	CustomerLast	
1	Maria	Anders	
2	Ana	Trujillo	
3	Antonio	Moreno	
4	Thomas	Hardy	
5	Christina	Berglund	
6	Hanna	Moos	

(24 rows)

The Employees table

	FirstName	LastName	
4	Olivia	Hernandez	
5	Robert	Aaronsen	
6	Denise	Watson	
7	Thomas	Hardy	
8	Rhea	O'Leary	
9	Paulo	Locario	

(9 rows)

A query that excludes rows from the first query if they also occur in the second query

```
    SELECT CustomerFirst, CustomerLast
    FROM Customers
EXCEPT
    SELECT FirstName, LastName
    FROM Employees
ORDER BY CustomerLast;
```

The result set

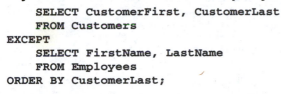

	CustomerFirst	CustomerLast	
4	Donna	Chelan	
5	Fred	Citeaux	
6	Karl	Jablonski	
7	Yoshi	Latimer	

(23 rows)

A query that only includes rows that occur in both queries

```
    SELECT CustomerFirst, CustomerLast
    FROM Customers
INTERSECT
    SELECT FirstName, LastName
    FROM Employees;
```

The result set

	CustomerFirst	CustomerLast
1	Thomas	Hardy

(1 row)

Description

- The number of columns must be the same in both SELECT statements.
- The data types for each column must be compatible.
- The column names in the final result set are taken from the first SELECT statement.

Figure 4-15   How to use the EXCEPT and INTERSECT operators

Perspective

In this chapter, you learned a variety of techniques for combining data from two or more tables into a single result set. In particular, you learned how to use the SQL-92 syntax for combining data using inner joins. Of all the techniques presented in this chapter, this is the one you'll use most often. So you'll want to be sure you understand it thoroughly before you go on.

Terms

join	interim table
join condition	implicit syntax
inner join	theta syntax
ad hoc relationship	outer join
qualified column name	left outer join
explicit syntax	right outer join
correlation name	full outer join
table alias	cross join
fully-qualified object name	Cartesian product
partially-qualified object name	union
self-join	set operator
interim result set	

Exercises

Unless otherwise stated, use the explicit join syntax.

1. Write a SELECT statement that returns all columns from the Vendors table inner-joined with the Invoices table.

2. Write a SELECT statement that returns four columns:

VendorName	From the Vendors table
InvoiceNumber	From the Invoices table
InvoiceDate	From the Invoices table
Balance	InvoiceTotal minus the sum of PaymentTotal and CreditTotal

   The result set should have one row for each invoice with a non-zero balance. Sort the result set by VendorName in ascending order.

3. Write a SELECT statement that returns three columns:

VendorName	From the Vendors table
DefaultAccountNo	From the Vendors table
AccountDescription	From the GLAccounts table

   The result set should have one row for each vendor, with the account number and account description for that vendor's default account number. Sort the result set by AccountDescription, then by VendorName.

4. Generate the same result set described in exercise 2, but use the implicit join syntax.

5. Write a SELECT statement that returns five columns from three tables, all using column aliases:

Vendor	VendorName column
Date	InvoiceDate column
Number	InvoiceNumber column
#	InvoiceSequence column
LineItem	InvoiceLineItemAmount column

    Assign the following correlation names to the tables:

v	Vendors table
i	Invoices table
li	InvoiceLineItems table

    Sort the final result set by Vendor, Date, Number, and #.

6. Write a SELECT statement that returns three columns:

VendorID	From the Vendors table
VendorName	From the Vendors table
Name	A concatenation of VendorContactFName and VendorContactLName, with a space in between

    The result set should have one row for each vendor whose contact has the same first name as another vendor's contact. Sort the final result set by Name.

    Hint: Use a self-join.

7. Write a SELECT statement that returns two columns from the GLAccounts table: AccountNo and AccountDescription. The result set should have one row for each account number that has never been used. Sort the final result set by AccountNo.

    Hint: Use an outer join to the InvoiceLineItems table.

8. Use the UNION operator to generate a result set consisting of two columns from the Vendors table: VendorName and VendorState. If the vendor is in California, the VendorState value should be "CA"; otherwise, the VendorState value should be "Outside CA." Sort the final result set by VendorName.

5

How to code summary queries

In this chapter, you'll learn how to code queries that summarize data. For example, you can use summary queries to report sales totals by vendor or state, or to get a count of the number of invoices that were processed each day of the month. You'll also learn how to use a special type of function called an aggregate function. Aggregate functions allow you to easily do jobs like figure averages or totals, or find the highest value for a given column. So you'll use them frequently in your summary queries.

How to work with aggregate functions

In chapter.3, you were introduced to *scalar functions*, which operate on a single value and return a single value. In this chapter, you'll learn how to use *aggregate functions*, which operate on a series of values and return a single summary value. Because aggregate functions typically operate on the values in columns, they are sometimes referred to as *column functions*. A query that contains one or more aggregate functions is typically referred to as a *summary query*.

How to code aggregate functions

Figure 5-1 presents the syntax of the most common aggregate functions. Since the purpose of these functions is self-explanatory, I'll focus mainly on how you use them.

All of the functions but one operate on an expression. In the query in this figure, for example, the expression that's coded for the SUM function calculates the balance due of an invoice using the InvoiceTotal, PaymentTotal, and CreditTotal columns. The result is a single value that represents the total amount due for all the selected invoices. If you look at the WHERE clause in this example, you'll see that it includes only those invoices with a balance due.

In addition to an expression, you can also code the ALL or DISTINCT keyword in these functions. ALL is the default, which means that all values are included in the calculation. The exceptions are null values, which are always excluded from these functions.

If you don't want duplicate values included, you can code the DISTINCT keyword. In most cases, you'll use DISTINCT only with the COUNT function. You'll see an example of that in the next figure. You won't use it with MIN or MAX because it has no effect on those functions. And it doesn't usually make sense to use it with the AVG and SUM functions.

Unlike the other aggregate functions, you can't use the ALL or DISTINCT keywords or an expression with COUNT(*). Instead, you code this function exactly as shown in the syntax. The value returned by this function is the number of rows in the base table that satisfy the search condition of the query, including rows with null values. The COUNT(*) function in the query in this figure, for example, indicates that the Invoices table contains 11 invoices with a balance due.

The syntax of the aggregate functions

Function syntax	Result
`AVG([ALL|DISTINCT] expression)`	The average of the non-null values in the expression.
`SUM([ALL|DISTINCT] expression)`	The total of the non-null values in the expression.
`MIN([ALL|DISTINCT] expression)`	The lowest non-null value in the expression.
`MAX([ALL|DISTINCT] expression)`	The highest non-null value in the expression.
`COUNT([ALL|DISTINCT] expression)`	The number of non-null values in the expression.
`COUNT(*)`	The number of rows selected by the query.

A summary query that counts unpaid invoices and calculates the total due

```
SELECT COUNT(*) AS NumberOfInvoices,
    SUM(InvoiceTotal - PaymentTotal - CreditTotal) AS TotalDue
FROM Invoices
WHERE InvoiceTotal - PaymentTotal - CreditTotal > 0;
```

The result set

	NumberOfInvoices	TotalDue
1	11	32020.42

Description

- *Aggregate functions*, also called *column functions*, perform a calculation on the values in a set of selected rows. You specify the values to be used in the calculation by coding an expression for the function's argument. In many cases, the expression is just the name of a column.

- A SELECT statement that includes an aggregate function can be called a *summary query*.

- The expression you specify for the AVG and SUM functions must result in a numeric value. The expression for the MIN, MAX, and COUNT functions can result in a numeric, date, or string value.

- By default, all values are included in the calculation regardless of whether they're duplicated. If you want to omit duplicate values, code the DISTINCT keyword. This keyword is typically used only with the COUNT function.

- All of the aggregate functions except for COUNT(*) ignore null values.

- Aggregate functions are often used with the GROUP BY clause of the SELECT statement, which is used to group the rows in a result set. See figure 5-3 for more information.

- If you code an aggregate function in the SELECT clause, that clause can't include non-aggregate columns from the base table unless the column is specified in a GROUP BY clause or the OVER clause is included for each aggregate function. See figure 5-10 for more information on the OVER clause.

Figure 5-1   How to code aggregate functions

Queries that use aggregate functions

Figure 5-2 presents four more queries that use aggregate functions. Before I describe these queries, you should know that with three exceptions, a SELECT clause that contains an aggregate function can contain only aggregate functions. The first exception is if the column specification results in a literal value. This is illustrated by the first column in the first two queries in this figure. The second exception is if the query includes a GROUP BY clause. Then, the SELECT clause can include any columns specified in the GROUP BY clause. The third exception is if the aggregate functions include the OVER clause. Then, the SELECT clause can include any columns from the base tables. You'll see how you use the GROUP BY and OVER clauses later in this chapter.

The first two queries in this figure use the COUNT(*) function to count the number of rows in the Invoices table that satisfy the search condition. In both cases, only those invoices with invoice dates after 9/1/2015 are included in the count. In addition, the first query uses the AVG function to calculate the average amount of those invoices and the SUM function to calculate the total amount of those invoices. In contrast, the second query uses the MIN and MAX functions to calculate the minimum and maximum invoice amounts.

Although the MIN, MAX, and COUNT functions are typically used on columns that contain numeric data, they can also be used on columns that contain character or date data. In the third query, for example, they're used on the VendorName column in the Vendors table. Here, the MIN function returns the name of the vendor that's lowest in the sort sequence, the MAX function returns the name of the vendor that's highest in the sort sequence, and the COUNT function returns the total number of vendors. Note that since the VendorName column can't contain null values, the COUNT(*) function would have returned the same result.

The fourth query illustrates how using the DISTINCT keyword can affect the result of a COUNT function. Here, the first COUNT function uses the DISTINCT keyword to count the number of vendors that have invoices dated 9/1/2015 or later in the Invoices table. To do that, it looks for distinct values in the VendorID column. In contrast, because the second COUNT function doesn't include the DISTINCT keyword, it counts every invoice after 9/1/2015. Of course, you could accomplish the same thing using the COUNT(*) function. I used COUNT(VendorID) here only to illustrate the difference between coding and not coding the DISTINCT keyword.

A summary query that uses the COUNT(*), AVG, and SUM functions

```
SELECT 'After 9/1/2015' AS SelectionDate, COUNT(*) AS NumberOfInvoices,
    AVG(InvoiceTotal) AS AverageInvoiceAmount,
    SUM(InvoiceTotal) AS TotalInvoiceAmount
FROM Invoices
WHERE InvoiceDate > '2015-09-01';
```

	SelectionDate	NumberOfInvoices	AverageInvoiceAmount	TotalInvoiceAmount
1	After 9/1/2015	114	1879.7413	214290.51

A summary query that uses the MIN and MAX functions

```
SELECT 'After 9/1/2015' AS SelectionDate, COUNT(*) AS NumberOfInvoices,
    MAX(InvoiceTotal) AS HighestInvoiceTotal,
    MIN(InvoiceTotal) AS LowestInvoiceTotal
FROM Invoices
WHERE InvoiceDate > '2015-09-01';
```

	SelectionDate	NumberOfInvoices	HighestInvoiceTotal	LowestInvoiceTotal
1	After 9/1/2015	114	37966.19	6.00

A summary query that works on non-numeric columns

```
SELECT MIN(VendorName) AS FirstVendor,
    MAX(VendorName) AS LastVendor,
    COUNT(VendorName) AS NumberOfVendors
FROM Vendors;
```

	FirstVendor	LastVendor	NumberOfVendors
1	Abbey Office Furnishings	Zylka Design	122

A summary query that uses the DISTINCT keyword

```
SELECT COUNT(DISTINCT VendorID) AS NumberOfVendors,
    COUNT(VendorID) AS NumberOfInvoices,
    AVG(InvoiceTotal) AS AverageInvoiceAmount,
    SUM(InvoiceTotal) AS TotalInvoiceAmount
FROM Invoices
WHERE InvoiceDate > '2015-09-01';
```

	NumberOfVendors	NumberOfInvoices	AverageInvoiceAmount	TotalInvoiceAmount
1	34	114	1879.7413	214290.51

Notes

- If you want to count all of the selected rows, you'll typically use the COUNT(*) function as illustrated by the first two examples above. An alternative is to code the name of any column in the base table that can't contain null values, as illustrated by the third example.

- If you want to count only the rows with unique values in a specified column, you can code the COUNT function with the DISTINCT keyword followed by the name of the column, as illustrated in the fourth example.

Figure 5-2   Queries that use aggregate functions

How to group and summarize data

Now that you understand how aggregate functions work, you're ready to learn how to group data and use aggregate functions to summarize the data in each group. To do that, you need to learn about two more clauses of the SELECT statement: GROUP BY and HAVING.

How to code the GROUP BY and HAVING clauses

Figure 5-3 presents the syntax of the SELECT statement with the GROUP BY and HAVING clauses. The GROUP BY clause determines how the selected rows are grouped, and the HAVING clause determines which groups are included in the final results. As you can see, these clauses are coded after the WHERE clause but before the ORDER BY clause. That makes sense because the search condition in the WHERE clause is applied before the rows are grouped, and the sort sequence in the ORDER BY clause is applied after the rows are grouped.

In the GROUP BY clause, you list one or more columns or expressions separated by commas. Then, the rows that satisfy the search condition in the WHERE clause are grouped by those columns or expressions in ascending sequence. That means that a single row is returned for each unique set of values in the GROUP BY columns. This will make more sense when you see the examples in the next figure that group by two columns. For now, take a look at the example in this figure that groups by a single column.

This example calculates the average invoice amount for each vendor who has invoices in the Invoices table that average over $2,000. To do that, it groups the invoices by VendorID. Then, the AVG function calculates the average of the InvoiceTotal column. Because this query includes a GROUP BY clause, this function calculates the average invoice total for each group rather than for the entire result set. In that case, the aggregate function is called a *vector aggregate*. In contrast, aggregate functions like the ones you saw earlier in this chapter that return a single value for all the rows in a result set are called *scalar aggregates*.

The example in this figure also includes a HAVING clause. The search condition in this clause specifies that only those vendors with invoices that average over $2,000 should be included. Note that this condition must be applied after the rows are grouped and the average for each group has been calculated.

In addition to the AVG function, the SELECT clause includes the VendorID column. That makes sense since the rows are grouped by this column. However, the columns used in the GROUP BY clause don't have to be included in the SELECT clause.

The syntax of the SELECT statement
with the GROUP BY and HAVING clauses

```
SELECT select_list
FROM table_source
[WHERE search_condition]
[GROUP BY group_by_list]
[HAVING search_condition]
[ORDER BY order_by_list]
```

A summary query that calculates the average invoice amount by vendor

```
SELECT VendorID, AVG(InvoiceTotal) AS AverageInvoiceAmount
FROM Invoices
GROUP BY VendorID
HAVING AVG(InvoiceTotal) > 2000
ORDER BY AverageInvoiceAmount DESC;
```

	VendorID	AverageInvoiceAmount
1	110	23978.482
2	72	10963.655
3	104	7125.34
4	99	6940.25
5	119	4901.26
6	122	2575.3288
7	86	2433.00
8	100	2184.50

Description

- The GROUP BY clause groups the rows of a result set based on one or more columns or expressions. It's typically used in SELECT statements that include aggregate functions.

- If you include aggregate functions in the SELECT clause, the aggregate is calculated for each set of values that result from the columns named in the GROUP BY clause.

- If you include two or more columns or expressions in the GROUP BY clause, they form a hierarchy where each column or expression is subordinate to the previous one.

- When a SELECT statement includes a GROUP BY clause, the SELECT clause can include aggregate functions, the columns used for grouping, and expressions that result in a constant value.

- A group-by list typically consists of the names of one or more columns separated by commas. However, it can contain any expression except for those that contain aggregate functions.

- The HAVING clause specifies a search condition for a group or an aggregate. This condition is applied after the rows that satisfy the search condition in the WHERE clause are grouped.

Figure 5-3   How to code the GROUP BY and HAVING clauses

Queries that use the GROUP BY and HAVING clauses

Figure 5-4 presents three more queries that group data. If you understood the query in the last figure, you shouldn't have any trouble understanding how the first query in this figure works. It groups the rows in the Invoices table by VendorID and returns a count of the number of invoices for each vendor.

The second query in this figure illustrates how you can group by more than one column. Here, a join is used to combine the VendorState and VendorCity columns from the Vendors table with a count and average of the invoices in the Invoices table. Because the rows are grouped by both state and city, a row is returned for each state and city combination. Then, the ORDER BY clause sorts the rows by city within state. Without this clause, the rows would be returned in no particular sequence.

The third query is identical to the second query except that it includes a HAVING clause. This clause uses the COUNT function to limit the state and city groups that are included in the result set to those that have two or more invoices. In other words, it excludes groups that have only one invoice.

A summary query that counts the number of invoices by vendor

```
SELECT VendorID, COUNT(*) AS InvoiceQty
FROM Invoices
GROUP BY VendorID;
```

	VendorID	InvoiceQty
1	34	2
2	37	3
3	48	1
4	72	2
5	80	2

(34 rows)

A summary query that calculates the number of invoices and the average invoice amount for the vendors in each state and city

```
SELECT VendorState, VendorCity, COUNT(*) AS InvoiceQty,
    AVG(InvoiceTotal) AS InvoiceAvg
FROM Invoices JOIN Vendors
    ON Invoices.VendorID = Vendors.VendorID
GROUP BY VendorState, VendorCity
ORDER BY VendorState, VendorCity;
```

	VendorState	VendorCity	InvoiceQty	InvoiceAvg
1	AZ	Phoenix	1	662.00
2	CA	Fresno	19	1208.7457
3	CA	Los Angeles	1	503.20
4	CA	Oxnard	3	188.00
5	CA	Pasadena	5	196.12

(20 rows)

A summary query that limits the groups to those with two or more invoices

```
SELECT VendorState, VendorCity, COUNT(*) AS InvoiceQty,
    AVG(InvoiceTotal) AS InvoiceAvg
FROM Invoices JOIN Vendors
    ON Invoices.VendorID = Vendors.VendorID
GROUP BY VendorState, VendorCity
HAVING COUNT(*) >= 2
ORDER BY VendorState, VendorCity;
```

	VendorState	VendorCity	InvoiceQty	InvoiceAvg
1	CA	Fresno	19	1208.7457
2	CA	Oxnard	3	188.00
3	CA	Pasadena	5	196.12
4	CA	Sacramento	7	253.0014
5	CA	San Francisco	3	1211.04

(12 rows)

Note

- You can use a join with a summary query to group and summarize the data in two or more tables.

Figure 5-4   Queries that use the GROUP BY and HAVING clauses

How the HAVING clause compares to the WHERE clause

As you've seen, you can limit the groups included in a result set by coding a search condition in the HAVING clause. In addition, you can apply a search condition to each row before it's included in a group. To do that, you code the search condition in the WHERE clause just as you would for any SELECT statement. To make sure you understand the differences between search conditions coded in the HAVING and WHERE clauses, figure 5-5 presents two examples.

In the first example, the invoices in the Invoices table are grouped by vendor name, and a count and average invoice amount are calculated for each group. Then, the HAVING clause limits the groups in the result set to those that have an average invoice total greater than $500.

In contrast, the second example includes a search condition in the WHERE clause that limits the invoices included in the groups to those that have an invoice total greater than $500. In other words, the search condition in this example is applied to every row. In the previous example, it was applied to each group of rows.

Beyond this, there are also two differences in the expressions that you can include in the WHERE and HAVING clauses. First, the HAVING clause can include aggregate functions as you saw in the first example in this figure, but the WHERE clause can't. That's because the search condition in a WHERE clause is applied before the rows are grouped. Second, although the WHERE clause can refer to any column in the base tables, the HAVING clause can only refer to columns included in the SELECT or GROUP BY clause. That's because it filters the summarized result set that's defined by the SELECT, FROM, WHERE, and GROUP BY clauses. In other words, it doesn't filter the base tables.

A summary query with a search condition in the HAVING clause

```
SELECT VendorName, COUNT(*) AS InvoiceQty,
    AVG(InvoiceTotal) AS InvoiceAvg
FROM Vendors JOIN Invoices
    ON Vendors.VendorID = Invoices.VendorID
GROUP BY VendorName
HAVING AVG(InvoiceTotal) > 500
ORDER BY InvoiceQty DESC;
```

	VendorName	InvoiceQty	InvoiceAvg
1	United Parcel Service	9	2575.3288
2	Zylka Design	8	867.5312
3	Malloy Lithographing Inc	5	23978.482
4	Data Reproductions Corp	2	10963.655
5	IBM	2	600.06

(19 rows)

A summary query with a search condition in the WHERE clause

```
SELECT VendorName, COUNT(*) AS InvoiceQty,
    AVG(InvoiceTotal) AS InvoiceAvg
FROM Vendors JOIN Invoices
    ON Vendors.VendorID = Invoices.VendorID
WHERE InvoiceTotal > 500
GROUP BY VendorName
ORDER BY InvoiceQty DESC;
```

	VendorName	InvoiceQty	InvoiceAvg
1	United Parcel Service	9	2575.3288
2	Zylka Design	7	946.6714
3	Malloy Lithographing Inc	5	23978.482
4	Ingram	2	1077.21
5	Pollstar	1	1750.00

(20 rows)

Description

- When you include a WHERE clause in a SELECT statement that uses grouping and aggregates, the search condition is applied before the rows are grouped and the aggregates are calculated. That way, only the rows that satisfy the search condition are grouped and summarized.

- When you include a HAVING clause in a SELECT statement that uses grouping and aggregates, the search condition is applied after the rows are grouped and the aggregates are calculated. That way, only the groups that satisfy the search condition are included in the result set.

- A HAVING clause can only refer to a column included in the SELECT or GROUP BY clause. A WHERE clause can refer to any column in the base tables.

- Aggregate functions can only be coded in the HAVING clause. A WHERE clause can't contain aggregate functions.

Figure 5-5   How the HAVING clause compares to the WHERE clause

How to code complex search conditions

You can code compound search conditions in a HAVING clause just as you can in a WHERE clause. This is illustrated by the first query in figure 5-6. This query groups invoices by invoice date and calculates a count of the invoices and the sum of the invoice totals for each date. In addition, the HAVING clause specifies three conditions. First, the invoice date must be between 1/1/2016 and 1/31/2016. Second, the invoice count must be greater than 1. And third, the sum of the invoice totals must be greater than $100.

Because the second and third conditions in the HAVING clause in this query include aggregate functions, they must be coded in the HAVING clause. The first condition, however, doesn't include an aggregate function, so it could be coded in either the HAVING or WHERE clause. The second statement in this figure, for example, shows this condition coded in the WHERE clause. Note that the query returns the same result set regardless of where you code this condition.

So how do you know where to code a search condition? In general, I think your code will be easier to read if you include all the search conditions in the HAVING clause. If, on the other hand, you prefer to code non-aggregate search conditions in the WHERE clause, that's OK, too.

Since a search condition in the WHERE clause is applied before the rows are grouped while a search condition in the HAVING clause isn't applied until after the grouping, you might expect a performance advantage by coding all search conditions in the HAVING clause. However, SQL Server takes care of this performance issue for you when it optimizes the query. To do that, it automatically moves search conditions to whichever clause will result in the best performance, as long as that doesn't change the logic of your query. As a result, you can code search conditions wherever they result in the most readable code without worrying about system performance.

A summary query with a compound condition in the HAVING clause

```
SELECT InvoiceDate, COUNT(*) AS InvoiceQty, SUM(InvoiceTotal) AS InvoiceSum
FROM Invoices
GROUP BY InvoiceDate
HAVING InvoiceDate BETWEEN '2016-01-01' AND '2016-01-31'
    AND COUNT(*) > 1
    AND SUM(InvoiceTotal) > 100
ORDER BY InvoiceDate DESC;
```

The same query coded with a WHERE clause

```
SELECT InvoiceDate, COUNT(*) AS InvoiceQty, SUM(InvoiceTotal) AS InvoiceSum
FROM Invoices
WHERE InvoiceDate BETWEEN '2016-01-01' AND '2016-01-31'
GROUP BY InvoiceDate
HAVING COUNT(*) > 1
    AND SUM(InvoiceTotal) > 100
ORDER BY InvoiceDate DESC;
```

The result set returned by both queries

	InvoiceDate	InvoiceQty	InvoiceSum
1	2016-01-31 00:00:00	2	453.75
2	2016-01-25 00:00:00	3	2201.15
3	2016-01-23 00:00:00	2	347.75
4	2016-01-21 00:00:00	2	8078.44
5	2016-01-13 00:00:00	3	1888.95
6	2016-01-11 00:00:00	2	5009.51
7	2016-01-03 00:00:00	2	866.87

Description

- You can use the AND and OR operators to code compound search conditions in a HAVING clause just as you can in a WHERE clause.

- If a search condition includes an aggregate function, it must be coded in the HAVING clause. Otherwise, it can be coded in either the HAVING or the WHERE clause.

- In most cases, your code will be easier to read if you code all the search conditions in the HAVING clause, but you can code non-aggregate search conditions in the WHERE clause if you prefer.

Figure 5-6   How to code complex search conditions

How to summarize data using SQL Server extensions

So far, this chapter has discussed standard SQL keywords and functions. However, you should also know about four extensions SQL Server provides for summarizing data: the ROLLUP, CUBE, and GROUPING SETS operators and the OVER clause.

How to use the ROLLUP operator

You can use the ROLLUP operator to add one or more summary rows to a result set that uses grouping and aggregates. The two examples in figure 5-7 illustrate how this works.

The first example shows how the ROLLUP operator works when you group by a single column. Here, the invoices in the Invoices table are grouped by VendorID, and an invoice count and invoice total are calculated for each vendor. Notice that because the WITH ROLLUP phrase is included in the GROUP BY clause, an additional row is added at the end of the result set. This row summarizes all the aggregate columns in the result set. In this case, it summarizes the InvoiceCount and InvoiceTotal columns. Because the VendorID column can't be summarized, it's assigned a null value.

The second query in this figure shows how the ROLLUP operator works when you group by two columns. This query groups the vendors in the Vendors table by state and city and counts the number of vendors in each group. Notice that in addition to a summary row at the end of the result set, summary rows are included for each state.

You should also notice the ORDER BY clause in this query. It causes the rows in the result set to be sorted by city in descending sequence within state in descending sequence. The reason these columns are sorted in descending sequence is that the sort is performed after the summary rows are added to the result set, and those rows have null values in the VendorCity column. In addition, the final summary row has a null value in the VendorState column. So if you sorted these columns in ascending sequence, the rows with null values would appear before the rows they summarize, which isn't what you want.

You can also use another function, the GROUPING function, to work with null columns in a summary row. However, this function is typically used in conjunction with the CASE function, which you'll learn about in chapter 9. So I'll present the GROUPING function in that chapter.

SQL Server 2008 introduced an alternate syntax that you can use for working with the ROLLUP operator, and it's shown below both of the examples. To use this syntax, you code the ROLLUP operator immediately after the GROUP BY keywords. Then, you code the columns within a set of parentheses. The advantage of this syntax is that it's more consistent with other SQL Server extensions. The disadvantage is that this syntax is not supported by earlier versions of SQL Server such as SQL Server 2005.

A summary query that includes a final summary row

```
SELECT VendorID, COUNT(*) AS InvoiceCount,
    SUM(InvoiceTotal) AS InvoiceTotal
FROM Invoices
GROUP BY VendorID WITH ROLLUP;
```

	VendorID	InvoiceCount	InvoiceTotal	
30	117	1	16.62	
31	119	1	4901.26	
32	121	8	6940.25	
33	122	9	23177.96	
34	123	47	4378.02	
35	NULL	114	214290.51	——— **Summary row**

Another way to code the GROUP BY clause (SQL Server 2008 or later)

```
GROUP BY ROLLUP(VendorID)
```

A summary query that includes a summary row for each grouping level

```
SELECT VendorState, VendorCity, COUNT(*) AS QtyVendors
FROM Vendors
WHERE VendorState IN ('IA', 'NJ')
GROUP BY VendorState, VendorCity WITH ROLLUP
ORDER BY VendorState DESC, VendorCity DESC;
```

	VendorState	VendorCity	QtyVendors	
1	NJ	Washington	1	
2	NJ	Fairfield	1	
3	NJ	East Brunswick	2	
4	NJ	NULL	4	——— **Summary row for state 'NJ'**
5	IA	Washington	1	
6	IA	Fairfield	1	
7	IA	NULL	2	——— **Summary row for state 'IA'**
8	NULL	NULL	6	——— **Summary row for all rows**

Another way to code the GROUP BY clause (SQL Server 2008 or later)

```
GROUP BY ROLLUP(VendorState, VendorCity)
```

Description

- The ROLLUP operator adds a summary row for each group specified. It also adds a summary row to the end of the result set that summarizes the entire result set. If the GROUP BY clause specifies a single group, only the final summary row is added.

- The sort sequence in the ORDER BY clause is applied after the summary rows are added. Because of that, you'll want to sort grouping columns in descending sequence so that the summary row for each group, which can contain null values, appears after the other rows in the group.

- When you use the ROLLUP operator, you can't use the DISTINCT keyword in any of the aggregate functions.

- You can use the GROUPING function with the ROLLUP operator to determine if a summary row has a null value assigned to a given column. See chapter 9 for details.

Figure 5-7   How to use the ROLLUP operator

How to use the CUBE operator

Figure 5-8 shows you how to use the CUBE operator. This operator is similar to the ROLLUP operator, except that it adds summary rows for every combination of groups. This is illustrated by the two examples in this figure. As you can see, these examples are the same as the ones in figure 5-7 except that they use the CUBE operator instead of the ROLLUP operator.

In the first example, the result set is grouped by a single column. In this case, a single summary row is added at the end of the result set that summarizes all the groups. In other words, this works the same as it does with the ROLLUP operator.

In the second example, however, you can see how CUBE differs from ROLLUP when you group by two or more columns. In this case, the result set includes a summary row for each state just as it did when the ROLLUP operator was used. In addition, it includes a summary row for each city. The eighth row in this figure, for example, indicates that there are two vendors in cities named Washington. If you look at the first and fifth rows in the result set, you'll see that one of those vendors is in Washington, New Jersey and one is in Washington, Iowa. The same is true of the city named Fairfield. There are also two vendors in the city of East Brunswick, but both are in New Jersey.

As with the ROLLUP operator, SQL Server 2008 introduced an alternate syntax that you can use for working with the CUBE operator. This syntax is shown below both of the examples. If you understand how this syntax works for the ROLLUP operator, you shouldn't have much trouble understanding how it works for the CUBE operator. Although this syntax won't work for versions of SQL Server prior to 2008, you can use it for new development.

Now that you've seen how the CUBE operator works, you may be wondering when you would use it. The fact is, you probably won't use it except to add a summary row to a result set that's grouped by a single column. And in that case, you could just as easily use the ROLLUP operator. In some unique cases, however, the CUBE operator can provide useful information that you can't get any other way.

A summary query that includes a final summary row

```
SELECT VendorID, COUNT(*) AS InvoiceCount,
    SUM(InvoiceTotal) AS InvoiceTotal
FROM Invoices
GROUP BY VendorID WITH CUBE;
```

	VendorID	InvoiceCount	InvoiceTotal	
30	117	1	16.62	
31	119	1	4901.26	
32	121	8	6940.25	
33	122	9	23177.96	
34	123	47	4378.02	
35	NULL	114	214290.51	Summary row

Another way to code the GROUP BY clause (SQL Server 2008 or later)

```
GROUP BY CUBE(VendorID)
```

A summary query that includes a summary row for each set of groups

```
SELECT VendorState, VendorCity, COUNT(*) AS QtyVendors
FROM Vendors
WHERE VendorState IN ('IA', 'NJ')
GROUP BY VendorState, VendorCity WITH CUBE
ORDER BY VendorState DESC, VendorCity DESC;
```

	VendorState	VendorCity	QtyVendors	
1	NJ	Washington	1	
2	NJ	Fairfield	1	
3	NJ	East Brunswick	2	
4	NJ	NULL	4	Summary row for state 'NJ'
5	IA	Washington	1	
6	IA	Fairfield	1	
7	IA	NULL	2	Summary row for state 'IA'
8	NULL	Washington	2	Summary row for city 'Washington'
9	NULL	Fairfield	2	Summary row for city 'Fairfield'
10	NULL	East Brunswick	2	Summary row for city 'East Brunswick'
11	NULL	NULL	6	Summary row for all rows

Another way to code the GROUP BY clause (SQL Server 2008 or later)

```
GROUP BY CUBE(VendorState, VendorCity)
```

Description

- The CUBE operator adds a summary row for every combination of groups specified. It also adds a summary row to the end of the result set that summarizes the entire result set.

- When you use the CUBE operator, you can't use the DISTINCT keyword in any of the aggregate functions.

- You can use the GROUPING function with the CUBE operator to determine if a summary row has a null value assigned to a given column. See chapter 9 for details.

Figure 5-8   How to use the CUBE operator

How to use the GROUPING SETS operator

Figure 5-9 shows you how to use the GROUPING SETS operator that was introduced with SQL Server 2008. This operator is similar to the ROLLUP and CUBE operators. However, the GROUPING SETS operator only includes summary rows, it only adds those summary rows for each specified group, and it uses a syntax that's similar to the 2008 syntax for the ROLLUP and CUBE operators.

The first example in this figure is similar to the second example that's presented in the previous two figures. However, this example uses the GROUPING SETS operator instead of the CUBE or ROLLUP operator. Here, the result set only includes summary rows for the two grouping elements: state and city. To start, it displays the summary rows for the states. Then, it displays the summary rows for the cities.

The second example in this figure shows some additional features that are available when you use the GROUPING SETS operator. To start, within the parentheses after the GROUPING SETS operator, you can add additional sets of parentheses to create composite groups that consist of multiple columns. In addition, you can add an empty set of parentheses to add a group for a summary row that summarizes the entire result set. In this example, the first group is the vendor's state and city, the second group is the vendor's zip code, and the third group is an empty set of parentheses that adds a summary row for the entire result set.

When you use composite groups, you should know that you can add additional summary rows by applying the ROLLUP and CUBE operators to a composite group. To do that, you code the ROLLUP or CUBE operator before the composite group. In this figure, for instance, the third example shows a GROUPING SETS clause that applies the ROLLUP operator to the composite state/city group. This adds a summary row for each state, and it adds a summary row that for the entire result set, much like the second example in figure 5-7. Although this may seem confusing at first, with a little experimentation, you should be able to get the result set you want.

A summary query with two groups

```
SELECT VendorState, VendorCity, COUNT(*) AS QtyVendors
FROM Vendors
WHERE VendorState IN ('IA', 'NJ')
GROUP BY GROUPING SETS(VendorState, VendorCity)
ORDER BY VendorState DESC, VendorCity DESC;
```

	VendorState	VendorCity	QtyVendors
1	NJ	NULL	4
2	IA	NULL	2
3	NULL	Washington	2
4	NULL	Fairfield	2
5	NULL	East Brunswick	2

A summary query with a composite grouping

```
SELECT VendorState, VendorCity, VendorZipCode,
       COUNT(*) AS QtyVendors
FROM Vendors
WHERE VendorState IN ('IA', 'NJ')
GROUP BY GROUPING SETS((VendorState, VendorCity), VendorZipCode, ())
ORDER BY VendorState DESC, VendorCity DESC;
```

	VendorState	VendorCity	VendorZipCode	QtyVendors
1	NJ	Washington	NULL	1
2	NJ	Fairfield	NULL	1
3	NJ	East Brunswick	NULL	2
4	IA	Washington	NULL	1
5	IA	Fairfield	NULL	1
6	NULL	NULL	07004	1
7	NULL	NULL	07882	1
8	NULL	NULL	08810	1
9	NULL	NULL	08816	1
10	NULL	NULL	52353	1
11	NULL	NULL	52556	1
12	NULL	NULL	NULL	6

A summary query with a group that uses the ROLLUP operator

```
GROUP BY GROUPING SETS(ROLLUP(VendorState, VendorCity), VendorZipCode)
```

Description

- The GROUPING SETS operator creates a summary row for each specified group.
- Within the parentheses after the GROUPING SETS operator, you can add additional sets of parentheses to create composite groups.
- Within the parentheses after the GROUPING SETS operator, you can add an empty set of parentheses to add a summary row that summarizes the entire result set.
- For a composite group, you can add the ROLLUP or CUBE operator to add additional summary rows. This performs the ROLLUP or CUBE operation on the composite group, which also adds a summary row that summarizes the entire result set.

Figure 5-9   How to use the GROUPING SETS operator

How to use the OVER clause

So far in this chapter, you've learned how to code summary queries that return just the summarized data. But what if you want to return the individual rows that are used to calculate the summaries along with the summary data? To do that, you can use the OVER clause as shown in figure 5-10.

In the syntax at the top of this figure, you can see that you code the OVER clause after the aggregate function, followed by a set of parentheses. Within the parentheses, you can code a PARTITION BY clause, an ORDER BY clause, or both of these clauses. This is illustrated by the three examples in this figure.

The first example calculates the total, count, and average of the invoices in the Invoices table. Here, I used the PARTITION BY clause to indicate that the invoices should be grouped by invoice date. If you look at the results of this query, you'll see that the Invoices table contains a single invoice for the first three dates. Because of that, the total, count, and average columns for those dates are calculated based on a single invoice. In contrast, the next three invoices are for the same date. In this case, the total, count, and average columns are calculated based on all three invoices.

The second example is similar, but it uses the ORDER BY clause instead of the PARTITION BY clause. Because of that, the calculations aren't grouped by the invoice date like they are in the first example. Instead, the summaries accumulate from one date to the next. For example, the total and average columns for the first invoice are the same as the invoice total because they're calculated based on just that total. The total and average columns for the second invoice, however, are calculated based on both the first and second invoices. The total and average columns for the third invoice are calculated based on the first, second, and third invoices. And so on. In addition, the count column indicates the sequence of the invoice date within the result set. A total that accumulates like this is called a *cumulative total*, and an average that's calculated based on a cumulative total is called a *moving average*.

If the result set contains more than one invoice for the same date, the summary values for all of the invoices are accumulated at the same time. This is illustrated by the fourth, fifth, and sixth invoices in this example. Here, the cumulative total column for each invoice includes the invoice totals for all three invoices for the same date, and the moving average is based on that cumulative total. Because the cumulative total now includes six rows, the count column is set to 6. In other words, the summary values for all three rows are the same.

The last example in this figure uses both the PARTITION BY and ORDER BY clauses. In this case, the invoices are grouped by terms ID and ordered by invoice date. Because of that, the summaries for each invoice date are accumulated separately within each terms ID. When one terms ID ends and the next one begins, the accumulation starts again.

The syntax of the OVER clause

```
aggregate_function OVER ([partition_by_clause] [order_by_clause])
```

A query that groups the summary data by date

```
SELECT InvoiceNumber, InvoiceDate, InvoiceTotal,
    SUM(InvoiceTotal) OVER (PARTITION BY InvoiceDate) AS DateTotal,
    COUNT(InvoiceTotal) OVER (PARTITION BY InvoiceDate) AS DateCount,
    AVG(InvoiceTotal) OVER (PARTITION BY InvoiceDate) AS DateAvg
FROM Invoices;
```

	InvoiceNumber	InvoiceDate	InvoiceTotal	DateTotal	DateCount	DateAvg
1	989319-457	2015-12-08 00:00:00	3813.33	3813.33	1	3813.33
2	263253241	2015-12-10 00:00:00	40.20	40.20	1	40.20
3	963253234	2015-12-13 00:00:00	138.75	138.75	1	138.75
4	2-000-2993	2015-12-16 00:00:00	144.70	202.95	3	67.65
5	963253251	2015-12-16 00:00:00	15.50	202.95	3	67.65
6	963253261	2015-12-16 00:00:00	42.75	202.95	3	67.65

A query that calculates a cumulative total and moving average

```
SELECT InvoiceNumber, InvoiceDate, InvoiceTotal,
    SUM(InvoiceTotal) OVER (ORDER BY InvoiceDate) AS CumTotal,
    COUNT(InvoiceTotal) OVER (ORDER BY InvoiceDate) AS Count,
    AVG(InvoiceTotal) OVER (ORDER BY InvoiceDate) AS MovingAvg
FROM Invoices;
```

	InvoiceNumber	InvoiceDate	InvoiceTotal	CumTotal	Count	MovingAvg
1	989319-457	2015-12-08 00:00:00	3813.33	3813.33	1	3813.33
2	263253241	2015-12-10 00:00:00	40.20	3853.53	2	1926.765
3	963253234	2015-12-13 00:00:00	138.75	3992.28	3	1330.76
4	2-000-2993	2015-12-16 00:00:00	144.70	4195.23	6	699.205
5	963253251	2015-12-16 00:00:00	15.50	4195.23	6	699.205
6	963253261	2015-12-16 00:00:00	42.75	4195.23	6	699.205

The same query grouped by TermsID

```
SELECT InvoiceNumber, TermsID, InvoiceDate, InvoiceTotal,
    SUM(InvoiceTotal)
        OVER (PARTITION BY TermsID ORDER BY InvoiceDate) AS CumTotal,
    COUNT(InvoiceTotal)
        OVER (PARTITION BY TermsID ORDER BY InvoiceDate) AS Count,
    AVG(InvoiceTotal)
        OVER (PARTITION BY TermsID ORDER BY InvoiceDate) AS MovingAvg
FROM Invoices;
```

	InvoiceNumber	TermsID	InvoiceDate	InvoiceTotal	CumTotal	Count	MovingAvg
22	97-1024A	2	2016-03-20 00:00:00	356.48	9415.08	16	588.4425
23	31361833	2	2016-03-21 00:00:00	579.42	9994.50	17	587.9117
24	134116	2	2016-03-28 00:00:00	90.36	10084.86	18	560.27
25	989319-457	3	2015-12-08 00:00:00	3813.33	3813.33	1	3813.33
26	263253241	3	2015-12-10 00:00:00	40.20	3853.53	2	1926.765
27	963253234	3	2015-12-13 00:00:00	138.75	3992.28	3	1330.76

Description

- When used with the aggregate functions, the OVER clause lets you summarize the data in a result set while still returning the rows used to calculate the summary.

Figure 5-10   How to use the OVER clause

Perspective

In this chapter, you learned how to code queries that group and summarize data. In most cases, you'll be able to use the techniques presented here to get the summary information you need. If not, you may want to find out about another tool provided by SQL Server 2016 called Analysis Services. This tool provides a graphical interface that lets you build complex data models based on cubes. Then, you can use those models to analyze the database using complex patterns and correlations. You can find out more about this tool by searching for "Analysis Services" in the documentation for SQL Server.

Terms

scalar function	scalar aggregate
aggregate function	vector aggregate
column function	cumulative total
summary query	moving average

Exercises

1. Write a SELECT statement that returns two columns from the Invoices table: VendorID and PaymentSum, where PaymentSum is the sum of the PaymentTotal column. Group the result set by VendorID.

2. Write a SELECT statement that returns two columns: VendorName and PaymentSum, where PaymentSum is the sum of the PaymentTotal column. Group the result set by VendorName. Return only 10 rows, corresponding to the 10 vendors who've been paid the most.

   Hint: Use the TOP clause and join Vendors to Invoices.

3. Write a SELECT statement that returns three columns: VendorName, InvoiceCount, and InvoiceSum. InvoiceCount is the count of the number of invoices, and InvoiceSum is the sum of the InvoiceTotal column. Group the result set by vendor. Sort the result set so that the vendor with the highest number of invoices appears first.

4. Write a SELECT statement that returns three columns: AccountDescription, LineItemCount, and LineItemSum. LineItemCount is the number of entries in the InvoiceLineItems table that have that AccountNo. LineItemSum is the sum of the InvoiceLineItemAmount column for that AccountNo. Filter the result set to include only those rows with LineItemCount greater than 1. Group the result set by account description, and sort it by descending LineItemCount.

   Hint: Join the GLAccounts table to the InvoiceLineItems table.

5. Modify the solution to exercise 4 to filter for invoices dated from December 1, 2015 to February 29, 2016.

   Hint: Join to the Invoices table to code a search condition based on InvoiceDate.

6. Write a SELECT statement that answers the following question: What is the total amount invoiced for each AccountNo? Use the WITH ROLLUP operator to include a row that gives the grand total.

   Hint: Use the InvoiceLineItemAmount column of the InvoiceLineItems table.

7. Write a SELECT statement that returns four columns: VendorName, AccountDescription, LineItemCount, and LineItemSum. LineItemCount is the row count, and LineItemSum is the sum of the InvoiceLineItemAmount column. For each vendor and account, return the number and sum of line items, sorted first by vendor, then by account description.

   Hint: Use a four-table join.

8. Write a SELECT statement that answers this question: Which vendors are being paid from more than one account? Return two columns: the vendor name and the total number of accounts that apply to that vendor's invoices.

   Hint: Use the DISTINCT keyword to count InvoiceLineItems.AccountNo.

9. Write a SELECT statement that returns six columns:

VendorID	From the Invoices table
InvoiceDate	From the Invoices table
InvoiceTotal	From the Invoices table
VendorTotal	The sum of the invoice totals for each vendor
VendorCount	The count of invoices for each vendor
VendorAvg	The average of the invoice totals for each vendor

   The result set should include the individual invoices for each vendor.

6

How to code subqueries

A subquery is a SELECT statement that's coded within another SQL statement. As a result, you can use subqueries to build queries that would be difficult or impossible to do otherwise. In this chapter, you'll learn how to use subqueries within SELECT statements. Then, in the next chapter, you'll learn how to use them when you code INSERT, UPDATE, and DELETE statements.

An introduction to subqueries

Since you know how to code SELECT statements, you already know how to code a *subquery*. It's simply a SELECT statement that's coded within another SQL statement. The trick to using subqueries, then, is knowing where and when to use them. You'll learn the specifics of using subqueries throughout this chapter. The two topics that follow, however, will give you an overview of where and when to use them.

How to use subqueries

In figure 6-1, you can see that a subquery can be coded, or *introduced*, in the WHERE, HAVING, FROM, or SELECT clause of a SELECT statement. The SELECT statement in this figure, for example, illustrates how you can use a subquery in the search condition of a WHERE clause. When it's used in a search condition, a subquery can be referred to as a *subquery search condition* or a *subquery predicate*.

The statement in this figure retrieves all the invoices from the Invoices table that have invoice totals greater than the average of all the invoices. To do that, the subquery calculates the average of all the invoices. Then, the search condition tests each invoice to see if its invoice total is greater than that average.

When a subquery returns a single value as it does in this example, you can use it anywhere you would normally use an expression. However, a subquery can also return a single-column result set with two or more rows. In that case, it can be used in place of a list of values, such as the list for an IN operator. In addition, if a subquery is coded within a FROM clause, it can return a result set with two or more columns. You'll learn about all of these different types of subqueries in this chapter.

You can also code a subquery within another subquery. In that case, the subqueries are said to be nested. Because *nested subqueries* can be difficult to read and can result in poor performance, you should use them only when necessary.

Four ways to introduce a subquery in a SELECT statement

1. In a WHERE clause as a search condition
2. In a HAVING clause as a search condition
3. In the FROM clause as a table specification
4. In the SELECT clause as a column specification

A SELECT statement that uses a subquery in the WHERE clause

```
SELECT InvoiceNumber, InvoiceDate, InvoiceTotal
FROM Invoices
WHERE InvoiceTotal >
    (SELECT AVG(InvoiceTotal)
     FROM Invoices)
ORDER BY InvoiceTotal;
```

The value returned by the subquery

```
1879.7413
```

The result set

	InvoiceNumber	InvoiceDate	InvoiceTotal	
1	989319-487	2016-02-20 00:00:00	1927.54	
2	97/522	2016-02-28 00:00:00	1962.13	
3	989319-417	2016-03-23 00:00:00	2051.59	
4	989319-427	2016-02-16 00:00:00	2115.81	
5	989319-477	2016-02-08 00:00:00	2184.11	

```
(21 rows)
```

Description

- A *subquery* is a SELECT statement that's coded within another SQL statement.

- A subquery can return a single value, a result set that contains a single column, or a result set that contains one or more columns.

- A subquery that returns a single value can be coded, or *introduced*, anywhere an expression is allowed. A subquery that returns a single column can be introduced in place of a list of values, such as the values for an IN phrase. And a subquery that returns one or more columns can be introduced in place of a table in the FROM clause.

- The syntax for a subquery is the same as for a standard SELECT statement. However, a subquery doesn't typically include the GROUP BY or HAVING clause, and it can't include an ORDER BY clause unless the TOP phrase is used.

- A subquery that's used in a WHERE or HAVING clause is called a *subquery search condition* or a *subquery predicate*. This is the most common use for a subquery.

- Although you can introduce a subquery in a GROUP BY or ORDER BY clause, you usually won't need to.

- Subqueries can be *nested* within other subqueries. However, subqueries that are nested more than two or three levels deep can be difficult to read and can result in poor performance.

Figure 6-1   How to use subqueries

How subqueries compare to joins

In the last figure, you saw an example of a subquery that returns an aggregate value that's used in the search condition of a WHERE clause. This type of subquery provides for processing that can't be done any other way. However, most subqueries can be restated as joins, and most joins can be restated as subqueries. This is illustrated by the SELECT statements in figure 6-2.

Both of the SELECT statements in this figure return a result set that consists of selected rows and columns from the Invoices table. In this case, only the invoices for vendors in California are returned. The first statement uses a join to combine the Vendors and Invoices table so that the VendorState column can be tested for each invoice. In contrast, the second statement uses a subquery to return a result set that consists of the VendorID column for each vendor in California. Then, that result set is used with the IN operator in the search condition so that only invoices with a VendorID in that result set are included in the final result set.

So if you have a choice, which technique should you use? In general, I recommend you use the technique that results in the most readable code. For example, I think that a join tends to be more intuitive than a subquery when it uses an existing relationship between two tables. That's the case with the Vendors and Invoices tables used in the examples in this figure. On the other hand, a subquery tends to be more intuitive when it uses an ad hoc relationship.

As your queries get more complex, you may find that they're easier to code by using subqueries, regardless of the relationships that are involved. On the other hand, a query with an inner join typically performs faster than the same query with a subquery. So if system performance is an issue, you may want to use inner joins instead of queries.

You should also realize that when you use a subquery in a search condition, its results can't be included in the final result set. For instance, the second example in this figure can't be changed to include the VendorName column from the Vendors table. That's because the Vendors table isn't named in the FROM clause of the outer query. So if you need to include information from both tables in the result set, you need to use a join.

A query that uses an inner join

```
SELECT InvoiceNumber, InvoiceDate, InvoiceTotal
FROM Invoices JOIN Vendors
    ON Invoices.VendorID = Vendors.VendorID
WHERE VendorState = 'CA'
ORDER BY InvoiceDate;
```

The same query restated with a subquery

```
SELECT InvoiceNumber, InvoiceDate, InvoiceTotal
FROM Invoices
WHERE VendorID IN
    (SELECT VendorID
    FROM Vendors
    WHERE VendorState = 'CA')
ORDER BY InvoiceDate;
```

The result set returned by both queries

	InvoiceNumber	InvoiceDate	InvoiceTotal	
1	125520-1	2015-12-24 00:00:00	95.00	
2	97/488	2015-12-24 00:00:00	601.95	
3	111-92R-10096	2015-12-30 00:00:00	16.33	
4	25022117	2016-01-01 00:00:00	6.00	

`(40 rows)`

Advantages of joins

- The result of a join operation can include columns from both tables. The result of a query that includes a subquery can only include columns from the table named in the outer query. It can't include columns from the table named in the subquery.

- A join tends to be more intuitive when it uses an existing relationship between the two tables, such as a primary key to foreign key relationship.

- A query with a join typically performs faster than the same query with a subquery, especially if the query uses only inner joins.

Advantages of subqueries

- You can use a subquery to pass an aggregate value to the outer query.

- A subquery tends to be more intuitive when it uses an ad hoc relationship between the two tables.

- Long, complex queries can sometimes be easier to code using subqueries.

Description

- Like a join, a subquery can be used to code queries that work with two or more tables.

- Most subqueries can be restated as joins and most joins can be restated as subqueries.

Figure 6-2   How subqueries compare to joins

How to code subqueries in search conditions

You can use a variety of techniques to work with a subquery in a search condition. You'll learn about those techniques in the topics that follow. As you read these topics, keep in mind that although all of the examples illustrate the use of subqueries in a WHERE clause, all of this information applies to the HAVING clause as well.

How to use subqueries with the IN operator

In chapter 3, you learned how to use the IN operator to test whether an expression is contained in a list of values. One way to provide that list of values is to use a subquery. This is illustrated in figure 6-3.

The example in this figure retrieves the vendors from the Vendors table that don't have invoices in the Invoices table. To do that, it uses a subquery to retrieve the VendorID of each vendor in the Invoices table. The result is a result set like the one shown in this figure that contains just the VendorID column. Then, this result set is used to filter the vendors that are included in the final result set.

You should notice two things about this subquery. First, it returns a single column. That's a requirement when a subquery is used with the IN operator. Second, the subquery includes the DISTINCT keyword. That way, if more than one invoice exists for a vendor, the VendorID for that vendor will be included only once. Note, however, that when the query is analyzed by SQL Server, this keyword will be added automatically. So you can omit it if you'd like to.

In the previous figure, you saw that a query that uses a subquery with the IN operator can be restated using an inner join. Similarly, a query that uses a subquery with the NOT IN operator can typically be restated using an outer join. The first query shown in this figure, for example, can be restated as shown in the second query. In this case, though, I think the query with the subquery is more readable. In addition, a query with a subquery will sometimes execute faster than a query with an outer join. That of course, depends on a variety of factors. In particular, it depends on the sizes of the tables and the relative number of unmatched rows. So if performance is an issue, you may want to test your query both ways to see which one executes faster.

The syntax of a WHERE clause that uses an IN phrase with a subquery

```
WHERE test_expression [NOT] IN (subquery)
```

A query that returns vendors without invoices

```
SELECT VendorID, VendorName, VendorState
FROM Vendors
WHERE VendorID NOT IN
    (SELECT DISTINCT VendorID
    FROM Invoices);
```

The result of the subquery

	VendorID
1	34
2	37
3	48
4	72
5	80
6	81

(34 rows)

The result set

	VendorID	VendorName	VendorState
32	33	Nielson	OH
33	35	Cal State Termite	CA
34	36	Graylift	CA
35	38	Venture Communications Int1	NY
36	39	Custom Printing Company	MO
37	40	Nat Assoc of College Stores	OH

(88 rows)

The query restated without a subquery

```
SELECT Vendors.VendorID, VendorName, VendorState
FROM Vendors LEFT JOIN Invoices
    ON Vendors.VendorID = Invoices.VendorID
WHERE Invoices.VendorID IS NULL;
```

Description

- You can introduce a subquery with the IN operator to provide the list of values that are tested against the test expression.

- When you use the IN operator, the subquery must return a single column of values.

- A query that uses the NOT IN operator with a subquery can typically be restated using an outer join.

Figure 6-3   How to use subqueries with the IN operator

How to compare the result of a subquery with an expression

Figure 6-4 illustrates how you can use the comparison operators to compare an expression with the result of a subquery. In the example in this figure, the subquery returns the average balance due of the invoices in the Invoices table that have a balance due greater than zero. Then, it uses that value to retrieve all the invoices that have a balance due that's less than the average.

When you use a comparison operator as shown in this figure, the subquery must return a single value. In most cases, that means that it uses an aggregate function. However, you can also use the comparison operators with subqueries that return two or more values. To do that, you use the SOME, ANY, or ALL keyword to modify the comparison operator. You'll learn more about these keywords in the next two topics.

The syntax of a WHERE clause that compares an expression with the value returned by a subquery

```
WHERE expression comparison_operator [SOME|ANY|ALL] (subquery)
```

A query that returns invoices with a balance due less than the average

```
SELECT InvoiceNumber, InvoiceDate, InvoiceTotal,
    InvoiceTotal - PaymentTotal - CreditTotal AS BalanceDue
FROM Invoices
WHERE InvoiceTotal - PaymentTotal - CreditTotal  > 0
    AND InvoiceTotal - PaymentTotal - CreditTotal <
    (SELECT AVG(InvoiceTotal - PaymentTotal - CreditTotal)
    FROM Invoices
    WHERE InvoiceTotal - PaymentTotal - CreditTotal > 0)
ORDER BY InvoiceTotal DESC;
```

The value returned by the subquery

```
2910.9472
```

The result set

	InvoiceNumber	InvoiceDate	InvoiceTotal	BalanceDue
1	31361833	2016-03-21 00:00:00	579.42	579.42
2	9982771	2016-03-24 00:00:00	503.20	503.20
3	547480102	2016-04-01 00:00:00	224.00	224.00
4	134116	2016-03-28 00:00:00	90.36	90.36
5	39104	2016-03-10 00:00:00	85.31	85.31

```
(9 rows)
```

Description

- You can use a comparison operator in a search condition to compare an expression with the results of a subquery.

- If you code a search condition without the ANY, SOME, and ALL keywords, the subquery must return a single value.

- If you include the ANY, SOME, or ALL keyword, the subquery can return a list of values. See figures 6-5 and 6-6 for more information on using these keywords.

Figure 6-4   How to compare the result of a subquery with an expression

How to use the ALL keyword

Figure 6-5 shows you how to use the ALL keyword. This keyword modifies the comparison operator so that the condition must be true for all the values returned by a subquery. This is equivalent to coding a series of conditions connected by AND operators. The table at the top of this figure describes how this works for some of the comparison operators.

If you use the greater than operator (>), the expression must be greater than the maximum value returned by the subquery. Conversely, if you use the less than operator (<), the expression must be less than the minimum value returned by the subquery. If you use the equal operator (=), the expression must be equal to all of the values returned by the subquery. And if you use the not equal operator (<>), the expression must not equal any of the values returned by the subquery. Note that a not equal condition could be restated using a NOT IN condition.

The query in this figure illustrates the use of the greater than operator with the ALL keyword. Here, the subquery selects the InvoiceTotal column for all the invoices with a VendorID value of 34. This results in a table with two rows, as shown in this figure. Then, the outer query retrieves the rows from the Invoices table that have invoice totals greater than all of the values returned by the subquery. In other words, this query returns all the invoices that have totals greater than the largest invoice for vendor number 34.

When you use the ALL operator, you should realize that if the subquery doesn't return any rows, the comparison operation will always be true. In contrast, if the subquery returns only null values, the comparison operation will always be false.

In many cases, a condition with the ALL keyword can be rewritten so it's easier to read and maintain. For example, the condition in the query in this figure could be rewritten to use the MAX function like this:

```
WHERE InvoiceTotal >
    (SELECT MAX(InvoiceTotal)
    FROM Invoices
    WHERE VendorID = 34)
```

Whenever you can, then, I recommend you replace the ALL keyword with an equivalent condition.

How the ALL keyword works

Condition	Equivalent expression	Description
`x > ALL (1, 2)`	`x > 2`	x must be greater than all the values returned by the subquery, which means it must be greater than the maximum value.
`x < ALL (1, 2)`	`x < 1`	x must be less than all the values returned by the subquery, which means it must be less than the minimum value.
`x = ALL (1, 2)`	`(x = 1) AND (x = 2)`	This condition can evaluate to True only if the subquery returns a single value or if all the values returned by the subquery are the same. Otherwise, it evaluates to False.
`x <> ALL (1, 2)`	`(x <> 1) AND (x <> 2)`	This condition is equivalent to: `x NOT IN (1, 2)`

A query that returns invoices larger than the largest invoice for vendor 34

```
SELECT VendorName, InvoiceNumber, InvoiceTotal
FROM Invoices JOIN Vendors ON Invoices.VendorID = Vendors.VendorID
WHERE InvoiceTotal > ALL
    (SELECT InvoiceTotal
    FROM Invoices
    WHERE VendorID = 34)
ORDER BY VendorName;
```

The result of the subquery

	Invoice Total
1	116.54
2	1083.58

The result set

	VendorName	Invoice Number	Invoice Total
1	Bertelsmann Industry Svcs. Inc	509786	6940.25
2	Cahners Publishing Company	587056	2184.50
3	Computerworld	367447	2433.00
4	Data Reproductions Corp	40318	21842.00
5	Dean Witter Reynolds	75C-90227	1367.50

`(25 rows)`

Description

- You can use the ALL keyword to test that a comparison condition is true for all of the values returned by a subquery. This keyword is typically used with the comparison operators <, >, <=, and >=.

- If no rows are returned by the subquery, a comparison that uses the ALL keyword is always true.

- If all of the rows returned by the subquery contain a null value, a comparison that uses the ALL keyword is always false.

Figure 6-5   How to use the ALL keyword

How to use the ANY and SOME keywords

Figure 6-6 shows how to use the ANY and SOME keywords. You use these keywords to test if a comparison is true for any, or some, of the values returned by a subquery. This is equivalent to coding a series of conditions connected with OR operators. Because these keywords are equivalent, you can use whichever one you prefer. The table at the top of this figure describes how these keywords work with some of the comparison operators.

The example in this figure shows how you can use the ANY keyword with the less than operator. This statement is similar to the one you saw in the previous figure, except that it retrieves invoices with invoice totals that are less than at least one of the invoice totals for a given vendor. Like the statement in the previous figure, this condition could be rewritten using the MAX function like this:

```
WHERE InvoiceTotal <
    (SELECT MAX(InvoiceTotal)
    FROM Invoices
    WHERE VendorID = 115)
```

Because you can usually replace an ANY condition with an equivalent condition that's more readable, you probably won't use ANY often.

How the ANY and SOME keywords work

Condition	Equivalent expression	Description
x > ANY (1, 2)	x > 1	x must be greater than at least one of the values returned by the subquery list, which means that it must be greater than the minimum value returned by the subquery.
x < ANY (1, 2)	x < 2	x must be less than at least one of the values returned by the subquery list, which means that it must be less than the maximum value returned by the subquery.
x = ANY (1, 2)	(x = 1) OR (x = 2)	This condition is equivalent to: x IN (1, 2)
x <> ANY (1, 2)	(x <> 1) OR (x <> 2)	This condition will evaluate to True for any non-empty result set containing at least one non-null value that isn't equal to x.

A query that returns invoices smaller than the largest invoice for vendor 115

```
SELECT VendorName, InvoiceNumber, InvoiceTotal
FROM Vendors JOIN Invoices ON Vendors.VendorID = Invoices.VendorID
WHERE InvoiceTotal < ANY
    (SELECT InvoiceTotal
    FROM Invoices
    WHERE VendorID = 115);
```

The result of the subquery

	InvoiceTotal
1	6.00
2	6.00
3	25.67
4	6.00

The result set

	VendorName	InvoiceNumber	InvoiceTotal
1	Abbey Office Furnishings	203339-13	17.50
2	Pacific Bell	111-92R-10096	16.33
3	Pacific Bell	111-92R-10097	16.33
4	Pacific Bell	111-92R-10094	19.67
5	Compuserve	21-4923721	9.95

(17 rows)

Description

- You can use the ANY or SOME keyword to test that a condition is true for one or more of the values returned by a subquery.

- ANY and SOME are equivalent keywords. SOME is the ANSI-standard keyword, but ANY is more commonly used.

- If no rows are returned by the subquery or all of the rows returned by the subquery contain a null value, a comparison that uses the ANY or SOME keyword is always false.

Figure 6-6   How to use the ANY and SOME keywords

How to code correlated subqueries

The subqueries you've seen so far in this chapter have been subqueries that are executed only once for the entire query. However, you can also code subqueries that are executed once for each row that's processed by the outer query. This type of query is called a *correlated subquery*, and it's similar to using a loop to do repetitive processing in a procedural programming language.

Figure 6-7 illustrates how correlated subqueries work. The example in this figure retrieves rows from the Invoices table for those invoices that have an invoice total that's greater than the average of all the invoices for the same vendor. To do that, the search condition in the WHERE clause of the subquery refers to the VendorID value of the current invoice. That way, only the invoices for the current vendor will be included in the average.

Each time a row in the outer query is processed, the value in the VendorID column for that row is substituted for the column reference in the subquery. Then, the subquery is executed based on the current value. If the VendorID value is 95, for example, this subquery will be executed:

```
SELECT AVG(InvoiceTotal)
FROM Invoices AS Inv_Sub
WHERE Inv_Sub.VendorID = 95;
```

After this subquery is executed, the value it returns is used to determine whether the current invoice is included in the result set. For example, the value returned by the subquery for vendor 95 is 28.5016. Then, that value is compared with the invoice total of the current invoice. If the invoice total is greater than that value, the invoice is included in the result set. Otherwise, it's not. This process is repeated until each of the invoices in the Invoices table has been processed.

As you study this example, notice how the column names in the WHERE clause of the inner query are qualified to indicate whether they refer to a column in the inner query or the outer query. In this case, the same table is used in both the inner and outer queries, so aliases, or correlation names, have been assigned to the tables. Then, those correlation names are used to qualify the column names. Although you have to qualify a reference to a column in the outer query, you don't have to qualify a reference to a column in the inner query. However, it's common practice to qualify both names, particularly if they refer to the same table.

Because correlated subqueries can be difficult to code, you may want to test a subquery separately before using it within another SELECT statement. To do that, however, you'll need to substitute a constant value for the variable that refers to a column in the outer query. That's what I did to get the average invoice total for vendor 95. Once you're sure that the subquery works on its own, you can replace the constant value with a reference to the outer query so you can use it within a SELECT statement.

A query that uses a correlated subquery to return each invoice that's higher than the vendor's average invoice

```
SELECT VendorID, InvoiceNumber, InvoiceTotal
FROM Invoices AS Inv_Main
WHERE InvoiceTotal >
    (SELECT AVG(InvoiceTotal)
    FROM Invoices AS Inv_Sub
    WHERE Inv_Sub.VendorID = Inv_Main.VendorID)
ORDER BY VendorID, InvoiceTotal;
```

The value returned by the subquery for vendor 95

```
28.5016
```

The result set

	VendorID	InvoiceNumber	InvoiceTotal
6	83	31359783	1575.00
7	95	111-92R-10095	32.70
8	95	111-92R-10093	39.77
9	95	111-92R-10092	46.21
10	110	P-0259	26881.40

```
(36 rows)
```

Description

- A *correlated subquery* is a subquery that is executed once for each row processed by the outer query. In contrast, a *noncorrelated subquery* is executed only once. All of the subqueries you've seen so far have been noncorrelated subqueries.

- A correlated subquery refers to a value that's provided by a column in the outer query. Because that value varies depending on the row that's being processed, each execution of the subquery returns a different result.

- To refer to a value in the outer query, a correlated subquery uses a qualified column name that includes the table name from the outer query. If the subquery uses the same table as the outer query, an alias, or *correlation name,* must be assigned to one of the tables to remove ambiguity.

Note

- Because a correlated subquery is executed once for each row processed by the outer query, a query with a correlated subquery typically takes longer to run than a query with a noncorrelated subquery.

Figure 6-7   How to code correlated subqueries

How to use the EXISTS operator

Figure 6-8 shows you how to use the EXISTS operator with a subquery. This operator tests whether or not the subquery returns a result set. In other words, it tests whether the result set exists. When you use this operator, the subquery doesn't actually return a result set to the outer query. Instead, it simply returns an indication of whether any rows satisfy the search condition of the subquery. Because of that, queries that use this operator execute quickly.

You typically use the EXISTS operator with a correlated subquery as illustrated in this figure. This query retrieves all the vendors in the Vendors table that don't have invoices in the Invoices table. Notice that this query returns the same vendors as the two queries you saw in figure 6-3 that use the IN operator with a subquery and an outer join. However, the query in this figure executes more quickly than either of the queries in figure 6-3.

In this example, the correlated subquery selects all of the invoices that have the same VendorID value as the current vendor in the outer query. Because the subquery doesn't actually return a result set, it doesn't matter what columns are included in the SELECT clause. So it's customary to just code an asterisk. That way, SQL Server will determine what columns to select for optimum performance.

After the subquery is executed, the search condition in the WHERE clause of the outer query uses NOT EXISTS to test whether any invoices were found for the current vendor. If not, the vendor row is included in the result set. Otherwise, it's not.

The syntax of a subquery that uses the EXISTS operator

```
WHERE [NOT] EXISTS (subquery)
```

A query that returns vendors without invoices

```
SELECT VendorID, VendorName, VendorState
FROM Vendors
WHERE NOT EXISTS
    (SELECT *
    FROM Invoices
    WHERE Invoices.VendorID = Vendors.VendorID);
```

The result set

	VendorID	VendorName	VendorState	
32	33	Nielson	OH	
33	35	Cal State Termite	CA	
34	36	Graylift	CA	
35	38	Venture Communications Int1	NY	
36	39	Custom Printing Company	MO	
37	40	Nat Assoc of College Stores	OH	

```
(88 rows)
```

Description

- You can use the EXISTS operator to test that one or more rows are returned by the subquery. You can also use the NOT operator along with the EXISTS operator to test that no rows are returned by the subquery.

- When you use the EXISTS operator with a subquery, the subquery doesn't actually return any rows. Instead, it returns an indication of whether any rows meet the specified condition.

- Because no rows are returned by the subquery, it doesn't matter what columns you specify in the SELECT clause. So you typically just code an asterisk (*).

- Although you can use the EXISTS operator with either a correlated or a noncorrelated subquery, it's used most often with correlated subqueries. That's because it's usually better to use a join than a noncorrelated subquery with EXISTS.

Figure 6-8   How to use the EXISTS operator

Other ways to use subqueries

Although you'll typically use subqueries in the WHERE or HAVING clause of a SELECT statement, you can also use them in the FROM and SELECT clauses. You'll learn how to do that in the topics that follow.

How to code subqueries in the FROM clause

Figure 6-9 shows you how to code a subquery in a FROM clause. As you can see, you can code a subquery in place of a table specification. In this example, the results of the subquery, called a *derived table*, are joined with another table. When you use a subquery in this way, it can return any number of rows and columns.

Subqueries are typically used in the FROM clause to create derived tables that provide summarized data to a summary query. The subquery in this figure, for example, creates a derived table that contains the VendorID values and the average invoice totals for the five vendors with the top invoice averages. To do that, it groups the invoices by VendorID, sorts them in descending sequence by average invoice total, and then returns the top five rows. The derived table is then joined with the Invoices table, and the resulting rows are grouped by VendorID. Finally, the maximum invoice date and average invoice total are calculated for the grouped rows, and the results are sorted by the maximum invoice date in descending sequence.

You should notice four things about this query. First, the derived table is assigned a table alias so that it can be referred to from the outer query. Second, the result of the AVG function in the subquery is assigned a column alias. This is because a derived table can't have unnamed columns. Third, since the subquery uses a TOP phrase, it also includes an ORDER BY clause. Fourth, although you might think that you could use the average invoice totals calculated by the subquery in the select list of the outer query, you can't. That's because the outer query includes a GROUP BY clause, so only aggregate functions, columns named in the GROUP BY clause, and constant values can be included in this list. Because of that, the AVG function is repeated in the select list.

When used in the FROM clause, a subquery is similar to a view. As you learned in chapter 1, a view is a predefined SELECT statement that's saved with the database. Because it's saved with the database, a view typically performs more efficiently than a derived table. However, it's not always practical to use a view. In those cases, derived tables can be quite useful. In addition, derived tables can be useful for testing possible solutions before creating a view. Then, once the derived table works the way you want it to, you can define the view based on the subquery you used to create the derived table.

A query that uses a derived table to retrieve the top 5 vendors by average invoice total

```
SELECT Invoices.VendorID, MAX(InvoiceDate) AS LatestInv,
    AVG(InvoiceTotal) AS AvgInvoice
FROM Invoices JOIN
    (SELECT TOP 5 VendorID, AVG(InvoiceTotal) AS AvgInvoice
    FROM Invoices
    GROUP BY VendorID
    ORDER BY AvgInvoice DESC) AS TopVendor
    ON Invoices.VendorID = TopVendor.VendorID
GROUP BY Invoices.VendorID
ORDER BY LatestInv DESC;
```

The derived table generated by the subquery

	VendorID	AvgInvoice
1	110	23978.482
2	72	10963.655
3	104	7125.34
4	99	6940.25
5	119	4901.26

The result set

	VendorID	LatestInv	AvgInvoice
1	110	2016-03-31 00:00:00	23978.482
2	72	2016-03-10 00:00:00	10963.655
3	99	2016-02-18 00:00:00	6940.25
4	104	2016-01-21 00:00:00	7125.34
5	119	2016-01-11 00:00:00	4901.26

Description

- A subquery that's coded in the FROM clause returns a result set called a *derived table*. When you create a derived table, you must assign an alias to it. Then, you can use the derived table within the outer query just as you would any other table.

- When you code a subquery in the FROM clause, you must assign names to any calculated values in the result set.

- Derived tables are most useful when you need to further summarize the results of a summary query.

- A derived table is like a view in that it retrieves selected rows and columns from one or more base tables. Because views are stored as part of the database, they're typically more efficient to use than derived tables. However, it may not always be practical to construct and save a view in advance.

Figure 6-9   How to code subqueries in the FROM clause

How to code subqueries in the SELECT clause

Figure 6-10 shows you how to use subqueries in the SELECT clause. As you can see, you can use a subquery in place of a column specification. Because of that, the subquery must return a single value.

In most cases, the subqueries you use in the SELECT clause will be correlated subqueries. The subquery in this figure, for example, calculates the maximum invoice date for each vendor in the Vendors table. To do that, it refers to the VendorID column from the Invoices table in the outer query.

Because subqueries coded in the SELECT clause are difficult to read, and because correlated subqueries are typically inefficient, you shouldn't use them unless you can't find another solution. In most cases, though, you can replace the subquery with a join. The first query shown in this figure, for example, could be restated as shown in the second query. This query joins the Vendors and Invoices tables, groups the rows by VendorName, and then uses the MAX function to calculate the maximum invoice date for each vendor. As you can see, this query is much easier to read than the one with the subquery. It will also execute more quickly.

A query that uses a correlated subquery in its SELECT clause to retrieve the most recent invoice for each vendor

```
SELECT DISTINCT VendorName,
    (SELECT MAX(InvoiceDate) FROM Invoices
    WHERE Invoices.VendorID = Vendors.VendorID) AS LatestInv
FROM Vendors
ORDER BY LatestInv DESC;
```

The result set

	VendorName	LatestInv
1	Federal Express Corporation	2016-04-02 00:00:00
2	Blue Cross	2016-04-01 00:00:00
3	Malloy Lithographing Inc	2016-03-31 00:00:00
4	Cardinal Business Media, Inc.	2016-03-28 00:00:00
5	Zylka Design	2016-03-25 00:00:00
6	Ford Motor Credit Company	2016-03-24 00:00:00
7	United Parcel Service	2016-03-24 00:00:00
8	Ingram	2016-03-21 00:00:00
9	Wakefield Co	2016-03-20 00:00:00

(122 rows)

The same query restated using a join

```
SELECT VendorName, MAX(InvoiceDate) AS LatestInv
FROM Vendors LEFT JOIN Invoices ON Vendors.VendorID = Invoices.VendorID
GROUP BY VendorName
ORDER BY LatestInv DESC;
```

Description

- When you code a subquery for a column specification in the SELECT clause, the subquery must return a single value.

- A subquery that's coded within a SELECT clause is typically a correlated subquery.

- A query that includes a subquery in its SELECT clause can typically be restated using a join instead of the subquery. Because a join is usually faster and more readable, subqueries are seldom coded in the SELECT clause.

Figure 6-10   How to code subqueries in the SELECT clause

Guidelines for working with complex queries

So far, the examples you've seen of queries that use subqueries have been relatively simple. However, these types of queries can get complicated in a hurry, particularly if the subqueries are nested. Because of that, you'll want to be sure that you plan and test these queries carefully. You'll learn a procedure for doing that in a moment. But first, you'll see a complex query that illustrates the type of query I'm talking about.

A complex query that uses subqueries

Figure 6-11 presents a query that uses three subqueries. The first subquery is used in the FROM clause of the outer query to create a derived table that contains the state, name, and total invoice amount for each vendor in the Vendors table. The second subquery is also used in the FROM clause of the outer query to create a derived table that's joined with the first table. This derived table contains the state and total invoice amount for the vendor in each state that has the largest invoice total. To create this table, a third subquery is nested within the FROM clause of the subquery. This subquery is identical to the first subquery.

After the two derived tables are created, they're joined based on the columns in each table that contain the state and the total invoice amount. The final result set includes the state, name, and total invoice amount for the vendor in each state with the largest invoice total. This result set is sorted by state.

As you can see, this query is quite complicated and difficult to understand. In fact, you might be wondering if there isn't an easier solution to this problem. For example, you might think that you could solve the problem simply by joining the Vendors and Invoices table and creating a grouped aggregate. If you grouped by vendor state, however, you wouldn't be able to include the name of the vendor in the result set. And if you grouped by vendor state and vendor name, the result set would include all the vendors, not just the vendor from each state with the largest invoice total.

If you think about how else you might solve this query, I think you'll agree that the solution presented here is fairly straightforward. However, in figure 6-13, you'll learn how to use a feature that was introduced with SQL Server 2005 to simplify this query. In particular, this feature allows you to code a single Summary subquery instead of coding the Summary1 and Summary2 subqueries shown here.

A query that uses three subqueries

```
SELECT Summary1.VendorState, Summary1.VendorName, TopInState.SumOfInvoices
FROM
        (SELECT V_Sub.VendorState, V_Sub.VendorName,
            SUM(I_Sub.InvoiceTotal) AS SumOfInvoices
        FROM Invoices AS I_Sub JOIN Vendors AS V_Sub
            ON I_Sub.VendorID = V_Sub.VendorID
        GROUP BY V_Sub.VendorState, V_Sub.VendorName) AS Summary1
    JOIN
        (SELECT Summary2.VendorState,
            MAX(Summary2.SumOfInvoices) AS SumOfInvoices
        FROM
            (SELECT V_Sub.VendorState, V_Sub.VendorName,
                SUM(I_Sub.InvoiceTotal) AS SumOfInvoices
            FROM Invoices AS I_Sub JOIN Vendors AS V_Sub
                ON I_Sub.VendorID = V_Sub.VendorID
            GROUP BY V_Sub.VendorState, V_Sub.VendorName) AS Summary2
        GROUP BY Summary2.VendorState) AS TopInState
    ON Summary1.VendorState = TopInState.VendorState AND
        Summary1.SumOfInvoices = TopInState.SumOfInvoices
ORDER BY Summary1.VendorState;
```

The result set

	VendorState	VendorName	SumOfInvoices
1	AZ	Wells Fargo Bank	662.00
2	CA	Digital Dreamworks	7125.34
3	DC	Reiter's Scientific & Pro Books	600.00
4	MA	Dean Witter Reynolds	1367.50
5	MI	Malloy Lithographing Inc	119892.41
6	NV	United Parcel Service	23177.96
7	OH	Edward Data Services	207.78
8	PA	Cardinal Business Media, Inc.	265.36

(10 rows)

How the query works

- This query retrieves the vendor from each state that has the largest invoice total. To do that, it uses three subqueries: Summary1, Summary2, and TopInState. The Summary1 and TopInState subqueries are joined together in the FROM clause of the outer query, and the Summary2 subquery is nested within the FROM clause of the TopInState subquery.

- The Summary1 and Summary2 subqueries are identical. They join data from the Vendors and Invoices tables and produce a result set that includes the sum of invoices for each vendor grouped by vendor name within state.

- The TopInState subquery produces a result set that includes the vendor state and the largest sum of invoices for any vendor in that state. This information is retrieved from the results of the Summary2 subquery.

- The columns listed in the SELECT clause of the outer query are retrieved from the result of the join between the Summary1 and TopInState subqueries, and the results are sorted by state.

Figure 6-11   A complex query that uses subqueries

A procedure for building complex queries

To build a complex query like the one in the previous figure, you can use a procedure like the one in figure 6-12. To start, you should state the problem to be solved so that you're clear about what you want the query to accomplish. In this case, the question is, "Which vendor in each state has the largest invoice total?"

Once you're clear about the problem, you should outline the query using *pseudocode*. Pseudocode is simply code that represents the intent of the query, but doesn't necessarily use SQL code. The pseudocode shown in this figure, for example, uses part SQL code and part English. Notice that this pseudocode identifies the two main subqueries. Because these subqueries define derived tables, the pseudocode also indicates the alias that will be used for each: Summary1 and TopInState. That way, you can use these aliases in the pseudocode for the outer query to make it clear where the data it uses comes from.

If it's not clear from the pseudocode how each subquery will be coded, or, as in this case, if a subquery is nested within another subquery, you can also write pseudocode for the subqueries. For example, the pseudocode for the TopInState query is presented in this figure. Because this subquery has a subquery nested in its FROM clause, that subquery is identified in this pseudocode as Summary2.

The next step in the procedure is to code and test the actual subqueries to be sure they work the way you want them to. For example, the code for the Summary1 and Summary2 queries is shown in this figure, along with the results of these queries and the results of the TopInState query. Once you're sure that the subqueries work the way you want them to, you can code and test the final query.

If you follow the procedure presented in this figure, I think you'll find it easier to build complex queries that use subqueries. Before you can use this procedure, of course, you need to have a thorough understanding of how subqueries work and what they can do. So you'll want to be sure to experiment with the techniques you learned in this chapter before you try to build a complex query like the one shown here.

A procedure for building complex queries

1. State the problem to be solved by the query in English.

2. Use pseudocode to outline the query. The pseudocode should identify the subqueries used by the query and the data they return. It should also include aliases used for any derived tables.

3. If necessary, use pseudocode to outline each subquery.

4. Code the subqueries and test them to be sure that they return the correct data.

5. Code and test the final query.

The problem to be solved by the query in figure 6-11

- Which vendor in each state has the largest invoice total?

Pseudocode for the query

```
SELECT Summary1.VendorState, Summary1.VendorName, TopInState.SumOfInvoices
FROM (Derived table returning VendorState, VendorName, SumOfInvoices)
        AS Summary1
    JOIN (Derived table returning VendorState, MAX(SumOfInvoices))
        AS TopInState
    ON Summary1.VendorState = TopInState.VendorState AND
        Summary1.SumOfInvoices = TopInState.SumOfInvoices
ORDER BY Summary1.VendorState;
```

Pseudocode for the TopInState subquery

```
SELECT Summary2.VendorState, MAX(Summary2.SumOfInvoices)
FROM (Derived table returning VendorState, VendorName, SumOfInvoices)
    AS Summary2
GROUP BY Summary2.VendorState;
```

The code for the Summary1 and Summary2 subqueries

```
SELECT V_Sub.VendorState, V_Sub.VendorName,
    SUM(I_Sub.InvoiceTotal) AS SumOfInvoices
FROM Invoices AS I_Sub JOIN Vendors AS V_Sub
    ON I_Sub.VendorID = V_Sub.VendorID
GROUP BY V_Sub.VendorState, V_Sub.VendorName;
```

The result of the Summary1 and Summary2 subqueries

	VendorState	VendorName	SumOfInvoices	
10	MA	Dean Witter Reynolds	1367.50	
11	CA	Digital Dreamworks	7125.34	
12	CA	Dristas Groom & McCormick	220.00	
13	OH	Edward Data Services	207.78	

(34 rows)

The result of the TopInState subquery

	VendorState	SumOfInvoices	
1	AZ	662.00	
2	CA	7125.34	
3	DC	600.00	
4	MA	1367.50	

(10 rows)

Figure 6-12   A procedure for building complex queries

How to work with common table expressions

A *common table expression* (*CTE*) is a feature that was introduced with SQL Server 2005 that allows you to code an expression that defines a derived table. You can use CTEs to simplify complex queries that use subqueries. This can make your code easier to read and maintain. In addition, you can use a CTE to loop through nested structures.

How to code a CTE

Figure 6-13 shows how to use a CTE to simplify the complex query presented in figure 6-11. To start, the statement for the query begins with the WITH keyword to indicate that you are about to define a CTE. Then, it specifies Summary as the name for the first table, followed by the AS keyword, followed by an opening parenthesis, followed by a SELECT statement that defines the table, followed by a closing parenthesis. In this figure, for example, this statement returns the same result set as the subqueries named Summary1 and Summary2 that were presented in figure 6-11.

After the first CTE is defined, this example continues by defining a second CTE named TopInState. To start, a comma is coded to separate the two CTEs. Then, this query specifies TopInState as the name for the second table, followed by the AS keyword, followed by an opening parenthesis, followed by a SELECT statement that defines the table, followed by a closing parenthesis. Here, this SELECT statement refers to the Summary table that was defined by the first CTE. When coding multiple CTEs like this, a CTE can reference any CTEs in the same WITH clause that are coded before it, but it can't reference CTEs coded after it. As a result, this statement wouldn't work if the two CTEs were coded in the reverse order.

Finally, the SELECT statement that's coded immediately after the two CTEs uses both of these CTEs just as if they were tables. To do that, this SELECT statement joins the two tables, specifies the columns to retrieve, and specifies the sort order. To avoid ambiguous references, each column is qualified by the name for the CTE. If you compare figure 6-13 with figure 6-11, I think you'll agree that the code in figure 6-13 is easier to read. That's partly because the tables defined by the subqueries aren't nested within the SELECT statement. In addition, I think you'll agree that the code in figure 6-13 is easier to maintain. That's because this query reduces code duplication by only coding the Summary query in one place, not in two places.

When using the syntax shown here to define CTEs, you must supply distinct names for all columns defined by the SELECT statement, including calculated values. That way, it's possible for other statements to reference the columns in the result set. Most of the time, that's all you need to know to be able to work with CTEs. For more information about working with CTEs, you can look up "WITH common_table_expression" in the documentation for SQL Server.

The syntax of a CTE

```
WITH cte_name1 AS (query_definition1)
[, cte_name2 AS (query_definition2)]
[...]
sql_statement
```

Two CTEs and a query that uses them

```
WITH Summary AS
(
    SELECT VendorState, VendorName, SUM(InvoiceTotal) AS SumOfInvoices
    FROM Invoices
        JOIN Vendors ON Invoices.VendorID = Vendors.VendorID
    GROUP BY VendorState, VendorName
),
TopInState AS
(
    SELECT VendorState, MAX(SumOfInvoices) AS SumOfInvoices
    FROM Summary
    GROUP BY VendorState
)
SELECT Summary.VendorState, Summary.VendorName, TopInState.SumOfInvoices
FROM Summary JOIN TopInState
    ON Summary.VendorState = TopInState.VendorState AND
        Summary.SumOfInvoices = TopInState.SumOfInvoices
ORDER BY Summary.VendorState;
```

The result set

	VendorState	VendorName	SumOfInvoices
1	AZ	Wells Fargo Bank	662.00
2	CA	Digital Dreamworks	7125.34
3	DC	Reiter's Scientific & Pro Books	600.00
4	MA	Dean Witter Reynolds	1367.50
5	MI	Malloy Lithographing Inc	119892.41
6	NV	United Parcel Service	23177.96
7	OH	Edward Data Services	207.78
8	PA	Cardinal Business Media, Inc.	265.36

```
(10 rows)
```

Description

- A *common table expression* (*CTE*) is an expression (usually a SELECT statement) that creates one or more temporary tables that can be used by the following query.

- To use a CTE with a query, you code the WITH keyword followed by the definition of the CTE. Then, immediately after the CTE, you code the statement that uses it.

- To code multiple CTEs, separate them with commas. Then, each CTE can refer to itself and any previously defined CTEs in the same WITH clause.

- You can use CTEs with SELECT, INSERT, UPDATE, and DELETE statements. However, you're most likely to use them with SELECT statements as shown in this figure and in figure 6-14.

Figure 6-13   How to code a CTE

How to code a recursive CTE

A *recursive query* is a query that is able to loop through a result set and perform processing to return a final result set. Recursive queries are commonly used to return hierarchical data such as an organizational chart in which a parent element may have one or more child elements, and each child element may have one or more child elements. Prior to SQL Server 2005, a recursive query required using derived tables, cursors, and logic to control the flow of the recursive steps. With SQL Server 2005 and later, you can use a *recursive CTE* to code recursive queries more easily. Figure 6-14 shows how.

The top of this figure shows an Employees table where the ManagerID column is used to identify the manager for each employee. Here, Cindy Smith is the top level manager since she doesn't have a manager, Elmer Jones and Paulo Locario report to Cindy, and so on.

The recursive CTE shown in this figure returns each employee according to their level in the organization chart for the company. To do that, this statement begins by defining a CTE named EmployeesCTE. Within this CTE, two SELECT statements are joined by the UNION ALL operator. Here, the first SELECT statement uses the IS NULL operator to return the first row of the result set. This statement is known as the *anchor member* of the recursive CTE.

Then, the second SELECT statement creates a loop by referencing itself. In particular, this query joins the Employees table to the EmployeesCTE table that's defined by the CTE. This statement is known as the *recursive member* and it loops through each row in the Employees table. With each loop, it adds 1 to the rank column and appends the current result set to the final result set. For example, on the first loop, it appends Elmer Jones and Paulo Locario to the final result set. On the second loop, it appends Ralph Simonian, Thomas Hardy, Olivia Hernandez, and Rhea O'Leary to the final result set. And so on.

When coding a recursive CTE, you must follow some rules. First, you must supply a name for each column defined by the CTE. To do that, you just need to make sure to specify a name for each column in the anchor member. Second, the rules for coding a union that you learned in chapter 4 still apply. In particular, the anchor member and the recursive member must have the same number of columns and the columns must have compatible data types.

Most of the time, that's all you need to know to be able to work with recursive CTEs. However, the goal of this figure is to show a simple recursive CTE to give you a general idea of how they work. If necessary, you can code much more complex recursive CTEs. For example, you can code multiple anchor members and multiple recursive members. For more information about working with recursive CTEs, you can start by looking up "recursive common table expressions" in the documentation for SQL Server.

If you find that you're often using recursive CTEs to return hierarchical data, you may want to learn more about the hierarchyid data type that was introduced with SQL Server 2008. This data type makes it easier to work with hierarchical data such as organization charts. To learn more about this data type, you can look up "hierarchyid (Transact-SQL)" in the documentation for SQL Server.

The Employees table

	EmployeeID	LastName	FirstName	ManagerID
1	1	Smith	Cindy	NULL
2	2	Jones	Elmer	1
3	3	Simonian	Ralph	2
4	4	Hernandez	Olivia	2
5	5	Aaronsen	Robert	3
6	6	Watson	Denise	3
7	7	Hardy	Thomas	2
8	8	O'Leary	Rhea	2
9	9	Locario	Paulo	1

A recursive CTE that returns hierarchical data

```
WITH EmployeesCTE AS
(
        -- Anchor member
        SELECT EmployeeID,
            FirstName + ' ' + LastName As EmployeeName,
            1 As Rank
        FROM Employees
        WHERE ManagerID IS NULL
    UNION ALL
        -- Recursive member
        SELECT Employees.EmployeeID,
            FirstName + ' ' + LastName,
            Rank + 1
        FROM Employees
            JOIN EmployeesCTE
            ON Employees.ManagerID = EmployeesCTE.EmployeeID
)
SELECT *
FROM EmployeesCTE
ORDER BY Rank, EmployeeID;
```

The final result set

	EmployeeID	EmployeeName	Rank
1	1	Cindy Smith	1
2	2	Elmer Jones	2
3	9	Paulo Locario	2
4	3	Ralph Simonian	3
5	4	Olivia Hernandez	3
6	7	Thomas Hardy	3
7	8	Rhea O'Leary	3
8	5	Robert Aaronsen	4
9	6	Denise Watson	4

Description

- A *recursive query* is a query that is able to loop through a result set and perform processing to return a final result set. A *recursive CTE* can be used to create a recursive query.

- A recursive CTE must contain at least two query definitions, an *anchor member* and a *recursive member*, and these members must be connected by the UNION ALL operator.

Figure 6-14   How to code a recursive CTE

Perspective

As you've seen in this chapter, subqueries provide a powerful tool for solving difficult problems. Before you use a subquery, however, remember that a subquery can often be restated more clearly by using a join. In addition, a query with a join often executes more quickly than a query with a subquery. Because of that, you'll typically use a subquery only when it can't be restated as a join or when it makes the query easier to understand without slowing it down significantly.

If you find yourself coding the same subqueries over and over, you should consider creating a view for that subquery as described in chapter 13. This will help you develop queries more quickly since you can use the view instead of coding the subquery again. In addition, since views execute more quickly than subqueries, this may improve the performance of your queries.

Terms

subquery	derived table
introduce a subquery	pseudocode
subquery search condition	common table expression (CTE)
subquery predicate	recursive query
nested subquery	recursive CTE
correlated subquery	anchor member
noncorrelated subquery	recursive member

Exercises

1. Write a SELECT statement that returns the same result set as this SELECT statement. Substitute a subquery in a WHERE clause for the inner join.

   ```
   SELECT DISTINCT VendorName
   FROM Vendors JOIN Invoices
       ON Vendors.VendorID = Invoices.VendorID
   ORDER BY VendorName;
   ```

2. Write a SELECT statement that answers this question: Which invoices have a PaymentTotal that's greater than the average PaymentTotal for all paid invoices? Return the InvoiceNumber and InvoiceTotal for each invoice.

3. Write a SELECT statement that answers this question: Which invoices have a PaymentTotal that's greater than the median PaymentTotal for all paid invoices? (The median marks the midpoint in a set of values; an equal number of values lie above and below it.) Return the InvoiceNumber and InvoiceTotal for each invoice.

   Hint: Begin with the solution to exercise 2, then use the ALL keyword in the WHERE clause and code "TOP 50 PERCENT PaymentTotal" in the subquery.

4. Write a SELECT statement that returns two columns from the GLAccounts table: AccountNo and AccountDescription. The result set should have one row for each account number that has never been used. Use a correlated subquery introduced with the NOT EXISTS operator. Sort the final result set by AccountNo.

5. Write a SELECT statement that returns four columns: VendorName, InvoiceID, InvoiceSequence, and InvoiceLineItemAmount for each invoice that has more than one line item in the InvoiceLineItems table.

    Hint: Use a subquery that tests for InvoiceSequence > 1.

6. Write a SELECT statement that returns a single value that represents the sum of the largest unpaid invoices submitted by each vendor. Use a derived table that returns MAX(InvoiceTotal) grouped by VendorID, filtering for invoices with a balance due.

7. Write a SELECT statement that returns the name, city, and state of each vendor that's located in a unique city and state. In other words, don't include vendors that have a city and state in common with another vendor.

8. Write a SELECT statement that returns four columns: VendorName, InvoiceNumber, InvoiceDate, and InvoiceTotal. Return one row per vendor, representing the vendor's invoice with the earliest date.

9. Rewrite exercise 6 so it uses a common table expression (CTE) instead of a derived table.

7

How to insert, update, and delete data

In the last four chapters, you learned how to code the SELECT statement to retrieve and summarize data. Now, you'll learn how to code the INSERT, UPDATE, and DELETE statements to modify the data in a table. When you're done with this chapter, you'll know how to code the four statements that are used every day by professional SQL programmers.

How to create test tables

As you learn to code INSERT, UPDATE, and DELETE statements, you need to make sure that your experimentation won't affect "live" data or a classroom database that is shared by other students. Two ways to get around that are presented next.

How to use the SELECT INTO statement

Figure 7-1 shows how to use the SELECT INTO statement to create test tables that are derived from the tables in a database. Then, you can experiment all you want with the test tables and delete them when you're done. When you use the SELECT INTO statement, the result set that's defined by the SELECT statement is simply copied into a new table.

The three examples in this figure show some of the ways you can use this statement. Here, the first example copies all of the columns from all of the rows in the Invoices table into a new table named InvoiceCopy. The second example copies all of the columns in the Invoices table into a new table, but only for rows where the balance due is zero. And the third example creates a table that contains summary data from the Invoices table.

For the examples in the rest of this chapter, I used the SELECT INTO statement to make copies of the Vendors and Invoices tables, and I named these tables VendorCopy and InvoiceCopy. If you do the same, you'll avoid corrupting the original database. Then, when you're done experimenting, you can use the DROP TABLE statement that's shown in this figure to delete the test tables.

When you use this technique to create tables, though, only the column definitions and data are copied, which means that definitions like those of primary keys, foreign keys, and default values aren't retained. As a result, the test results that you get with the copied tables may be slightly different than the results you would get with the original tables. You'll understand that better after you read chapters 10 and 11.

How to use a copy of the database

If you download the files for this book as described in appendix A, you can create copies of the databases used in this book on your local server by running the provided database creation scripts. As a result, you can modify the tables within these databases without worrying about how much you change them. Then, when you're done testing, you can restore these databases by running the database creation scripts again.

However, when you create a copy of the entire database instead of making copies of tables within a database, the definitions of primary keys, foreign keys, and default values are retained, so your results may be slightly different than the ones shown in the examples. If, for example, you try to add a row with an invalid foreign key, SQL Server won't let you do that. You'll learn more about that in chapters 10 and 11.

The syntax of the SELECT INTO statement

```
SELECT select_list
INTO table_name
FROM table_source
[WHERE search_condition]
[GROUP BY group_by_list]
[HAVING search_condition]
[ORDER BY order_by_list]
```

A statement that creates a complete copy of the Invoices table

```
SELECT *
INTO InvoiceCopy
FROM Invoices;
```

```
(114 row(s) affected)
```

A statement that creates a partial copy of the Invoices table

```
SELECT *
INTO OldInvoices
FROM Invoices
WHERE InvoiceTotal - PaymentTotal - CreditTotal = 0;
```

```
(103 row(s) affected)
```

A statement that creates a table with summary rows

```
SELECT VendorID, SUM(InvoiceTotal) AS SumOfInvoices
INTO VendorBalances
FROM Invoices
WHERE InvoiceTotal - PaymentTotal - CreditTotal <> 0
GROUP BY VendorID;
```

```
(7 row(s) affected)
```

A statement that deletes a table

```
DROP TABLE InvoiceCopy;
```

Description

- The INTO clause is a SQL Server extension that lets you create a new table based on the result set defined by the SELECT statement. Since the definitions of the columns in the new table are based on the columns in the result set, the column names assigned in the SELECT clause must be unique.

- You can code the other clauses of the SELECT INTO statement just as you would for any other SELECT statement.

- If you use calculated values in the select list, you must name the column since that name is used in the definition of the new table.

- The table you name in the INTO clause must not exist. If it does, you must delete it using the DROP TABLE statement before you execute the SELECT INTO statement.

Warning

- When you use the SELECT INTO statement to create a table, only the column definitions and data are copied. That means that definitions of primary keys, foreign keys, indexes, default values, and so on are not included in the new table.

Figure 7-1   How to use the SELECT INTO statement to create test tables

How to insert new rows

To add new rows to a table, you use the INSERT statement. This statement lets you insert a single row or multiple rows.

How to insert a single row

Figure 7-2 shows how to code an INSERT statement to insert a single row. The two examples in this figure insert a row into the InvoiceCopy table. The data this new row contains is defined near the top of this figure.

In the first example, you can see that you name the table in which the row will be inserted in the INSERT clause. Then, the VALUES clause lists the values to be used for each column. You should notice three things about this list. First, it includes a value for every column in the table except for the InvoiceID column. This value is omitted because the InvoiceID column is defined as an identity column. Because of that, its value will be generated by SQL Server. Second, the values are listed in the same sequence that the columns appear in the table. That way, SQL Server knows which value to assign to which column. And third, a null value is assigned to the last column, PaymentDate, using the NULL keyword. You'll learn more about using this keyword in the next topic.

The second INSERT statement in this figure includes a column list in the INSERT clause. Notice that this list doesn't include the PaymentDate column since it allows a null value. In addition, the columns aren't listed in the same sequence as the columns in the InvoiceCopy table. When you include a list of columns, you can code the columns in any sequence you like. Then, you just need to be sure that the values in the VALUES clause are coded in the same sequence.

When you specify the values for the columns to be inserted, you must be sure that those values are compatible with the data types of the columns. For example, you must enclose literal values for dates and strings within single quotes. However, you don't need to enclose literal values for numbers in single quotes. You'll learn more about data types and how to work with them in the next chapter. For now, just realize that if any of the values aren't compatible with the data types of the corresponding columns, an error will occur and the row won't be inserted.

How to insert multiple rows

SQL Server 2008 extended the syntax for the INSERT statement to allow a single INSERT statement to insert multiple rows. To do that, you just use a comma to separate the multiple value lists as shown in the third INSERT statement. Although this syntax doesn't provide a performance gain, it does provide a more concise way to write the code than coding multiple INSERT statements.

The syntax of the INSERT statement

```
INSERT [INTO] table_name [(column_list)]
[DEFAULT] VALUES (expression_1 [, expression_2]...)
[, (expression_1 [, expression_2]...)...]
```

The values for a new row to be added to the Invoices table

Column	Value	Column	Value
InvoiceID	(Next available unique ID)	PaymentTotal	0
VendorID	97	CreditTotal	0
InvoiceNumber	456789	TermsID	1
InvoiceDate	4/01/2016	InvoiceDueDate	4/31/2016
InvoiceTotal	8,344.50	PaymentDate	null

An INSERT statement that adds the new row without using a column list

```
INSERT INTO InvoiceCopy
VALUES (97, '456789', '2016-04-01', 8344.50, 0, 0, 1, '2016-04-30', NULL);
```

An INSERT statement that adds the new row using a column list

```
INSERT INTO InvoiceCopy
    (VendorID, InvoiceNumber, InvoiceTotal, PaymentTotal, CreditTotal,
    TermsID, InvoiceDate, InvoiceDueDate)
VALUES
    (97, '456789', 8344.50, 0, 0, 1, '2016-04-01', '2016-04-30');
```

The response from the system

```
(1 row(s) affected)
```

An INSERT statement that adds three new rows

```
INSERT INTO InvoiceCopy
VALUES
    (95, '111-10098', '2016-04-01', 219.50, 0, 0, 1, '2016-04-30', NULL),
    (102, '109596', '2016-04-01', 22.97, 0, 0, 1, '2016-04-30', NULL),
    (72, '40319', '2016-04-01', 173.38, 0, 0, 1, '2016-04-30', NULL);
```

The response from the system

```
(3 row(s) affected)
```

Description

- You specify the values to be inserted in the VALUES clause. The values you specify depend on whether you include a column list.

- If you don't include a column list, you must specify the column values in the same order as they appear in the table, and you must code a value for each column in the table. The exception is an identity column, which must be omitted.

- If you include a column list, you must specify the column values in the same order as they appear in the column list. You can omit columns with default values and columns that accept null values, and you must omit identity columns.

Figure 7-2   How to insert one or more rows

How to insert default values and null values

If a column allows null values, you'll want to know how to insert a null value into that column. Similarly, if a column is defined with a default value, you'll want to know how to insert that value. The technique you use depends on whether the INSERT statement includes a column list, as shown by the examples in figure 7-3.

All of these INSERT statements use a table named ColorSample. This table contains the three columns shown at the top of this figure. The first column, ID, is defined as an identity column. The second column, ColorNumber, is defined with a default value of 0. And the third column, ColorName, is defined so that it allows null values.

The first two statements illustrate how you assign a default value or a null value using a column list. To do that, you simply omit the column from the list. In the first statement, for example, the column list names only the ColorNumber column, so the ColorName column is assigned a null value. Similarly, the column list in the second statement names only the ColorName column, so the ColorNumber is assigned its default value.

The next three statements show how you assign a default or null value to a column without including a column list. As you can see, you do that by using the DEFAULT and NULL keywords. For example, the third statement specifies a value for the ColorName column, but uses the DEFAULT keyword for the ColorNumber column. Because of that, SQL Server will assign a value of zero to this column. The fourth statement assigns a value of 808 to the ColorNumber column, and it uses the NULL keyword to assign a null value to the ColorName column. The fifth statement uses both the DEFAULT and NULL keywords.

Finally, in the sixth statement, the DEFAULT keyword is coded in front of the VALUES clause. When you use the DEFAULT keyword this way, any column that has a default value will be assigned that value, and all other columns (except the identity column) will be assigned a null value. Because of that, you can use this technique only when every column in the table is defined as either an identity column, a column with a default value, or a column that allows null values.

The definition of the ColorSample table

Column name	Data Type	Length	Identity	Allow Nulls	Default Value
ID	Int	4	Yes	No	No
ColorNumber	Int	4	No	No	0
ColorName	VarChar	10	No	Yes	No

Six INSERT statements for the ColorSample table

```
INSERT INTO ColorSample (ColorNumber)
VALUES (606);

INSERT INTO ColorSample (ColorName)
VALUES ('Yellow');

INSERT INTO ColorSample
VALUES (DEFAULT, 'Orange');

INSERT INTO ColorSample
VALUES (808, NULL);

INSERT INTO ColorSample
VALUES (DEFAULT, NULL);

INSERT INTO ColorSample
DEFAULT VALUES;
```

The ColorSample table after the rows are inserted

	ID	ColorNumber	ColorName
1	1	606	NULL
2	2	0	Yellow
3	3	0	Orange
4	4	808	NULL
5	5	0	NULL
6	6	0	NULL

Description

- If a column is defined so that it allows null values, you can use the NULL keyword in the list of values to insert a null value into that column.

- If a column is defined with a default value, you can use the DEFAULT keyword in the list of values to insert the default value for that column.

- If all of the columns in a table are defined as either identity columns, columns with default values, or columns that allow null values, you can code the DEFAULT keyword at the beginning of the VALUES clause and then omit the list of values.

- If you include a column list, you can omit columns with default values and null values. Then, the default value or null value is assigned automatically.

Figure 7-3   How to insert default values and null values

How to insert rows selected from another table

Instead of using the VALUES clause of the INSERT statement to specify the values for a single row, you can use a subquery to select the rows you want to insert from another table. Figure 7-4 shows you how to do that.

Both examples in this figure retrieve rows from the InvoiceCopy table and insert them into a table named InvoiceArchive. This table is defined with the same columns as the InvoiceCopy table. However, the InvoiceID column isn't defined as an identity column, and the PaymentTotal and CreditTotal columns aren't defined with default values. Because of that, you must include values for these columns.

The first example in this figure shows how you can use a subquery in an INSERT statement without coding a column list. In this example, the SELECT clause of the subquery is coded with an asterisk so that all the columns in the InvoiceCopy table will be retrieved. Then, after the search condition in the WHERE clause is applied, all the rows in the result set are inserted into the InvoiceArchive table.

The second example shows how you can use a column list in the INSERT clause when you use a subquery to retrieve rows. Just as when you use the VALUES clause, you can list the columns in any sequence. However, the columns must be listed in the same sequence in the SELECT clause of the subquery. In addition, you can omit columns that are defined with default values or that allow null values.

Notice that the subqueries in these statements aren't coded within parentheses as a subquery in a SELECT statement is. That's because they're not coded within a clause of the INSERT statement. Instead, they're coded in place of the VALUES clause.

Before you execute INSERT statements like the ones shown in this figure, you'll want to be sure that the rows and columns retrieved by the subquery are the ones you want to insert. To do that, you can execute the SELECT statement by itself. Then, when you're sure it retrieves the correct data, you can add the INSERT clause to insert the rows in the derived table into another table.

The syntax of the INSERT statement for inserting rows selected from another table

```
INSERT [INTO] table_name [(column_list)]
SELECT column_list
FROM table_source
[WHERE search_condition]
```

An INSERT statement that inserts paid invoices in the InvoiceCopy table into the InvoiceArchive table

```
INSERT INTO InvoiceArchive
SELECT *
FROM InvoiceCopy
WHERE InvoiceTotal - PaymentTotal - CreditTotal = 0;

(103 row(s) affected)
```

The same INSERT statement with a column list

```
INSERT INTO InvoiceArchive
    (InvoiceID, VendorID, InvoiceNumber, InvoiceTotal, CreditTotal,
    PaymentTotal, TermsID, InvoiceDate, InvoiceDueDate)
SELECT
    InvoiceID, VendorID, InvoiceNumber, InvoiceTotal, CreditTotal,
    PaymentTotal, TermsID, InvoiceDate, InvoiceDueDate
FROM InvoiceCopy
WHERE InvoiceTotal - PaymentTotal - CreditTotal = 0;

(103 row(s) affected)
```

Description

- To insert rows selected from one or more tables into another table, you can code a subquery in place of the VALUES clause. Then, the rows in the derived table that result from the subquery are inserted into the table.

- If you don't code a column list in the INSERT clause, the subquery must return values for all the columns in the table where the rows will be inserted, and the columns must be returned in the same order as they appear in that table. The exception is an identity column, which must be omitted.

- If you include a column list in the INSERT clause, the subquery must return values for those columns in the same order as they appear in the column list. You can omit columns with default values and columns that accept null values, and you must omit identity columns.

Figure 7-4   How to insert rows selected from another table

How to modify existing rows

To modify the data in one or more rows of a table, you use the UPDATE statement. Although most of the UPDATE statements you code will perform simple updates like the ones you'll see in the next figure, you can also code more complex UPDATE statements that include subqueries and joins. You'll learn how to use these features after you learn how to perform a basic update operation.

How to perform a basic update operation

Figure 7-5 presents the syntax of the UPDATE statement. As you can see in the examples, most UPDATE statements include just the UPDATE, SET, and WHERE clauses. The UPDATE clause names the table to be updated, the SET clause names the columns to be updated and the values to be assigned to those columns, and the WHERE clause specifies the condition a row must meet to be updated. Although the WHERE clause is optional, you'll almost always include it. If you don't, all of the rows in the table will be updated, which usually isn't what you want.

The first UPDATE statement in this figure modifies the values of two columns in the InvoiceCopy table: PaymentDate and PaymentTotal. Because the WHERE clause in this statement identifies a specific invoice number, only the columns in that invoice will be updated. Notice in this example that the values to be assigned to the two columns are coded as literals. You should realize, however, that you can assign any valid expression to a column as long as it results in a value that's compatible with the data type of the column. You can also use the NULL keyword to assign a null value to a column that allows nulls, and you can use the DEFAULT keyword to assign the default value to a column that's defined with one.

The second UPDATE statement modifies a single column in the InvoiceCopy table: TermsID. This time, however, the WHERE clause specifies that all the rows for vendor 95 should be updated. Because this vendor has six rows in the InvoiceCopy table, all six rows will be updated.

The third UPDATE statement illustrates how you can use an expression to assign a value to a column. In this case, the expression increases the value of the CreditTotal column by 100. Like the first UPDATE statement, this statement updates a single row.

Before you execute an UPDATE statement, you'll want to be sure that you've selected the correct rows. To do that, you can execute a SELECT statement with the same search condition. Then, if the SELECT statement returns the correct rows, you can change it to an UPDATE statement.

In addition to the UPDATE, SET, and WHERE clauses, an UPDATE statement can also include a FROM clause. This clause is an extension to the SQL standards, and you'll see how to use it in the next two figures.

The syntax of the UPDATE statement

```
UPDATE table_name
SET column_name_1 = expression_1 [, column_name_2 = expression_2]...
[FROM table_source [[AS] table_alias]
[WHERE search_condition]
```

An UPDATE statement that assigns new values to two columns of a single row in the InvoiceCopy table

```
UPDATE InvoiceCopy
SET PaymentDate = '2016-05-21',
    PaymentTotal = 19351.18
WHERE InvoiceNumber = '97/522';

(1 row(s) affected)
```

An UPDATE statement that assigns a new value to one column of all the invoices for a vendor

```
UPDATE InvoiceCopy
SET TermsID = 1
WHERE VendorID = 95;

(6 row(s) affected)
```

An UPDATE statement that uses an arithmetic expression to assign a value to a column

```
UPDATE InvoiceCopy
SET CreditTotal = CreditTotal + 100
WHERE InvoiceNumber = '97/522';

(1 row(s) affected)
```

Description

- You use the UPDATE statement to modify one or more rows in the table named in the UPDATE clause.

- You name the columns to be modified and the value to be assigned to each column in the SET clause. You can specify the value for a column as a literal or an expression.

- You can provide additional criteria for the update operation in the FROM clause, which is a SQL Server extension. See figures 7-6 and 7-7 for more information.

- You can specify the conditions that must be met for a row to be updated in the WHERE clause.

- You can use the DEFAULT keyword to assign the default value to a column that has one, and you can use the NULL keyword to assign a null value to a column that allows nulls.

- You can't update an identity column.

Warning

- If you omit the WHERE clause, all the rows in the table will be updated.

Figure 7-5   How to perform a basic update operation

How to use subqueries in an update operation

Figure 7-6 presents four more UPDATE statements that illustrate how you can use subqueries in an update operation. In the first statement, a subquery is used in the SET clause to retrieve the maximum invoice due date from the InvoiceCopy table. Then, that value is assigned to the InvoiceDueDate column for invoice number 97/522.

In the second statement, a subquery is used in the WHERE clause to identify the invoices to be updated. This subquery returns the VendorID value for the vendor in the VendorCopy table with the name "Pacific Bell." Then, all the invoices with that VendorID value are updated.

The third UPDATE statement also uses a subquery in the WHERE clause. This subquery returns a list of the VendorID values for all the vendors in California, Arizona, and Nevada. Then, the IN operator is used to update all the invoices with VendorID values in that list. Note that although the subquery returns 80 vendors, many of these vendors don't have invoices. As a result, the UPDATE statement only affects 51 invoices.

The fourth example in this figure shows how you can use a subquery in the FROM clause of an UPDATE statement to create a derived table. In this case, the subquery returns a table that contains the InvoiceID values of the ten invoices with the largest balances of $100 or more. (Because this UPDATE statement will apply a credit of $100 to these invoices, you don't want to retrieve invoices with balances less than that amount.) Then, the WHERE clause specifies that only those invoices should be updated. You can also use a column from a derived table in an expression in the SET clause to update a column in the base table.

An UPDATE statement that assigns the maximum due date in the InvoiceCopy table to a specific invoice

```
UPDATE InvoiceCopy
SET CreditTotal = CreditTotal + 100,
    InvoiceDueDate = (SELECT MAX(InvoiceDueDate) FROM InvoiceCopy)
WHERE InvoiceNumber = '97/522';

(1 row(s) affected)
```

An UPDATE statement that updates all the invoices for a vendor based on the vendor's name

```
UPDATE InvoiceCopy
SET TermsID = 1
WHERE VendorID =
    (SELECT VendorID
     FROM VendorCopy
     WHERE VendorName = 'Pacific Bell');

(6 row(s) affected)
```

An UPDATE statement that changes the terms of all invoices for vendors in three states

```
UPDATE InvoiceCopy
SET TermsID = 1
WHERE VendorID IN
    (SELECT VendorID
     FROM VendorCopy
     WHERE VendorState IN ('CA', 'AZ', 'NV'));

(51 row(s) affected)
```

An UPDATE statement that applies a $100 credit to the 10 invoices with the largest balances

```
UPDATE InvoiceCopy
SET CreditTotal = CreditTotal + 100
FROM
    (SELECT TOP 10 InvoiceID
     FROM InvoiceCopy
     WHERE InvoiceTotal - PaymentTotal - CreditTotal >= 100
     ORDER BY InvoiceTotal - PaymentTotal - CreditTotal DESC) AS TopInvoices
WHERE InvoiceCopy.InvoiceID = TopInvoices.InvoiceID;

(5 rows(s) affected)
```

Description

- You can code a subquery in the SET, FROM, or WHERE clause of an UPDATE statement.

- You can use a subquery in the SET clause to return the value that's assigned to a column.

- You can use a subquery in the FROM clause to identify the rows that are available for update. Then, you can refer to the derived table in the SET and WHERE clauses.

- You can code a subquery in the WHERE clause to provide one or more values used in the search condition.

Figure 7-6   How to use subqueries in an update operation

How to use joins in an update operation

In addition to subqueries, you can use joins in the FROM clause of an UPDATE statement. Joins provide an easy way to base an update on data in a table other than the one that's being updated. The two examples in figure 7-7 illustrate how this works.

The first example in this figure updates the TermsID column in all the invoices in the InvoiceCopy table for the vendor named "Pacific Bell." This is the same update operation you saw in the second example in the previous figure. Instead of using a subquery to retrieve the VendorID value for the vendor, however, this UPDATE statement joins the InvoiceCopy and VendorCopy tables on the VendorID column in each table. Then, the search condition in the WHERE clause uses the VendorName column in the VendorCopy table to identify the invoices to be updated.

The second example in this figure shows how you can use the columns in a table that's joined with the table being updated to specify values in the SET clause. Here, the VendorCopy table is joined with a table named ContactUpdates. As you can see in the figure, this table includes VendorID, LastName, and FirstName columns. After the two tables are joined on the VendorID column, the SET clause uses the LastName and FirstName columns from the ContactUpdates table to update the VendorContactLName and VendorContactFName columns in the VendorCopy table.

An UPDATE statement that changes the terms of all the invoices for a vendor

```
UPDATE InvoiceCopy
SET TermsID = 1
FROM InvoiceCopy JOIN VendorCopy
    ON InvoiceCopy.VendorID = VendorCopy.VendorID
WHERE VendorName = 'Pacific Bell';

(6 row(s) affected)
```

An UPDATE statement that updates contact names in the VendorCopy table based on data in the ContactUpdates table

```
UPDATE VendorCopy
SET VendorContactLName = LastName,
    VendorContactFName = FirstName
FROM VendorCopy JOIN ContactUpdates
    ON VendorCopy.VendorID = ContactUpdates.VendorID;

(8 row(s) affected)
```

The ContactUpdates table

	VendorID	LastName	FirstName
1	5	Davison	Michelle
2	12	Mayteh	Kendall
3	17	Onandonga	Bruce
4	44	Antavius	Anthony
5	76	Bradlee	Danny
6	94	Suscipe	Reynaldo
7	101	O'Sullivan	Geraldine
8	123	Bucket	Charles

Description

- If you need to specify column values or search conditions that depend on data in a table other than the one named in the UPDATE clause, you can use a join in the FROM clause.

- You can use columns from the joined tables in the values you assign to columns in the SET clause or in the search condition of a WHERE clause.

Figure 7-7   How to use joins in an update operation

How to delete existing rows

To delete one or more rows from a table, you use the DELETE statement. Just as you can with the UPDATE statement, you can use subqueries and joins in a DELETE statement to help identify the rows to be deleted. You'll learn how to use subqueries and joins after you learn how to perform a basic delete operation.

How to perform a basic delete operation

Figure 7-8 presents the syntax of the DELETE statement along with three examples that illustrate some basic delete operations. As you can see, you specify the name of the table that contains the rows to be deleted in the DELETE clause. You can also code the FROM keyword in this clause, but this keyword is optional and is usually omitted.

To identify the rows to be deleted, you code a search condition in the WHERE clause. Although this clause is optional, you'll almost always include it. If you don't, all of the rows in the table are deleted. This is a common coding mistake, and it can be disastrous.

You can also include a FROM clause in the DELETE statement to join additional tables with the base table. Then, you can use the columns of the joined tables in the search condition of the WHERE clause. The FROM clause is an extension to the standard SQL syntax. You'll see how to use it in the next figure.

The first DELETE statement in this figure deletes a single row from the InvoiceCopy table. To do that, it specifies the InvoiceID value of the row to be deleted in the search condition of the WHERE clause. The second statement is similar, but it deletes all the invoices with a VendorID value of 37. In this case, three rows are deleted.

The third DELETE statement shows how you can use an expression in the search condition of the WHERE clause. In this case, the InvoiceTotal, PaymentTotal, and CreditTotal columns are used to calculate the balance due. Then, if the balance due is zero, the row is deleted. You might use a statement like this after inserting the paid invoices into another table as shown in figure 7-4.

Finally, the fourth DELETE statement shows how easy it is to delete all the rows from a table. Because the WHERE clause has been omitted from this statement, all the rows in the InvoiceCopy table will be deleted, which probably isn't what you want.

Because you can't restore rows once they've been deleted, you'll want to be sure that you've selected the correct rows. One way to do that is to issue a SELECT statement with the same search condition. Then, if the correct rows are retrieved, you can be sure that the DELETE statement will work as intended.

The syntax of the DELETE statement

```
DELETE [FROM] table_name
[FROM table_source]
[WHERE search_condition]
```

A DELETE statement that removes a single row from the InvoiceCopy table

```
DELETE InvoiceCopy
WHERE InvoiceID = 115;
```

```
(1 row(s) affected)
```

A DELETE statement that removes all the invoices for a vendor

```
DELETE InvoiceCopy
WHERE VendorID = 37;
```

```
(3 row(s) affected)
```

A DELETE statement that removes all paid invoices

```
DELETE InvoiceCopy
WHERE InvoiceTotal - PaymentTotal - CreditTotal = 0;
```

```
(103 row(s) affected)
```

A DELETE statement that removes all the rows from the InvoiceCopy table

```
DELETE InvoiceCopy;
```

```
(114 row(s) affected)
```

Description

- You can use the DELETE statement to delete one or more rows from the table you name in the DELETE clause.
- You specify the conditions that must be met for a row to be deleted in the WHERE clause.
- You can specify additional criteria for the delete operation in the FROM clause. See figure 7-9 for more information.

Warning

- If you omit the WHERE clause from a DELETE statement, all the rows in the table will be deleted.

Figure 7-8   How to perform a basic delete operation

How to use subqueries and joins in a delete operation

The examples in figure 7-9 illustrate how you can use subqueries and joins in a DELETE statement. Because you've seen code like this in other statements, you shouldn't have any trouble understanding these examples.

The first two examples delete all the invoices from the InvoiceCopy table for the vendor named "Blue Cross." To accomplish that, the first example uses a subquery in the WHERE clause to retrieve the VendorID value from the VendorCopy table for this vendor. In contrast, the second example joins the InvoiceCopy and VendorCopy tables. Then, the WHERE clause uses the VendorName column in the VendorCopy table to identify the rows to be deleted.

The third DELETE statement deletes all vendors that don't have invoices. To do that, it uses a subquery to return a list of the VendorID values in the InvoiceCopy table. Then, it deletes all vendors that aren't in that list.

The fourth DELETE statement shows how you can use the FROM clause to join the base table named in the DELETE clause with a derived table. Here, the subquery creates a derived table based on the InvoiceCopy table. This subquery groups the invoices in this table by vendor and calculates the total invoice amount for each vendor. Then, after the derived table is joined with the VendorCopy table, the results are filtered by the total invoice amount. Because of that, only those vendors that have invoices totaling $100 or less will be deleted from the VendorCopy table.

A DELETE statement that deletes all invoices for a vendor based on the vendor's name

```
DELETE InvoiceCopy
WHERE VendorID =
    (SELECT VendorID
     FROM VendorCopy
     WHERE VendorName = 'Blue Cross');
```

```
(3 row(s) affected)
```

The same DELETE statement using a join

```
DELETE InvoiceCopy
FROM InvoiceCopy JOIN VendorCopy
    ON InvoiceCopy.VendorID = VendorCopy.VendorID
WHERE VendorName = 'Blue Cross';
```

```
(3 row(s) affected)
```

A DELETE statement that deletes vendors that don't have invoices

```
DELETE VendorCopy
WHERE VendorID NOT IN
    (SELECT DISTINCT VendorID FROM InvoiceCopy);
```

```
(88 row(s) affected)
```

A DELETE statement that deletes vendors whose invoices total $100 or less

```
DELETE VendorCopy
FROM VendorCopy JOIN
        (SELECT VendorID, SUM(InvoiceTotal) AS TotalOfInvoices
         FROM InvoiceCopy
         GROUP BY VendorID) AS InvoiceSum
    ON VendorCopy.VendorID = InvoiceSum.VendorID
WHERE TotalOfInvoices <= 100;
```

```
(6 row(s) affected)
```

Description

- You can use subqueries and joins in the FROM clause of a DELETE statement to base the delete operation on the data in tables other than the one named in the DELETE clause.

- You can use any of the columns returned by a subquery or a join in the WHERE clause of the DELETE statement.

- You can also use subqueries in the WHERE clause to provide one or more values used in the search condition.

Note

- The FROM clause is a SQL Server extension.

Figure 7-9   How to use subqueries and joins in a delete operation

A review of the SQL data types

A column's *data type* specifies the kind of information the column is intended to store. In addition, a column's data type determines the operations that can be performed on the column.

Data type overview

The SQL Server data types can be divided into the four categories shown in the first table in figure 8-1. The *string data types* are intended for storing a string of one or more characters, which can include letters, numbers, symbols, or special characters. The terms *character*, *string*, and *text* are used interchangeably to describe this type of data.

The *numeric data types* are intended for storing numbers that can be used for mathematical calculations. As you'll see in the next topic, SQL Server can store numbers in a variety of formats.

The *temporal data types* are used to store dates and times. These data types are typically referred to as *date/time*, or *date*, *data types*.

Historically, most databases have stored string, numeric, and temporal data. That's why this book focuses on working with these data types. However, it's becoming more common to store other types of data such as images, sound, and video in databases. That's why SQL Server 2005 introduced new data types for working with these types of data. For more information about working with large character and binary values, see figure 8-5.

SQL Server 2005 also introduced an xml data type that provides new functionality for storing XML in a database. To learn more about working with the xml data type, see chapter 18.

Beyond that, SQL Server 2008 introduced several more data types. It introduced several new date/time data types that are described later in this chapter. In addition, it introduced a geometry data type for storing geometric data such as points, lines, and polygons. It introduced a geography data type that works similarly to the geometry type, except that it uses longitude and latitude to specify points on the earth's surface. And, it introduced the hierarchyid data type for storing hierarchical data such as organization charts.

Most of the SQL Server data types correspond to the ANSI-standard data types. These data types are listed in the second table in this figure. Here, the second column lists the SQL Server data type names, and the first column lists the synonyms SQL Server provides for the ANSI-standard data types. Although you can use these synonyms instead of the SQL Server data types, you're not likely to do that. If you do, SQL Server simply maps the synonyms to the corresponding SQL Server data types.

The only synonym I recommend you use is rowversion, which is a synonym for the timestamp data type. This data type is used to store unique numbers that are generated by SQL Server and that are typically used to identify various versions of a row in a table. Microsoft plans to modify the timestamp data type

The four data type categories

Category	Description
String	Strings of character data
Numeric	Integers, floating point numbers, currency, and other numeric data
Temporal (date/time)	Dates, times, or both
Other	Large character and binary values, XML, geometric data, geographic data, hierarchical data

ANSI-standard data types and SQL Server equivalents

Synonym for ANSI-standard data type	SQL Server data type used
binary varying	varbinary
char varying character varying	varchar
character	char
dec	decimal
double precision	float
float	real or float
integer	int
national char national character	nchar
national char varying national character varying	nvarchar
national text	ntext
rowversion	timestamp

Description

- SQL Server defines dozens of *data types* that are divided into the four categories shown above.

- The *temporal data types* are typically referred to as *date/time data types*, or simply *date data types*.

- SQL Server supports most, but not all, of the ANSI-standard data types.

- SQL Server provides a synonym for each of the supported ANSI-standard data types. Although you can use these synonyms, I recommend you use the SQL Server data types instead. The exception is rowversion, which you should use instead of timestamp.

- When you use the synonym for an ANSI data type, it's mapped to the appropriate SQL Server data type indicated in the table above.

Figure 8-1   Data type overview

in a future release so that it's compatible with the timestamp data type defined by the standards. When it does that, it will also replace the current timestamp data type with a new rowversion data type. Because of that, you'll want to use the rowversion synonym instead of the timestamp data type.

The numeric data types

Figure 8-2 presents the numeric data types supported by SQL Server. As you can see, these can be divided into three groups: integer, decimal, and real.

Integer data types store whole numbers, which are numbers with no digits to the right of the decimal point. The five integer data types differ in the amount of storage they use and the range of values they can store. Notice that the bigint, int, and smallint data types can store positive or negative numbers. In contrast, the tinyint and bit data types can store only positive numbers or zero.

To store numbers with digits to the right of the decimal point, you use the *decimal data types*. These data types have a fixed decimal point, which means that the number of digits to the right of the decimal point doesn't vary. The number of digits a value has to the right of the decimal point is called its *scale,* and the total number of digits is called its *precision.* Notice that the money and smallmoney data types have a fixed precision and scale. These data types are intended for storing units of currency. In contrast, you can customize the precision and scale of the decimal and numeric data types so they're right for the data to be stored. Although the decimal and numeric data types are synonymous, decimal is more commonly used.

In contrast to the *fixed-point numbers* stored by the decimal data types, the *real data types* are used to store *floating-point numbers*. These data types provide for very large and very small numbers, but with a limited number of *significant digits*. The real data type can be used to store a *single-precision number*, which provides for numbers with up to 7 significant digits. And the float data type can be used to store a *double-precision number*, which provides for numbers with up to 15 significant digits. Because the real data type is equivalent to float(24), the float data type is typically used for floating-point numbers.

To express the value of a floating-point number, you can use *scientific notation*. To use this notation, you type the letter E followed by a power of 10. For instance, 3.65E+9 is equal to 3.65×10^9, or 3,650,000,000. If you have a mathematical background, of course, you're already familiar with this notation.

Because the precision of all the integer and decimal data types is exact, these data types are considered *exact numeric data types*. In contrast, the real data types are considered *approximate numeric data types* because they may not represent a value exactly. That can happen, for example, when a number is rounded to the appropriate number of significant digits. For business applications, you will most likely use only the exact numeric types, as there's seldom the need to work with the very large and very small numbers that the real data types are designed for.

The integer data types

Type	Bytes	Description
bigint	8	Large integers from -9,223,372,036,854,775,808 through 9,223,372,036,854,775,807.
int	4	Integers from -2,147,483,648 through 2,147,483,647.
smallint	2	Small integers from -32,768 through 32,767.
tinyint	1	Very small positive integers from 0 through 255.
bit	1	Integers with a value of 1 or 0.

The decimal data types

Type	Bytes	Description
decimal[(p[,s])]	5-17	Decimal numbers with fixed precision (p) and scale (s) from $-10^{38}+1$ through $10^{38}-1$. The precision can be any number between 1 and 38; the default is 18. The scale can be any number between 0 and the precision; the default is 0.
numeric[(p[,s])]	5-17	Synonymous with decimal.
money	8	Monetary values with four decimal places from -922,337,203,685,477.5808 through 922,337,203,685,477.5807. Synonymous with decimal(19,4).
smallmoney	4	Monetary values with four decimal places from -214,748.3648 through 214,748.3647. Synonymous with decimal(10,4).

The real data types

Type	Bytes	Description
float[(n)]	4 or 8	Double-precision floating-point numbers from -1.79×10^{308} through 1.79×10^{308}. n represents the number of bits used to store the decimal portion of the number (the mantissa): n=24 is single-precision; n=53 is double-precision. The default is 53.
real	4	Single-precision floating point numbers from -3.4×10^{38} through 3.4×10^{38}. Synonymous with float(24).

Description

- The *integer data types* are used to store whole numbers, which are numbers without any digits to the right of the decimal point.

- The *decimal data types* are used to store decimal values, which can include digits to the right of the decimal point. The *precision* of a decimal value indicates the total number of digits that can be stored, and the *scale* indicates the number of digits that can be stored to the right of the decimal point.

- The integer and decimal data types are considered *exact numeric data types* because their precision is exact.

- The *real data types* are used to store *floating-point numbers*, which have a limited number of *significant digits*. These data types are considered *approximate numeric data types* because they may not represent a value exactly.

Figure 8-2   The numeric data types

The string data types

Figure 8-3 presents the four most common string data types supported by SQL Server. The char and varchar data types store strings of standard characters using one byte per character. The nchar and nvarchar data types store strings of *Unicode characters* that require two bytes per character. You'll learn more about the *Unicode specification* in a moment. In the ANSI standards, two-byte characters are known as *national characters*, hence the prefix *n* on the data types.

You use the char and nchar data types to store *fixed-length strings*. Data stored using these data types always occupies the same number of bytes regardless of the actual length of the string. These data types are typically used to define columns that have a fixed number of characters. For example, the VendorState column in the Vendors table is defined with the char(2) data type because it always contains two characters.

You use the varchar and nvarchar data types to store *variable-length strings*. Data stored using these data types occupies only the number of bytes needed to store the string. They're typically used to define columns whose lengths vary from one row to the next. In general, variable-length strings are more efficient than fixed-length strings.

Although you typically store numeric values using numeric data types, the string data types may be a better choice for some numeric values. For example, you typically store zip codes, telephone numbers, and social security numbers in string columns even if they contain only numbers. That's because their values aren't used in arithmetic operations. In addition, if you stored these numbers in numeric columns, leading zeros would be stripped, which isn't what you want.

As I said, when you use the char and varchar data types, each character is stored in a single byte. Because a byte consists of eight *bits* and because eight bits can be combined in 256 different ways, each byte can represent one of 256 different characters. These characters are assigned numeric codes from 0 to 255. Most systems use the same codes for the first 128 characters. These are the codes defined by the *ASCII* (*American Standard Code for Information Interchange*) system. The other codes, however, may be unique on your system.

When you use the nchar and nvarchar data types to store Unicode characters, each character is stored in two bytes, which provides for 63,536 different characters. That allows for all of the characters used by most of the world's languages, and all systems associate the same numeric codes with the same characters. Because of that, you should use the nchar and nvarchar data types if your database will be used in a multi-language environment. Otherwise, you should use the char and varchar data types to keep storage requirements to a minimum.

The string data types used to store standard characters

Type	Bytes	Description
char[(n)]	n	Fixed-length strings of character data. *n* is the number of characters between 1 and 8000. The default is 1.
varchar[(n)]		Variable-length strings of character data. *n* is the maximum number of characters between 1 and 8000. The default is 1. The number of bytes used to store the string depends on the actual length of the string.

The string data types used to store Unicode characters

Type	Bytes	Description
nchar(n)	2×n	Fixed-length strings of Unicode character data. *n* is the number of characters between 1 and 4000. The default is 1.
nvarchar(n)		Variable-length strings of Unicode character data. *n* is the maximum number of characters between 1 and 4000. The default is 1. The number of bytes used to store the string depends on the actual length of the string. Two bytes are needed to store each character.

Description

- The string data types can be used to store standard characters that use a single byte of storage or *Unicode characters* that use two bytes of storage.

- The char and nchar data types are typically used for *fixed-length strings*. These data types use the same amount of storage regardless of the actual length of the string.

- The varchar and nvarchar data types are typically used for *variable-length strings*. These data types use only the amount of storage needed for a given string.

- Unless your system is used in a multi-language environment, you should use the char and varchar data types rather than nchar and nvarchar data types.

Note

- The *Unicode specification* is a scheme that's used to encode characters used in languages around the world. This reduces the possibility that a receiving system will translate the characters incorrectly. The Unicode data types support a wider range of characters than the standard character data types, but they require twice as much space per character.

Figure 8-3   The string data types

The date/time data types

Figure 8-4 starts by presenting the two date/time data types supported prior to SQL Server 2008. These data types differ by the amount of storage they use and the range of values they can store. In particular, the datetime type supports a wider range of dates and more precise time values than the smalldatetime type. However, it also requires more bytes.

After the older data types, this figure presents the four date/time data types that were introduced with SQL Server 2008. These data types offer several advantages over the older date/time types. As a result, for new development, you will probably want to use the data types that were introduced with SQL Server 2008 instead of the older date/time data types. Of course, for existing databases, you can continue to use the older date/time types.

If you want to store date values without storing a time component, you can use the date data type. This data type is appropriate for many date/time values where the time component isn't necessary such as birthdays. In addition, compared to the datetime type, the date type reduces storage requirements, allows for a wider range of dates, and makes it easier to search a range of dates.

Conversely, if you want to store a time value without storing a date component, you can use the time data type. When you work with this type, you can specify the precision for the fractional seconds from 0 to 7 digits. Then, the amount of disk space that's required varies from 3 to 5 bytes depending on the precision that's specified. For example, the time(1) type can only store 1 digit of fractional seconds and requires 3 bytes. At the other end of the spectrum, the time(7) type can store 7 digits of fractional seconds and requires 5 bytes.

The datetime2 data type combines the date and time data types into a single type that stores both a date and a time component. This allows you to use the techniques for specifying the precision for fractional seconds with the datetime2 data type. For example, compared to the datetime type, the datetime2(3) type stores a wider range of date values with more precise time values and uses less storage (only 6 bytes).

The datetimeoffset data type works like the datetime2 data type. However, this data type also stores a time zone offset that specifies the number of hours that the value is ahead or behind *Greenwich Mean Time (GMT)*, which is also known as *Universal Time Coordinate* (*UTC*). Although this can make it easier to work with time zones, it requires another 2 bytes of storage.

When you work with date/time values, you need to know how to code date and time literals. This figure presents some of the most common formats for dates and times. All SQL Server systems recognize dates in the yyyy-mm-dd format, which is why I've used this format in most of the examples in this book. Most systems recognize the other date and time formats shown here as well. Since the supported formats depend on system settings, however, you may need to check and see which ones are acceptable on your system.

You also need to be aware of the two-digit year cutoff that's defined on your system when you work with date literals. When you code a two-digit year, the two-digit year cutoff determines whether the year is interpreted as a year

The date/time data types prior to SQL Server 2008

Type	Bytes	Description
datetime	8	Dates and times from January 1, 1753 through December 31, 9999, with an accuracy af 3.33 milliseconds.
smalldatetime	4	Dates and times from January 1, 1900 through June 6, 2079, with an accuracy of one minute.

The date/time data types introduced with SQL Server 2008

Type	Bytes	Description
date	3	Dates only (no time part) from January 1, 0001 through December 31, 9999.
time(n)	3-5	Times only (no date part) from 00:00:00.0000000 through 23:59:59.9999999, with an accuracy of .0000001 seconds. *n* is the number of digits from 0 to 7 that are used for fractional second precision.
datetime2(n)	6-8	Dates from January 1, 0001 through December 31, 9999 with time values from 00:00:00.0000000 through 23:59:59.9999999.
datetimeoffset(n)	8-10	An extension of the datetime2 type that also includes a time zone offset from -14 to +14.

Common date formats

Format	Example
yyyy-mm-dd	2016-04-30
mm/dd/yyyy	4/30/2016
mm-dd-yy	4-30-16
Month dd, yyyy	April 30, 2016
Mon dd, yy	Apr 30, 16
dd Mon yy	30 Apr 16

Common time formats

Format	Example
hh:mi	16:20
hh:mi am/pm	4:20 pm
hh:mi:ss	4:20:36
hh:mi:ss:mmm	4:20:36:12
hh:mi:ss.nnnnnnn	4:20:36.1234567

Description

- You can specify a date/time value by coding a date/time literal. To code a date/time literal, enclose the date/time value in single quotes.

- If you don't specify a time when storing a date value, the time defaults to 12:00 a.m. If you don't specify a date when storing a time value, the date defaults to January 1, 1900.

- By default, the two-digit year cutoff is 50, which means that 00 to 49 are interpreted as 2000 to 2049 and 50 through 99 are interpreted as 1950 through 1999.

- You can specify a time using either a 12-hour or a 24-hour clock. For a 12-hour clock, am is the default.

Figure 8-4   The date/time data types

in the 20th or the 21st century. By default, SQL Server interprets the years 00 through 49 as 2000 through 2049, and it interprets the years 50 through 99 as 1950 through 1999. Because the two-digit year cutoff can be modified, however, you'll want to find out what it is on your system before you use date literals with two-digit years. Then, if you code a date literal outside the range, you'll have to use a four-digit year. Of course, you can always code all of your date literals with four-digit years, just to be sure.

The large value data types

Figure 8-5 presents the data types introduced in SQL Server 2005 that make it easier to work with large values, such as image and sound files. To start, SQL Server provides a max specifier that can be used with the varchar and nvarchar data types described in figure 8-3. This allows you to store up to 2 gigabytes of character data in a column. In addition, the max specifier can be used with the varbinary data type. This allows you to store up to 2 gigabytes of binary data in a column. Since these data types allow you to store large values, they're known as the *large value data types*.

Prior to SQL Server 2005, you could use the text, ntext, and image data types to store this type of data. However, these data types have been deprecated and will be removed in a future version of Microsoft SQL Server. As a result, you should avoid using these data types for any new development. Instead, you should use the corresponding large value data type.

One advantage of the large value data types is that they work like their smaller counterparts. As a result, once you learn how to use the smaller counterparts, you can use the same skills to work with the large value data types. For example, once you understand how to work with the varchar data type, you can use the same skills for working with the varchar(max) data type. However, since the large value data types may store up to 2 gigabytes of data in a column, you may not want to read or write the entire value at once. In that case, you can use the SUBSTRING function that you'll learn about in the next chapter to read the data in chunks, and you can use the .WRITE clause of the UPDATE statement to update the value in chunks. For more information about using the .WRITE clause of the UPDATE statement, you can look up the UPDATE statement in the documentation for SQL Server.

A second advantage of the large value data types is that they don't have as many restrictions as the old text, ntext, and image data types. For example, they can be used as variables in batches and scripts.

In recent years, it has become increasingly common to store large binary values such as images, sounds, and video within a database. That's why chapter 19 shows how to use the varbinary(max) type to store large binary values within a database. Once you learn how to work with this type, you can apply similar skills to the varchar(max) and nvarchar(max) types if you need to do that.

The large value data types for SQL Server 2005 and later

Type	Description
`varchar(max)`	Works the same as the varchar type described in figure 8-3, but the max specifier allows this data type to store up to 2,147,483,648 bytes of data.
`nvarchar(max)`	Works the same as the nvarchar type described in figure 8-3, but the max specifier allows this data type to store up to 2,147,483,648 bytes of data.
`varbinary(max)`	Stores variable-length binary data up to a maximum of 2,147,483,648 bytes. The number of bytes used to store the data depends on the actual length of the data.

How the large value data types map to the old large object types

SQL Server 2005 and later	Prior to 2005
`varchar(max)`	`text`
`nvarchar(max)`	`ntext`
`varbinary(max)`	`image`

Description

- The max specifier can be used with the varchar, nvarchar, and varbinary data types to increase the storage capacity of the column so it can store up to 2 gigabytes of data.

- The varchar(max), nvarchar(max), and varbinary(max) data types are known as the *large value data types*, and these data types can be used to store images and other types of large character or binary data. For more information about working with the varbinary(max) data type, see chapter 19.

- The text, ntext, and image data types that were used prior to SQL Server 2005 have been deprecated and will be removed in a future version of Microsoft SQL Server. As a result, you should avoid using these data types for any new development.

- The large value data types work like their smaller counterparts. As a result, once you learn how to use the smaller counterparts, you can use the same skills to work with the large value data types. In addition, the large value data types don't have as many restrictions as the old text, ntext, and image data types.

Figure 8-5   The large value data types

How to convert data

As you work with the various data types, you'll find that you frequently need to convert a value with one data type to another data type. Although SQL Server does many conversions automatically, it doesn't always do them the way you want. Because of that, you need to be aware of how data conversion works, and you need to know when and how to specify the type of conversion you want to do.

How data conversion works

Before SQL Server can operate on two values, it must convert those values to the same data type. To do that, it converts the value that has the data type with the lowest precedence to the data type of the other value. Figure 8-6 presents the order of precedence for some common SQL Server data types.

To illustrate how this works, consider the three expressions shown in this figure. The first expression multiplies the InvoiceTotal column, which is defined with the money data type, by a decimal value. Because the decimal data type has a higher precedence than the money data type, the value in the InvoiceTotal column is converted to a decimal before the multiplication is performed. Then, the result of the operation is also a decimal value. Similarly, the integer literal in the second expression is converted to the money data type before it's subtracted from the PaymentTotal column, and the result of the operation is a money value.

The third example shows that data conversion is also used when a value is assigned to a column. In this case, a date literal is assigned to the PaymentDate column. Because this column is defined with the smalldatetime data type, the literal must be converted to this data type before it can be assigned to the column.

When SQL Server performs a conversion automatically, it's called an *implicit conversion*. However, not all conversions can be done implicitly. Some of the conversions that can't be done implicitly are listed in this figure. These conversions must be done explicitly. To perform an *explicit conversion*, you use the CAST and CONVERT functions you'll learn about in the next two topics.

Before I go on, you should realize that you won't usually code expressions with literal values like the ones shown in this figure. Instead, you'll use column names that contain the appropriate values. I used literal values here so that it's clear what data types are being evaluated.

Order of precedence for common SQL Server data types

Precedence	Category	Data type
Highest	Date/time	datetime
		smalldatetime
	Numeric	float
		real
		decimal
		money
		smallmoney
		int
		smallint
		tinyint
		bit
	String	nvarchar
		nchar
		varchar
Lowest		char

Conversions that can't be done implicitly

From data type	To data type
char, varchar, nchar, nvarchar	money, smallmoney
datetime, smalldatetime	decimal, numeric, float, real, bigint, int, smallint, tinyint, money, smallmoney, bit
money, smallmoney	char, varchar, nchar, nvarchar

Expressions that use implicit conversion

```
InvoiceTotal * .0775        -- InvoiceTotal (money) converted to decimal
PaymentTotal - 100          -- Numeric literal converted to money
PaymentDate = '2016-04-05'  -- Date literal converted to smalldatetime value
```

Description

- If you assign a value with one data type to a column with another data type, SQL Server converts the value to the data type of the column using *implicit conversion*. Not all data types can be converted implicitly to all other data types.

- SQL Server also uses implicit conversion when it evaluates an expression that involves values with different data types. In that case, it converts the value whose data type has lower precedence to the data type that has higher precedence. The result of the expression is returned in this same data type.

- Each combination of precision and scale for the decimal and numeric values is considered a different data type, with higher precision and scale taking precedence.

- If you want to perform a conversion that can't be done implicitly or you want to convert a data type with higher precedence to a data type with lower precedence, you can use the CAST or CONVERT function to perform an *explicit conversion*.

Figure 8-6   How data conversion works

How to convert data using the CAST function

Figure 8-7 presents the syntax of the CAST function. This function lets you convert, or *cast*, an expression to the data type you specify.

The SELECT statement in this figure illustrates how this works. Here, the third column in the result set shows what happens when the smalldatetime values that are stored in the InvoiceDate column are cast as varchar values. As you can see, this conversion causes the date to be displayed in an alphanumeric format. The fourth column in the result set shows what happens when the money values in the InvoiceTotal column are cast as integer values. Before the digits to the right of the decimal point are dropped, the numbers are rounded to the nearest whole number. Finally, the last column in the result set shows the values from the InvoiceTotal column cast as varchar values. In this case, the result looks the same even though the data has been converted from the money type to the varchar type.

This figure also illustrates a problem that can occur when you perform integer division without explicit conversion. In the first example, the number 50 is divided by the number 100 giving a result of 0. This happens because the result of the division of two integers must be an integer. For this operation to return an accurate result, then, you must explicitly convert one of the numbers to a decimal. Then, because the data type of the other value will be lower in the order of precedence, that value will be converted to a decimal value as well and the result will be a decimal. This is illustrated in the second example, where the value 100 is converted to a decimal. As you can see, the result is .5, which is what you want.

The syntax of the CAST function

```
CAST(expression AS data_type)
```

A SELECT statement that uses the CAST function

```
SELECT InvoiceDate, InvoiceTotal,
    CAST(InvoiceDate AS varchar) AS varcharDate,
    CAST(InvoiceTotal AS int) AS integerTotal,
    CAST(InvoiceTotal AS varchar) AS varcharTotal
FROM Invoices;
```

	InvoiceDate	InvoiceTotal	varcharDate	integerTotal	varcharTotal
1	2015-12-08 00:00:00	3813.33	Dec 8 2015 12:00AM	3813	3813.33
2	2015-12-10 00:00:00	40.20	Dec 10 2015 12:00AM	40	40.20
3	2015-12-13 00:00:00	138.75	Dec 13 2015 12:00AM	139	138.75
4	2015-12-16 00:00:00	144.70	Dec 16 2015 12:00AM	145	144.70

How to convert data when performing integer division

Operation	Result
50/100	0
50/CAST(100 AS decimal(3))	.500000

Description

- You can use the CAST function to explicitly convert, or *cast*, an expression from one data type to another.

- When you perform a division operation on two integers, the result is an integer. To get a more accurate result, you can cast one of the integer values as a decimal. That way, the result will be a decimal.

- CAST is an ANSI-standard function and is used more frequently than CONVERT, which is unique to SQL Server. You should use CONVERT when you need the additional formatting capabilities it provides. See figure 8-8 for details.

Figure 8-7   How to convert data using the CAST function

How to convert data using the CONVERT function

Although the CAST function is an ANSI-standard function, SQL Server provides another function you can use to convert data: CONVERT. Figure 8-8 shows you how to use this function.

In the syntax at the top of this figure, you can see that the CONVERT function provides an optional style argument. You can use this argument to specify the format you want to use when you convert date/time, real, or money data to character data. Some of the common style codes are presented in this figure. For a complete list of codes, please refer to the documentation for SQL Server.

The SELECT statement in this figure shows several examples of the CONVERT function. The first thing you should notice here is that if you don't code a style argument, the CONVERT function works just like CAST. This is illustrated by the first and fourth columns in the result set. Because of that, you'll probably use CONVERT only when you need to use one of the formats provided by the style argument.

The second and third columns both use the CONVERT function to format the InvoiceDate column. The second column uses a style code of 1, so the date is returned in the mm/dd/yy format. In contrast, the third column uses a style code of 107, so the date is returned in the Mon dd, yyyy format. Notice that neither of these formats includes a time. Finally, the fifth column uses the CONVERT function to format the InvoiceTotal column with two digits to the right of the decimal point and commas to the left.

The syntax of the CONVERT function

```
CONVERT(data_type, expression [, style])
```

A SELECT statement that uses the CONVERT function

```
SELECT CONVERT(varchar, InvoiceDate) AS varcharDate,
    CONVERT(varchar, InvoiceDate, 1) AS varcharDate_1,
    CONVERT(varchar, InvoiceDate, 107) AS varcharDate_107,
    CONVERT(varchar, InvoiceTotal) AS varcharTotal,
    CONVERT(varchar, InvoiceTotal, 1) AS varcharTotal_1
FROM Invoices;
```

	varcharDate	varcharDate_1	varcharDate_107	varcharTotal	varcharTotal_1
1	Dec 8 2015 12:00AM	12/08/15	Dec 08, 2015	3813.33	3,813.33
2	Dec 10 2015 12:00AM	12/10/15	Dec 10, 2015	40.20	40.20
3	Dec 13 2015 12:00AM	12/13/15	Dec 13, 2015	138.75	138.75
4	Dec 16 2015 12:00AM	12/16/15	Dec 16, 2015	144.70	144.70

Common style codes for converting date/time data to character data

Code	Output format
0 or **100** (default)	`Mon dd yyyy hh:miAM/PM`
1 or **101**	`mm/dd/yy or mm/dd/yyyy`
7 or **107**	`Mon dd, yy or Mon dd, yyyy`
8 or **108**	`hh:mi:ss`
10 or **110**	`mm-dd-yy or mm-dd-yyyy`
12 or **112**	`yymmdd or yyyymmdd`
14 or **114**	`hh:mi:ss:mmm (24-hour clock)`

Common style codes for converting real data to character data

Code	Output
0 (default)	6 digits maximum
1	8 digits; must use scientific notation
2	16 digits; must use scientific notation

Common style codes for converting money data to character data

Code	Output
0 (default)	2 digits to the right of the decimal point; no commas to the left
1	2 digits to the right of the decimal point; commas to the left
2	4 digits to the right of the decimal point; no commas to the left

Description

- You can use the CONVERT function to explicitly convert an expression from one data type to another.

- You can use the optional style argument to specify the format to be used for date/time, real, and money values converted to character data. For a complete list of codes, search for "cast and convert" in the SQL Server documentation.

Figure 8-8   How to convert data using the CONVERT function

How to use the TRY_CONVERT function

When you use the CAST or CONVERT function, SQL Server returns an error if the expression can't be converted to the data type you specify. If that's not what you want, you can use the TRY_CONVERT function instead. Figure 8-9 shows how this function works.

If you compare the SELECT statement in this figure to the one in figure 8-8, you'll notice two differences. First, it uses the TRY_CONVERT function instead of the CONVERT function. If you look at the results of the first five columns, you'll see that they're identical to the results of the CONVERT function.

Second, a sixth column has been added to the SELECT clause. This column uses a TRY_CONVERT function that attempts to convert an invalid date to the date data type. As you can see, this function returns a value of NULL instead of generating an error. This is particularly useful if you need to test the value of a variable within a script. For more information on coding scripts, please see chapter 14.

The syntax of the TRY_CONVERT function

```
TRY_CONVERT(data_type, expression [, style ])
```

A SELECT statement that uses the CONVERT function

```
SELECT TRY_CONVERT(varchar, InvoiceDate) AS varcharDate,
    TRY_CONVERT(varchar, InvoiceDate, 1) AS varcharDate_1,
    TRY_CONVERT(varchar, InvoiceDate, 107) AS varcharDate_107,
    TRY_CONVERT(varchar, InvoiceTotal) AS varcharTotal,
    TRY_CONVERT(varchar, InvoiceTotal, 1) AS varcharTotal_1,
    TRY_CONVERT(date, 'Feb 29 2015') AS invalidDate
FROM Invoices;
```

	varcharDate	varcharDate_1	varcharDate_107	varcharTotal	varcharTotal_1	invalidDate
1	Dec 8 2015 12:00AM	12/08/15	Dec 08, 2015	3813.33	3,813.33	NULL
2	Dec 10 2015 12:00AM	12/10/15	Dec 10, 2015	40.20	40.20	NULL
3	Dec 13 2015 12:00AM	12/13/15	Dec 13, 2015	138.75	138.75	NULL
4	Dec 16 2015 12:00AM	12/16/15	Dec 16, 2015	144.70	144.70	NULL
5	Dec 16 2015 12:00AM	12/16/15	Dec 16, 2015	15.50	15.50	NULL
6	Dec 16 2015 12:00AM	12/16/15	Dec 16, 2015	42.75	42.75	NULL
7	Dec 21 2015 12:00AM	12/21/15	Dec 21, 2015	172.50	172.50	NULL
8	Dec 24 2015 12:00AM	12/24/15	Dec 24, 2015	95.00	95.00	NULL

Description

- You can use the TRY_CONVERT function to explicitly convert an expression from one data type to another.

- If the TRY_CONVERT function can't convert the expression to the specified data type, it returns a NULL value instead of generating an error.

- You can use the optional style argument to specify the format to be used for date/time, real, and money values converted to character data. See figure 8-8 for more information.

Figure 8-9   How to convert data using the TRY_CONVERT function

How to use other data conversion functions

Although CAST, CONVERT, and TRY_CONVERT are the conversion functions you'll use most often, SQL Server provides some additional functions to perform special types of conversions. These functions are presented in figure 8-10.

You can use the first function, STR, to convert a floating-point value to a character value. You can think of this function as two conversion functions combined into one. First, it converts a floating-point value to a decimal value with the specified length and number of digits to the right of the decimal point. Then, it converts the decimal value to a character value. The function in this figure, for example, converts the number 1234.5678 to a string with a maximum length of seven characters and one digit to the right of the decimal point. Notice that the decimal digits are rounded rather than truncated.

The other four functions are used to convert characters to their equivalent numeric code and vice versa. CHAR and ASCII work with standard character strings that are stored one byte per character. The CHAR function shown in this figure, for example, converts the number 79 to its equivalent ASCII code, the letter O. Conversely, the ASCII function converts the letter O to its numeric equivalent of 79. Notice that although the string in the ASCII function can include more than one character, only the first character is converted.

The NCHAR and UNICODE functions convert Unicode characters to and from their numeric equivalents. You can see how these functions work in the examples. Notice in the last example that to code a Unicode character as a literal value, you have to precede the literal with the letter N.

CHAR is frequently used to output ASCII control characters that can't be typed on your keyboard. The three most common control characters are presented in this figure. These characters can be used to format output so it's easy to read. The SELECT statement in this figure, for example, uses the CHAR(13) and CHAR(10) control characters to start new lines after the vendor name and vendor address in the output.

Other data conversion functions

Function	Description
`STR(float[,length[,decimal]])`	Converts a floating-point number to a character string with the given length and number of digits to the right of the decimal point. The length must include one character for the decimal point and one character for the sign. The sign is blank if the number is positive.
`CHAR(integer)`	Converts the ASCII code represented by an integer between 0 and 255 to its character equivalent.
`ASCII(string)`	Converts the leftmost character in a string to its equivalent ASCII code.
`NCHAR(integer)`	Converts the Unicode code represented by an integer between 0 and 65535 to its character equivalent.
`UNICODE(string)`	Converts the leftmost character in a UNICODE string to its equivalent UNICODE code.

Examples that use the data conversion functions

Function	Result
`STR(1234.5678, 7, 1)`	`1234.6`
`CHAR(79)`	`O`
`ASCII('Orange')`	`79`
`NCHAR(332)`	`O`
`UNICODE(N'Or')`	`332`

ASCII codes for common control characters

Control character	Value
Tab	`Char(9)`
Line feed	`Char(10)`
Carriage return	`Char(13)`

A SELECT statement that uses the CHAR function to format output

```
SELECT VendorName + CHAR(13) + CHAR(10)
    + VendorAddress1 + CHAR(13) + CHAR(10)
    + VendorCity + ', ' + VendorState + ' ' + VendorZipCode
FROM Vendors
WHERE VendorID = 1;
```

```
US Postal Service
Attn:  Supt. Window Services
Madison, WI 53707
```

Description

- The CHAR function is typically used to insert control characters into a character string.
- To code a Unicode value as a literal, precede the value with the character N.

Figure 8-10   How to use other data conversion functions

Perspective

In this chapter, you learned about the different SQL Server data types. In addition, you learned how to use some functions for converting data from one type to another. In the next chapter, you'll learn about some of the additional functions for working with data.

Terms

data type	exact numeric data types
string data type	approximate numeric data types
numeric data type	Unicode character
temporal data type	Unicode specification
date/time data type	national character
date data type	fixed-length string
integer data type	variable-length string
decimal data type	bit
scale	ASCII (American Standard Code
precision	for Information Interchange)
real data type	large value data types
fixed-point number	implicit conversion
floating-point number	explicit conversion
significant digits	cast
single-precision number	Universal Time Coordinate (UTC)
double-precision number	Greenwich Mean Time
scientific notation	

Exercises

1. Write a SELECT statement that returns four columns based on the InvoiceTotal column of the Invoices table:

   - Use the CAST function to return the first column as data type decimal with 2 digits to the right of the decimal point.

   - Use CAST to return the second column as a varchar.

   - Use the CONVERT function to return the third column as the same data type as the first column.

   - Use CONVERT to return the fourth column as a varchar, using style 1.

2. Write a SELECT statement that returns four columns based on the InvoiceDate column of the Invoices table:

   - Use the CAST function to return the first column as data type varchar.

   - Use the CONVERT function to return the second and third columns as a varchar, using style 1 and style 10, respectively.

   - Use the CAST function to return the fourth column as data type real.

9

How to use functions

In chapter 3, you were introduced to some of the scalar functions that you can use in a SELECT statement. Now, this chapter expands on that coverage by presenting many more of the scalar functions. When you complete this chapter, you'll have a thorough understanding of the functions that you can use with SQL Server.

How to work with string data

SQL Server provides a number of functions for working with string data. You'll learn how to use some of those functions in the topics that follow. In addition, you'll learn how to solve two common problems that can occur when you work with string data.

A summary of the string functions

Part 1 of figure 9-1 summarizes the string functions that are available with SQL Server. Most of these functions are used to perform string manipulation. For example, you can use the LEN function to get the number of characters in a string. Note that this function counts spaces at the beginning of the string (leading spaces), but not spaces at the end of the string (trailing spaces). If you want to remove leading or trailing spaces from a string, you can use the LTRIM or RTRIM function.

You can use the LEFT and RIGHT functions to get the specified number of characters from the beginning and end of a string. You can use the SUBSTRING function to get the specified number of characters from anywhere in a string. You can use the REPLACE function to replace a substring within a string with another substring. And you can use the REVERSE function to reverse the order of the characters in a string.

The CHARINDEX function lets you locate the first occurrence of a substring within another string. The return value is a number that indicates the position of the substring. Note that you can start the search at a position other than the beginning of the string by including the start argument.

The PATINDEX function is similar to CHARINDEX. Instead of locating a string, however, it locates a string pattern. Like the string patterns you learned about in chapter 3 for use with the LIKE operator, the string patterns you use with the PATINDEX function can include wildcard characters. You can refer back to chapter 3 if you need to refresh your memory on how to use these characters.

The CONCAT function lets you concatenate two or more values into a single string. Although this function is similar to the concatenation operator, it lets you concatenate values other than strings. To do that, it implicitly converts all values to strings. That includes null values, which it converts to empty strings.

The last three functions should be self-explanatory. You use the LOWER and UPPER functions to convert the characters in a string to lower or upper case. And you use the SPACE function to return a string that has the specified number of spaces.

Some of the string functions

Function	Description
`LEN(string)`	Returns the number of characters in the string. Leading spaces are included, but trailing spaces are not.
`LTRIM(string)`	Returns the string with any leading spaces removed.
`RTRIM(string)`	Returns the string with any trailing spaces removed.
`LEFT(string,length)`	Returns the specified number of characters from the beginning of the string.
`RIGHT(string,length)`	Returns the specified number of characters from the end of the string.
`SUBSTRING(string,start,length)`	Returns the specified number of characters from the string starting at the specified position.
`REPLACE(search,find,replace)`	Returns the search string with all occurrences of the find string replaced with the replace string.
`REVERSE(string)`	Returns the string with the characters in reverse order.
`CHARINDEX(find,search[,start])`	Returns an integer that represents the position of the first occurrence of the find string in the search string starting at the specified position. If the starting position isn't specified, the search starts at the beginning of the string. If the string isn't found, the function returns zero.
`PATINDEX(find,search)`	Returns an integer that represents the position of the first occurrence of the find pattern in the search string. If the pattern isn't found, the function returns zero. The find pattern can include wildcard characters. If the pattern begins with a wildcard, the value returned is the position of the first non-wildcard character.
`CONCAT(value1,value2[,value3]...`	Returns a string that contains a concatenation of the specified values. The values are implicitly converted to strings. A null value is converted to an empty string.
`LOWER(string)`	Returns the string converted to lowercase letters.
`UPPER(string)`	Returns the string converted to uppercase letters.
`SPACE(integer)`	Returns a string with the specified number of space characters (blanks).

Notes

- The start argument must be an integer from 1 to the length of the string.
- The ANSI standards specify a TRIM function that removes both leading and trailing spaces from a string. Although this function isn't supported by SQL Server, you can get the same result by combining LTRIM and RTRIM (see the example in part 2 of this figure).

Figure 9-1   A summary of the string functions (part 1 of 2)

Part 2 of figure 9-1 presents examples of most of the string functions. If you study the examples at the top of this figure, you shouldn't have any trouble figuring out how they work. If you're confused by any of them, though, you can refer back to part 1 to check the syntax.

The SELECT statement shown in this figure illustrates how you can use the LEFT and RIGHT functions to format columns in a result set. In this case, the LEFT function is used to retrieve the first character of the VendorContactFName column in the Vendors table, which contains the first name of the vendor contact. In other words, this function retrieves the first initial of the vendor contact. Then, this initial is combined with the last name of the vendor contact and two literal values. You can see the result in the second column of the result set.

The third column in the result set lists the vendor's phone number without an area code. To accomplish that, this column specification uses the RIGHT function to extract the eight rightmost characters of the VendorPhone column. This assumes, of course, that all of the phone numbers are stored in the same format, which isn't necessarily the case since the VendorPhone column is defined as varchar(50).

This SELECT statement also shows how you can use a function in the search condition of a WHERE clause. This condition uses the SUBSTRING function to select only those rows with an area code of 559. To do that, it retrieves three characters from the VendorPhone column starting with the second character. Again, this assumes that the phone numbers are all in the same format and that the area code is enclosed in parentheses.

String function examples

Function	Result
LEN('SQL Server')	10
LEN(' SQL Server ')	12
LEFT('SQL Server', 3)	'SQL'
LTRIM(' SQL Server ')	'SQL Server '
RTRIM(' SQL Server ')	' SQL Server'
LTRIM(RTRIM(' SQL Server '))	'SQL Server'
LOWER('SQL Server')	'sql server'
UPPER('ca')CA	
PATINDEX('%v_r%', 'SQL Server')	8
CHARINDEX('SQL', ' SQL Server')	3
CHARINDEX('-', '(559) 555-1212')	10
SUBSTRING('(559) 555-1212', 7, 8)	555-1212
REPLACE(RIGHT('(559) 555-1212', 13), ') ', '-')	559-555-1212
CONCAT('Run time: ',1.52,' seconds')	Run time: 1.52 seconds

A SELECT statement that uses the LEFT, RIGHT, and SUBSTRING functions

```
SELECT VendorName, VendorContactLName + ', ' + LEFT(VendorContactFName, 1)
    + '.' AS ContactName, RIGHT(VendorPhone, 8) AS Phone
FROM Vendors
WHERE SUBSTRING(VendorPhone, 2, 3) = 559
ORDER BY VendorName;
```

	VendorName	ContactName	Phone
1	Abbey Office Furnishings	Francis, K.	555-8300
2	BFI Industries	Kaleigh, E.	555-1551
3	Bill Marvin Electric Inc	Hostlery, K.	555-5106
4	Cal State Termite	Hunter, D.	555-1534
5	California Business Machines	Rohansen, A.	555-5570
6	California Data Marketing	Jonessen, M.	555-3801
7	City Of Fresno	Mayte, K.	555-9999
8	Coffee Break Service	Smitzen, J.	555-8700

Figure 9-1   A summary of the string functions (part 2 of 2)

How to solve common problems that occur with string data

Figure 9-2 presents solutions to two common problems that occur when you work with string data. The first problem occurs when you store numeric data in a character column and then want to sort the column in numeric sequence.

To illustrate, look at the first example in this figure. Here, the columns in the StringSample table are defined with character data types. The first SELECT statement shows the result of sorting the table by the first column, which contains a numeric ID. As you can see, the rows are not in numeric sequence. That's because SQL Server interprets the values as characters, not as numbers.

One way to solve this problem is to convert the values in the ID column to integers for sorting purposes. This is illustrated in the second SELECT statement in this example. As you can see, the rows are now sorted in numeric sequence.

Another way to solve this problem is to pad the numbers with leading zeros or spaces so that the numbers are aligned on the right. This is illustrated by the AltID column in this table, which is padded with zeros. If you sorted by this column instead of the first column, the rows would be returned in numeric sequence.

The second problem you'll encounter when working with string data occurs when two or more values are stored in the same string. For example, both a first and a last name are stored in the Name column of the StringSample table. If you want to work with the first and last names independently, you have to parse the string using the string functions. This is illustrated by the SELECT statement in the second example in this figure.

To extract the first name, this statement uses the LEFT and CHARINDEX functions. First, it uses the CHARINDEX function to locate the first space in the Name column. Then, it uses the LEFT function to extract all of the characters up to that space. Notice that one is subtracted from the value that's returned by the CHARINDEX function, so the space itself isn't included in the first name.

To extract the last name, this statement uses the RIGHT, LEN, and CHARINDEX functions. It uses the LEN function to get the number of characters in the Name column. Then, it uses the CHARINDEX function to locate the first space in the Name column, and it subtracts that value from the value returned by the LEN function. The result is the number of characters in the last name. That value is then used in the RIGHT function to extract the last name from the Name column.

As you review this example, you should keep in mind that I kept it simple so that you can focus on how the string functions are used. You should realize, however, that this code won't work for all names. If, for example, a first name contains a space, such as in the name Jean Paul, this code won't work properly. That illustrates the importance of designing a database so that this type of problem doesn't occur. You'll learn more about that in the next chapter. For now, just realize that if a database is designed correctly, you won't have to worry about this type of problem. Instead, this problem should occur only if you're importing data from another file or database system.

How to use the CAST function to sort by a string column that contains numbers

The StringSample table sorted by the ID column

```
SELECT * FROM StringSample
ORDER BY ID;
```

	ID	Name	AltID
1	1	Lizbeth Darien	01
2	17	Lance Pinos-Potter	17
3	2	Darnell O'Sullivan	02
4	20	Jean Paul Renard	20
5	3	Alisha von Strump	03

The StringSample table sorted by the ID column cast to an integer

```
SELECT * FROM StringSample
ORDER BY CAST(ID AS int);
```

	ID	Name	AltID
1	1	Lizbeth Darien	01
2	2	Darnell O'Sullivan	02
3	3	Alisha von Strump	03
4	17	Lance Pinos-Potter	17
5	20	Jean Paul Renard	20

How to use the string functions to parse a string

```
SELECT Name,
    LEFT(Name, CHARINDEX(' ', Name) - 1) AS First,
    RIGHT(Name, LEN(Name) - CHARINDEX(' ', Name) ) AS Last
FROM StringSample;
```

	Name	First	Last
1	Lizbeth Darien	Lizbeth	Darien
2	Darnell O'Sullivan	Darnell	O'Sullivan
3	Lance Pinos-Potter	Lance	Pinos-Potter
4	Jean Paul Renard	Jean	Paul Renard
5	Alisha von Strump	Alisha	von Strump

Description

- If you sort by a string column that contains numbers, you may receive unexpected results. To avoid that, you can convert the string column to a numeric value in the ORDER BY clause.

- If a string consists of two or more components, you can parse it into its individual components. To do that, you can use the CHARINDEX function to locate the characters that separate the components. Then, you can use the LEFT, RIGHT, SUBSTRING, and LEN functions to extract the individual components.

Figure 9-2   How to solve common problems that occur with string data

How to work with numeric data

In addition to the string functions, SQL Server provides several numeric functions. Although you'll probably use only a couple of these functions on a regular basis, you should be aware of all of them in case you ever need them. After you learn about these functions, I'll show you how you can use them and some of the other functions you've learned about in this chapter to solve common problems that occur when you work with numeric data.

A summary of the numeric functions

Figure 9-3 summarizes eight of the numeric functions SQL Server provides. The function you'll probably use most often is ROUND. This function rounds a number to the precision specified by the length argument. Note that you can round the digits to the left of the decimal point by coding a negative value for this argument. However, you're more likely to code a positive number to round the digits to the right of the decimal point. You can also use the ROUND function to truncate a number to the specified length. To do that, you can code any integer value other than zero for the optional function argument.

The first set of examples in this figure shows how the ROUND function works. The first example rounds the number 12.5 to a precision of zero, which means that the result has no significant digits to the right of the decimal point. Note that this function does not change the precision of the value. The result still has one digit to the right of the decimal point. The number has just been rounded so that the digit is insignificant. To make that point clear, the second example rounds a number with four decimal places to a precision of zero. Notice that the result still has four digits to the right of the decimal point; they're just all zero.

The next three examples show variations of the first two examples. The third example rounds a number with four decimal places to a precision of 1, and the fourth example rounds the digits to the left of the decimal point to a precision of one. Finally, the last example truncates a number to a precision of zero.

The other function you're likely to use is ISNUMERIC. This function returns a Boolean value that indicates if an expression is numeric. This is illustrated by the next set of examples in this figure. This function can be useful for testing the validity of a value before saving it in a table.

You can use the next three functions, ABS, CEILING, and FLOOR, to get the absolute value of a number, the smallest integer greater than or equal to a number, or the largest integer less than or equal to a number. If you study the examples, you shouldn't have any trouble figuring out how these functions work.

The next two functions, SQUARE and SQRT, are used to calculate the square and square root of a number. And the last function, RAND, generates a floating-point number with a random value between 0 and 1. SQL Server provides a variety of functions like these for performing mathematical calculations, but you're not likely to use them. For a complete list of these functions, you can search for "mathematical functions" in the SQL Server documentation.

Some of the numeric functions

Function	Description
ROUND(number,length [,function])	Returns the number rounded to the precision specified by length. If length is positive, the digits to the right of the decimal point are rounded. If it's negative, the digits to the left of the decimal point are rounded. To truncate the number rather than round it, code a non-zero value for function.
ISNUMERIC(expression)	Returns a value of 1 (true) if the expression is a numeric value; returns a value of 0 (false) otherwise.
ABS(number)	Returns the absolute value of the number.
CEILING(number)	Returns the smallest integer that is greater than or equal to the number.
FLOOR(number)	Returns the largest integer that is less than or equal to the number.
SQUARE(float_number)	Returns the square of a floating-point number.
SQRT(float_number)	Returns the square root of a floating-point number.
RAND([integer])	Returns a random floating-point number between 0 and 1. If integer is coded, it provides a starting value for the function. Otherwise, the function will return the same number each time it's invoked within the same query.

Examples that use the numeric functions

Function	Result
ROUND(12.5,0)	13.0
ROUND(12.4999,0)	12.0000
ROUND(12.4999,1)	12.5000
ROUND(12.4999,-1)	10.0000
ROUND(12.5,0,1)	12.0
ISNUMERIC(-1.25)	1
ISNUMERIC('SQL Server')	0
ISNUMERIC('2016-09-30')	0
ABS(-1.25) 1.25	
CEILING(-1.25)	-1
FLOOR(-1.25)	-2
CEILING(1.25)	2
FLOOR(1.25)1	
SQUARE(5.2786)	27.86361796
SQRT(125.43)	11.199553562531
RAND()	0.243729

Note

- To calculate the square or square root of a number with a data type other than float or real, you must cast it to a floating-point number.

Figure 9-3   A summary of the numeric functions

How to solve common problems that occur with numeric data

In the previous chapter, you learned that numbers with the real data types don't contain exact values. The details of why that is are beyond the scope of this book. From a practical point of view, though, that means that you don't want to search for exact values when you're working with real numbers. If you do, you'll miss values that are in essence equal to the value you're looking for.

To illustrate, consider the RealSample table shown in figure 9-4. This table includes a column named R that's defined with the float(53) data type. Now, consider what would happen if you selected all the rows where the value of R is equal to 1. The result set would include only the second row, even though the table contains two other rows that have values approximately equal to 1.

When you perform a search on a column with a real data type, then, you usually want to search for an approximate value. This figure shows two ways to do that. First, you can search for a range of values. The first SELECT statement in this figure, for example, searches for values between .99 and 1.01. Second, you can search for values that round to an exact value. This is illustrated by the second SELECT statement. Both of these statements return the three rows in the RealSample table that are approximately equal to 1. In fact, the value in the first row is so close to 1 that the Management Studio removes the decimal places from this number when it displays the results.

Although both of the SELECT statements shown here return the same results, the first statement is more efficient than the second one. That's because SQL Server isn't able to optimize a query that uses a function in its search condition. Because of that, I recommend you use the range technique to search for a real value whenever possible.

Another problem you may face is formatting numeric values so that they're easy to read. One way to do that is to format them so they're aligned on the right, as shown in the third SELECT statement. To do this, the real numbers in the R column are first cast as decimal numbers to give them a consistent scale. Then, the decimal values are cast as character data and padded on the left with spaces to right-align the data as shown in the column named R_Formatted.

If you look at the expression for the last column, you'll see that it's quite complicated. If you break it down into its component parts, however, you shouldn't have much trouble understanding how it works. To help you break it down, the third, fourth, and fifth columns in the result set show the interim results returned by portions of the expression.

To align the values at the right, the last column specification assumes a column width of nine characters. Then, the length of the number to be formatted is subtracted from nine, and the SPACE function is used to create a string with the resulting number of spaces. Finally, the number is concatenated to the string of spaces after it's converted to a string value. The result is a string column with the numbers aligned at the right. However, this formatting isn't displayed properly when you use the Management Studio to view the results in the grid. As a result, to view this formatting, you must click on the Results to Text button to view the results as text as shown in this figure.

The RealSample table

ID	R
1	1.0000000000000011
2	1
3	0.999999999999999
4	1234.56789012345
5	999.04440209348
6	24.04849

How to search for approximate real values

A SELECT statement that searches for a range of values

```
SELECT * FROM RealSample
WHERE R BETWEEN 0.99 AND 1.01;
```

A SELECT statement that searches for rounded values

```
SELECT * FROM RealSample
WHERE ROUND(R,2) = 1;
```

	ID	R
1	1	1
2	2	1
3	3	0.999999999999999

A SELECT statement that formats real numbers

```
SELECT ID, R, CAST(R AS decimal(9,3)) AS R_decimal,
    CAST(CAST(R AS decimal(9,3)) AS varchar(9)) AS R_varchar,
    LEN(CAST(CAST(R AS decimal(9,3)) AS varchar(9))) AS R_LEN,
    SPACE(9 - LEN(CAST(CAST(R AS decimal(9,3)) AS varchar(9)))) +
        CAST(CAST(R AS decimal(9,3)) AS varchar(9)) AS R_Formatted
FROM RealSample;
```

R_decimal	R_varchar	R_LEN	R_Formatted
1.000	1.000	5	1.000
1.000	1.000	5	1.000
1.000	1.000	5	1.000
1234.568	1234.568	8	1234.568
999.044	999.044	7	999.044
24.048	24.048	6	24.048

100 %

Description

- Because real values are approximate, you'll want to search for approximate values when retrieving real data. To do that, you can specify a range of values, or you can use the ROUND function to search for rounded values.

- When you display real or decimal values, you may want to format them so they're aligned on the right.

Figure 9-4   How to solve common problems that occur with numeric data

How to work with date/time data

In the topics that follow, you'll learn how to use some of the functions SQL Server provides for working with dates and times. As you'll see, these include functions for extracting different parts of a date/time value and for performing operations on dates and times. In addition, you'll learn how to perform different types of searches on date/time values.

A summary of the date/time functions

Figure 9-5 presents a summary of the date/time functions and shows how some of them work. One of the functions you'll use frequently is GETDATE, which gets the current local date and time from your system. GETUTCDATE is similar, but it returns the Universal Time Coordinate (UTC) date, also known as Greenwich Mean Time (GMT).

Although you probably won't use the GETUTCDATE function often, it's useful if your system will operate in different time zones. That way, the date/time values will always reflect Greenwich Mean Time, regardless of the time zone in which they're entered. For example, a date/time value entered at 11:00 a.m. Los Angeles time would be given the same value as a date/time value entered at 2:00 p.m. New York time. That makes it easy to compare and operate on these values.

The next three functions (SYSDATETIME, SYSUTCDATETIME, and SYSDATETIMEOFFSET) work similarly to the first two functions. However, they return the datetime2 and datetimeoffset types that were introduced with SQL Server 2008. As a result, these functions return a more precise fractional second value. In addition, the SYSDATETIMEOFFSET function returns a value that includes a time zone offset. Note that the time zone offset is not adjusted for daylight savings time.

The next five functions (DAY, MONTH, YEAR, DATENAME, and DATEPART) let you extract different parts of a date value. For more information about these functions, you can refer to figure 9-6. For now, just realize that when you use the DATEPART and DATENAME functions, you can retrieve any of the date parts listed in part 2 of this figure.

The DATEADD and DATEDIFF functions let you perform addition and subtraction operations on date/time values. As you can see, these functions let you specify the date part to be added. For more information about these functions, you can refer to figure 9-7.

The TODATETIMEOFFSET and SWITCHOFFSET functions let you work with the datetimeoffset data type. In particular, you can use the TODATETIMEOFFSET function to add a time zone offset to a datetime2 value and return a datetimeoffset value. In addition, you can use the SWITCHOFFSET function to specify a new time zone offset value for a datetimeoffset value.

The next two functions, EOMONTH and DATEFROMPARTS, were introduced with SQL Server 2012. The EOMONTH function gets the last day of the month for the specified date. This can be helpful for determining what days are valid for a given month. The DATEFROMPARTS function lets you create

Some of the date/time functions

Function	Description
GETDATE()	Returns a datetime value for the current local date and time based on the system's clock.
GETUTCDATE()	Returns a datetime value for the current UTC date and time based on the system's clock and time zone setting.
SYSDATETIME()	Returns a datetime2(7) value for the current local date and time based on the system's clock.
SYSUTCDATETIME()	Returns a datetime2(7) value for the current UTC date and time based on the system's clock and time zone setting.
SYSDATETIMEOFFSET()	Returns a datetimeoffset(7) value for the current UTC date and time based on the system's clock and time zone setting with a time zone offset that is *not* adjusted for daylight savings time.
DAY(date)	Returns the day of the month as an integer.
MONTH(date)	Returns the month as an integer.
YEAR(date)	Returns the 4-digit year as an integer.
DATENAME(datepart,date)	Returns the part of the date specified by datepart as a character string.
DATEPART(datepart,date)	Returns the part of the date specified by datepart as an integer.
DATEADD(datepart,number,date)	Returns the date that results from adding the specified number of datepart units to the date.
DATEDIFF(datepart,startdate,enddate)	Returns the number of datepart units between the specified start and end dates.
TODATETIMEOFFSET(datetime2,tzoffset)	Returns a datetimeoffset value that results from adding the specified time zone offset to the specified datetime2 value.
SWITCHOFFSET(datetimeoffset,tzoffset)	Returns a datetimeoffset value that results from switching the time zone offset for the specified datetimeoffset value to the specified offset.
EOMONTH(startdate[,months])	Returns a date for the last day of the month specified by the start date. If months is specified, the number of months is added to the start date before the end-of-month date is calculated.
DATEFROMPARTS(year,month,day)	Returns a date for the specified year, month, and day.
ISDATE(expression)	Returns a value of 1 (true) if the expression is a valid date/time value; returns a value of 0 (false) otherwise.

Figure 9-5   A summary of the date/time functions (part 1 of 2)

a date value for a given year, month, and day. In addition to this function, SQL Server 2012 introduced other functions that let you create datetime, smalldatetime, time, datetime2, and datetimeoffset values. For more information, please search for "date and time functions" in the SQL Server documentation.

The last function (ISDATE) returns a Boolean value that indicates whether an expression can be cast as a valid date/time value. This function is useful for testing the validity of a date/time value before it's saved to a table. This is illustrated by the last set of examples. Here, you can see that the first and third expressions are valid dates, but the second and fourth expressions aren't. The second expression isn't valid because the month of September has only 30 days. And the fourth expression isn't valid because a time value can have a maximum of 59 minutes and 59 seconds. Note that this function checks for both a valid date/time format and a valid date/time value.

The first two sets of examples illustrate the differences between the functions that return date/time values. To start, there's a 7 hour difference between the datetime value that's returned by the GETDATE and GETUTCDATE functions. That's because I ran these functions from California, which is 7 hours behind the Universal Time Coordinate (UTC). In addition, note that the datetime2(7) value that's returned by the SYSDATETIME function provides more precise fractional second values than the datetime value that's returned by the GETDATE and GETUTCDATE functions. Finally, note that the SYSDATETIMEOFFSET function returns a datetimeoffset value that includes a time zone offset.

The third set of examples shows how you can use the date parts with the DATEPART and DATENAME functions. To start, you don't need to specify a date part when you use the MONTH function to return an integer value for the month. However, you can get the same result with the DATEPART function by specifying the month date part as the first argument. Or, if you want to return the name of the month as a string of characters, you can specify the month date part as the first argument of the DATENAME function. Finally, you can use an abbreviation for a date part whenever that makes sense. However, I generally prefer to avoid abbreviations as they tend to make the code more difficult to read and understand.

The fourth set of examples shows how to use the EOMONTH and DATEFROMPARTS functions that were introduced with SQL Server 2012. Here, the first expression uses the EOMONTH function to return a date for the last day of the month for February 1, 2016. Since 2016 is a leap year, this returns February 29, 2016. The second expression is similar, but it adds two months to the specified date. Finally, the last expression uses the DATEFROMPARTS function to create a date with a year value of 2016, a month value of 4, and a day value of 3.

Date part values and abbreviations

Argument	Abbreviations
year	yy, yyyy
quarter	qq, q
month	mm, m
dayofyear	dy, y
day	dd, d
week	wk, ww
weekday	dw
hour	hh
minute	mi, n
second	ss, s
millisecond	ms
microsecond	mcs
nanosecond	ns
tzoffset	tz

Examples that use date/time functions

Function	Result
GETDATE()	2016-09-30 14:10:13.813
GETUTCDATE()	2016-09-30 21:10:13.813
SYSDATETIME()	2016-09-30 14:10:13.8160822
SYSUTCDATETIME()	2016-09-30 21:10:13.8160822
SYSDATETIMEOFFSET()	2016-09-30 14:10:13.8160822 -07.00
MONTH('2016-09-30')	9
DATEPART(month,'2016-09-30')	9
DATENAME(month,'2016-09-30')	September
DATENAME(m,'2016-09-30')	September
EOMONTH('2016-02-01')	2016-02-29
EOMONTH('2016-02-01',2)	2016-04-30
DATEFROMPARTS(2016,4,3)	2016-04-03
ISDATE('2016-09-30')	1
ISDATE('2016-09-31')	0
ISDATE('23:59:59')	1
ISDATE('23:99:99')	0

Figure 9-5   A summary of the date/time functions (part 2 of 2)

How to parse dates and times

Figure 9-6 shows you how to use the DAY, MONTH, YEAR, DATEPART, and DATENAME functions to parse dates and times. If you just need to get an integer value for a day, month, or year, you should use the DAY, MONTH, and YEAR functions as shown in the examples at the top of this figure since these are ANSI-standard functions. If you need to extract another part of a date or time as an integer, however, you'll need to use the DATEPART function. And if you need to extract a date part as a string, you'll need to use the DATENAME function.

This figure shows the result of using each of the date part values with the DATEPART and DATENAME functions. As you can see, many of the values returned by the two functions appear to be the same. Keep in mind, however, that all of the values returned by DATEPART are integers. In contrast, all of the values returned by DATENAME are strings. That's why the month and week day are returned as names rather than numbers when you use DATENAME. The function you use, then, will depend on what you need to do with the date part. If you need to use it in an arithmetic operation, for example, you'll want to use the DATEPART function. But if you need to use it in a concatenation, you'll want to use the DATENAME function.

Finally, it's important to note the difference between the DATEPART and DATENAME functions when working with the tzoffset date part. With this part, the DATEPART function returns an integer value for the number of minutes for the time zone offset, and the DATENAME function returns a string value that specifies the hours and minutes.

Examples that use the DAY, MONTH, and YEAR functions

Function	Result
DAY('2016-09-30')	30
MONTH('2016-09-30')	9
YEAR('2016-09-30')	2016

Examples that use the DATEPART function

Function	Result
DATEPART(day, '2016-09-30 11:35:00')	30
DATEPART(month, '2016-09-30 11:35:00')	9
DATEPART(year, '2016-09-30 11:35:00')	2016
DATEPART(hour, '2016-09-30 11:35:00')	11
DATEPART(minute, '2016-09-30 11:35:00')	35
DATEPART(second, '2016-09-30 11:35:00')	0
DATEPART(quarter, '2016-09-30 11:35:00')	3
DATEPART(dayofyear, '2016-09-30 11:35:00')	274
DATEPART(week, '2016-09-30 11:35:00')	40
DATEPART(weekday, '2016-09-30 11:35:00')	1
DATEPART(millisecond, '11:35:00.1234567')	123
DATEPART(microsecond, '11:35:00.1234567')	123456
DATEPART(nanosecond, '11:35:00.1234567')	123456700
DATEPART(tzoffset, '11:35:00.1234567 -07:00')	-420

Examples that use the DATENAME function

Function	Result
DATENAME(day, '2016-09-30 11:35:00')	30
DATENAME(month, '2016-09-30 11:35:00')	September
DATENAME(year, '2016-09-30 11:35:00')	2016
DATENAME(hour, '2016-09-30 11:35:00')	11
DATENAME(minute, '2016-09-30 11:35:00')	35
DATENAME(second, '2016-09-30 11:35:00')	0
DATENAME(quarter, '2016-09-30 11:35:00')	3
DATENAME(dayofyear, '2016-09-30 11:35:00')	274
DATENAME(week, '2016-09-30 11:35:00')	40
DATENAME(weekday, '2016-09-30 11:35:00')	Sunday
DATENAME(millisecond, '11:35:00.1234567')	123
DATENAME(microsecond, '11:35:00.1234567')	123456
DATENAME(nanosecond, '11:35:00.1234567')	123456700
DATENAME(tzoffset, '11:35:00.1234567 -07:00')	-07:00

Notes

- When you use weekday with the DATEPART function, it returns an integer that indicates the day of the week where 1=Sunday, 2=Monday, etc.
- The DAY, MONTH, and YEAR functions are ANSI-standard functions. The DATEPART and DATENAME functions are more general-purpose functions provided by SQL Server.

Figure 9-6   How to parse dates and times

How to perform operations on dates and times

Figure 9-7 shows you how to use the DATEADD and DATEDIFF functions to perform operations on dates and times. You can use the DATEADD function to add a specified number of date parts to a date. The first eight DATEADD functions in this figure, for example, show how you can add one day, month, year, hour, minute, second, quarter, and week to a date/time value. If you want to subtract date parts from a date/time value, you can do that with the DATEADD function too. Just code the number argument as a negative value, as illustrated by the next to last DATEADD function. The last DATEADD function illustrates that you can't add a fractional number of date parts to a date/time value. If you try to, the fractional portion is ignored.

If you need to find the difference between two date/time values, you can use the DATEDIFF function as illustrated by the second set of examples in this figure. As you can see, the result is expressed in the date part units you specify. The first function, for example, returns the number of days between two dates, and the second example returns the number of months between the same two dates.

In most cases, the earlier date is specified as the second argument in the DATEDIFF function and the later date is specified as the third argument. That way, the result of the function is a positive value. However, you can also code the later date first. Then, the result is a negative value as you can see in the last DATEDIFF function in this figure.

If you use the DATEDIFF function, you should realize that it returns the number of date/time boundaries crossed, which is not necessarily the same as the number of intervals between two dates. To understand this, consider the third DATEDIFF function. This function returns the difference in years between the dates 2015-12-01 and 2016-09-30. Since the second date is less than one year after the first date, you might expect this function to return a value of zero. As you can see, however, it returns a value of 1 because it crossed the one-year boundary between the years 2015 and 2016. Because this is not intuitive, you'll want to use this function carefully.

The last three examples in this figure show how you can perform operations on dates and times without using the DATEADD and DATEDIFF functions. The first expression, for example, adds one day to a date/time value, and the second expression subtracts one day from the same value. When you use this technique, SQL Server assumes you're adding or subtracting days. So you can't add or subtract other date parts unless you express them as multiples or fractions of days.

The last expression shows how you can subtract two date/time values to calculate the number of days between them. Notice that after the dates are subtracted, the result is converted to an integer. That's necessary because the result of the subtraction operation is implicitly cast as a date/time value that represents the number of days after January 1, 1900. For this reason, the integer difference of 304 days is interpreted as the following date/time value: 1900-10-31 00:00:00:000.

Examples that use the DATEADD function

Function	Result
DATEADD(day, 1, '2016-09-30 11:35:00')	2016-10-01 11:35:00.000
DATEADD(month, 1, '2016-09-30 11:35:00')	2016-10-30 11:35:00.000
DATEADD(year, 1, '2016-09-30 11:35:00')	2017-09-30 11:35:00.000
DATEADD(hour, 1, '2016-09-30 11:35:00')	2016-09-30 12:35:00.000
DATEADD(minute, 1, '2016-09-30 11:35:00')	2016-09-30 11:36:00.000
DATEADD(second, 1, '2016-09-30 11:35:00')	2016-09-30 11:35:01.000
DATEADD(quarter, 1, '2016-09-30 11:35:00')	2016-12-30 11:35:00.000
DATEADD(week, 1, '2016-09-30 11:35:00')	2016-10-07 11:35:00.000
DATEADD(month, -1, '2016-09-30 11:35:00')	2016-08-30 11:35:00.000
DATEADD(year, 1.5, '2016-09-30 11:35:00')	2017-09-30 11:35:00.000

Examples that use the DATEDIFF function

Function	Result
DATEDIFF(day, '2015-12-01', '2016-09-30')	304
DATEDIFF(month, '2015-12-01', '2016-09-30')	9
DATEDIFF(year, '2015-12-01', '2016-09-30')	1
DATEDIFF(hour, '06:46:45', '11:35:00')	5
DATEDIFF(minute, '06:46:45', '11:35:00')	289
DATEDIFF(second, '06:46:45', '11:35:00')	17295
DATEDIFF(quarter, '2015-12-01', '2016-09-30')	3
DATEDIFF(week, '2015-12-01', '2016-09-30')	44
DATEDIFF(day, '2016-09-30', '2015-12-01')	-304

Examples that use the addition and subtraction operators

Operation	Result
CAST('2016-09-30 11:35:00' AS smalldatetime) + 1	2016-10-01 11:35:00
CAST('2016-09-30 11:35:00' AS smalldatetime) - 1	2016-09-29 11:35:00
CAST(CAST('2016-09-30' AS datetime) - CAST('2015-12-01' AS datetime) AS int)	304

Description

- You can use the DATEADD function to subtract a specified number of date parts from a date by coding the number of date parts as a negative value.

- If the number of date parts you specify in the DATEADD function isn't an integer, the fractional portion of the number is ignored.

- If the end date you specify in a DATEDIFF function is before the start date, the function will return a negative value.

- You can also use the addition and subtraction operators to add and subtract days from a date value. To add and subtract days from a date string, cast the string to a date/time value.

- You can also calculate the number of days between two dates by subtracting the date/time values and converting the result to an integer.

Figure 9-7   How to perform operations on dates and times

How to perform a date search

Because date/time values often contain both a date and a time component, searching for specific dates and times can be difficult. In this topic, you'll learn a variety of ways to ignore the time component when you search for a date value. And in the next topic, you'll learn how to ignore date components when you search for time values.

Before I go on, you should realize that the problems described here can sometimes be avoided by designing the database differently. For example, if you don't need to include a time component, you can use the date data type for the column that stores the date. That way, there's no time component to complicate your date searches. Conversely, if you don't need to include a date component, you can use the time data type for the column that holds the time. Of course, since these data types were introduced with SQL Server 2008, you'll need to use a different technique for prior versions of SQL Server.

Figure 9-8 illustrates the problem you can encounter when searching for dates. The examples in this figure use a table named DateSample. This table includes an ID column that contains an integer value and a StartDate column that contains a datetime value. Notice that the time components in the first three rows in this table have a zero value. In contrast, the time components in the next three rows have non-zero time components.

The problem occurs when you try to search for a date value. The first SELECT statement in this figure, for example, searches for rows in the DateSample table with the date 2011-10-28. Because a time component isn't specified, a zero time component is added when the date string is converted to a datetime value. However, because the row with this date has a non-zero time value, no rows are returned by this statement.

To solve this problem, you can use one of the five techniques shown in this figure. Of these techniques, the first technique is usually the easiest to use. Here, you use the CONVERT function to convert the datetime value to a date value. Of course, this only works for SQL Server 2008 or later.

As a result, if you need to work with a prior version of SQL Server, you'll need to use one of the other techniques. For example, you can use the second technique to search for dates that are greater than or equal to the date you're looking for and less than the date that follows the date you're looking for. Or, you can use the third technique to search for the values that are returned by the MONTH, DAY, and YEAR functions.

The fourth technique is to use the CAST function to convert the value in the StartDate column to an 11-character string. That causes the time portion of the date to be truncated (if you look back at figure 8-7, you'll see that when a date/time data type is cast to a string data type, the date portion contains 11 characters in the format "Mon dd yyyy"). Then, the string is converted back to a datetime value, which adds a zero time component.

The last technique is similar, but it uses the CONVERT function instead of the CAST function. The style code used in this function converts the datetime value to a 10-character string that doesn't include the time. Then, the string is converted back to a date with a zero time component.

The contents of the DateSample table

	ID	StartDate
1	1	1982-11-01 00:00:00.000
2	2	2002-10-28 00:00:00.000
3	3	2007-06-30 00:00:00.000
4	4	2008-10-28 10:00:00.000
5	5	2011-10-28 13:58:32.823
6	6	2011-11-01 09:02:25.000

A search condition that fails to return a row

```
SELECT * FROM DateSample
WHERE StartDate = '2011-10-28';
```

Five SELECT statements that ignore time values

A SELECT statement that uses the date type to remove time values (SQL Server 2008 or later)

```
SELECT * FROM DateSample
WHERE CONVERT(date, StartDate) = '2011-10-28';
```

A SELECT statement that searches for a range of dates

```
SELECT * FROM DateSample
WHERE StartDate >= '2011-10-28' AND StartDate < '2011-10-29';
```

A SELECT statement that searches for month, day, and year components

```
SELECT * FROM DateSample
WHERE MONTH(StartDate) = 10 AND
      DAY(StartDate) = 28 AND
      YEAR(StartDate) = 2011;
```

A SELECT statement that uses the CAST function to remove time values

```
SELECT * FROM DateSample
WHERE CAST(CAST(StartDate AS char(11)) AS datetime) = '2011-10-28';
```

A SELECT statement that uses the CONVERT function to remove time values

```
SELECT * FROM DateSample
WHERE CONVERT(datetime, CONVERT(char(10), StartDate, 110)) = '2011-10-28';
```

The result set

	ID	StartDate
1	5	2011-10-28 13:58:32.823

Description

- If you perform a search using a date string that doesn't include the time, the date string is converted implicitly to a date/time value with a zero time component. Then, if the date columns you're searching have non-zero time components, you have to accommodate the times in the search condition.

Figure 9-8   How to perform a date search

Note that the second technique (searching for a range of dates) is the only technique that doesn't use any functions in the WHERE clause. Because of that, this is the most efficient technique for searching for dates. As a result, you may want to use it even if you're using SQL Server 2008 or later.

How to perform a time search

When you search for a time value without specifying a date component, SQL Server automatically uses the default date of January 1, 1900. That's why neither of the first two SELECT statements in figure 9-9 return any rows. Even though at least one row has the correct time value for each search condition, those rows don't have the correct date value.

To solve this problem, you can use a SELECT statement like the one shown in the third or fourth example. In the third example, the CONVERT function is used to convert the datetime value to a time value. Of course, since the time data type was introduced with SQL Server 2008, this won't work for earlier versions of SQL Server.

As a result, if you need to use an earlier version of SQL Server, you can use a SELECT statement like the one shown in the fourth example. In this statement, the search condition uses the CONVERT function to convert the datetime values in the StartDate column to string values without dates. To do that, it uses a style argument of 8. Then, it converts the string values back to datetime values, which causes the default date to be used. That way, the date will match the dates that are added to the date literals.

The contents of the DateSample table

	ID	StartDate
1	1	1982-11-01 00:00:00.000
2	2	2002-10-28 00:00:00.000
3	3	2007-06-30 00:00:00.000
4	4	2008-10-28 10:00:00.000
5	5	2011-10-28 13:58:32.823
6	6	2011-11-01 09:02:25.000

Two search conditions that fail to return a row

```
SELECT * FROM DateSample
WHERE StartDate = CAST('10:00:00' AS datetime);

SELECT * FROM DateSample
WHERE StartDate >= '09:00:00' AND
    StartDate < '12:59:59:999';
```

Two SELECT statements that ignore date values

A SELECT statement that removes date values (SQL Server 2008 or later)

```
SELECT * FROM DateSample
WHERE CONVERT(time, StartDate) >= '09:00:00' AND
    CONVERT(time, StartDate) < '12:59:59:999';
```

A SELECT statement that removes date values (prior to SQL Server 2008)

```
SELECT * FROM DateSample
WHERE CONVERT(datetime, CONVERT(char(12), StartDate, 8)) >= '09:00:00' AND
    CONVERT(datetime, CONVERT(char(12), StartDate, 8)) < '12:59:59:999';
```

The result set

	ID	StartDate
1	4	2008-10-28 10:00:00.000
2	6	2011-11-01 09:02:25.000

Description

- If you perform a search using a date string that includes only a time, the date is converted implicitly to a date/time value with a default date component of 1900-01-01. Then, if the date columns you're searching have other dates, you have to accommodate those dates in the search condition.

Figure 9-9   How to perform a time search

Other functions you should know about

In addition to the conversion functions and the functions for working with specific types of data, SQL Server provides some other general purpose functions you should know about. Several of these functions are described in the topics that follow.

How to use the CASE function

Figure 9-10 presents the two formats of the CASE function. This function returns a value that's determined by the conditions you specify. The easiest way to describe how this function works is to look at the two examples shown in this figure.

The first example uses a simple CASE function. When you use this function, SQL Server compares the input expression you code in the CASE clause with the expressions you code in the WHEN clauses. In this example, the input expression is a value in the TermsID column of the Invoices table, and the when expressions are the valid values for this column. When SQL Server finds a when expression that's equal to the input expression, it returns the expression specified in the matching THEN clause. If the value of the TermsID column is 3, for example, this function returns the value "Net due 30 days." Although it's not shown in this example, you can also code an ELSE clause at the end of the CASE function. Then, if none of the when expressions are equal to the input expression, the function returns the value specified in the ELSE clause.

The simple CASE function is typically used with columns that can contain a limited number of values, such as the TermsID column used in this example. In contrast, the searched CASE function can be used for a wide variety of purposes. For example, you can test for conditions other than equal with this function. In addition, each condition can be based on a different column or expression. The second example in this figure illustrates how this function works.

This example determines the status of the invoices in the Invoices table. To do that, the searched CASE function uses the DATEDIFF function to get the number of days between the current date and the invoice due date. If the difference is greater than 30, the CASE function returns the value "Over 30 days past due." Similarly, if the difference is greater than 0, the function returns the value "1 to 30 days past due." Notice that if an invoice is 45 days old, both of these conditions are true. In that case, the function returns the expression associated with the first condition since this condition is evaluated first. In other words, the sequence of the conditions is critical to getting logical results. If neither of the conditions is true, the function returns the value "Current."

Because the WHEN clauses in this example use greater than conditions, this CASE function couldn't be coded using the simple syntax. Of course, CASE functions can be more complicated than what's shown here, but this should give you an idea of what you can do with this function.

The syntax of the simple CASE function

```
CASE input_expression
    WHEN when_expression_1 THEN result_expression_1
    [WHEN when_expression_2 THEN result_expression_2]...
    [ELSE else_result_expression]
END
```

The syntax of the searched CASE function

```
CASE
    WHEN conditional_expression_1 THEN result_expression_1
    [WHEN conditional_expression_2 THEN result_expression_2]...
    [ELSE else_result_expression]
END
```

A SELECT statement that uses a simple CASE function

```
SELECT InvoiceNumber, TermsID,
    CASE TermsID
        WHEN 1 THEN 'Net due 10 days'
        WHEN 2 THEN 'Net due 20 days'
        WHEN 3 THEN 'Net due 30 days'
        WHEN 4 THEN 'Net due 60 days'
        WHEN 5 THEN 'Net due 90 days'
    END AS Terms
FROM Invoices;
```

	InvoiceNumber	TermsID	Terms
6	963253261	3	Net due 30 days
7	963253237	3	Net due 30 days
8	125520-1	1	Net due 10 days

A SELECT statement that uses a searched CASE function

```
SELECT InvoiceNumber, InvoiceTotal, InvoiceDate, InvoiceDueDate,
    CASE
        WHEN DATEDIFF(day, InvoiceDueDate, GETDATE()) > 30
            THEN 'Over 30 days past due'
        WHEN DATEDIFF(day, InvoiceDueDate, GETDATE()) > 0
            THEN '1 to 30 days past due'
        ELSE 'Current'
    END AS Status
FROM Invoices
WHERE InvoiceTotal - PaymentTotal - CreditTotal > 0;
```

	InvoiceNumber	InvoiceTotal	InvoiceDate	InvoiceDueDate	Status
9	134116	90.36	2016-03-28 00:00:00	2016-04-17 00:00:00	Current
10	0-2436	10976.06	2016-03-31 00:00:00	2016-04-30 00:00:00	Current
11	547480102	224.00	2016-04-01 00:00:00	2016-04-30 00:00:00	Current

Description

- The simple CASE function tests the expression in the CASE clause against the expressions in the WHEN clauses. Then, the function returns the result expression associated with the first test that results in an equal condition.

- The searched CASE function tests the conditional expression in each WHEN clause in sequence and returns the result expression for the first condition that evaluates to true.

Figure 9-10   How to use the CASE function

How to use the IIF and CHOOSE functions

Figure 9-11 shows how to use the two *logical functions* that were introduced with SQL Server 2012. The IIF function returns one of two values depending on the result of a conditional expression, and the CHOOSE function returns a value from a list of values depending on the index you specify.

The SELECT statement in the first example in this figure illustrates how the IIF function works. This statement groups the rows in the Invoices table by the VendorID column and returns three columns. The first column contains the VendorID for each vendor, and the second column contains the sum of the invoice totals for that vendor. Then, the third column contains a value that indicates if the sum of invoice totals is less than 1000 or greater than or equal to 1000. To do that, the first argument of the IIF function tests if the sum of invoice totals is less than 1000. If it is, a value of "Low" is returned. Otherwise, a value of "High" is returned.

If you compare the IIF function with the searched CASE function in the previous figure, you'll see that it provides another way to test a conditional expression that can result in one of two values. In fact, SQL Server translates IIF functions to CASE functions before processing them. For example, SQL Server would translate the IIF function in this figure so it looks something like this:

```
SELECT VendorID, SUM(InvoiceTotal) AS SumInvoices,
    CASE
        WHEN SUM(InvoiceTotal) < 1000
            THEN 'Low'
        ELSE
            'High'
    END AS InvoiceRange
FROM Invoices
GROUP BY VendorID;
```

The technique you use is mostly a matter of preference.

The second SELECT statement in this figure illustrates how to use the CHOOSE function. Although this functions isn't as useful as some of the other functions presented in this book, it can be useful in certain situations. In this example, it's used to return a description of the due days for the invoices in the Invoices table with a balance due based on the value of the TermsID column. This works because the TermsID column is an int type.

The syntax of the IIF function

```
IIF(conditional_expression, true_value, false_value)
```

The syntax of the CHOOSE function

```
CHOOSE(index, value1, value2 [,value3]...)
```

A SELECT statement that uses the IIF function

```
SELECT VendorID, SUM(InvoiceTotal) AS SumInvoices,
    IIF(SUM(InvoiceTotal) < 1000, 'Low', 'High') AS InvoiceRange
FROM Invoices
GROUP BY VendorID;
```

	VendorID	SumInvoices	InvoiceRange
1	34	1200.12	High
2	37	564.00	Low
3	48	856.92	Low
4	72	21927.31	High
5	80	265.36	Low
6	81	936.93	Low
7	82	600.00	Low
8	83	2154.42	High

A SELECT statement that uses the CHOOSE function

```
SELECT InvoiceNumber, InvoiceDate, InvoiceTotal,
    CHOOSE(TermsID, '10 days', '20 days', '30 days', '60 days', '90 days')
        AS NetDue
FROM Invoices
WHERE InvoiceTotal - PaymentTotal - CreditTotal > 0;
```

	InvoiceNumber	InvoiceDate	InvoiceTotal	NetDue
1	39104	2016-03-10 00:00:00	85.31	30 days
2	963253264	2016-03-18 00:00:00	52.25	30 days
3	31361833	2016-03-21 00:00:00	579.42	20 days
4	263253268	2016-03-21 00:00:00	59.97	30 days
5	263253270	2016-03-22 00:00:00	67.92	30 days

Description

- The IIF and CHOOSE functions are known as *logical functions*, and they were introduced with SQL Server 2012.

- The IIF function lets you test an expression and return one value if the expression is true and another value if the expression is false. It provides a shorthand way of coding a searched CASE function with a single WHEN clause and an ELSE clause.

- The CHOOSE function provides an index into a list of values. The index value must be a type that can be converted to an int value and it must range from 1 to the number of values in the list.

Figure 9-11   How to use the IIF and CHOOSE functions

How to use the COALESCE and ISNULL functions

Figure 9-12 presents two functions that you can use to work with null values: COALESCE and ISNULL. Both of these functions let you substitute non-null values for null values. Although these two functions are similar, COALESCE is more flexible because it lets you specify a list of values. Then, it returns the first non-null value in the list. In contrast, the ISNULL function uses only two expressions. It returns the first expression if that expression isn't null. Otherwise, it returns the second expression.

The examples in this figure illustrate how these functions work. The first example uses the COALESCE function to return the value of the PaymentDate column, if that column doesn't contain a null value. Otherwise, it returns the date 1900-01-01. The second example performs the operation using the ISNULL function. Note that when you use either of these functions, all of the expressions must have the same data type. So, for example, you couldn't substitute the string "Not Paid" for a null payment date.

The third example shows how you can work around this restriction. In this example, the value of the InvoiceTotal column is converted to a character value. That way, if the InvoiceTotal column contains a null value, the COALESCE function can substitute the string "No invoices" for this value. Notice that this example uses an outer join to combine all of the rows in the Vendors table with the rows for each vendor in the Invoices table. Because of that, a null value will be returned for the InvoiceTotal column for any vendor that doesn't have invoices. As you can see, then, this function is quite useful with outer joins.

The syntax of the COALESCE function

```
COALESCE(expression_1 [, expression_2]...)
```

The syntax of the ISNULL function

```
ISNULL(check_expression, replacement_value)
```

A SELECT statement that uses the COALESCE function

```
SELECT PaymentDate,
    COALESCE(PaymentDate, '1900-01-01') AS NewDate
FROM Invoices;
```

The same SELECT statement using the ISNULL function

```
SELECT PaymentDate,
    ISNULL(PaymentDate, '1900-01-01') AS NewDate
FROM Invoices;
```

The result set

	PaymentDate	NewDate
111	2016-05-03 00:00:00	2016-05-03 00:00:00
112	NULL	1900-01-01 00:00:00
113	NULL	1900-01-01 00:00:00
114	2016-05-04 00:00:00	2016-05-04 00:00:00

A SELECT statement that substitutes a different data type

```
SELECT VendorName,
    COALESCE(CAST(InvoiceTotal AS varchar), 'No invoices') AS InvoiceTotal
FROM Vendors LEFT JOIN Invoices
    ON Vendors.VendorID = Invoices.VendorID
ORDER BY VendorName;
```

	VendorName	InvoiceTotal
1	Abbey Office Furnishings	17.50
2	American Booksellers Assoc	No invoices
3	American Express	No invoices
4	ASC Signs	No invoices
5	Ascom Hasler Mailing Syst...	No invoices

Description

- The COALESCE and ISNULL functions let you substitute non-null values for null values.

- The COALESCE function returns the first expression in a list of expressions that isn't null. All of the expressions in the list must have the same data type. If all of the expressions are null, this function returns a null value.

- The ISNULL function returns the expression if it isn't null. Otherwise, it returns the value you specify. The expression and the value must have the same data type.

- COALESCE is not an ANSI-standard function, but it's more widely supported than ISNULL, which is unique to SQL Server.

Figure 9-12   How to use the COALESCE and ISNULL functions

How to use the GROUPING function

In chapter 5, you learned how to use the ROLLUP and CUBE operators to add summary rows to a summary query. You may recall that when you do that, a null value is assigned to any column in a summary row that isn't being summarized. If you need to, you can refer back to figures 5-7 and 5-8 to refresh your memory on how this works.

If you want to assign a value other than null to these columns, you can do that using the GROUPING function as illustrated in figure 9-13. This function accepts the name of a column as its argument. The column you specify must be one of the columns named in a GROUP BY clause that includes the ROLLUP or CUBE operator.

The example in this figure shows how you can use the GROUPING function in a summary query that summarizes vendors by state and city. This is the same summary query you saw back in figure 5-7. Instead of simply retrieving the values of the VendorState and VendorCity columns from the base table, however, this query uses the GROUPING function within a CASE function to determine the values that are assigned to those columns. If a row is added to summarize the VendorState column, for example, the value of the GROUPING function for that column is 1. Then, the CASE function assigns the value "All" to that column. Otherwise, it retrieves the value of the column from the Vendors table. Similarly, if a row is added to summarize the VendorCity column, the value "All" is assigned to that column. As you can see in the result set shown here, this makes it more obvious what columns are being summarized.

This technique is particularly useful if the columns you're summarizing can contain null values. In that case, it would be difficult to determine which rows are summary rows and which rows simply contain null values. Then, you may not only want to use the GROUPING function to replace the null values in summary rows, but you may want to use the COALESCE or ISNULL function to replace null values retrieved from the base table.

The syntax of the GROUPING function

```
GROUPING(column_name)
```

A summary query that uses the GROUPING function

```
SELECT
    CASE
        WHEN GROUPING(VendorState) = 1 THEN 'All'
        ELSE VendorState
    END AS VendorState,
    CASE
        WHEN GROUPING(VendorCity) = 1 THEN 'All'
        ELSE VendorCity
    END AS VendorCity,
    COUNT(*) AS QtyVendors
FROM Vendors
WHERE VendorState IN ('IA', 'NJ')
GROUP BY VendorState, VendorCity WITH ROLLUP
ORDER BY VendorState DESC, VendorCity DESC;
```

The result set

	VendorState	VendorCity	QtyVendors
1	NJ	Washington	1
2	NJ	Fairfield	1
3	NJ	East Brunswick	2
4	NJ	All	4
5	IA	Washington	1
6	IA	Fairfield	1
7	IA	All	2
8	All	All	6

Description

- You can use the GROUPING function to determine when a null value is assigned to a column as the result of the ROLLUP or CUBE operator. The column you name in this function must be one of the columns named in the GROUP BY clause.

- If a null value is assigned to the specified column as the result of the ROLLUP or CUBE operator, the GROUPING function returns a value of 1. Otherwise, it returns a value of 0.

- You typically use the GROUPING function with the CASE function. Then, if the GROUPING function returns a value of 1, you can assign a value other than null to the column.

Figure 9-13   How to use the GROUPING function

How to use the ranking functions

Figure 9-14 shows how to use four *ranking functions* that were introduced with SQL Server 2005. These functions provide a variety of ways that you can rank the rows that are returned by a result set. All four of these functions have a similar syntax and work similarly.

The first example shows how to use the ROW_NUMBER function. Here, the SELECT statement retrieves two columns from the Vendors table. The first column uses the ROW_NUMBER function to sort the result set by VendorName and to number each row in the result set. To show that the first column has been sorted and numbered correctly, the second column displays the VendorName.

To accomplish the sorting and numbering, you code the name of the ROW_NUMBER function, followed by a set of parentheses, followed by the OVER keyword and a second set of parentheses. Within the second set of parentheses, you code the required ORDER BY clause that specifies the sort order that's used by the function. In this example, for instance, the ORDER BY clause sorts by VendorName in ascending order. However, you can code more complex ORDER BY clauses whenever that's necessary. In addition, when necessary, you can code an ORDER BY clause that applies to the entire result set. In that case, the ORDER BY clause within the ranking function is used to number the rows and the ORDER BY clause outside the ranking function is used to sort the rows after the numbering has been applied.

The second example shows how to use the optional PARTITION BY clause of a ranking function. This clause allows you to specify a column that's used to divide the result set into groups. In this example, for instance, the PARTITION BY clause uses a column within the Vendors table to group vendors by state and to sort these vendors by name within each state.

However, you can also use the PARTITION BY clause when a SELECT statement joins one or more tables like this:

```
SELECT VendorName, InvoiceNumber,
    ROW_NUMBER() OVER(PARTITION BY VendorName
    ORDER BY InvoiceNumber) As RowNumber
FROM Vendors JOIN Invoices
    ON Vendors.VendorID = Invoices.VendorID;
```

Here, the invoices will be grouped by vendor and sorted within each vendor by invoice number. As a result, if a vendor has three invoices, these invoices will be sorted by invoice number and numbered from 1 to 3.

The syntax for the four ranking functions

```
ROW_NUMBER()              OVER ([partition_by_clause] order_by_clause)
RANK()                    OVER ([partition_by_clause] order_by_clause)
DENSE_RANK()              OVER ([partition_by_clause] order_by_clause)
NTILE(integer_expression) OVER ([partition_by_clause] order_by_clause)
```

A query that uses the ROW_NUMBER function

```
SELECT ROW_NUMBER() OVER(ORDER BY VendorName) AS RowNumber, VendorName
FROM Vendors;
```

The result set

	RowNumber	VendorName
1	1	Abbey Office Furnishings
2	2	American Booksellers Assoc
3	3	American Express
4	4	ASC Signs
5	5	Ascom Hasler Mailing Systems

A query that uses the PARTITION BY clause

```
SELECT ROW_NUMBER() OVER(PARTITION BY VendorState
    ORDER BY VendorName) As RowNumber, VendorName, VendorState
FROM Vendors;
```

The result set

	RowNumber	VendorName	VendorState
1	1	AT&T	AZ
2	2	Computer Library	AZ
3	3	Wells Fargo Bank	AZ
4	1	Abbey Office Furnishings	CA
5	2	American Express	CA
6	3	ASC Signs	CA

Description

- The ROW_NUMBER, RANK, DENSE_RANK, and NTILE functions are known as *ranking functions*, and they were introduced with SQL Server 2005.

- The ROW_NUMBER function returns the sequential number of a row within a partition of a result set, starting at 1 for the first row in each partition.

- The ORDER BY clause of a ranking function specifies the sort order in which the ranking function is applied.

- The optional PARTITION BY clause of a ranking function specifies the column that's used to divide the result set into groups.

Figure 9-14   How to use the ranking functions (part 1 of 2)

The third example shows how the RANK and DENSE_RANK functions work. You can use these functions to rank the rows in a result set. In this example, both the RANK and the DENSE_RANK functions sort all invoices in the Invoices table by the invoice total. Since the first three rows have the same invoice total, both of these functions give these three rows the same rank, 1. However, the fourth row has a different value. To calculate the value for this row, the RANK function adds 1 to the total number of previous rows. In other words, since the first three rows are tied for first place, the fourth row gets fourth place and is assigned a rank of 4.

The DENSE_RANK function, on the other hand, calculates the value for the fourth row by adding 1 to the rank for the previous row. As a result, this function assigns a rank of 2 to the fourth row. In other words, since the first three rows are tied for first place, the fourth row gets second place.

The fourth example shows how the NTILE function works. You can use this function to divide the rows in a partition into the specified number of groups. When the rows can be evenly divided into groups, this function is easy to understand. For example, if a result set returns 100 rows, you can use the NTILE function to divide this result set into 10 groups of 10. However, when the rows can't be evenly divided into groups, this function is a little more difficult to understand. In this figure, for example, the NTILE function is used to divide a result set that contains 5 rows. Here, the first NTILE function divides this result into 2 groups with the first having 3 rows and the second having 2 rows. The second NTILE function divides this result set into 3 groups with the first having 2 rows, the second having 2 rows, and the third having 1 row. And so on. Although this doesn't result in groups with even numbers of rows, the NTILE function creates the number of groups specified by its argument.

In this figure, the examples for the RANK, DENSE_RANK, and NTILE functions don't include PARTITION BY clauses. As a result, these functions are applied to the entire result set. However, whenever necessary, you can use the PARTITION BY clause to divide the result set into groups just as shown in the second example for the ROW_NUMBER function.

A query that uses the RANK and DENSE_RANK functions

```
SELECT RANK() OVER (ORDER BY InvoiceTotal) As Rank,
       DENSE_RANK() OVER (ORDER BY InvoiceTotal) As DenseRank,
       InvoiceTotal, InvoiceNumber
FROM Invoices;
```

The result set

	Rank	DenseRank	InvoiceTotal	InvoiceNumber
1	1	1	6.00	25022117
2	1	1	6.00	24863706
3	1	1	6.00	24780512
4	4	2	9.95	21-4923721
5	4	2	9.95	21-4748363
6	6	3	10.00	4-321-2596

Description

- The RANK and DENSE_RANK functions both return the rank of each row within the partition of a result set.
- If there is a tie, both of these functions give the same rank to all rows that are tied.
- To determine the rank for the next distinct row, the RANK function adds 1 to the total number of rows, while the DENSE_RANK function adds 1 to the rank for the previous row.

A query that uses the NTILE function

```
SELECT TermsDescription,
    NTILE(2) OVER (ORDER BY TermsID) AS Tile2,
    NTILE(3) OVER (ORDER BY TermsID) AS Tile3,
    NTILE(4) OVER (ORDER BY TermsID) AS Tile4
FROM Terms;
```

The result set

	TermsDescription	Tile2	Tile3	Tile4
1	Net due 10 days	1	1	1
2	Net due 20 days	1	1	1
3	Net due 30 days	1	2	2
4	Net due 60 days	2	2	3
5	Net due 90 days	2	3	4

Description

- The NTILE function divides the rows in a partition into the specified number of groups.
- If the rows can't be evenly divided into groups, the later groups may have one less row than the earlier groups.

Figure 9-14   How to use the ranking functions (part 2 of 2)

How to use the analytic functions

Figure 9-15 shows how to use the *analytic functions* that were introduced with SQL Server 2012. These functions let you perform calculations on ordered sets of data. Note that all of the examples in this figure use the SalesReps and SalesTotals tables that are summarized in this figure. These tables are related by the RepID column in each table.

The FIRST_VALUE and LAST_VALUE functions let you return the first and last values in an ordered set of values. The first example in this figure uses these functions to return the name of the sales rep with the highest and lowest sales for each year. To do that, the OVER clause is used to group the result set by year and sort the rows within each year by sales total in descending sequence. Then, the expression that's specified for the functions causes the name for the first rep within each year to be returned.

For the LAST_VALUE function to return the value you want, you also have to include the RANGE clause as shown here. This clause indicates that the rows should be unbounded within the partition. In other words, all of the rows in the partition should be included in the calculation. If you don't include this clause, the LAST_VALUE function will return the last value for each group specified by the ORDER BY clause. In this case, that means that the function would return the last rep name for each sales total. Since all of the sales totals are different, though, the function would simply return the name of the rep in each row, which isn't what you want. So, you would typically use this clause only if you sorted the result set by a column that contains duplicate values. In that case, you can typically omit the PARTITION BY clause.

Instead of the RANGE clause, you can code a ROWS clause on a FIRST_VALUE or LAST_VALUE function. This clause lets you specify the rows to include relative to the current row. For more information on how to code this clause and the RANGE clause, please search for it in the SQL Server documentation.

The syntax of the analytic functions

```
{FIRST_VALUE|LAST_VALUE}(scalar_expression)
    OVER ([partition_by_clause] order_by_clause [rows_range_clause])

{LEAD|LAG}(scalar_expression [, offset [, default]])
    OVER ([partition_by_clause] order_by_clause)

{PERCENT_RANK()|CUME_DIST} OVER ([partition_by_clause] order_by_clause)

{PERCENTILE_CONT|PERCENTILE_DISC}(numeric_literal)
    WITHIN GROUP (ORDER BY expression [ASC|DESC]) OVER (partition_by_clause)
```

The columns in the SalesReps and SalesTotals tables

Column name	Data type	Column name	Data type
RepID	int	RepID	int
RepFirstName	varchar(50)	SalesYear	char(4)
RepLastName	varchar(50)	SalesTotal	money

A query that uses the FIRST_VALUE and LAST_VALUE functions

```
SELECT SalesYear, RepFirstName + ' ' + RepLastName AS RepName, SalesTotal,
    FIRST_VALUE(RepFirstName + ' ' + RepLastName)
        OVER (PARTITION BY SalesYear ORDER BY SalesTotal DESC)
        AS HighestSales,
    LAST_VALUE(RepFirstName + ' ' + RepLastName)
        OVER (PARTITION BY SalesYear ORDER BY SalesTotal DESC
            RANGE BETWEEN UNBOUNDED PRECEDING AND UNBOUNDED FOLLOWING)
        AS LowestSales
FROM SalesTotals JOIN SalesReps
  ON SalesTotals.RepID = SalesReps.RepID;
```

	SalesYear	RepName	SalesTotal	HighestSales	LowestSales
1	2014	Jonathon Thomas	1274856.38	Jonathon Thomas	Sonja Martinez
2	2014	Andrew Markasian	1032875.48	Jonathon Thomas	Sonja Martinez
3	2014	Sonja Martinez	978465.99	Jonathon Thomas	Sonja Martinez
4	2015	Andrew Markasian	1132744.56	Andrew Markasian	Lydia Kramer
5	2015	Sonja Martinez	974853.81	Andrew Markasian	Lydia Kramer
6	2015	Jonathon Thomas	923746.85	Andrew Markasian	Lydia Kramer
7	2015	Phillip Winters	655786.92	Andrew Markasian	Lydia Kramer
8	2015	Lydia Kramer	422847.86	Andrew Markasian	Lydia Kramer
9	2016	Jonathon Thomas	998337.46	Jonathon Thomas	Lydia Kramer
10	2016	Sonja Martinez	887695.75	Jonathon Thomas	Lydia Kramer
11	2016	Phillip Winters	72443.37	Jonathon Thomas	Lydia Kramer
12	2016	Lydia Kramer	45182.44	Jonathon Thomas	Lydia Kramer

Description

- The FIRST_VALUE, LAST_VALUE, LEAD, LAG, PERCENT_RANK, CUME_DIST, PERCENTILE_CONT, and PERCENTILE_DISC functions are known as *analytic functions*. They were introduced with SQL Server 2012.

- The FIRST_VALUE function returns the first value in a sorted set of values, and the LAST_VALUE function returns the last value in a sorted set of values. When you use the PARTITION BY clause with LAST_VALUE, you typically include the ROWS or RANGE clause as well.

Figure 9-15   How to use the analytic functions (part 1 of 2)

The LEAD and LAG functions let you refer to values in other rows of the result set. The LAG function is illustrated in the second example in this figure. Here, the OVER clause is used to group the result set by rep ID and sort it by year. Then, the LAG function in the fourth column gets the sales total from one row prior to the current row (the offset). Since the rows are sorted by year for each sales rep, that means that the function retrieves the sales rep's sales for the previous year. The fifth column uses the same function, but it subtracts the result of this function from the current sales to show the change in sales from the previous year. The LEAD function is similar, but it lets you refer to values in following rows rather than preceding rows.

Notice that the value of the LAG function for the first row for each sales rep is 0.00. That's because there isn't a row for the prior year. By default, this value is NULL. Because I wanted to calculate the change for each row in the result set, though, I set the third argument of the LAG function (default) to 0.

The third example in this figure shows how to use all four of the remaining functions. Each of these functions groups the rows by year and sorts them by sales total in ascending sequence. Notice, though, that the ORDER BY clause for the PERCENTILE_CONT and PERCENTILE_DISC functions isn't specified on the OVER clause. Instead, it's specified on the WITHIN GROUP clause, which, unlike the OVER clause, allows for the result set to be sorted only by a single column.

The PERCENT_RANK function calculates a percent that indicates the rank of each row within a group. The result of this function is always a value between 0 and 1. If you study the results in this example, you shouldn't have any trouble understanding how this function works.

The CUME_DIST function is similar, but it calculates the percent of values that are less than or equal to the current value. This function represents the *cumulative distribution* of the values. The cumulative distribution is calculated by dividing the number of rows with the current value or a lower value by the total number of rows in the group.

The PERCENTILE_CONT and PERCENTILE_DISC functions calculate the value at the percentile you specify. The difference between these two functions is that PERCENTILE_CONT is based on a *continuous distribution* of values, and PERCENTILE_DISC is based on a *discrete distribution* of values. This means that the value returned by PERCENTILE_CONT doesn't need to appear in the result set, but the value returned by PERCENTILE_DISC does.

In this example, these functions are used to calculate the median of the sales totals for each year (the value in the middle). Because there are an odd number of rows for 2014 and 2015, both functions return the value in the middle row. Because there are an even number of rows for 2016, though, there isn't a middle value. In that case, the PERCENTILE_CONT function calculates the median by adding the two middle values together and dividing by 2. As you can see, the resulting value doesn't exist in the result set. In contrast, the PERCENTILE_DISC function uses the CUME_DIST function to identify the row with a cumulative distribution of .5 (the same percentile specified by the PERCENTILE_DISC function), and it uses the value of that row as the result.

A query that uses the LAG function

```
SELECT RepID, SalesYear, SalesTotal AS CurrentSales,
    LAG(SalesTotal, 1, 0) OVER (PARTITION BY RepID ORDER BY SalesYear)
        AS LastSales,
    SalesTotal - LAG(SalesTotal, 1, 0)
        OVER (PARTITION BY REPID ORDER BY SalesYear) AS Change
FROM SalesTotals;
```

	RepID	SalesYear	CurrentSales	LastSales	Change
1	1	2014	1274856.38	0.00	1274856.38
2	1	2015	923746.85	1274856.38	-351109.53
3	1	2016	998337.46	923746.85	74590.61
4	2	2014	978465.99	0.00	978465.99
5	2	2015	974853.81	978465.99	-3612.18
6	2	2016	887695.75	974853.81	-87158.06

A query that uses the PERCENT_RANK, CUME_DIST, PERCENTILE_CONT, and PERCENTILE_DISC functions

```
SELECT SalesYear, RepID, SalesTotal,
    PERCENT_RANK() OVER (PARTITION BY SalesYear ORDER BY SalesTotal)
        AS PctRank,
    CUME_DIST() OVER (PARTITION BY SalesYear ORDER BY SalesTotal)
        AS CumeDist,
    PERCENTILE_CONT(.5) WITHIN GROUP (ORDER BY SalesTotal)
        OVER (PARTITION BY SalesYear) AS PercentileCont,
    PERCENTILE_DISC(.5) WITHIN GROUP (ORDER BY SalesTotal)
        OVER (PARTITION BY SalesYear) AS PercentileDisc
FROM SalesTotals;
```

	SalesYear	RepID	SalesTotal	PctRank	CumeDist	PercentileCont	PercentileDisc
1	2014	2	978465.99	0	0.333333333333333	1032875.48	1032875.48
2	2014	3	1032875.48	0.5	0.666666666666667	1032875.48	1032875.48
3	2014	1	1274856.38	1	1	1032875.48	1032875.48
4	2015	5	422847.86	0	0.2	923746.85	923746.85
5	2015	4	655786.92	0.25	0.4	923746.85	923746.85
6	2015	1	923746.85	0.5	0.6	923746.85	923746.85
7	2015	2	974853.81	0.75	0.8	923746.85	923746.85
8	2015	3	1132744.56	1	1	923746.85	923746.85
9	2016	5	45182.44	0	0.25	480069.56	72443.37
10	2016	4	72443.37	0.3333...	0.5	480069.56	72443.37
11	2016	2	887695.75	0.6666...	0.75	480069.56	72443.37
12	2016	1	998337.46	1	1	480069.56	72443.37

Description

- The LEAD function retrieves data from a subsequent row in a result set, and the LAG function retrieves data from a previous row in a result set.

- The PERCENT_RANK function calculates the rank of the values in a sorted set of values as a percent. The CUME_DIST function calculates the percent of the values in a sorted set of values that are less than or equal to the current value.

- The PERCENTILE_CONT and PERCENTILE_DISC functions calculate the value at the specified percentile for a sorted set of values. PERCENTILE_CONT returns an exact percentile, and PERCENTILE_DIST returns a value that exists in the sorted column.

Figure 9-15   How to use the analytic functions (part 2 of 2)

Perspective

In this chapter, you learned about many of the functions that you can use to operate on SQL Server data. At this point, you have all of the essential skills you need to develop SQL code at a professional level.

However, there's a lot more to learn about SQL Server. In the next section of this book, then, you'll learn the basic skills for designing a database. Even if you never need to design your own database, understanding this material will help you work more efficiently with databases that have been designed by others.

Terms

logical functions

ranking functions

analytic functions

cumulative distribution

continuous distribution

discrete distribution

Exercises

1. Write a SELECT statement that returns two columns based on the Vendors table. The first column, Contact, is the vendor contact name in this format: first name followed by last initial (for example, "John S.") The second column, Phone, is the VendorPhone column without the area code. Only return rows for those vendors in the 559 area code. Sort the result set by first name, then last name.

2. Write a SELECT statement that returns the InvoiceNumber and balance due for every invoice with a non-zero balance and an InvoiceDueDate that's less than 30 days from today.

3. Modify the search expression for InvoiceDueDate from the solution for exercise 2. Rather than 30 days from today, return invoices due before the last day of the current month.

4. Write a summary query WITH CUBE that returns LineItemSum (which is the sum of InvoiceLineItemAmount) grouped by Account (an alias for AccountDescription) and State (an alias for VendorState). Use the CASE and GROUPING function to substitute the literal value "*ALL*" for the summary rows with null values.

5. Add a column to the query described in exercise 2 that uses the RANK() function to return a column named BalanceRank that ranks the balance due in descending order.

Section 3

Database design and implementation

In large programming shops, database administrators are usually responsible for designing the databases that are used by production applications, and they may also be responsible for the databases that are used for testing those applications. Often, though, programmers are asked to design, create, or maintain small databases that are used for testing. And in a small shop, programmers may also be responsible for the production databases.

So whether you're a database administrator or a SQL programmer, you need the skills and knowledge presented in this section. That's true even if you aren't ever called upon to design or maintain a database. By understanding what's going on behind the scenes, you'll be able to use SQL more effectively.

So, in chapter 10, you'll learn how to design a SQL Server database. In chapter 11, you'll learn how to use the Data Definition Language (DDL) statements to create and maintain the SQL Server objects of a database. And in chapter 12, you'll learn how to use the Management Studio to do the same tasks.

10

How to design a database

In this chapter, you'll learn how to design a new database. This is useful information for the SQL programmer whether or not you ever design a database on your own. To illustrate this process, I'll use the accounts payable (AP) system that you've seen throughout this book because that will make it easier for you to understand the design techniques.

How to design a data structure

Databases are often designed by database administrators (DBAs) or design specialists. This is especially true for large, multiuser databases. How well this is done can directly affect your job as a SQL programmer. In general, a well designed database is easy to query, while a poorly designed database is difficult to work with. In fact, when you work with a poorly designed database, you will often need to figure out how it is designed before you can code your queries appropriately.

The topics that follow will teach you a basic approach for designing a *data structure*. We use that term to refer to a model of the database rather than the database itself. Once you design the data structure, you can use the techniques presented in the next two chapters to create a database with that design.

The basic steps for designing a data structure

In many cases, you can design a data structure based on an existing real-world system. The illustration at the top of figure 10-1 presents a conceptual view of how this works. Here, you can see that all of the information about the people, documents, and facilities within a real-world system is mapped to the tables, columns, and rows of a database system.

As you design a data structure, each table represents one object, or *entity*, in the real-world system. Then, within each table, each column stores one item of information, or *attribute*, for the entity, and each row stores one occurrence, or *instance*, of the entity.

This figure also presents the six steps you can follow to design a data structure. You'll learn more about each of these steps in the topics that follow. In general, though, step 1 is to identify all the data elements that need to be stored in the database. Step 2 is to break complex elements down into smaller components whenever that makes sense. Step 3 is to identify the tables that will make up the system and to determine which data elements are assigned as columns in each table. Step 4 is to define the relationships between the tables by identifying the primary and foreign keys. Step 5 is to normalize the database to reduce data redundancy. And step 6 is to identify the indexes that are needed for each table.

To model a database system after a real-world system, you can use a technique called *entity-relationship (ER) modeling*. Because this is a complex subject of its own, I won't present it in this book. However, I have applied some of the basic elements of this technique to the design diagrams presented in this chapter. In effect, then, you'll be learning some of the basics of this modeling technique.

A database system is modeled after a real-world system

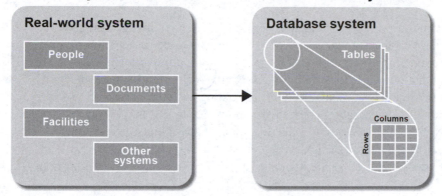

The six basic steps for designing a data structure

Step 1:   Identify the data elements

Step 2:   Subdivide each element into its smallest useful components

Step 3:   Identify the tables and assign columns

Step 4:   Identify the primary and foreign keys

Step 5:   Review whether the data structure is normalized

Step 6:   Identify the indexes

Description

- A relational database system should model the real-world environment where it's used. The job of the designer is to analyze the real-world system and then map it onto a relational database system.

- A table in a relational database typically represents an object, or *entity*, in the real world. Each column of a table is used to store an *attribute* associated with the entity, and each row represents one *instance* of the entity.

- To model a database and the relationships between its tables after a real-world system, you can use a technique called *entity-relationship (ER) modeling*. Some of the diagrams you'll see in this chapter apply the basic elements of ER modeling.

Figure 10-1   The basic steps for designing a data structure

How to identify the data elements

The first step for designing a data structure is to identify the data elements required by the system. You can use several techniques to do that, including analyzing the existing system if there is one, evaluating comparable systems, and interviewing anyone who will be using the system. One particularly good source of information are the documents used by an existing system.

In figure 10-2, for example, you can see an invoice that's used by an accounts payable system. We'll use this document as the main source of information for the database design presented in this chapter. Keep in mind, though, that you'll want to use all available resources when you design your own database.

If you study this document, you'll notice that it contains information about three different entities: vendors, invoices, and line items. First, the form itself has preprinted information about the vendor who issued the invoice, such as the vendor's name and address. If this vendor were to issue another invoice, this information wouldn't change.

This document also contains specific information about the invoice. Some of this information, such as the invoice number, invoice date, and invoice total, is general in nature. Although the actual information will vary from one invoice to the next, each invoice will include this information. In addition to this general information, each invoice includes information about the items that were purchased. Although each line item contains similar information, each invoice can contain a different number of line items.

One of the things you need to consider as you review a document like this is how much information your system needs to track. For an accounts payable system, for example, you may not need to store detailed data such as the information about each line item. Instead, you may just need to store summary data like the invoice total. As you think about what data elements to include in the database, then, you should have an idea of what information you'll need to get back out of the system.

An invoice that can be used to identify data elements

Acme Fabrication, Inc.

Custom Contraptions, Contrivances and Confabulations

1234 West Industrial Way   East Los Angeles   California 90022

800.555.1212   fax 562.555.1213   www.acmefabrication.com

Invoice Number:	I01-1088
Invoice Date:	06/05/12
Terms:	Net 30

Part No.	Qty.	Description	Unit Price	Extension
CUST345	12	Design service, hr	100.00	1200.00
457332	7	Baling wire, 25x3ft roll	79.90	559.30
50173	4375	Duct tape, black, yd	1.09	4768.75
328771	2	Rubber tubing, 100ft roll	4.79	9.58
CUST281	7	Assembly, hr	75.00	525.00
CUST917	2	Testing, hr	125.00	250.00
		Sales Tax		245.20

Your salesperson:	Ruben Goldberg, ext 4512
Accounts receivable:	Inigo Jones, ext 4901

$7,557.83
PLEASE PAY THIS AMOUNT

Thanks for your business!

The data elements identified on the invoice document

Vendor name	Invoice date	Item extension
Vendor address	Invoice terms	Vendor sales contact name
Vendor phone number	Item part number	Vendor sales contact extension
Vendor fax number	Item quantity	Vendor AR contact name
Vendor web address	Item description	Vendor AR contact extension
Invoice number	Item unit price	Invoice total

Description

- Depending on the nature of the system, you can identify data elements in a variety of ways, including interviewing users, analyzing existing systems, and evaluating comparable systems.

- The documents used by a real-world system, such as the invoice shown above, can often help you identify the data elements of the system.

- As you identify the data elements of a system, you should begin thinking about the entities that those elements are associated with. That will help you identify the tables of the database later on.

Figure 10-2   How to identify the data elements

How to subdivide the data elements

Some of the data elements you identify in step 1 of the design procedure will consist of multiple components. The next step, then, is to divide these elements into their smallest useful values. Figure 10-3 shows how you can do that.

The first example in this figure shows how you can divide the name of the sales contact for a vendor. Here, the name is divided into two elements: a first name and a last name. When you divide a name like this, you can easily perform operations like sorting by last name and using the first name in a salutation, such as "Dear Ruben." In contrast, if the full name is stored in a single column, you have to use the string functions to extract the component you need. And, as you learned in the last chapter, that can lead to inefficient and complicated code. In general, then, you should separate a name like this whenever you'll need to use the name components separately. Later, when you need to use the full name, you can combine the first and last names using concatenation.

The second example shows how you typically divide an address. Notice in this example that the street number and street name are stored in a single column. Although you could store these components in separate columns, that usually doesn't make sense since these values are typically used together. That's what I mean when I say the data elements should be divided into their smallest *useful* values.

With that guideline in mind, you might even need to divide a single string into two or more components. A bulk mail system, for example, might require a separate column for the first three digits of the zip code. And a telephone number might require two columns: one for the area code and another for the rest of the number. Historically, the area code was a useful value as it provided information about the geographical location of the phone. However, now that so many phone numbers are mobile numbers, this value has become less useful.

As in the previous step, knowledge of the real-world system and of the information that will be extracted from the database is critical. In some circumstances, it may be okay to store data elements with multiple components in a single column. That can simplify your design and reduce the overall number of columns. In general, though, most designers divide data elements as much as possible. That way, it's easy to accommodate almost any query, and you don't have to change the database design later on when you realize that you need to use just part of a column value.

A name that's divided into first and last names

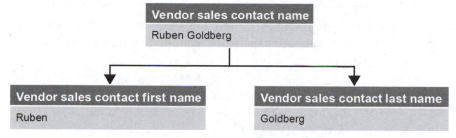

An address that's divided into street address, city, state, and zip code

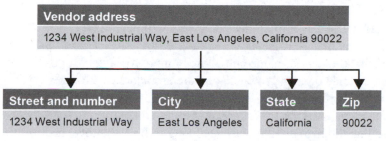

Description

- If a data element contains two or more components, you should consider subdividing the element into those components. That way, you won't need to parse the element each time you use it.

- The extent to which you subdivide a data element depends on how it will be used. Because it's difficult to predict all future uses for the data, most designers subdivide data elements as much as possible.

- When you subdivide a data element, you can easily rebuild it when necessary by concatenating the individual components.

Figure 10-3   How to subdivide the data elements

How to identify the tables and assign columns

Figure 10-4 presents the three main entities for the accounts payable system and lists the possible data elements that can be associated with each one. In most cases, you'll recognize the main entities that need to be included in a data structure as you identify the data elements. As I reviewed the data elements represented on the invoice document in figure 10-2, for example, I identified the three entities shown in this figure: vendors, invoices, and invoice line items. Although you may identify additional entities later on in the design process, it's sufficient to identity the main entities at this point. These entities will become the tables of the database.

After you identify the main entities, you need to determine which data elements are associated with each entity. These elements will become the columns of the tables. In many cases, the associations are obvious. For example, it's easy to determine that the vendor name and address are associated with the vendors entity and the invoice date and invoice total are associated with the invoices entity. Some associations, however, aren't so obvious. In that case, you may need to list a data element under two or more entities. In this figure, for example, you can see that the invoice number is included in both the invoices and invoice line items entities and the account number is included in all three entities. Later, when you normalize the data structure, you may be able to remove these repeated elements. For now, though, it's okay to include them.

Before I go on, I want to point out the notation I used in this figure. To start, any data elements I included that weren't identified in previous steps are shown in italics. Although you should be able to identify most of the data elements in the first two steps of the design process, you'll occasionally think of additional elements during the third step. In this case, since the initial list of data elements was based on a single document, I added several data elements to this list.

Similarly, you may decide during this step that you don't need some of the data elements you've identified. For example, I decided that I didn't need the fax number or web address of each vendor. So I used the strikethrough feature of my word processor to indicate that these data elements should not be included.

Finally, I identified the data elements that are included in two or more tables by coding an asterisk after them. Although you can use any notation you like for this step of the design process, you'll want to be sure that you document your design decisions. For a complicated design, you may even want to use a *CASE (computer-aided software engineering)* tool.

By the way, a couple of the new data elements I added may not be clear to you if you haven't worked with a corporate accounts payable system before. "Terms" refers to the payment terms that the vendor offers. For example, the terms might be net 30 (the invoice must be paid in 30 days) or might include a discount for early payment. "Account number" refers to the general ledger accounts that a company uses to track its expenses. For example, one account number might be assigned for advertising expenses, while another might be for office supplies. Each invoice that's paid is assigned to an account, and in some cases, different line items on an invoice are assigned to different accounts.

Possible tables and columns for an accounts payable system

Vendors	Invoices	Invoice line items
Vendor name	Invoice number*	Invoice number*
Vendor address	Invoice date	~~Item part number~~
Vendor city	Terms*	Item quantity
Vendor state	Invoice total	Item description
Vendor zip code	*Payment date*	Item unit price
Vendor phone number	*Payment total*	Item extension
~~Vendor fax number~~	*Invoice due date*	Account number*
~~Vendor web address~~	*Credit total*	*Sequence number*
Vendor contact first name	*Account number**	
Vendor contact last name		
~~Vendor contact phone~~		
~~Vendor AR first name~~		
~~Vendor AR last name~~		
~~Vendor AR phone~~		
*Terms**		
*Account number**		

Description

- After you identify and subdivide all of the data elements for a database, you should group them by the entities with which they're associated. These entities will later become the tables of the database, and the elements will become the columns.

- If a data element relates to more than one entity, you can include it under all of the entities it relates to. Then, when you normalize the database, you may be able to remove the duplicate elements.

- As you assign the elements to entities, you should omit elements that aren't needed, and you should add any additional elements that are needed.

The notation used in this figure

- Data elements that were previously identified but aren't needed are crossed out.
- Data elements that were added are displayed in italics.
- Data elements that are related to two or more entities are followed by an asterisk.
- You can use a similar notation or develop one of your own. You can also use a *CASE* (*computer-aided software engineering*) tool if one is available to you.

Figure 10-4   How to identify the tables and assign columns

How to identify the primary and foreign keys

Once you identify the entities and data elements of a system, the next step is to identify the relationships between the tables. To do that, you need to identify the primary and foreign keys as shown in figure 10-5.

As you know, a primary key is used to uniquely identify each row in a table. In some cases, you can use an existing column as the primary key. For example, you might consider using the VendorName column as the primary key of the Vendors table. Because the values for this column can be long, however, and because it would be easy to enter a value incorrectly, that's not a good candidate. Instead, an identity column is used as the primary key.

Similarly, you might consider using the InvoiceNumber column as the primary key of the Invoices table. However, it's possible for different vendors to use the same invoice number, so this value isn't necessarily unique. Because of that, an identity column is used as the primary key of this table as well.

To uniquely identify the rows in the InvoiceLineItems table, this design uses a *composite key*. This composite key uses two columns to uniquely identify each row. The first column is the InvoiceID column from the Invoices table, and the second column is the InvoiceSequence column. This is necessary because this table may contain more than one row (line item) for each invoice. And that means that the InvoiceID value by itself won't be unique.

This book uses the composite key in the InvoiceLineItems table to show how to work with composite keys. However, it usually makes more sense to use a single column as the primary key. For example, the InvoiceLineItems table could start with an InvoiceLineItemID column that uniquely identifies each row in the table. Then, you could use that column as the primary key, and you could consider dropping the InvoiceSequence column.

After you identify the primary key of each table, you need to identify the relationships between the tables and add foreign key columns as necessary. In most cases, two tables will have a one-to-many relationship with each other. For example, each vendor can have many invoices, and each invoice can have many line items. To identify the vendor that each invoice is associated with, a VendorID column is included in the Invoices table. Because the InvoiceLineItems table already contains an InvoiceID column, it's not necessary to add another column to this table.

The diagram at the top of this figure illustrates the relationships I identified between the tables in the accounts payable system. As you can see, the primary keys are displayed in bold. Then, the lines between the tables indicate how the primary key in one table is related to the foreign key in another table. Here, a small, round connector indicates the "one" side of the relationship, and the triangular connector indicates the "many" side of the relationship.

In addition to the one-to-many relationships shown in this diagram, you can also use many-to-many relationships and one-to-one relationships. The second diagram in this figure, for example, shows a many-to-many relationship between an Employees table and a Committees table. As you can see, this type of relationship can be implemented by creating a *linking table*, also called a

The relationships between the tables in the accounts payable system

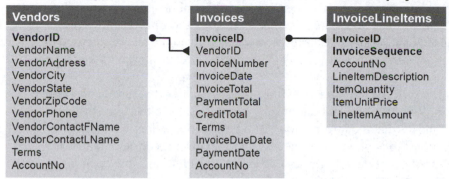

Two tables with a many-to-many relationship

Two tables with a one-to-one relationship

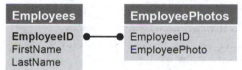

Description

- Most tables should have a primary key that uniquely identifies each row. If necessary, you can use a *composite key* that uses two or more columns to uniquely identify each row.

- The values of the primary keys should seldom, if ever, change. The values should also be short and easy to enter correctly.

- If a suitable column doesn't exist, you can create an identity column that can be used as the primary key.

- If two tables have a one-to-many relationship, you may need to add a foreign key column to the table on the "many" side. The foreign key column must have the same data type as the primary key column it's related to.

- If two tables have a many-to-many relationship, you'll need to define a *linking table* to relate them. Then, each of the tables in the many-to-many relationship will have a one-to-many relationship with the linking table. The linking table doesn't usually have a primary key.

- If two tables have a one-to-one relationship, they should be related by their primary keys. This type of relationship is typically used to improve performance. Then, columns with large amounts of data can be stored in a separate table.

Figure 10-5   How to identify the primary and foreign keys

connecting table or an *associate table*. This table contains the primary key columns from the two tables. Then, each table has a one-to-many relationship with the linking table. Notice that the linking table doesn't have its own primary key. Because this table doesn't correspond to an entity and because it's used only in conjunction with the Employees and Committees tables, a primary key isn't needed.

The third example in figure 10-5 illustrates two tables that have a one-to-one relationship. With this type of relationship, both tables have the same primary key, which means that the information could be stored in a single table. This type of relationship is often used when a table contains one or more columns with large amounts of data. In this case, the EmployeePhotos table contains a large binary column with a photo of each employee. Because this column is used infrequently, storing it in a separate table will make operations on the Employees table more efficient. Then, when this column is needed, it can be combined with the columns in the Employees table using a join.

How to enforce the relationships between tables

Although the primary keys and foreign keys indicate how the tables in a database are related, SQL Server doesn't enforce those relationships automatically. Because of that, any of the operations shown in the table at the top of figure 10-6 would violate the *referential integrity* of the tables. If you deleted a row from a primary key table, for example, and the foreign key table included rows related to that primary key, the referential integrity of the two tables would be destroyed. In that case, the rows in the foreign key table that no longer have a related row in the primary key table would be *orphaned*. Similar problems can occur when you insert a row into the foreign key table or update a primary key or foreign key value.

To enforce those relationships and maintain the referential integrity of the tables, you can use one of two features provided by SQL Server: declarative referential integrity or triggers. To use *declarative referential integrity* (*DRI*), you define *foreign key constraints* that indicate how the referential integrity between the tables is enforced. You'll learn more about defining foreign key constraints in the next two chapters. For now, just realize that these constraints can prevent all of the operations listed in this figure that violate referential integrity.

Operations that can violate referential integrity

This operation...	Violates referential integrity if...
Delete a row from the primary key table	The foreign key table contains one or more rows related to the deleted row
Insert a row in the foreign key table	The foreign key value doesn't have a matching primary key value in the related table
Update the value of a foreign key	The new foreign key value doesn't have a matching primary key value in the related table
Update the value of a primary key	The foreign key table contains one or more rows related to the row that's changed

Description

- *Referential integrity* means that the relationships between tables are maintained correctly. That means that a table with a foreign key doesn't have rows with foreign key values that don't have matching primary key values in the related table.

- In SQL Server, you can enforce referential integrity by using declarative referential integrity or by defining triggers.

- To use *declarative referential integrity (DRI)*, you define *foreign key constraints*. You'll learn how to do that in the next two chapters.

- When you define foreign key constraints, you can specify how referential integrity is enforced when a row is deleted from the primary key table. The options are to return an error or to delete the related rows in the foreign key table.

- You can also specify how referential integrity is enforced when the primary key of a row is changed and foreign key constraints are in effect. The options are to return an error or to change the foreign keys of all the related rows to the new value.

- If referential integrity isn't enforced and a row is deleted from the primary key table that has related rows in the foreign key table, the rows in the foreign key table are said to be *orphaned*.

- The three types of errors that can occur when referential integrity isn't enforced are called the *deletion anomaly*, the *insertion anomaly*, and the *update anomaly*.

Figure 10-6   How to enforce the relationships between tables

How normalization works

The next step in the design process is to review whether the data structure is *normalized*. To do that, you look at how the data is separated into related tables. If you follow the first four steps for designing a database that are presented in this chapter, your database will already be partially normalized when you get to this step. However, almost every design can be normalized further.

Figure 10-7 illustrates how *normalization* works. The first two tables in this figure show some of the problems caused by an *unnormalized* data structure. In the first table, you can see that each row represents an invoice. Because an invoice can have one or more line items, however, the ItemDescription column must be repeated to provide for the maximum number of line items. But since most invoices have fewer line items than the maximum, this can waste storage space.

In the second table, each line item is stored in a separate row. That eliminates the problem caused by repeating the ItemDescription column, but it introduces a new problem: the invoice number must be repeated in each row. This, too, can cause storage problems, particularly if the repeated column is large. In addition, it can cause maintenance problems if the column contains a value that's likely to change. Then, when the value changes, each row that contains the value must be updated. And if a repeated value must be reentered for each new row, it would be easy for the value to vary from one row to another.

To eliminate the problems caused by *data redundancy*, you can normalize the data structure. To do that, you apply the *normal forms* you'll learn about later in this chapter. As you'll see, there are a total of seven normal forms. However, it's common to apply only the first three.

The diagram in this figure, for example, shows the accounts payable system in third normal form. Here, the Terms table stores data that's needed by the Vendors and Invoices tables. Similarly, the GLAccounts table stores data that's needed by the Vendors and InvoiceLineItems tables. Storing terms and accounts data in one table instead of in multiple tables reduces data redundancy. At this point, it might not be clear to you how this works, but it should become clearer as you learn about the different normal forms.

A table that contains repeating columns

	InvoiceNumber	ItemDescription1	ItemDescription2	ItemDescription3
1	112897	VB ad	SQL ad	Library directory
2	97/552	Catalogs	SQL flyer	NULL
3	97/533B	Card revision	NULL	NULL

A table that contains redundant data

	InvoiceNumber	ItemDescription -
1	112897	VB ad
2	112897	SQL ad
3	112897	Library directory
4	97/522	Catalogs
5	97/522	SQL flyer
6	97/533B	Card revision

The accounts payable system in third normal form

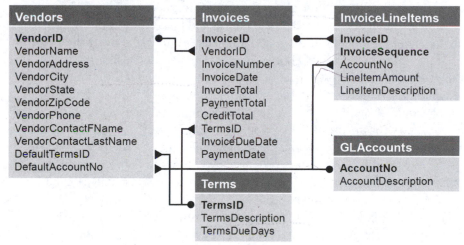

Description

- *Normalization* is a formal process you can use to separate the data in a data structure into related tables. Normalization reduces *data redundancy*, which can cause storage and maintenance problems.

- In an *unnormalized data structure*, a table can contain information about two or more entities. It can also contain repeating columns, columns that contain repeating values, and data that's repeated in two or more rows.

- In a *normalized data structure*, each table contains information about a single entity, and each piece of information is stored in exactly one place.

- To normalize a data structure, you apply the *normal forms* in sequence. Although there are a total of seven normal forms, a data structure is typically considered normalized if the first three normal forms are applied.

Figure 10-7   How normalization works

How to identify the columns to be indexed

The last step in the design process is to identify the columns that should be indexed. An *index* is a structure that provides for locating one or more rows directly. Without an index, SQL Server has to perform a *table scan*, which involves searching through the entire table. Just as the index of a book has page numbers that direct you to a specific subject, a database index has pointers that direct the system to a specific row. This can speed performance not only when you're searching for rows based on a search condition, but when you're joining data from tables as well. If a join is done based on a primary key to foreign key relationship, for example, and an index is defined for the foreign key column, SQL Server can use that index to locate the rows for each primary key value.

In general, a column should meet the guidelines listed at the top of figure 10-8 before you consider creating an index for it. To start, you should index a column if it will be used frequently in search conditions or joins. Since you use foreign keys in most joins, you should typically index each foreign key column. The column should also contain mostly distinct values, and the values in the column should be updated infrequently. If these conditions aren't met, the overhead of maintaining the index will probably outweigh the advantages of using it.

SQL Server provides for two types of indexes. A *clustered index* defines the sequence in which the rows of the table are stored. Because of that, each table can contain a single clustered index. Although SQL Server creates a clustered index automatically for the primary key, you can change that if you need to. The second list in this figure presents some guidelines you can use to determine when to change the clustered index from the primary key column to another column. If you review these guidelines, you'll see that the primary key is usually the best column to use for the clustered index.

The other type of index is a *nonclustered index*. You can define up to 249 nonclustered indexes for each table. You should be aware, however, that the indexes must be updated each time you add, update, or delete a row. Because of that, you don't want to define more indexes than you need.

As you identify the indexes for a table, keep in mind that, like a key, an index can consist of two or more columns. This type of index is called a *composite index*. A special type of composite index that includes all of the columns used by a query is called a *covering index*. Although a covering index speeds retrieval, the overhead to maintain this type of index is significant, particularly if the table is updated frequently. Because of that, you won't usually define covering indexes.

Since you don't want to add unnecessary indexes, some database designers recommend adding indexes later when the database is in testing or production. That way, you can test the queries that are commonly run against the database and see how they perform. Then, if they don't perform well, you can add indexes.

Management Studio includes a feature that can help you identify and add indexes that would improve performance. To do that, enter a commonly run query into a Query Editor window. Then, select the Query→Display Estimated Execution Plan command. This should show any missing indexes that would improve performance. If you want to add the missing index, you can right-click it and select the Missing Index Details command to generate a script for creating that index.

When to create an index

- When the column is a foreign key
- When the column is used frequently in search conditions or joins
- When the column contains a large number of distinct values
- When the column is updated infrequently

When to reassign the clustered index

- When the column is used in almost every search condition
- When the column contains mostly distinct values
- When the column is small
- When the column values seldom, if ever, change
- When most queries against the column will return large result sets

Description

- An *index* provides a way for SQL Server to locate information more quickly. When it uses an index, SQL Server can go directly to a row rather than having to search through all the rows until it finds the ones you want.

- An index can be either *clustered* or *nonclustered*. Each table can have one clustered index and up to 249 nonclustered indexes.

- The rows of a table are stored in the sequence of the clustered index. By default, SQL Server creates a clustered index for the primary key. If you don't identify a primary key, the rows of the table are stored in the order in which they're entered.

- Indexes speed performance when searching and joining tables. However, they can't be used in search conditions that use the LIKE operator with a pattern that starts with a wildcard. And they can't be used in search conditions that include functions or expressions.

- You can create *composite indexes* that include two or more columns. You should use this type of index when the columns in the index are updated infrequently or when the index will cover almost every search condition on the table.

- Because indexes must be updated each time you add, update, or delete a row, you shouldn't create more indexes than you need.

Figure 10-8   How to identify the columns to be indexed

How to normalize a data structure

The topics that follow describe the seven normal forms and teach you how to apply the first three. As I said earlier, you apply these three forms to some extent in the first four database design steps, but these topics will give you more insight into the process. Then, the last topic explains when and how to denormalize a data structure. When you finish these topics, you'll have the basic skills for designing databases that are efficient and easy to use.

The seven normal forms

Figure 10-9 summarizes the seven normal forms. Each normal form assumes that the previous forms have already been applied. Before you can apply the third normal form, for example, the design must already be in the second normal form.

Strictly speaking, a data structure isn't normalized until it's in the fifth or sixth normal form. However, the normal forms past the third normal form are applied infrequently. Because of that, I won't present those forms in detail here. Instead, I'll just describe them briefly so you'll have an idea of how to apply them if you need to.

The *Boyce-Codd normal form* is a slightly stronger version of the third normal form that can be used to eliminate *transitive dependencies*. With this type of dependency, one column depends on another column, which depends on a third column. Most tables that are in the third normal form are also in the Boyce-Codd normal form.

The fourth normal form can be used to eliminate multiple *multivalued dependencies* from a table. A multivalued dependency is one where a primary key column has a one-to-many relationship with a non-key column. This normal form gets rid of misleading many-to-many relationships.

To apply the fifth normal form, you continue to divide the tables of the data structure into smaller tables until all redundancy has been removed. When further splitting would result in tables that couldn't be used to reconstruct the original table, the data structure is in fifth normal form. In this form, most tables consist of little more than key columns with one or two data elements.

The *domain-key normal form*, sometimes called the sixth normal form, is only of academic interest since no database system has implemented a way to apply it. For this reason, even normalization purists might consider a database to be normalized in fifth normal form.

This figure also lists the benefits of normalizing a data structure. To summarize, normalization produces smaller, more efficient tables. In addition, it reduces data redundancy, which makes the data easier to maintain and reduces the amount of storage needed for the database. Because of these benefits, you should always consider normalizing your data structures.

You should also be aware that the subject of normalization is a contentious one in the database community. In the academic study of computer science, normalization is considered a form of design perfection that should always be strived for. In practice, though, database designers and DBAs tend to use normalization as a flexible design guideline.

The seven normal forms

Normal form	Description
First (1NF)	The value stored at the intersection of each row and column must be a scalar value, and a table must not contain any repeating columns.
Second (2NF)	Every non-key column must depend on the primary key.
Third (3NF)	Every non-key column must depend *only* on the primary key.
Boyce-Codd (BCNF)	A non-key column can't be dependent on another non-key column. This prevents *transitive dependencies*, where column A depends on column C and column B depends on column C. Since both A and B depend on C, A and B should be moved into another table with C as the key.
Fourth (4NF)	A table must not have more than one *multivalued dependency*, where the primary key has a one-to-many relationship to non-key columns. This form gets rid of misleading many-to-many relationships.
Fifth (5NF)	The data structure is split into smaller and smaller tables until all redundancy has been eliminated. If further splitting would result in tables that couldn't be joined to recreate the original table, the structure is in fifth normal form.
Domain-key (DKNF) or Sixth (6NF)	Every constraint on the relationship is dependent only on key constraints and *domain* constraints, where a domain is the set of allowable values for a column. This form prevents the insertion of any unacceptable data by enforcing constraints at the level of a relationship, rather than at the table or column level. DKNF is less a design model than an abstract "ultimate" normal form. SQL Server has no way to implement the constraints required for DKNF.

The benefits of normalization

- Since a normalized database has more tables than an unnormalized database, and since each table can have a clustered index, the database has more clustered indexes. That makes data retrieval more efficient.
- Since each table contains information about a single entity, each index has fewer columns (usually one) and fewer rows. That makes data retrieval and insert, update, and delete operations more efficient.
- Each table has fewer indexes, which makes insert, update, and delete operations more efficient.
- Data redundancy is minimized, which simplifies maintenance and reduces storage.
- Queries against the database run faster.

Description

- Each normal form assumes that the design is already in the previous normal form.
- A database is typically considered to be normalized if it is in third normal form. The other four forms are not commonly used and are not covered in detail in this book.

Figure 10-9   The seven normal forms

How to apply the first normal form

Figure 10-10 illustrates how you apply the first normal form to an unnormalized invoice data structure consisting of the data elements that are shown in figure 10-2. The first two tables in this figure illustrate structures that aren't in first normal form. Both of these tables contain a single row for each invoice. Because each invoice can contain one or more line items, however, the first table allows for repeating values in the ItemDescription column. The second table is similar, except it includes a separate column for each line item description. Neither of these structures is acceptable in first normal form.

The third table in this figure has eliminated the repeating values and columns. To do that, it includes one row for each line item. Notice, however, that this has increased the data redundancy. Specifically, the vendor name and invoice number are now repeated for each line item. This problem can be solved by applying the second normal form.

Before I describe the second normal form, I want you to realize that I intentionally omitted many of the columns in the invoice data structure from the examples in this figure and the next figure. In addition to the columns shown here, for example, each of these tables would also contain the vendor address, invoice date, invoice total, etc. By eliminating these columns, it will be easier for you to focus on the columns that are affected by applying the normal forms.

The invoice data with a column that contains repeating values

	VendorName	InvoiceNumber	ItemDescription
1	Cahners Publishing	112897	VB ad, SQL ad, Library directory
2	Zylka Design	97/522	Catalogs, SQL flyer
3	Zylka Design	97/533B	Card revision

The invoice data with repeating columns

	VendorName	InvoiceNumber	ItemDescription1	ItemDescription2	ItemDescription3
1	Cahners Publishing	112897	VB ad	SQL ad	Library directory
2	Zylka Design	97/522	Catalogs	SQL flyer	NULL
3	Zylka Design	97/533B	Card revision	NULL	NULL

The invoice data in first normal form

	VendorName	InvoiceNumber	ItemDescription
1	Cahners Publishing	112897	VB ad
2	Cahners Publishing	112897	SQL ad
3	Cahners Publishing	112897	Library directory
4	Zylka Design	97/522	Catalogs
5	Zylka Design	97/522	SQL flyer
6	Zylka Design	97/533B	Card revision

Description

- For a table to be in first normal form, its columns must not contain repeating values. Instead, each column must contain a single, scalar value. In addition, the table must not contain repeating columns that represent a set of values.

- A table in first normal form often has repeating values in its rows. This can be resolved by applying the second normal form.

Figure 10-10   How to apply the first normal form

How to apply the second normal form

Figure 10-11 shows how to apply the second normal form. To be in second normal form, every column in a table that isn't a key column must depend on the entire primary key. This form only applies to tables that have composite primary keys, which is often the case when you start with data that is completely unnormalized. The table at the top of this figure, for example, shows the invoice data in first normal form after key columns have been added. In this case, the primary key consists of the InvoiceID and InvoiceSequence columns.

Now, consider the three non-key columns shown in this table. Of these three, only one, ItemDescription, depends on the entire primary key. The other two, VendorName and InvoiceNumber, depend only on the InvoiceID column. Because of that, these columns should be moved to another table. The result is a data structure like the second one shown in this figure. Here, all of the information related to an invoice is stored in the Invoices table, and all of the information related to an individual line item is stored in the InvoiceLineItems table.

Notice that the relationship between these tables is based on the InvoiceID column. This column is the primary key of the Invoices table, and it's the foreign key in the InvoiceLineItems table that relates the rows in that table to the rows in the Invoices table. This column is also part of the primary key of the InvoiceLineItems table.

When you apply second normal form to a data structure, it eliminates some of the redundant row data in the tables. In this figure, for example, you can see that the invoice number and vendor name are now included only once for each invoice. In first normal form, this information was included for each line item.

The invoice data in first normal form with keys added

	InvoiceID	VendorName	InvoiceNumber	InvoiceSequence	ItemDescription
1	1	Cahners Publishing	112897	1	VB ad
2	1	Cahners Publishing	112897	2	SQL ad
3	1	Cahners Publishing	112897	3	Library directory
4	2	Zylka Design	97/522	1	Catalogs
5	2	Zylka Design	97/522	2	SQL flyer
6	3	Zylka Design	97/533B	1	Card revision

The invoice data in second normal form

	InvoiceNumber	VendorName	InvoiceID
1	112897	Cahners Publishing	1
2	97/522	Zylka Design	2
3	97/533B	Zylka Design	3

	InvoiceID	InvoiceSequence	ItemDescription
1	1	1	VB ad
2	1	2	SQL ad
3	1	3	Library directory
4	2	1	Catalogs
5	2	2	SQL flyer
6	3	1	Card revision

Description

- For a table to be in second normal form, every non-key column must depend on the entire primary key. If a column doesn't depend on the entire key, it indicates that the table contains information for more than one entity. This is reflected by the table's composite key.

- To apply second normal form, you move columns that don't depend on the entire primary key to another table and then establish a relationship between the two tables.

- Second normal form helps remove redundant row data, which can save storage space, make maintenance easier, and reduce the chance of storing inconsistent data.

Figure 10-11   How to apply the second normal form

How to apply the third normal form

To apply the third normal form, you make sure that every non-key column depends *only* on the primary key. Figure 10-12 illustrates how you can apply this form to the data structure for the accounts payable system. At the top of this figure, you can see all of the columns in the Invoices and InvoiceLineItems tables in second normal form. Then, you can see a list of questions that you might ask about some of the columns in these tables when you apply third normal form.

First, does the vendor information depend only on the InvoiceID column? Another way to phrase this question is, "Will the information for the same vendor change from one invoice to another?" If the answer is no, the vendor information should be stored in a separate table. That way, you can be sure that the vendor information for each invoice for a vendor will be the same. In addition, you will reduce the redundancy of the data in the Invoices table. This is illustrated by the diagram in this figure that shows the accounts payable system in third normal form. Here, a Vendors table has been added to store the information for each vendor. This table is related to the Invoices table by the VendorID column, which has been added as a foreign key to the Invoices table.

Second, does the Terms column depend only on the InvoiceID column? The answer to that question depends on how this column is used. In this case, it's used not only to specify the terms for each invoice, but also to specify the default terms for a vendor. Because of that, the terms information could be stored in both the Vendors and the Invoices tables. To avoid redundancy, however, the information related to different terms can be stored in a separate table, as illustrated by the Terms table in this figure. As you can see, the primary key of this table is an identity column named TermsID. Then, a foreign key column named DefaultTermsID has been added to the Vendors table, and a foreign key column named TermsID has been added to the Invoices table.

Third, does the AccountNo column depend only on the InvoiceID column? Again, that depends on how this column is used. In this case, it's used to specify the general ledger account number for each line item, so it depends on the InvoiceID and the InvoiceSequence columns. In other words, this column should be stored in the InvoiceLineItems table. In addition, each vendor has a default account number, which should be stored in the Vendors table. Because of that, another table named GLAccounts has been added to store the account numbers and account descriptions. Then, foreign key columns have been added to the Vendors and InvoiceLineItems tables to relate them to this table.

Fourth, can the InvoiceDueDate column in the Invoices table and the InvoiceLineItemAmount column in the InvoiceLineItems table be derived from other data in the database? If so, they depend on the columns that contain that data rather than on the primary key columns. In this case, the value of the InvoiceLineItemAmount column can always be calculated from the ItemQuantity and ItemUnitPrice columns. Because of that, this column could be omitted. Alternatively, you could omit the ItemQuantity and ItemUnitPrice columns and keep just the InvoiceLineItemAmount column. That's what I did in the data structure shown in this figure. The solution you choose, however, depends on how the data will be used.

The accounts payable system in second normal form

Invoices

InvoiceID	
VendorName	InvoiceDate
VendorAddress	InvoiceTotal
VendorCity	PaymentTotal
VendorState	CreditTotal
VendorZipCode	Terms
VendorPhone	InvoiceDueDate
VendorContactFName	PaymentDate
VendorContactLName	AccountNo
InvoiceNumber	

InvoiceLineItems

InvoiceID
InvoiceSequence
AccountNo
InvoiceLineItemDescription
ItemQuantity
ItemUnitPrice
InvoiceLineItemAmount

Questions about the structure

1. Does the vendor information (VendorName, VendorAddress, etc.) depend only on the InvoiceID column?

2. Does the Terms column depend only on the InvoiceID column?

3. Does the AccountNo column depend only on the InvoiceID column?

4. Can the InvoiceDueDate and InvoiceLineItemAmount columns be derived from other data?

The accounts payable system in third normal form

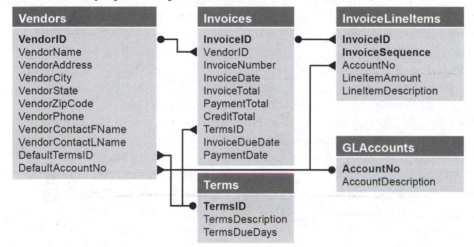

Description

- For a table to be in third normal form, every non-key column must depend only on the primary key.

- If a column doesn't depend only on the primary key, it implies that the column is assigned to the wrong table or that it can be computed from other columns in the table. A column that can be computed from other columns contains *derived data*.

Figure 10-12   How to apply the third normal form

In contrast, although the InvoiceDueDate column could be calculated from the InvoiceDate column in the Invoices table and the TermsDueDays column in the related row of the Terms table, the system also allows this date to be overridden. Because of that, the InvoiceDueDate column should not be omitted. If the system didn't allow this value to be overridden, however, this column could be safely omitted.

When and how to denormalize a data structure

Denormalization is the deliberate deviation from the normal forms. Most denormalization occurs beyond the third normal form. In contrast, the first three normal forms are almost universally applied.

To illustrate when and how to denormalize a data structure, figure 10-13 presents the design of the accounts payable system in fifth normal form. Here, notice that the vendor addresses are stored in a separate table that contains the address, city, state, and zip code for each vendor. In addition, the vendor contacts are stored in a separate table that contains the first name, last name, and phone number for each vendor contact.

Since this allows you to use the same address or contact for multiple vendors, this reduces data redundancy if multiple vendors share the same address or contact person. However, since vendor address and contact information is now split across three tables, a query that retrieves vendor addresses and contact information requires two joins. In contrast, if you left the address and contact information in the Vendors table, no joins would be required, but the Vendors table would be larger.

In general, you should denormalize based on the way the data will be used. In this case, the system rarely needs to query vendors without address and contact information. In addition, it's rare that multiple vendors would have the same address or contact information. For these reasons, I've denormalized my design by eliminating the Addresses and Contacts tables.

You might also consider denormalizing a table if the data it contains is updated infrequently. In that case, redundant data isn't as likely to cause problems.

Finally, you should consider including derived data in a table if that data is used frequently in search conditions. For example, if you frequently query the Invoices table based on invoice balances, you might consider including a column that contains the balance due. That way, you won't have to calculate this value each time it's queried. Keep in mind, though, that if you store derived data, it's possible for it to deviate from the derived value. For this reason, you may need to protect the derived column so it can't be updated directly. Alternatively, you could update the table periodically to reset the value of the derived column.

Because normalization eliminates the possibility of data redundancy errors and optimizes the use of storage, you should carefully consider when and how to denormalize a data structure. In general, you should denormalize only when the increased efficiency outweighs the potential for redundancy errors and storage problems. Of course, your decision to denormalize should also be based on your knowledge of the real-world environment in which the system will be used. If you've carefully analyzed the real-world environment as outlined in this chapter, you'll have a good basis for making that decision.

The accounts payable system in fifth normal form

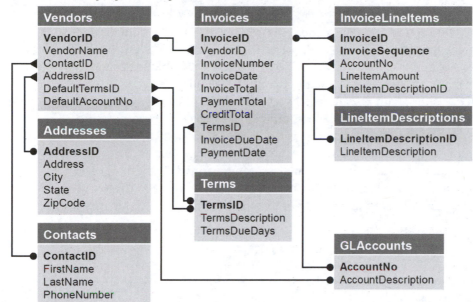

When to denormalize

- When a column from a joined table is used repeatedly in search criteria, you should consider moving that column to the primary key table if it will eliminate the need for a join.

- If a table is updated infrequently, you should consider denormalizing it to improve efficiency. Because the data remains relatively constant, you don't have to worry about data redundancy errors once the initial data is entered and verified.

- Include columns with derived values when those values are used frequently in search conditions. If you do that, you need to be sure that the column value is always synchronized with the value of the columns it's derived from.

Description

- Data structures that are normalized to the fourth normal form and beyond typically require more joins than tables normalized to the third normal form.

- Most designers *denormalize* data structures to some extent, usually to the third normal form.

- *Denormalization* can result in larger tables, redundant data, and reduced performance.

- Only denormalize when necessary. It is better to adhere to the normal forms unless it is clear that performance will be improved by denormalizing.

Figure 10-13   When and how to denormalize a data structure

Perspective

Database design is a complicated subject. Because of that, it's impossible to teach you everything you need to know in a single chapter. With the skills you've learned in this chapter, however, you should now be able to design simple databases of your own. More important, you should now be able to evaluate the design of any database that you work with. That way, you can be sure that the queries you code will be as efficient and as effective as possible.

One aspect of database design that isn't covered in this chapter is designing the security of the database. Among other things, that involves creating login IDs and database users and assigning permissions. It may also involve organizing the tables and other objects in the database into two or more schemas. You'll learn more about how to implement database security in chapter 17.

Terms

data structure	deletion anomaly
entity	normalization
attribute	data redundancy
instance	unnormalized data structure
entity-relationship (ER) modeling	normalized data structure
CASE (computer-aided software engineering)	normal forms
	index
composite key	table scan
linking table	clustered index
connecting table	nonclustered index
associate table	composite index
referential integrity	covering index
declarative referential integrity (DRI)	Boyce-Codd normal form
	transitive dependency
foreign key constraints	multivalued dependency
triggers	domain-key normal form
orphaned row	derived data
update anomaly	denormalized data structure
insertion anomaly	denormalization

Exercises

1. Design a database diagram for a product orders database with four tables. Indicate the relationships between tables and identify the primary key and foreign keys in each table. Explain your design decisions.

Customers
CustomerID
CustomerName
CustomerAddress
CustomerPhone
...

Orders
OrdersID
CustomerID
OrderDate
ShipAddress
ShipDate
...

OrderLineItems
OrderID
OrderSequence
ProductID
Quantity
UnitPrice

Products
ProductID
ProductName
QtyPerUnit
UnitPrice
InStock
OnOrder
...

2. Add the two tables below into the design for exercise 1. Create additional tables and columns, if necessary. Explain your design decisions.

Shippers
ShipperID
ShipperName
ShipperAddress
ShipperPhone
...

Employees
EmployeeID
FirstName
LastName
SSN
HireDate
...

3. Modify your design for exercise 2 to identify the columns that should be indexed, and explain your decision.

4. Design a database diagram that allows individuals to be assigned membership in one or more groups. Each group can have any number of individuals and each individual can belong to any number of groups. Create additional tables and columns, if necessary. Explain your design decisions.

5. Modify your design for exercise 4 to keep track of the *role* served by each individual in each group. Each individual can only serve one role in each group. Each group has a unique set of roles that members can fulfill. Create additional tables and columns, if necessary. Explain your design decisions.

11

How to create a database and its tables with SQL statements

Now that you've learned how to design a database, you're ready to learn how to implement your design. To do that, you use the set of SQL statements that are known as the data definition language (DDL). As an application programmer, you can use the DDL statements to create and modify the database objects such as tables and sequences that you need for testing. Beyond that, knowing what these statements do will give you a better appreciation for how a database works.

An introduction to DDL

All of the SQL statements that you've seen so far have been part of the data manipulation language, or DML. But now, you'll learn how to use the SQL statements that are part of the data definition language. You use these statements to define the objects of a database.

The SQL statements for data definition

Figure 11-1 summarizes the *data definition language*, or *DDL*, statements that you use to create, delete, or change the *objects* of a database. In this chapter, you'll learn how to use the statements that work with databases, tables, indexes, and sequences. You'll learn how to use the statements that work with other objects in later chapters.

To work with the objects of a database, you often use the Management Studio that comes with SQL Server. This tool lets you create and change database objects using a graphical user interface. To do that, it generates and executes the DDL statements that implement the changes you've made. You'll learn how to use the Management Studio to work with database objects in chapter 12.

But first, this chapter teaches you how to code the DDL statements yourself. This is useful for two reasons. First, you sometimes need to examine and verify the DDL that's generated by the Management Studio. This is especially true for large database projects. Second, knowing the DDL statements helps you use the DML statements more effectively. Beyond that, if you ever use a DBMS that doesn't offer a graphical tool like the Management Studio, you have to code the DDL yourself.

Because the syntax of each of the DDL statements is complex, this chapter doesn't present complete syntax diagrams for the statements. Instead, the diagrams present only the most commonly used clauses. If you're interested in the complete syntax of any statement, of course, you can find it the SQL Server documentation.

If you're working on a large database project, you probably won't have the option of coding DDL statements at all because that will be handled by a database administrator (DBA). This is a common practice because the DDL statements can destroy data if they're used incorrectly. In addition, many of the optional clauses for these statements are used for tuning the performance of the system, which is typically the role of a DBA.

For small projects, though, the SQL programmer may often have to serve as the DBA too. And even for large databases, the SQL programmer often uses the DDL to create and work with smaller databases that are needed for testing or for special projects.

DDL statements to create, modify, and delete objects

Statement	Description
CREATE DATABASE	Creates a new database.
CREATE TABLE	Creates a new table in the current database.
CREATE INDEX	Creates a new index for the specified table.
CREATE SEQUENCE	Creates a new sequence in the current database.
CREATE FUNCTION	Creates a new function in the current database.
CREATE PROCEDURE	Creates a new stored procedure in the current database.
CREATE TRIGGER	Creates a new trigger in the current database.
CREATE VIEW	Creates a new view in the current database.
ALTER TABLE	Modifies the structure of the specified table.
ALTER SEQUENCE	Modifies the attributes of a sequence.
ALTER FUNCTION	Modifies the specified function.
ALTER PROCEDURE	Modifies the specified stored procedure.
ALTER TRIGGER	Modifies the specified trigger.
ALTER VIEW	Modifies the specified view.
DROP DATABASE	Deletes the specified database.
DROP TABLE	Deletes the specified table.
DROP SEQUENCE	Deletes the specified sequence.
DROP INDEX	Deletes the specified index.
DROP FUNCTION	Deletes the specified function.
DROP PROCEDURE	Deletes the specified stored procedure.
DROP TRIGGER	Deletes the specified trigger.
DROP VIEW	Deletes the specified view.

Description

- You use the *data definition language* (*DDL*) statements to create, modify, and delete database objects such as the database itself, the tables contained in a database, and the indexes for those tables.

- Typically, a database administrator is responsible for using the DDL statements on production databases in a large database system. However, every SQL programmer should be comfortable using these statements so that they can create and work with small databases for testing.

- In most cases, you'll use the graphical user interface of the Management Studio to create and maintain database objects as described in chapter 12. Although the Management Studio generates DDL statements for you, you may need to verify or correct these statements. To do that, you need to understand their syntax and use.

- If you use a SQL database other than SQL Server, it may not have a graphical tool for managing database objects. In that case, you must use the DDL statements.

Figure 11-1   The SQL statements for data definition

Rules for coding object names

When you create most database objects, you give them names. In SQL Server, the name of an object is its *identifier*. Each identifier can be up to 128 characters in length. To code an identifier, you typically follow the formatting rules presented in figure 11-2.

As you can see, the formatting rules limit the characters you can use in an identifier. For example, the first character of an identifier can be a letter, an underscore, an at sign, or a number sign. The characters that can be used in the remainder of the identifier include all of the characters allowed as the first character, plus numbers and dollar signs. Note that a regular identifier can't include spaces and can't be a Transact-SQL reserved keyword, which is a word that's reserved for use by SQL Server.

The first set of examples in this figure presents some valid regular identifiers. Notice that the identifier in the second example starts with a number sign. This type of identifier is used for a temporary table or procedure. Similarly, an identifier that starts with an at sign as in the fifth example is used for a local variable or parameter. You'll learn about these special types of identifiers in chapters 14 and 15.

In most cases, you'll create objects with identifiers that follow the formatting rules shown here. If you're working with an existing database, however, the identifiers may not follow these rules. In that case, you have to delimit the identifiers to use them in SQL statements. You can code a delimited identifier by enclosing it in either brackets or double quotes. The second set of examples shows how this works. Here, two of the identifiers are enclosed in brackets and one is enclosed in double quotes. The identifier in the first example must be delimited because it starts with a percent sign. The identifier in the second example must be delimited because it includes spaces. The third example illustrates that even when a name follows the formatting rules, you can delimit it. In most cases, though, there's no reason to do that.

Formatting rules for identifiers

- The first character of an identifier must be a letter as defined by the Unicode Standard 2.0, an underscore (_), an at sign (@), or a number sign (#).

- All characters after the first must be a letter as defined by the Unicode Standard 2.0, a number, an at sign, a dollar sign ($), a number sign, or an underscore.

- An identifier can't be a Transact-SQL reserved keyword.

- An identifier can't contain spaces or special characters other than those already mentioned.

Valid regular identifiers

```
Employees
#PaidInvoices
ABC$123
Invoice_Line_Items
@TotalDue
```

Valid delimited identifiers

```
[%Increase]
"Invoice Line Items"
[@TotalDue]
```

Description

- The name of an object in SQL Server is called its *identifier*. Most objects are assigned an identifier when they're created. Then, the identifier can be used to refer to the object.

- SQL Server provides for two classes of identifiers. Regular identifiers follow the formatting rules for identifiers. Delimited identifiers are enclosed in brackets ([]) or double quotation marks ("") and may or may not follow the formatting rules. If an identifier doesn't follow the formatting rules, it must be delimited.

- An identifier can contain from 1 to 128 characters.

- An at sign (@) at the beginning of an identifier indicates that the identifier is a local variable or parameter, a number sign (#) indicates that the identifier is a temporary table or procedure, and two number signs (##) indicates that the identifier is a global temporary object. See chapters 14 and 15 for details.

Figure 11-2   Rules for coding object names

How to create databases, tables, and indexes

The primary role of the DDL statements is to define database objects on the server. So to start, the three topics that follow will teach you how to code the DDL statements that you use to create databases, tables, and indexes.

How to create a database

Figure 11-3 presents the basic syntax of the CREATE DATABASE statement. This statement creates a new database on the current server. In many cases, you'll code this statement with just a database name to create the database with the default options. This is illustrated by the first example in this figure.

The CREATE DATABASE statement in this example creates a database named New_AP. When you issue a statement like this one, SQL Server creates two files and allocates space for them. The first file, New_AP.mdf, will hold the data for the database. The second file, New_AP_log.ldf, will keep a log of any changes made to the database.

If you want to use a database that was created on another server, you can copy the mdf file to your server, but at that point, it's simply a data file. To be able to use the database, you have to *attach* it to your server. To do that, you use two of the optional clauses in the CREATE DATABASE statement, ON PRIMARY and FOR ATTACH. As you can see in the second example, you specify the name of the file that contains the database in the ON PRIMARY clause. Then, instead of creating a new database, SQL Server simply makes the existing database available from the current server.

In this figure, the statement that attaches the database doesn't specify an existing transaction log file for the database. As a result, SQL Server attempts to use an ldf file with the same name as the database followed by "_log". For example, for the data stored in the file named Test_AP.mdf, SQL Server will attempt to use the log data stored in the file named Test_AP_log.ldf. If a log file with that name doesn't exist, SQL Server will create a new log file with that name. However, it will also return an error message that indicates that a new log file was created.

Most of the clauses that aren't included in the syntax shown here are used to tune the database by changing the locations of the database files. For small databases, though, this tuning usually isn't necessary. If you want to learn about these options, you can refer to the description of this statement in the SQL Server documentation.

The basic syntax of the CREATE DATABASE statement

```
CREATE DATABASE database_name
    [ON [PRIMARY] (FILENAME = 'file_name')]
    [FOR ATTACH]
```

A statement that creates a new database

```
CREATE DATABASE New_AP;
```

The response from the system
```
Command(s) completed successfully.
```

A statement that attaches an existing database file

```
CREATE DATABASE Test_AP
    ON PRIMARY (FILENAME =
        'C:\Murach\SQL Server 2016\Databases\Test_AP.mdf')
    FOR ATTACH;
```

The response from the system
```
Command(s) completed successfully.
```

Description

- The CREATE DATABASE statement creates a new, empty database on the current server. Although the ANSI standards don't include this statement, it's supported by virtually all SQL database systems. The optional clauses shown here, however, are supported only by SQL Server.

- If you code this statement without any options, the new database is created using the default settings and the database files are stored in the default directory on the hard drive. For most small database projects, these settings are acceptable.

- One of the files SQL Server creates when it executes the CREATE DATABASE statement is a *transaction log file*. This file is used to record modifications to the database. SQL Server generates the name for this file by appending "_log" to the end of the database name. The database name is limited to 123 characters.

- If you have a copy of a database file that you'd like to work with on your server, you can use the FOR ATTACH clause in addition to the ON PRIMARY clause to *attach* the file as a database to the current server.

- Most of the optional clauses that have been omitted from this syntax are used to specify the underlying file structure of the database. These clauses are used by DBAs to tune the performance of the database. See the SQL Server documentation for details.

Warning

- On some systems, the CREATE DATABASE statement can overwrite an existing database. Because of that, you'll want to check with the DBA before using this statement.

Figure 11-3   How to create a database

How to create a table

Figure 11-4 presents the basic syntax of the CREATE TABLE statement. By default, this statement creates a new table in the default schema, dbo, within the current database. If that's not what you want, you can qualify the table name with the schema name or the database name.

All of the clauses and keywords for the CREATE TABLE statement can be divided into two categories: attributes that affect a single column and attributes that affect the entire table. This figure summarizes some of the common column attributes. You'll learn about the table attributes later in this chapter.

In its simplest form, the CREATE TABLE statement consists of the name of the new table followed by the names and data types of its columns. This is illustrated by the first example of this figure. Notice that the column definitions are enclosed in parentheses. In most cases, you'll code one or more attributes for each column as illustrated by the second example in this figure.

To identify whether a column can accept null values, you code either the NULL or NOT NULL keyword. If you omit both keywords, the default value is NULL unless the column is also defined as the primary key, in which case the default is NOT NULL.

The PRIMARY KEY keywords identify the primary key for the table. To create a primary key based on a single column, you can code these keywords as an attribute of that column. To create a primary key based on two or more columns, however, you must code PRIMARY KEY as a table attribute. You'll see how to do that in a later figure.

When you identify a column as the primary key, two of the column's attributes are changed automatically. First, the column is forced to be NOT NULL. Second, the column is forced to contain a unique value for each row. In addition, a clustered index is automatically created based on the column.

In addition to a primary key, you can also define one or more unique keys using the UNIQUE keyword. Unlike a primary key column, a unique key column can contain null values. And instead of creating a clustered index for the key, SQL Server creates a nonclustered index. Like the PRIMARY keyword, you can code the UNIQUE keyword at either the column or the table level.

NOT NULL, PRIMARY KEY, and UNIQUE are examples of *constraints*. Constraints are special attributes that restrict the data that can be stored in the columns of a table. You'll learn how to code other constraints in a moment.

The IDENTITY keyword defines a column as an identity column. As you know, SQL Server assigns an identity column a unique integer value. This value is generated by incrementing the previous value for the column. SQL Server allows only one identity column per table, and that column is typically used as the primary key.

The DEFAULT attribute specifies a default value for a column. This value is used if another value isn't specified. The default value that's specified must correspond to the data type for the column.

The last attribute, the SPARSE attribute, optimizes the storage of null values for a column. Since this optimization requires more overhead to retrieve non-null

The basic syntax of the CREATE TABLE statement

```
CREATE TABLE table_name
(column_name_1 data_type [column_attributes]
[, column_name_2 data_type [column_attributes]]...
[, table_attributes])
```

Common column attributes

Attribute	Description
NULL|NOT NULL	Indicates whether or not the column can accept null values. If omitted, NULL is the default unless PRIMARY KEY is specified.
PRIMARY KEY|UNIQUE	Identifies the primary key or a unique key for the table. If PRIMARY is specified, the NULL attribute isn't allowed.
IDENTITY	Identifies an identity column. Only one identity column can be created per table.
DEFAULT default_value	Specifies a default value for the column.
SPARSE	Optimizes storage of null values for the column. This attribute was introduced with SQL Server 2008.

A statement that creates a table without column attributes

```
CREATE TABLE Vendors
(VendorID        INT,
VendorName       VARCHAR(50));
```

A statement that creates a table with column attributes

```
CREATE TABLE Invoices
(InvoiceID       INT                 PRIMARY KEY IDENTITY,
VendorID         INT                 NOT NULL,
InvoiceDate      SMALLDATETIME       NULL,
InvoiceTotal     MONEY               NULL DEFAULT 0);
```

A column definition that uses the SPARSE attribute

```
VendorAddress2      VARCHAR(50)      SPARSE NULL
```

Description

- The CREATE TABLE statement creates a table based on the column definitions, column attributes, and table attributes you specify. A database can contain as many as two billion tables.

- A table can contain between one and 1,024 columns. Each column must have a unique name and must be assigned a data type. In addition, you can assign one or more of the column attributes shown above.

- You can also assign one or more constraints to a column or to the entire table. See figures 11-7, 11-8, and 11-9 for details.

- For the complete syntax of the CREATE TABLE statement, refer to the SQL Server documentation.

Figure 11-4   How to create a table

values, you should only use it when a column contains a high percentage of null values. As a general guideline, it usually makes sense to use the SPARSE attribute when at least 60% of the column's values are null.

How to create an index

Figure 11-5 presents the basic syntax of the CREATE INDEX statement, which creates an index based on one or more columns of a table. This syntax omits some of the optional clauses that you can use for tuning the indexes for better performance. This tuning is often done by DBAs working with large databases, but usually isn't necessary for small databases.

In the last chapter, you learned that a table can have one clustered index and up to 249 nonclustered indexes. By default, SQL Server creates a clustered index based on the primary key of a table, which is usually what you want. Because of that, you'll rarely create a clustered index.

To create an index, you name the table and columns that the index will be based on in the ON clause. For each column, you can specify the ASC or DESC keyword to indicate whether you want the index sorted in ascending or descending sequence. If you don't specify a sort order, ASC is the default.

The first example in this figure creates an index based on the VendorID column in the Invoices table. Because none of the optional keywords are specified, this creates a nonclustered index that is sorted in ascending sequence.

The second example creates a nonclustered index based on two columns in the Invoices table: InvoiceDate and InvoiceTotal. Notice here that the InvoiceDate column is sorted in descending sequence. That way, the most recent invoices will occur first.

For most databases, you can achieve adequate performance using indexes like the ones shown in the first two examples. Since these indexes index every row in the table, they are known as *full-table indexes*. However, when a database becomes very large, you may be able to improve performance by creating *filtered indexes*, which are indexes that use a WHERE clause to filter the rows in the index.

In general, it makes sense to create a filtered index when the number of rows in the index is small compared to the total number of rows in the table as shown in the third and fourth examples. That way, it's easier for the database engine to use and maintain the index, which results in better performance. Otherwise, a full-table index may yield better performance.

You should also notice the names that are assigned to the indexes in these examples. Although you can name an index anything you like, SQL Server's convention is to prefix index names with the characters *IX_*. So I recommend you do that too. Then, if the index is based on a single column, you can follow the prefix with the name of that column as shown in the first example. Or, if an index is based on two or more columns, you can use the table name instead of the column names as shown in the second example. If necessary, you can add additional information to identify the index as shown in the last two examples.

The basic syntax of the CREATE INDEX statement

```
CREATE [CLUSTERED|NONCLUSTERED] INDEX index_name
    ON table_name (col_name_1 [ASC|DESC] [, col_name_2 [ASC|DESC]]...)
    [WHERE filter-condition]
```

A statement that creates a nonclustered index based on a single column

```
CREATE INDEX IX_VendorID
    ON Invoices (VendorID);
```

A statement that creates a nonclustered index based on two columns

```
CREATE INDEX IX_Invoices
    ON Invoices (InvoiceDate DESC, InvoiceTotal);
```

A statement that creates a filtered index for a subset of data in a column

```
CREATE INDEX IX_InvoicesPaymentFilter
    ON Invoices (InvoiceDate DESC, InvoiceTotal)
WHERE PaymentDate IS NULL;
```

A statement that creates a filtered index for categories in a column

```
CREATE INDEX IX_InvoicesDateFilter
    ON Invoices (InvoiceDate DESC, InvoiceTotal)
WHERE InvoiceDate > '2016-02-01';
```

Description

- You use the CREATE INDEX statement to create an index for a table. An index can improve performance when SQL Server searches for rows in the table.

- SQL Server automatically creates a clustered index for a table's primary key. If that's not what you want, you can drop the primary key constraint using the ALTER TABLE statement shown in figure 11-11 and then recreate the primary key with a nonclustered index.

- Each table can have a single clustered index and up to 999 nonclustered indexes. SQL Server automatically creates a nonclustered index for each unique key other than the primary key.

- By default, an index is sorted in ascending sequence. If that's not what you want, you can code the DESC keyword. The sequence you use should be the sequence in which the rows are retrieved most often when using that index.

- A *full-table index* is an index that applies to every row in the table.

- A *filtered index* is a type of nonclustered index that includes a WHERE clause that filters the rows that are included in the index. Filtered indexes were introduced with SQL Server 2008.

- A filtered index can improve performance when the number of rows in the index is small compared to the total number of rows in the table.

- For more details about working with filtered indexes, refer to the SQL Server documentation.

Figure 11-5   How to create an index

How to use snippets to create database objects

Now that you're familiar with the statements for creating tables and indexes, you should know that you don't have to start these statements from scratch when you use the SQL Server Management Studio. Instead, you can use a feature introduced with SQL Server 2012 called Transact-SQL *snippets* that provide the basic structure of the statements for creating these objects as well as many others. Figure 11-6 shows how snippets work.

To insert a snippet, you use the *snippet picker*. The easiest way to display this picker is to right-click in the Query Editor window and then select the Insert Snippet command from the shortcut menu. When you do, a list of folders that correspond with different types of database objects is displayed. Then, you can double-click the folder for the type of object you want to create to display a list of the snippets for that object. Finally, you can double-click a snippet to insert it into your code. In this figure, I inserted the snippet for the CREATE TABLE statement.

After you insert a snippet, you need to replace the highlighted portions of code so the object is defined appropriately. For the CREATE TABLE statement shown here, for example, you'll want to change the name of the table, and you'll want to change the definitions for the two columns. You may also want to change the schema name. In addition, you'll typically need to add code to the snippet. To create a table, for example, you'll need to enter the definitions for any additional columns.

The snippet picker with a list of database object folders

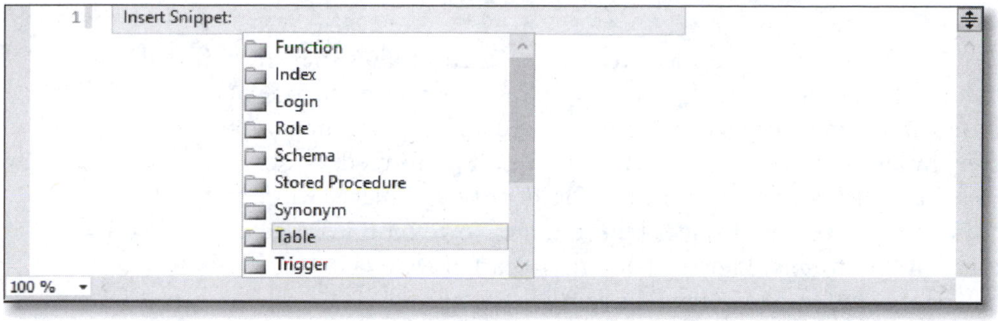

```
1    Insert Snippet:
                        📁 Function
                        📁 Index
                        📁 Login
                        📁 Role
                        📁 Schema
                        📁 Stored Procedure
                        📁 Synonym
                        📁 Table
                        📁 Trigger
100 %  ▼
```

The snippet picker with the list of snippets for a table

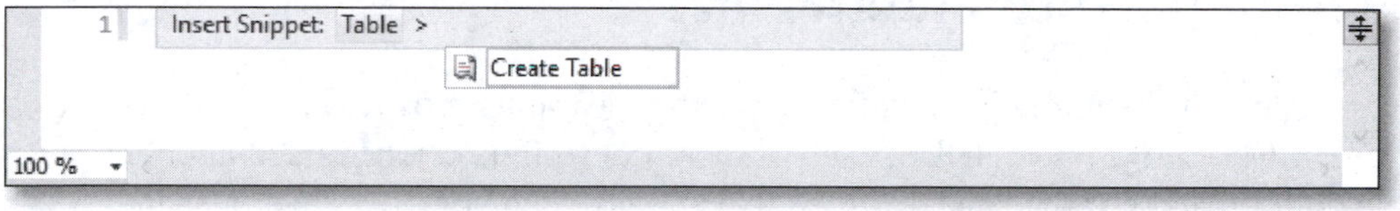

```
1    Insert Snippet:  Table  >
                        📄 Create Table

100 %  ▼
```

The CREATE TABLE snippet after it has been inserted

```
1    CREATE TABLE dbo.Sample_Table
2    (
3        column_1 int NOT NULL,
4        column_2 int NULL
5    );
100 %  ▼
```

Description

- Transact-SQL *snippets* help you write statements for creating database objects.

- To insert a Transact-SQL snippet, right-click in the Query Editor window and select the Insert Snippet command from the resulting menu. Then, use the *snippet picker* to select a snippet.

- To select a snippet using the snippet picker, double-click on the folder for the object you want to create, then double-click on a snippet in the list that's displayed. Alternatively, you can select the folder or snippet and then press the Tab or Enter key.

- Once a snippet has been inserted, you can replace the highlighted portions with your own code and add any other required code. To move from one highlighted portion of code to the next, press the Tab key. To move to the previous highlighted portion, press the Shift+Tab keys.

Figure 11-6   How to use snippets to create database objects

How to use constraints

As you've already learned, you can code constraints to restrict the values that can be stored in a table. These constraints are tested before a new row is added to a table or an existing row is updated. Then, if one or more of the constraints aren't satisfied, the operation isn't performed.

The constraints you've seen so far identify a primary key or unique key column or prevent null values in a column. Now you'll learn how to code other types of constraints. In particular, you'll learn how to code constraints to validate data and to enforce referential integrity.

An introduction to constraints

Figure 11-7 summarizes the five types of constraints provided by SQL Server. Except for NOT NULL, each of these constraints can be coded at either the column level or the table level. You've already seen how to code a primary key constraint at the column level, and you can code a unique key constraint in the same way. Now, the first example in this figure shows how to code a primary key constraint at the table level.

In this example, the primary key consists of two columns. Because of that, it can't be defined at the column level. Notice that when you code a constraint at the table level, you must code a comma at the end of the preceding column definition. If you don't, SQL Server will try to associate the constraint with the preceding column, and an error will result.

Two types of constraints you haven't seen yet are *check constraints* and *foreign key constraints*. You'll learn more about these types of constraints in the next two topics. To illustrate the difference between *column-level constraints* and *table-level constraints*, however, the second and third examples in this figure show two ways you can code the same two check constraints. The first example uses column-level constraints to limit the values in the InvoiceTotal and PaymentTotal columns to numbers greater than or equal to zero. The second example uses a compound condition to specify both constraints at the table level. Although the first technique is preferred, the second example illustrates that a table-level constraint can refer to any of the columns in a table. In contrast, a column-level constraint can refer only to the column that contains the constraint.

Column and table constraints

Constraint	Used as a column-level constraint	Used as a table-level constraint
NOT NULL	Prevents null values from being stored in the column.	n/a
PRIMARY KEY	Requires that each row in the table have a unique value in the column. Null values are not allowed.	Requires that each row in the table have a unique set of values over one or more columns. Null values are not allowed.
UNIQUE	Requires that each row in the table have a unique value in the column.	Requires that each row in the table have a unique set of values over one or more columns.
CHECK	Limits the values for a column.	Limits the values for one or more columns.
[FOREIGN KEY] REFERENCES	Enforces referential integrity between a column in the new table and a column in a related table.	Enforces referential integrity between one or more columns in the new table and one or more columns in the related table.

A statement that creates a table with a two-column primary key constraint

```
CREATE TABLE InvoiceLineItems1
(InvoiceID                INT        NOT NULL,
 InvoiceSequence          SMALLINT   NOT NULL,
 InvoiceLineItemAmount    MONEY      NOT NULL,
 PRIMARY KEY (InvoiceID, InvoiceSequence));
```

A statement that creates a table with two column-level check constraints

```
CREATE TABLE Invoices1
(InvoiceID      INT   NOT NULL IDENTITY PRIMARY KEY,
 InvoiceTotal   MONEY NOT NULL CHECK (InvoiceTotal >= 0),
 PaymentTotal   MONEY NOT NULL DEFAULT 0 CHECK (PaymentTotal >= 0));
```

The same statement with the check constraints coded at the table level

```
CREATE TABLE Invoices2
(InvoiceID      INT     NOT NULL IDENTITY PRIMARY KEY,
 InvoiceTotal   MONEY   NOT NULL,
 PaymentTotal   MONEY   NOT NULL DEFAULT 0,
 CHECK ((InvoiceTotal >= 0) AND (PaymentTotal >= 0)));
```

Description

- *Constraints* are used to enforce the integrity of the data in a table by defining rules about the values that can be stored in the columns of the table. Constraints can be used at the column level to restrict the value of a single column or at the table level to restrict the value of one or more columns.

- You code a *column-level constraint* as part of the definition of the column it constrains. You code a *table-level constraint* as if it were a separate column definition, and you name the columns it constrains within that definition.

- Constraints are tested before a new row is added to a table or an existing row is updated. If the new or modified row meets all of the constraints, the operation succeeds. Otherwise, an error occurs and the operation fails.

Figure 11-7   An introduction to constraints

How to use check constraints

To code a check constraint, you use the syntax presented in figure 11-8. As you can see, you code the CHECK keyword followed by the condition that the data must satisfy. This condition is evaluated as a Boolean expression. The insert or update operation that's being performed is allowed only if this expression evaluates to a True value.

The first example in this figure uses a column-level check constraint to limit the values in the InvoiceTotal column to numbers greater than zero. This is similar to the constraints you saw in the previous figure. Notice that if you try to store a negative value in this column as illustrated by the INSERT statement in this example, the system responds with an error and the insert operation is terminated.

The second example shows how you can use a check constraint to limit a column to values that have a specific format. Note that although this constraint limits the values in a single column, it's coded at the table level because it refers to a column other than the one being constrained. The first part of the condition in this check constraint uses a LIKE expression to restrict the VendorCode column to six characters, consisting of two alphabetic characters followed by four numeric characters. Then, the second part of the condition restricts the first two characters of the VendorCode column to the first two characters of the VendorName column.

In general, you should use check constraints to restrict the values in a column whenever possible. In some situations, however, check constraints can be too restrictive. As an example, consider a telephone number that's constrained to the typical "(000) 000-0000" format used for US phone numbers. The problem with this constraint is that it wouldn't let you store phone numbers with extensions (although you could store extensions in a separate column) or phone numbers with an international format.

For this reason, check constraints aren't used by all database designers. That way, the database can store values with formats that weren't predicted when the database was designed. However, this flexibility comes at the cost of allowing some invalid data. For some systems, this tradeoff is acceptable.

Keep in mind, too, that application programs that add and update data can also include data validation. In that case, check constraints may not be necessary. Because you can't always assume that an application program will check for valid data, though, you should include check constraints whenever that makes sense.

The syntax of a check constraint

```
CHECK (condition)
```

A column-level check constraint that limits invoices to positive amounts

A statement that defines the check constraint

```
CREATE TABLE Invoices3
(InvoiceID      INT    NOT NULL IDENTITY PRIMARY KEY,
InvoiceTotal    MONEY NOT NULL CHECK (InvoiceTotal > 0));
```

An INSERT statement that fails due to the check constraint

```
INSERT Invoices3
VALUES (-100);
```

The response from the system

```
The INSERT statement conflicted with the CHECK constraint "CK__Invoices3__
Invoi__0BC6C43E". The conflict occurred in database "New_AP", table "dbo.
Invoices3", column 'InvoiceTotal'.
The statement has been terminated.
```

A table-level check constraint that limits vendor IDs to a specific format

A statement that defines the check constraint

```
CREATE TABLE Vendors1
(VendorCode     CHAR(6)     NOT NULL PRIMARY KEY,
VendorName      VARCHAR(50) NOT NULL,
CHECK          ((VendorCode LIKE '[A-Z][A-Z][0-9][0-9][0-9][0-9]') AND
                (LEFT(VendorCode,2) = LEFT(VendorName,2))));
```

An INSERT statement that fails due to the check constraint

```
INSERT Vendors1
VALUES ('Mc4559','Castle Printers, Inc.');
```

The response from the system

```
The INSERT statement conflicted with the CHECK constraint "CK__
Vendors1__164452B1". The conflict occurred in database "New_AP", table
"dbo.Vendors1".
The statement has been terminated.
```

Description

- *Check constraints* limit the values that can be stored in the columns of a table.

- The condition you specify for a check constraint is evaluated as a Boolean expression. If the expression is true, the insert or update operation proceeds. Otherwise, it fails.

- A check constraint that's coded at the column level can refer only to that column. A check constraint that's coded at the table level can refer to any column in the table.

Figure 11-8   How to use check constraints

How to use foreign key constraints

Figure 11-9 presents the syntax of a foreign key constraint, also known as a *reference constraint*. This type of constraint is used to define the relationships between tables and to enforce referential integrity.

To create a foreign key constraint at the column level, you code the REFERENCES keyword followed by the name of the related table and the name of the related column in parentheses. Although you can also code the FOREIGN KEY keywords, these keywords are optional and are usually omitted. After the REFERENCES clause, you can code the ON DELETE and ON UPDATE clauses. I'll have more to say about these clauses in a moment.

The first two statements in this figure show how to create two related tables. The first statement creates the primary key table, a table named Vendors9. Then, the second statement creates the foreign key table, named Invoices9. Notice that the VendorID column in this table includes a REFERENCES clause that identifies the VendorID column in the Vendors9 table as the related column.

The next statement in this figure is an INSERT statement that attempts to insert a row into the Invoices9 table. Because the Vendors9 table doesn't contain a row with the specified VendorID value, however, the insert operation fails.

Before I go on, you should realize that although the foreign key of one table is typically related to the primary key of another table, that doesn't have to be the case. Instead, a foreign key can be related to any unique key. For the purposes of this topic, though, I'll assume that the related column is a primary key column.

By default, you can't delete a row from the primary key table if related rows exist in a foreign key table. Instead, you have to delete the related rows from the foreign key table first. If that's not what you want, you can code the ON DELETE clause with the CASCADE option. Then, when you delete a row from the primary key table, the delete is *cascaded* to the related rows in the foreign key table. Because a *cascading delete* can destroy valuable data if it's used improperly, you should use it with caution.

The ON UPDATE clause is similar. If you code the CASCADE keyword in this clause, a change to the value of a primary key is automatically cascaded to the related rows in the foreign key table. Otherwise, the change isn't allowed. Since most tables are designed so their primary key values don't change, you won't usually code the ON UPDATE clause.

When you code a foreign key constraint at the column level, you relate a single column in the foreign key table to a single column in the primary key table. If the keys consist of two or more columns, however, you have to code the constraint at the table level. For example, suppose that a foreign key consists of two columns named CustomerID2 and CustomerID4 and that the foreign key is related to two columns with the same name in a table named Customers. Then, you would define the foreign key constraint like this:

```
FOREIGN KEY (CustomerID2, CustomerID4)
    REFERENCES Customers (CustomerID2, CustomerID4)
```

In this case, you must include the FOREIGN KEY keywords.

The syntax of a column-level foreign key constraint

```
[FOREIGN KEY] REFERENCES ref_table_name (ref_column_name)
    [ON DELETE {CASCADE|NO ACTION}]
    [ON UPDATE {CASCADE|NO ACTION}]
```

The syntax of a table-level foreign key constraint

```
FOREIGN KEY (column_name_1 [, column_name_2]...)
    REFERENCES ref_table_name (ref_column_name_1 [, ref_column_name_2]...)
    [ON DELETE {CASCADE|NO ACTION}]
    [ON UPDATE {CASCADE|NO ACTION}]
```

A foreign key constraint defined at the column level

A statement that creates the primary key table

```
CREATE TABLE Vendors9
(VendorID        INT NOT NULL PRIMARY KEY,
VendorName       VARCHAR(50) NOT NULL);
```

A statement that creates the foreign key table

```
CREATE TABLE Invoices9
(InvoiceID       INT NOT NULL PRIMARY KEY,
VendorID         INT NOT NULL REFERENCES Vendors9 (VendorID),
InvoiceTotal     MONEY NULL);
```

An INSERT statement that fails because a related row doesn't exist

```
INSERT Invoices9
VALUES (1, 99, 100);
```

The response from the system

```
The INSERT statement conflicted with the FOREIGN KEY constraint
"FK__Invoices9__Vendo__1367E606". The conflict occurred in database "New_AP",
table "dbo.Vendors9", column 'VendorID'.
The statement has been terminated.
```

Description

- You use the FOREIGN KEY clause to define a *foreign key constraint*, also called a *reference constraint*. A foreign key constraint defines the relationship between two tables and enforces referential integrity.

- A foreign key constraint that's coded at the column level can only relate a single column in the new table to a single column in the related table. A constraint that's coded at the table level can relate two tables by two or more columns.

- Typically, a foreign key constraint refers to the primary key of the related table. However, it can also refer to a unique key.

- The ON DELETE clause specifies what happens to rows in the table if the row in the related table with the same key value is deleted. The ON UPDATE clause specifies what happens to rows in the table if the key of the related row is updated.

- The CASCADE keyword causes the rows in this table to be deleted or updated to match the row in the related table. This is known as a *cascading delete* or a *cascading update*.

- The NO ACTION keyword prevents the row in the related table from being deleted or updated and causes an error to be raised. This is usually the preferred option.

Figure 11-9   How to use foreign key constraints

How to change databases and tables

After you create a database, you may need to change it. For example, you may need to add a new table or index. To do that, you can use the CREATE statements that you've already learned. If you need to modify an existing table, however, or if you need to delete an existing index, table, or database, you'll need to use the statements that follow.

How to delete an index, table, or database

Figure 11-10 presents the syntax of the three DROP statements you use to delete an index, a table, or a database. You can use these statements to delete one or more indexes, tables, or databases on the current server. Note that the syntax of the DROP INDEX statement changed with SQL Server 2005. Because the syntax that was used with previous versions of SQL Server has been deprecated, you should use the syntax shown in this figure for all new development work.

If other objects depend on the object you're trying to delete, SQL Server won't allow the deletion. For example, you can't delete a table if a foreign key constraint in another table refers to that table, and you can't delete an index if it's based on a primary key or a unique key. In addition, you can't drop a database that's currently in use.

You should also know that when you delete a table, many of the objects related to that table are deleted as well. That includes any indexes, triggers, or constraints defined for the table. In contrast, any views or stored procedures that are associated with a deleted table are not deleted. Instead, you have to delete these objects explicitly using the statements you'll learn in chapter 15.

Because the DROP statements delete objects permanently, you'll want to use them cautiously. In fact, you may want to create a backup copy of the database before using any of these statements. That way, you can restore the database if necessary.

The syntax of the DROP INDEX statement

```
DROP INDEX index_name_1 ON table_name_1 [, index_name_2 ON table_name_2]...
```

The syntax of the DROP TABLE statement

```
DROP TABLE table_name_1 [, table_name_2]...
```

The syntax of the DROP DATABASE statement

```
DROP DATABASE database_name_1 [, database_name_2]...
```

Statements that delete database objects

A statement that deletes an index from the Invoices table

```
DROP INDEX IX_Invoices ON Invoices;
```

A statement that deletes a table from the current database

```
DROP TABLE Vendors1;
```

A statement that qualifies the table to be deleted

```
DROP TABLE New_AP.dbo.Vendors1;
```

A statement that deletes a database

```
DROP DATABASE New_AP;
```

Description

- You can use the DROP INDEX statement to delete one or more indexes from one or more tables in any database on the current server.

- You can use the DROP TABLE statement to delete one or more tables from any database on the current server. To delete a table from a database other than the current database, you must qualify the table name with the database name.

- You can use the DROP DATABASE statement to delete one or more databases from the current server.

- You can't delete a table if a foreign key constraint in another table refers to that table.

- When you delete a table, all of the data, indexes, triggers, and constraints are deleted. Any views or stored procedures associated with the table must be deleted explicitly.

- You can't delete an index that's based on a primary key or unique key constraint. To do that, you have to use the ALTER TABLE statement. See figure 11-11 for details.

Warnings

- You can't undo a delete operation. For this reason, you may want to back up the database before you use any of these statements so you can restore it if necessary.

- You should never use these statements on a production database without first consulting the DBA.

Figure 11-10   How to delete an index, table, or database

How to alter a table

Figure 11-11 presents the basic syntax of the ALTER TABLE statement. You can use this statement to modify an existing table in one of several ways. The clauses shown here are the ones you're most likely to use.

The first example in this figure shows how to add a new column to a table. As you can see, you code the column definition the same way you do when you create a new table: You specify the column name, followed by its data type and its attributes.

The second example shows how to drop an existing column. Note that SQL Server prevents you from dropping some columns. For example, you can't drop a column if it's the primary key column, if it's used in a check constraint or in a foreign key constraint, or if an index is based on it.

The third and fourth examples show how to add constraints to a table. The third example adds a check constraint, and the fourth example adds a foreign key constraint. You can use the same technique to add a primary key or unique constraint. Note that you use this technique regardless of whether the constraint refers to a single column or to two or more columns. That's because the ALTER COLUMN clause only lets you change the data type or the NULL or NOT NULL attribute of an existing column. You can't use it to add column constraints.

When you add a table constraint, SQL Server automatically checks that existing data meets the constraint. If that's not what you want, you can include the WITH NOCHECK keywords in the ALTER statement. This is illustrated in the third example.

In addition to adding constraints, you can use the ALTER TABLE statement to delete constraints. To do that, you have to know the name of the constraint. Although you can name a constraint when you create it, you don't usually do that. That's why I didn't include that information in the syntax for creating constraints. Instead, you usually let SQL Server generate a constraint name for you. Then, if you need to delete the constraint, you can use the Management Studio as described in the next chapter to find out what name SQL Server assigned to it.

The last example shows how to modify the data type of an existing column. In this case, a column that was defined as VARCHAR(100) is changed to VARCHAR(200). Because the new data type is wider than the old data type, you can be sure that the existing data will still fit. However, that's not always the case. Because of that, SQL Server checks to be sure that no data will be lost before it changes the data type. If the change will result in a loss of data, it's not allowed.

The basic syntax of the ALTER TABLE statement

```
ALTER TABLE table_name [WITH CHECK|WITH NOCHECK]
{ADD new_column_name data_type [column_attributes] |
 DROP COLUMN column_name |
 ALTER COLUMN column_name new_data_type [NULL|NOT NULL] |
 ADD [CONSTRAINT] new_constraint_definition |
 DROP [CONSTRAINT] constraint_name}
```

Examples of the ALTER TABLE statement

A statement that adds a new column

```
ALTER TABLE Vendors
ADD LastTranDate SMALLDATETIME NULL;
```

A statement that drops a column

```
ALTER TABLE Vendors
DROP COLUMN LastTranDate;
```

A statement that adds a new check constraint

```
ALTER TABLE Invoices WITH NOCHECK
ADD CHECK (InvoiceTotal >= 1);
```

A statement that adds a foreign key constraint

```
ALTER TABLE InvoiceLineItems WITH CHECK
ADD FOREIGN KEY (AccountNo) REFERENCES GLAccounts(AccountNo);
```

A statement that changes the data type of a column

```
ALTER TABLE InvoiceLineItems
ALTER COLUMN InvoiceLineItemDescription VARCHAR(200);
```

Description

- You use the ALTER TABLE statement to modify an existing table. You can use this statement to add columns or constraints, drop columns or constraints, or change the definition of an existing column, including changing the column's data type.

- Before SQL Server changes the data type of a column, it checks to be sure that no data will be lost. If it will, the operation isn't performed.

- You can modify a column to allow null values as long as the column isn't defined as the primary key. You can modify a column so that it doesn't allow null values as long as none of the existing rows contain null values in that column.

- You can add a column that doesn't allow null values only if you specify a default value for that column.

- To delete a constraint, you must know its name. If you let SQL Server generate the name for you, you can use the Management Studio as shown in the next chapter to look up the name.

- By default, SQL Server verifies that existing data satisfies a new check or foreign key constraint. If that's not what you want, you can code the WITH NOCHECK keywords.

Warning

- You should never alter a table in a production database without first consulting the DBA.

Figure 11-11   How to alter a table

How to work with sequences

A *sequence* is a type of database object introduced with SQL Server 2012 that automatically generates a sequence of integer values. Because you can use the IDENTITY attribute for the primary key of a table to generate a simple sequence of numbers that starts with 1 and is incremented by 1, you won't typically use a sequence for that purpose. Instead, you'll use a sequence only if you want to generate a more complex sequence of numbers or if you want to share the sequence between multiple tables.

How to create a sequence

Figure 11-12 shows how to create a sequence. Most of the time, you can create a sequence by coding the CREATE SEQUENCE statement followed by the name of the sequence and the starting value. In the first example, for instance, the CREATE SEQUENCE statement creates a sequence named TestSequence1. This sequence starts with a value of 1, is incremented by a value of 1, has minimum and maximum values that are determined by the data type (bigint by default). In addition, this sequence doesn't cycle back to the minimum value when it reaches the last number in the sequence, and it doesn't cache any sequence numbers. (Although CACHE is the default, a cache size must be specified to use it.) In most cases, these settings are adequate.

If you need to create a sequence that works differently, you can use any of the other clauses of the CREATE SEQUENCE statement to modify the sequence. For example, you can use the INCREMENT BY clause as shown in the second example to increment the sequence numbers by a value other than 1. Although you'll typically code a positive increment value to create an ascending sequence, you can also code a negative value to create a descending sequence.

The third example shows how to create a sequence using all of the optional clauses. This example generates a sequence of int values that begins with 100, is incremented by a value of 10, has a minimum value of 0, has a maximum value of 1,000,000, stores 10 values in the cache at a time, and cycles back to the beginning of the sequence when it reaches the end. Note that a sequence cycles back to the minimum value for the sequence (the maximum value for a descending sequence) even if a starting value is specified. Because of that, you'll want to be sure to specify a minimum value when you use the CYCLE keyword.

How to use a sequence

Once you've created a sequence, you can use it in a variety of ways. For example, you can use it to specify the default value for a column in a table. You can also use it in an INSERT statement as the value for a column. This is illustrated in the second set of examples in figure 11-12. Here, the first example creates a table that contains an int column named SequenceNo. Then, the second example inserts two rows into the table. Here, the NEXT VALUE FOR function

How to create a sequence

The syntax of the CREATE SEQUENCE statement

```
CREATE SEQUENCE sequence_name
    [AS integer_type]
    [START WITH starting_integer]
    [INCREMENT BY increment_integer]
    [{MINVALUE minimum_integer | NO MINVALUE}]
    [{MAXVALUE maximum_integer | NO MAXVALUE}]
    [{CYCLE|NOCYCLE}]
    [{CACHE cache_size|NOCACHE}]
```

A statement that creates a sequence that starts with 1

```
CREATE SEQUENCE TestSequence1
    START WITH 1;
```

A statement that specifies a starting value and an increment for a sequence

```
CREATE SEQUENCE TestSequence2
    START WITH 10
    INCREMENT BY 10;
```

A statement that specifies all optional parameters for a sequence

```
CREATE SEQUENCE TestSequence3
    AS int
    START WITH 100 INCREMENT BY 10
    MINVALUE 0 MAXVALUE 1000000
    CYCLE CACHE 10;
```

How to use a sequence

A statement that creates a test table

```
CREATE TABLE SequenceTable(
    SequenceNo      INT,
    Description     VARCHAR(50));
```

Statements that get the next value for a sequence

```
INSERT INTO SequenceTable
VALUES (NEXT VALUE FOR TestSequence3, 'First inserted row')
INSERT INTO SequenceTable
VALUES (NEXT VALUE FOR TestSequence3, 'Second inserted row');
```

A statement that gets the current value of the sequence

```
SELECT current_value FROM sys.sequences WHERE name = 'TestSequence3';
```

	current_value
1	110

Description

- You use the CREATE SEQUENCE statement to generate integer values for a column in one or more tables.

- By default, the CREATE SEQUENCE statement creates a sequence with the bigint data type that starts with the minimum value for the data type, is incremented by a value of 1, has minimum and maximum values based on the data type, doesn't specify the cache size, and doesn't restart the sequence when the end is reached.

- You can use the NEXT VALUE FOR function to get the next value in the sequence.

- You can query the sys.sequences table to get information about a sequence.

Figure 11-12   How to create and use a sequence

gets the next value from the sequence named TestSequence3 so it can be inserted into the SequenceNo column.

The last example in figure 11-12 shows how to use the sys.sequences catalog view to get information about a sequence. You'll learn about catalog views in chapter 13. For now, just realize that the SELECT statement shown here retrieves the current value for the sequence from this view. If you review the starting value and the increment for the sequence, you'll see how this works.

How to delete a sequence

When you delete a table, all indexes related to the table are also deleted. However, the sequences that are used by the table aren't deleted since they're independent of any table. As a result, if you want to delete a sequence, you must use the DROP SEQUENCE statement shown in figure 11-13. Here, the first example drops the sequence named TestSequence2 that was created in figure 11-12.

How to alter a sequence

Once you've created a sequence, you can use the ALTER SEQUENCE statement to alter the attributes of the sequence as shown in figure 11-13. This statement is similar to the CREATE SEQUENCE statement. The two differences are that you can't change the data type for a sequence, and you use the RESTART clause to set a new starting number for the sequence. In addition, you can't set the minimum and maximum values so they don't make sense. For example, if the starting value of the sequence is 1, you can't set the minimum value to 2 without resetting the starting value so it's greater than or equal to 2. Similarly, if the current value of the sequence is 99, you can't set the maximum value to 98 without resetting the starting value so it's less than or equal to 98.

The syntax of the DROP SEQUENCE statement

```
DROP SEQUENCE sequence_name1[, sequence_name2]...
```

A statement that drops a sequence

```
DROP SEQUENCE TestSequence2;
```

The syntax of the ALTER SEQUENCE statement

```
ALTER SEQUENCE sequence_name
    [RESTART [WITH starting_integer]]
    [INCREMENT BY increment_integer]
    [{MINVALUE minimum_integer | NO MINVALUE}]
    [{MAXVALUE maximum_integer | NO MAXVALUE}]
    [{CYCLE|NOCYCLE}]
    [{CACHE cache_size|NOCACHE}]
```

A statement that alters a sequence

```
ALTER SEQUENCE TestSequence1
    INCREMENT BY 9
    MINVALUE 1 MAXVALUE 999999
    CACHE 9
    CYCLE;
```

Description

- You can use the DROP SEQUENCE statement to delete a sequence. A sequence can't be deleted if it's used as the default value for a column.

- You can use the ALTER SEQUENCE statement to alter the attributes of a sequence. However, you can't change the data type, and you can't set the minimum and maximum values so they don't make sense.

- If you omit the WITH value of the RESTART clause, the sequence is restarted based on the current definition of the sequence.

Figure 11-13   How to delete and alter a sequence

The script used to create the AP database

To complete this chapter, figure 11-14 presents the DDL statements that I used to create the AP database that's used in the examples throughout this book. By studying these DDL statements, you'll get a better idea of how a database is actually implemented. Note, however, that these statements are coded as part of a script. So before I describe the DDL statements, I'll introduce you to scripts.

How the script works

In this figure, all of the DDL statements are coded as part of a *script*, which consists of one or more SQL statements that are stored in a file. This is typically the way that all of the objects for a database are created. In chapter 14, you'll learn the details of coding scripts, but here are some basic concepts.

A script consists of one or more *batches*. The script shown in the two parts of this figure, for example, consists of two batches. Each batch consists of one or more SQL statements that are executed as a unit. To signal the end of a batch and execute the statements it contains, you use the GO command. As you can see, then, the first batch shown in this figure consists of a single CREATE DATABASE statement, and the second batch consists of several CREATE TABLE and CREATE INDEX statements. Notice that a GO command isn't required at the end of the second batch, which is the last batch in this script.

To create and execute a script, you can use the Management Studio. Although you may not be aware of it, you're creating a script each time you enter a SQL statement into the Management Studio. So far, though, the scripts you've created have consisted of a single batch.

The reason for breaking a script like the one shown here into batches is that some of the statements must be executed before others can execute successfully. Before any tables can be created in the AP database, for example, the database itself must be created.

The only other statement used in this script that you're not familiar with is the USE statement. You use this statement to change the current database. That way, after the script creates the AP database, the statements that follow will operate on that database rather than on the one that's selected in the Management Studio toolbar.

How the DDL statements work

Notice that each CREATE TABLE statement in this script lists the primary key column (or columns) first. Although this isn't required, it's a conventional coding practice. Also note that the order in which you declare the columns defines the default order for the columns. That means that when you use a SELECT * statement to retrieve all of the columns, they're returned in this order. For that reason, you'll want to define the columns in a logical sequence.

The SQL script that creates the AP database

```
CREATE DATABASE AP;
GO

USE AP;
CREATE TABLE Terms
(TermsID                  INT            NOT NULL PRIMARY KEY,
TermsDescription          VARCHAR(50)    NOT NULL,
TermsDueDays              SMALLINT       NOT NULL);

CREATE TABLE GLAccounts
(AccountNo                INT            NOT NULL PRIMARY KEY,
AccountDescription        VARCHAR(50)    NOT NULL);

CREATE TABLE Vendors
(VendorID                 INT            NOT NULL IDENTITY PRIMARY KEY,
VendorName                VARCHAR(50)    NOT NULL,
VendorAddress1            VARCHAR(50)    NULL,
VendorAddress2            VARCHAR(50)    SPARSE NULL,
VendorCity                VARCHAR(50)    NOT NULL,
VendorState               CHAR(2)        NOT NULL,
VendorZipCode             VARCHAR(20)    NOT NULL,
VendorPhone               VARCHAR(50)    NULL,
VendorContactLName        VARCHAR(50)    NULL,
VendorContactFName        VARCHAR(50)    NULL,
DefaultTermsID            INT            NOT NULL
                          REFERENCES Terms(TermsID),
DefaultAccountNo          INT            NOT NULL
                          REFERENCES GLAccounts(AccountNo));
```

Basic script concepts

- Instead of creating database objects one at a time, you can write a *script* that contains all of the statements needed to create the database and its tables and indexes.

- A script is a set of one or more *batches* that can be stored in a file. A batch is a sequence of SQL statements that are executed as a unit. You can use the Management Studio to create and execute script files.

- The GO command signals the end of the batch and causes all of the statements in the batch to be executed. You should issue a GO command when the execution of the next statement depends on the successful completion of the previous statements.

- SQL Server executes the last batch in a script automatically, so a final GO command isn't required.

- To change the current database within a script, you use the USE statement.

Note

- The Terms and GLAccounts tables are created first so the other tables can define foreign keys that refer to them. Similarly, the Vendors table is created before the Invoices table, and the Invoices table is created before the InvoiceLineItems table (see part 2).

Figure 11-14   The script used to create the AP database (part 1 of 2)

Also notice that most of the columns in this database are assigned the NOT NULL constraint. The exceptions are the VendorAddress1, VendorAddress2, VendorPhone, VendorContactLName, and VendorContactFName columns in the Vendors table and the PaymentDate column in the Invoices table. Because not all vendor addresses will require two lines and because some vendors won't provide a street address at all, a null value can be assigned to both address columns to indicate that they're not applicable. Similarly, you may not have a phone number and contact information for each vendor. For this reason, you could assign a null value to one of these columns to indicate an unknown value. Finally, an invoice wouldn't be assigned a payment date until it was paid. Until that time, you could assign a null value to the PaymentDate column to indicate that it hasn't been paid.

I could also have used a default date to indicate an unpaid invoice. To do that, I could have defined the PaymentDate column like this:

```
PaymentDate SMALLDATETIME NOT NULL DEFAULT '1900-01-01'
```

In this case, the date January 1, 1900 would be stored in the PaymentDate column unless another value was assigned to that column. Usually, a null value is a more intuitive representation of an unknown value than a default such as this, but either representation is acceptable. Keep in mind, though, that the technique you use will affect how you query the table.

Since at least 60% of the values for the VendorAddress2 column are likely to contain a null value, this column uses the SPARSE attribute to optimize storage of null values. Although this attribute isn't critical, it can significantly reduce the amount of storage required for this column.

Because each of the five tables in this database has a primary key, SQL Server creates a clustered index for each table based on that key. In addition, this script creates seven additional indexes to improve the performance of the database. The first five of these indexes are based on the foreign keys that each referring table uses to relate to another table. For example, since the VendorID column in the Invoices table references the VendorID column in the Vendors table, I created a nonclustered index on VendorID in the Invoices table. Similarly, I created indexes for TermsID in the Invoices table, DefaultTermsID and DefaultAccountNo in the Vendors table, and AccountNo in the InvoiceLineItems table. Finally, I created indexes for the VendorName column in the Vendors table and the InvoiceDate column in the Invoices table because these columns are frequently used to search for rows in these tables.

As you may have noticed, I created an index for each column that appears in a foreign key constraint except one: the InvoiceID column in the InvoiceLineItems table. Since this column is part of the composite primary key for this table, it's already included in the clustered index. For this reason, the addition of a nonclustered index on InvoiceID by itself won't improve performance.

The SQL script that creates the AP database   Page 2

```
CREATE TABLE Invoices
(InvoiceID                 INT             NOT NULL IDENTITY PRIMARY KEY,
 VendorID                  INT             NOT NULL
                           REFERENCES Vendors(VendorID),
 InvoiceNumber             VARCHAR(50)     NOT NULL,
 InvoiceDate               SMALLDATETIME   NOT NULL,
 InvoiceTotal              MONEY           NOT NULL,
 PaymentTotal              MONEY           NOT NULL DEFAULT 0,
 CreditTotal               MONEY           NOT NULL DEFAULT 0,
 TermsID                   INT             NOT NULL
                           REFERENCES Terms(TermsID),
 InvoiceDueDate            SMALLDATETIME   NOT NULL,
 PaymentDate               SMALLDATETIME   NULL);

CREATE TABLE InvoiceLineItems
(InvoiceID                 INT             NOT NULL
                           REFERENCES Invoices(InvoiceID),
 InvoiceSequence           SMALLINT        NOT NULL,
 AccountNo                 INT             NOT NULL
                           REFERENCES GLAccounts(AccountNo),
 InvoiceLineItemAmount     MONEY           NOT NULL,
 InvoiceLineItemDescription VARCHAR(100)   NOT NULL,
 PRIMARY KEY (InvoiceID, InvoiceSequence));

CREATE INDEX IX_Invoices_VendorID
    ON Invoices (VendorID);
CREATE INDEX IX_Invoices_TermsID
    ON Invoices (TermsID);
CREATE INDEX IX_Vendors_TermsID
    ON Vendors (DefaultTermsID);
CREATE INDEX IX_Vendors_AccountNo
    ON Vendors (DefaultAccountNo);
CREATE INDEX IX_InvoiceLineItems_AccountNo
    ON InvoiceLineItems (AccountNo);
CREATE INDEX IX_VendorName
    ON Vendors (VendorName);
CREATE INDEX IX_InvoiceDate
    ON Invoices (InvoiceDate DESC);
```

Notes

- The InvoiceLineItems table has a composite primary key that consists of the InvoiceID and InvoiceSequence columns. For this reason, the PRIMARY KEY constraint must be defined as a table-level constraint.

- In addition to the five indexes that SQL Server automatically creates for the primary key of each table, this script creates seven additional indexes. The first five are indexes for the foreign keys that are used in the REFERENCES constraints. The last two create indexes on the VendorName column and the InvoiceDate column since these columns are used frequently in search conditions.

Figure 11-14   The script used to create the AP database (part 2 of 2)

Perspective

Now that you've completed this chapter, you should be able to create and modify databases, tables, and indexes by coding DDL statements. This provides a valuable background for working with any database. In practice, though, you may sometimes want to use the Management Studio to perform the functions that are done by DDL statements, so that's what you'll learn to do in the next chapter.

Terms

data definition language (DDL)	column-level constraint
database objects	table-level constraint
identifier	check constraint
transaction log file	foreign key constraint
attach a database	reference constraint
full-table index	cascading delete
filtered index	cascading update
snippet	sequence
snippet picker	script
constraint	batch

Exercises

1. Create a new database named Membership.

2. Write the CREATE TABLE statements needed to implement the following design in the Membership database. Include foreign key constraints. Define IndividualID and GroupID as identity columns. Decide which columns should allow null values, if any, and explain your decision. Define the Dues column with a default of zero and a check constraint to allow only positive values.

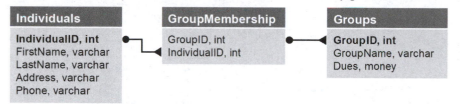

3. Write the CREATE INDEX statements to create a clustered index on the GroupID column and a nonclustered index on the IndividualID column of the GroupMembership table.

4. Write an ALTER TABLE statement that adds a new column, DuesPaid, to the Individuals table. Use the bit data type, disallow null values, and assign a default Boolean value of False.

5. Write an ALTER TABLE statement that adds two new check constraints to the Invoices table of the AP database. The first should allow (1) PaymentDate to be null only if PaymentTotal is zero and (2) PaymentDate to be not null only if PaymentTotal is greater than zero. The second constraint should prevent the sum of PaymentTotal and CreditTotal from being greater than InvoiceTotal.

6. Delete the GroupMembership table from the Membership database. Then, write a CREATE TABLE statement that recreates the table, this time with a unique constraint that prevents an individual from being a member in the same group twice.

12

How to create a database and its tables with the Management Studio

Now that you've learned how to code all of the essential SQL statements for data definition, you're ready to learn how to use the Management Studio to generate this code for you. The Management Studio makes it easy to perform common tasks, and you'll use it frequently to create, modify, and delete the objects of a database. Once you learn how to use the Management Studio to create or modify the design of a database, you can decide when it makes sense to use it and when it makes sense to code the DDL statements yourself.

How to work with a database

In chapter 2, you learned how to use the Management Studio to attach the files for an existing database to the SQL Server engine. Now, you'll learn how to use the Management Studio to create a new database from scratch.

How to create a database

Figure 12-1 shows the New Database dialog box that's used to create a new database. To display this dialog box, you can start the Management Studio, right-click on the Databases folder, and select the New Database command. Then, you can use the New Database dialog box to enter a name for the database. When you do, the names for the data and log files are automatically updated in the Database Files pane. In this figure, for example, I entered New_AP for the database name. As a result, the New Database dialog box automatically changed the name for the data file to New_AP, and it changed the name of the log file to New_AP_log. Although it's possible to alter these names, I recommend using this naming convention.

Since the default properties for a database are set correctly for most databases, that's usually all you need to do to create a new database. However, if necessary, you can use the New Database dialog box to change any default properties that are used by SQL Server. If you want to change the initial size for the data file for a database, you can click in the Initial Size column and enter a new initial size. If you want to change the owner of the database from the default owner, you can click on the button to the right of the Owner text box. If you want to change other properties, you can display the Options page and change the properties that are available from this page. And so on.

By default, the data and log files for a new database are stored in the directory shown in this figure, which is usually what you want. If it isn't, you can detach, move, and reattach the database files as described in chapter 2.

How to delete a database

If you want to delete a database, you can right-click on the database in the Management Studio, select the Delete command, and click OK in the resulting dialog box. Keep in mind, however, that this permanently deletes the data and log files for the database. Because of that, you may want to create a backup copy of the database before you delete it as described in chapter 2. That way, you can restore the database later if necessary. Alternatively, you may want to detach the database from the server instead of deleting it. That way, the database files aren't deleted and can be attached again later if necessary.

The New Database dialog box

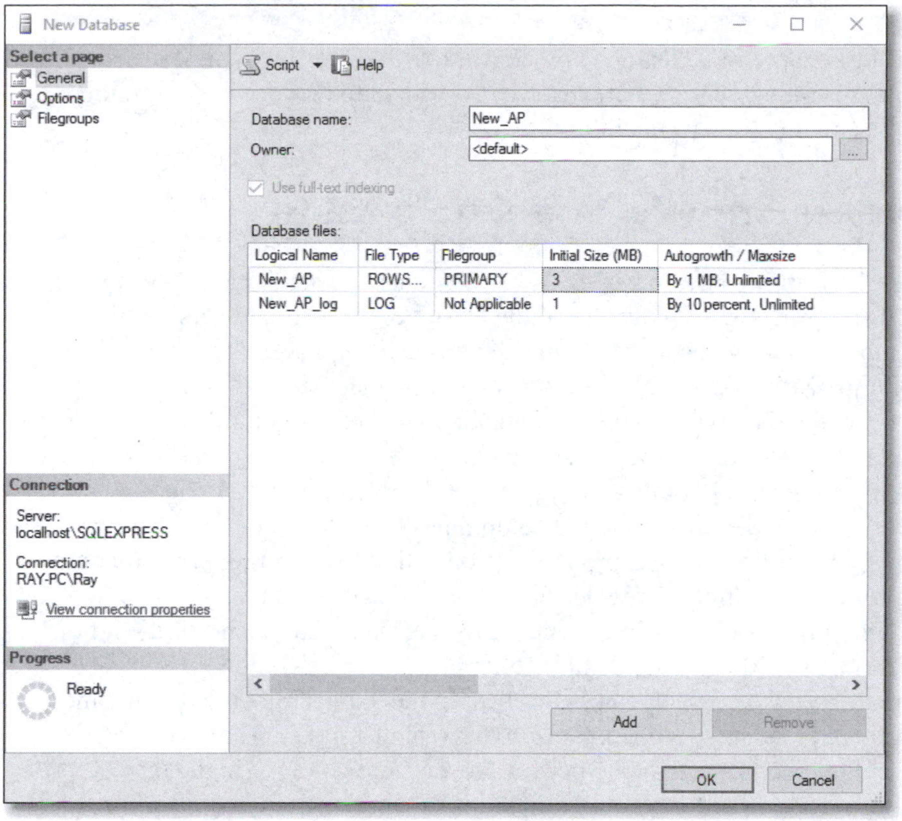

The default directory for SQL Server 2016 databases

```
C:\Program Files\Microsoft SQL Server\MSSQL13.SQLEXPRESS\MSSQL\DATA
```

How to create a new database

- To create a new database, right-click on the Databases folder in the Management Studio and select the New Database command to display the New Database dialog box shown above. Then, enter a name for the database. This updates the names for the data and log files that are displayed in the Database Files pane. Finally, click OK to create the database and its files.

How to delete a database

- To delete a database, expand the Databases folder, right-click on the database, and select the Delete command to display the Delete Object dialog box. Then, click OK to delete the database and its files.

Figure 12-1   How to create or delete a database

How to work with tables

In the last chapter, you learned how to work with tables, keys, indexes, and constraints by coding DDL statements. Now you'll learn how to work with these objects by using the Management Studio.

How to create, modify, or delete a table

Figure 12-2 shows how to use the Table Designer to create, modify, or delete a table. To start, this figure shows the Table Designer for a simple version of the Invoices table that only has four columns. Here, each column in the table is listed in the column grid that's at the top of the Table Designer. This grid includes the column name, the data type for the column, and whether the column allows null values. In addition to these properties, you can use the Column Properties pane that appears at the bottom of this window to set the other column properties. In this figure, for example, the InvoiceID column has been defined as an identity column. As you modify column properties, you'll find that the properties that are available for each column change depending on the properties that are specified in the column grid. For example, since the InvoiceDate column isn't of the int type, it can't be specified as an identity column.

To create a new table, you can right-click on the Tables folder and select the Table command to display a blank table in the Table Designer. Then, you can enter the column names and data types for one or more columns in the table. When you save the table for the first time, the Management Studio will prompt you with a dialog box that allows you to enter a name for the table.

To edit the design of an existing table, you can expand the Tables folder, right-click on the table, and select the Design command. This displays the table in the Table Designer. In addition, the Management Studio automatically displays the Table Designer toolbar. You can use this toolbar to work with the keys, relationships, indexes, and constraints defined by a table.

To set the primary key for a table, for example, you can click on the box to the left of the key column to select it and then click on the Set Primary Key button that's available from the Table Designer toolbar. If the key consists of two or more columns, you can hold down the Ctrl key and click multiple columns to select them. When you set the primary key, a key icon appears to the left of the key column or columns. In this figure, for example, a key icon appears to the left of the InvoiceID column.

By default, you can't use the Table Designer to modify a table in such a way that requires dropping and recreating the table. For example, you can't modify the identity column for an existing table. Since dropping the table deletes all data in the table, this isn't usually what you want. However, in some cases, you may want to allow this type of change. To do that, you can pull down the Tools menu, select the Options command, expand the Designers group, select the Table and Database Designers group, and deselect the "Prevent saving changes that require table re-creation" option.

The Table Designer for the Invoices table

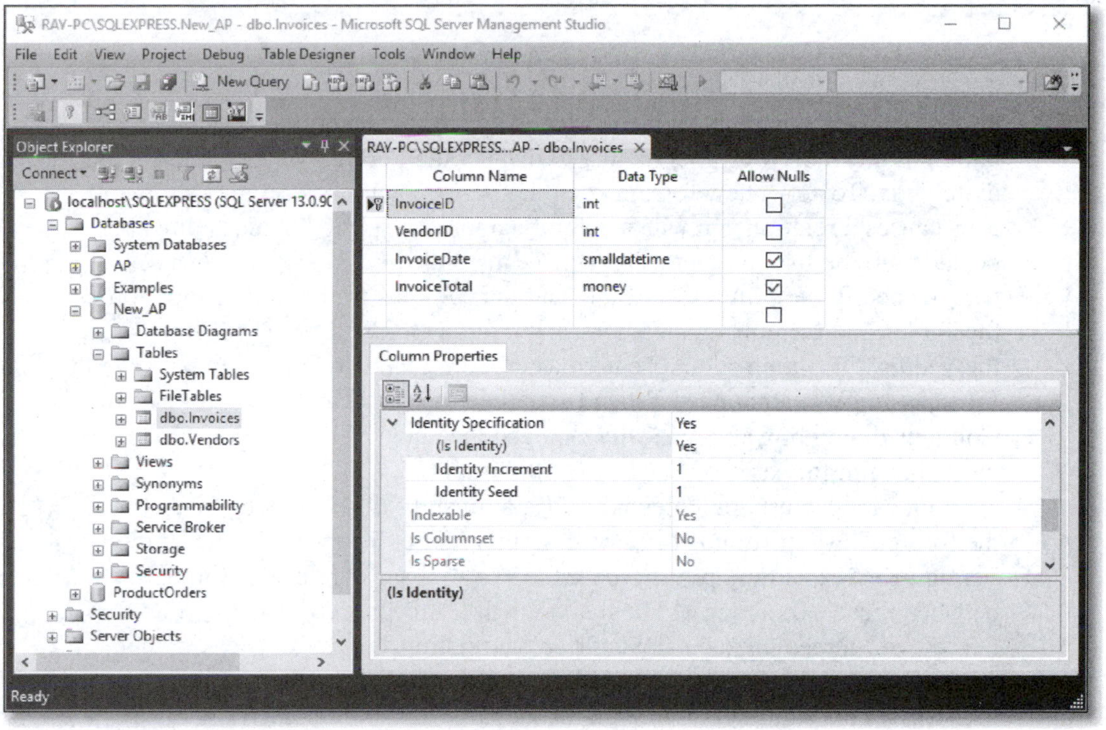

How to create or modify the design of a table

- To create a new table, right-click on the Tables folder and select the Table command to display a new table in the Table Designer. Then, when you click on the Save button in the toolbar, you can supply a name for the table.

- To edit the design of an existing table, expand the Tables folder, right-click on the table, and select the Design command to display the table in the Table Designer.

- To set the basic properties for each column, use the grid at the top of the Table Designer to specify the column name, data type, and whether or not the column allows nulls.

- To set other column properties, such as the identity column or a default value, use the Column Properties pane.

- To set the primary key, select the column or columns and click the Set Primary Key button in the Table Designer toolbar. Then, a key icon appears to the left of key columns.

How to delete a table

- To delete a table, expand the Tables folder, right-click on the table, select the Delete command, and click the OK button in the Delete Object dialog box that's displayed.

Note

- When you create a table using the Management Studio, the table is automatically stored in the default schema. If you want to transfer the table to a different schema, you can use the ALTER SCHEMA statement. See chapter 17 for details.

Figure 12-2   How to create, modify, or delete a table

How to work with foreign key relationships

Figure 12-3 shows how to specify foreign key relationships between tables. To start, you display the table that you want to contain the foreign key in the Table Designer as shown in figure 12-2. Then, you click on the Relationships button in the Table Designer toolbar to display the Foreign Key Relationships dialog box. To add a new foreign key relationship, you click on the Add button. This causes a relationship with a default name such as FK_Invoices_Invoices to be added to the list box on the left side of the dialog box.

To specify the primary key table and the columns for a relationship, you use the Tables and Columns dialog box shown in this figure. Here, I specified that the VendorID column should be used as the foreign key relationship between the Invoices and Vendors tables. When I specified this relationship, the Tables and Columns dialog box automatically changed the name of the relationship to the more meaningful name of FK_Invoices_Vendors.

You can also use the Foreign Key Relationships dialog box to control how the foreign key constraint is enforced. In this figure, for example, the Enforce Foreign Key Constraint property is set to Yes so that the referential integrity between these two tables will be maintained. If this property was set to No, SQL Server would recognize but not enforce the relationship. In most cases, then, you'll want to be sure this property is set to Yes.

You'll also want to be sure that the Delete Rule and Update Rule properties are set the way you want them. In this figure, these properties, which appear in the INSERT and UPDATE Specification group, are set to No Action. That means that primary keys in the Vendors table can't be changed if related records exist in the Invoices table, and a row can't be deleted from the Vendors table if related rows exist in the Invoices table. In most cases, that's what you want. In other cases, though, you'll want to change these properties to Cascade so that update and delete operations are cascaded to the foreign key table.

Although these properties are the ones you're most likely to change, you can also use the Check Existing Data On Creation Or Re-Enabling property to control whether SQL Server checks existing data to be sure that it satisfies the constraint. By default, this property is set to Yes, which is usually what you want. In addition, by default, the Enforce For Replication property is set to Yes, which causes the relationship to be enforced when the database is replicated. *Replication* is a technique that's used to create multiple copies of the same database in different locations. By using replication, SQL Server can keep the various copies of a database synchronized. Because this feature is only used by DBAs for enterprise systems, a complete presentation is beyond the scope of this book.

The Foreign Key Relationships dialog box for the Invoices table

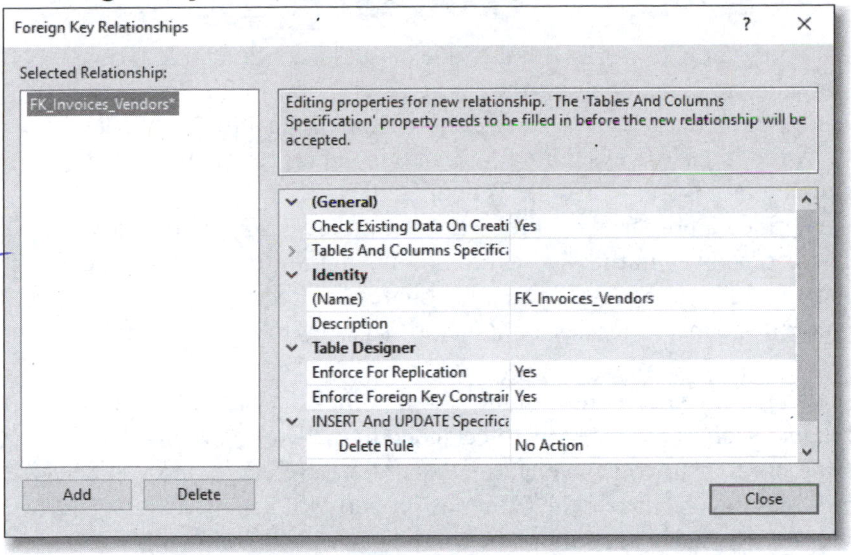

The Tables and Columns dialog box

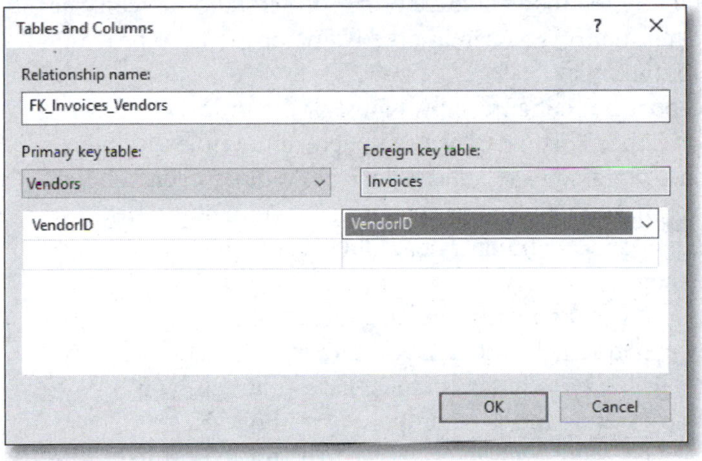

Description

- To display the Foreign Key Relationships dialog box for a table, display the table in the Table Designer and click on the Relationships button in the toolbar.

- To add a new foreign key relationship, click on the Add button. To delete an existing relationship, select the relationship and click on the Delete button.

- To specify the tables and columns that define the relationship, select the relationship, select the Tables And Columns Specification property, and click the button that appears to display the Tables and Columns dialog box. Then, use this dialog box to specify the primary key table and the appropriate columns in both tables.

- To set other properties for a relationship, select the relationship and use the properties grid to change the properties.

Figure 12-3   How to work with foreign key relationships

How to work with indexes and keys

Figure 12-4 shows how to work with the indexes and keys of a table. To start, you display the table that contains the foreign key in the Table Designer. Then, you click on the Manage Indexes and Keys button in the Table Designer toolbar to display the Indexes/Keys dialog box. In this figure, for example, the Indexes/Keys dialog box is shown for the Vendors table.

If you have defined a primary key as described in figure 12-2, the primary key for the table is displayed in this dialog box. In this figure, for example, the primary key is named PK_Vendors. If you click on this key to select it and view its properties, you'll see that it defines a unique primary key with a clustered index.

To add a new index, you can click on the Add button. This causes an index with a default name such as IX_Vendors to be added to the list box on the left side of the dialog box. Then, you can click on this index to select it, and you can set its properties. Here, you can use the Columns property to display a dialog box that allows you to specify the column or columns to index along with a sort order for each column. You can set the Type property to Index or Unique Key. If you set this property to Unique Key, the Is Unique property will automatically be set to Yes and grayed out. And finally, you can use the Name property to provide a more meaningful name for the index.

The Index/Keys dialog box in this figure shows most of the properties for an index named IX_VendorName. This index uses a nonclustered index to index the VendorName column in ascending order, and it does not require each vendor name to be unique. However, if you change the Type property to Unique Key, this index will define a unique key constraint. Then, SQL Server requires each vendor to have a unique name.

You can also create an index that enforces the uniqueness of its values without using a unique key constraint. To do that, you set the Is Unique property to Yes, and you set the Type property to Index. In most cases, though, you'll want to enforce uniqueness by setting the Type property to Unique Key.

By default, the Create As Clustered property is set to Yes for the primary key of the table, which is usually what you want. This causes the primary key to use a clustered index. Since a table can only have one clustered index, SQL Server grays out this property for all other indexes. If a table doesn't have a primary key, however, you can set the Create As Clustered property to Yes to create a clustered index for one index in the table.

The Indexes/Keys dialog box

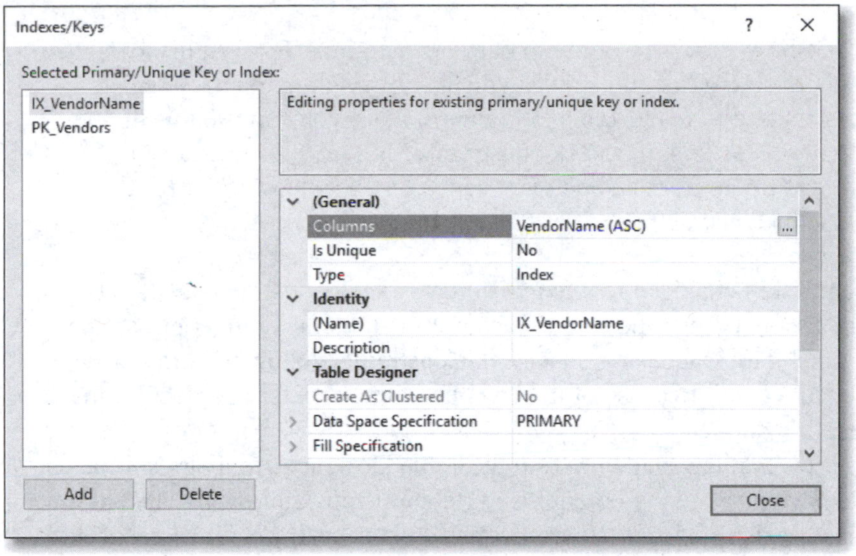

Description

- To display the Indexes/Keys dialog box for a table, display the table in the Table Designer and click on the Indexes and Keys button in the Table Designer toolbar.

- To add a new index, click the Add button, use the Columns property to specify the column name and sort order for each column in the index, and use the Name property to enter the name you want to use for the index.

- To view or edit an existing index, select the index from the list box on the left side of the dialog box. Then, you can view its properties on the right side of the dialog box.

- To create a unique key and an index that's based on that key, use the Type property to select the Unique Index option. When you do, the Is Unique property will automatically be set to Yes.

- To create an index without creating a unique key, use the Type property to select the Index option and set the Is Unique property to No.

- To create a clustered index, set the Create As Clustered property to Yes. If a table already contains a clustered index, this property is grayed out to show that it isn't available.

- The other options in this dialog box are used for performance tuning. In most cases, the default values for these options are acceptable. For more information, see Books Online.

Figure 12-4 How to work with indexes and keys

How to work with check constraints

Figure 12-5 shows how to work with check constraints. To start, it shows the Check Constraints dialog box that you can display by clicking on the Manage Check Constraints button in the Table Designer toolbar. You can use this dialog box to modify or delete existing check constraints for a table or to add new constraints. In this figure, for example, you can see a check constraint for the Invoices table. This constraint specifies that the InvoiceTotal column must be greater than zero.

As you learned in chapter 11, when you create check constraints using DDL, you can define them at either the column level or the table level. In contrast, the check constraints you create using the Check Constraints dialog box are always defined at the table level. Because of that, a constraint can refer to any column in the table where it's defined.

The properties that are available from the Table Designer group are similar to the properties you saw in the Foreign Key Relationships dialog box. The first one determines if existing data is checked when a new constraint is created. The second one determines if constraints are enforced when rows are inserted or updated. The third one determines if constraints are enforced when the database is replicated. In most cases, you'll set all three of these properties to Yes. If you want to temporarily disable a constraint during testing, however, you can do that by setting one or more of these properties to No.

The Check Constraints dialog box

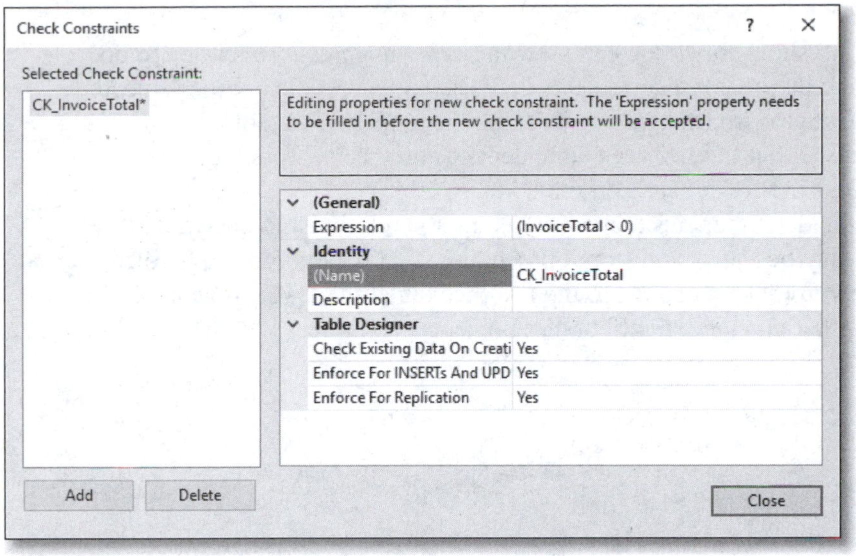

Description

- To display the Check Constraints dialog box for a table, display the table in the Table Designer and click on the Check Constraints button in the Table Designer toolbar.

- To add a new constraint to the table, click the Add button. Then, you must enter the expression that defines the constraint in the Expression property, and you usually want to use the Name property to provide a meaningful name for the constraint.

- To delete a constraint, select the constraint and click the Delete button.

- To view or edit the properties for an existing constraint, select the constraint from the list that's displayed on the left side of the dialog box.

- By default, SQL Server checks existing data when you add a new check constraint to be sure it satisfies the constraint. If that's not what you want, you can set the Check Existing Data On Creation Or Re-Enabling property to No.

- By default, SQL Server enforces the constraint for insert and update operations. If that's not what you want, you can set the Enforce For INSERTs And UPDATEs property to No.

- By default, SQL Server enforces the constraint when the database is replicated. If that's not what you want, you can set the Enforce For Replication property to No.

Figure 12-5   How to work with check constraints

How to examine table dependencies

Figure 12-6 shows how you can view the *dependencies* for a table. To do that, right-click on the table and select View Dependencies. Then, the Object Dependencies dialog box lists the objects that depend on that table. In this case, you can see that the Invoices table depends on the Vendors table, and the InvoiceLineItems table depends on the Invoices table.

Besides the dependencies that are based on the relationships between the tables, there may be views and stored procedures that depend on the Invoices table. Before you make a change to the Invoices table, then, you'll want to consider how that change will affect these objects.

The Object Dependencies dialog box for the Vendors table

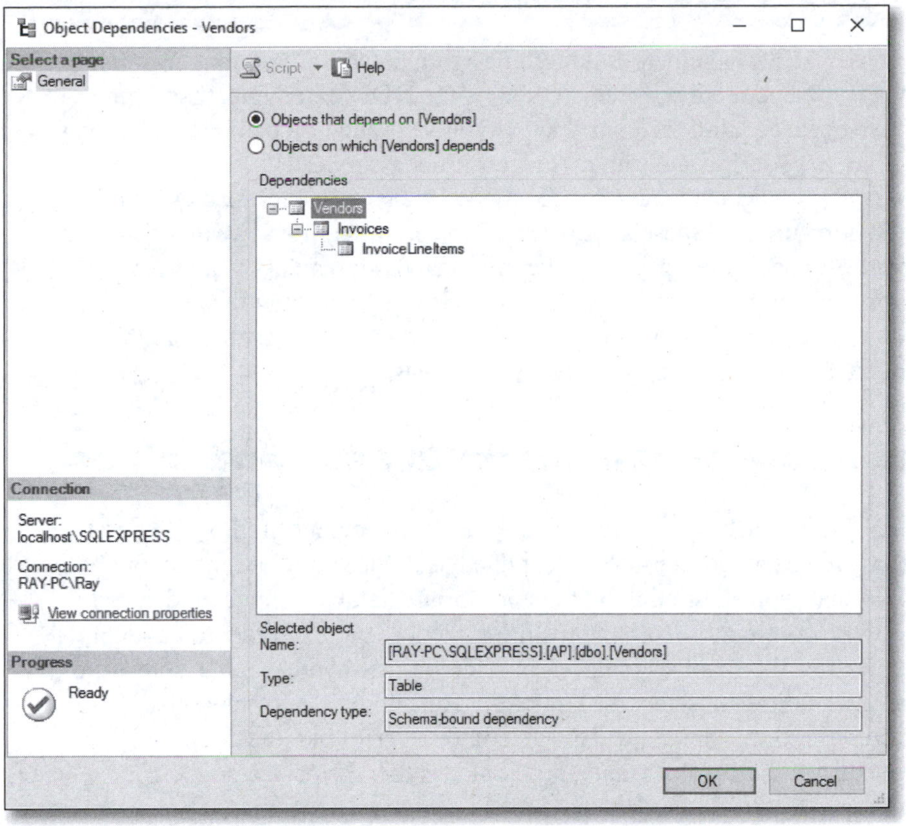

Description

- To view the *dependencies* for a table, right-click the table and select View Dependencies to display the Object Dependencies dialog box.

- To expand or collapse a dependency, click on the plus (+) or minus sign (-) that's displayed to the left of the dependency.

- You should check table dependencies before you delete or modify a column or an entire table.

Figure 12-6   How to examine table dependencies

How to generate scripts

If you use the Management Studio to design a database, you may eventually need or want to generate a script that contains the DDL statements that define the database or that record the changes that you've made to a database. That way, you can save these scripts and run them later if necessary.

Fortunately, the Management Studio makes it easy to generate these types of scripts. Unfortunately, these scripts are often formatted in a way that's not easy to read. Worse, these scripts often contain DDL statements that are more complex than if you had coded them yourself. Still, by studying these DDL statements, you can learn a lot, and you can see the DDL statements that the Management Studio uses to create or alter a database.

How to generate scripts for databases and tables

Figure 12-7 describes how you can use the Management Studio to generate a script that creates, drops, or alters most database objects including the database itself. To do that, you right-click on the appropriate database object and select the appropriate commands from the resulting menus. For example, to create a script that creates the Invoices table, right-click on the Invoices table, select the Script Table as submenu, select the CREATE To submenu, and select the New Query Editor Window command. This generates a script like the one in this figure that creates the Invoices table, and it places this script in a new Query Editor window.

If you study this script, you'll see that it uses nearly a full page of DDL statements to create a simple Invoices table that only contains four columns. In addition, this script encloses all names in square brackets ([]) even though that's not required, it qualifies table names with the default schema even though that's not required, and it uses separate ALTER TABLE statements to define the foreign key relationship constraint, check constraints, and default constraint even though that isn't necessary. Compared with the script presented at the end of chapter 11, I think you'll agree that this script is unwieldy and difficult to read even though it's for a simple table that contains only four columns. But that's one of the downsides of using a graphical tool like the Management Studio instead of coding the DDL statements yourself.

Although the CREATE scripts are the ones that you'll want to generate most often, you can also generate other scripts such as ALTER and DROP scripts for most objects. In addition, you can generate SELECT, INSERT, UPDATE, and DELETE scripts for some objects such as tables, and you can generate EXECUTE scripts for other objects such as stored procedures. Some of these scripts are essentially templates that you'll need to modify before they become functional. Still, they can give you a good start for creating certain types of statements. With a little experimentation, you should be able to figure out how this works.

A generated script that creates a simple Invoices table

```
USE [New_AP]
GO

SET ANSI_NULLS ON
GO

SET QUOTED_IDENTIFIER ON
GO

CREATE TABLE [dbo].[Invoices]
(
    [InvoiceID] [int] IDENTITY(1,1) NOT NULL,
    [VendorID] [int] NOT NULL,
    [InvoiceDate] [smalldatetime] NULL,
    [InvoiceTotal] [money] NULL,
    CONSTRAINT [PK_Invoices] PRIMARY KEY CLUSTERED ([InvoiceID] ASC)
    WITH (PAD_INDEX = OFF, STATISTICS_NORECOMPUTE = OFF, IGNORE_DUP_KEY = OFF,
    ALLOW_ROW_LOCKS = ON, ALLOW_PAGE_LOCKS = ON) ON [PRIMARY]
)
ON [PRIMARY]
GO

ALTER TABLE [dbo].[Invoices] ADD  CONSTRAINT [DF_Invoices_InvoiceTotal]
    DEFAULT ((0)) FOR [InvoiceTotal]
GO

ALTER TABLE [dbo].[Invoices]  WITH CHECK ADD  CONSTRAINT [FK_Invoices_Vendors]
    FOREIGN KEY([VendorID]) REFERENCES [dbo].[Vendors] ([VendorID])
GO

ALTER TABLE [dbo].[Invoices]
    CHECK CONSTRAINT [FK_Invoices_Vendors]
GO

ALTER TABLE [dbo].[Invoices]  WITH CHECK ADD  CONSTRAINT [CK_InvoiceTotal]
    CHECK  (([InvoiceTotal]>(0)))
GO

ALTER TABLE [dbo].[Invoices]
    CHECK CONSTRAINT [CK_InvoiceTotal]
GO
```

Description

- You can use the Management Studio to generate scripts to create, drop, or alter most objects that are contained in the database. You can send each script to Management Studio's Query Editor, a file, or to the clipboard.

- To generate a script that creates a database, right-click on the database and select Script Database as→CREATE To. Then, select New Query Editor Window, File, or Clipboard.

- To generate a script that creates a table, right-click on the table and select Script Table as→CREATE To. Then, select New Query Editor Window, File, or Clipboard.

Figure 12-7   How to generate scripts for databases and tables

If you experiment with scripts, you'll find that you can send them to a new Query Editor window, to a file, or to the clipboard. Most of the time, it's easiest to send the generated script to a Query Editor window. Then, you can review the script before you run it, save it, or copy it to the clipboard. In some cases, though, you may want to send a script directly to a file without viewing it first. Or, you may want to send the script to the clipboard without viewing it first so you can paste it into another tool and use that tool to view, save, or run the script.

How to generate a change script when you modify a table

When you use the Table Designer to modify the design of a table, a Generate Change Script button becomes available in the Table Designer toolbar. If you want, you can click on this button to display the Save Change Script dialog box shown in figure 12-8. Then, you can use this dialog box to examine or save the SQL script that the Management Studio uses to alter the table. Most of the time, this isn't necessary. However, if you want to keep a permanent record of the change, or if you want to apply the change to other databases, you can save this script. Then, if necessary, you can run it against other databases.

If you want to generate and save a change script every time you modify a table, you can check the Automatically Generate Change Script On Every Save option. Then, every time you attempt to save changes to the design of a table, the Management Studio will prompt you with a Save Change Script dialog box like the one in this figure. To save the script, you can click Yes and respond to the resulting Save dialog box.

The Save Change Script dialog box

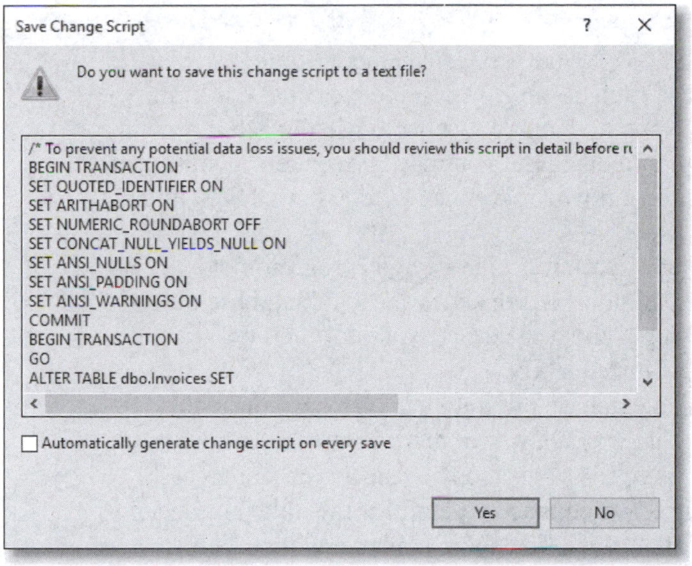

Description

- If you use the Table Designer to modify the design of a table, you can click the Generate Change Script button in the toolbar to display the Save Change Script dialog box shown above. You can use this dialog box to examine or save the SQL script that the Management Studio uses to alter the table.

- If you check the Automatically Generate Change Script On Every Save box, the Management Studio will prompt you with a Save Change Script dialog box each time you attempt to save changes to the design of a table.

Figure 12-8   How to generate a change script when you modify a table

Perspective

In this chapter, you learned how to use the Management Studio to create and work with database objects, such as tables, keys, indexes, and constraints as well as the database itself. Now that you know how to use the Management Studio to work with the design of a database, you may be wondering when you should use it for database design and when you should code the DDL statements yourself.

Although it's often a matter of preference, most SQL programmers find it easier to use the Management Studio to create and work with database objects. That way, they don't have to worry about the exact syntax of the DDL statements, which they may use infrequently.

However, some experienced database programmers prefer to enter the DDL statements themselves. That way, they have more control over how these scripts are coded. In addition, they can save a copy of the script that creates the database for future reference, which may be helpful if the database design ever needs to be ported to another type of database management system such as Oracle, DB2, or MySQL.

Terms

Table Designer
replication
dependencies

Exercises

1. Use the Management Studio to create a new database called Membership2 using the default settings. (If the database already exists, use the Management Studio to delete it and then recreate it.)

2. Use the Management Studio to create the following tables and relationships in the Membership database. Define IndividualID and GroupID as IDENTITY columns. Allow Address and Phone to accept null values; none of the other columns should allow null values. Define the Dues column with a default of zero and a check constraint to allow only positive values. Define the DuesPaid column with a default Boolean value of False.

3. Use the Management Studio to index the GroupMembership table. Create a clustered index on the GroupID column, a nonclustered index on the IndividualID column, and a unique index and constraint on both columns.

Section 4

Advanced SQL skills

This section teaches SQL skills that go beyond the essentials. After you read all of the chapters in this section, you'll have the skills of a professional SQL programmer. To make these chapters as easy to use as possible, they're designed as independent modules. That means that you can read them in any order you prefer.

In chapter 13, you can learn how to work with views, which let you simplify and restrict access to the data in a database. In chapter 14, you can learn how to use scripts to control the processing of SQL statements that you execute from a client tool like the Management Studio. Scripts are just one type of procedural program you can create in SQL Server. In chapter 15, you can learn how to use the other types of procedural programs: stored procedures, triggers, and functions.

In chapter 16, you can learn how to use transactions and locking to prevent data errors in a multi-user environment. In chapter 17, you can learn how to secure a database to restrict who has access to it. In chapter 18, you can learn how to work with XML. In chapter 19, you can learn how to work with large binary values such as images, sound, and video. Finally, in chapter 20, you'll get an introduction to CLR integration.

How to work with views

As you've seen throughout this book, SELECT queries can be complicated, particularly if they use multiple joins, subqueries, or complex functions. Because of that, you may want to save the queries you use regularly. One way to do that is to store the statement in a file using the Management Studio. Another way is to create a view.

Unlike a file you create with the Management Studio, a view is stored as part of the database. That means it can be used not only by SQL programmers, but by users and application programs that have access to the database. This provides some distinct advantages over using tables directly, as you'll see in this chapter.

An introduction to views

In chapter 1, you learned the basics of how views work. In the next topic, then, I'll just review this information. Then, I'll present some of the benefits of views so you'll know when and why you should use them.

How views work

A view is a SELECT statement that's stored with the database. To create a view, you use a CREATE VIEW statement like the one shown in figure 13-1. This statement creates a view named VendorsMin that retrieves the VendorName, VendorState, and VendorPhone columns from the Vendors table.

You can think of a view as a virtual table that consists only of the rows and columns specified in its CREATE VIEW statement. The table or tables that are listed in the FROM clause are called the base tables for the view. Since the view refers back to the base tables, it doesn't store any data itself, and it always reflects the most current data in the base tables.

To use a view, you refer to it from another SQL statement. The SELECT statement in this figure, for example, uses the VendorsMin view in the FROM clause instead of a table. As a result, this SELECT statement extracts its result set from the virtual table that the view represents. In this case, all the rows for vendors in California are retrieved from the view.

Because a view is stored as an object in a database, it can be used by anyone who has access to the database. That includes users who have access to the database through end-user programs such as programs that provide for ad hoc queries and report generation, and application programs that are written specifically to work with the data in the database. In fact, views are often designed to be used with these types of programs. In the next topic, you'll learn why.

A CREATE VIEW statement for a view named VendorsMin

```
CREATE VIEW VendorsMin AS
    SELECT VendorName, VendorState, VendorPhone
    FROM Vendors;
```

The virtual table that's represented by the view

	VendorName	VendorState	VendorPhone
1	US Postal Service	WI	(800) 555-1205
2	National Information Data Ctr	DC	(301) 555-8950
3	Register of Copyrights	DC	NULL
4	Jobtrak	CA	(800) 555-8725
5	Newbrige Book Clubs	NJ	(800) 555-9980
6	California Chamber Of Commerce	CA	(916) 555-6670
7	Towne Advertiser's Mailing Svcs	CA	NULL
8	BFI Industries	CA	(559) 555-1551

`(122 rows)`

A SELECT statement that uses the VendorsMin view

```
SELECT * FROM VendorsMin
WHERE VendorState = 'CA'
ORDER BY VendorName;
```

The result set that's returned by the SELECT statement

	VendorName	VendorState	VendorPhone
1	Abbey Office Furnishings	CA	(559) 555-8300
2	American Express	CA	(800) 555-3344
3	ASC Signs	CA	NULL
4	Aztek Label	CA	(714) 555-9000
5	Bertelsmann Industry Svcs. Inc	CA	(805) 555-0584
6	BFI Industries	CA	(559) 555-1551
7	Bill Jones	CA	NULL
8	Bill Marvin Electric Inc	CA	(559) 555-5106

`(75 rows)`

Description

- A *view* consists of a SELECT statement that's stored as an object in the database. The tables referenced in the SELECT statement are called the *base tables* for the view.

- When you create a view, the query on which it's based is optimized by SQL Server before it's saved in the database. Then, you can refer to the view anywhere you would normally use a table in any of the data manipulation statements: SELECT, INSERT, UPDATE, and DELETE.

- Although a view behaves like a virtual table, it doesn't store any data. Since the view refers back to its base tables, it always returns current data.

- A view can also be referred to as a *viewed table* because it provides a view to the underlying base tables.

Figure 13-1   How views work

Benefits of using views

Figure 13-2 describes some of the advantages of using views. To start, the data that you access through a view isn't dependent on the structure of the database. To illustrate, suppose a view refers to a table that you've decided to divide into two tables. To accommodate this change, you simply modify the view; you don't have to modify any statements that refer to the view. That means that users who query the database using the view don't have to be aware of the change in the database structure, and application programs that use the view don't have to be modified.

You can also use views to restrict access to a database. To do that, you include just the columns and rows you want a user or application program to have access to in the views. Then, you let the user or program access the data only through the views. The view shown in this figure, for example, restricts access to a table that contains information on investors. In this case, the view provides access to name and address information that might be needed by the support staff that maintains the table. In contrast, another view that includes investment information could be used by the consultants who manage the investments.

Views are also flexible. Because views can be based on almost any SELECT statement, they can be used to provide just the data that's needed for specific situations. In addition, views can hide the complexity of a SELECT statement. That makes it easier for end users and application programs to retrieve the data they need. Finally, views can be used not only to retrieve data, but to modify data as well. You'll see how that works later in this chapter.

Some of the benefits provided by views

Benefit	Description
Design independence	Data that's accessed through a view is independent of the underlying database structure. That means that you can change the design of a database and then modify the view as necessary so that the queries that use it don't need to be changed.
Data security	You can create views that provide access only to the data that specific users are allowed to see.
Flexibility	You can create custom views to accommodate different needs.
Simplified queries	You can create views that hide the complexity of retrieval operations. Then, the data can be retrieved using simple SELECT statements.
Updatability	With certain restrictions, a view can be used to update, insert, and delete data from a base table.

The data in a table of investors

	InvestorID	LastName	FirstName	Address	City	State	ZipCode	Phone	Investments	NetGain
1	1	Anders	Maria	345 Winchell Pl	Anderson	IN	46014	(765) 555-7878	15000.00	1242.57
2	2	Trujilo	Ana	1298 E Smathers St.	Benton	AR	72018	(510) 555-7733	43500.00	8497.44
3	3	Moreno	Antonio	6925 N Parkland Ave.	Puyallup	WA	98373	(253) 555-8332	22900.00	2338.87
4	4	Hardy	Thomas	83 d'Urberville Ln.	Casterbridge	GA	31209	(478) 555-1139	5000.00	-245.69
5	5	Berglund	Christina	22717 E 73rd Ave.	Dubuque	IA	52004	(319) 555-1139	11750.00	865.77

`(5 rows)`

A view that restricts access to certain columns

```
CREATE VIEW InvestorsGeneral
AS
SELECT InvestorID, LastName, FirstName, Address,
    City, State, ZipCode, Phone
FROM Investors;
```

The data retrieved by the view

	InvestorID	LastName	FirstName	Address	City	State	ZipCode	Phone
1	1	Anders	Maria	345 Winchell Pl	Anderson	IN	46014	(765) 555-7878
2	2	Trujilo	Ana	1298 E Smathers St.	Benton	AR	72018	(510) 555-7733
3	3	Moreno	Antonio	6925 N Parkland Ave.	Puyallup	WA	98373	(253) 555-8332
4	4	Hardy	Thomas	83 d'Urberville Ln.	Casterbridge	GA	31209	(478) 555-1139
5	5	Berglund	Christina	22717 E 73rd Ave.	Dubuque	IA	52004	(319) 555-1139

`(5 rows)`

Description

- You can create a view based on almost any SELECT statement. That means that you can code views that join tables, summarize data, and use subqueries and functions.

- You can restrict access to the data in a table by including selected columns in the SELECT clause for a view, or by including a WHERE clause in the SELECT statement so that only selected rows are retrieved by the view.

Figure 13-2   Benefits of using views

How to create and manage views

Now that you understand how views work and what benefits they provide, you're ready to learn how to create and manage them. That's what you'll learn in the topics that follow.

How to create a view

Figure 13-3 presents the CREATE VIEW statement you use to create a view. In its simplest form, you code the name of the view in the CREATE VIEW clause followed by the AS keyword and the SELECT statement that defines the view. The statement shown in this figure, for example, creates a view named VendorShortList. This view includes selected columns from the Vendors table for all vendors with invoices. When this statement is executed, the view is added to the current database and a message like the one shown in this figure is displayed to indicate that the statement was successful.

Because a SELECT statement can refer to a view, the SELECT statement you code within the definition of a view can also refer to another view. In other words, views can be nested. I recommend you avoid using nested views, however, because the dependencies between tables and views can become confusing, which can make problems difficult to locate.

The SELECT statement for a view can use any of the features of a normal SELECT statement with two exceptions. First, it can't include an ORDER BY clause unless it also uses a TOP clause or the OFFSET and FETCH clauses. That means that if you want to sort the result set that's extracted from a view, you have to include an ORDER BY clause in the SELECT statement that refers to the view. Second, it can't include the INTO keyword. That's because a view can't be used to create a permanent table.

By default, the columns in a view are given the same names as the columns in the base tables. If a view contains a calculated column, however, you'll want to name that column just as you do in other SELECT statements. In addition, you'll need to rename columns from different tables that have the same name. To do that, you can use the AS clause in the SELECT statement or you can code the column names in the CREATE VIEW clause. You'll see examples of both of these techniques in the next figure.

The CREATE VIEW statement also provides three optional clauses: WITH ENCRYPTION, WITH SCHEMABINDING, and WITH CHECK OPTION. The WITH ENCRYPTION clause prevents other users from examining the SELECT statement on which the view is based. In general, though, you don't need to use this option unless your system requires enhanced security.

The WITH SCHEMABINDING clause protects a view by binding it to the database structure, or schema. This prevents the underlying base tables from being deleted or modified in any way that affects the view. You'll typically use this option for production databases, but not for databases you're using for testing.

The WITH CHECK OPTION clause prevents a row in a view from being updated if that would cause the row to be excluded from the view. I'll have more to say about this clause in the topic on updating rows using a view.

The syntax of the CREATE VIEW statement

```
CREATE VIEW view_name [(column_name_1 [, column_name_2]...)]
[WITH {ENCRYPTION|SCHEMABINDING|ENCRYPTION,SCHEMABINDING}]
AS
select_statement
[WITH CHECK OPTION]
```

A CREATE VIEW statement that creates a view of vendors that have invoices

```
CREATE VIEW VendorShortList
AS
SELECT VendorName, VendorContactLName, VendorContactFName, VendorPhone
FROM Vendors
WHERE VendorID IN (SELECT VendorID FROM Invoices);
```

The response from the system

```
Command(s) completed successfully.
```

Description

- You use the CREATE VIEW statement to create a view. The name you give the view must not be the same as the name of any existing table or view.

- The SELECT statement within the view can refer to as many as 256 tables, and it can use any valid combination of joins, unions, or subqueries.

- You can create a view that's based on another view rather than on a table, called a *nested view*. SQL Server views can be nested up to 32 levels deep.

- The SELECT statement for a view can't include an INTO clause, and it can't include an ORDER BY clause unless the TOP clause or the OFFSET and FETCH clauses are also used. To sort the rows in a view, you have to include the ORDER BY clause in the SELECT statement that uses the view.

- You can name the columns in a view by coding a list of names in parentheses following the view name or by coding the new names in the SELECT clause. A column must be named if it's calculated from other columns or if a column with the same name already exists. Otherwise, the name from the base table can be used.

- You can use the WITH ENCRYPTION clause to keep users from examining the SQL code that defines the view.

- You can use the WITH SCHEMABINDING clause to bind a view to the *database schema*. Then, you can't drop the tables on which the view is based or modify the tables in a way that would affect the view.

- If you include the WITH SCHEMABINDING clause, you can't use the all columns operator (*) in the SELECT statement. In addition, you must qualify the names of tables and views in the FROM clause with the name of the schema that contains them.

- You can use the WITH CHECK OPTION clause to prevent a row from being updated through a view if it would no longer be included in the view. See figure 13-7 for details.

Figure 13-3   How to create a view

Examples that create views

To help you understand the flexibility that views provide, figure 13-4 presents several CREATE VIEW statements. The first statement creates a view that joins data from the Vendors and Invoices tables. The second statement creates a view that retrieves the top five percent of invoices in the Invoices table. Notice that this SELECT statement includes an ORDER BY clause that sorts the rows in descending sequence so the invoices with the largest amounts are retrieved. This is one of only two cases in which you can use the ORDER BY clause. The other is if you include the OFFSET and FETCH clauses on the ORDER BY clause.

The third and fourth statements illustrate the two ways that you can name the columns in a view. In both cases, the SELECT statement retrieves a calculated column, so a name must be assigned to this column. The third statement shows how you would do this using the CREATE VIEW clause. Notice that even if you only want to name one column, you have to include the names for all the columns even if they're the same as the names in the base tables. In contrast, if you name this column in the SELECT clause as shown in the fourth example, you can let the other column names default to the column names in the base table. Since this syntax is easier to use, you'll use it most of the time. Keep in mind, though, that the ANSI standards don't support this syntax for naming view columns.

The fifth statement creates a view that summarizes the rows in the Invoices table by vendor. This illustrates the use of the aggregate functions and the GROUP BY clause in a view. In this case, the rows are grouped by vendor name, and a count of the invoices and the invoice total are calculated for each vendor.

Like the first statement, the last statement joins data from the Vendors and Invoices table. Unlike the first statement, though, this statement includes the WITH SCHEMABINDING clause. That means that neither the Vendors nor the Invoices table can be deleted without first deleting the view. In addition, no changes can be made to these tables that would affect the view. Notice that the table names in the FROM clause are qualified with the name of the table's schema, in this case, dbo. If you include the WITH SCHEMABINDING clause, you must qualify the table names in this way.

A CREATE VIEW statement that uses a join

```
CREATE VIEW VendorInvoices
AS
SELECT VendorName, InvoiceNumber, InvoiceDate, InvoiceTotal
FROM Vendors JOIN Invoices ON Vendors.VendorID = Invoices.VendorID;
```

A CREATE VIEW statement that uses TOP and ORDER BY clauses

```
CREATE VIEW TopVendors
AS
SELECT TOP 5 PERCENT VendorID, InvoiceTotal
FROM Invoices
ORDER BY InvoiceTotal DESC;
```

Two CREATE VIEW statements that name the columns in a view

A statement that names all the view columns in its CREATE VIEW clause

```
CREATE VIEW OutstandingInvoices
    (InvoiceNumber, InvoiceDate, InvoiceTotal, BalanceDue)
AS
SELECT InvoiceNumber, InvoiceDate, InvoiceTotal,
    InvoiceTotal - PaymentTotal - CreditTotal
FROM Invoices
WHERE InvoiceTotal - PaymentTotal - CreditTotal > 0;
```

A statement that names just the calculated column in its SELECT clause

```
CREATE VIEW OutstandingInvoices
AS
SELECT InvoiceNumber, InvoiceDate, InvoiceTotal,
    InvoiceTotal - PaymentTotal - CreditTotal AS BalanceDue
FROM Invoices
WHERE InvoiceTotal - PaymentTotal - CreditTotal > 0;
```

A CREATE VIEW statement that summarizes invoices by vendor

```
CREATE VIEW InvoiceSummary
AS
SELECT VendorName, COUNT(*) AS InvoiceQty, SUM(InvoiceTotal) AS InvoiceSum
FROM Vendors JOIN Invoices ON Vendors.VendorID = Invoices.VendorID
GROUP BY VendorName;
```

A CREATE VIEW statement that uses the WITH SCHEMABINDING option

```
CREATE VIEW VendorsDue
WITH SCHEMABINDING
AS
SELECT InvoiceDate AS Date, VendorName AS Name,
    VendorContactFName + ' ' + VendorContactLName AS Contact,
    InvoiceNumber AS Invoice,
    InvoiceTotal - PaymentTotal - CreditTotal AS BalanceDue
FROM dbo.Vendors JOIN dbo.Invoices
    ON Vendors.VendorID = Invoices.VendorID
WHERE InvoiceTotal - PaymentTotal - CreditTotal > 0;
```

Note

- If you name the columns of a view in the CREATE VIEW clause, you have to name all of the columns. In contrast, if you name the columns in the SELECT clause, you can name just the columns you need to rename.

Figure 13-4   CREATE VIEW examples

How to create an updatable view

Once you create a view, you can refer to it in a SELECT statement as you saw in figure 13-1. In addition, you can refer to it in INSERT, UPDATE, and DELETE statements to modify an underlying table. To do that, the view must be updatable. Figure 13-5 lists the requirements for creating updatable views.

The first three requirements have to do with what you can code in the select list of the SELECT statement that defines the view. As you can see, the select list can't include the DISTINCT or TOP clause, it can't include aggregate functions, and it can't include calculated columns. In addition, the SELECT statement can't include a GROUP BY or HAVING clause, and two SELECT statements can't be joined by a union operation.

The first CREATE VIEW statement in this figure creates a view that's updatable. This view adheres to all of the requirements for updatable views. That means that you can refer to it in an INSERT, UPDATE, or DELETE statement. For example, you could use the UPDATE statement shown in this figure to update the CreditTotal column in the Invoices base table.

In contrast, the second CREATE VIEW statement in this figure creates a read-only view. This view is read-only because the select list contains a calculated value.

In general, using INSERT, UPDATE, and DELETE statements to update data through a view is inflexible and prone to errors. Because of that, you should avoid this technique whenever possible. Instead, you should consider using INSTEAD OF triggers to update data through a view. You'll learn about this type of trigger in chapter 15.

Requirements for creating updatable views

- The select list can't include a DISTINCT or TOP clause.
- The select list can't include an aggregate function.
- The select list can't include a calculated value.
- The SELECT statement can't include a GROUP BY or HAVING clause.
- The view can't include the UNION operator.

A CREATE VIEW statement that creates an updatable view

```
CREATE VIEW InvoiceCredit
AS
SELECT InvoiceNumber, InvoiceDate, InvoiceTotal, PaymentTotal, CreditTotal
FROM Invoices
WHERE InvoiceTotal - PaymentTotal - CreditTotal > 0;
```

An UPDATE statement that updates the view

```
UPDATE InvoiceCredit
SET CreditTotal = CreditTotal + 200
WHERE InvoiceTotal - PaymentTotal - CreditTotal >= 200;
```

A CREATE VIEW statement that creates a read-only view

```
CREATE VIEW OutstandingInvoices
AS
SELECT InvoiceNumber, InvoiceDate, InvoiceTotal,
    InvoiceTotal - PaymentTotal - CreditTotal AS BalanceDue
FROM Invoices
WHERE InvoiceTotal - PaymentTotal - CreditTotal > 0;
```

Description

- An *updatable view* is one that can be used in an INSERT, UPDATE, or DELETE statement to modify the contents of a base table that the view refers to. If a view is not updatable, it's called a *read-only view*.
- The requirements for coding updatable views are more restrictive than for coding read-only views. That's because SQL Server must be able to unambiguously determine which base tables and which columns are affected.
- You can also insert, update, and delete data through a view using an INSTEAD OF trigger. See chapter 15 for details.

Figure 13-5   How to create an updatable view

How to delete or modify a view

Figure 13-6 presents the statements you use to delete or modify a view. To delete a view, you use the DROP VIEW statement. In this statement, you simply name the view you want to delete. Like the other statements for deleting database objects, this statement deletes the view permanently. So you may want to make a backup copy of the database first if there's any chance that you may want to restore the view later.

To modify a view, you can use the ALTER VIEW statement. Notice that the syntax of this statement is the same as the syntax of the CREATE VIEW statement. If you understand the CREATE VIEW statement, then, you won't have any trouble using the ALTER VIEW statement.

Instead of using the ALTER VIEW statement to modify a view, you can delete the view and then recreate it. If you've defined permissions for the view, you should know that those permissions are deleted when the view is deleted. If that's not what you want, you should use the ALTER VIEW statement instead.

The examples in this figure show how you can use the DROP VIEW and ALTER VIEW statements. The first example is a CREATE VIEW statement that creates a view named Vendors_SW. This view retrieves rows from the Vendors table for vendors located in four states. Then, the second example is an ALTER VIEW statement that modifies this view so it includes vendors in two additional states. Finally, the third example is a DROP VIEW statement that deletes this view.

In the last chapter, you learned how to display the dependencies for a table. Before you delete a table, you should display its dependencies to determine if any views are dependent on the table. If so, you should delete the views along with the tables. If you don't, a query that refers to the view will cause an error. To prevent this problem, you can bind the view to the database schema by specifying the WITH SCHEMABINDING option in the CREATE VIEW or ALTER VIEW statement. Then, you won't be able to delete the base table without deleting the views that depend on it first.

The syntax of the DROP VIEW statement

```
DROP VIEW view_name
```

The syntax of the ALTER VIEW statement

```
ALTER VIEW view_name [(column_name_1 [, column_name_2]...)]
[WITH {ENCRYPTION|SCHEMABINDING|ENCRYPTION,SCHEMABINDING}]
AS
select_statement
[WITH CHECK OPTION]
```

A statement that creates a view

```
CREATE VIEW Vendors_SW
AS
SELECT *
FROM Vendors
WHERE VendorState IN ('CA','AZ','NV','NM');
```

A statement that modifies the view

```
ALTER VIEW Vendors_SW
AS
SELECT *
FROM Vendors
WHERE VendorState IN ('CA','AZ','NV','NM','UT','CO');
```

A statement that deletes the view

```
DROP VIEW Vendors_SW;
```

Description

- To delete a view from the database, use the DROP VIEW statement.

- To modify the definition of a view, you can delete the view and then create it again, or you can use the ALTER VIEW statement to specify the new definition.

- When you delete a view, any permissions that are assigned to the view are also deleted.

- If you delete a table, you should also delete any views that are based on that table. Otherwise, an error will occur when you run a query that refers to one of those views. To find out what views are dependent on a table, display the table's dependencies as described in chapter 12.

- If you specify the WITH SCHEMABINDING option when you create or modify a view, you won't be able to delete the base tables without first deleting the view.

Note

- ALTER VIEW isn't an ANSI-standard statement. Although it's supported on other SQL-based systems, its behavior on each system is different.

Figure 13-6   How to delete or modify a view

How to use views

So far, you've seen how to use views in SELECT statements to retrieve data from one or more base tables. But you can also use views in INSERT, UPDATE, and DELETE statements to modify the data in a base table. You'll learn how to do that in the topics that follow. In addition, you'll learn how to use some views provided by SQL Server to get information about the database schema.

How to update rows through a view

Figure 13-7 shows how you can update rows in a table through a view. To do that, you simply name the view that refers to the table in the UPDATE statement. Note that for this to work, the view must be updatable as described in figure 13-5. In addition, the UPDATE statement can only update the data in a single base table, even if the view refers to two or more tables.

The examples in this figure illustrate how this works. First, the CREATE VIEW statement creates an updatable view named VendorPayment that joins data from the Vendors and Invoices tables. The data that's retrieved by this view is shown in this figure. Then, the UPDATE statement uses this view to modify the PaymentDate and PaymentTotal columns for a specific vendor and invoice. As you can see, the Invoices table reflects this update.

Notice, however, that the row that was updated is no longer included in the view. That's because the row no longer meets the criteria in the WHERE clause of the SELECT statement that defines the view. If that's not what you want, you can include the WITH CHECK OPTION clause in the CREATE VIEW statement. Then, an update through the view isn't allowed if it causes the row to be excluded from the view. If the WITH CHECK OPTION clause had been included in the definition of the VendorPayment view, for example, the UPDATE statement in this figure would have resulted in an error message like the one shown.

A statement that creates an updatable view

```
CREATE VIEW VendorPayment
AS
SELECT VendorName, InvoiceNumber, InvoiceDate, PaymentDate,
    InvoiceTotal, CreditTotal, PaymentTotal
FROM Invoices JOIN Vendors ON Invoices.VendorID = Vendors.VendorID
WHERE InvoiceTotal - PaymentTotal - CreditTotal > 0;
```

The data retrieved by the view before the update

	VendorName	InvoiceNumber	InvoiceDate	PaymentDate	Invoice Total	Credit Total	Payment Total	
6	Federal Express Corporation	263253273	2016-03-22 00:00:00	NULL	30.75	0.00	0.00	
7	Malloy Lithographing Inc	P-0608	2016-03-23 00:00:00	NULL	20551.18	1200.00	0.00	
8	Ford Motor Credit Company	9982771	2016-03-24 00:00:00	NULL	503.20	0.00	0.00	
9	Cardinal Business Media, I...	134116	2016-03-28 00:00:00	NULL	90.36	0.00	0.00	
10	Malloy Lithographing Inc	0-2436	2016-03-31 00:00:00	NULL	10976.06	0.00	0.00	

A statement that updates the Invoices table through the view

```
UPDATE VendorPayment
SET PaymentTotal = 19351.18, PaymentDate = '2016-04-02'
WHERE VendorName = 'Malloy Lithographing Inc' AND InvoiceNumber = 'P-0608';
```

The updated Invoices table

	InvoiceID	VendorID	InvoiceNumber	InvoiceDate	Invoice Total	Payment Total	Credit Total	TermsID	InvoiceDueD	
102	102	110	P-0608	2016-03-23 00:00:00	20551.18	19351.18	1200.00	3	2016-04-22 (	
103	103	122	989319-417	2016-03-23 00:00:00	2051.59	2051.59	0.00	3	2016-04-22 (	
104	104	123	263253243	2016-03-23 00:00:00	44.44	44.44	0.00	3	2016-04-22 (	
105	105	106	9982771	2016-03-24 00:00:00	503.20	0.00	0.00	3	2016-04-23 (	
106	106	110	0-2060	2016-03-24 00:00:00	23517.58	21221.63	2295.95	3	2016-04-23 (	

The data retrieved by the view after the update

	VendorName	InvoiceNumber	InvoiceDate	PaymentDate	Invoice Total	Credit Total	Payment Total	
6	Federal Express Corporation	263253273	2016-03-22 00:00:00	NULL	30.75	0.00	0.00	
7	Ford Motor Credit Company	9982771	2016-03-24 00:00:00	NULL	503.20	0.00	0.00	
8	Cardinal Business Media, I...	134116	2016-03-28 00:00:00	NULL	90.36	0.00	0.00	
9	Malloy Lithographing Inc	0-2436	2016-03-31 00:00:00	NULL	10976.06	0.00	0.00	

The response if WITH CHECK OPTION is specified for the view

```
The attempted insert or update failed because the target view either
specifies WITH CHECK OPTION or spans a view that specifies WITH CHECK OPTION
and one or more rows resulting from the operation did not qualify under the
CHECK OPTION constraint.
The statement has been terminated.
```

Description

- You can use the UPDATE statement to update a table through a view. To do that, you name the view in the UPDATE clause.

- The view you name in the UPDATE statement must be updatable. In addition, the UPDATE statement can't update data in more than one base table.

- If you don't specify WITH CHECK OPTION when you create a view, a change you make through the view can cause the modified rows to no longer be included in the view.

- If you specify WITH CHECK OPTION when you create a view, an error will occur if you try to modify a row in such a way that it would no longer be included in the view.

Figure 13-7   How to update rows through a view

How to insert rows through a view

To insert rows through a view, you use the INSERT statement as shown in figure 13-8. At the top of this figure, you can see a CREATE VIEW statement for a view named IBM_Invoices. This view retrieves columns and rows from the Invoices table for the vendor named IBM. Then, the INSERT statement attempts to insert a row into the Invoices table through this view.

This insert operation fails, though, because the view and the INSERT statement don't include all of the required columns for the Invoices table. In this case, a value is required for the InvoiceNumber, InvoiceDate, InvoiceTotal, TermsID, and InvoiceDueDate columns. In contrast, the InvoiceID column can be omitted because it's an identity column; the PaymentTotal and CreditTotal columns can be omitted because they have default values; and the PaymentDate column can be omitted because it allows null values.

In addition to providing values for all the required columns in a table, you should know that the INSERT statement can insert rows into only one table. That's true even if the view is based on two or more tables and all of the required columns for those tables are included in the view. In that case, you could use a separate INSERT statement to insert rows into each table through the view.

How to delete rows through a view

Figure 13-8 also shows how to delete rows through a view. To do that, you use DELETE statements like the ones shown here. To start, the first DELETE statement attempts to delete an invoice from the Invoices table through the IBM_Invoices view. However, this DELETE statement fails because the InvoiceLineItems table contains rows related to the invoice. This causes an error message like the one in this figure to be displayed. To get this DELETE statement to work, you must first delete the related line items for the invoice. This is illustrated by the last two DELETE statements in this figure.

A statement that creates an updatable view

```
CREATE VIEW IBM_Invoices
AS
SELECT InvoiceNumber, InvoiceDate, InvoiceTotal
FROM Invoices
WHERE VendorID = (SELECT VendorID FROM Vendors WHERE VendorName = 'IBM');
```

The contents of the view

	InvoiceNumber	InvoiceDate	InvoiceTotal
1	QP58872	2016-01-07 00:00:00	116.54
2	Q545443	2016-02-09 00:00:00	1083.58

An INSERT statement that fails due to columns with null values

```
INSERT INTO IBM_Invoices
    (InvoiceNumber, InvoiceDate, InvoiceTotal)
VALUES ('RA23988', '2016-05-04', 417.34);
```

The response from the system

```
Cannot insert the value NULL into column 'VendorID', table 'AP.dbo.Invoices';
column does not allow nulls. INSERT fails.
The statement has been terminated.
```

A DELETE statement that fails due to a foreign key constraint

```
DELETE FROM IBM_Invoices
WHERE InvoiceNumber = 'Q545443';
```

The response from the system

```
The DELETE statement conflicted with the REFERENCE constraint
"FK_InvoiceLineItems_Invoices". The conflict occurred in database
"AP_AllObjects", table "dbo.InvoiceLineItems", column 'InvoiceID'.
The statement has been terminated.
```

Two DELETE statements that succeed

```
DELETE FROM InvoiceLineItems
WHERE InvoiceID = (SELECT InvoiceID FROM Invoices
                   WHERE InvoiceNumber = 'Q545443');

DELETE FROM IBM_Invoices
WHERE InvoiceNumber = 'Q545443';
```

The response from the system

```
(1 row(s) affected)
```

Description

- You can use the INSERT statement to insert rows into a base table through a view. To do that, you name the view in the INSERT clause. Both the view and the INSERT statement must include all of the columns from the base table that require a value.

- If the view names more than one base table, an INSERT statement can insert data into only one of those tables.

- You can use the DELETE statement to delete rows from a base table through a view. To do that, you name the table in the DELETE clause. For this to work, the view must be based on a single table.

Figure 13-8   How to insert or delete rows through a view

How to use the catalog views

The ANSI standards specify that a SQL database must maintain an online *system catalog* that lists all of the objects in a database. Although SQL Server lets you query the system catalogs directly, I don't recommend you do that. That's because if you do, you have to code queries that are dependent on the structure of the system tables that make up the system catalog. So if the system tables change in a future release of SQL Server, you have to change your queries.

Instead of querying the system tables directly, you can use the *catalog views* provided by SQL Server. Because these views are independent of the structure of the system tables, you don't have to worry about changing the queries that refer to them if the structure changes. Figure 13-9 lists some of these views and shows you how to use them.

To display the data defined by a catalog view, you use a SELECT statement just as you would for any other view. The SELECT statement shown in this figure, for example, displays the name and schema of every table in the current database. To do that, it joins the sys.tables and sys.schemas views on the schema_id column in each view.

If you look up the sys.tables view in the SQL Server documentation, you'll notice that this table doesn't include the name column that's retrieved by the SELECT statement in this figure. Instead, this column is inherited from the sys. objects view. A view like this that contains columns that can be inherited by other views is called a *base view*, and the view that inherits the columns is called the *derived view*. Because the columns of the base view are inherited automatically, you can think of these columns as part of the derived view.

Catalog views were introduced with SQL Server 2005. With previous releases of SQL Server, you used *information schema views* to query the system catalog. Although these views are still available, we recommend you use the catalog views instead. That's because unlike the information schema views, the catalog views provide access to all of the data in the system catalogs. In addition, the catalog views are more efficient than the information schema views. If you use the information schema views, however, you should know that some of them have changed. Because of that, SQL statements you've written previously that use information schema views may no longer work. To get more information about a particular information schema view, you can look it up by name in the SQL Server documentation.

At this point, you may be wondering why you would want to use the catalog or information schema views. After all, you can get the same information using the Management Studio. The answer is that you may occasionally need to get information about the objects in a database from a script. You'll learn how to do that in the next chapter.

Some of the SQL Server catalog views

View name	Contents
sys.schemas	One row for each schema in the current database.
sys.sequences	One row for each sequence in the current database.
sys.tables	One row for each table in the current database.
sys.views	One row for each view in the current database.
sys.columns	One row for each column in each table, view, or table-valued function in the current database.
sys.key_constraints	One row for each primary or unique key in each table in the current database.
sys.foreign_keys	One row for each foreign key.
sys.foreign_key_columns	One row for each column or set of columns that make up a foreign key.
sys.objects	One row for each user-defined object in the current database, except for triggers.

A SELECT statement that retrieves the name and schema of each table

```
SELECT sys.tables.name AS TableName, sys.schemas.name AS SchemaName
FROM sys.tables INNER JOIN sys.schemas
ON sys.tables.schema_id = sys.schemas.schema_id;
```

The result set

	TableName	SchemaName
1	ContactUpdates	dbo
2	GLAccounts	dbo
3	InvoiceArchive	dbo
4	InvoiceLineIte...	dbo
5	Invoices	dbo
6	Terms	dbo
7	Vendors	dbo
8	sysdiagrams	dbo
9	VendorCopy	dbo

Description

- You can use the *catalog views* to examine the *system catalog*, which lists all of the system objects that define a database, including tables, views, columns, keys, and constraints. Catalog views were introduced with SQL Server 2005.

- Some catalog views inherit columns from other catalog views. In that case, the catalog view from which the columns are inherited is called the *base view*, and the catalog view that inherits the columns is called the *derived view*.

- For a complete listing of the catalog views, refer to SQL Server documentation.

Note

- You can also use *information schema views*, which were available with earlier releases of SQL Server, to examine the system catalog. However, we recommend you use the catalog views instead.

Figure 13-9   How to use the catalog views

How to use the View Designer

The Management Studio provides a graphical tool called the View Designer that you can use to work with views. However, many programmers prefer to use the Query Editor to manually code the SQL for views as described earlier. As a result, this topic only provides a brief description of the View Designer.

How to create or modify a view

You can use the View Designer to create or modify a view as described in figure 13-10. This figure shows a view named VendorPayment in the View Designer. This tool is similar to the Query Designer that was briefly introduced in chapter 2.

To create a new view, right-click on the Views folder and select the New View command. When you do, the View Designer prompts you to select the tables that the view will be based on. Then, it displays the tables that you select in the Diagram pane of the View Designer. When appropriate, the Diagram pane includes a link icon that shows the relationships between these tables. When you save the view for the first time, the Management Studio prompts you with a dialog box that allows you to enter a name for the view.

To edit the design of an existing view, you can expand the Views folder, right-click on the view, and select the Design command to display the view in the View Designer. If necessary, you can use the Add Table button in the View Designer toolbar to add new tables to the Diagram pane.

Once you display the tables for the view in the Diagram pane, you can use that pane to select the columns that are displayed in the Criteria pane. Then, you can use the Criteria pane to set the criteria and sort sequence for the query. In this figure, for example, the Criteria pane shows the columns that will be included in the view, and it shows that the last column, which is a calculated column and is not included in the result set, must be greater than zero.

As you work in the Diagram and Criteria panes, the View Designer generates a SQL statement and displays it in the SQL pane. When you have the statement the way you want it, you can test the view by clicking on the Execute SQL button in the View Designer toolbar. Then, the data that's returned by the view is displayed in the Results pane. In this figure, for example, the Results pane displays the results as read-only because the view that's defined by the SQL statement uses a calculated column.

How to delete a view

You can also use the Management Studio to delete a view. You do that using the same technique you use to delete any other type of database object. To start, right-click on the view and select Delete. Then, select OK to confirm the delete.

The Management Studio with a view displayed in the View Designer

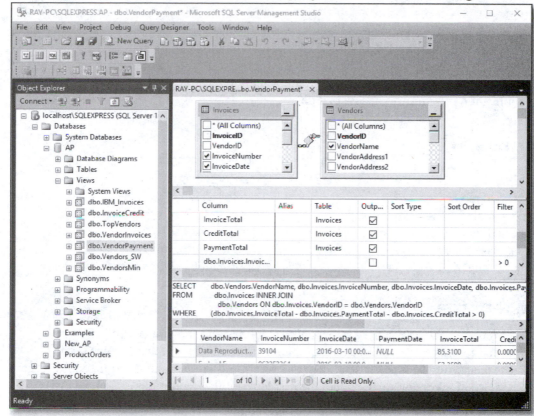

How to create or modify the design of a view

- To create a new view, right-click on the Views folder and select the New View command to display a new view in the View Designer. Then, when you click on the Save button in the toolbar, you can supply a name for the view.

- To edit the design of an existing view, expand the Views folder, right-click on the view, and select the Design command to display the view in the View Designer.

- To add tables to the Diagram pane, click on the Add Table button in the View Designer toolbar.

- To select the columns for a view, use the Diagram pane.

- To specify the selection criteria and sort order for the view, use the Criteria pane.

- To view the code that's generated for the view or to modify the generated code, use the SQL pane.

- To display the results of the view in the Results pane, click on the Execute SQL button in the View Designer toolbar.

How to delete a view

- To delete a view, expand the Views folder, right-click on the view, select the Delete command, and click OK in the resulting Delete Object dialog box.

Figure 13-10   How to use the Management Studio to work with views

Perspective

In this chapter, you learned how to create and use views. As you've seen, views provide a powerful and flexible way to predefine the data that can be retrieved from a database. By using them, you can restrict the access to a database while providing a consistent and simplified way for end users and application programs to access that data.

Terms

view	read-only view
viewed table	catalog views
base table	base view
nested view	derived view
database schema	system catalog
updatable view	information schema view

Exercises

1. Write a CREATE VIEW statement that defines a view named InvoiceBasic that returns three columns: VendorName, InvoiceNumber, and InvoiceTotal. Then, write a SELECT statement that returns all of the columns in the view, sorted by VendorName, where the first letter of the vendor name is N, O, or P.

2. Create a view named Top10PaidInvoices that returns three columns for each vendor: VendorName, LastInvoice (the most recent invoice date), and SumOfInvoices (the sum of the InvoiceTotal column). Return only the 10 vendors with the largest SumOfInvoices and include only paid invoices.

3. Create an updatable view named VendorAddress that returns the VendorID, both address columns, and the city, state, and zip code columns for each vendor. Then, write a SELECT query to examine the result set where VendorID=4. Next, write an UPDATE statement that changes the address so that the suite number (Ste 260) is stored in VendorAddress2 rather than in VendorAddress1. To verify the change, rerun your SELECT query.

4. Write a SELECT statement that selects all of the columns for the catalog view that returns information about foreign keys. How many foreign keys are defined in the AP database?

5. Using the Management Studio, modify the InvoiceBasic view created in exercise 1 to sort the result set by VendorName. What clause does the system automatically code to allow the use of an ORDER BY clause in the view?

How to code scripts

At the end of chapter 11, you saw a simple script that defines the AP database and the tables it contains. Now, this chapter teaches you how to code more complex scripts. With the skills you'll learn in this chapter, you'll be able to code scripts with functionality that's similar to the functionality provided by procedural programming languages like C#, Visual Basic, and Java.

If you have experience with another procedural programming language, you shouldn't have any trouble with the skills presented in this chapter. However, you should know that the programming power of Transact-SQL is limited when compared to other languages. That's because Transact-SQL is designed specifically to work with SQL Server databases rather than as a general-purpose programming language. For its intended use, Transact-SQL programming is powerful and flexible.

An introduction to scripts

To start, this chapter reviews and expands on the script concepts you learned in chapter 11. Then, it summarizes the Transact-SQL statements you can use within scripts. Most of these statements will be presented in detail later in this chapter.

How to work with scripts

Most of the *scripts* you've created so far in this book have consisted of a single SQL statement. However, a script can include any number of statements, and those statements can be divided into one or more *batches*. To indicate the end of a batch, you code a GO command. The script in figure 14-1, for example, consists of two batches. The first one creates a database, and the second one creates three tables in that database.

Because the new database must exist before you can add tables to it, the CREATE DATABASE statement must be coded in a separate batch that's executed before the CREATE TABLE statements. In contrast, the three CREATE TABLE statements don't have to be in separate batches. However, notice that these three statements are coded in a logical sequence within the second batch. In this case, the CommitteeAssignments table references the other two tables, so I created the other tables first. If I'd created the CommitteeAssignments table first, I couldn't have declared the foreign key constraints. In that case, I would have had to add these constraints in an ALTER TABLE statement after the other two tables were created.

Although you don't have to code the CREATE TABLE statement in a separate batch, you do have to code the five statements listed in this figure in separate batches. Each of these statements must be the first and only statement in the batch. You learned how to code the CREATE VIEW statement in the last chapter, you'll learn how to code the CREATE PROCEDURE, CREATE FUNCTION, and CREATE TRIGGER statements in the next chapter, and you'll learn how to code the CREATE SCHEMA statement in chapter 17.

Before I go on, you should realize that GO isn't a Transact-SQL statement. Instead, it's a command that's interpreted by two of the software tools that are included with SQL Server: the Management Studio and the SQLCMD utility. When one of these tools encounters a GO command, it sends the preceding statements to the server to be executed. You already know how to use the Management Studio, and you'll learn the basics of working with the SQLCMD utility later in this chapter.

A script with two batches

```
/*
Creates three tables in a database named ClubRoster.
Author:   Bryan Syverson
Created:  2008-08-12
Modified: 2016-09-26
*/

CREATE DATABASE ClubRoster;
GO

USE ClubRoster;

CREATE TABLE Members
(MemberID int NOT NULL IDENTITY PRIMARY KEY,
LastName varchar(75) NOT NULL,
FirstName varchar(50) NOT NULL,
MiddleName varchar(50) NULL);

CREATE TABLE Committees
(CommitteeID int NOT NULL IDENTITY PRIMARY KEY,
CommitteeName varchar(50) NOT NULL);

CREATE TABLE CommitteeAssignments
(MemberID int NOT NULL REFERENCES Members(MemberID),
CommitteeID int NOT NULL REFERENCES Committees(CommitteeID));
```

Statements that must be in their own batch

```
CREATE VIEW          CREATE PROCEDURE        CREATE FUNCTION
CREATE TRIGGER       CREATE SCHEMA
```

Description

- A *script* is a series of SQL statements that you can store in a file. Each script can contain one or more *batches* that are executed as a unit.

- To signal the end of a batch, you use the GO command. A GO command isn't required after the last batch in a script or for a script that contains a single batch.

- If a statement must be executed before the statements that follow can succeed, you should include a GO command after it.

- The statements within a batch are executed in the order that they appear in the batch. Because of that, you need to code statements that depend on other statements after the statements they depend on.

- If you create a database within a script, you have to execute the batch that contains the CREATE DATABASE statement before you can execute other statements that refer to the database.

- The five statements listed above (CREATE VIEW, CREATE PROCEDURE, CREATE FUNCTION, CREATE TRIGGER, and CREATE SCHEMA) can't be combined with other statements in a batch.

- If a script will be used with a production database, you should include documentation as shown above. Additional information should be included when appropriate.

Figure 14-1   How to work with scripts

The Transact-SQL statements for script processing

Figure 14-2 presents the Transact-SQL statements used to process scripts. These statements, which are sometimes referred to as *T-SQL statements*, are specific to SQL Server. You'll learn how to code many of these statements throughout this chapter.

Two statements I want to present right now are USE and PRINT. You can see both of these statements in the script presented in this figure. You use the USE statement to change the current database within a script. In this example, the USE statement makes the AP database the current database. That way, you don't have to worry about setting the current database using the drop-down list in the Management Studio. And when you create stored procedures, functions, and triggers as you'll learn in the next chapter, you have to use the USE statement.

You use the PRINT statement to return a message to the client. If the client is the Management Studio, for example, the message is displayed in the Messages tab of the Query Editor. The script in this figure includes two PRINT statements. Notice that the first statement uses concatenation to combine a literal string with the value of a variable. You'll learn how to work with variables as well as the other statements in this script in a moment.

Two statements I won't present in this chapter are GOTO and RETURN. I recommend that you don't use the GOTO statement because it can make your scripts difficult to follow. And the RETURN statement is used most often with stored procedures, so I'll present it in the next chapter.

Transact-SQL statements for controlling the flow of execution

Keyword	Description
IF...ELSE	Controls the flow of execution based on a condition.
BEGIN...END	Defines a statement block.
WHILE	Repeats statements while a specific condition is true.
BREAK	Exits the innermost WHILE loop.
CONTINUE	Returns to the beginning of a WHILE loop.
TRY...CATCH	Controls the flow of execution when an error occurs.
GOTO	Unconditionally changes the flow of execution.
RETURN	Exits unconditionally.

Other Transact-SQL statements for script processing

Keyword	Description
USE	Changes the database context to the specified database.
PRINT	Returns a message to the client.
DECLARE	Declares a local variable.
SET	Sets the value of a local variable or a session variable.
EXEC	Executes a dynamic SQL statement or stored procedure.

The syntax of the USE statement

```
USE database
```

The syntax of the PRINT statement

```
PRINT string_expression
```

A script that uses some of the statements shown above

```
USE AP;
DECLARE @TotalDue money;
SET @TotalDue = (SELECT SUM(InvoiceTotal - PaymentTotal - CreditTotal)
    FROM Invoices);
IF @TotalDue > 0
    PRINT 'Total invoices due = $' + CONVERT(varchar,@TotalDue,1);
ELSE
    PRINT 'Invoices paid in full';
```

Description

- These statements are used within SQL scripts to add functionality similar to that provided by procedural programming languages.

- These statements are part of the Transact-SQL, or *T-SQL*, language and aren't available on SQL-based systems other than SQL Server.

Figure 14-2   The Transact-SQL statements for script processing

How to work with variables and temporary tables

If you need to store values within a script, you can store them in scalar variables, table variables, or temporary tables. You'll learn how to use all three of these techniques in the topics that follow. In addition, you'll see a comparison of the different types of SQL Server objects that you can use to work with table data so you'll know when to use each type.

How to work with scalar variables

Figure 14-3 presents the DECLARE and SET statements that you use to work with *variables*. Specifically you use these statements to work with *scalar variables*, which can contain a single value. You use the DECLARE statement to create a variable and specify the type of data it can contain, and you use the SET statement to assign a value to a variable.

The variables you create using the DECLARE statement are also known as *local variables*. That's because a variable's scope is limited to a single batch. In other words, you can't refer to a variable from outside the batch. Variables are also described as local to distinguish them from *global variables*, which is an obsolete term for system functions. You'll learn about some of the system functions later in this chapter.

You can also assign a value to a variable within the select list of a SELECT statement. To do that, you use the alternate syntax shown in this figure. Although you can accomplish the same thing by using a SET statement to assign the result of a SELECT query to the variable, the alternate syntax usually results in more readable code. In addition, when you use a SELECT statement, you can assign values to two or more variables with a single statement.

The script shown in this figure uses five variables to calculate the percent difference between the minimum and maximum invoices for a particular vendor. This script starts by declaring all of these variables. Then, it assigns values to two of the variables using SET statements. Notice that the second SET statement assigns the result of a SELECT statement to the variable, and the value of the first variable is used in the WHERE clause of that SELECT statement. The SELECT statement that follows this SET statement uses the alternate syntax to assign values to two more variables. Then, the next SET statement assigns the result of an arithmetic expression to the final variable. Finally, PRINT statements are used to display the values of four of the variables.

Although you can use a variable in any expression, you can't use it in place of a keyword or an object name. For example, this use is invalid:

```
DECLARE @TableNameVar varchar(128);
SET @TableNameVar = 'Invoices';
SELECT * FROM @TableNameVar;
```

Later in this chapter, however, you'll learn how to execute a SQL statement like this one using dynamic SQL.

The syntax of the DECLARE statement for scalar variables

```
DECLARE @variable_name_1 data_type [, @variable_name_2 data_type]...
```

The syntax of the SET statement for a scalar variable

```
SET @variable_name = expression
```

An alternate syntax for setting a variable's value in a select list

```
SELECT @variable_name_1 = column_specification_1
    [, @variable_name_2 = column_specification_2]...
```

A SQL script that uses variables

```
USE AP;
DECLARE @MaxInvoice money, @MinInvoice money;
DECLARE @PercentDifference decimal(8,2);
DECLARE @InvoiceCount int, @VendorIDVar int;

SET @VendorIDVar = 95;
SET @MaxInvoice = (SELECT MAX(InvoiceTotal) FROM Invoices
    WHERE VendorID = @VendorIDVar);
SELECT @MinInvoice = MIN(InvoiceTotal), @InvoiceCount = COUNT(*)
FROM Invoices
WHERE VendorID = @VendorIDVar;
SET @PercentDifference = (@MaxInvoice - @MinInvoice) / @MinInvoice * 100;

PRINT 'Maximum invoice is $' + CONVERT(varchar,@MaxInvoice,1) + '.';
PRINT 'Minimum invoice is $' + CONVERT(varchar,@MinInvoice,1) + '.';
PRINT 'Maximum is ' + CONVERT(varchar,@PercentDifference) +
    '% more than minimum.';
PRINT 'Number of invoices: ' + CONVERT(varchar,@InvoiceCount) + '.';
```

The response from the system

```
Maximum invoice is $46.21.
Minimum invoice is $16.33.
Maximum is 182.97% more than minimum.
Number of invoices: 6.
```

Description

- A *variable* is used to store data. To create a variable, you use the DECLARE statement. The initial value of a variable is always null.

- A *scalar variable* is defined with a standard data type and contains a single value. You can also create table variables to store an entire result set.

- The name of a variable must always start with an at sign (@). Whenever possible, you should use long, descriptive names for variables.

- The scope of a variable is the batch in which it's defined, which means that it can't be referred to from outside that batch. Because of that, variables are often called *local variables*.

- To assign a value to a variable, you can use the SET statement. Alternatively, you can use the SELECT statement to assign a value to one or more variables.

- You can use a variable in any expression, but you can't use it in place of an object name or a keyword.

Figure 14-3 How to work with scalar variables

How to work with table variables

Figure 14-4 presents the syntax of the DECLARE statement you use to create table variables. A *table variable* is a variable that can store the contents of an entire table. To create this type of variable, you specify the table data type in the DECLARE statement rather than one of the standard SQL data types. Then, you define the columns and constraints for the table using the same syntax that you use for the CREATE TABLE statement.

The script shown in this figure illustrates how you might use a table variable. Here, a DECLARE statement is used to create a table variable named @BigVendors that contains two columns: VendorID and VendorName. Then, an INSERT statement is used to insert all of the rows from the Vendors table for vendors that have invoices totaling over $5000 into this table variable. Finally, a SELECT statement is used to retrieve the contents of the table variable.

Notice that the table variable in this example is used in place of a table name in the INSERT and SELECT statements. You can also use a table variable in place of a table name in an UPDATE or DELETE statement. The only place you can't use a table variable instead of a table name is in the INTO clause of a SELECT INTO statement.

The syntax of the DECLARE statement for a table variable

```
DECLARE @table_name TABLE
(column_name_1 data_type [column_attributes]
[, column_name_2 data_type [column_attributes]]...
[, table_attributes])
```

A SQL script that uses a table variable

```
USE AP;

DECLARE @BigVendors table
(VendorID int,
VendorName varchar(50));

INSERT @BigVendors
SELECT VendorID, VendorName
FROM Vendors
WHERE VendorID IN
    (SELECT VendorID FROM Invoices WHERE InvoiceTotal > 5000);

SELECT * FROM @BigVendors;
```

The result set

	VendorID	VendorName
1	72	Data Reproductions Corp
2	99	Bertelsmann Industry Svcs. Inc
3	104	Digital Dreamworks
4	110	Malloy Lithographing Inc

Description

- A *table variable* can store an entire result set rather than a single value. To create a table variable, use a DECLARE statement with the table data type.
- You use the same syntax for defining the columns of a table variable as you do for defining a new table with the CREATE TABLE statement. See figure 11-4 in chapter 11 for details.
- Like a scalar variable, a table variable has local scope, so it's available only within the batch where it's declared.
- You can use a table variable like a standard table within SELECT, INSERT, UPDATE, and DELETE statements. The exception is that you can't use it within the INTO clause of a SELECT INTO statement.

Figure 14-4   How to work with table variables

How to work with temporary tables

In addition to table variables, you can use *temporary tables* to store table data within a script. Temporary tables are useful for storing table data within a complex script. In addition, they provide a way for you to test queries against temporary data rather than permanent data.

Unlike a table variable, a temporary table exists for the duration of the database session in which it's created. If you create a temporary table in the Management Studio's Query Editor, for example, it exists as long as the Query Editor is open. As a result, you can refer to the table from more than one script.

Figure 14-5 presents two scripts that use temporary tables. The first script creates a temporary table named #TopVendors using a SELECT INTO query. This temporary table contains the VendorID and average invoice total for the vendor with the greatest average. Then, the second SELECT statement joins the temporary table with the Invoices table to get the date of the most recent invoice for that vendor. Note, however, that you could have created the same result set using a derived table like this:

```
WITH TopVendors AS
(
    SELECT TOP 1 VendorID, AVG(InvoiceTotal) AS AvgInvoice
    FROM Invoices
    GROUP BY VendorID
    ORDER BY AvgInvoice DESC
)
SELECT Invoices.VendorID, MAX(InvoiceDate) AS LatestInv
FROM Invoices JOIN TopVendors
    ON Invoices.VendorID = TopVendors.VendorID
GROUP BY Invoices.VendorID;
```

Because derived tables are more efficient to use than temporary tables, you should use them whenever possible.

The second script in this figure shows another use of a temporary table. This script creates a temporary table that contains two columns: an identity column and a character column with a nine-digit default value that's generated using the RAND function. Then, the script inserts two rows into this table using the default values. Finally, the script uses a SELECT statement to retrieve the contents of the table. A script like this can be useful during testing.

In these examples, the name of a temporary table begins with a number sign (#). If the name begins with a single number sign, the table is defined as a *local temporary table*, which means that it's visible only to the database session in which it's created. However, you can also create temporary tables that are visible to all open database sessions, called *global temporary tables*. To create a global temporary table, code two number signs at the beginning of the table name.

When a database session ends, any temporary tables created during that session are deleted. If you want to delete a temporary table before the session ends, however, you can do that by issuing a DROP TABLE statement.

A script that uses a local temporary table instead of a derived table

```
SELECT TOP 1 VendorID, AVG(InvoiceTotal) AS AvgInvoice
INTO #TopVendors
FROM Invoices
GROUP BY VendorID
ORDER BY AvgInvoice DESC;

SELECT Invoices.VendorID, MAX(InvoiceDate) AS LatestInv
FROM Invoices JOIN #TopVendors
    ON Invoices.VendorID = #TopVendors.VendorID
GROUP BY Invoices.VendorID;
```

The result set

	VendorID	LatestInv
1	110	2016-03-31 00:00:00

A script that creates a global temporary table of random numbers

```
CREATE TABLE ##RandomSSNs
(
  SSN_ID int       IDENTITY,
  SSN     char(9) DEFAULT
          LEFT(CAST(CAST(CEILING(RAND()*10000000000)AS bigint)AS varchar),9)
);

INSERT ##RandomSSNs VALUES (DEFAULT);
INSERT ##RandomSSNs VALUES (DEFAULT);

SELECT * FROM ##RandomSSNs;
```

The result set

	SSN_ID	SSN
1	1	419741221
2	2	327280021

Description

- A *temporary table* exists only during the current database session. In the Management Studio, that means that the table is available until you close the window where you created the table.

- Temporary tables are stored in the system database named tempdb.

- If you need to drop a temporary table before the end of the current session, you can do that using the DROP TABLE statement.

- Temporary tables are useful for testing queries or for storing data temporarily in a complex script.

- A *local temporary table* is visible only within the current session, but a *global temporary table* is visible to all sessions. To identify a local temporary table, you prefix the name with a number sign (#). To identify a global temporary table, you prefix the name with two number signs (##). Temporary table names are limited to 116 characters.

- Because derived tables result in faster performance than temporary tables, you should use derived tables whenever possible. See figure 14-6 for details.

Figure 14-5   How to work with temporary tables

A comparison of the five types of Transact-SQL table objects

Now that you've learned about table variables and temporary tables, you might want to consider when you'd use them within a script and when you'd create a new standard table or view or simply use a derived table instead. Figure 14-6 presents a comparison of these five types of table objects. Note that although a view isn't technically a table, I've included it in this figure because it can be used in place of a table.

One of the biggest differences between these objects is their *scope*, which determines where it can be used in a script. Because standard tables and views are stored permanently within a database, they have the broadest scope and can be used anywhere, including in other scripts on the current connection or other scripts on other connections. In contrast, a derived table exists only while the query that creates it is executing. Because of that, a derived table can't be referred to from outside the query. As you've just learned, temporary tables and table variables fall somewhere in between.

Another difference between the five table types is where they're stored. Like standard tables, temporary tables are stored on disk. In contrast, table variables and derived tables are stored in memory if they're relatively small. Because of that, table variables and derived tables usually take less time to create and access than standard or temporary tables.

Although a view is also stored on disk, it can be faster to use than any of the other table objects. That's because it's simply a precompiled query, so it takes less time to create and access than an actual table. However, with the other table objects, you can insert, update, or delete data without affecting any of the base tables in your database, which isn't true of a view. For this reason, you can't use a view in the same way as the other table objects. But if you find that you're creating a table object that doesn't need to be modified within your script, then you should be defining it as a view instead.

In most scripts, table variables and temporary tables can be used interchangeably. Since a script that uses a table variable will outperform the same script with a temporary table, you should use table variables whenever possible. However, table variables are dropped when the batch finishes execution. So if you need to use the table in other batches, you'll need to use a temporary table instead.

The five types of Transact-SQL table objects

Type	Scope
Standard table	Available within the system until explicitly deleted.
Temporary table	Available within the system while the current database session is open.
Table variable	Available within a script while the current batch is executing.
Derived table	Available within a statement while the current statement is executing.
View	Available within the system until explicitly deleted.

Description

- Within a Transact-SQL script, you often need to work with table objects other than the base tables in your database.

- The *scope* of a table object determines what code has access to that table.

- Standard tables and views are stored permanently on disk until they are explicitly deleted, so they have the broadest scope and are therefore always available for use.

- Derived tables and table variables are generally stored in memory, so they can provide the best performance. In contrast, standard tables and temporary tables are always stored on disk and therefore provide slower performance.

- To improve the performance of your scripts, use a derived table instead of creating a table variable. However, if you need to use the table in other batches, create a temporary table. Finally, if the data needs to be available to other connections to the database, create a standard table or, if possible, a view.

- Although a view isn't a table, it can be used like one. Views provide fast performance since they're predefined, and high availability since they're permanent objects. For these reasons, you should try to use a view rather than create a table whenever that's possible. However, if you need to insert, delete, or update the data in the table object without affecting the base tables of your database, then you can't use a view.

- A common table expression (CTE) is a type of derived table. For more information about CTEs, see chapter 6.

Figure 14-6   A comparison of the five types of Transact-SQL tables

How to control the execution of a script

The ability to control the execution of a program is an essential feature of any procedural programming language. T-SQL provides three basic control structures that you can use within scripts. You can use the first one to perform conditional processing, you can use the second one to perform repetitive processing, and you can use the third one to handle errors. You'll learn how to use the statements that implement these structures in the topics that follow.

How to perform conditional processing

To execute a statement or a block of statements based on a condition, you use the IF…ELSE statement. This statement is presented in figure 14-7. When an IF…ELSE statement is executed, SQL Server evaluates the conditional expression after the IF keyword. If this condition is true, the statement or block of statements after the IF keyword is executed. Otherwise, the statement or block of statements after the ELSE keyword is executed if this keyword is included.

The first script in this figure uses a simple IF statement to test the value of a variable that's assigned in a SELECT statement. This variable contains the oldest invoice due date in the Invoices table. If this value is less than the current date, the PRINT statement that follows the IF keyword is executed. Otherwise, no action is taken.

In the second script, the logic of the first script has been enhanced. Here, a block of statements is executed if the oldest due date is less than the current date. Notice that this block of statements begins with the BEGIN keyword and ends with the END keyword. In addition, an ELSE clause has been added. Then, if the oldest due date is greater than or equal to the current date, a PRINT statement is executed to indicate that none of the invoices are overdue.

Notice the comment that follows the ELSE keyword. This comment describes the expression that would result in this portion of code being executed. Although it isn't required, this programming practice makes it easier to find and debug logical errors, especially if you're *nesting* IF...ELSE statements within other IF...ELSE statements.

The syntax of the IF...ELSE statement

```
IF Boolean_expression
    {statement|BEGIN...END}
[ELSE
    {statement|BEGIN...END}]
```

A script that tests for outstanding invoices with an IF statement

```
USE AP;
DECLARE @EarliestInvoiceDue smalldatetime;
SELECT @EarliestInvoiceDue = MIN(InvoiceDueDate) FROM Invoices
    WHERE InvoiceTotal - PaymentTotal - CreditTotal > 0;
IF @EarliestInvoiceDue < GETDATE()
    PRINT 'Outstanding invoices overdue!';
```

The response from the system

```
Outstanding invoices overdue!
```

An enhanced version of the same script that uses an IF...ELSE statement

```
USE AP;
DECLARE @MinInvoiceDue money, @MaxInvoiceDue money;
DECLARE @EarliestInvoiceDue smalldatetime, @LatestInvoiceDue smalldatetime;
SELECT @MinInvoiceDue = MIN(InvoiceTotal - PaymentTotal - CreditTotal),
    @MaxInvoiceDue = MAX(InvoiceTotal - PaymentTotal - CreditTotal),
    @EarliestInvoiceDue = MIN(InvoiceDueDate),
    @LatestInvoiceDue = MAX(InvoiceDueDate)
FROM Invoices
WHERE InvoiceTotal - PaymentTotal - CreditTotal > 0;
IF @EarliestInvoiceDue < GETDATE()
    BEGIN
        PRINT 'Outstanding invoices overdue!';
        PRINT 'Dated ' + CONVERT(varchar,@EarliestInvoiceDue,1) +
            ' through ' + CONVERT(varchar,@LatestInvoiceDue,1) + '.';
        PRINT 'Amounting from $' + CONVERT(varchar,@MinInvoiceDue,1) +
            ' to $' + CONVERT(varchar,@MaxInvoiceDue,1) + '.';
    END;
ELSE --@EarliestInvoiceDue >= GETDATE()
    PRINT 'No overdue invoices.';
```

The response from the system

```
Outstanding invoices overdue!
Dated 04/09/16 through 04/30/16.
Amounting from $30.75 to $19,351.18.
```

Description

- You use the IF...ELSE statement to test a conditional expression. If that expression is true, the statements that follow the IF keyword are executed. Otherwise, the statements that follow the ELSE keyword are executed if that keyword is included.

- If you need to execute two or more SQL statements within an IF or ELSE clause, enclose them within a BEGIN...END block.

- You can *nest* IF...ELSE statements within other IF...ELSE statements. Although SQL Server doesn't limit the number of nested levels, you should avoid nesting so deeply that your script becomes difficult to read.

Figure 14-7   How to perform conditional processing

How to test for the existence of a database object

Frequently, you'll need to write scripts that create and work with database objects. If you try to create an object that already exists, SQL Server will return an error. Similarly, SQL Server will return an error if you try to work with an object that doesn't exist. To avoid these types of errors, you should check for the existence of an object before you create or work with it.

If you're working with SQL Server 2016 or later, you can add the IF EXISTS clause to a DROP statement to check whether the object exists before you drop it. In figure 14-8, for instance, the first example adds this clause to a DROP statement that drops a database. As a result, if this database exists, it's dropped. If not, the script continues without returning an error. Although this example shows how to work with a database, the IF EXISTS clause also works with statements that drop other database objects such as tables, views, stored procedures, user-defined functions, and triggers.

This example begins with a USE statement to change the current database to something other than the database you're testing. That's because a database can't be deleted if it's currently in use.

If you're working with an older version of SQL Server, or if you want to perform another task besides dropping an object, you can use the OBJECT_ID function to check for the existence of a table, view, stored procedure, user-defined function, or trigger. Or, you use the DB_ID function to check for the existence of a database. If the specified object exists, these functions return the unique identification number assigned to that object by SQL Server. Otherwise, they return a null value.

You can use these functions within an IF...ELSE statement to test for a null return value. For instance, the second example uses the DB_ID function to test for the existence of a database. If the database already exists, this example executes a DROP DATABASE statement to delete it.

The third example tests for the existence of a table name InvoiceCopy. Then, if the table exists, the example executes a DROP TABLE statement to delete it. However, when you use the OBJECT_ID function, you may not know what type of object you're dealing with. For example, InvoiceCopy could also be the name of a view or a stored procedure. In that case, the DROP TABLE statement would cause an error.

To avoid this situation, you can use the technique shown in the fourth example. Instead of using a function, this example uses information in the catalog view named tables to determine if a table named InvoiceCopy exists. If it does, the table is deleted. Otherwise, no action is taken. You can use similar code to check for the existence of a view using the sys.views catalog view.

The last example tests for the existence of a temporary table. Here, the table name is qualified with the name of the database that contains temporary tables, tempdb. You can omit the schema qualification, though, since this is a system database.

The syntax for the IF EXISTS clause (SQL Server 2016 and later)

```
DROP OBJECT_TYPE IF EXISTS object_name;
```

An example that uses the IF EXISTS clause

```
USE master;
DROP DATABASE IF EXISTS TestDB;
```

The syntax of the OBJECT_ID function

```
OBJECT_ID('object')
```

The syntax of the DB_ID function

```
DB_ID('database')
```

Examples that use the OBJECT_ID and DB_ID functions

Code that tests whether a database exists before it deletes it

```
USE master;
IF DB_ID('TestDB') IS NOT NULL
    DROP DATABASE TestDB;

CREATE DATABASE TestDB;
```

Code that tests for the existence of a table

```
IF OBJECT_ID('InvoiceCopy') IS NOT NULL
    DROP TABLE InvoiceCopy;
```

Another way to test for the existence of a table

```
IF EXISTS (SELECT * FROM sys.tables
            WHERE name = 'InvoiceCopy')
    DROP TABLE InvoiceCopy;
```

Code that tests for the existence of a temporary table

```
IF OBJECT_ID('tempdb..#AllUserTables') IS NOT NULL
    DROP TABLE #AllUserTables;
```

Description

- With SQL Server 2016 and later, you can add the IF EXISTS clause to a DROP statement to check whether an object exists before you drop it.

- With earlier versions of SQL Server, you can use the OBJECT_ID and DB_ID functions within IF statements to check whether an object exists.

- You can use the OBJECT_ID function to check for the existence of a table, view, stored procedure, user-defined function, or trigger. You use the DB_ID function to check for the existence of a database. Both functions return a null value if the object doesn't exist. Otherwise, they return the object's identification number.

- To test for the existence of a temporary table, you must qualify the table name with the database that contains it: tempdb. Since this is a system database, though, you can omit the schema name as shown above.

Figure 14-8   How to test for the existence of a database object

How to perform repetitive processing

In some cases, you'll need to repeat a statement or a block of statements while a condition is true. To do that, you use the WHILE statement that's presented in figure 14-9. This coding technique is referred to as a *loop*.

The script in this figure illustrates how the WHILE statement works. Here, a WHILE loop is used to adjust the credit amount of each invoice in the Invoices table that has a balance due until the total balance due is less than $20,000. Although this example is unrealistic, it will help you understand how the WHILE statement works. A more realistic example would be to use a WHILE statement to process cursors, which you'll learn about in the next figure.

This script starts by creating a copy of the Invoices table named InvoiceCopy that contains just the invoices that have a balance due. Since the WHILE statement will change the data in the table, this prevents corruption of the data in the source table. Then, the expression in the WHILE statement uses a SELECT statement to retrieve the sum of the invoice balances in this table. If the sum is greater than or equal to 20,000, the block of statements that follows is executed. Otherwise, the loop ends.

The UPDATE statement within the WHILE loop adds five cents to the CreditTotal column of each invoice that has a balance due. (Although the table initially contains only invoices that have a balance due, that may change as credits are applied to the invoices within the loop.) Then, an IF statement tests the maximum credit amount in the table to see if it's more than 3000. If it is, a BREAK statement is used to terminate the loop. Because this statement can make your scripts difficult to read and debug, I recommend you use it only when necessary. In this case, it's used only for illustrative purposes.

If the maximum credit total is less than or equal to 3000, the CONTINUE statement is executed. This statement causes control to return to the beginning of the loop. Then, the condition for the loop is tested again, and if it's true, the statements within the loop are processed again.

Note that because the CONTINUE statement is the last statement in the loop, it's not required. That's because control will automatically return to the beginning of the loop after the last statement in the loop is executed. For example, this code would produce the same result:

```
BEGIN
    ...
    IF (SELECT MAX(CreditTotal) FROM #InvoiceCopy) > 3000
        BREAK;
END;
```

Sometimes, though, the CONTINUE statement can clarify the logic of an IF statement, as it does in the example in this figure. In addition, since this statement returns control to the beginning of the loop, it can be used in an IF clause to bypass the remaining statements in the loop. However, like the BREAK statement, this makes your code confusing to read, so I recommend you code your IF statements in such a way that you avoid using the CONTINUE statement whenever possible.

The syntax of the WHILE statement

```
WHILE expression
    {statement|BEGIN...END}
    [BREAK]
    [CONTINUE]
```

A script that tests and adjusts credit amounts with a WHILE loop

```
USE AP;
IF OBJECT_ID('tempdb..#InvoiceCopy') IS NOT NULL
    DROP TABLE #InvoiceCopy;

SELECT * INTO #InvoiceCopy FROM Invoices
WHERE InvoiceTotal - CreditTotal - PaymentTotal > 0;

WHILE (SELECT SUM(InvoiceTotal - CreditTotal - PaymentTotal)
        FROM #InvoiceCopy) >= 20000
    BEGIN
        UPDATE #InvoiceCopy
        SET CreditTotal = CreditTotal + .05
        WHERE InvoiceTotal - CreditTotal - PaymentTotal > 0;

        IF (SELECT MAX(CreditTotal) FROM #InvoiceCopy) > 3000
            BREAK;
        ELSE --(SELECT MAX(CreditTotal) FROM #InvoiceCopy) <= 3000
            CONTINUE;
    END;

SELECT InvoiceDate, InvoiceTotal, CreditTotal
FROM #InvoiceCopy;
```

The result set

	InvoiceDate	InvoiceTotal	CreditTotal
1	2016-03-10 00:00:00	85.31	0.00
2	2016-03-18 00:00:00	52.25	0.00
3	2016-03-21 00:00:00	579.42	0.00
4	2016-03-21 00:00:00	59.97	0.00

Description

- To execute a SQL statement repeatedly, you use the WHILE statement. This statement is executed as long as the conditional expression in the WHILE clause is true.

- If you need to execute two or more SQL statements within a WHILE *loop*, enclose the statements within BEGIN and END keywords.

- To exit from a WHILE loop immediately without testing the expression, use the BREAK statement. To return to the beginning of a WHILE loop without executing any additional statements in the loop, use the CONTINUE statement.

Warning

- This script takes a few seconds to execute.

Figure 14-9   How to perform repetitive processing

How to use a cursor

By default, SQL statements work with an entire result set rather than individual rows. However, you may sometimes need to work with the data in a result set one row at a time. To do that, you can use a *cursor* as described in figure 14-10.

In this figure, the script begins by declaring three variables. Then, it assigns a value of 0 to the third variable, the @UpdateCount variable.

After declaring the variables, this code declares a variable for the CURSOR named Invoices_Cursor. Within this declaration, this code uses a SELECT statement to define the result set for this cursor. This result set contains two columns from the Invoices table and all of the rows that have a balance due.

After declaring the cursor, this code uses the OPEN statement to open the cursor. Then, it uses a FETCH statement to get the column values from the first row and store them in the variables declared earlier in the script.

After getting the values from the first row, this script uses a WHILE loop to loop through each row in the cursor. To do that, this WHILE loop checks the value of the @@FETCH_STATUS system function at the top of the loop. If this function returns a value that is not equal to -1, the loop continues. Otherwise, the end of the result set has been reached, so the loop exits. This loop works correctly because a second FETCH statement is coded at the end of the loop.

Within the loop, an IF statement checks whether the value of the InvoiceTotal column for the current row is greater than 1000. If it is, an UPDATE statement adds 10% of the InvoiceTotal column to the CreditTotal column for the row, and a SET statement increments the count of the number of rows that have been updated.

After the WHILE loop, this code closes and deallocates the cursor. Then, the first PRINT statement prints a blank line, and the second PRINT statements prints the number of rows that have been updated.

Before you use a cursor to work with individual rows in a result set, you should consider other solutions. That's because standard database access is faster and uses fewer server resources than cursor-based access. For example, you can accomplish the same update as the stored procedure in this figure with this UPDATE statement:

```
UPDATE Invoices
SET CreditTotal = CreditTotal + (InvoiceTotal * .1)
WHERE InvoiceTotal - PaymentTotal - CreditTotal > 0
AND InvoiceTotal > 1000
```

However, if you encounter a situation where it makes sense to use a cursor, the skills presented in this figure should help you do that.

The syntax

Declare a cursor

```
DECLARE cursor_name CURSOR FOR select_statement;
```

Open the cursor

```
OPEN cursor_name;
```

Get column values from the row and store them in a series of variables

```
FETCH NEXT FROM cursor_name INTO @variable1[, @variable2][, @variable3]...;
```

Close and deallocate the cursor

```
CLOSE cursor_name;

DEALLOCATE cursor_name;
```

A script that uses a cursor

```
USE AP;

DECLARE @InvoiceIDVar int, @InvoiceTotalVar money, @UpdateCount int;
SET @UpdateCount = 0;

DECLARE Invoices_Cursor CURSOR
FOR
    SELECT InvoiceID, InvoiceTotal  FROM Invoices
    WHERE InvoiceTotal - PaymentTotal - CreditTotal > 0;

OPEN Invoices_Cursor;

FETCH NEXT FROM Invoices_Cursor INTO @InvoiceIDVar, @InvoiceTotalVar;
WHILE @@FETCH_STATUS <> -1
    BEGIN
        IF @InvoiceTotalVar > 1000
        BEGIN
            UPDATE Invoices
            SET CreditTotal = CreditTotal + (InvoiceTotal * .1)
            WHERE InvoiceID = @InvoiceIDVar;

            SET @UpdateCount = @UpdateCount + 1;
        END;
        FETCH NEXT FROM Invoices_Cursor INTO @InvoiceIDVar, @InvoiceTotalVar;
    END;

CLOSE Invoices_Cursor;
DEALLOCATE Invoices_Cursor;

PRINT '';
PRINT CONVERT(varchar, @UpdateCount) + ' row(s) updated.';
```

The response from the system when the script is run

```
2 row(s) updated.
```

Description

- The @@FETCH_STATUS system function returns 0 if the row was fetched successfully or -1 if the row can't be fetched because the end of the result set has been reached.

Figure 14-10   How to use a cursor

How to handle errors

SQL Server 2005 introduced a TRY...CATCH statement that makes it much easier to handle errors than it was in previous versions of SQL Server. Handling errors is often referred to as *error handling* or *exception handling*, and the TRY...CATCH statement works similarly to the exception handling statements that are available from the .NET languages such as C# and Visual Basic. Figure 14-11 shows how you can use the TRY...CATCH statement to handle errors.

To start, you code the TRY block around any statements that might cause an error to be raised. A TRY block begins with the BEGIN TRY keywords and ends with the END TRY keywords. In this figure, for example, you can see that a TRY block is coded around an INSERT statement and a PRINT statement.

Immediately following the TRY block, you must code a single CATCH block. A CATCH block begins with the BEGIN CATCH keywords and ends with the END CATCH keywords. Within the CATCH block, you can include any statements that handle the error that might be raised in the TRY block. In this figure, for example, the first statement in the CATCH block uses a PRINT statement to display a simple message that indicates that the INSERT statement in the TRY block did not execute successfully. Then, the second PRINT statement uses two functions that are designed to work within a CATCH block to provide more detailed information about the error. All four of the functions you can use within a CATCH block are presented in this figure. Although it's common to use a CATCH block to display information to the user, you can also use a CATCH block to perform other error handling tasks such as writing information about the error to a log table or rolling back a transaction.

In this figure, the INSERT statement that's coded within the TRY block provides a vendor ID that doesn't exist. As a result, when SQL Server attempts to execute this statement, a foreign key constraint will be violated and an error will be raised. Then, program execution will skip over the PRINT statement that follows the INSERT statement and jump into the CATCH block. This causes the message that's shown in this figure to be displayed. However, if the INSERT statement had executed successfully, program execution would have continued by executing the PRINT statement immediately following the INSERT statement and skipping the CATCH block. In that case, this code would have displayed a message indicating that the INSERT statement executed successfully.

When coding TRY...CATCH statements, you may find that some types of errors aren't handled. In particular, errors with a low severity are considered warnings and aren't handled. Conversely, errors with a high severity often cause the database connection to be closed, which prevents them from being handled.

Another thing to keep in mind when coding TRY...CATCH statements is that they must be coded within a single batch, stored procedure, or trigger. In other words, you can't code a TRY block that spans multiple batches within a script. However, you can nest one TRY...CATCH statement within another. For example, if a CATCH block contains complex code that inserts error data into a log table, you may want to code a TRY...CATCH statement within that CATCH block to catch any errors that might occur there.

The syntax of the TRY...CATCH statement

```
BEGIN TRY
    {sql_statement|statement_block}
END TRY
BEGIN CATCH
    {sql_statement|statement_block}
END CATCH
```

Functions you can use within a CATCH block

Function	Description
`ERROR_NUMBER()`	Returns the error number.
`ERROR_MESSAGE()`	Returns the error message.
`ERROR_SEVERITY()`	Returns the severity of the error.
`ERROR_STATE()`	Returns the state of the error.

A script that uses a TRY...CATCH statement

```
BEGIN TRY
    INSERT Invoices
    VALUES (799, 'ZXK-799', '2016-05-07', 299.95, 0, 0,
            1, '2016-06-06', NULL);
    PRINT 'SUCCESS: Record was inserted.';
END TRY
BEGIN CATCH
    PRINT 'FAILURE: Record was not inserted.';
    PRINT 'Error ' + CONVERT(varchar, ERROR_NUMBER(), 1)
        + ': ' + ERROR_MESSAGE();
END CATCH;
```

The message that's displayed

```
FAILURE: Record was not inserted.
Error 547: The INSERT statement conflicted with the FOREIGN KEY constraint
"FK_Invoices_Vendors". The conflict occurred in database "AP", table
"dbo.Vendors", column 'VendorID'.
```

Description

- SQL Server 2005 introduced a TRY...CATCH statement that you can use to provide *error handling* (also known as *exception handling*). This works similarly to exception handling statements provided by C# and Visual Basic.

- A TRY block must be followed immediately by a single CATCH block.

- When an error occurs in a statement within a TRY block, control is passed to the CATCH block where the error can be processed. If no error occurs inside the TRY block, the CATCH block is skipped.

- Errors that have a severity of 10 or lower are considered warnings and are not handled by TRY...CATCH blocks. Errors that have a severity of 20 or higher and cause the database connection to be closed are not handled by TRY...CATCH blocks.

- Within a CATCH block, you can use the functions shown in this figure to return data about the error that caused the CATCH block to be executed.

Figure 14-11   How to handle errors

How to use surround-with snippets

In chapter 11, you learned how to use snippets to help you code statements for creating database objects. In addition to these snippets, you can use *surround-with snippets* to enclose a block of statements in a BEGIN...END, IF, or WHILE statement. Figure 14-12 shows how surround-with snippets work.

The first screen in this figure shows part of the code from the script in figure 14-9. If you look back at that figure, you'll see that the UPDATE and IF... ELSE statements were executed within a WHILE loop. In this figure, I used a surround-with snippet to add the WHILE statement. To do that, I selected the statements I wanted to include in the loop and then selected the snippet for the WHILE statement as described in this figure.

When you insert a snippet for an IF or WHILE statement, a BEGIN...END statement is added automatically. That's true regardless of the number of statements you selected. That makes it easy to add statements to the block later on.

After you insert a snippet for an IF or WHILE statement, you have to enter a condition for the statement. To make that easy to do, the placeholder for the condition is highlighted. Then, you can just replace the placeholder with the appropriate condition.

The list of surround-with snippets

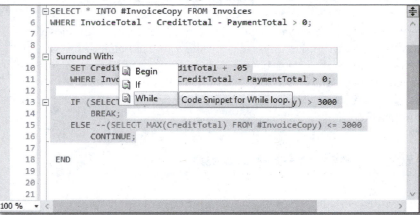

The code after the snippet is inserted

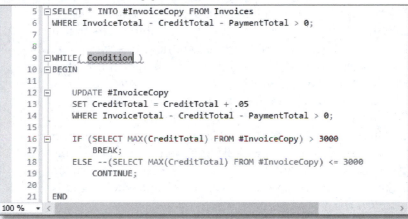

Description

- *Surround-with snippets* make it easy to enclose a block of statements in a BEGIN... END, IF, or WHILE statement.

- To insert a surround-with snippet, select the statements you want to enclose. Then, right-click on the statements, select the Surround With command from the resulting menu, and select the snippet you want to insert from the list that's displayed.

- To select a snippet from the list, double-click on it. Alternatively, you can use the Up and Down arrow keys to select the snippet and then press the Tab or Enter key.

- If you insert a snippet for an IF or WHILE statement, you will need to complete the statement by replacing the highlighted condition. You can also enter an ELSE clause for an IF statement.

- When you insert a snippet for an IF or WHILE statement, a BEGIN...END statement is added automatically.

Figure 14-12 How to use surround-with snippets

Advanced scripting techniques

The remaining topics of this chapter present some additional techniques you can use in the scripts you write. Here, you'll learn how to use some of the system functions that come with SQL Server, change some of the settings for the current session, use dynamic SQL, and use a command line utility to execute SQL statements and scripts. In addition, you'll see a complete script that uses many of the techniques presented in this chapter.

How to use the system functions

Figure 14-13 presents some of the Transact-SQL *system functions*. These functions are particularly helpful for writing Transact-SQL scripts. For example, the script shown in this figure illustrates how you might use the @@IDENTITY and @@ROWCOUNT functions. This script starts by inserting a row into the Vendors table. Because the VendorID column in that table is defined as an identity column, SQL Server generates the value of this column automatically. Then, the script uses the @@IDENTITY function to retrieve this value so it can insert an invoice for the new vendor. Before it does that, though, it uses the @@ROWCOUNT function to determine if the vendor was inserted successfully.

Notice that this script stores the values returned by the @@IDENTITY and @@ROWCOUNT functions in variables named @MyIdentity and @MyRowCount. Alternatively, the script could have used the system functions directly in the IF and VALUES clauses. However, the values returned by these functions can change each time a SQL statement is executed on the system, so it usually makes sense to store these values in variables immediately after you execute a SQL statement.

You can use the @@ERROR function to get the error number returned by the most recent SQL statement. If you use the TRY…CATCH statement as shown in the previous figure, you won't need to use this function. However, you may see it used in scripts that were written with earlier versions of SQL Server.

The other functions I want to point out right now are the @@SERVERNAME, HOST_NAME, and SYSTEM_USER functions. The values returned by these functions can vary depending on who enters them and where they're entered. Because of that, they're often used to identify who entered or modified a row. For example, you could define a table with a column that defaults to the SYSTEM_USER function like this:

```
CREATE TABLE #SysFunctionEx
(EntryDBUser varchar(128) DEFAULT SYSTEM_USER);
```

This would cause the user name to be inserted automatically when each new row was added to the table.

At this point, you may be wondering why the names of some of the system functions start with two at signs (@@) and some don't. Those with @@ in their names have been a part of the T-SQL dialect for a long time and used to be called *global variables*. As of version 7.0, however, that term is no longer used. The other system functions have been added to T-SQL more recently.

Some of the Transact-SQL system functions

Function name	Description
`@@IDENTITY`	Returns the last value generated for an identity column on the server. Returns NULL if no identity value was generated.
`IDENT_CURRENT('tablename')`	Similar to @@IDENTITY, but returns the last identity value that was generated for a specified table.
`@@ROWCOUNT`	Returns the number of rows affected by the most recent SQL statement.
`@@ERROR`	Returns the error number generated by the execution of the most recent SQL statement. Returns 0 if no error occurred.
`@@SERVERNAME`	Returns the name of the local server.
`HOST_NAME()`	Returns the name of the current workstation.
`SYSTEM_USER`	Returns the name of the current user.

A script that inserts a new vendor and a new invoice

```
USE AP;
DECLARE @MyIdentity int, @MyRowCount int;

INSERT Vendors (VendorName, VendorAddress1, VendorCity, VendorState,
    VendorZipCode, VendorPhone, DefaultTermsID, DefaultAccountNo)
VALUES ('Peerless Binding', '1112 S Windsor St', 'Hallowell', 'ME',
    '04347', '(207) 555-1555', 4, 400);

SET @MyIdentity = @@IDENTITY;
SET @MyRowCount = @@ROWCOUNT;

IF @MyRowCount = 1
    INSERT Invoices
    VALUES (@MyIdentity, 'BA-0199', '2016-05-01', 4598.23,
        0, 0, 4, '2016-06-30', NULL);
```

The response from the system

```
(1 row(s) affected)

(1 row(s) affected)
```

Description

- The *system functions* return information about SQL Server values, objects, and settings. They can be used anywhere an expression is allowed.

- System functions are useful in writing scripts. In addition, some of these functions can be used to provide a value for a DEFAULT constraint on a column.

- System functions used to be called *global variables*, but that name is no longer used.

- In general, it's better to store the value returned by a system function in a variable than to use the system function directly. That's because the value of a system function can change when subsequent statements are executed.

Figure 14-13   How to use the system functions

How to change the session settings

Each time you start a new session, SQL Server sets the settings for that session to the defaults. If that's not what you want, you can change the settings using the SET statements presented in figure 14-14. Although SQL Server provides a variety of other statements, these are the ones you're most likely to use. And you're likely to use these only under special circumstances.

For example, because the default format for entering dates is "mdy," 05/06/12 is interpreted as May 6, 2012. If this date is being inserted from another data source, however, that data source could have used a date format where the year is entered first, followed by the month and the day. In that case, you could use a SET statement like the one shown in this figure to change the date format of the current session to "ymd." Then, the date would be interpreted as June 12, 2005.

The ANSI_NULLS option determines how null values are compared. By default, this option is set to ON, in which case you can't compare a value to the NULL keyword using a comparison operator. In that case,

```
PaymentDate = NULL
```

is always Unknown rather than True or False, even if PaymentDate contains a null value. To determine if a column contains a null value, you must use the IS NULL or IS NOT NULL clause. If you set the ANSI_NULLS option to OFF, however, the expression shown above would return True if PaymentDate contains a null value, and it would return False otherwise. Because a future version of SQL Server will require that the ANSI_NULLS option is always set to on, I recommend that you don't set this option to OFF.

The SET ROWCOUNT statement limits the number of rows that are processed by subsequent queries. For a SELECT query, this works the same as coding a TOP clause. However, since most other dialects of SQL don't support the TOP clause, you'll often see SET ROWCOUNT used in the code of other SQL programmers. Be aware, though, that this session setting affects all queries, including action queries and queries stored within views and stored procedures. Since this can cause unexpected results, I recommend that you avoid modifying this session setting and use the TOP clause instead.

Note that with a future version of SQL Server, SET ROWCOUNT won't affect actions queries. Because of that, you'll have to use the TOP clause to limit the rows processed by INSERT, UPDATE, and DELETE statements. Since you don't typically use the TOP clause with these statements, though, we don't present it in this book. If you want to learn more about using it with these statements, you can refer to the SQL Server documentation.

Transact-SQL statements for changing session settings

Statement	Description
`SET DATEFORMAT format`	Sets the order of the parts of a date (month/day/year) for entering date/time data. The default is mdy, but any permutation of m, d, and y is valid.
`SET NOCOUNT {ON|OFF}`	Determines whether SQL Server returns a message indicating the number of rows that were affected by a statement. OFF is the default.
`SET ANSI_NULLS {ON|OFF}`	Determines how SQL Server handles equals (=) and not equals (<>) comparisons with null values. The default is ON, in which case "WHERE column = NULL" will always return an empty result set, even if there are null values in the column.
`SET ANSI_PADDING {ON|OFF}`	Determines how SQL Server stores char and varchar values that are smaller than the maximum size for a column or that contain trailing blanks. Only affects new column definitions. The default is ON, which causes char values to be padded with blanks. In addition, trailing blanks in varchar values are not trimmed. If this option is set to OFF, char values that don't allow nulls are padded with blanks, but blanks are trimmed from char values that allow nulls as well as from varchar values.
`SET ROWCOUNT number`	Limits the number of rows that are processed by a query. The default setting is 0, which causes all rows to be processed.

A statement that changes the date format

```
SET DATEFORMAT ymd;
```

Description

- You use the SET statement to change configuration settings for the current session. These settings control the way queries and scripts execute.

- If the ANSI_NULLS option is set to ON, you can only test for null values in a column by using the IS NULL clause. See figure 3-15 in chapter 3 for details.

- In a future version of SQL Server, the ANSI_NULLS and ANSI_PADDING options will always be on and you won't be able to turn them off. Because of that, you shouldn't use these options in new scripts that you write.

- Instead of using the SET ROWCOUNT statement to limit the numbers of rows that are processed by a query, you should use the TOP clause. See chapter 3 for information on how to use this clause with the SELECT statement. For information on how to use it with the INSERT, UPDATE, and DELETE statements, see the SQL Server documentation.

- In a future version of SQL Server, the SET ROWCOUNT statement won't affect INSERT, UPDATE, and DELETE statements.

- For a complete list of the Transact-SQL statements for changing session settings, see the topic on the SET statement in the SQL Server documentation.

Figure 14-14   How to change the session settings

How to use dynamic SQL

So far, the scripts you've seen in this chapter have contained predefined SQL statements. In other words, the statements don't change from one execution of the script to another other than for the values of variables used in the statements. However, you can also define an SQL statement as a script executes. Then, you use the EXEC statement shown in figure 14-15 to execute the *dynamic SQL*. Notice that EXEC is an abbreviation for EXECUTE.

The EXEC statement executes a string that contains a SQL statement. To illustrate, the first script in this figure executes a SELECT statement against a table that's specified at run time. To do that, it concatenates the literal string "SELECT * FROM " with the value of a variable named @TableNameVar. If you think about it, you'll realize that there's no other way to do this in SQL. Of course, it would have been easier to submit the simple query shown here directly rather than to use dynamic SQL. However, a more complex script might use an IF...ELSE statement to determine the table that's used in the query. In that case, dynamic SQL can make the script easier to code.

The second script in this figure is more complicated. It creates a table with columns that represent each vendor with outstanding invoices. That means that the number of columns in the new table will vary depending on the current values in the Invoices table.

This script starts by creating a variable named @DynamicSQL that will store the SQL string that's executed. Next, the new table to be created is deleted if it already exists. Then, a SET statement assigns the beginning of the SQL string to @DynamicSQL, which includes the CREATE TABLE statement, the name of the new table, and an opening parenthesis. The SELECT statement that follows concatenates the name of each column (the name of the current vendor) and data type to the SQL string. Finally, the second SET statement concatenates a closing parenthesis and a semicolon to the string, and the string is executed.

Notice that for each row retrieved by the SELECT statement, the variable @DynamicSQL is concatenated with its previous value. Although this syntax is valid for any query, it isn't useful except when generating dynamic SQL as shown here. Also notice that the name of each vendor is enclosed in brackets. That's because many of the vendors have spaces or other special characters in their names, which aren't allowed in column names unless they're delimited.

This figure also shows the SQL statement that's created by one execution of this script along with the contents of the table that's created. Although this table isn't useful the way it is, it could be used to cross-tabulate data based on the Vendors table. For example, each row of this table could represent a date and the Boolean value in each column could represent whether the vendor has an invoice that's due on that date. Since more than one vendor's invoice can be due on the same date, a cross-tabulation is a good representation of this data.

As you may have noticed, the SQL string that's generated by this script has an extra comma following the last column specification. Fortunately, the CREATE TABLE statement ignores this extra comma without generating an error. However, if you wanted to, you could eliminate this comma by using the LEFT function before concatenating the closing parenthesis.

The syntax of the EXEC statement

```
{EXEC|EXECUTE} ('SQL_string')
```

A script that uses an EXEC statement

```
USE AP;
DECLARE @TableNameVar varchar(128);
SET @TableNameVar = 'Invoices';
EXEC ('SELECT * FROM ' + @TableNameVar + ';');
```

The contents of the SQL string at execution

```
SELECT * FROM Invoices;
```

A script that creates a table with one column for each vendor with a balance due

```
USE AP;
DECLARE @DynamicSQL varchar(8000);

IF OBJECT_ID('XtabVendors') IS NOT NULL
    DROP TABLE XtabVendors;

SET @DynamicSQL = 'CREATE TABLE XtabVendors ('
    SELECT @DynamicSQL = @DynamicSQL + '[' + VendorName + '] bit,'
    FROM Vendors
    WHERE VendorID IN
        (SELECT VendorID
        FROM Invoices
        WHERE InvoiceTotal - CreditTotal - PaymentTotal > 0)
    ORDER BY VendorName;
SET @DynamicSQL = @DynamicSQL + ');';

EXEC (@DynamicSQL);

SELECT * FROM XtabVendors;
```

The contents of the SQL string

```
CREATE TABLE XtabVendors ([Blue Cross] bit,[Cardinal Business Media, Inc.]
bit,[Data Reproductions Corp] bit,[Federal Express Corporation] bit,[Ford
Motor Credit Company] bit,[Ingram] bit,[Malloy Lithographing Inc] bit,);
```

The result set

Blue Cross	Cardinal Business Media, Inc.	Data Reproductions Corp	Federal Express Corporation	Ford M

Description

- The EXEC statement executes the SQL statement contained in a string. Because you define the SQL string within the script, you can create and execute SQL code that changes each time the script is run. This is called *dynamic SQL*.

- You can use dynamic SQL to perform operations that can't be accomplished using any other technique.

Figure 14-15   How to use dynamic SQL

A script that summarizes the structure of a database

Figure 14-16 presents a script that you can use to summarize the structure of a database. This script illustrates many of the techniques you learned in this chapter. It also shows how you might use some of the catalog views you learned about in the last chapter.

This script starts by dropping the temporary table named #TableSummary if it already exists. Then, it recreates this table using a SELECT INTO statement and data from three catalog views named tables, columns, and types. The tables view provides information about the tables in the current database. The columns view provides information about the columns in the current database, including the ID of the table that contains the column and the ID of the column's data type. And the types view contains information about data types.

As you can see in this figure, the tables and columns catalog views are joined to get the name of the table that contains a column. In addition, the columns and types catalog views are joined together to get the name of a column's data type. Then, the WHERE clause excludes three tables by name, including the two temporary tables created by this script and the system table named dtproperties.

Next, this script drops and recreates another temporary table named #AllUserTables. This table will be used to generate the row count for each table. It has two columns: an identity column and a column for the table name. The INSERT statement that follows populates this table with the same list of table names that was inserted into the #TableSummary table.

A script that creates a summary of the tables in a database   Page 1

```
/*
Creates and queries a table, #TableSummary, that lists
the columns for each user table in the database, plus
the number of rows in each table.

Author:    Bryan Syverson
Created:   2008-07-02
Modified:  2016-07-16
*/

USE AP;

IF OBJECT_ID('tempdb..#TableSummary') IS NOT NULL
    DROP TABLE #TableSummary;

SELECT sys.tables.name AS TableName, sys.columns.name AS ColumnName,
    sys.types.name AS Type
INTO #TableSummary
FROM sys.tables
    JOIN sys.columns ON sys.tables.object_id = sys.columns.object_id
    JOIN sys.types ON sys.columns.system_type_id = sys.types.system_type_id
WHERE sys.tables.name IN
    (SELECT name
    FROM sys.tables
    WHERE name NOT IN ('dtproperties', 'TableSummary', 'AllUserTables'));

IF OBJECT_ID('tempdb..#AllUserTables') IS NOT NULL
    DROP TABLE #AllUserTables;

CREATE TABLE #AllUserTables
(TableID int IDENTITY, TableName varchar(128));
GO

INSERT #AllUserTables (TableName)
SELECT name
FROM sys.tables
WHERE name NOT IN ('dtproperties', 'TableSummary', 'AllUserTables');
```

Description

- A SELECT INTO statement is used to retrieve information from the tables, columns, and types catalog views and store it in a temporary table named #TableSummary. This table has one row for each column in each table of the database that includes the table name, column name, and data type.

- A CREATE TABLE statement is used to create a temporary table named #AllUserTables. Then, an INSERT statement is used to insert rows into this table that contain the name of each table in the database. This information is retrieved from the catalog view named tables. Each row also contains a sequence number that's generated by SQL Server.

- The system table named dtproperties and the two temporary tables themselves are omitted from both SELECT queries.

Figure 14-16   A script that summarizes the structure of a database (part 1 of 2)

Part 2 of this script includes a WHILE loop that uses dynamic SQL to insert an additional row into #TableSummary for each table in #AllUserTables. Each of these rows indicates the total number of rows in one of the base tables. The @LoopMax variable used by this loop is set to the maximum value of the TableID column in #AllUserTables. The @LoopVar variable is set to 1, which is the minimum value of TableID. The WHILE loop uses @LoopVar to step through the rows of #AllUserTables.

Within the loop, the SELECT statement sets @TableNameVar to the value of the TableName column for the current table. Then, @ExecVar is built by concatenating each of the clauses of the final SQL string. This string consists of three statements. The DECLARE statement is used to create a variable named @CountVar that will store the number of rows in the current table. Note that because this variable is created within the dynamic SQL statement, its scope is limited to the EXEC statement. In other words, it isn't available to the portion of the script outside of the EXEC statement.

The SELECT statement within the dynamic SQL statement retrieves the row count from the current table and stores it in the @CountVar variable. Then, the INSERT statement inserts a row into the #TableSummary table that includes the table name, a literal value that indicates that the row contains the row count, and the number of rows in the table. You can see the contents of the SQL string that's created for one table, the ContactUpdates table, in this figure.

After the SQL string is created, it's executed using an EXEC statement. Then, @LoopVar is increased by 1 and the loop is executed again. When the loop completes, the script executes a SELECT statement that retrieves the data from the #TableSummary table. That result set is also shown in this figure.

A script that creates a summary of the tables in a database   Page 2

```
DECLARE @LoopMax int, @LoopVar int;
DECLARE @TableNameVar varchar(128), @ExecVar varchar(1000);

SELECT @LoopMax = MAX(TableID) FROM #AllUserTables;

SET @LoopVar = 1;

WHILE @LoopVar <= @LoopMax
    BEGIN
        SELECT @TableNameVar = TableName
            FROM #AllUserTables
            WHERE TableID = @LoopVar;
        SET @ExecVar = 'DECLARE @CountVar int; ';
        SET @ExecVar = @ExecVar + 'SELECT @CountVar = COUNT(*) ';
        SET @ExecVar = @ExecVar + 'FROM ' + @TableNameVar + '; ';
        SET @ExecVar = @ExecVar + 'INSERT #TableSummary ';
        SET @ExecVar = @ExecVar + 'VALUES (''' + @TableNameVar + ''',';
        SET @ExecVar = @ExecVar + '''*Row Count*'',';
        SET @ExecVar = @ExecVar + ' @CountVar);';
        EXEC (@ExecVar);
        SET @LoopVar = @LoopVar + 1;
    END;

SELECT * FROM #TableSummary
ORDER BY TableName, ColumnName;
```

The contents of the SQL string for one iteration of the loop

```
DECLARE @CountVar int; SELECT @CountVar = COUNT(*) FROM ContactUpdates;
INSERT #TableSummary VALUES ('ContactUpdates','*Row Count*', @CountVar);
```

The result set

	TableName	ColumnName	Type
30	InvoiceLineItems	*Row Count*	118
31	InvoiceLineItems	AccountNo	int
32	InvoiceLineItems	InvoiceID	int
33	InvoiceLineItems	InvoiceLineItemA…	money
34	InvoiceLineItems	InvoiceLineItemD…	varchar
35	InvoiceLineItems	InvoiceSequence	smallint
36	Invoices	*Row Count*	114
37	Invoices	CreditTotal	money

Description

- The WHILE statement loops through the tables in the #AllUserTables table. For each table, it creates a dynamic SQL string that contains a SELECT statement and an INSERT statement. The SELECT statement retrieves the number of rows in the table, and the INSERT statement inserts a new row into the #TableSummary table that indicates the number of rows.

- The final SELECT statement retrieves all of the rows and columns from the #TableSummary table sorted by column name within table name.

Figure 14-16   A script that summarizes the structure of a database (part 2 of 2)

How to use the SQLCMD utility

SQL Server 2005 introduced a command line utility known as the *SQLCMD utility* that replaced the *OSQL utility* that was available from previous versions of SQL Server. Unlike the Management Studio you've used throughout this book, the SQLCMD utility lets you enter and execute scripts from a command line. One advantage of the SQLCMD utility is that it provides a way to run a SQL script from a DOS batch file.

Figure 14-17 presents an example of a Command Prompt window running a SQLCMD session. To open a session, you enter "sqlcmd" at the command prompt, followed by the appropriate command line switches. To start a session, you must begin by using the -S switch to specify a valid server. Then, if you want to connect to SQL Server using Windows authentication, the only command line switch you need is -E as shown in this figure. If you connect using SQL Server authentication, though, you'll need to enter switches for the user name and password like this:

```
sqlcmd -S localhost\SQLExpress -U joel -P Top$Secret
```

You can also omit the password switch and the SQLCMD utility will prompt you for your password. This improves security because, unlike the Command Prompt window, the SQLCMD utility doesn't display the password on the screen.

Once you're connected, you can type one SQL statement per line as shown. Then, to execute the statement you've entered, you enter a GO command. When you're done, you can close the SQLCMD session by entering the EXIT command. Then, you're returned to the command prompt.

You can also execute a script that's stored in a file on disk. To do that, you use the -i switch. To save the response from the server to a file, you use the -o switch. For example, this command would execute the script contained in a file named test.sql and save the result set in a file named test.txt:

```
sqlcmd -S localhost\SQLExpress -i test.sql -o test.txt
```

Note that the response also includes any result sets that are created. As a result, if the script stored in the test.sql file contains a SELECT statement, the result set returned by that SELECT statement will be stored in text format in the test.txt file.

Although the SQLCMD utility provides an easy way to run T-SQL scripts from a DOS command line, SQL Server 2008 introduced support for Microsoft's command line tool, *Microsoft Windows PowerShell*. PowerShell is a powerful scripting tool that makes it possible to automate complex administrative tasks across multiple servers. However, due to its power and complexity, PowerShell has a steep learning curve. As a result, if you aren't familiar with it already, you'll only want to use it if you can't accomplish the task using a DOS batch file and a T-SQL script.

A Command Prompt window running the SQLCMD utility

Command line switches

Switch	Function
-?	Show a summary of all command line switches.
-E	Use a trusted connection (Windows authentication mode).
-L	List the names of the available servers.
-S server_name	Log in to a specific server.
-U user_name	Log in as a specific user (SQL Server authentication mode).
-P password	Specify the password in the command line (SQL Server authentication mode).
-Q "query"	Execute the specified query, then exit.
-i file_name	Specify the name of the script file to be executed.
-o file_name	Specify an output file in which to save responses from the system.

Description

- You can use the *SQLCMD utility* to run T-SQL scripts from a command line. This provides a way to use a DOS batch file to run a script.

- To open a Command Prompt window, select Command Prompt from the Start menu. On Windows 7, it's in the All Programs→Accessories group. On Windows 10, it's in the All Apps→Windows System group.

- To start the SQLCMD utility, enter "sqlcmd" at the C:\> prompt along with the appropriate command line switches.

- You must begin most commands with the -S switch to specify the name of a valid server.

- To log in, you can use the -E switch for Windows authentication, or you can use the -U and -P switches for SQL Server authentication.

- Once you've started the SQLCMD utility and logged in, you can enter the statements you want to execute followed by the GO command.

- To exit from the SQLCMD utility, enter "exit" at the SQLCMD prompt.

Figure 14-17   How to use the SQLCMD utility

Perspective

In this chapter, you've learned how to code procedural scripts in T-SQL. By using the techniques you've learned here, you'll be able to code scripts that are more general, more useful, and less susceptible to failure. In particular, when you use dynamic SQL, you'll be able to solve problems that can't be solved using any other technique.

In the next chapter, you'll expand on what you've learned here by learning how to code stored procedures, functions, and triggers. These objects are basically one-batch scripts that are stored with the database. But they provide special functionality that gives you greater control over a database, who has access to it, and how they can modify it.

Terms

script	WHILE loop
batch	cursor
T-SQL statement	error handling
variable	exception handling
scalar variable	surround-with snippets
local variable	system function
table variable	global variable
temporary table	dynamic SQL
local temporary table	SQLCMD
global temporary table	OSQL
scope	Windows PowerShell
nested IF...ELSE statements	

Exercises

1. Write a script that declares and sets a variable that's equal to the total outstanding balance due. If that balance due is greater than $10,000.00, the script should return a result set consisting of VendorName, InvoiceNumber, InvoiceDueDate, and Balance for each invoice with a balance due, sorted with the oldest due date first. If the total outstanding balance due is less than $10,000.00, the script should return the message "Balance due is less than $10,000.00."

2. The following script uses a derived table to return the date and invoice total of the earliest invoice issued by each vendor. Write a script that generates the same result set but uses a temporary table in place of the derived table. Make sure your script tests for the existence of any objects it creates.

    ```
    USE AP;

    SELECT VendorName, FirstInvoiceDate, InvoiceTotal
    FROM Invoices JOIN
       (SELECT VendorID, MIN(InvoiceDate) AS FirstInvoiceDate
        FROM Invoices
        GROUP BY VendorID) AS FirstInvoice
       ON (Invoices.VendorID = FirstInvoice.VendorID AND
           Invoices.InvoiceDate = FirstInvoice.FirstInvoiceDate)
    JOIN Vendors
       ON Invoices.VendorID = Vendors.VendorID
    ORDER BY VendorName, FirstInvoiceDate;
    ```

3. Write a script that generates the same result set as the code shown in exercise 2, but uses a view instead of a derived table. Also write the script that creates the view. Make sure that your script tests for the existence of the view. The view doesn't need to be redefined each time the script is executed.

4. Write a script that uses dynamic SQL to return a single column that represents the number of rows in the first table in the current database. The script should automatically choose the table that appears first alphabetically, and it should exclude tables named dtproperties and sysdiagrams. Name the column CountOfTable, where Table is the chosen table name.

    Hint: Use the sys.tables catalog view.

15

How to code stored procedures, functions, and triggers

Now that you've learned how to work with scripts, you know that procedural statements can help you manage a database and automate tasks. In this chapter, you'll learn how to extend this functionality by creating database objects that store program code within a database. The three types of programs discussed in this chapter provide a powerful and flexible way to control how a database is used.

Procedural programming options in Transact-SQL

Figure 15-1 presents the four types of procedural programs you can code using Transact-SQL. Each program type contains SQL statements. However, they differ by how they're stored and executed.

Scripts

Of the four types of procedural programs, only scripts can contain two or more batches. That's because only scripts can be executed by SQL Server tools such as the Management Studio and the SQLCMD utility. In addition, only scripts are stored in files outside of the database. For these reasons, scripts tend to be used most often by SQL Server programmers and database administrators.

Stored procedures, user-defined functions, and triggers

The other three types of procedural programs—*stored procedures*, *user-defined functions*, and *triggers*—are executable database objects. This means that each is stored within the database. To create these objects, you use the DDL statements you'll learn about in this chapter. Then, these objects remain as a part of the database until they're explicitly dropped.

Stored procedures, user-defined functions, and triggers differ by how they're executed. Stored procedures and user-defined functions can be run from any database connection that can run a SQL statement. In contrast, triggers run automatically in response to the execution of an action query on a specific table.

Stored procedures are frequently written by SQL programmers for use by end users or application programmers. If you code stored procedures in this way, you can simplify the way these users interact with a database. In addition, you can provide access to a database exclusively through stored procedures. This gives you tight control over the security of the data.

Both user-defined functions and triggers are used more often by SQL programmers than by application programmers or end users. SQL programmers often use their own functions within the scripts, stored procedures, and triggers they write. Since triggers run in response to an action query, programmers use them to help prevent errors caused by inconsistent or invalid data.

Stored procedures, functions, and triggers also differ by whether or not they can use parameters. *Parameters* are values that can be passed to or returned from a procedure. Both stored procedures and user-defined functions can use parameters, but triggers can't.

A comparison of the different types of procedural SQL programs

Type	Batches	How it's stored	How it's executed	Accepts parameters
Script	Multiple	In a file on a disk	From within a client tool such as the Management Studio or SQLCMD	No
Stored procedure	One only	In an object in the database	By an application or within a SQL script	Yes
User-defined function	One only	In an object in the database	By an application or within a SQL script	Yes
Trigger	One only	In an object in the database	Automatically by the server when a specific action query is executed	No

Description

- You can write procedural programs with Transact-SQL using scripts, stored procedures, user-defined functions, and triggers.

- Scripts are useful for those users with access to the SQL Server client tools, such as the Management Studio. Typically, these tools are used by SQL programmers and DBAs, not by application programmers or end users.

- Stored procedures, user-defined functions, and triggers are all executable database objects that contain SQL statements. Although they differ in how they're executed and by the kinds of values they can return, they all provide greater control and better performance than a script.

- *Stored procedures* give the SQL programmer control over who accesses the database and how. Since some application programmers don't have the expertise to write certain types of complex SQL queries, stored procedures can simplify their use of the database.

- *User-defined functions* are most often used by SQL programmers within the stored procedures and triggers that they write, although they can also be used by application programmers and end users.

- *Triggers* are special procedures that execute when an action query, such as an INSERT, UPDATE, or DELETE statement, is executed. Like constraints, you can use triggers to prevent database errors, but triggers give you greater control and flexibility.

- Since procedures, functions, and triggers are database objects, the SQL statements you use to create, delete, and modify them are considered part of the DDL.

Figure 15-1   Procedural programming options in Transact-SQL

How to code stored procedures

A *stored procedure* is a database object that contains one or more SQL statements. In the topics that follow, you'll learn how to create and use stored procedures. In addition, you'll learn how to use some of the stored procedures provided by SQL Server.

An introduction to stored procedures

Figure 15-2 presents a script that creates a stored procedure, also called an *sproc* or just a *procedure*. To do that, you use the CREATE PROC statement. You'll learn the details of coding this statement in a moment.

The first time a procedure is executed, each SQL statement it contains is compiled and executed to create an *execution plan*. Then, the procedure is stored in compiled form within the database. For each subsequent execution, the SQL statements are executed without compilation, because they're *precompiled*. This makes the execution of a stored procedure faster than the execution of an equivalent SQL script.

To execute, or *call*, a stored procedure, you use the EXEC statement. If the EXEC statement is the first line in a batch, you can omit the EXEC keyword and just code the procedure name. Since this can lead to code that's confusing to read, however, I recommend that you include the EXEC keyword.

The script in this figure creates a stored procedure named spInvoiceReport. This procedure consists of a single statement: a SELECT statement that retrieves data from the Vendors and Invoices tables. As you'll see in the topics that follow, however, a stored procedure can contain more than one statement, along with the same procedural code used in scripts.

When you execute the script in this figure, you create the stored procedure. The response from the system shows that the procedure was created successfully. Then, when you execute the stored procedure, the result set retrieved by the SELECT statement is returned.

As you can see, a user or program that calls this procedure doesn't need to know the structure of the database to use the stored procedure. This simplifies the use of the database by eliminating the need to know SQL and the need to understand the structure of the database.

As you'll learn in chapter 17, you can allow a user or program to call specific stored procedures but not to execute other SQL statements. By doing this, you can secure your database by restricting access to only those rows, columns, and tables that you provide access to through the stored procedures. For those systems where security is critical, this can be the best way to secure the data.

A script that creates a stored procedure

```
USE AP;
GO
CREATE PROC spInvoiceReport
AS

SELECT VendorName, InvoiceNumber, InvoiceDate, InvoiceTotal
FROM Invoices JOIN Vendors
     ON Invoices.VendorID = Vendors.VendorID
WHERE InvoiceTotal - CreditTotal - PaymentTotal > 0
ORDER BY VendorName;
```

The response from the system

```
Command(s) completed successfully.
```

A statement that calls the procedure

```
EXEC spInvoiceReport;
```

The result set created by the procedure

	VendorName	InvoiceNumber	InvoiceDate	InvoiceTotal
1	Blue Cross	547480102	2016-04-01 00:00:00	224.00
2	Cardinal Business Media, Inc.	134116	2016-03-28 00:00:00	90.36
3	Data Reproductions Corp	39104	2016-03-10 00:00:00	85.31
4	Federal Express Corporation	963253264	2016-03-18 00:00:00	52.25
5	Federal Express Corporation	263253268	2016-03-21 00:00:00	59.97

Description

- A stored procedure is an executable database object that contains SQL statements. A stored procedure is also called a *sproc* (pronounced either as one word or as "ess-proc") or a *procedure*.

- Stored procedures are *precompiled*. That means that the *execution plan* for the SQL code is compiled the first time the procedure is executed and is then saved in its compiled form. For this reason, stored procedures execute faster than an equivalent SQL script.

- You use the EXEC statement to run, or *call*, a procedure. If this statement is the first line in a batch, you can omit the EXEC keyword and code just the procedure name. To make your code easier to read, however, you should always include the EXEC keyword.

- You can call a stored procedure from within another stored procedure. You can even call a stored procedure from within itself. This technique, called a *recursive call* or *recursion*, is seldom used in SQL programming.

- One of the advantages of using procedures is that application programmers and end users don't need to know the structure of the database or how to code SQL.

- Another advantage of using procedures is that they can restrict and control access to a database. If you use procedures in this way, you can prevent both accidental errors and malicious damage.

Figure 15-2   An introduction to stored procedures

How to create a stored procedure

Figure 15-3 presents the syntax of the CREATE PROC statement you use to create a stored procedure. You code the name of the procedure in the CREATE PROC clause. Note that stored procedure names can't be the same as the name of any other object in the database. To help distinguish a stored procedure from other database objects, it's a good practice to prefix its name with the letters *sp*.

When the CREATE PROC statement is executed, the syntax of the SQL statements within the procedure is checked. If you've made a coding error, the system responds with an appropriate message and the procedure isn't created.

Because the stored procedure is created in the current database, you need to change the database context by coding a USE statement before the CREATE PROC statement. In addition, CREATE PROC must be the first and only statement in the batch. Since the script in this figure creates the procedure after a USE and DROP PROC statement, for example, it has a GO command just before the CREATE PROC statement.

In addition to stored procedures that are stored in the current database, you can create *temporary stored procedures* that are stored in the tempdb database. These procedures exist only while the current database session is open, so they aren't used often. To identify a temporary stored procedure, prefix the name with one number sign (#) for a *local procedure* and two number signs (##) for a *global procedure*.

After the name of the procedure, you code declarations for any parameters it uses. You'll learn more about that in the figures that follow.

You can also code the optional WITH clause with the RECOMPILE option, the ENCRYPTION option, the EXECUTE_AS_clause option, or any combination of these options. The RECOMPILE option prevents the system from precompiling the procedure. That means that the execution plan for the procedure must be compiled each time it's executed, which will slow down most procedures. For this reason, you should generally omit this option.

Some procedures, however, might make use of unusual or atypical values. If so, the first compilation may result in an execution plan that isn't efficient for subsequent executions. In that case, the additional overhead involved in recompiling the procedure may be offset by the reduced query execution time. If you find that a stored procedure you've written performs erratically, you may want to try this option.

ENCRYPTION is a security option that prevents the user from being able to view the declaration of a stored procedure. Since the system stores the procedure as an object in the database, it also stores the code for the procedure. If this code contains information that you don't want the user to examine, you should use this option.

The EXECUTE_AS_clause option allows you to specify an EXECUTE AS clause to allow users to execute the stored procedure with a specified security context. For example, you can use this clause to allow users to execute the stored procedure with the same security permissions as you. That way, you can be sure that the stored procedure will work for the caller even if the caller doesn't have permissions to access all of the objects that you used within the stored procedure.

The syntax of the CREATE PROC statement

```
CREATE {PROC|PROCEDURE} procedure_name
[parameter_declarations]
[WITH [RECOMPILE] [, ENCRYPTION] [, EXECUTE_AS_clause]]
AS sql_statements
```

A script that creates a stored procedure that copies a table

```
USE AP;
IF OBJECT_ID('spCopyInvoices') IS NOT NULL
    DROP PROC spCopyInvoices;
GO

CREATE PROC spCopyInvoices
AS
    IF OBJECT_ID('InvoiceCopy') IS NOT NULL
        DROP TABLE InvoiceCopy;
    SELECT *
    INTO InvoiceCopy
    FROM Invoices;
```

Description

- You use the CREATE PROC statement to create a stored procedure in the current database. The name of a stored procedure can be up to 128 characters and is typically prefixed with the letters *sp*.

- The CREATE PROC statement must be the first and only statement in a batch. If you're creating the procedure within a script, then, you must code a GO command following any statements that precede the CREATE PROC statement.

- To create a *temporary stored procedure*, prefix the procedure name with a number sign (#) for a *local procedure* or two number signs (##) for a *global procedure*. A temporary stored procedure only exists while the current database session is open.

- You can use *parameters* to pass one or more values from the calling program to the stored procedure or from the procedure to the calling program. See figures 15-4 and 15-5 for more information on working with parameters.

- The AS clause contains the SQL statements to be executed by the stored procedure. Since a stored procedure must consist of a single batch, a GO command is interpreted as the end of the CREATE PROC statement.

- The RECOMPILE option prevents the system from precompiling the procedure, which means that it has to be compiled each time it's run. Since that reduces system performance, you don't typically use this option.

- The ENCRYPTION option prevents users from viewing the code in a stored procedure. See figure 15-11 for more information on viewing stored procedures.

- The EXECUTE_AS_clause option was introduced with SQL Server 2005. You can use this option to allow users to execute the stored procedure with the permissions specified by the EXECUTE AS clause. For more information, look up "EXECUTE AS clause" in the SQL Server documentation.

Figure 15-3   How to create a stored procedure

How to declare and work with parameters

Figure 15-4 presents the syntax for declaring parameters in a CREATE PROC statement. Like a local variable, the name of a parameter must begin with an at sign (@). The data type for a parameter can be any valid SQL Server data type except for the table data type.

Stored procedures provide for two different types of parameters: input parameters and output parameters. An *input parameter* is passed to the stored procedure from the calling program. An *output parameter* is returned to the calling program from the stored procedure. You identify an output parameter with the OUTPUT keyword. If this keyword is omitted, the parameter is assumed to be an input parameter.

You can declare an input parameter so it requires a value or so its value is optional. The value of a *required parameter* must be passed to the stored procedure from the calling program or an error occurs. The value of an *optional parameter* doesn't need to be passed from the calling program. You identify an optional parameter by assigning a default value to it. Then, if a value isn't passed from the calling program, the default value is used. Although you can also code a default value for an output parameter, there's usually no reason for doing that.

You can also use output parameters as input parameters. That is, you can pass a value from the calling program to the stored procedure through an output parameter. However, that's an unusual way to use output parameters. To avoid confusion, you should use output parameters strictly for output.

Within the procedure, you use parameters like variables. Although you can change the value of an input parameter within the procedure, that change isn't returned to the calling program and has no effect on it. Instead, when the procedure ends, the values of any output parameters are returned to the calling program.

The syntax for declaring parameters

```
@parameter_name_1 data_type [= default] [OUTPUT]
[, @parameter_name_2 data_type [= default] [OUTPUT]]...
```

Typical parameter declarations

```
@DateVar smalldatetime            -- Input parameter that accepts
                                  -- a date/time value
@VendorVar varchar(40) = NULL     -- Optional input parameter that accepts
                                  -- a character value
@InvTotal money OUTPUT            -- Output parameter that returns
                                  -- a monetary value
```

A CREATE PROC statement that uses an input and an output parameter

```
CREATE PROC spInvTotal1
        @DateVar smalldatetime,
        @InvTotal money OUTPUT
AS
SELECT @InvTotal = SUM(InvoiceTotal)
FROM Invoices
WHERE InvoiceDate >= @DateVar;
```

A CREATE PROC statement that uses an optional parameter

```
CREATE PROC spInvTotal2
        @DateVar smalldatetime = NULL
AS
IF @DateVar IS NULL
    SELECT @DateVar = MIN(InvoiceDate) FROM Invoices;
SELECT SUM(InvoiceTotal)
FROM Invoices
WHERE InvoiceDate >= @DateVar;
```

Description

- To declare a parameter within a stored procedure, you code the name of the parameter followed by its data type. The parameter name must start with an at sign (@), and the data type can be any type except table. Parameters are always local to the procedure.

- *Input parameters* accept values passed from the calling program.

- *Output parameters* store values that are passed back to the calling program. You identify an output parameter by coding the OUTPUT keyword after the parameter name and data type

- *Optional parameters* are parameters that do not require that a value be passed from the calling program. To declare an optional parameter, you assign it a default value. Then, that value is used if one isn't passed from the calling program.

- A stored procedure can declare up to 2100 parameters. If you declare two or more parameters, the declarations must be separated by commas.

- It's a good programming practice to code your CREATE PROC statements so they list required parameters first, followed by optional parameters.

Figure 15-4   How to declare and work with parameters

How to call procedures with parameters

Figure 15-5 shows how you call procedures that use parameters. The stored procedure in this figure accepts two input parameters and returns one output parameter. As you can see, both of the input parameters are optional because each has a default value.

To pass parameter values to a stored procedure, you code the values in the EXEC statement after the procedure name. You can pass parameters to a stored procedure either by position or by name. The first EXEC statement in this figure passes the parameters *by position*. When you use this technique, you don't include the names of the parameters. Instead, the parameters are listed in the same order as they appear in the CREATE PROC statement. This is the most common way to call stored procedures that have a short list of parameters.

The second EXEC statement shows how you can pass the parameters *by name*. To do that, you include the names of the parameters as defined in the CREATE PROC statement. When you use this technique, you can list parameters in any order. If the procedure has many parameters, particularly if some of them are optional, passing parameters by name is usually easier than passing parameters by position.

The third EXEC statement in this figure shows how you can omit an optional parameter when you pass the parameters by name. To do that, you simply omit the optional parameter. In contrast, when you pass parameters by position, you can omit them only if they appear after the required parameters. This is illustrated by the last EXEC statement in this figure.

Notice that in all four of these examples, the EXEC statement is preceded by a DECLARE statement that creates a variable named @MyInvTotal. This variable is used to store the value of the output parameter that's returned from the stored procedure. As you can see, the name of this variable is included in each of the EXEC statements in this figure. In addition, the variable name is followed by the OUTPUT keyword, which identifies it as an output parameter.

A CREATE PROC statement that includes three parameters

```
CREATE PROC spInvTotal3
        @InvTotal money OUTPUT,
        @DateVar smalldatetime = NULL,
        @VendorVar varchar(40) = '%'
AS

IF @DateVar IS NULL
    SELECT @DateVar = MIN(InvoiceDate) FROM Invoices;

SELECT @InvTotal = SUM(InvoiceTotal)
FROM Invoices JOIN Vendors
    ON Invoices.VendorID = Vendors.VendorID
WHERE (InvoiceDate >= @DateVar) AND
      (VendorName LIKE @VendorVar);
```

Code that passes the parameters by position

```
DECLARE @MyInvTotal money;
EXEC spInvTotal3 @MyInvTotal OUTPUT, '2016-02-01', 'P%';
```

Code that passes the parameters by name

```
DECLARE @MyInvTotal money;
EXEC spInvTotal3 @DateVar = '2016-02-01', @VendorVar = 'P%',
    @InvTotal = @MyInvTotal OUTPUT;
```

Code that omits one optional parameter

```
DECLARE @MyInvTotal money;
EXEC spInvTotal3 @VendorVar = 'M%', @InvTotal = @MyInvTotal OUTPUT;
```

Code that omits both optional parameters

```
DECLARE @MyInvTotal money;
EXEC spInvTotal3 @MyInvTotal OUTPUT;
```

Description

- To call a procedure that accepts parameters, you pass values to the procedure by coding them following the procedure name. You can pass the parameters by position or by name.

- To pass parameters *by position*, list them in the same order as they appear in the CREATE PROC statement and separate them with commas. When you use this technique, you can omit optional parameters only if they're declared after any required parameters.

- To pass parameters *by name*, code the name of the parameter followed by an equal sign and the value. You can separate multiple parameters with commas. When you use this technique, you can list the parameters in any order and you can easily omit optional parameters.

- To use an output parameter in the calling program, you must declare a variable to store its value. Then, you use the name of that variable in the EXEC statement, and you code the OUTPUT keyword after it to identify it as an output parameter.

Figure 15-5   How to call procedures with parameters

How to work with return values

In addition to passing output parameters back to the calling program, stored procedures also pass back a *return value*. By default, this value is zero. However, you can use a RETURN statement to return another number. For example, if a stored procedure updates rows, you may want to return the number of rows that have been updated. To do that, you can use the @@ROWCOUNT function described in chapter 14.

In figure 15-6, the stored procedure named spInvCount returns a count of the number of invoices that meet the conditions specified by the input parameters. These parameters are identical to the input parameters used by the stored procedure in figure 15-5. However, since this procedure uses a RETURN statement to return an integer value, there's no need to use an output parameter.

The script that calls the procedure uses a variable to store the return value. To do that, the name of the variable is coded after the EXEC keyword, followed by an equals sign and the name of the stored procedure. After the procedure returns control to the script, the script uses a PRINT statement to print the return value.

In this figure, the script gets the count of invoices where the invoice date is after February 1, 2016 and the vendor's name begins with P. Here, the return value indicates that 6 invoices match these specifications.

So, when should you use the RETURN statement to return values and when should you use output parameters? If a stored procedure needs to return a single integer value, many programmers prefer using a RETURN statement since the syntax for returning a value is more concise and intuitive than using output parameters. However, if a stored procedure needs to return other types of data, or if it needs to return multiple values, then a RETURN statement won't work. In that case, you can use output parameters, or you can use a function to return other data types (including result sets) as described later in this chapter. Of course, you can always use a RETURN statement together with output parameters whenever that makes sense.

The syntax of the RETURN statement for a stored procedure

```
RETURN [integer_expression]
```

A stored procedure that returns a value

```
CREATE PROC spInvCount
      @DateVar smalldatetime = NULL,
      @VendorVar varchar(40) = '%'
AS

IF @DateVar IS NULL
   SELECT @DateVar = MIN(InvoiceDate) FROM Invoices;

DECLARE @InvCount int;

SELECT @InvCount = COUNT(InvoiceID)
FROM Invoices JOIN Vendors
     ON Invoices.VendorID = Vendors.VendorID
WHERE (InvoiceDate >= @DateVar) AND
      (VendorName LIKE @VendorVar);

RETURN @InvCount;
```

A script that calls the stored procedure

```
DECLARE @InvCount int;
EXEC @InvCount = spInvCount '2016-02-01', 'P%';
PRINT 'Invoice count: ' + CONVERT(varchar, @InvCount);
```

The response from the system

```
Invoice count: 6
```

Description

- The RETURN statement immediately exits the procedure and returns an optional integer value to the calling program. If you don't specify a value in this statement, the *return value* is zero.

- To use the return value in the calling program, you must declare a variable to store its value. Then, you code that variable name followed by an equals sign and the name of the procedure in the EXEC statement.

Figure 15-6   How to work with return values

How to validate data and raise errors

In addition to using the TRY...CATCH statement to handle errors after they occur, you can also prevent errors before they occur by checking data before it's used to make sure it's valid. Checking data before it's used is often referred to as *data validation*, and it often makes sense to perform data validation within a stored procedure. Then, if the data is not valid, you can execute code that makes it valid, or you can return an error to the calling program. To return an error, it's often helpful to use the THROW statement. Then, if the calling program contains a TRY...CATCH statement, it can catch and handle the error. Otherwise, the client connection is terminated immediately.

Figure 15-7 presents the syntax of the THROW statement. The first parameter is the error number you want to assign to the error. The value of this parameter must be 50000 or greater, which identifies it as a custom error. You can use this value to indicate the type of error that occurred. The second parameter is simply the error message you want to display if the error is raised. And the third parameter is the state that you want to associate with the error. The state code is strictly informational and has no system meaning. You can use any value between 0 and 255 to represent the state that the system was in when the error was raised. In most cases, you'll just code 1 for this argument.

The stored procedure in this figure illustrates how the THROW statement works. This procedure checks the VendorID that's passed from the calling program before it performs the insert operation that's specified by the INSERT statement. That way, the system error that's raised when you try to insert a row with an invalid foreign key will never occur. Instead, if the VendorID value is invalid, the THROW statement will raise a custom error that provides a user-friendly message. In this case, the custom error contains a short message that indicates that the VendorID is not valid.

The calling script in this figure attempts to insert a row into the Invoices table with VendorID 799. Since this VendorID doesn't exist in the Vendors table, the insertion causes the custom error to be raised. As a result, program execution jumps into the CATCH block of the TRY...CATCH statement. This CATCH block prints a message that indicates that an error occurred, and it prints the message that's stored in the custom error. Then, the catch block uses an IF statement to check if the error number is greater than or equal to 50000. If so, it prints a message on the third line that indicates that the error is a custom error.

When you code a THROW statement within a block of statements, you should be aware that it must always be preceded by a semicolon. That's true even if the THROW statement is the first or only statement in the block. This is illustrated in the last example in this figure. Here, you can see that I've coded a semicolon on the line before the THROW statement. Of course, if the THROW statement is preceded by another statement in the block, you can just code the semicolon at the end of that statement.

The THROW statement was introduced with SQL Server 2012. In previous versions of SQL Server, you used the RAISERROR statement to perform a similar function. In addition to raising custom errors, this statement lets you raise system errors. It also lets you specify a severity level that indicates whether

The syntax of the THROW statement

```
THROW [error_number, message, state]
```

A stored procedure that tests for a valid foreign key

```
CREATE PROC spInsertInvoice
        @VendorID     int,              @InvoiceNumber  varchar(50),
        @InvoiceDate smalldatetime, @InvoiceTotal    money,
        @TermsID      int,              @InvoiceDueDate smalldatetime
AS

IF EXISTS(SELECT * FROM Vendors WHERE VendorID = @VendorID)
    INSERT Invoices
    VALUES (@VendorID, @InvoiceNumber,
            @InvoiceDate, @InvoiceTotal, 0, 0,
            @TermsID, @InvoiceDueDate, NULL);
ELSE
    THROW 50001, 'Not a valid VendorID!', 1;
```

A script that calls the procedure

```
BEGIN TRY
    EXEC spInsertInvoice
        799,'ZXK-799','2016-05-01',299.95,1,'2016-06-01';
END TRY
BEGIN CATCH
    PRINT 'An error occurred.';
    PRINT 'Message: ' + CONVERT(varchar, ERROR_MESSAGE());
    IF ERROR_NUMBER() >= 50000
        PRINT 'This is a custom error message.';
END CATCH;
```

The response from the system

```
An error occurred.
Message: Not a valid VendorID!
This is a custom error message.
```

The THROW statement coded within a block

```
BEGIN
    ;
    THROW 50001, 'Not a valid VendorID!', 1;
END;
```

Description

- The process of checking the values in one or more columns is known as *data validation*. It's a good practice to validate the data within a stored procedure whenever possible.

- The THROW statement manually raises an error. Unless this error is caught by a TRY…CATCH statement within the stored procedure, the error will be returned to the caller just like an error that's raised by the database engine.

- You use the state argument to identify how serious an error is. The severity of an error that's raised with the THROW statement is always 16.

- A THROW statement that's coded within a block must be preceded by a semicolon.

- A THROW statement that doesn't include any parameters must be coded in a CATCH block.

Figure 15-7   How to validate data and raise errors

the error is informational, whether program execution should jump into a CATCH block, or whether the client connection should be terminated. Because you shouldn't throw system errors, though, and because you'll almost always want an error to be caught and handled, you can simplify your error handling by using THROW statements instead of RAISERROR statements.

A stored procedure
that manages insert operations

Figure 15-8 presents a stored procedure that might be used by an application program that inserts new invoices into the Invoices table. This should give you a better idea of how you can use stored procedures.

This procedure starts with a comment that documents the stored procedure. This documentation includes the author's name, the date the procedure was created, the dates it was modified, who it was modified by, and a general description of the procedure's purpose. Since this procedure returns a value, the return value is briefly described in the comments too. Of course, you can include any other information that you feel is useful.

This procedure uses nine parameters that correspond to nine of the columns in the Invoices table. All of these parameters are input parameters, and each parameter is assigned the same data type as the matching column in the Invoices table. This means that if the calling program passes a value that can't be cast into the proper data type, an error will be raised as the procedure is called. In other words, this type of error won't be caught by the procedure.

If the calling program was to pass a value of 13-15-89 to the @InvoiceDate parameter, for example, an error would occur because this value can't be cast as a date. To handle this type of error within the procedure, you could define each parameter with the varchar data type. Then, the procedure could test for invalid data types and raise appropriate errors when necessary.

All of the input parameters are also assigned a default value of NULL. Since most of the columns in the Invoices table can't accept null values, this might seem like a problem. As you'll see in a minute, however, the procedure tests the value of each parameter before the insertion is attempted. Then, if the parameter contains an invalid value, an appropriate error is returned to the calling program and the insert operation is never performed. By coding the procedure this way, you can fix some errors by supplying default values, and you can return custom error messages for other errors.

A stored procedure that validates the data in a new invoice   Page 1

```
/*
Handles insertion of new invoices into AP database,
including data validation.
Author:         Bryan Syverson
Created:        2002-07-17
Modified:       2008-07-29 by Joel Murach
                2016-05-09 by Ray Halliday
Return value:   InvoiceID for the new row if successful,
                0 if unsuccessful
*/

USE AP;
GO

IF OBJECT_ID('spInsertInvoice') IS NOT NULL
    DROP PROC spInsertInvoice;
GO

CREATE PROC spInsertInvoice
        @VendorID        int = NULL,
        @InvoiceNumber   varchar(50) = NULL,
        @InvoiceDate     smalldatetime = NULL,
        @InvoiceTotal    money = NULL,
        @PaymentTotal    money = NULL,
        @CreditTotal     money = NULL,
        @TermsID         int = NULL,
        @InvoiceDueDate  smalldatetime = NULL,
        @PaymentDate     smalldatetime = NULL
    AS
```

Description

- The nine parameters used in this procedure correspond nine of the columns in the Invoices table.

Figure 15-8   A stored procedure that manages insert operations (part 1 of 3)

After the AS keyword, a series of IF statements are used to test the values in each input parameter. The first IF statement, for example, tests the value of @VendorID to determine if that vendor exists in the Vendors table. If not, a THROW statement is used to raise a custom error that indicates that the VendorID is invalid. This statement also exits the stored procedure and returns the custom error to the calling program.

For the first IF statement, the custom error contains a short message that says, "Invalid VendorID." However, this message could easily be enhanced to display a more helpful and descriptive message such as "The specified VendorID value does not exists in the Vendors table. Please specify a valid VendorID."

The next five IF statements check for null values. In addition, the IF statement for the @InvoiceDate parameter checks to be sure that it falls between the current date and 30 days prior to the current date, and the IF statement for the @InvoiceTotal parameter checks to be sure that it's greater than zero. If not, a custom error is raised.

Instead of returning an error if the @CreditTotal or @PaymentTotal parameter contains a null value, this procedure sets the value of the parameter to zero. It also checks that the credit total isn't greater than the invoice total, and it checks that the payment total isn't greater than the invoice total minus the credit total.

The next IF statement checks the value of the @TermsID parameter to see if a row with this value exists in the Terms table. If not, this parameter is set to the value of the DefaultTermsId column for the vendor if the parameter contains a null value. If it contains any other value, though, a custom error is raised.

This procedure also sets the @InvoiceDueDate parameter if a due date isn't passed to the procedure. To do that, it adds the value of the TermsDueDays column in the Terms table to the value in the @InvoiceDate parameter. If a due date is passed to the procedure, the procedure checks that the date is after the invoice date but isn't more than 180 days after the invoice date. Finally, the procedure checks the @PaymentDate parameter to be sure that it's not less than the invoice date or more than 14 days before the current date.

As you can see, some of the data validation performed by this procedure duplicates the constraints for the Invoices table. If you didn't check the VendorID to be sure that it existed in the Vendors table, for example, the foreign key constraint would cause an error to occur when the row was inserted. By testing for the error before the insertion, however, the stored procedure can raise a custom error message that might be more easily handled by the calling program.

Some of the data validation performed by this procedure goes beyond the constraints for the columns in the table. For example, all three of the date values are tested to determine whether they fall within an appropriate range. This illustrates the flexibility provided by using stored procedures to validate data.

A stored procedure that validates the data in a new invoice   Page 2

```
IF NOT EXISTS (SELECT * FROM Vendors WHERE VendorID = @VendorID)
    THROW 50001, 'Invalid VendorID.', 1;
IF @InvoiceNumber IS NULL
    THROW 50001, 'Invalid InvoiceNumber.', 1;
IF @InvoiceDate IS NULL OR @InvoiceDate > GETDATE()
        OR DATEDIFF(dd, @InvoiceDate, GETDATE()) > 30
    THROW 50001, 'Invalid InvoiceDate.', 1;
IF @InvoiceTotal IS NULL OR @InvoiceTotal <= 0
    THROW 50001, 'Invalid InvoiceTotal.', 1;
IF @PaymentTotal IS NULL
    SET @PaymentTotal = 0;
IF @CreditTotal IS NULL
    SET @CreditTotal = 0;
IF @CreditTotal > @InvoiceTotal
    THROW 50001, 'Invalid CreditTotal.', 1;
IF @PaymentTotal > @InvoiceTotal - @CreditTotal
    THROW 50001, 'Invalid PaymentTotal.', 1;
IF NOT EXISTS (SELECT * FROM Terms WHERE TermsID = @TermsID)
    IF @TermsID IS NULL
        SELECT @TermsID = DefaultTermsID
        FROM Vendors
        WHERE VendorID = @VendorID;
    ELSE  -- @TermsID IS NOT NULL
        THROW 50001, 'Invalid TermsID.', 1;
IF @InvoiceDueDate IS NULL
    SET @InvoiceDueDate = @InvoiceDate +
        (SELECT TermsDueDays FROM Terms WHERE TermsID = @TermsID);
ELSE  -- @InvoiceDueDate IS NOT NULL
    IF @InvoiceDueDate < @InvoiceDate OR
            DATEDIFF(dd, @InvoiceDueDate, @InvoiceDate) > 180
        THROW 50001, 'Invalid InvoiceDueDate.', 1;
IF @PaymentDate < @InvoiceDate OR
        DATEDIFF(dd, @PaymentDate, GETDATE()) > 14
    THROW 50001, 'Invalid PaymentDate.', 1;
```

Description

- A series of IF statements is used to validate the data in each column of the new invoice row. If the value in a column is invalid, a THROW statement is used to return a custom error to the calling program. This terminates the stored procedure.

- Some of the conditions tested by this code could be accomplished using constraints. However, testing these conditions before the INSERT statement is executed prevents system errors from occurring and allows you to return a user-friendly custom error message. Other conditions tested by this code can't be enforced using constraints.

Figure 15-8   A stored procedure that manages insert operations (part 2 of 3)

If the input parameters pass all of the validation tests, the INSERT statement is executed. Since the data has already been validated, the INSERT statement should execute successfully most of the time and insert the row. Then, the following statement uses the @@IDENTITY function to get the new invoice ID value that's generated when the row is inserted, and it returns that value to the calling program.

However, even though the data for the insert has been validated, it's still possible for an unexpected system error to occur. In that case, SQL Server will raise a system error and end the stored procedure.

In most cases, a stored procedure like this would be called from an application program. Since the details of doing that are beyond the scope of this book, however, this figure presents a SQL script that calls the procedure. This script includes processing similar to what might be used in an application program. In short, this script uses a TRY...CATCH statement to catch any errors that have been raised and to handle them appropriately. In many cases, handling an error is as simple as displaying a message that describes the error and indicates what can be done to fix the problem. In this figure, for example, the CATCH block uses three PRINT statements to indicate that an error occurred, to display the error number, and to display the error message. In other cases, though, error handling can include additional processing such as saving data or exiting the program as gracefully as possible.

A stored procedure that validates the data in a new invoice   **Page 3**

```
INSERT Invoices
VALUES (@VendorID, @InvoiceNumber, @InvoiceDate, @InvoiceTotal,
        @PaymentTotal, @CreditTotal, @TermsID, @InvoiceDueDate,
        @PaymentDate);
RETURN @@IDENTITY;
```

A SQL script that calls the stored procedure

```
BEGIN TRY
    DECLARE @InvoiceID int;
    EXEC @InvoiceID = spInsertInvoice
        @VendorID = 799,
        @InvoiceNumber = 'RZ99381',
        @InvoiceDate = '2016-04-12',
        @InvoiceTotal = 1292.45;
    PRINT 'Row was inserted.';
    PRINT 'New InvoiceID: ' + CONVERT(varchar, @InvoiceID);
END TRY
BEGIN CATCH
    PRINT 'An error occurred. Row was not inserted.';
    PRINT 'Error number: ' + CONVERT(varchar, ERROR_NUMBER());
    PRINT 'Error message: ' + CONVERT(varchar, ERROR_MESSAGE());
END CATCH;
```

The response from the system for a successful insert

```
Row was inserted.
New InvoiceID: 115
```

The response from the system when a validation error occurs

```
An error occurred. Row was not inserted.
Error number: 50001
Error message: Invalid VendorID.
```

Description

- If the data in all of the columns of the new row is valid, the procedure executes an INSERT statement to insert the row. If the insert succeeds, this procedure gets the new InvoiceID value and returns it to the calling program, which ends the procedure. Otherwise, the database engine raises a system error, returns a value of zero, and ends the procedure.

- If this procedure was called by an application program, the program would need to handle any errors that occur. This includes custom errors raised by this stored procedure and unexpected system errors raised by SQL Server if it can't execute the INSERT statement.

Figure 15-8   A stored procedure that manages insert operations (part 3 of 3)

How to pass a table as a parameter

So far, all of the stored procedures shown in this chapter have accepted scalar values as parameters. However, there are times when you may want to pass an entire table to a stored procedure. For example, you may want to pass multiple invoices or line items to a stored procedure for processing.

Prior to SQL Server 2008, programmers were left to develop their own workarounds for passing a table as a parameter. Unfortunately, this often resulted in custom code that was difficult to develop and maintain. With SQL Server 2008 and later, you can pass a table as a parameter as shown in figure 15-9.

Before you can pass a table as a parameter, you must define a data type for the table. In other words, you must create a *user-defined table type*. To do that, you can code a CREATE TYPE statement like the one shown in this figure. This statement defines a data type named LineItems for a table that contains columns similar to the columns of the InvoiceLineItems table, including the same definition for the primary key. However, foreign keys aren't allowed for user-defined table types. As a result, the column definitions in this figure don't include foreign keys.

Once you define a table type, you can create a stored procedure that accepts this data type as a parameter. In this figure, for example, the CREATE PROC statement creates a procedure that accepts a single parameter named @LineItems of the LineItems type. As a result, the body of the stored procedure can treat this parameter just as if it was a table variable. In this figure, for example, an INSERT statement inserts all of the rows stored in the @LineItems parameter into the InvoiceLineItems table. This works because the LineItems type contains the same number and type of columns as the InvoiceLineItems table.

When you code a stored procedure that accepts a table as a parameter, you must use the READONLY keyword to identify this parameter as read-only. As a result, you can't modify the data that's stored in the parameter. However, outside of the stored procedure, you can modify the data that's stored in a variable of a user-defined table type. In this figure, for example, the code that passes the table to the stored procedure begins by declaring a variable of the LineItems type. Then, it uses three INSERT statements to insert three rows into the table. Finally, it uses an EXEC statement to pass this table to the procedure.

If you need to, you can also join a table that's passed as a parameter with another table. For example, suppose you want to update the InvoiceLineItems table with data from the @LineItems table. To do that, you could code a s tatement like this:

```
UPDATE InvoiceLineItems
SET InvoiceLineItemAmount = li.ItemAmount
FROM InvoiceLineItems i JOIN @LineItems li
    ON i.InvoiceID = li.InvoiceID
    AND i.InvoiceSequence = li.InvoiceSequence;
```

Here, the InvoiceLineItems table has a primary key that's defined by two columns. As a result, tables are joined based on both of these columns.

The syntax for creating a user-defined table type

```
CREATE TYPE TableTypeName AS
TABLE
table_definition
```

A statement that creates a user-defined table type

```
CREATE TYPE LineItems AS
TABLE
(InvoiceID         INT           NOT NULL,
InvoiceSequence   SMALLINT      NOT NULL,
AccountNo         INT           NOT NULL,
ItemAmount        MONEY         NOT NULL,
ItemDescription   VARCHAR(100)  NOT NULL,
PRIMARY KEY (InvoiceID, InvoiceSequence));
```

A statement that creates a stored procedure that accepts a table as a parameter

```
CREATE PROC spInsertLineItems
    @LineItems LineItems READONLY
AS
    INSERT INTO InvoiceLineItems
    SELECT *
    FROM @LineItems;
```

Statements that pass a table to a stored procedure

```
DECLARE @LineItems LineItems;

INSERT INTO @LineItems VALUES (114, 1, 553, 127.75, 'Freight');
INSERT INTO @LineItems VALUES (114, 2, 553, 29.25, 'Freight');
INSERT INTO @LineItems VALUES (114, 3, 553, 48.50, 'Freight');

EXEC spInsertLineItems @LineItems;
```

The response from the system

```
(1 row(s) affected)
(1 row(s) affected)
(1 row(s) affected)
(3 row(s) affected)
```

Description

- If you want to pass a table as a parameter to a stored procedure or a user-defined function, you must create a *user-defined table type* for the table.

- A user-defined table type can only be used as an input parameter, not as an output parameter.

- Creating a user-defined table type is similar to creating a regular table. However, you can't define foreign keys for the table.

Figure 15-9   How to pass a table as a parameter

How to delete or change a stored procedure

Figure 15-10 presents the syntax of the DROP PROC statement. You use this statement to delete one or more stored procedures from the database. As with the other statements you've learned that delete objects from the database, the deletion is permanent.

This figure also presents the syntax of the ALTER PROC statement. You use this statement to redefine an existing stored procedure. As you can see, the syntax is the same as the syntax of the CREATE PROC statement.

Like the ALTER VIEW statement, ALTER PROC completely replaces the previous definition for the stored procedure. Because of that, you'll usually change the definition of a stored procedure by deleting the procedure and then recreating it. If you've assigned security permissions to restrict the users who can call the procedure, however, those permissions are lost when you delete the procedure. If you want to retain the permissions, then, you should use the ALTER PROC statement instead.

The examples in this figure show how you might use the ALTER PROC and DROP PROC statements. The first example creates a stored procedure named spVendorState that selects vendors from the state specified by the @State parameter. Because the SELECT statement will fail if a state isn't specified, this parameter is required. In the second example, however, an ALTER PROC statement is used to modify this procedure so the state is optional. The last example deletes this procedure.

If you delete a table or view used by a stored procedure, you should be sure to delete the stored procedure as well. If you don't, the stored procedure can still be called by any user or program that has access to it. Then, an error will occur because the table or view has been deleted.

The syntax of the DROP PROC statement

```
DROP {PROC|PROCEDURE} procedure_name [, ...]
```

The syntax of the ALTER PROC statement

```
ALTER {PROC|PROCEDURE} procedure_name
[parameter declarations]
[WITH [RECOMPILE] [, ENCRYPTION] [, EXECUTE_AS_clause]]
AS sql_statements
```

A statement that creates a procedure

```
CREATE PROC spVendorState
      @State varchar(20)
AS
SELECT VendorName
FROM Vendors
WHERE VendorState = @State;
```

A statement that changes the parameter defined by the procedure

```
ALTER PROC spVendorState
      @State varchar(20) = NULL
AS
IF @State IS NULL
   SELECT VendorName
   FROM Vendors;
ELSE
   SELECT VendorName
   FROM Vendors
   WHERE VendorState = @State;
```

A statement that deletes the procedure

```
DROP PROC spVendorState;
```

Description

- To delete a stored procedure from the database, use the DROP PROC statement.

- To modify the definition of a procedure, you can delete the procedure and then create it again, or you can use the ALTER PROC statement to specify the new definition.

- When you delete a procedure, any security permissions that are assigned to the procedure are also deleted. If that's not what you want, you can use the ALTER PROC statement to modify the procedure and preserve the permissions.

Figure 15-10   How to delete or change a stored procedure

How to work with system stored procedures

SQL Server comes with hundreds of *system stored procedures* that you can use to manage and maintain your databases. These procedures are stored in the Master database, but you can call them from any database. Figure 15-11 presents a table of commonly used system stored procedures.

This figure also presents a script that calls the sp_HelpText system stored procedure. This procedure returns the SQL code that was specified by the CREATE statement for a view, stored procedure, user-defined function, or trigger. If the object was created with the WITH ENCRYPTION option, however, the SQL code can't be returned. Because the code for system stored procedures is never encrypted, you can examine the code in these procedures too.

You can use the system stored procedures to simplify your administrative tasks. However, you may want to avoid using these procedures in production programs. That's because each time a new version of SQL Server is released, some of these stored procedures may change. Then, you may have to rewrite the programs that use them.

In addition to the system stored procedures provided by SQL Server, you can also create your own system stored procedures. To do that, you create the procedure in the Master database, and you give the procedure a name that starts with *sp_*.

Commonly used system stored procedures

Procedure	Description
sp_Help [name]	Returns information about the specified database object or data type. Without a parameter, returns a summary of all objects in the current database.
sp_HelpText name	Returns the text of an unencrypted stored procedure, user-defined function, trigger, or view.
sp_HelpDb [database_name]	Returns information about the specified database or, if no parameter is specified, all databases.
sp_Who [login_ID]	Returns information about who is currently logged in and what processes are running. If no parameter is specified, information on all active users is returned.
sp_Columns name	Returns information about the columns defined in the specified table or view.

How to use the sp_HelpText system stored procedure

```
USE AP;
EXEC sp_HelpText spInvoiceReport;
```

The results returned by the procedure

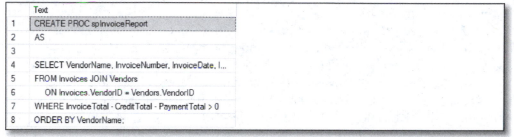

	Text
1	CREATE PROC spInvoiceReport
2	AS
3	
4	SELECT VendorName, InvoiceNumber, InvoiceDate, I...
5	FROM Invoices JOIN Vendors
6	ON Invoices.VendorID = Vendors.VendorID
7	WHERE InvoiceTotal - CreditTotal - PaymentTotal > 0
8	ORDER BY VendorName;

The results if WITH ENCRYPTION is included in the procedure definition

```
The text for object 'spInvoiceReport' is encrypted.
```

Description

- Microsoft SQL Server includes many *system stored procedures* that you can use to perform useful tasks on a database. These procedures are identified by the prefix *sp_*. You can use these procedures in the scripts and procedures you write.

- System stored procedures are stored in the Master database, but you can execute them on any database. These procedures operate within the current database context that you've set with the USE statement.

- SQL Server has hundreds of system stored procedures. To view the complete list, look up "system stored procedures" in the SQL Server documentation.

- You can also create your own system stored procedures. To do that, give the procedure a name that begins with *sp_* and create it in the Master database.

Figure 15-11 How to work with system stored procedures

How to code user-defined functions

In addition to the SQL Server functions you've learned about throughout this book, you can also create your own functions, called user-defined functions. To do that, you use code that's similar to the code you use to create a stored procedure. There are some distinct differences between stored procedures and user-defined functions, however. You'll learn about those differences in the topics that follow.

An introduction to user-defined functions

Figure 15-12 summarizes the three types of user-defined functions, also called *UDFs*, or just *functions*, that you can create using Transact-SQL. *Scalar-valued functions* are like the functions you learned about in chapter 9 that return a single value. In addition to scalar-valued functions, however, you can also create *table-valued functions*. As its name implies, a table-valued function returns an entire table. A table-valued function that's based on a single SELECT statement is called a *simple table-valued function*. In contrast, a table-valued function that's based on multiple SQL statements is called a *multi-statement table-valued function*.

Like a stored procedure, a UDF can accept one or more input parameters. The function shown in this figure, for example, accepts a parameter named @VendorName. However, a UDF can't be defined with output parameters. Instead, the RETURN statement must be used to pass a value back to the calling program. The value that's returned must be compatible with the data type that's specified in the RETURNS clause. In this example, an integer that contains a VendorID value selected from the Vendors table is returned.

To call, or *invoke*, a scalar-valued function, you include it in an expression. Then, the value returned by the function is substituted for the function. The first SELECT statement in this figure, for example, uses the value returned by the fnVendorID function in its WHERE clause. Note that when you refer to a user-defined function, you must include the name of the schema. In this case, the schema is dbo.

To invoke a table-valued function, you refer to it anywhere you would normally code a table or view name. The second SELECT statement in this figure, for example, uses a function named fnTopVendorsDue in the FROM clause. You'll see the definition of this function later in this chapter.

Unlike a stored procedure, a UDF can't make permanent changes to the objects in a database. For example, it can't issue INSERT, UPDATE, and DELETE statements against tables or views in the database. However, within the code for a function, you can create a table, a temporary table, or a table variable. Then, the function can perform insert, update, and delete operations on that table.

The three types of user-defined functions

Function type	Description
Scalar-valued function	Returns a single value of any T-SQL data type.
Simple table-valued function	Returns a table that's based on a single SELECT statement.
Multi-statement table-valued function	Returns a table that's based on multiple statements.

A statement that creates a scalar-valued function

```
CREATE FUNCTION fnVendorID
    (@VendorName varchar(50))
    RETURNS int
BEGIN
    RETURN (SELECT VendorID FROM Vendors WHERE VendorName = @VendorName);
END;
```

A statement that invokes the scalar-valued function

```
SELECT InvoiceDate, InvoiceTotal
FROM Invoices
WHERE VendorID = dbo.fnVendorID('IBM');
```

A statement that invokes a table-valued function

```
SELECT * FROM dbo.fnTopVendorsDue(5000);
```

Description

- A user-defined function, also called a *UDF* or just a *function*, is an executable database object that contains SQL statements.

- The name of a function can be up to 128 characters and is typically prefixed with the letters *fn*.

- Functions always return a value. A *scalar-valued function* returns a single value of any T-SQL data type. A *table-valued function* returns an entire table.

- A table-valued function can be based on a single SELECT statement, in which case it's called a *simple table-valued function*, or it can be based on two or more statements, in which case it's called a *multi-statement table-valued function*.

- A function can't have a permanent effect on the database. In other words, it can't run an action query against the database.

- You can call, or *invoke*, a scalar-valued function from within any expression. You can invoke a table-valued function anywhere you'd refer to a table or a view.

- Unlike other database objects, you must specify the name of the schema when invoking a UDF.

Figure 15-12   An introduction to user-defined functions

How to create a scalar-valued function

Figure 15-13 presents the syntax of the CREATE FUNCTION statement you use to create a scalar-valued function. The CREATE FUNCTION clause names the function and declares the input parameters. If you don't specify the schema name as part of the name, the function is stored in the schema that's associated with the current user.

The syntax you use to declare parameters for a function is similar to the syntax you use to declare parameters for stored procedures. For a function, however, the declarations must be enclosed in parentheses. In addition, because a function can't have output parameters, the OUTPUT keyword isn't allowed.

To invoke a function that has parameters, you must pass the parameters by position. You can't pass them by name as you can when you call a stored procedure. For this reason, you should code required parameters first, followed by optional parameters. Furthermore, you can't simply omit optional parameters when invoking a function as you can with a stored procedure. Instead, you must use the DEFAULT keyword as a placeholder for the optional parameter. You'll see an example of that in figure 15-14.

The RETURNS clause specifies the data type of the value that's returned by the function. Because the value must be scalar, you can't specify the table data type. In addition, you can't specify text, ntext, image, or timestamp.

You code the statements for the function within a BEGIN...END block. Within that block, the RETURN statement specifies the value that's passed back to the invoking program. Since this statement causes the function to terminate, it's usually coded at the end of the function. Notice that unlike a RETURN statement you code within a stored procedure, a RETURN statement you code within a function can return a value with any data type. Within a specific function, however, it must return a value with a data type that's compatible with the data type specified by the RETURNS clause.

The scalar-valued function that's shown in this figure doesn't accept any input parameters and returns a value with the money data type. In this case, the code for the function consists of a single SELECT statement coded within the RETURN statement. However, a function can include as many statements as are necessary to calculate the return value.

If you find yourself repeatedly coding the same expression, you may want to create a scalar-valued function for the expression. Then, you can use that function in place of the expression, which can save you coding time and make your code easier to maintain. Most SQL programmers create a set of useful UDFs each time they work on a new database.

The syntax for creating a scalar-valued function

```
CREATE FUNCTION [schema_name.]function_name
    ([@parameter_name data_type [= default]] [, ...])
    RETURNS data_type
    [WITH [ENCRYPTION] [, SCHEMABINDING] [, EXECUTE_AS_clause]]
    [AS]
BEGIN
    [sql_statements]
    RETURN scalar_expression
END
```

A statement that creates a scalar-valued function that returns the total invoice amount due

```
CREATE FUNCTION fnBalanceDue()
    RETURNS money
BEGIN
    RETURN (SELECT SUM(InvoiceTotal - PaymentTotal - CreditTotal)
            FROM Invoices
            WHERE InvoiceTotal - PaymentTotal - CreditTotal > 0);
END;
```

A script that invokes the function

```
PRINT 'Balance due: $' + CONVERT(varchar, dbo.fnBalanceDue(), 1);
```

The response from the system

```
Balance due: $32,020.42
```

Description

- Functions can be defined with from zero to 1024 input parameters. You specify these parameters in parentheses after the name of the function in the CREATE FUNCTION statement. Each parameter can be assigned an optional default value.

- A function can't contain output parameters. Instead, you specify the data type of the data to be returned by the function in the RETURNS clause.

- You code the statements that define the function within a BEGIN…END block. This block includes a RETURN statement that specifies the value to be returned.

- When you invoke a function, you list the parameters within parentheses after the name of the function. To use the default value of a parameter, code the DEFAULT keyword in place of the parameter value. You can't pass function parameters by name.

- When you create a function, it's stored in the schema associated with the current user if you don't specify a schema name. When you invoke the function, however, you must specify the schema name.

- The SCHEMABINDING option binds the function to the database schema. This prevents you from dropping or altering tables or views that are used by the function. This option is more commonly used for table-valued functions.

- The ENCRYPTION option prevents users from viewing the code in the function.

- The EXECUTE_AS_clause option specifies the security context under which the function is executed.

Figure 15-13   How to create and use a scalar-valued function

How to create a simple table-valued function

Figure 15-14 presents the syntax for creating a simple table-valued function, also called an *inline table-valued function*. You use this syntax if the result set can be returned from a single SELECT statement. Otherwise, you'll need to use the syntax that's presented in the next figure.

To declare the function as table-valued, you code the table data type in the RETURNS clause. Then, you code the SELECT statement that defines the table in parentheses in the RETURN statement. Note that because a table can't have any unnamed columns, you must assign a name to every calculated column in the result set.

The function shown in this figure returns a table that contains the vendor name and total balance due for each vendor with a balance due. The one input parameter, @CutOff, is an optional parameter because it's assigned a default value of 0. This parameter is used in the HAVING clause to return only those vendors with total invoices that are greater than or equal to the specified amount. The first SELECT statement shown in this figure, for example, returns vendors with total invoices greater than or equal to $5,000.

The second SELECT statement shows how you can join the result of a table-valued function with another table. Notice that to avoid having to code the function in both the FROM and ON clauses, the function is assigned a correlation name. Also notice in this example that a value isn't specified for the optional parameter. Instead, the DEFAULT keyword is specified so the default value of the parameter will be used.

A table-valued function like the one shown here acts like a dynamic view. Because a function can accept parameters, the result set it creates can be modified. This is a powerful extension to standard SQL functionality.

The syntax for creating a simple table-valued function

```
CREATE FUNCTION [schema_name.]function_name
    ([@parameter_name data_type [= default]] [, ...])
    RETURNS TABLE
    [WITH [ENCRYPTION] [, SCHEMABINDING]]
    [AS]
RETURN [(] select_statement [)]
```

A statement that creates a simple table-valued function

```
CREATE FUNCTION fnTopVendorsDue
    (@CutOff money = 0)
    RETURNS table
RETURN
    (SELECT VendorName, SUM(InvoiceTotal) AS TotalDue
    FROM Vendors JOIN Invoices ON Vendors.VendorID = Invoices.VendorID
    WHERE InvoiceTotal - CreditTotal - PaymentTotal > 0
    GROUP BY VendorName
    HAVING SUM(InvoiceTotal) >= @CutOff);
```

A SELECT statement that invokes the function

```
SELECT * FROM dbo.fnTopVendorsDue(5000);
```

The result set

	VendorName	TotalDue
1	Malloy Lithographing Inc	31527.24

A SELECT statement that uses the function in a join operation

```
SELECT Vendors.VendorName, VendorCity, TotalDue
FROM Vendors JOIN dbo.fnTopVendorsDue(DEFAULT) AS TopVendors
    ON Vendors.VendorName = TopVendors.VendorName;
```

The result set

	VendorName	VendorCity	TotalDue
1	Blue Cross	Oxnard	224.00
2	Cardinal Business Media, Inc.	Philadelphia	90.36
3	Data Reproductions Corp	Auburn Hills	85.31
4	Federal Express Corporation	Memphis	210.89
5	Ford Motor Credit Company	Los Angeles	503.20
6	Ingram	Dallas	579.42
7	Malloy Lithographing Inc	Ann Arbor	31527.24

Description

- You create a simple table-valued function, also called an *inline table-valued function*, by coding the table data type in the RETURNS clause of the CREATE FUNCTION statement. Then, you code a SELECT statement that defines the table in the RETURN statement.

- To use a simple table-valued function, code the function name in place of a table name or a view name. If you use a table-valued function in a join operation, you'll want to assign a correlation name to it as shown above.

Figure 15-14   How to create and use a simple table-valued function

How to create a multi-statement table-valued function

Figure 15-15 presents the syntax for creating a multi-statement table-valued function. Although you should know about this syntax, you'll probably never need to use it. That's because a single SELECT statement with joins and subqueries can fulfill almost every query need.

Since a multi-statement table-valued function creates a new table, you must define the structure of that table. To do that, you declare a table variable in the RETURNS clause and then define the columns for the new table. The syntax you use to define the columns is similar to the syntax you use to define the columns of a table variable.

You code the SQL statements that create the table within a BEGIN...END block. This blocks ends with a RETURN keyword with no argument. This terminates the function and returns the table variable to the invoking program.

The function shown in this figure returns a table with one row for each invoice with a balance due. This function calculates the credit adjustment that would be necessary to reduce the total balance due to the threshold amount that's passed to the function. This function is similar to the script you saw in figure 14-9 in chapter 14 that uses a temporary table.

This function starts by using an INSERT statement to copy all the rows in the Invoices table with a balance due to the @OutTable table variable. Then, a WHILE statement is used to increment the CreditTotal column of each row in this table by one cent until the total amount due for all invoices falls below the threshold. The SELECT statement that uses this function summarizes the CreditTotal column by vendor.

The syntax for creating a multi-statement table-valued function

```
CREATE FUNCTION [schema_name.]function_name
    ([@parameter_name data_type [= default]] [, ...])
    RETURNS @return_variable TABLE
    (column_name_1 data_type [column_attributes]
    [, column_name_2 data_type [column_attributes]]...)
    [WITH [ENCRYPTION] [, SCHEMABINDING] [, EXECUTE_AS_clause]]
    [AS]
BEGIN
    sql_statements
    RETURN
END
```

A statement that creates a multi-statement table-valued function

```
CREATE FUNCTION fnCreditAdj (@HowMuch money)
    RETURNS @OutTable table
            (InvoiceID int, VendorID int, InvoiceNumber varchar(50),
             InvoiceDate smalldatetime, InvoiceTotal money,
             PaymentTotal money, CreditTotal money)
BEGIN
    INSERT @OutTable
        SELECT InvoiceID, VendorID, InvoiceNumber, InvoiceDate,
               InvoiceTotal, PaymentTotal, CreditTotal
        FROM Invoices
        WHERE InvoiceTotal - CreditTotal - PaymentTotal > 0;
    WHILE (SELECT SUM(InvoiceTotal - CreditTotal - PaymentTotal)
           FROM @OutTable) >= @HowMuch
        UPDATE @OutTable
        SET CreditTotal = CreditTotal + .01
        WHERE InvoiceTotal - CreditTotal - PaymentTotal > 0;
    RETURN;
END;
```

A SELECT statement that uses the function

```
SELECT VendorName, SUM(CreditTotal) AS CreditRequest
FROM Vendors JOIN dbo.fnCreditAdj(25000) AS CreditTable
    ON Vendors.VendorID = CreditTable.VendorID
GROUP BY VendorName;
```

The response from the system

	VendorName	CreditRequest
1	Blue Cross	224.00
2	Cardinal Business Media, Inc.	90.36
3	Data Reproductions Corp	85.31
4	Federal Express Corporation	210.89
5	Ford Motor Credit Company	503.20
6	Ingram	579.42
7	Malloy Lithographing Inc	6527.26

Warning

- Because this code must loop through the Invoices table thousands of times, this function can take a long time to execute.

Figure 15-15   How to create and use a multi-statement table-valued function

How to delete or change a function

Figure 15-16 presents the syntax of the DROP FUNCTION and ALTER FUNCTION statements. The DROP FUNCTION statement permanently deletes one or more user-defined functions from the database. In addition, it drops any security permissions defined for the function along with any dependencies between the function and the tables and views it uses.

The ALTER FUNCTION statement modifies the definition of a user-defined function. You should use this statement if you need to preserve permissions and dependencies that would be lost if you dropped the function and then recreated it. Just like the CREATE FUNCTION statement, the ALTER FUNCTION statement has three syntax variations for the three types of functions you can create.

The syntax of the DROP FUNCTION statement

```
DROP FUNCTION [schema_name.]function_name [, ...]
```

The syntax of the ALTER FUNCTION statement
for a scalar-valued function

```
ALTER FUNCTION [schema_name.]function_name
    ([@parameter_name data_type [= default]] [, ...])
    RETURNS data_type
    [WITH [ENCRYPTION] [, SCHEMABINDING] [, EXECUTE_AS_clause]]
BEGIN
    [sql_statements]
    RETURN scalar_expression
END
```

The syntax for altering a simple table-valued function

```
ALTER FUNCTION [schema_name.]function_name
    ([@parameter_name data_type [= default]] [, ...])
    RETURNS TABLE
    [WITH [ENCRYPTION] [, SCHEMABINDING]]
RETURN [(] select_statement [)]
```

The syntax for altering a multi-statement table-valued function

```
ALTER FUNCTION [schema_name.]function_name
    ([@parameter_name data_type [= default]] [, ...])
    RETURNS @return_variable TABLE
    (column_name_1 data_type [column_attributes]
    [, column_name_2 data_type [column_attributes]]...)
    [WITH [ENCRYPTION] [, SCHEMABINDING] [, EXECUTE_AS_clause]]
BEGIN
    sql_statements
    RETURN
END
```

Description

- To delete a user-defined function from the database, use the DROP FUNCTION statement.

- To modify the definition of a function, you can delete the function and then create it again, or you can use the ALTER FUNCTION statement to specify the new definition.

- When you delete a function, any security permissions that are assigned to the function and any dependencies between the function and the tables and views it uses are also deleted. If that's not what you want, you can use the ALTER FUNCTION statement to modify the function and preserve the permissions and dependencies.

Figure 15-16   How to delete or change a function

How to code triggers

A trigger is a special type of procedure that's invoked, or *fired*, automatically when an action query is executed on a table or view. Triggers provide a powerful way to control how action queries modify the data in your database. If necessary, you can use triggers to enforce design rules, implement business logic, and prevent data inconsistency. However, triggers can cause locking and performance problems. In addition, there's often a better way to accomplish a task than by using a trigger. As a result, I recommend you use them sparingly.

How to create a trigger

Figure 15-17 presents the syntax of the CREATE TRIGGER statement you use to create a trigger. Notice in this syntax that a trigger can't use parameters. In addition, a trigger can't return a value.

The CREATE TRIGGER statement provides for two types of triggers: AFTER triggers and INSTEAD OF triggers. Both types of triggers can be defined to fire for an insert, update, or delete operation or any combination of these operations. If an action query has an AFTER trigger, the trigger fires after the action query. If an action query has an INSTEAD OF trigger, the trigger is fired instead of the action query. In other words, the action query is never executed.

In addition to AFTER and INSTEAD OF, you can code the FOR keyword in the CREATE TRIGGER statement. A FOR trigger is identical to an AFTER trigger. FOR is an ANSI-standard keyword, and it was the only keyword allowed prior to SQL Server 2000. For these reasons, FOR is more commonly used than AFTER. However, this book uses AFTER since it more clearly describes when the trigger fires.

Each trigger is associated with the table or view named in the ON clause. Although each trigger is associated with a single table or view, a single table can have any number of AFTER triggers. Since two or more triggers for the same table can be confusing to manage and debug, however, I recommend you have no more than one trigger for each action. Each table or view can also have one INSTEAD OF trigger for each action. A view can't have AFTER triggers.

The CREATE TRIGGER statement in this figure defines an AFTER trigger for the Vendors table. Notice that the name of this trigger reflects the table it's associated with and the operations that will cause it to fire. This is a common naming convention. In this case, the trigger fires after an insert or update operation is performed on the table. As you can see, the trigger updates the VendorState column so state codes are in uppercase letters.

Notice that the WHERE clause in the trigger uses a subquery that's based on a table named Inserted. This is a special table that's created by SQL Server during an insert operation. It contains the rows that are being inserted into the table. Since this table only exists while the trigger is executing, you can only refer to it in the trigger code.

The syntax of the CREATE TRIGGER statement

```
CREATE TRIGGER trigger_name
    ON {table_name|view_name}
    [WITH [ENCRYPTION] [,] [EXECUTE_AS_clause]]
    {FOR|AFTER|INSTEAD OF} [INSERT] [,] [UPDATE] [,] [DELETE]
AS sql_statements
```

A CREATE TRIGGER statement that corrects mixed-case state names

```
CREATE TRIGGER Vendors_INSERT_UPDATE
    ON Vendors
    AFTER INSERT,UPDATE
AS
    UPDATE Vendors
    SET VendorState = UPPER(VendorState)
    WHERE VendorID IN (SELECT VendorID FROM Inserted);
```

An INSERT statement that fires the trigger

```
INSERT Vendors
VALUES ('Peerless Uniforms, Inc.', '785 S Pixley Rd', NULL,
        'Piqua', 'Oh', '45356', '(937) 555-8845', NULL, NULL, 4, 550);
```

The new row that's inserted into the Vendors table

	VendorID	VendorName	VendorAddress1	VendorAddress2	VendorCity	VendorState	VendorZip
1	125	Peerless Uniforms, Inc.	785 S Pixley Rd	NULL	Piqua	OH	45356

Description

- A trigger is a special kind of procedure that executes, or *fires*, in response to an action query. Unlike a stored procedure, you can't invoke a trigger directly, you can't pass parameters to a trigger, and a trigger can't pass back a return value.

- A trigger is associated with a single table or view, which you identify in the ON clause. The trigger can be set to fire on INSERT, UPDATE, or DELETE statements or on a combination of these statements.

- A trigger can be set to fire after the action query (AFTER) or instead of the action query (INSTEAD OF). A FOR trigger is the same as an AFTER trigger.

- A table can have multiple AFTER triggers, even for the same action. A view can't have an AFTER trigger. A table or view can have only one INSTEAD OF trigger for each action.

- To hide the code for the trigger from the user, include the ENCRYPTION option.

- To execute a trigger under a specific security context, include the EXECUTE_AS_clause option.

- It's a common programming practice to name triggers based on the table or view and the actions that will cause the trigger to fire.

- Within a trigger, you can refer to two tables that are created by the system: Inserted and Deleted. The Inserted table contains the new rows for insert and update operations. The Deleted table contains the original rows for update and delete operations.

Figure 15-17   How to create a trigger

Similarly, a table named Deleted is created by SQL Server during a delete operation that contains the rows that are being deleted. For an update operation, SQL Server creates both tables. In that case, the Inserted table contains the rows with the updated data, and the Deleted table contains the original data from the rows that are being updated.

How to use AFTER triggers

Figure 15-18 shows another example of an AFTER trigger. This trigger archives all rows deleted from the Invoices table by inserting the deleted rows into another table named InvoiceArchive.

The CREATE TRIGGER statement shown in this figure begins by specifying a name of Invoices_DELETE. Then, it specifies that this trigger should execute after a DELETE statement is executed against the Invoices table. The body of this trigger uses an INSERT statement to insert the rows that have been deleted from the Invoices table into the InvoiceArchive table. To accomplish this, this trigger uses a SELECT statement to retrieve columns from the Deleted table.

The DELETE statement shown in this figure deletes three rows from Invoices table. This causes the Invoices_DELETE trigger to fire. As a result, the trigger inserts these three rows into the InvoiceArchive table after the DELETE statement executes.

Because an AFTER trigger fires after the action query is executed, the trigger doesn't fire if the action query causes an error. Usually, that's what you want. In this figure, for example, you wouldn't want to archive deleted rows if the DELETE statement caused an error and didn't execute successfully.

An AFTER trigger that archives deleted data

```
CREATE TRIGGER Invoices_DELETE
    ON Invoices
    AFTER DELETE
AS
INSERT INTO InvoiceArchive
    (InvoiceID, VendorID, InvoiceNumber, InvoiceDate, InvoiceTotal,
        PaymentTotal, CreditTotal, TermsID, InvoiceDueDate, PaymentDate)
    SELECT InvoiceID, VendorID, InvoiceNumber, InvoiceDate, InvoiceTotal,
        PaymentTotal, CreditTotal, TermsID, InvoiceDueDate, PaymentDate
    FROM Deleted
```

A DELETE statement that causes the AFTER trigger to fire

```
DELETE Invoices
WHERE VendorID = 37
```

The rows inserted into the InvoiceArchive table

	InvoiceID	VendorID	InvoiceNumber	InvoiceDate	InvoiceTotal	PaymentTotal	CreditTotal	Ter
1	113	37	547480102	2016-04-01 00:00:00	224.00	0.00	0.00	3
2	50	37	547479217	2016-02-07 00:00:00	116.00	116.00	0.00	3
3	46	37	547481328	2016-02-03 00:00:00	224.00	224.00	0.00	3

Description

- An AFTER trigger fires after the action query is executed. If the action query causes an error, the AFTER trigger never fires.
- AFTER triggers can be used to archive deleted data.

Figure 15-18 How to use AFTER triggers

How to use INSTEAD OF triggers

An INSTEAD OF trigger can be associated with either a table or a view. However, INSTEAD OF triggers are used most often to provide better control of updatable views.

Figure 15-19 presents an INSTEAD OF trigger that's used to control an insert operation through a view named IBM_Invoices. This view selects the InvoiceNumber, InvoiceDate, and InvoiceTotal from the Invoices table for the vendor named "IBM." If you look at the design of the Invoices table you'll see that there are six additional columns that don't allow null values. The problem is, how do you insert values into these six additional columns when the view isn't aware of their existence?

Three of the six columns (InvoiceID, PaymentTotal, and CreditTotal) don't need to be inserted through the view. That's because the design of the Invoices table automatically handles null values for these columns. InvoiceID is an identity column, so the database automatically inserts the value for that column. The other two columns have a default value of 0, so the database uses this default value.

This leaves three columns (VendorID, TermsID, and InvoiceDueDate) that must be updated when you insert data through the view. If you attempt to insert a row through the view, you can't specify these required columns, and the insert operation fails.

This trigger accommodates these missing columns by calculating their values based on three logical assumptions. First, the VendorID can be assumed because this view is explicitly for invoices for vendor "IBM." Second, the terms for the invoice can be assumed to be the default terms for the vendor. Third, the due date for the invoice can be calculated based on the invoice date and the terms.

After it declares the variables it uses, the trigger queries the Inserted table to get a count of the number of rows that are being inserted. Since this trigger will work only if a single row is being inserted, an error is raised if the row count is greater than one. Otherwise, the trigger queries the Inserted table to get the values of the three columns that were specified in an INSERT statement like the one shown in this figure. The SELECT statement assigns these values to three of the variables. Then, if all three variables contain values other than null, the trigger calculates the values of the missing columns.

Since an INSTEAD OF trigger is executed instead of the action query that caused it to fire, the action will never occur unless you code it as part of the trigger. For this reason, the last statement in this trigger is an INSERT statement that inserts the new row into the Invoices table. Without this statement, the row would never be inserted.

An INSTEAD OF INSERT trigger for a view

```
CREATE TRIGGER IBM_Invoices_INSERT
    ON IBM_Invoices
    INSTEAD OF INSERT
AS
DECLARE @InvoiceDate smalldatetime, @InvoiceNumber varchar(50),
        @InvoiceTotal money, @VendorID int,
        @InvoiceDueDate smalldatetime, @TermsID int,
        @DefaultTerms smallint, @TestRowCount int;
SELECT @TestRowCount = COUNT(*) FROM Inserted;
IF @TestRowCount = 1
    BEGIN
        SELECT @InvoiceNumber = InvoiceNumber, @InvoiceDate = InvoiceDate,
            @InvoiceTotal = InvoiceTotal
        FROM Inserted;
        IF (@InvoiceDate IS NOT NULL AND @InvoiceNumber IS NOT NULL AND
            @InvoiceTotal IS NOT NULL)
            BEGIN
                SELECT @VendorID = VendorID, @TermsID = DefaultTermsID
                FROM Vendors
                WHERE VendorName = 'IBM';

                SELECT @DefaultTerms = TermsDueDays
                FROM Terms
                WHERE TermsID = @TermsID;

                SET @InvoiceDueDate = @InvoiceDate + @DefaultTerms;

                INSERT Invoices
                    (VendorID, InvoiceNumber, InvoiceDate, InvoiceTotal,
                    TermsID, InvoiceDueDate, PaymentDate)
                VALUES (@VendorID, @InvoiceNumber, @InvoiceDate,
                    @InvoiceTotal, @TermsID, @InvoiceDueDate, NULL);
            END;
    END;
ELSE
    THROW 50027, 'Limit INSERT to a single row.', 1;
```

An INSERT statement that succeeds due to the trigger

```
INSERT IBM_Invoices
VALUES ('RA23988', '2016-05-09', 417.34);
```

Description

- An INSTEAD OF trigger is executed instead of the action query that causes it to fire. Because the action query is never executed, the trigger typically contains code that performs the operation.

- INSTEAD OF triggers are typically used to provide for updatable views. They can also be used to prevent errors, such as constraint violations, before they occur.

- Each table or view can have only one INSTEAD OF trigger for each type of action. However, if a table is defined with a foreign key constraint that specifies the CASCADE UPDATE or CASCADE DELETE option, INSTEAD OF UPDATE and INSTEAD OF DELETE triggers can't be defined for the table.

Figure 15-19   How to use INSTEAD OF triggers

How to use triggers to enforce data consistency

Triggers can also be used to enforce data consistency. For example, the sum of line item amounts in the InvoiceLineItems table should always be equal to the invoice total for the invoice in the Invoices table. Unfortunately, you can't enforce this rule using a constraint on either the Invoices table or the InvoiceLineItems table. However, you can use a trigger like the one in figure 15-20 to enforce this rule when a payment amount is updated.

The trigger shown here fires after an update operation on the Invoices table. Since you can assume that posting a payment is likely to be the last action taken on an invoice, firing a trigger on this action is a good way to verify that all of the data is valid. If an update operation changes the PaymentTotal column, the rest of the trigger verifies that the sum of the line items is equal to the invoice total. If the data isn't valid, the trigger raises an error and rolls back the update.

Notice the two IF statements shown in this figure. They use the EXISTS keyword to test for the existence of the data specified by the subqueries that follow. In chapter 6, you saw how to use the EXISTS keyword in the WHERE clause. Because this keyword returns a Boolean value, however, you can use it in an IF statement as well.

You can use triggers like the one shown here to enforce business rules or verify data consistency. Since you can program a trigger to accommodate virtually any situation, triggers are more flexible than constraints. As a result, some programmers prefer to use triggers rather than constraints to enforce data consistency and sometimes even check constraints and defaults.

In addition, prior to version 6.5, way back in the early 1990s, SQL Server didn't support foreign key constraints. In those days, triggers were the only way to enforce referential integrity. As a result, if you're working on a legacy system, it's possible that you may come across a database that uses triggers rather than foreign key constraints to enforce referential integrity.

A trigger that validates line item amounts when posting a payment

```
CREATE TRIGGER Invoices_UPDATE
    ON Invoices
    AFTER UPDATE
AS
IF EXISTS              --Test whether PaymentTotal was changed
  (SELECT *
   FROM Deleted JOIN Invoices
     ON Deleted.InvoiceID = Invoices.InvoiceID
   WHERE Deleted.PaymentTotal <> Invoices.PaymentTotal)
  BEGIN
    IF EXISTS          --Test whether line items total and InvoiceTotal match
      (SELECT *
       FROM Invoices JOIN
          (SELECT InvoiceID, SUM(InvoiceLineItemAmount) AS SumOfInvoices
           FROM InvoiceLineItems
           GROUP BY InvoiceID) AS LineItems
        ON Invoices.InvoiceID = LineItems.InvoiceID
       WHERE (Invoices.InvoiceTotal <> LineItems.SumOfInvoices) AND
           (LineItems.InvoiceID IN (SELECT InvoiceID FROM Deleted)))
      BEGIN
        ;
        THROW 50113, 'Correct line item amounts before posting payment.', 1;
        ROLLBACK TRAN;
      END;
  END;
```

An UPDATE statement that fires the trigger

```
UPDATE Invoices
SET PaymentTotal = 662, PaymentDate = '2016-05-09'
WHERE InvoiceID = 98;
```

The response from the system

```
Msg 50113, Level 16, State 1, Procedure Invoices_UPDATE, Line 23
Correct line item amounts before posting payment.
```

Description

- Triggers can be used to enforce database rules for data consistency that can't be enforced by constraints.

- Triggers can also be used to enforce the same rules as constraints, but with more flexibility.

Figure 15-20   How to use triggers to enforce data consistency

How to use triggers to work with DDL statements

So far, this chapter has only shown you how to create triggers for DML statements such as the INSERT, UPDATE, and DELETE statements since that's typically how triggers are used. However, you can also create triggers for DDL statements such as the CREATE TABLE statement. For example, figure 15-21 shows a trigger that is executed when any CREATE TABLE or DROP TABLE statement is executed on the current database.

Although the syntax for this trigger is similar to a trigger for a DML statement, the ON clause works a little differently. To start, you can code the DATABASE keyword after the ON keyword to fire the trigger when the specified DDL actions are executed on the current database. Or, you can code the ALL SERVER keywords after the ON keyword to fire the trigger when the specified DDL actions are executed on any database on the current server. However, only a handful of DDL actions apply to a server-level trigger. As a result, a server-level trigger can only be fired by certain actions that apply to the server such as the CREATE DATABASE statement.

To specify the DDL actions for the trigger, you can begin by coding the AFTER or INSTEAD OF keywords just as you do for any type of trigger. Then, you can specify one or more DDL statements, separated by commas. When you code the name of the DDL statement, replace any spaces with underscores. In this figure, for example, the statement uses CREATE_TABLE and DROP_TABLE to specify that the trigger fires after a CREATE TABLE or DROP TABLE statement is executed.

Next, two variables are declared, @EventData with an xml data type and @EventType with a varchar data type. Then, the @EventData variable is filled using a special function called EVENTDATA. This function is available from within the body of a trigger for a DDL statement, and it returns an XML document that contains data about the event that caused the trigger to fire.

After that, the @EventType variable is filled by parsing the character data that's stored in the @EventData variable. This returns information about what type of DDL statement was executed. For now, don't worry if you don't understand the code that parses the @EventData variable. It should make more sense after you've read chapter 18. Finally, the code inserts the data stored in the @EventData and @EventType variables into the corresponding columns in the AuditDDL table.

This figure shows the data in the AuditDDL table after a user has created a table named VendorsTest. If you are using Management Studio, and you click on the XML in the EventData column, Management Studio displays the XML for the event. This XML should be similar to the XML shown in this figure.

If you want to make it easier to access any of this data, you can store it in the columns of the AuditDDL table. To do that, create the necessary columns in the AuditDDL table. Then, use the techniques described in chapter 18 to parse the @EventData variable and store each piece of data in the appropriate column. For example, you might want to store the PostTime and UserName values in their own columns. That way, you could easily query the AuditDDL table to determine when the DDL statement was executed and who executed it.

A trigger that works with DDL statements

```
CREATE TRIGGER Database_CreateTable_DropTable
    ON DATABASE
    AFTER CREATE_TABLE, DROP_TABLE
AS
    DECLARE @EventData xml;
    DECLARE @EventType varchar(20);

    SELECT @EventData = EVENTDATA();
    SET @EventType =
        @EventData.value('(/EVENT_INSTANCE/EventType)[1]', 'varchar(100)');

    INSERT INTO AuditDDL (EventType, EventData)
        VALUES(@EventType, @EventData);
```

A CREATE TABLE statement that fires the trigger

```
CREATE TABLE VendorsTest (VendorID int, VendorName varchar(50));
```

The row inserted into the AuditDDL table

	EventType	EventData
1	CREATE_TABLE	<EVENT_INSTANCE><EventType>CREATE_TABLE</EventTy...

The XML saved in the EventData column

```
<EVENT_INSTANCE>
  <EventType>CREATE_TABLE</EventType>
  <PostTime>2016-01-05T12:38:23.147</PostTime>
  <SPID>54</SPID>
  <ServerName>RAY-PC\SQLEXPRESS</ServerName>
  <LoginName>Ray-PC\Ray</LoginName>
  <UserName>dbo</UserName>
  <DatabaseName>AP</DatabaseName>
  <SchemaName>dbo</SchemaName>
  <ObjectName>VendorsTest</ObjectName>
  <ObjectType>TABLE</ObjectType>
  <TSQLCommand>
      <SetOptions ANSI_NULLS="ON" ANSI_NULL_DEFAULT="ON" ANSI_PADDING="ON"
          QUOTED_IDENTIFIER="ON" ENCRYPTED="FALSE" />
      <CommandText>
          CREATE TABLE VendorsTest
          (VendorID int, VendorName varchar(50));
      </CommandText>
  </TSQLCommand>
</EVENT_INSTANCE>
```

Description

- In the ON clause, you can specify the DATABASE keyword to fire the trigger only for the current database, or you can specify the ALL SERVER keywords to fire the trigger for any database on the current server.

- To specify a DDL statement for a trigger, you can code the name of the DDL statement, replacing any spaces with underscores.

- The EVENTDATA function returns an XML document of the xml data type. If necessary, you can use the skills presented in chapter 18 to parse this document.

Figure 15-21   A trigger that works with DDL statements

How to delete or change a trigger

Figure 15-22 presents the syntax of the DROP TRIGGER and ALTER TRIGGER statements. DROP TRIGGER permanently deletes one or more triggers along with any security permissions associated with the trigger.

If you want to change the definition of a trigger without affecting permissions, you can use the ALTER TRIGGER statement. The statement shown in this figure, for example, modifies the trigger you saw in figure 15-17. This trigger now removes spaces from the beginning and end of the address columns in addition to converting the state code to upper case.

The syntax of the DROP TRIGGER statement

```
DROP TRIGGER trigger_name [, ...]
```

The syntax of the ALTER TRIGGER statement

```
ALTER TRIGGER trigger_name
ON {table_name|view_name}
[WITH [ENCRYPTION] [,] [EXECUTE_AS_clause]]
{FOR|AFTER|INSTEAD OF} [INSERT] [,] [UPDATE] [,] [DELETE]
AS sql_statements
```

A statement that modifies the trigger in figure 15-17

```
ALTER TRIGGER Vendors_INSERT_UPDATE
    ON Vendors
    AFTER INSERT,UPDATE
AS

UPDATE Vendors
SET VendorState = UPPER(VendorState),
    VendorAddress1 = LTRIM(RTRIM(VendorAddress1)),
    VendorAddress2 = LTRIM(RTRIM(VendorAddress2))
WHERE VendorID IN (SELECT VendorID FROM Inserted);
```

A statement that deletes the trigger

```
DROP TRIGGER Vendors_INSERT_UPDATE;
```

Description

- To delete a trigger from the database, use the DROP TRIGGER statement.

- To modify the definition of a trigger, you can locate the trigger in the Object Explorer of SQL Server Management Studio by expanding the table the trigger is associated with and then expanding the Triggers folder. Finally, you can right-click on the trigger and choose modify.

- To modify the definition of a DDL trigger, you can locate the trigger in the Object Explorer by expanding the Programmability folder and then expanding the Database Triggers folder. Finally, you can right-click on the trigger and choose modify.

- When you delete a trigger, any security permissions that are assigned to the trigger are also deleted. If that's not what you want, you can use the ALTER TRIGGER statement to modify the trigger and preserve the permissions.

- Unless a trigger and its corresponding table or view belong to the default schema, you must include the schema name on the DROP TRIGGER and ALTER TRIGGER statements.

Figure 15-22   How to delete or change a trigger

Perspective

In this chapter, you've learned how to create the three types of executable database objects supported by SQL Server using SQL statements. Stored procedures are the most flexible of the three because you can use them in so many different ways. You can code procedures to simultaneously simplify and restrict a user's access to the database, to verify data integrity, and to ease your own administrative tasks.

Although they're generally less flexible than stored procedures, functions and triggers are powerful objects. You can use them to solve problems that otherwise would be difficult or impossible to solve. In particular, table-valued functions are one of the most useful extensions provided by Transact-SQL because they behave like views but can accept parameters that can change the result set.

In addition to using SQL statements to work with stored procedures, functions, and triggers, you can use the Management Studio. You'll find all three of these object types in folders within the Programmability folder for a database. Then, you can add, modify, and delete objects using the menus that appear when you right-click on a folder or object. You can use this same technique to work with the user-defined table types you use with stored procedures.

Terms

stored procedure	required parameter
user-defined function (UDF)	optional parameter
trigger	passing parameters by position
sproc	passing parameters by name
call a procedure	return value
precompiled	data validation
execution plan	user-defined table type
recursive call	system stored procedure
recursion	scalar-valued function
temporary stored procedure	table-valued function
local procedure	simple table-valued function
global procedure	multi-statement table-valued function
parameter	invoke a function
input parameter	inline table-valued function
output parameter	fire a trigger

Exercises

1. Create a stored procedure named spBalanceRange that accepts three optional parameters. The procedure should return a result set consisting of VendorName, InvoiceNumber, and Balance for each invoice with a balance due, sorted with largest balance due first. The parameter @VendorVar is a mask that's used with a LIKE operator to filter by vendor name, as shown in figure 15-5. @BalanceMin and @BalanceMax are parameters used to specify the requested range of balances due. If called with no parameters or with a maximum value of 0, the procedure should return all invoices with a balance due.

2. Code three calls to the procedure created in exercise 1:
   (a) passed by position with @VendorVar='M%' and no balance range
   (b) passed by name with @VendorVar omitted and a balance range from $200 to $1000
   (c) passed by position with a balance due that's less than $200 filtering for vendors whose names begin with C or F

3. Create a stored procedure named spDateRange that accepts two parameters, @DateMin and @DateMax, with data type varchar and default value null. If called with no parameters or with null values, raise an error that describes the problem. If called with non-null values, validate the parameters. Test that the literal strings are valid dates and test that @DateMin is earlier than @DateMax. If the parameters are valid, return a result set that includes the InvoiceNumber, InvoiceDate, InvoiceTotal, and Balance for each invoice for which the InvoiceDate is within the date range, sorted with earliest invoice first.

4. Code a call to the stored procedure created in exercise 3 that returns invoices with an InvoiceDate between December 10 and December 20, 2015. This call should also catch any errors that are raised by the procedure and print the error number and description.

5. Create a scalar-valued function named fnUnpaidInvoiceID that returns the InvoiceID of the earliest invoice with an unpaid balance. Test the function in the following SELECT statement:

```
SELECT VendorName, InvoiceNumber, InvoiceDueDate,
       InvoiceTotal - CreditTotal - PaymentTotal AS Balance
FROM Vendors JOIN Invoices
  ON Vendors.VendorID = Invoices.VendorID
WHERE InvoiceID = dbo.fnUnpaidInvoiceID();
```

6. Create a table-valued function named fnDateRange, similar to the stored procedure of exercise 3. The function requires two parameters of data type smalldatetime. Don't validate the parameters. Return a result set that includes the InvoiceNumber, InvoiceDate, InvoiceTotal, and Balance for each invoice for which the InvoiceDate is within the date range. Invoke the function from within a SELECT statement to return those invoices with InvoiceDate between December 10 and December 20, 2015.

7. Use the function you created in exercise 6 in a SELECT statement that returns five columns: VendorName and the four columns returned by the function.

8. Create a trigger for the Invoices table that automatically inserts the vendor name and address for a paid invoice into a table named ShippingLabels. The trigger should fire any time the PaymentTotal column of the Invoices table is updated. The structure of the ShippingLabels table is as follows:

```
CREATE TABLE ShippingLabels
(VendorName        varchar(50),
 VendorAddress1    varchar(50),
 VendorAddress2    varchar(50),
 VendorCity        varchar(50),
 VendorState       char(2),
 VendorZipCode     varchar(20));
```

Use this UPDATE statement to test the trigger:

```
UPDATE Invoices
SET PaymentTotal = 67.92, PaymentDate = '2016-04-23'
WHERE InvoiceID = 100;
```

9. Write a trigger that prohibits duplicate values *except for nulls* in the NoDupName column of the following table:

```
CREATE TABLE TestUniqueNulls
(RowID       int  IDENTITY  NOT NULL,
 NoDupName   varchar(20)     NULL);
```

(Note that you can't do this by using a unique constraint because the constraint wouldn't allow duplicate null values.) If an INSERT or UPDATE statement creates a duplicate value, roll back the statement and return an error message.

Write a series of INSERT statements that tests that duplicate null values are allowed but duplicates of other values are not.

16

How to manage transactions and locking

If you've been working with a stand-alone copy of SQL Server, you've been the only user of your database. In the real world, though, a database is typically used by many users working simultaneously. Then, what happens when two users try to update the same data at the same time?

In this chapter, you'll learn how SQL Server manages concurrent changes. But first, you'll learn how to combine related SQL statements into a single unit, called a transaction. By learning these skills, you'll be able to write code that anticipates these conflicts.

How to work with transactions

A *transaction* is a group of database operations that you combine into a single logical unit. By combining operations in this way, you can prevent certain kinds of database errors. In the topics that follow, you'll learn the SQL statements for managing transactions.

How transactions maintain data integrity

Figure 16-1 presents an example of three INSERT statements that are good candidates for a transaction. As you can see, the first INSERT statement adds a new invoice to the Invoices table. Next, a SET statement assigns the identity value for the newly inserted invoice to the @InvoiceID variable. Then, the last two INSERT statements insert rows into the InvoiceLineItems table that represent the two line items associated with the invoice.

What would happen if one or more of these INSERT statements failed? If the first statement failed, @InvoiceID wouldn't be assigned a valid value, so the last two insertions would also fail. However, if the first statement succeeded and one or both of the other INSERT statements failed, the Invoices and InvoiceLineItems tables wouldn't match. Specifically, the total of the InvoiceLineItemAmount columns in the InvoiceLineItems table wouldn't equal the InvoiceTotal column in the Invoices table, so the data would be invalid.

Now, suppose that these three INSERT statements were executed as part of the same transaction as illustrated in the second example in this figure. Here, you can see that a BEGIN TRAN statement is executed before the first INSERT statement. Then, after all three INSERT statements are executed, a COMMIT TRAN statement *commits* the changes to the database making them permanent. Because these statements are coded within a TRY block, however, the COMMIT TRAN statement is never executed if any of the INSERT statements fail. Instead, execution jumps into the CATCH block. This block executes a ROLLBACK TRAN statement to undo, or *rollback*, all of the changes made since the beginning of the transaction.

By grouping these SQL statements together in a single transaction, you can control whether and how changes are made to the database. Since all three INSERT statements must succeed for the transaction to be committed, a failure of any of the statements will cause the entire transaction to be rolled back. Note, however, that once you commit the transaction, you can't roll it back. Likewise, once you roll a transaction back, you can't commit it.

In this particular example, an error in one of the INSERT statements wouldn't be catastrophic. If a statement failed because you coded it incorrectly, you could easily correct the error by resubmitting the failed INSERT statement. If the failure was due to a system error such as a server crash, however, you wouldn't discover the error unless you looked for it after the server was restored.

Three INSERT statements that work with related data

```
DECLARE @InvoiceID int;
INSERT Invoices
    VALUES (34,'ZXA-080','2016-04-30',14092.59,0,0,3,'2016-05-30',NULL);
SET @InvoiceID = @@IDENTITY;
INSERT InvoiceLineItems VALUES (@InvoiceID,1,160,4447.23,'HW upgrade');
INSERT InvoiceLineItems VALUES (@InvoiceID,2,167,9645.36,'OS upgrade');
```

The same statements coded as a transaction

```
DECLARE @InvoiceID int;
BEGIN TRY
    BEGIN TRAN;
    INSERT Invoices
      VALUES (34,'ZXA-080','2016-04-30',14092.59,0,0,3,'2016-05-30',NULL);
    SET @InvoiceID = @@IDENTITY;
    INSERT InvoiceLineItems VALUES (@InvoiceID,1,160,4447.23,'HW upgrade');
    INSERT InvoiceLineItems VALUES (@InvoiceID,2,167,9645.36,'OS upgrade');
    COMMIT TRAN;
END TRY
BEGIN CATCH
    ROLLBACK TRAN;
END CATCH;
```

When to use explicit transactions

- When you code two or more action queries that affect related data
- When you update foreign key references
- When you move rows from one table to another table
- When you code a SELECT query followed by an action query and the values inserted in the action query are based on the results of the SELECT query
- When a failure of any set of SQL statements would violate data integrity

Description

- A *transaction* is a group of database operations that are combined into a logical unit. By default, each SQL statement is treated as a separate transaction. However, you can combine any number of SQL statements into a single transaction as shown above.

- When you *commit* a transaction, the operations performed by the SQL statements become a permanent part of the database. Until it's committed, you can undo all of the changes made to the database since the beginning of the transaction by *rolling back* the transaction.

- A transaction is either committed or rolled back in its entirety. Once you commit a transaction, it can't be rolled back.

Figure 16-1   How transactions maintain data integrity

For some systems, however, a violation of data integrity such as this one is critical. For instance, consider the classic example of a transfer between two accounts in a banking system. In that case, one update reduces the balance in the first account and another update increases the balance in the second account. If one of these updates fails, either the bank or the customer gets an unexpected windfall. Because an error like this could cause problems even during the short period of time it may take to fix it, these two updates should be coded as a transaction.

SQL statements for handling transactions

Figure 16-2 summarizes the SQL statements used to process transactions. As you can see, you can code either the TRAN or the TRANSACTION keyword in each of these statements, although TRAN is used more commonly. You can also omit this keyword entirely from the COMMIT and ROLLBACK statements. However, it's customary to include this keyword since it makes your code easier to read.

The BEGIN TRAN statement explicitly marks the starting point of a transaction. If you don't code this statement, SQL Server implicitly starts a new transaction for each SQL statement you code. If the statement succeeds, the implicit transaction is committed automatically. For this reason, this mode is called *autocommit* mode. Note that you can't use the COMMIT TRAN statement to commit an implicit transaction.

However, you can code a ROLLBACK TRAN statement to roll back an implicit transaction. You saw examples of that in some of the triggers presented in chapter 15. The triggers in figure 15-18 rolled back an action query if it violated referential integrity between the Vendors and Invoices tables. And the trigger in figure 15-20 rolled back an UPDATE statement if it caused the data in the Invoices and InvoiceLineItems tables to be inconsistent.

You can also use the SAVE TRAN statement to declare one or more *save points* within a transaction. Then, you can roll back part of a transaction by coding the save point name in the ROLLBACK TRAN statement. You'll learn more about how that works in a moment.

This figure presents another script that uses a transaction. This script deletes the invoices for a particular vendor and then deletes the vendor. Notice that the script tests the value of the @@ROWCOUNT system function after rows are deleted from the Invoices table to see if more than one invoice was deleted. If so, the transaction is rolled back, so the deletion from the Invoices table is undone. If only one invoice was deleted, however, the transaction is committed, so the deletion is made permanent.

Before I go on, you should realize that you can also name a transaction in the BEGIN TRAN statement, and you can refer to that name in the COMMIT TRAN and ROLLBACK TRAN statements. Since there's usually no reason to do that, however, I've omitted that option from the syntax shown in this figure and from the examples shown in this chapter.

Summary of the SQL statements for processing transactions

Statement	Description
`BEGIN {TRAN|TRANSACTION}`	Marks the starting point of a transaction.
`SAVE {TRAN|TRANSACTION} save_point`	Sets a new save point within a transaction.
`COMMIT [TRAN|TRANSACTION]`	Marks the end of a transaction and makes the changes within the transaction a permanent part of the database.
`ROLLBACK [[TRAN|TRANSACTION]` `    [save_point]]`	Rolls back a transaction to the starting point or to the specified save point.

A script that performs a test before committing the transaction

```
BEGIN TRAN;

DELETE Invoices
WHERE VendorID = 34;

IF @@ROWCOUNT > 1
    BEGIN
        ROLLBACK TRAN;
        PRINT 'More invoices than expected. Deletions rolled back.';
    END;
ELSE
    BEGIN
        COMMIT TRAN;
        PRINT 'Deletions committed to the database.';
    END;
```

The response from the system

```
(3 row(s) affected)
More invoices than expected. Deletions rolled back.
```

Description

- Although you can omit the TRAN keyword from the COMMIT and ROLLBACK statements, it's generally included for readability.

- By default, SQL Server is in *autocommit mode*. Then, unless you explicitly start a transaction using the BEGIN TRAN statement, each statement is automatically treated as a separate transaction. If the statement causes an error, it's automatically rolled back. Otherwise, it's automatically committed.

- Even if you don't explicitly start a transaction, you can roll it back using the ROLLBACK TRAN statement. However, you can't explicitly commit an implicit transaction.

- When you use *save points*, you can roll a transaction back to the beginning or to a particular save point. See figure 16-4 for details on using save points.

- Although you can name a transaction in the BEGIN TRAN statement and you can refer to that name in the COMMIT TRAN and ROLLBACK TRAN statements, you're not likely to do that.

Figure 16-2   SQL statements for handling transactions

How to work with nested transactions

A *nested transaction* is a transaction that's coded within another transaction. In other words, a BEGIN TRAN statement is coded after another BEGIN TRAN statement but before the COMMIT TRAN or ROLLBACK TRAN statement that ends the first transaction. Since there are few problems that can only be solved using nested transactions, it's unlikely that you'll ever need to code them. However, you should understand how the COMMIT TRAN statement behaves when you code it within a nested transaction. Figure 16-3 presents a script that illustrates how this works.

This example uses the @@TRANCOUNT system function, which returns the number of explicit transactions that are active on the current connection. If you haven't coded a BEGIN TRAN statement, @@TRANCOUNT returns zero. Then, each BEGIN TRAN statement increments @@TRANCOUNT by one, so its value indicates how deeply you've nested the transactions.

If the current value of @@TRANCOUNT is one, the COMMIT TRAN statement closes the current transaction and commits the changes to the database as you've seen in the last two figures. But if @@TRANCOUNT is greater than one, COMMIT TRAN simply decrements @@TRANCOUNT by 1. In other words, within a nested transaction, the COMMIT TRAN statement doesn't commit a transaction.

This counterintuitive behavior is illustrated by the script in this figure. Here, the COMMIT TRAN statement that follows the DELETE statement that deletes all the rows in the Vendors table decrements @@TRANCOUNT, but doesn't commit the deletion. That's because this COMMIT TRAN statement is coded within a nested transaction.

On the other hand, the ROLLBACK TRAN statement always rolls back all of the uncommitted statements, whether or not they're coded within a nested transaction. In this script, for example, the ROLLBACK TRAN statement rolls back both DELETE statements. As you can see from the results of the last five statements in this script, neither DELETE statement was committed.

A script with nested transactions

```
BEGIN TRAN;
PRINT 'First Tran  @@TRANCOUNT: ' + CONVERT(varchar,@@TRANCOUNT);
DELETE Invoices;
   BEGIN TRAN;
      PRINT 'Second Tran @@TRANCOUNT: ' + CONVERT(varchar,@@TRANCOUNT);
      DELETE Vendors;
   COMMIT TRAN;             -- This COMMIT decrements @@TRANCOUNT.
                            -- It doesn't commit 'DELETE Vendors'.
   PRINT 'COMMIT      @@TRANCOUNT: ' + CONVERT(varchar,@@TRANCOUNT);
ROLLBACK TRAN;
PRINT 'ROLLBACK    @@TRANCOUNT: ' + CONVERT(varchar,@@TRANCOUNT);

PRINT ' ';
DECLARE @VendorsCount int, @InvoicesCount int;
SELECT @VendorsCount = COUNT (*) FROM Vendors;
SELECT @InvoicesCount = COUNT (*) FROM Invoices;
PRINT 'Vendors Count:  ' + CONVERT (varchar , @VendorsCount);
PRINT 'Invoices Count: ' + CONVERT (varchar , @InvoicesCount);
```

The response from the system

```
First Tran  @@TRANCOUNT: 1

(114 row(s) affected)
Second Tran @@TRANCOUNT: 2

(122 row(s) affected)
COMMIT      @@TRANCOUNT: 1
ROLLBACK    @@TRANCOUNT: 0

Vendors count:  122
Invoices count: 114
```

Description

- You can *nest* transactions by coding nested BEGIN TRAN statements. Each time this statement is executed, it increments the @@TRANCOUNT system function by 1. Then, you can query this function to determine how many levels deep the transactions are nested.

- If you execute a COMMIT TRAN statement when @@TRANCOUNT is equal to 1, all of the changes made to the database during the transaction are committed and @@TRANCOUNT is set to zero. If @@TRANCOUNT is greater than 1, however, the changes aren't committed. Instead, @@TRANCOUNT is simply decremented by 1.

- The ROLLBACK TRAN statement rolls back all active transactions regardless of the nesting level where it's coded. It also sets the value of @@TRANCOUNT back to 0.

- Since there are few programming problems that you can only solve using nested transactions, you probably won't use them often.

Figure 16-3   How to work with nested transactions

How to work with save points

You can create save points within a transaction by coding the SAVE TRAN statement. In that case, you can roll back the transaction to that particular point by coding the save point name in the ROLLBACK TRAN statement. Figure 16-4 presents a script that shows how this works.

First, this script creates a temporary table named #VendorCopy that contains a copy of the VendorIDs and names and for the first four vendors in the Vendors table. After beginning a transaction, the script deletes a row and then sets a save point named Vendor1. Then the script deletes a second row, sets another save point named Vendor2, and deletes a third row. The result of the first SELECT statement that follows illustrates that only one row is left in the #VendorCopy table.

Next, a ROLLBACK TRAN statement rolls back the transaction to the Vendor2 save point. This rolls back the third delete, as illustrated by the second SELECT statement in this figure. The next ROLLBACK TRAN statement rolls the transaction back to the Vendor1 save point, which rolls back the second delete. At that point, the #VendorCopy table contains three rows, as illustrated by the third SELECT statement. Finally, a COMMIT TRAN statement commits the transaction. Since the only statement that hasn't already been rolled back is the statement that deleted the first row, this row is deleted permanently. The last SELECT statement illustrates the final result of this code.

You should note that if you don't code a save point name in the ROLLBACK TRAN statement, it ignores any save points and rolls back the entire transaction. In addition, you should notice that you can't code a save point name in a COMMIT TRAN statement. This means that you can't partially commit a transaction. Instead, a COMMIT TRAN statement ignores save points completely and commits the entire transaction.

As with nested transactions, you'll probably never need to use save points since there are few problems that can be solved by using them. Unlike the way that nested transactions work, however, save points work in an intuitive way, so coding them is less confusing.

A transaction with two save points

```
IF OBJECT_ID('tempdb..#VendorCopy') IS NOT NULL
    DROP TABLE tempdb.. #VendorCopy;
SELECT VendorID, VendorName
INTO #VendorCopy
FROM Vendors
WHERE VendorID < 5;
BEGIN TRAN;
  DELETE #VendorCopy WHERE VendorID = 1;
  SAVE TRAN Vendor1;
    DELETE #VendorCopy WHERE VendorID = 2;
    SAVE TRAN Vendor2;
      DELETE #VendorCopy WHERE VendorID = 3;
      SELECT * FROM #VendorCopy;
    ROLLBACK TRAN Vendor2;
    SELECT * FROM #VendorCopy;
  ROLLBACK TRAN Vendor1;
  SELECT * FROM #VendorCopy;
COMMIT TRAN;
SELECT * FROM #VendorCopy;
```

The response from the system

	VendorID	VendorName
1	4	Jobtrak

	VendorID	VendorName
1	3	Register of Copyrights
2	4	Jobtrak

	VendorID	VendorName
1	2	National Information Data Ctr
2	3	Register of Copyrights
3	4	Jobtrak

	VendorID	VendorName
1	2	National Information Data Ctr
2	3	Register of Copyrights
3	4	Jobtrak

Description

- You can partially roll back a transaction if you use save points. If you code a save point name in the ROLLBACK TRAN statement, the system rolls back all of the statements to that save point.

- If you don't code a save point name, the ROLLBACK TRAN statement rolls back the entire transaction.

- Since you can't code a save point name in a COMMIT TRAN statement, the system always commits the entire transaction.

- As with nested transactions, there are few practical programming problems that you can solve using save points.

Figure 16-4   How to work with save points

An introduction to concurrency and locking

When two or more users have access to the same database, it's possible for them to be working with the same data at the same time. This is called *concurrency*. Concurrency isn't a problem when two users retrieve the same data at the same time. If they then try to update that data, however, that can be a problem. In the topics that follow, you'll learn more about concurrency and how SQL Server uses locking to prevent concurrency problems. You'll also learn how you can control the types of problems that are allowed.

How concurrency and locking are related

Figure 16-5 presents two transactions that select and then update data from the same row in the same table. If these two transactions are submitted at the same time, the one that executes first will be overwritten by the one that executes second. Since this means that one of the two updates is lost, this is known as a *lost update*.

This figure shows the result if the update operation in transaction A is executed first, in which case its update is lost when the update in transaction B is executed. Because transaction A is unaware that its update has been lost, however, this can leave the data in an unpredictable state that affects the integrity of the data. For the AP database, it's unlikely that a lost update will adversely affect the system. For some database systems, however, this sort of unpredictability can be disastrous.

If your database has a relatively small number of users, the likelihood of concurrency problems is low. However, the larger the system, the greater the number of users and transactions. For a large system, then, you should expect concurrency, and therefore concurrency problems, to occur more frequently.

One way to avoid concurrency problems is to use *locking*. By holding a lock on the data, the transaction prevents others from using that data. Then, after the transaction releases the lock, the next transaction can work with that data.

Since SQL Server automatically enables and manages locking, it may prevent most of the concurrency problems on your system. If the number of users of your system grows, however, you may find that the default locking mechanism is insufficient. In that case, you may need to override the default locking behavior. You'll learn how to do that in a moment. But first, you need to understand the four concurrency problems that locks can prevent.

Two transactions that retrieve and then modify the data in the same row

Transaction A

```
BEGIN TRAN;
DECLARE @InvoiceTotal money, @PaymentTotal money, @CreditTotal money;
SELECT @InvoiceTotal = InvoiceTotal, @CreditTotal = CreditTotal,
       @PaymentTotal = PaymentTotal FROM Invoices WHERE InvoiceID = 112;
UPDATE Invoices
  SET InvoiceTotal = @InvoiceTotal, CreditTotal = @CreditTotal + 317.40,
      PaymentTotal = @PaymentTotal WHERE InvoiceID = 112;
COMMIT TRAN;
```

Transaction B

```
BEGIN TRAN;
DECLARE @InvoiceTotal money, @PaymentTotal money, @CreditTotal money;
SELECT @InvoiceTotal = InvoiceTotal, @CreditTotal = CreditTotal,
       @PaymentTotal = PaymentTotal FROM Invoices WHERE InvoiceID = 112;
UPDATE Invoices
  SET InvoiceTotal = @InvoiceTotal, CreditTotal = @CreditTotal,
      PaymentTotal = @InvoiceTotal - @CreditTotal,
      PaymentDate = GetDate() WHERE InvoiceID = 112;
COMMIT TRAN;
```

The initial values for the row

	InvoiceTotal	CreditTotal	PaymentTotal	PaymentDate
1	10976.06	0.00	0.00	NULL

The values after transaction A executes

	InvoiceTotal	CreditTotal	PaymentTotal	PaymentDate
1	10976.06	317.40	0.00	NULL

The values after transaction B executes, losing transaction A's updates

	InvoiceTotal	CreditTotal	PaymentTotal	PaymentDate
1	10976.06	0.00	10976.06	2016-02-24 16:10:00

Description

- *Concurrency* is the ability of a system to support two or more transactions working with the same data at the same time.

- Because small systems have few users, concurrency isn't generally a problem on these systems. On large systems with many users and many transactions, however, you may need to account for concurrency in your SQL code.

- Concurrency is a problem only when the data is being modified. When two or more transactions simply read the same data, the transactions don't affect each other.

- You can avoid some database concurrency problems by using *locks*, which delay the execution of a transaction if it conflicts with a transaction that's already running. Then, the second transaction can't use the data until the first transaction releases the lock.

- Although SQL Server automatically enforces locking, you can write more efficient code by understanding and customizing locking in your programs.

Figure 16-5   An introduction to concurrency and locking

The four concurrency problems
that locks can prevent

Figure 16-6 describes the four types of concurrency problems. You've already learned about the first problem: lost updates. In a moment, you'll see how locking can be used to prevent all four of these problems.

Like lost updates, the other three problems may not adversely affect a database. That depends on the nature of the data. In fact, for many systems, these problems happen infrequently. Then, when they do occur, they can be corrected by simply resubmitting the query that caused the problem. On some database systems, however, these problems can affect data integrity in a serious way.

Although locks can prevent the problems listed in this figure, SQL Server's default locking behavior won't. If your transaction could adversely affect data integrity on your system, then, you should consider changing the default locking behavior by setting the transaction isolation level.

The four types of concurrency problems

Problem	Description
Lost updates	Occur when two transactions select the same row and then update the row based on the values originally selected. Since each transaction is unaware of the other, the later update overwrites the earlier update.
Dirty reads (uncommitted dependencies)	Occur when a transaction selects data that isn't committed by another transaction. For example, transaction A changes a row. Transaction B then selects the changed row before transaction A commits the change. If transaction A then rolls back the change, transaction B has selected a row that doesn't exist in the database.
Nonrepeatable reads (inconsistent analysis)	Occur when two SELECT statements of the same data result in different values because another transaction has updated the data in the time between the two statements. For example, transaction A selects a row. Transaction B then updates the row. When transaction A selects the same row again, the data is different.
Phantom reads	Occur when you perform an update or delete on a set of rows when another transaction is performing an insert or delete that affects one or more rows in that same set of rows. For example, transaction A updates the payment total for each invoice that has a balance due. Transaction B inserts a new, unpaid invoice while transaction A is still running. After transaction A finishes, there is still an invoice with a balance due.

Description

- In a large system with many users, you should expect for these kinds of problems to occur. In general, you don't need to take any action except to anticipate the problem. In many cases, if the query is resubmitted, the problem goes away.

- On some systems, if two transactions overwrite each other, the validity of the database is compromised and resubmitting one of the transactions will not eliminate the problem. If you're working on such a system, you must anticipate these concurrency problems and account for them in your code.

- You should consider these locking problems as you write your code. If one of these problems would affect data integrity, you can change the default locking behavior by setting the transaction isolation level as shown in the next figure.

Figure 16-6   The four concurrency problems that locks can prevent

How to set the transaction isolation level

The simplest way to prevent concurrency problems is to reduce concurrency. To do that, you need to change SQL Server's default locking behavior. Figure 16-7 shows you how.

To change the default locking behavior, you use the SET TRANSACTION ISOLATION LEVEL statement to set the *transaction isolation level* for the current session. As you can see, this statement accepts one of five options. The table in this figure lists which of the four concurrency problems each option will prevent or allow. For example, if you code the SERIALIZABLE option, all four concurrency problems will be prevented.

When you set the isolation level to SERIALIZABLE, each transaction is completely isolated from every other transaction and concurrency is severely restricted. The server does this by locking each resource, preventing other transactions from accessing it. Since each transaction must wait for the previous transaction to commit, the transactions are executed serially, one after another.

Since the SERIALIZABLE isolation level eliminates all possible concurrency problems, you may think that this is the best option. However, this option requires more server overhead to manage all of the locks. In addition, access time for each transaction is increased, since only one transaction can work with the data at a time. For most systems, this will actually eliminate few concurrency problems but will cause severe performance problems.

The lowest isolation level is READ UNCOMMITTED, which allows all four of the concurrency problems to occur. It does this by performing SELECT queries without setting any locks and without honoring any existing locks. Since this means that your SELECT statements will always execute immediately, this setting provides the best performance. Since other transactions can retrieve and modify the same data, however, this setting can't prevent concurrency problems.

The default isolation level, READ COMMITTED, is acceptable for most applications. However, the only concurrency problem it prevents is dirty reads. Although it can prevent some lost updates, it doesn't prevent them all.

The REPEATABLE READ level allows more concurrency than the SERIALIZABLE level but less than the READ COMMITTED level. As you might expect, then, it results in faster performance than SERIALIZABLE and permits fewer concurrency problems than READ COMMITTED.

SQL Server 2005 introduced another isolation level, SNAPSHOT, that uses a feature called *row versioning*. With row versioning, any data that's retrieved by a transaction that uses SNAPSHOT isolation is consistent with the data that existed at the start of the transaction. To accomplish that, SQL Server stores the original version of a row in the tempdb database each time it's modified.

You can also use row versioning with the READ COMMITTED isolation level. Then, each statement within a transaction works with a snapshot of the data as it existed at the start of the statement.

When you use row versioning, locks are not required for read operations, which improves concurrency. However, the need to maintain row versions requires additional resources and can degrade performance. In most cases, then, you'll use row versioning only when data consistency is imperative.

The syntax of the SET TRANSACTION ISOLATION LEVEL statement

```
SET TRANSACTION ISOLATION LEVEL
    {READ UNCOMMITTED|READ COMMITTED|REPEATABLE READ|SNAPSHOT|SERIALIZABLE}
```

The concurrency problems prevented by each transaction isolation level

Isolation level	Dirty reads	Lost updates	Nonrepeatable reads	Phantom reads
READ UNCOMMITTED	Allows	Allows	Allows	Allows
READ COMMITTED	Prevents	Allows	Allows	Allows
REPEATABLE READ	Prevents	Prevents	Prevents	Allows
SNAPSHOT	Prevents	Prevents	Prevents	Prevents
SERIALIZABLE	Prevents	Prevents	Prevents	Prevents

Description

- Since SQL Server manages locking automatically, you can't control every aspect of locking for your transactions. However, you can set the isolation level in your code.

- The *transaction isolation level* controls the degree to which transactions are isolated from one another. The server isolates transactions by using more restrictive locking behavior. If you isolate your transactions from other transactions, concurrency problems are reduced or eliminated.

- You specify the transaction isolation level by changing the ISOLATION LEVEL session setting. The default transaction isolation level is READ COMMITTED. At this level, some lost updates can occur, but this is acceptable for most transactions.

- The READ UNCOMMITTED isolation level doesn't set any locks and ignores locks that are already held. Setting this level results in the highest possible performance for your query, but at the risk of every kind of concurrency problem. For this reason, you should only use this level for data that is rarely updated.

- The REPEATABLE READ level places locks on all data that's used in a transaction, preventing other users from updating that data. However, this isolation level still allows inserts, so phantom reads can occur.

- The SNAPSHOT level was introduced with SQL Server 2005. It uses *row versioning* rather than locks to provide read consistency. To use this level, you use the ALTER DATABASE statement to set the ALLOW_SNAPSHOT_ISOLATION option on.

- The SERIALIZABLE level places a lock on all data that's used in a transaction. Since each transaction must wait for the previous transaction to commit, the transactions are handled in sequence. This is the most restrictive of the five isolation levels.

- You can also use row versioning with the READ COMMITTED isolation level. To do that, you must set the READ_COMMITTED_SNAPSHOT database option on.

- With row versioning, each time a transaction modifies a row, SQL Server stores an image of the row as it existed before the modification. That way, read operations that use row versioning retrieve the row as it existed at the start of the transaction (SNAPSHOT) or statement (READ COMMITTED).

Figure 16-7   How to set the transaction isolation level

How SQL Server manages locking

SQL Server automatically manages locking by setting a lock on the data used by each transaction. By understanding how this process works, you'll be able to write better SQL code.

Lockable resources and lock escalation

A transaction like the one shown in figure 16-5 affects only one row in one table. In contrast, a transaction that uses DDL statements to change the design of a database can affect every object in the database. To accommodate these differences, SQL Server can lock data resources at ten different levels. These levels are presented in figure 16-8.

A resource's *granularity* refers to the relative amount of data it includes. For example, a row is a *fine-grain resource* and has higher granularity than a database, which is a *coarse-grain resource*. As you can see, the resources listed in this figure are listed in order of increasing granularity.

The SQL Server *lock manager* automatically assigns locks for each transaction. Since a coarse-grain lock will lock out more transactions than a fine-grain lock, the lock manager always tries to lock resources at the highest possible granularity. However, it takes greater server resources to maintain several fine-grain locks compared to one coarse-grain lock. For this reason, the lock manager detects when several fine-grain locks apply to a single coarse-grain resource. Then it converts, or *escalates*, the fine-grain locks to a single coarse-grain lock.

The ten levels of lockable resources

Granularity	Resource	Description
Coarse	Database	Locks an entire database.
	Allocation unit	Locks a collection of pages that contains a particular type of data.
	Metadata	Locks the data in the system catalog.
	File	Locks an entire database file.
	Table	Locks an entire table, including indexes.
	Heap or B-tree	Locks the index pages (B-tree) for a table with a clustered index or the data pages (heap) for a table with no clustered index.
	Extent	Locks a contiguous group of eight pages.
	Page	Locks one page (8 KB) of data.
	Key	Locks a key or range of keys in an index.
Fine	Row	Locks a single row within a table.

Description

- SQL Server can lock data at various levels, known as *lockable resources*. The ten levels form a hierarchy based on *granularity*, which refers to the amount of data the resource encompasses. A resource that encompasses more data than another resource is said to be less granular, or *coarser*, than the other resource.

- A *coarse-grain lock* affects more data than a *fine-grain lock*. For this reason, more transactions are locked out when the lock is less granular. Since this slows database performance, the server assigns locks of the finest possible granularity.

- Locking is automatically enabled and controlled by a SQL Server application called the *lock manager*. This program generates locking events and handles the setting and releasing of locks.

- Maintaining several fine-grain locks requires greater server resources than maintaining one coarse-grain lock. For this reason, the lock manager will automatically convert multiple fine-grain locks on the same resource into a single coarse-grain lock. This is known as *lock escalation*.

Figure 16-8   Lockable resources and lock escalation

Lock modes and lock promotion

In addition to assigning a resource level, the lock manager also assigns a *lock mode* to your transaction. Figure 16-9 presents the most common lock modes used by SQL Server. Although nine different lock modes are listed, each mode can be categorized as either a shared lock or an exclusive lock.

A *shared lock* doesn't prevent other shared locks from being granted on the same resource. For example, if you submit the query

```
SELECT * FROM Invoices;
```

the lock manager grants your transaction a Shared (S) lock on the Invoices table. If, while your query is executing, another user submits a query on the same table, your lock doesn't prevent the lock manager from granting a second S lock on the same table.

An *exclusive lock* on a resource, however, is granted exclusively to a single transaction. If another transaction requests a lock on the same resource, it must wait until the transaction that holds the exclusive lock has finished and its lock is released. If you submit an INSERT statement against the Invoices table, for example, the lock manager requests an Exclusive (X) lock on the Invoices table. If no other transaction has an exclusive lock on that table, the lock is granted. While that transaction holds that lock, no other transaction can be granted a lock.

A single transaction can include various SQL statements that each require a different lock mode. In that case, a shared lock may need to be *promoted* to an exclusive lock. If, while the transaction is still executing, an exclusive lock can't be acquired, the transaction must wait until the lock is available. If the lock never becomes available, the transaction can never commit.

To prevent this problem, an Update (U) lock is assigned for some transactions. For example, consider the locks needed for an UPDATE query. First, the query must determine which row or rows are being updated based on the WHERE clause. For this part of the query, only a shared lock is needed. Then, when the actual update takes place, the lock must be promoted to an exclusive lock. Since this kind of lock promotion occurs with virtually every action query, the lock manager first assigns a U lock, which prevents another transaction from gaining a shared lock.

The Schema lock modes place a lock on a table's design. For this reason, they can't be placed at resource levels other than the table level. Interestingly, these lock modes represent both the least restrictive and the most restrictive mode. A Schema Stability (Sch-S) lock is placed when a query is compiling to prevent changes to the table's design. A Schema Modification (Sch-M) lock is placed when a query includes DDL statements that modify a table's design.

If another transaction requests a lock on the same resource but at a lower granularity, your finer-grain lock must still be honored. In other words, if your transaction holds an X lock on a page of data, you wouldn't want the lock manager to grant another transaction an X lock on the entire table. To manage this, the three intent lock modes are used as placeholders for locks on finer-grained resources.

Common SQL Server lock modes

Category	Lock mode	What the lock owner can do
Shared	Schema Stability (Sch-S)	Compile a query
	Intent Shared (IS)	Read but not change data
	Shared (S)	Read but not change data
	Update (U)	Read but not change data until promoted to an Exclusive (X) lock
Exclusive	Shared with Intent Exclusive (SIX)	Read and change data
	Intent Exclusive (IX)	Read and change data
	Exclusive (X)	Read and change data
	Bulk Update (BU)	Bulk-copy data into a table
	Schema Modification (Sch-M)	Modify the database schema

Description

- SQL Server automatically determines the appropriate *lock mode* for your transaction. In general, retrieval operations acquire *shared locks*, and update operations acquire *exclusive locks*. As a single transaction is being processed, its lock may have to be converted, or *promoted*, from one lock mode to a more exclusive lock mode.

- An Update (U) lock is acquired during the first part of an update, when the data is being read. Later, if the data is changed, the Update lock is promoted to an Exclusive (X) lock. This can prevent a common locking problem called a deadlock.

- An *intent lock* indicates that SQL Server intends to acquire a shared lock or an exclusive lock on a finer-grain resource. For example, an Intent Shared (IS) lock acquired at the table level means that the transaction intends to acquire shared locks on pages or rows within that table. This prevents another transaction from acquiring an exclusive lock on the table containing that page or row.

- *Schema locks* are placed on a table's design. Schema Modification (Sch-M) locks are acquired when the design is being changed with a DDL statement. Schema Stability (Sch-S) locks are acquired when compiling a query to prevent a schema change while the query is compiling.

- The Bulk Update (BU) lock mode is acquired for the BULK INSERT statement and by the bulk copy program (bcp). Since these operations are typically done by DBAs, neither is presented in this book.

Figure 16-9   Lock modes and lock promotion

The three *intent locks* differ based on the portion of the resource and the type of lock that the transaction intends to acquire. An Intent Shared (IS) lock indicates that the transaction intends to acquire a shared lock on some, but not all, of the finer-grained resource. Likewise, an Intent Exclusive (IX) lock indicates an intent to acquire an exclusive lock on some, but not all, of the resource. Finally, a Shared with Intent Exclusive (SIX) lock indicates an intent to acquire both an exclusive lock on some of the resource and a shared lock on the entire resource.

The Bulk Update (BU) lock mode is used exclusively for copying large amounts of data in bulk into a database using either the BULK INSERT statement or the bulk copy program. Since bulk copies are usually done by DBAs to create databases based on other sources, they're not presented in this book.

Lock mode compatibility

Figure 16-10 presents a table that shows the compatibility between the different lock modes. When a transaction tries to acquire a lock on a resource, the lock manager must first determine whether another transaction already holds a lock on that resource. If a lock is already in place, the lock manager will grant the new lock only if it's compatible with the current lock. Otherwise, the transaction will have to wait.

For example, if a transaction currently holds a U lock on a table and another transaction requests a U lock on the same table, the lock manager doesn't grant the second transaction's request. Instead, the second transaction must wait until the first transaction commits and releases its lock.

As you can see, Sch-S lock mode is compatible with every other lock mode except Sch-M. For this reason, the only lock that can delay the compilation of a query is the lock placed by a DDL statement that's changing the table's design.

Notice that the IS and S locks are compatible. This means that any number of SELECT queries can execute concurrently. All of the other locks, however, are incompatible to some extent. That's because each of these other modes indicates that data is already being modified by a current transaction.

Although the intent locks are similar to the standard shared and exclusive locks, they result in improved performance. That's because when the lock manager grants an intent lock, it locks a resource at a higher level than it would if it granted shared or exclusive locks. In other words, it grants a more coarse-grained lock. Then, to determine if a resource is already locked, the lock manager needs to look only at the coarse-grained resource rather than every fine-grained resource it contains.

Compatibility between lock modes

Current lock mode		Requested lock mode								
		Sch-S	IS	S	U	SIX	IX	X	BU	Sch-M
Schema Stability	Sch-S	√	√	√	√	√	√	√	√	
Intent Shared	IS	√	√	√	√	√	√			
Shared	S	√	√	√	√					
Update	U	√	√	√						
Shared w/Intent Exclusive	SIX	√	√							
Intent Exclusive	IX	√	√				√			
Exclusive	X	√								
Bulk Update	BU	√								
Schema Modification	Sch-M									

Description

- If a resource is already locked by a transaction, a request by another transaction to acquire a lock on the same resource will be granted or denied depending on the compatibility of the two lock modes.

- For example, if a transaction has a Shared (S) lock on a table and another transaction requests an Exclusive (X) lock on the same table, the lock isn't granted. The second transaction must wait until the first transaction releases its lock.

- Intent locks can help improve performance since the server only needs to examine the high-level locks rather than examining every low-level lock.

Figure 16-10   Lock mode compatibility

How to prevent deadlocks

A *deadlock* occurs when two transactions are simultaneously holding and requesting a lock on each other's resource. Since deadlocks can occur more frequently at higher isolation levels, you need to understand how they come about and how you can prevent them.

Two transactions that deadlock

Figure 16-11 presents two transactions that are executed simultaneously. As you can see, transaction A queries the InvoiceLineItems table to determine the sum of all line item amounts for a specific invoice. Then, the WAITFOR DELAY statement causes the transaction to wait five seconds before continuing. (This statement is included only so you can actually cause the deadlock to occur.) Next, an UPDATE statement updates the InvoiceTotal column in the Invoices table with the value retrieved by the SELECT statement.

When this transaction executes, it requests several different locks. In particular, when the SELECT statement is executed, it requests an S lock on one page of the InvoiceLineItems table. And when the UPDATE statement is executed, it requests an X lock on a page of the Invoices table.

Now take a look at transaction B, which queries the Invoices table and then updates the InvoiceLineItems table for the same invoice as transaction A. In this case, the transaction requests an S lock on the Invoices table when the SELECT statement is executed, and it requests an X lock on the InvoiceLineItems table when the UPDATE statement is executed. Because transaction A has an S lock on the InvoiceLineItems table, however, the X lock isn't granted. Similarly, the X lock on the Invoices table isn't granted to transaction A because transaction B has an S lock on it. Because neither UPDATE can execute, neither transaction can commit and neither can release the resource needed by the other. In other words, the two transactions are deadlocked.

SQL Server automatically detects deadlocks and keeps them from tying up the system. It does this by selecting one of the transactions as the *deadlock victim*, which is rolled back and receives an error message. The other transaction runs to completion and commits. In the example in this figure, transaction B is the deadlock victim, as you can see by the system response.

Note that these two transactions will deadlock only if you set the transaction isolation level to REPEATABLE READ or SERIALIZABLE. Otherwise, the S lock acquired by each transaction is released after the SELECT statement completes. Since this doesn't prevent the other transaction from acquiring an X lock, each transaction can commit but causes the other to suffer from a dirty read.

Two transactions that deadlock

A
```
SET TRANSACTION ISOLATION LEVEL
    REPEATABLE READ;

DECLARE @InvoiceTotal money;

BEGIN TRAN;
  SELECT @InvoiceTotal =
    SUM(InvoiceLineItemAmount)
  FROM InvoiceLineItems
  WHERE InvoiceID = 101;


WAITFOR DELAY '00:00:05';

  UPDATE Invoices
  SET InvoiceTotal =
    @InvoiceTotal
  WHERE InvoiceID = 101;


COMMIT TRAN;
```

B
```
SET TRANSACTION ISOLATION LEVEL
    REPEATABLE READ;

DECLARE @InvoiceTotal money;

BEGIN TRAN;
    SELECT @InvoiceTotal =
        InvoiceTotal
    FROM Invoices
    WHERE InvoiceID = 101;



    UPDATE InvoiceLineItems
    SET InvoiceLineItemAmount =
        @InvoiceTotal
    WHERE InvoiceID = 101 AND
        InvoiceSequence = 1;

COMMIT TRAN;
```

The response from the system

```
(1 row(s) affected)
```

```
Msg 1205, Level 13, State 51, Line
11
Transaction (Process ID 53) was
deadlocked on lock resources with
another process and has been chosen
as the deadlock victim. Rerun the
transaction.
```

How the deadlock occurs

1. Transaction A requests and acquires a shared lock on the InvoiceLineItems table.

2. Transaction B requests and acquires a shared lock on the Invoices table.

3. Transaction A tries to acquire an exclusive lock on the Invoices table to perform the update. Since transaction B already holds a shared lock on this table, transaction A must wait for the exclusive lock.

4. Transaction B tries to acquire an exclusive lock on the InvoiceLineItems table, but must wait because transaction A holds a shared lock on that table.

Description

*   A *deadlock* occurs when neither of two transactions can be committed because they each have a lock on a resource needed by the other.

*   SQL Server automatically detects deadlocks and allows one of the transactions to commit. The other transaction is rolled back and raises error number 1205. This transaction is known as the *deadlock victim*.

Note

*   To test this example, you must execute transaction A first and then execute transaction B within five seconds.

Figure 16-11   Two transactions that deadlock

Coding techniques that prevent deadlocks

Deadlocks slow system performance and cause transactions to become deadlock victims. For these reasons, you should try to avoid deadlocks as much as possible. Figure 16-12 presents a summary of the techniques you can use to do that.

First, you shouldn't leave transactions open any longer than is necessary. That's because the longer a transaction remains open and uncommitted, the more likely it is that another transaction will need to work with that same resource. Second, you shouldn't use a higher isolation level than you need. That's because the higher you set the isolation level, the more likely it is that two transactions will be unable to work concurrently on the same resource. Third, you should schedule transactions that modify a large number of rows to run when no other transactions, or only a small number of other transactions, will be running. That way, it's less likely that the transactions will try to change the same rows at the same time.

Finally, you should consider how a program you code could cause a deadlock. To illustrate, consider the UPDATE statements shown in this figure that transfer money between two accounts. The first example transfers money from a savings to a checking account. Notice that the savings account is updated first. The second example transfers money from a checking to a savings account. In this example, the checking account is updated first, which could cause a deadlock if the first transaction already has an X lock on the data. To prevent this situation, you should always update the same account first, regardless of which is being debited and which is being credited. This is illustrated by the third example in this figure.

Don't allow transactions to remain open for very long

- Keep transactions short.
- Keep SELECT statements outside of the transaction except when absolutely necessary.
- Never code requests for user input during an open transaction.

Use the lowest possible transaction isolation level

- The default level of READ COMMITTED is almost always sufficient.
- Reserve the use of higher levels for short transactions that make changes to data where integrity is vital.

Make large changes when you can be assured of nearly exclusive access

- If you need to change millions of rows in an active table, don't do so during hours of peak usage.
- If possible, give yourself exclusive access to the database before making large changes.

Consider locking when coding your transactions

- If you need to code two or more transactions that update the same resources, code the updates in the same order in each transaction.

UPDATE statements that transfer money between two accounts

From savings to checking
```
UPDATE Savings SET Balance = Balance - @TransferAmt;
UPDATE Checking SET Balance = Balance + @TransferAmt;
```

From checking to savings
```
UPDATE Checking SET Balance = Balance - @TransferAmt;
UPDATE Savings SET Balance = Balance + @TransferAmt;
```

From checking to savings in reverse order to prevent deadlocks
```
UPDATE Savings SET Balance = Balance + @TransferAmt;
UPDATE Checking SET Balance = Balance - @TransferAmt;
```

Figure 16-12   Coding techniques that prevent deadlocks

Perspective

In this chapter, you've learned the ways that SQL Server protects your data from the problems that can occur on a real-world system. Since the failure of one or more related SQL statements can violate data integrity, you learned how to prevent these problems by grouping the statements into transactions. Since multiple transactions can simultaneously modify the same data, you learned how to prevent concurrency problems by setting the transaction isolation level to change the default locking behavior. And since changing the isolation level can increase the chances of deadlocks, you learned defensive programming techniques to prevent deadlocks.

Terms

transaction	row versioning
commit a transaction	granularity
roll back a transaction	fine-grain lock
autocommit mode	coarse-grain lock
nested transactions	lock manager
save point	lock escalation
concurrency	lock mode
locking	shared lock
lost update	exclusive lock
dirty read	intent lock
nonrepeatable read	schema lock
phantom read	lock promotion
transaction isolation level	deadlock
lockable resource	deadlock victim

Exercises

1. Write a set of action queries coded as a transaction to reflect the following change: United Parcel Service has been purchased by Federal Express Corporation and the new company is named FedUP. Rename one of the vendors and delete the other after updating the VendorID column in the Invoices table.

2. Write a set of action queries coded as a transaction to move rows from the Invoices table to the InvoiceArchive table. Insert all paid invoices from Invoices into InvoiceArchive, but only if the invoice doesn't already exist in the InvoiceArchive table. Then, delete all paid invoices from the Invoices table, but only if the invoice exists in the InvoiceArchive table.

17

How to manage database security

If you've been using a stand-alone copy of SQL Server installed on your own computer, the security of the system hasn't been of concern. When you install SQL Server for use in a production environment, however, you must configure security to prevent misuse of your data. In this chapter, you'll learn how to do that using either the Management Studio or Transact-SQL.

How to work with SQL Server login IDs

Before a user can work with the data in a database, he must have a valid *login ID* so that he can log on to SQL Server. Then, he must have access to the database itself. In the topics that follow, you'll learn how to work with login IDs and how to give a user access to a database. But first, I'll present an overview of how SQL Server manages database security.

An introduction to SQL Server security

Figure 17-1 illustrates how a user gains access to a SQL Server database. First, the user must connect and log on to the server using either an application program or the Management Studio. As you can see, the login ID can be authenticated in one of two ways, which I'll discuss in a moment.

Once the user is logged on to SQL Server, the data he has access to and the operations he can perform depend on the *permissions* that have been granted to him. You can grant *object permissions* so the user can perform specific actions on a specific database object, you can grant *schema permissions* so the user can perform actions on every object in the schema, you can grant *database permissions* so the user can perform specific database operations, and you can grant *server permissions* so the user can perform specific actions at the server level. In addition, you can define a collection of permissions called a *role*. Then, you can assign users to that role to grant them all of the permissions associated with that role. This reduces the number of permissions you must grant each user and makes it easier to manage security. For this reason, roles are used on most systems.

This figure also summarizes the two ways you can manage SQL Server security. First, you can do that by executing SQL statements and system stored procedures from the Query Editor or using the SQLCMD utility. Second, you can use the graphical interface of the Management Studio. You'll learn how to use both of these techniques in this chapter. The technique you use is mostly a matter of preference. However, even if you intend to use the Management Studio, you should still read the topics on using the SQL statements and stored procedures. These topics will help you understand the underlying structure of SQL Server security, which will help you use the Management Studio better.

Although the Management Studio's graphical interface makes it easier to work with security, it can also slow you down. For example, if you need to set up a new database with hundreds of users, you'll have to create those users one at a time using the Management Studio. On the other hand, if you've read chapter 14 and know how to code dynamic SQL, you can code a script that will manage the entire process. For this reason, many experienced system administrators prefer to manage security using Transact-SQL.

Before I go on, you should know about two terms that are used frequently when talking about security. The first term, *principal*, refers to a user, group, login, or role that has access to a database. The second term, *securable*, refers to a SQL Server entity that can be secured. That includes tables, schemas, databases, and the server itself. You'll learn more about principals and securables as you progress through this chapter.

How users gain access to a SQL Server database

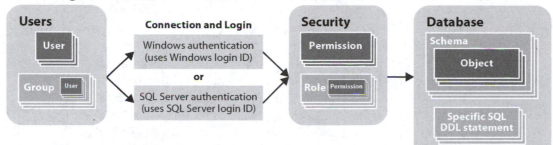

Two ways to configure SQL Server security

Method	Description
Transact-SQL	Use Transact-SQL statements to manage login IDs, database users, permissions, and roles.
Management Studio	Use the Management Studio to configure all aspects of system security.

Description

- Typically, a network user must log on to the network at a PC using a *login ID* and password. If the client PC uses Windows, SQL Server can use the Windows login ID defined for the user. Otherwise, you can create a separate SQL Server login ID.

- Once a user is logged on to SQL Server, the security configuration determines which database objects the user can work with and which SQL statements the user can execute.

- *Permissions* determine the actions a user can take on a database object, such as a table, view, or stored procedure, on the objects in a schema, on a database, and on a server.

- A *role* is a collection of permissions that you can assign to a user by assigning the user to that role.

- You can create a collection of users in Windows called a *group*. Then you can assign permissions and roles either to individual users or to a group of users.

- The users, groups, logins, and roles that have access to a server are called *principals*. The entities that can be secured on a server, including the server itself, are called *securables*.

- If you need to set up a new system with many users, it's often easier to code SQL scripts using the SQL security statements. The Management Studio is better for making changes to an existing system or for setting up a small system.

- Even if you use the Management Studio to manage security, you should know how to manage security with Transact-SQL statements. That will help you understand the underlying structure of SQL Server security.

Figure 17-1   An introduction to SQL Server security

How to change the authentication mode

As you learned in chapter 2, you can log on to SQL Server using one of two types of login authentication: *Windows authentication* or *SQL Server authentication*. To accommodate these two types of authentication, a server can be configured to run in one of two *authentication modes*: Windows Authentication mode or Mixed mode. Figure 17-2 summarizes these authentication modes and shows you how you can change from one to the other.

When you install SQL Server, Windows Authentication mode is the default. Then, when a user logs on to SQL Server, authentication is handled by the security that's integrated into Windows. In other words, the login ID and password that the user enters to log on to Windows are also used to log on to SQL Server.

If you use Mixed mode authentication, users can log on using either Windows authentication or SQL Server authentication. When SQL Server authentication is used, the user must enter a SQL Server user ID and password to log on to SQL Server. This user ID and password are separate from the Windows user ID and password, which means that the user must enter two IDs and passwords to access SQL Server. Since non-Windows clients can't use Windows authentication, it's likely that the only time you'll use SQL Server authentication is to support access by non-Windows clients.

To change the authentication mode, you use the Security page of the Server Properties dialog box shown in this figure. The two available options are listed under the Server Authentication heading. The SQL Server and Windows Authentication Mode option corresponds to Mixed mode.

If you change the authentication mode, the Management Studio warns you that the change won't take effect until you stop and restart SQL Server. Before you stop SQL Server, though, you'll want to be sure that there aren't any transactions currently executing. If there are and you stop SQL Server, those transactions won't be committed. If you're working on a desktop server or on a new server with no users, this shouldn't be a problem. If you're working on an active server, however, you shouldn't restart the server until you're sure that no users are connected.

If you install SQL Server with Windows Authentication mode, you should know that the default system administrator login ID, sa, is disabled. That's because this login can only connect using SQL Server authentication. If you later change to Mixed mode, however, the sa login ID isn't automatically enabled. So you'll have to enable it manually. You'll learn how to enable and disable login IDs later in this chapter.

The Security tab of the SQL Server Properties dialog box

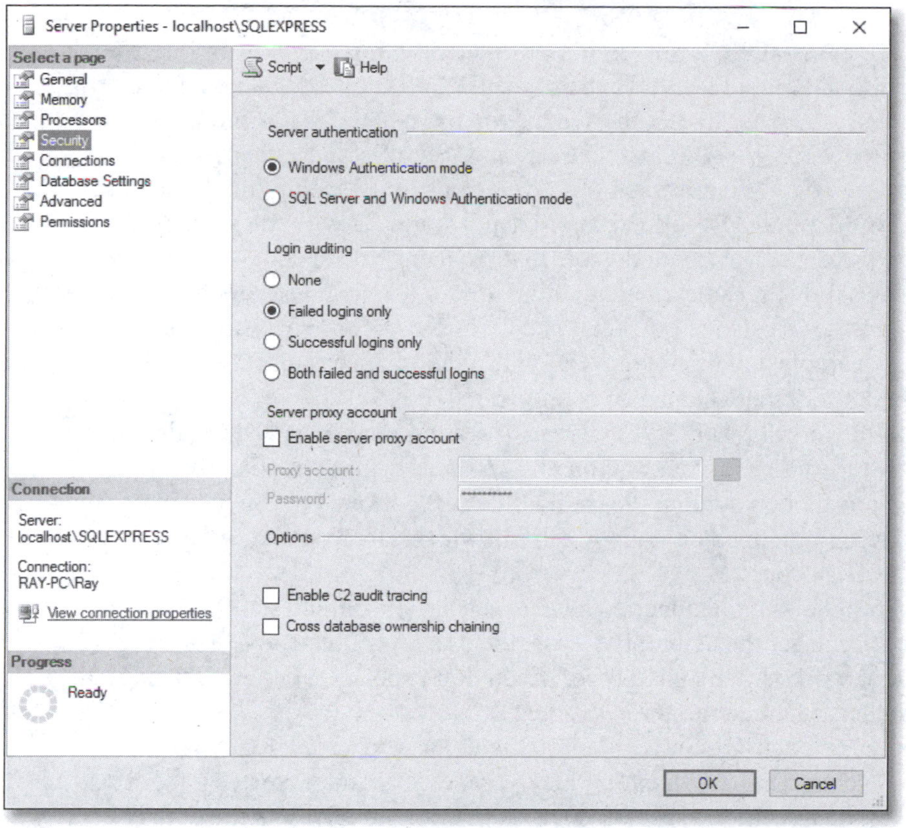

The two SQL Server authentication modes

Mode	Description
Windows Authentication mode	Only Windows authentication is allowed. This is the default.
Mixed mode	Both Windows authentication and SQL Server authentication are allowed. To use this mode, select the SQL Server and Windows Authentication Mode option. If your database needs to be accessed by non-Windows clients, you must use Mixed mode.

Description

- To change the SQL Server *authentication mode*, right-click on the server in the Object Explorer of the Management Studio, select the Properties command to display the Server Properties dialog box, then display the Security page.

- When you use *Windows authentication*, access to SQL Server is controlled via the security integrated into Windows. This simplifies login because Windows users only have to log on once.

- When you use *SQL Server authentication*, access to SQL Server is controlled via the separate security built into SQL Server. The user has a login ID and password that are distinct from their Windows login ID and password, so they have to log on twice.

Figure 17-2 How to change the authentication mode

How to create login IDs

When you install SQL Server, it's configured with some built-in IDs. Then, to add additional login IDs, you can use the CREATE LOGIN statement shown in figure 17-3. As you can see, the syntax you use depends on whether you're creating a login for Windows authentication or SQL Server authentication.

To create a new Windows login ID, you can simply specify the login name and the FROM WINDOWS keywords. Then, a login ID with the same name as the Windows login ID is created. Note that the name you specify must include the Windows domain name along with the user or group name, and the name must be enclosed in square brackets. The first CREATE LOGIN statement in this figure, for example, creates a login ID for a Windows user named SusanRoberts in the Windows domain named Accounting.

If you're working with SQL Server Express on your own system, the domain name is just the name of your computer. In that case, though, you probably won't need to set up additional login IDs. The exception is if you have more than one user account defined on your system, in which case you can set up a separate login for each account.

In addition to the login name, you can specify the default database and language. If you set the default database, the user won't have to execute a USE statement to work with that database. If you don't specify a default database, the system database named master is the default.

To create a new SQL Server login ID, you must specify a login name and password. The second statement in this figure, for example, creates a login ID for user JohnDoe with the password "pt8806FG$B". It also sets the default database to AP.

The last two options determine how password policies are enforced. If the CHECK_EXPIRATION option is on, users are reminded to change passwords, and SQL Server disables IDs that have expired passwords. If the CHECK_POLICY option is on, password policies are enforced, and the CHECK_EXPIRATION option is also on unless it's explicitly turned off.

In most cases, you'll leave these options at their defaults so the password policies specified for the server are enforced. Among other things, the default password policies for SQL Server 2012 and later require that SQL Server logins use *strong passwords*, which are difficult for someone to guess. This figure lists the guidelines for coding strong passwords, and the example in this figure that creates a SQL Server login ID illustrates a strong password.

Another option you can use with the CREATE LOGIN statement is MUST_CHANGE. If you include this option, the user will be prompted for a new password the first time the new login is used. That way, users can set their own passwords. If you specify the MUST_CHANGE option, the CHECK_EXPIRATION and CHECK_POLICY options must also be on.

By the way, you should know that the CREATE LOGIN statement, as well as many of the other statements presented in this chapter, were introduced with SQL Server 2005. These statements replace stored procedures that were used in previous versions of SQL Server. For example, you used the sp_AddLogin

The syntax of the CREATE LOGIN statement

For Windows authentication

```
CREATE LOGIN login_name FROM WINDOWS
    [WITH [DEFAULT_DATABASE = database]
        [, DEFAULT_LANGUAGE = language]]
```

For SQL Server authentication

```
CREATE LOGIN login_name WITH PASSWORD = 'password' [MUST_CHANGE]
        [, DEFAULT_DATABASE = database]
        [, DEFAULT_LANGUAGE = language]
        [, CHECK_EXPIRATION = {ON|OFF}]
        [, CHECK_POLICY = {ON|OFF}]
```

A statement that creates a new login ID from a Windows account

```
CREATE LOGIN [Accounting\SusanRoberts] FROM WINDOWS;
```

A statement that creates a new SQL Server login ID

```
CREATE LOGIN JohnDoe WITH PASSWORD = 'pt8806FG$B',
    DEFAULT_DATABASE = AP;
```

Guidelines for strong passwords

- Cannot be blank or null or the values "Password", "Admin", "Administrator", "sa", or "sysadmin"

- Cannot be the name of the current user or the machine name

- Must contain more than 8 characters

- Must contain at least three of the following: uppercase letters, lowercase letters, numbers, and non-alphanumeric characters (#, %, &, etc.)

Description

- You use the CREATE LOGIN statement to create a new SQL Server login ID or to create a new login ID from a Windows account. This statement was introduced with SQL Server 2005.

- If you don't specify a default database when you create a login, the default is set to master. If you don't specify a default language, the default is set to the default language of the server. Unless it's been changed, the server language default is English.

- The password you specify for a SQL Server login ID should be a *strong password*. A strong password is not easy to guess and cannot easily be hacked. A password can have up to 128 characters.

- If you include the MUST_CHANGE option, SQL Server will prompt the user for a new password the first time the login ID is used.

- The CHECK_EXPIRATION option determines whether SQL Server enforces password expiration policy. The CHECK_POLICY option determines if password policies, such as strong passwords, are enforced. These options are enforced only if SQL Server is running on Windows Server 2003 or later.

Figure 17-3   How to create login IDs

stored procedure to add a new SQL Server login ID. Although these stored procedures are still supported by SQL Server 2016, they will be dropped in a future release of SQL Server. So you should use the statements presented in this chapter instead of the equivalent stored procedures.

How to delete or change login IDs or passwords

To change an existing login ID, you can use the ALTER LOGIN statement shown in figure 17-4. A common task you can perform with this statement is to change the password for a SQL Server Login ID. This is illustrated in the first example in this figure. Notice in this example that you can change the password without specifying the old password. You can also force the user to enter a new password the next time the login is used by coding the MUST_CHANGE option.

Another common task that you can perform with the ALTER LOGIN statement is to disable or enable a login ID as illustrated in the second example. Here, the login ID for a Windows account is being disabled. That means that the user will no longer have access to SQL Server.

The third example in this figure shows how you can use the ALTER LOGIN statement to change a login name. This is useful if a user's name actually changes. It's also useful if one employee replaces another. Then, you can give the new employee the same permissions as the old employee simply by changing the login name.

To delete a login ID, you use the DROP LOGIN statement. This is illustrated in the fourth example in this figure.

The syntax of the DROP LOGIN statement

```
DROP LOGIN login_name
```

The syntax of the ALTER LOGIN statement

For Windows authentication

```
ALTER LOGIN login_name {{ENABLE|DISABLE}|WITH
        [NAME = login_name]
     [, DEFAULT_DATABASE = database]
     [, DEFAULT_LANGUAGE = language]}
```

For SQL Server authentication

```
ALTER LOGIN login_name {{ENABLE|DISABLE}|WITH
        [PASSWORD = 'password' [OLD_PASSWORD = 'oldpassword']
        [MUST_CHANGE]]
     [, NAME = login_name]
     [, DEFAULT_DATABASE = database]
     [, DEFAULT_LANGUAGE = language]
     [, CHECK_EXPIRATION = {ON|OFF}]
     [, CHECK_POLICY = {ON|OFF}]}
```

Statements that use the ALTER LOGIN and DROP LOGIN statements

A statement that changes the password for a SQL Server login ID

```
ALTER LOGIN JohnDoe WITH PASSWORD = 'lg22A%G45x';
```

A statement that disables a Windows login ID

```
ALTER LOGIN [Accounting\SusanRoberts] DISABLE;
```

A statement that changes a login name

```
ALTER LOGIN JohnDoe WITH NAME = JackWilliams;
```

A statement that deletes a SQL Server login ID

```
DROP LOGIN JackWilliams;
```

Description

- You use the ALTER LOGIN statement to enable or disable a login ID, change the name for a login ID, or change the default database or language. For a SQL Server login ID, you can also change the password and the password options.

- You use the DROP LOGIN statement to drop a login ID.

- The ALTER LOGIN and DROP LOGIN statements were introduced with SQL Server 2005.

Figure 17-4   How to delete or change login IDs or passwords

How to work with database users

Each database maintains a list of the users that are authorized to access that database. This list is distinct from the list of login IDs that's maintained by the server. Figure 17-5 presents the SQL statements you use to maintain the list of users for a database.

You use the CREATE USER statement to create a database user. On this statement, you code the name of the user, which is usually the same as the login name. In that case, you don't need to specify the login name. This is illustrated in the first example in this figure. If you want to use a user name that's different from the login name, however, you can include the FOR LOGIN clause to specify the login name that the user name is mapped to.

In most cases, it's not a good idea to use two different names for the same user. For this reason, the FOR LOGIN clause is generally omitted. However, since login IDs generated from Windows user names include the domain name, those login IDs can be quite long. If all of your users are on the same Windows domain, then, you may want to use just the user names for the database users. This is illustrated in the second example in this figure, which creates a database user named SusanRoberts for the login ID Accounting\SusanRoberts.

You can also specify a default schema for a database user as illustrated in the third example in this figure. Then, when SQL Server searches for an object for that user, it will look for the object in the user's default schema before it looks in the dbo schema.

After you create a database user, the user can set the database as the current database using the USE statement but can't perform any operations on the database or the objects it contains. To do that, the user must be granted object and database permissions. You'll learn how to grant these permissions in a moment.

If you need to change a database user, you can use the ALTER USER statement. This statement lets you change the user name or the default schema for the user. The fourth statement in this figure, for example, changes the name of a database user from SusanRoberts to SusanStanley, and the fifth statement changes the default schema for a user to Marketing.

Finally, if you need to delete a database user, you use the DROP USER statement as illustrated in the last example. The only information you specify on this statement is the user name.

Note that all three of these statements work with the current database. For this reason, you must be sure to change the database context to the database you want to work with before you execute any of these statements. If you don't, you may inadvertently create, change, or delete a user in the wrong database.

The syntax of the CREATE USER statement

```
CREATE USER user_name
    [{FOR|FROM} LOGIN login_name]
    [WITH DEFAULT_SCHEMA = schema_name]
```

The syntax of the ALTER USER statement

```
ALTER USER user_name WITH
        [NAME = new_user_name]
    [, DEFAULT_SCHEMA = schema_name]
```

The syntax of the DROP USER statement

```
DROP USER user_name
```

Statements that work with database users

A statement that creates a database user with the same name as a login ID

```
CREATE USER JohnDoe;
```

A statement that creates a database user for a Windows user account

```
CREATE USER SusanRoberts FOR LOGIN [Accounting\SusanRoberts];
```

A statement that creates a database user and assigns a default schema

```
CREATE USER SusanRoberts FOR LOGIN [Accounting\SusanRoberts]
    WITH DEFAULT_SCHEMA = Accounting;
```

A statement that changes a user name

```
ALTER USER SusanRoberts WITH NAME = SusanStanley;
```

A statement that assigns a default schema to a user

```
ALTER USER JohnDoe WITH DEFAULT_SCHEMA = Marketing;
```

A statement that deletes a database user

```
DROP USER JohnDoe;
```

Description

- You use the CREATE USER statement to create a user for a login ID for the current database. If the login name is the same as the user name, you can omit the FOR LOGIN clause.

- When you create a database user, you can specify a default schema. Then, SQL Server will look in this schema when it searches for objects for the database user before it looks in the default schema (dbo).

- The ALTER USER statement lets you change the name of an existing database user or change the default schema for a user.

- You use the DROP USER statement to delete a user from the current database.

- Since all three of these statements work on the current database, you must change the database context using the USE statement before executing any of these statements.

- The CREATE USER, ALTER USER, and DROP USER statements were introduced with SQL Server 2005.

Figure 17-5   How to work with database users

How to work with schemas

As you know, the tables, views, functions, and procedures of a database are stored in schemas. If you don't specify a schema when you create these objects, they're stored in the default schema.

One advantage of using schemas is that you can grant permissions to all the objects in a schema by granting permissions to the schema. Another advantage is that users don't own database objects, they own schemas. Because of that, if you need to delete a user, you can just transfer the schemas that user owns to another user rather than having to transfer the ownership of each individual object.

Figure 17-6 presents the SQL statements for working with schemas. To create a schema, you use the CREATE SCHEMA statement. The only information you must include on this statement is the schema name. This is illustrated in the first CREATE SCHEMA statement in this figure, which creates a schema named Accounting.

When you create a schema, you can also create tables and views within that schema, and you can grant, revoke, and deny permissions to those tables and views. For example, the second CREATE SCHEMA statement shown here creates a schema named Marketing. In addition, it creates a table named Contacts within the Marketing schema. Notice that because the CREATE TABLE statement is coded within the CREATE SCHEMA statement, it isn't necessary to specify the schema on the CREATE TABLE statement. For this to work, the CREATE SCHEMA statement must be coded as a separate batch.

By default, a schema is owned by the owner of the database. In most cases, that's what you want. If you want to assign a different owner to a schema, however, you can include the AUTHORIZATION clause with the name of the user or role you want to own the schema on the CREATE SCHEMA statement.

The ALTER SCHEMA statement lets you transfer a securable from one schema to another. For example, the ALTER SCHEMA statement in this figure transfers the Contacts table in the Marketing schema that was created by the second statement to the Accounting schema that was created by the first statement. Note that you can't transfer an object to a different schema if any views or functions are schema-bound to the object. Because of that, you'll want to make sure an object is in the correct schema before you create any views or functions that are bound to it.

To delete a schema from a database, you use the DROP SCHEMA statement. The last statement in this figure, for example, deletes the Marketing schema. Keep in mind that before you delete a schema, you must delete any objects it contains or transfer them to another schema.

The syntax of the CREATE SCHEMA statement

```
CREATE SCHEMA schema_name [AUTHORIZATION owner_name]
    [table_definition]...
    [view_definition]...
    [grant_statement]...
    [revoke_statement]...
    [deny_statement]...
```

The syntax of the ALTER SCHEMA statement

```
ALTER SCHEMA schema_name TRANSFER securable_name
```

The syntax of the DROP SCHEMA statement

```
DROP SCHEMA schema_name
```

Statements that work with schemas

A statement that creates a schema

```
CREATE SCHEMA Accounting;
```

A statement that creates a schema and a table within that schema

```
CREATE SCHEMA Marketing
    CREATE TABLE Contacts
    (ContactID    INT        NOT NULL IDENTITY PRIMARY KEY,
    ContactName  VARCHAR(50) NOT NULL,
    ContactPhone VARCHAR(50) NULL,
    ContactEmail VARCHAR(50) NULL);
```

A statement that transfers a table from one schema to another

```
ALTER SCHEMA Accounting TRANSFER Marketing.Contacts;
```

A statement that deletes a schema

```
DROP SCHEMA Marketing;
```

Description

- You use the CREATE SCHEMA statement to create a schema in the current database. You can also create tables and views within the new schema, and you can grant, revoke, or deny permissions for those tables and views.

- After you create a schema, you can create any object within that schema by qualifying the object name with the schema name.

- You use the ALTER SCHEMA statement to transfer an object from one schema to another.

- You can't transfer an object from one schema to another if any views or functions are bound to it.

- When you transfer an object from one schema to another, all the permissions that were associated with that object are dropped.

- You use the DROP SCHEMA statement to delete a schema. The schema you delete must not contain any objects.

- The CREATE SCHEMA, ALTER SCHEMA, and DROP SCHEMA statements were introduced with SQL Server 2005.

Figure 17-6   How to work with schemas

How to work with permissions

Now that you understand how to create login IDs and database users, you need to learn how to grant users permission to work with a database and the objects it contains. That's what you'll learn in the topics that follow. In addition, you'll learn how to grant login IDs permission to work with the server.

How to grant or revoke object permissions

Figure 17-7 presents the GRANT and REVOKE statements you use to grant or revoke permissions to use an object in the current database. In the GRANT clause, you list the permissions you want to grant. You'll see a list of the standard permissions in the next figure.

You code the name of the object for which this permission is granted in the ON clause. This object can be a table, a view, a stored procedure, or a user-defined function. If the object is contained in a schema other than the default schema, you must specify the schema name along with the object name. Note that you can only grant permissions for a single object with the GRANT statement.

In the TO clause, you code one or more database principal names to which you're granting the permission. Typically, this is the database user name. The statement in this figure, for example, grants permission for the user SusanRoberts to select data from the Invoices table. You can also use this statement to assign permissions to a database role. You'll learn more about database roles later in this chapter.

If you code the GRANT statement with the optional WITH GRANT OPTION clause, you delegate to this user the permission to GRANT this same permission to others. Since it's simpler to have a single person or group managing the security for a database, I don't recommend that you use this option. If you do, however, you should keep good records so you can later revoke this permission if you begin to have security problems.

The syntax of the REVOKE statement is similar to the syntax of the GRANT statement. You code a list of the permissions you're revoking in the REVOKE clause, the object name in the ON clause, and one or more database principal names in the FROM clause. The statement in this figure, for example, revokes the SELECT permission for the Invoices table that was granted to user SusanRoberts by the GRANT statement.

You can code two optional clauses in the REVOKE statement. These clauses are related to the WITH GRANT OPTION clause you can code in the GRANT statement. The GRANT OPTION FOR clause revokes the user's permission to grant this permission to others. The CASCADE clause revokes this permission from all of the users to whom this user has granted permission. If you avoid using the WITH GRANT OPTION clause, you won't have to use these clauses.

How to grant object permissions

The syntax of the GRANT statement for object permissions

```
GRANT permission [, ...]
ON [schema_name.]object_name [(column [, ...])]
TO database_principal [, ...]
[WITH GRANT OPTION]
```

A GRANT statement that grants SELECT permission for the Invoices table

```
GRANT SELECT
ON Invoices
TO SusanRoberts;
```

How to revoke object permissions

The syntax of the REVOKE statement for object permissions

```
REVOKE [GRANT OPTION FOR] permission [, ...]
ON [schema_name.]object_name [(column [, ...])]
FROM database_principal [, ...]
[CASCADE]
```

A REVOKE statement that revokes SELECT permission

```
REVOKE SELECT
ON Invoices
FROM SusanRoberts;
```

Description

- You use this GRANT statement format to give a user permission to work with a database object. This format of the REVOKE statement takes object permissions away. See figure 17-8 for a list of the standard permissions that can be granted for objects.

- The object_name argument specifies the object for which the permission is being granted or revoked and can specify a table, a view, a stored procedure, or a user-defined function. If you specify a table, a view, or a table-valued function, you can also list the columns for which SELECT, UPDATE, or REFERENCES permissions are granted or revoked.

- The database_principal argument in the TO and FROM clauses can be the name of a database user or a user-defined role.

- The WITH GRANT OPTION clause gives a user permission to grant this permission to other users.

- The REVOKE statement includes two clauses that undo WITH GRANT OPTION. GRANT OPTION FOR revokes the user's permission to grant the permission to others. CASCADE revokes the permission from any other users who were given the permission by this user.

- Since both the GRANT and REVOKE statements work on the current database, you must first change the database context using the USE statement.

Figure 17-7   How to grant or revoke object permissions

The SQL Server object permissions

Figure 17-8 lists the specific object permissions that you can code in either the GRANT or REVOKE statement. The first four permissions let the user execute the corresponding SQL statement: SELECT, UPDATE, INSERT, or DELETE. The fifth permission, EXECUTE, lets the user run an executable database object.

Each permission can be granted only for certain types of objects. For example, you can grant SELECT permission only to an object from which you can select data, such as a table or view. Likewise, you can grant EXECUTE permission only to an object that you can execute, such as a stored procedure or scalar function.

The REFERENCES permission lets a user refer to an object, even if the user doesn't have permission to use that object directly. For example, to create a FOREIGN KEY constraint that refers to another table, the user would need to have REFERENCES permission on that other table. Of course, he'd also need permission to create a table. You'll see how to grant permissions like this in a moment.

You also need to assign the REFERENCES permission to objects that are referenced by a function or view that's created with the WITH SCHEMABINDING clause. Since this permission is only needed for users who'll be creating database objects, you'll probably never assign it individually. Instead, you'll include it with other permissions in a database role as you'll learn later in this chapter.

The last permission, ALTER, lets the user change the definition of an object. This permission is typically given to users who are responsible for designing a database. That includes database administrators and, in many cases, programmers.

In addition to the permissions shown here, SQL Server 2016 continues to support the deprecated ALL permission. Because this permission may not work in future versions of SQL Server, you should avoid using it. If you do use it, though, you should know that despite its name, this permission doesn't always grant all permissions that are applicable to the object. For example, when working with database permissions as shown in figure 17-10, the ALL permission doesn't include the CREATE SCHEMA permission.

The standard permissions for SQL Server objects

Permission	Description	Applies to
SELECT	Lets the user select the data.	Tables, views, and table-valued functions
UPDATE	Lets the user update existing data.	Tables, views, and table-valued functions
INSERT	Lets the user insert new data.	Tables, views, and table-valued functions
DELETE	Lets the user delete existing data.	Tables, views, and table-valued functions
EXECUTE	Lets the user execute a procedure or function.	Stored procedures and scalar and aggregate functions
REFERENCES	Lets the user create objects that refer to the object.	Tables, views, and functions
ALTER	Lets the user modify an object.	Tables, procedures, functions, and sequences

A GRANT statement that grants permission to run action queries

```
GRANT INSERT, UPDATE, DELETE
ON Invoices
TO SusanRoberts;
```

A REVOKE statement that revokes the DELETE permission

```
REVOKE DELETE
ON Invoices
FROM SusanRoberts;
```

A GRANT statement that grants permission to execute a stored procedure

```
GRANT EXECUTE
ON spInvoiceReport
TO [Payroll\MarkThomas], JohnDoe, TomAaron;
```

A GRANT statement that grants SELECT permission to specific columns

```
GRANT SELECT
ON Vendors (VendorName,VendorAddress1,VendorCity,VendorState,VendorZipCode)
TO TomAaron, [Payroll\MarkThomas];
```

A GRANT statement that grants REFERENCES permission to the Contacts table in the Accounting schema

```
GRANT REFERENCES
ON Accounting.Contacts
To JohnDoe;
```

A GRANT statement that grants permission to alter a table

```
GRANT ALTER
ON Vendors
To JoelMurach;
```

Description

- You can only grant permissions that are appropriate for the object or schema.
- You can grant or revoke SELECT, UPDATE, or REFERENCES permission to specific columns in a table, view, or table-valued function. However, a view is typically a better way to limit access to specific columns.

Figure 17-8   The SQL Server object permissions

How to grant or revoke schema permissions

In addition to granting or revoking permissions to individual objects in a database, you can grant or revoke permissions to all the objects in a schema. To do that, you use the formats of the GRANT and REVOKE statements shown in figure 17-9.

The main difference between the formats shown here and the formats shown in figure 17-7 is that the ON clause uses a class name and a *scope qualifier* (::). In this case, the class name is SCHEMA. You can also use a class name and scope qualifier when you grant or revoke object permissions. For example, I could have coded the GRANT statement in figure 17-7 like this:

```
GRANT SELECT
ON OBJECT :: Invoices
TO SusanRoberts;
```

However, because the class name and scope qualifier aren't required when you grant or revoke object permissions, I've omitted them from the syntax of the GRANT and REVOKE statements shown in figure 17-7.

Before you go on, you should realize that to delete an object from a schema, a user must have ALTER permission to the schema. A user must also have ALTER permission to a schema to create an object in the schema. In addition, the user must have permission to create the object in the database. The exception is that you can create a sequence simply by granting the CREATE SEQUENCE permission to the schema. To alter an object in the schema, the user only needs to have ALTER permission on the object.

How to grant schema permissions

The syntax of the GRANT statement for schema permissions

```
GRANT permission [, ...]
ON SCHEMA :: schema_name
TO database_principal [, ...]
[WITH GRANT OPTION]
```

A GRANT statement that grants UPDATE permission for the Accounting schema

```
GRANT UPDATE
ON SCHEMA :: Accounting
TO JohnDoe;
```

A GRANT statement that grants ALTER permission to a schema

```
GRANT ALTER
ON SCHEMA :: Marketing
TO JudyTaylor;
```

How to revoke schema permissions

The syntax of the REVOKE statement for schema permissions

```
REVOKE [GRANT OPTION FOR] permission [, ...]
ON SCHEMA :: schema_name
FROM database_principal [, ...]
[CASCADE]
```

A REVOKE statement that revokes UPDATE permission

```
REVOKE UPDATE
ON SCHEMA :: Accounting
FROM JohnDoe;
```

Description

- You use this format of the GRANT statement to give a user permission to work with all the objects in a database schema. This format of the REVOKE statement takes schema permissions away. These statements work just as they do for object permissions.

- To create an object in a schema or to delete an object from a schema, the user must have ALTER permission to the schema. To create an object, the user must also have CREATE permission to the database that contains the object. See figure 17-10 for information on database permissions.

- You can also grant or revoke the CREATE SEQUENCE permission on a schema.

- The ON clause in the GRANT and REVOKE statements includes a class name (SCHEMA) and a *scope qualifier* (::). Although class names and scope qualifiers can be used with other Transact-SQL statements, they're not usually required.

Figure 17-9   How to grant or revoke schema permissions

How to grant or revoke database permissions

Figure 17-10 presents the syntax of the GRANT and REVOKE statements you use to work with database permissions. In the GRANT clause, you list the statements you want to grant a user permission to execute. Some of the statements you can include in this list are shown in this figure. Then, in the TO clause, you list the users you want to have these permissions. The GRANT statement in this figure, for example, grants two users permission to create views. Remember that to create a view, though, the user must also have permission to alter the schema that contains it.

The syntax of the REVOKE statement is identical except that you code the user names in the FROM clause. The REVOKE statement shown in this figure, for example, revokes permission for the specified user to create databases or tables.

How to grant database permissions

The syntax of the GRANT statement for database permissions

```
GRANT permission [, ...]
TO database_principal [, ...]
[WITH GRANT OPTION]
```

A GRANT statement that gives permission to create views

```
GRANT CREATE VIEW
TO JohnDoe, SusanRoberts;
```

How to revoke database permissions

The syntax of the REVOKE statement for database permissions

```
REVOKE permission [, ...]
FROM database_principal [, ...]
[CASCADE]
```

A REVOKE statement that revokes permission to create databases and tables

```
REVOKE CREATE DATABASE, CREATE TABLE
FROM SylviaJones;
```

Some of the permissions that can be explicitly permitted

```
CREATE DATABASE
CREATE TABLE
CREATE VIEW
CREATE PROCEDURE
CREATE FUNCTION
CREATE SCHEMA
```

Description

- In addition to granting or revoking permissions for objects and schemas, you can grant or revoke permissions for databases.
- The list of SQL statements shown above only includes those discussed in this book. For a complete list, refer to the "GRANT Database Permissions (Transact-SQL)" topic in the SQL Server documentation.

Figure 17-10   How to grant or revoke database permissions

How to grant or revoke server permissions

The highest level at which you can grant or revoke permissions is the server level. Server permissions are typically reserved for system and database administrators. Figure 17-11 lists some of the permissions that are available and shows how to grant and revoke them.

Because the GRANT and REVOKE statements for server permissions are similar to the GRANT and REVOKE statements for other types of permissions, I'll just point out the main difference here. That is, because the permission is for the server and not the current database, the TO and FROM clauses must name a server principal instead of a database principal. A server principal can be either a login ID or a user-defined server role. In this figure, for example, both statements refer to a login ID. You'll learn more about server roles in just a minute.

How to grant server permissions

The syntax of the GRANT statement for server permissions

```
GRANT permission [, ...]
TO server_principal [, ...]
[WITH GRANT OPTION]
```

A GRANT statement that gives permission to create, alter, and drop databases

```
GRANT ALTER ANY DATABASE
TO JoelMurach;
```

How to revoke server permissions

The syntax of the REVOKE statement for server permissions

```
REVOKE permission [, ...]
FROM server_principal [, ...]
[CASCADE]
```

A REVOKE statement that revokes permission to create server roles

```
REVOKE CREATE SERVER ROLE
FROM [Administration\SylviaJones];
```

Some of the permissions that can be explicitly permitted

Permission	Description
CONTROL SERVER	Can perform any activity on the server.
CREATE ANY DATABASE	Can create databases.
CREATE SERVER ROLE	Can create server roles.
ALTER ANY DATABASE	Can create, alter, and drop databases.
ALTER ANY LOGIN	Can create, alter, and drop logins.
ALTER ANY SERVER ROLE	Can create, alter, and drop server roles.
VIEW ANY DATABASE	Can view database properties.

Description

- You can also use the GRANT and REVOKE statements to grant and revoke permissions for the entire server. When you do that, you specify a login or server role on the TO or FROM clause.

- For a complete list of server permissions, refer to the "GRANT Server Permissions (Transact-SQL)" topic in the SQL Server documentation.

Figure 17-11   How to grant or revoke server permissions

How to work with roles

Now that you've learned how to grant object and database permissions to a user, you can set up security on your database. If a system has many users, however, granting and revoking all of these permissions one by one would require a lot of coding. To help reduce the amount of coding and to help you keep your database security organized, you can use roles.

As you know, a role is a collection of permissions. When you assign a user to a particular role, you grant them all of the permissions associated with that role. SQL Server supports two different types of roles: fixed roles and user-defined roles. You'll learn how to work with both of these types of roles in the topics that follow.

How to work with the fixed server roles

Fixed roles are roles that are built into SQL Server. These roles can't be deleted and the permissions associated with them can't be modified. SQL Server provides two types of fixed roles: *fixed server roles* and *fixed database roles*. Figure 17-12 shows you how to work with the fixed server roles. You'll learn how to work with the fixed database roles later in this chapter.

The fixed server roles typically include users who manage the server. For example, the sysadmin role is intended for system administrators. For this reason, it grants permission to perform any task on the server. If you're a member of the Windows BUILTIN\Administrators group, you're a member of this role by default.

The securityadmin role is intended for those users who need to be able to manage security. The members of this role are allowed to work with login IDS and passwords. The dbcreator role is intended for those users who need to be able to work with database objects. The members of this role can create, alter, and drop databases. Although SQL Server provides other server roles, these are the ones you'll use most often.

To assign a user to a server role or to remove a user from a server role, you use the ALTER SERVER ROLE statement. On this statement, you specify the name of the server role. Then, to assign a user to the role, you specify the login ID of the user on the ADD MEMBER clause. To remove a user from the role, you specify the login ID on the DROP MEMBER clause. The first statement in this figure, for example, adds user JohnDoe to the sysadmin server role. The second statement drops this user from that role.

You can also use the ALTER SERVER ROLE statement to rename a server role. However, you can't rename fixed server roles, only user-defined server roles. You'll see an example of that in the next figure.

One additional fixed server role you should know about is the public server role. Each login that's created on the server is automatically assigned to this role and can't be removed. Then, the default permission for this role, VIEW ANY DATABASE, lets any login view the properties of any database on the server. If that's not what you want, you can revoke this permission from the role. To do that, you code the role name on the TO clause of the REVOKE statement. In most cases, though, it's not necessary to change the permissions for this role.

The syntax of the ALTER SERVER ROLE statement

```
ALTER SERVER ROLE role_name
{
ADD MEMBER server_principal |
DROP MEMBER server_principal |
WITH NAME = new_role_name
}
```

A statement that assigns a user to a server role

```
ALTER SERVER ROLE sysadmin ADD MEMBER JohnDoe;
```

A statement that removes a user from a server role

```
ALTER SERVER ROLE sysadmin DROP MEMBER JohnDoe;
```

Some of the SQL Server fixed server roles

Role	Description
sysadmin	Can perform any activity on the server. By default, all members of the Windows BUILTIN\Administrators group are members of this role.
securityadmin	Can manage login IDs and passwords for the server and can grant, deny, and revoke database permissions.
dbcreator	Can create, alter, drop, and restore databases.

Description

- A role is a collection of permissions you can assign to a user or group of users. By assigning a user to a role, you grant that user all of the permissions of the role. You can use roles to simplify user and security administration.

- SQL Server has built-in, or *fixed*, roles defined at the server level and at the database level. In addition, you can create user-defined roles for your server or database.

- Each role is assigned a set of permissions. For example, the dbcreator role can execute CREATE DATABASE, ALTER DATABASE, DROP DATABASE, and RESTORE DATABASE statements. This role can also add new members to the role.

- You use the ALTER SERVER ROLE statement to add a user to or remove a user from a server role. You can also use this statement to rename a user-defined server role.

- The fixed server roles are intended for users who are involved in the administration of the server. For a complete list of the fixed server roles, see the "Server-level Roles" topic in the SQL Server documentation.

- The ALTER SERVER ROLE statement was introduced with SQL Server 2012. In previous versions of SQL Server, you used the sp_AddSrvRoleMember system stored procedure to add a user to a server role, and you used the sp_DropSrvRoleMember procedure to remove a user from a server role.

Figure 17-12   How to work with the fixed server roles

How to work with user-defined server roles

In addition to fixed server roles, SQL Server 2012 and later lets you create *user-defined server roles*. Like the fixed server roles, a user-defined server role consists of a set of permissions that you can grant to a user by giving them membership in that role. Unlike the fixed server roles, you can create your own user-defined server roles, you can modify the permissions associated with those roles, and you can delete the roles when necessary. Figure 17-13 presents the two SQL statements you use to create and delete user-defined server roles.

The CREATE SERVER ROLE statement creates a new role on the server. The role name you specify on this statement must be unique: It can't be the same as another user-defined server role, fixed server role, or login name. The first statement in this figure, for example, creates a new server role named Consultant.

By default, a user-defined server role is owned by the login that creates it. If that's not what you want, you can include the AUTHORIZATION clause on the CREATE SERVER ROLE statement. This clause names the login or fixed server role that will own the new role.

Once a role is defined, you can use the GRANT statement to grant permissions to that role. To do that, you simply code the role name in the TO clause instead of a user name. The GRANT statement in this figure, for example, grants the Consultant role ALTER ANY LOGIN permission. Note that because these permissions can only be assigned at the server level, the current database must be set to master when they're executed.

The next statement in this figure assigns a user to the new role. That means that this user now has the ALTER ANY LOGIN permission that was assigned to the role by the previous GRANT statement. In addition, the next statement assigns the new role as a member of the dbcreator role. If you look back to figure 17-12, you'll see that this role grants any member of the role permission to create, alter, drop, and restore databases. Since the member itself is a role, any member of that role now has permission to create, alter, drop, and restore databases.

The next statement shows how to change the name of a user-defined server role. To do that, you use the WITH NAME clause of the ALTER SERVER ROLE statement. The statement shown here, for example, renames the Consultant role to DBConsultant.

To drop a user-defined server role, you use the DROP SERVER ROLE statement. Before you do that, however, you must delete all of the members of the role. The last two statements in this figure, for example, drop the member of the DBConsultant role and then drop the role.

Because the fixed server roles that SQL Server provides are adequate for most systems, you won't usually need to create user-defined server roles. That's because a limited number of users are typically given permissions at the server level. However, many users can be given permissions at the database level. Because of that, you're more likely to create user-defined database roles. You'll learn how to do that in a minute. But first, you should know how to display information about server roles and how to work with fixed database roles.

The syntax of the CREATE SERVER ROLE statement

```
CREATE SERVER ROLE role_name [AUTHORIZATION server_principal]
```

The syntax of the DROP SERVER ROLE statement

```
DROP SERVER ROLE role_name
```

Statements that work with a user-defined server role

A statement that creates a new server role

```
CREATE SERVER ROLE Consultant;
```

A statement that grants permissions to the new role

```
GRANT ALTER ANY LOGIN
TO Consultant;
```

A statement that assigns a user to the new role

```
ALTER SERVER ROLE Consultant ADD MEMBER JohnDoe;
```

A statement that assigns the new role to a fixed server role

```
ALTER SERVER ROLE dbcreator ADD MEMBER Consultant;
```

A statement that changes the name of the new role

```
ALTER SERVER ROLE Consultant WITH NAME = DBConsultant;
```

Statements that delete the new role

```
ALTER SERVER ROLE DBConsultant DROP MEMBER JohnDoe;
DROP SERVER ROLE DBConsultant;
```

Description

- You use the CREATE SERVER ROLE statement to create a *user-defined server role*. Role names can be up to 128 characters in length and can include letters, symbols, and numbers, but not the backslash (\) character.

- The AUTHORIZATION clause lets you specify a login or fixed server role that owns the user-defined role. If you omit this clause, the role will be owned by the login that executes the statement.

- Once you create a server role, you can grant permissions to or revoke permissions from the role. To do that, the current database must be master.

- To add members to a user-defined server role or delete members from the role, you use the ALTER SERVER ROLE statement shown in figure 17-12.

- You use the DROP SERVER ROLE statement to delete a user-defined server role. You can't delete a fixed server role or the public server role.

- Before you can delete a server role, you must delete all of its members. To find out how to list the members of a role, see figure 17-14.

- The CREATE SERVER ROLE and DROP SERVER ROLE statements were introduced with SQL Server 2012.

Figure 17-13   How to work with user-defined server roles

How to display information about server roles and role members

After you set the role membership for the fixed and user-defined server roles, you may want to review the role and membership information. One way to do that is to use the Management Studio. However, SQL Server also provides two catalog views that contain information about server roles and members. Figure 17-14 illustrates how you can use these catalog views.

To start, you can use the sys.server_principals catalog view to get a list of the server roles. In the first example in this figure, for instance, I used a SELECT statement to retrieve the name, principal_id, and is_fixed_role columns from this table. I also restricted the rows that were retrieved to roles (type = 'R'), since logins and Windows groups are also server principals. In the result set, you can see that all of the roles except for the first one and the last one are fixed roles. The first role is the public server role, and the last role is the user-defined Consultant role that I created in figure 17-13.

To list the members of a role, you have to join the sys.server_role_members catalog view with the sys.server_principals catalog view. The sys.server_role_members view contains every combination of server role principal ID and member principal ID. Then, you can join the member_principal_id column in that view with the principal_id column in the sys.server_principals view to get results like those shown in the second example in this figure.

If you only need to get information about fixed server roles and members, you can use two system stored procedures instead of the catalog views. The third example in this figure shows how to use the sp_HelpSrvRole procedure to get information about the server roles. That information includes the name and description for each server role. Although you can code a role name as a parameter so information for a single role is displayed, you're more likely to omit this parameter.

To get information about the members of a fixed server role, you can use the sp_HelpSrvRoleMember stored procedure. In this figure, for example, the stored procedure will return information about the members of the sysadmin role. If you omit the role name, this procedure will return information about the members in all of the fixed server roles that have at least one member.

How to display information for any server role

```
SELECT name, principal_id, is_fixed_role
FROM sys.server_principals
WHERE type = 'R';
```

	name	principal_id	is_fixed_role
1	public	2	0
2	sysadmin	3	1
3	securityadmin	4	1
4	serveradmin	5	1
5	setupadmin	6	1
6	processadmin	7	1
7	diskadmin	8	1
8	dbcreator	9	1
9	bulkadmin	10	1
10	Consultant	271	0

How to display member information for any server role

```
SELECT member_principal_id, name
FROM sys.server_role_members AS srm
JOIN sys.server_principals AS sp
  ON srm.member_principal_id = sp.principal_id
WHERE srm.role_principal_id = 267;
```

	member_principal_id	name
1	268	JohnDoe

How to display information for fixed server roles
The syntax for sp_HelpSrvRole

```
sp_HelpSrvRole [[@srvrolename = ] 'server_role_name']
```

A statement that lists the fixed server roles

```
EXEC sp_HelpSrvRole;
```

How to display member information for fixed server roles
The syntax for sp_HelpSrvRoleMember

```
sp_HelpSrvRoleMember [[@srvrolename = ] 'server_role_name']
```

A statement that lists the members of the sysadmin role

```
EXEC sp_HelpSrvRoleMember sysadmin;
```

Description

- The sys.server_principals catalog view contains information about each principal defined on the server. To display information about just the server roles, use a SELECT statement with a WHERE clause that checks for a type of 'R'.

- The sys.server_role_members catalog view contains a list of each role principal/member principal combination. To display information about the members of a server role, join this view with the sys.server_role_member view and restrict the results to the principal ID of the role whose members you want to display.

- To display information about just the fixed server roles and members, you can use the sp_HelpSrvRole and sp_HelpSrvRoleMember system stored procedures.

Figure 17-14   How to display information about server roles and role members

How to work with the fixed database roles

Figure 17-15 lists the fixed database roles and shows you how to work with them. These roles are added automatically to each new database you create. In addition, when you create a database, you're automatically added to the db_owner database role.

To add a member to a database role or to delete a member from a database role, you use the ALTER ROLE statement. This statement is similar to the ALTER SERVER ROLE statement you saw earlier in this chapter. The main difference is that you specify a database principal on the ADD MEMBER and DROP MEMBER clauses. A database principal can be a database user, a Windows user or group name, or a user-defined database role. You'll see how to create user-defined database roles in a moment. For now, just realize that the ability to assign user-defined database roles as members of fixed database roles makes assigning permissions flexible and convenient.

Like the ALTER SERVER ROLE statement, you can also use the ALTER ROLE statement to rename a user-defined database role. You'll see an example of that in the next figure.

In addition to the fixed database roles listed in this figure, SQL Server includes a special fixed database role named public. This role is included in every database, and every database user is automatically a member of this role. This role has no permissions by default, however, so you don't need to be concerned about security violations due to the existence of this role. You can't add or drop members from this role, nor can you delete the role from a database. If you want all users to have some basic permissions on a database, however, you can assign those permissions to this role.

The syntax of the ALTER ROLE statement

```
ALTER ROLE role_name
{
ADD MEMBER database_principal |
DROP MEMBER database_principal |
WITH NAME = new_name
}
```

A statement that assigns a user to a database role

```
ALTER ROLE db_owner ADD MEMBER JohnDoe;
```

A statement that removes a user from a database role

```
ALTER ROLE db_owner DROP MEMBER JohnDoe;
```

The SQL Server fixed database roles

Role	Description
db_owner	Has all permissions for the database.
db_accessadmin	Can add or remove login IDs for the database.
db_securityadmin	Can manage object permissions, database permissions, roles, and role memberships.
db_ddladmin	Can issue all DDL statements except GRANT, REVOKE, and DENY.
db_datawriter	Can insert, delete, or update data from any user table in the database.
db_datareader	Can select data from any user table in the database.
db_denydatawriter	Can't insert, delete, or update data from any user table in the database.
db_denydatareader	Can't select data from any user table in the database.
db_backupoperator	Can back up the database and run consistency checks on the database.

Description

- The *fixed database roles* are added to each database you create. You can add and delete members from these roles, but you can't delete the roles.

- You use the ALTER ROLE statement to assign a user to or remove a user from a database role in the current database. You can also use this statement to change the name of a user-defined database role.

- The database_principal parameter can be the name of a database user, a user-defined database role, or a Windows login or group. If you specify a Windows login or group that doesn't have a corresponding database user, a database user is created.

- The users you specify are assigned to or removed from the role you name in the current database. Because of that, you should be sure to change the database context before executing one of these stored procedures.

- SQL Server also provides a public database role. Any user that's not given specific permissions on a securable is given the permissions assigned to the public role.

- Prior to SQL Server 2012, you could use the ALTER ROLE statement only to change the name of a user-defined database role. To add or drop a role, you used the sp_AddRoleMember or sp_DropRoleMember system stored procedure.

Figure 17-15   How to work with the fixed database roles

How to work with user-defined database roles

Figure 17-16 presents the two SQL statements you use to create and delete user-defined database roles. If you compare these statements with the statements for creating and deleting user-defined server roles, you'll see that they're almost identical. The only difference is that you can specify a user name or role on the AUTHORIZATION clause of the CREATE ROLE statement to indicate the owner of the role. If you omit this clause, the role is owned by the user who creates it.

The CREATE ROLE statement creates a new role in the current database. The role name you specify on this statement must be unique: It can't be the same as another user-defined database role, fixed database role, or database user name. The first statement in this figure, for example, creates a new role named InvoiceEntry.

To grant permissions to a user-defined database role, you use the GRANT statement. The two GRANT statements in this figure, for example, grant the InvoiceEntry role INSERT and UPDATE permissions to the Invoices and InvoiceLineItems tables in the AP database. (You can assume that AP is the current database for these examples.)

The next two statements in this figure assign two users to the new role. That means that these two users now have the INSERT and UPDATE permissions that were assigned to the role. Then, the next statement assigns the new role as a member of the db_datareader role. This role grants any member of the role permission to select data from any user table in the database. Since the member itself is a role, any member of that role now has permission to select data from the database.

The next statement in this figure uses the ALTER ROLE statement to rename the InvoiceEntry role to InvEntry. Then, the last group of statements deletes the two members from this role and then deletes the role.

As you can see, using roles can significantly simplify security management. If you assign roles as members of other roles, however, managing the various roles and permissions can quickly get out of hand. For example, suppose you added a new table to the AP database. Then, the two users that are members of the InvoiceEntry role would automatically be able to select data from that table because the InvoiceEntry role is a member of the db_datareader role. If that's not what you want, you'd need to remove InvoiceEntry from the db_datareader role and then grant SELECT permission to that role for each of the tables in the database that you want the users to have access to. If you plan to assign roles to other roles, then, you'll want to plan it out carefully to avoid having to redesign the security in the future.

The syntax of the CREATE ROLE statement

```
CREATE ROLE role_name [AUTHORIZATION owner_name]
```

The syntax of the DROP ROLE statement

```
DROP ROLE role_name
```

Statements that work with user-defined database roles

A statement that creates a new user-defined database role

```
CREATE ROLE InvoiceEntry;
```

Statements that grant permissions to the new role

```
GRANT INSERT, UPDATE
ON Invoices
TO InvoiceEntry;

GRANT INSERT, UPDATE
ON InvoiceLineItems
TO InvoiceEntry;
```

Statements that assign users to the new role

```
ALTER ROLE InvoiceEntry ADD MEMBER JohnDoe;
ALTER ROLE InvoiceEntry ADD MEMBER SusanRoberts;
```

A statement that assigns the new role to a fixed database role

```
ALTER ROLE db_datareader ADD MEMBER InvoiceEntry;
```

A statement that changes the name of the new role

```
ALTER ROLE InvoiceEntry WITH NAME = InvEntry;
```

Statements that delete the new role

```
ALTER ROLE InvEntry DROP MEMBER JohnDoe;
ALTER ROLE InvEntry DROP MEMBER SusanRoberts;
DROP ROLE InvEntry;
```

Description

- You use the CREATE ROLE statement to create a *user-defined database role*. Role names can be up to 128 characters in length and can include letters, symbols, and numbers, but not the backslash (\) character.

- Once you create a database role, you can grant permissions to or revoke permissions from the role. Then, you grant or revoke permissions for every member of the role.

- To add members to a user-defined database role, delete members from the role, or rename the role, you use the ALTER ROLE statement shown in figure 17-15.

- You use the DROP ROLE statement to delete user-defined database roles. You can't delete a fixed database role or the public database role.

- Before you can delete a database role, you must delete all of its members. To find out how to list the members of a role, see figure 17-17.

- The CREATE ROLE and DROP ROLE statements were introduced with SQL Server 2005.

Figure 17-16   How to work with user-defined database roles

How to display information about database roles and role members

As you might expect, most systems have many database users and many database roles. Some users belong to several roles, and some roles belong to other roles. For this reason, keeping track of security permissions can be a complex task. Since the Management Studio provides an easy way to examine current role settings, most security managers use this tool rather than using Transact-SQL. However, SQL Server provides some system stored procedures that can be helpful for managing database roles. Figure 17-17 presents two of these procedures.

The sp_HelpRole procedure returns information about the database roles defined for the current database. If you code a valid role name as a parameter, this procedure returns information about that one role. Otherwise it returns information about all the roles in the database. That includes both user-defined database roles and fixed database roles. In most cases, you'll use this function just to list the roles in a database, so you'll omit the role name.

The information that's returned by this procedure includes the role name, the role ID, and an indication of whether or not the role is an application role. The role ID is the internal object identification number that's assigned to the role. An application role is a special kind of role that's typically used to provide secure access to an application program rather than a user. You'll learn more about application roles later in this chapter.

The sp_HelpRoleMember stored procedure returns information about the current members of a database role. If you include a role name as a parameter, it returns information about the members of that role. Otherwise, it returns information about the members in all the roles in the current database that have at least one member.

In most cases, the information provided by the sp_HelpRole and sp_HelpRoleMember stored procedures is all you need. If you need additional information, though, you can find it in the sys.database_principals and sys.database_role_members catalog views. These catalog views are similar to the catalog views that you use to get information about server roles and role members as shown in figure 17-14. To learn more about these catalog views, see the SQL Server documentation.

How to display database role information

The syntax for sp_HelpRole

```
sp_HelpRole [[@rolename = ] 'database_role_name']
```

A statement that lists the roles for the current database

```
EXEC sp_HelpRole;
```

The response from the system

	RoleName	RoleId	IsAppRole
1	public	0	0
2	InvoiceEntry	6	0
3	AppInvoiceQuery	8	1
4	db_owner	16384	0
5	db_accessadmin	16385	0
6	db_securityadmin	16386	0
7	db_ddladmin	16387	0
8	db_backupoperator	16389	0
9	db_datareader	16390	0
10	db_datawriter	16391	0
11	db_denydatareader	16392	0
12	db_denydatawriter	16393	0

How to display database role member information

The syntax for sp_HelpRoleMember

```
sp_HelpRoleMember [[@rolename = ] database_role_name']
```

A statement that lists the members of the InvoiceEntry role

```
EXEC sp_HelpRoleMember InvoiceEntry;
```

The response from the system

	DbRole	MemberName	MemberSID
1	InvoiceEntry	JohnDoe	0x7E3BB643D227244AA02DA4213C0C9978
2	InvoiceEntry	MartinRey	0x4333E01D011965459F45A85D3F956780

Description

- To display information about the roles defined in the current database, use the sp_HelpRole system stored procedure. If you don't specify a role name on this procedure, information about all of the roles in the database is returned.

- To display information about the members of a database role, use the sp_HelpRoleMember system stored procedure. If you don't specify the role name on this procedure, information about the members of all of the roles in the database that have at least one member is returned.

- You can display additional information about database roles using the sys.database_principals and sys.database_role_members catalog views. These views are similar to the sys.server_principals and sys.server_role_members views described in figure 17-14.

Figure 17-17   How to display information about database roles and role members

How to deny permissions granted by role membership

A user's permissions include those that are granted explicitly to that user plus permissions that are granted by that user's membership in one or more roles. That means that if you revoke a permission from the user but the same permission is granted by a role to which the user belongs, the user still has that permission. Since this might not be what you want, SQL Server provides a DENY statement that you can use to deny a user permission that's granted by the user's membership in a role. This statement is presented in figure 17-18.

The syntax of the DENY statement is similar to the syntax of the REVOKE statement. To deny object permissions, you specify the permissions you want to deny, the object to which you want to deny permissions, and the users and roles whose permissions you want to deny. To deny permissions to all of the objects in the schema, you specify the permissions you want to deny, the schema that contains the objects to which you want to deny permissions, and the users and roles whose permissions you want to deny. To deny database permissions, you specify the permissions you want to deny and the users and roles whose permissions you want to deny. And to deny server permissions, you specify the permissions you want to deny and the login IDs and roles whose permissions you want to deny.

The two examples in this figure illustrate how this works. The script in the first example adds the user named MartinRey to the InvoiceEntry role. Since InvoiceEntry is a member of the db_datareaders fixed database role, MartinRey can retrieve data from any table in the database. This is illustrated by the successful completion of the SELECT statement that follows, which retrieves data from the GLAccounts table.

The script in the second example uses a DENY statement to deny the user named MartinRey SELECT permission on the GLAccounts table. As a result, when this user executes a SELECT statement against the GLAccounts table, the system responds with an error. That's because the DENY statement specifically denied this user permission to retrieve data from this table even though that permission is granted by the db_datareaders role.

The syntax of the DENY statement for object permissions

```
DENY permission [, ...]
ON [schema_name.]object_name [(column [, ...])]
TO database_principal [, ...]
[CASCADE]
```

The syntax of the DENY statement for schema permissions

```
DENY permission [, ...]
ON SCHEMA :: schema_name
TO database_principal [, ...]
[CASCADE]
```

The syntax of the DENY statement for database permissions

```
DENY permission [, ...]
TO database_principal [, ...]
[CASCADE]
```

The syntax of the DENY statement for server permissions

```
DENY permission [, ...]
TO server_principal [, ...]
[CASCADE]
```

A script that assigns membership to the InvoiceEntry role

```
ALTER ROLE InvoiceEntry ADD MEMBER MartinRey;
```

A SELECT statement entered by the user

```
SELECT * FROM GLAccounts;
```

The response from the system

	AccountNo	AccountDescription
1	100	Cash
2	110	Accounts Receivable
3	120	Book Inventory

A script that denies SELECT permission to GLAccounts

```
DENY SELECT
ON GLAccounts
TO MartinRey;
```

A SELECT statement entered by the user

```
SELECT * FROM GLAccounts;
```

The response from the system

```
Server: Msg 229, Level 14, State 5, Line 1
SELECT permission was denied on object 'GLAccounts', database 'AP', schema 'dbo'.
```

Description

- The permissions granted to individual users are granted by two sources: permissions granted to their user names or login IDs and permissions granted through any roles to which they are members.

- The DENY statement differs from the REVOKE statement in that DENY prevents the permission from being granted by role membership. A denied permission can't be granted by role membership, but a revoked permission can.

Figure 17-18   How to deny permissions granted by role membership

How to work with application roles

An *application role* is a special kind of user-defined database role. Unlike other roles, you can't assign members to an application role. Instead, you activate the role for a connection. Then, the normal security for the login ID that was used to open the connection is replaced by the security that's specified by the application role.

Figure 17-19 presents SQL statements and system stored procedures for working with application roles. To create a new application role, you use the CREATE APPLICATION ROLE statement. This statement requires a role name and a password. The first statement in this figure, for example, creates an application role named AppInvoiceQuery that has a password of "appqrypw". You can also specify a default schema for an application role.

After you create an application role, you can use it in GRANT, REVOKE, or DENY statements just as you would any other role. The second statement in this figure, for example, grants the application role permission to retrieve data from the Invoices table.

To activate an application role, you execute the sp_SetAppRole procedure. Once activated, the connection is granted the permissions associated with the application role instead of the permissions associated with the login ID. Since the connection takes on an entirely new set of permissions, it's almost as if the user logged off and then logged back on under a different login ID.

You can see how this works in the script in this figure. First, assume that the login ID that was used to log on to the server doesn't have SELECT permission for the Invoices table. For this reason, the first SELECT statement in this script fails and returns an error message. Next, the script activates the AppInvoiceQuery application role. Because this role has permission to select data from the Invoices table, the SELECT statement that follows now succeeds.

Notice that you can also create a cookie when you activate an application role. This cookie is stored in an OUTPUT parameter that must be defined as VARBINARY(8000). If you create a cookie, you can use the sp_UnsetAppRole stored procedure to deactivate the application role. Otherwise, the role remains in effect until the connection is closed.

Application roles are intended for use by application programs that manage their own security. Typically, an application like this will open a limited number of connections to a database and then share those connections among many application users. Then, the application role controls the application's access to the database, and the application controls the users that are allowed to use the connections it establishes.

You can also use application roles to provide for more flexible security. For example, suppose a user needs to access a database both through the Management Studio and through an application. Also suppose that the user needs broader permissions to use the application than you want to give him through the Management Studio. To do that, you could assign the user standard permissions through his login ID and role memberships, and you could give the application enhanced permissions through an application role.

SQL statements for working with application roles

The syntax of the CREATE APPLICATION ROLE statement

```
CREATE APPLICATION ROLE role_name WITH PASSWORD = 'password'
    [, DEFAULT_SCHEMA = schema_name]
```

The syntax of the DROP APPLICATION ROLE statement

```
DROP APPLICATION ROLE role_name
```

System stored procedures for working with application roles

The syntax for sp_SetAppRole

```
sp_SetAppRole [@rolename = ] 'role_name',
              [@password = ] 'password'
          [, [@fCreateCookie = ] {True|False}]
          [, [@cookie = ] @cookie OUTPUT]
```

The syntax for sp_UnsetAppRole

```
sp_UnsetAppRole @cookie
```

Statements that create an application role and give it permissions

```
CREATE APPLICATION ROLE AppInvoiceQuery WITH PASSWORD = 'appqrypw';

GRANT SELECT
ON Invoices
TO AppInvoiceQuery;
```

A script that tests the application role

```
SELECT * FROM Invoices;
EXEC sp_SetAppRole AppInvoiceQuery, appqrypw;
SELECT * FROM Invoices;
```

The response from the system

```
Server: Msg 229, Level 14, State 5, Line 1
SELECT permission was denied on object 'Invoices', database 'AP', schema 'dbo'.
```

	InvoiceID	VendorID	InvoiceNumber	InvoiceDate	InvoiceTotal	PaymentTotal	CreditTotal	
1	1	122	989319-457	2015-12-08 00:00:00	3813.33	3813.33	0.00	
2	2	123	263253241	2015-12-10 00:00:00	40.20	40.20	0.00	

Description

- An *application role* is a special type of user-define database role. It can't contain any members, but it's activated when a connection executes the sp_SetAppRole system stored procedure.

- Once the connection activates an application role, the normal security for the login ID set by the permissions for the ID and its roles is ignored. Instead, the connection assumes a new security profile as defined by the permissions for the application role.

- Once a connection activates an application role, the application role remains in effect until the connection is closed or until the sp_UnsetAppRole procedure is executed. To use sp_UnsetAppRole, you must create a cookie when you execute sp_SetAppRole.

- Application roles are typically used by application programs that manage their own security. Then, those programs can control the users that can log on to the server.

Figure 17-19   How to work with application roles

How to manage security using the Management Studio

Now that you understand how SQL Server security works, you're ready to learn how to manage security using the Management Studio. The topics that follow present the basic skills for doing that. If you want to learn additional skills, you shouldn't have any trouble doing that on your own.

How to work with login IDs

Figure 17-20 presents the General page of the Login - New dialog box. You use this page to specify the basic settings for a new login. To start, you select which type of authentication you want to use. If you select Windows authentication, you can click the Search button to the right of the Login Name box to select a domain and a user or group. Alternatively, you can enter a domain name and a user or group name in the Login Name box.

If you select SQL Server authentication, you must enter the new login name in the Login Name box. In addition, you must enter a password for the user in both the Password and Confirm Password boxes. You can also set the three password options shown here. These options are equivalent to the CHECK_POLICY, CHECK_EXPIRATION, and MUST_CHANGE options that you can include on the CREATE LOGIN statement.

In addition to setting the authentication mode and password options, you can use this page to set the default database and the default language for the user. If you don't select another database, the master database is used. And if you don't select a specific language, the default language for the server is used.

After you create a login ID, you can modify it using the Login Properties dialog box. The General page of this dialog box is almost identical to the General page of the Login - New dialog box shown in this figure. The main difference is that you can't change the type of authentication that's used from this page. To do that, you have to delete the login ID and create a new one with the authentication you want.

The Status page of the Login Properties dialog box lets you grant or deny a login ID permission to connect to SQL Server. It also lets you enable or disable a login ID. Although these options are similar, they differ in how they're implemented.

The General page of the Login - New dialog box

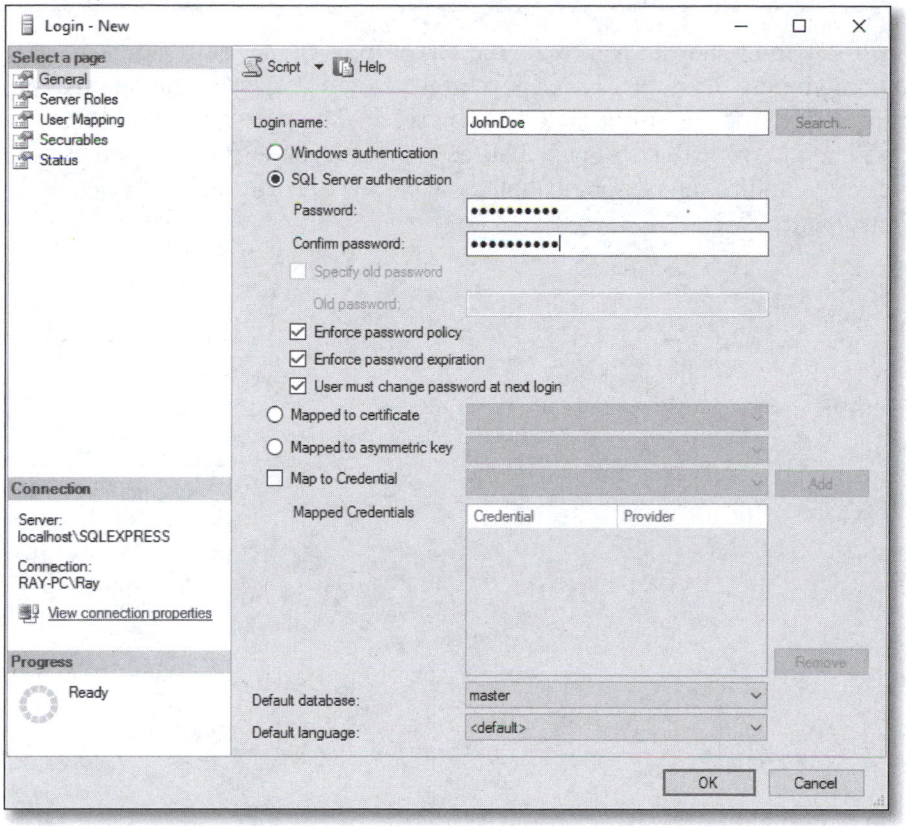

Description

- To create a new login ID, expand the Security folder for the server in the Object Explorer. Then, right-click the Logins folder and select New Login to display the Login - New dialog box.

- Select the type of authentication you want to use and then specify the appropriate settings. The settings that are available depend on whether you select Windows or SQL Server authentication.

- To modify a login ID, right-click the ID in the Object Explorer and select Properties to display the Login Properties dialog box. The General page of this dialog box lets you change all the settings for the login ID except for the login name and the authentication mode.

- You can use the options on the Status page of the Login Properties dialog box to deny or grant a login ID permission to connect to SQL Server. You can also disable or enable a login ID.

- To delete a login ID, right-click the ID in the Object Explorer and select Delete to display the Delete Object dialog box. Click the OK button to delete the login ID.

Figure 17-20 How to work with login IDs

How to work with the server roles for a login ID

Figure 17-21 shows how to work with the server roles for a specific login ID. To do that, you use the Server Roles page of the Login Properties dialog box. This page lists all of the server roles and lets you select the ones you want the login ID assigned to. Note that this page lists user-defined server roles as well as fixed server roles. In this figure, for example, you can see the user-defined role named Consultant.

The dialog box for working with server roles

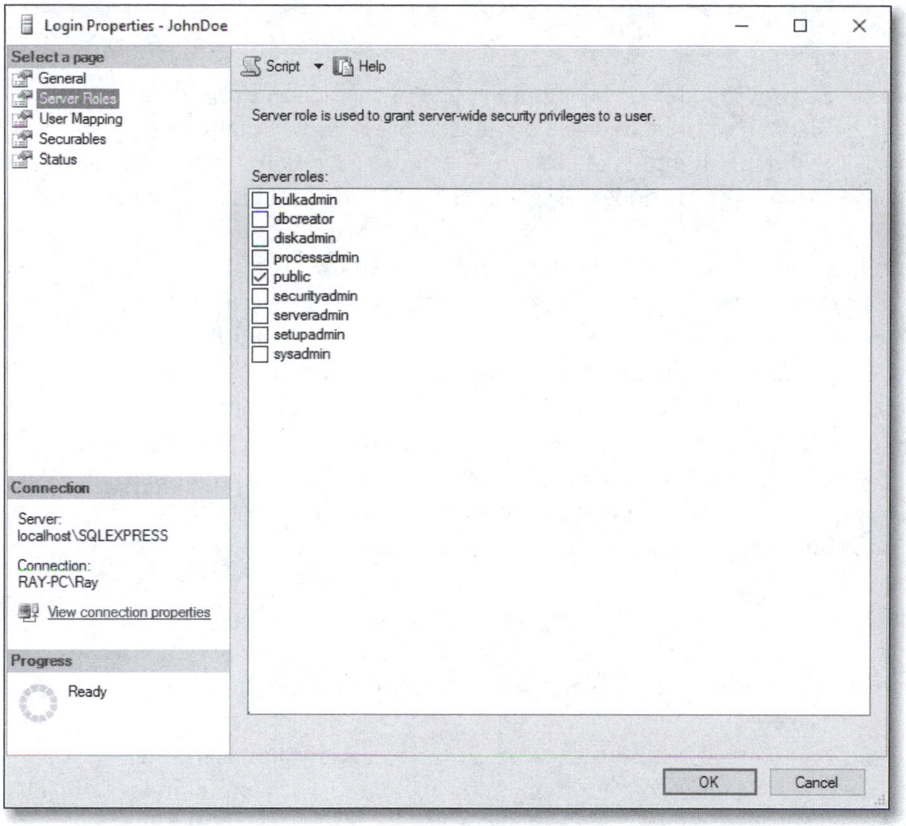

Description

- To work with the server roles for a login ID, right-click the ID in the Object Explorer and select Properties to display the Login Properties dialog box. Then, display the Server Roles page. The roles that the login ID is currently assigned to are checked in the list that's displayed.

- To add or remove a login ID from a server role, select or deselect the role.

Figure 17-21   How to work with the server roles for a login ID

How to assign database access and roles by login ID

Figure 17-22 presents the User Mapping page of the Login Properties dialog box. This page lists all of the databases on the server and all of the database roles defined for the highlighted database. You can use this dialog box to grant database access to a login ID and to assign a login ID membership in one or more database roles.

To grant or revoke database access, simply select or deselect the check box to the left of the database name. If you grant a login ID access to a database, the name of the associated database user is displayed in the User column, and the default schema for the user is displayed in the Default Schema column. If no user is associated with the login ID, the user name is set to the login name by default and no default schema is specified. If that's not what you want, you can enter a different name for the user and select a schema. Then, when you click the OK button, a new user is created with the name and default schema you specified. This is a quick and easy way to create a user at the same time that you grant database access.

If you want to create a user before granting access to one or more databases, you can do that using the Database User - New dialog box. To display this dialog box, expand the database in the Object Explorer, right-click on the Users folder, and select New User.

After you grant a user access to a database, you can add that user as a member of any of the database roles defined for the database. That includes both the fixed database roles and any user-defined roles. To do that, just highlight the database and then select the check boxes to the left of the database roles to add the user to those roles.

The User Mapping page of the Login Properties dialog box

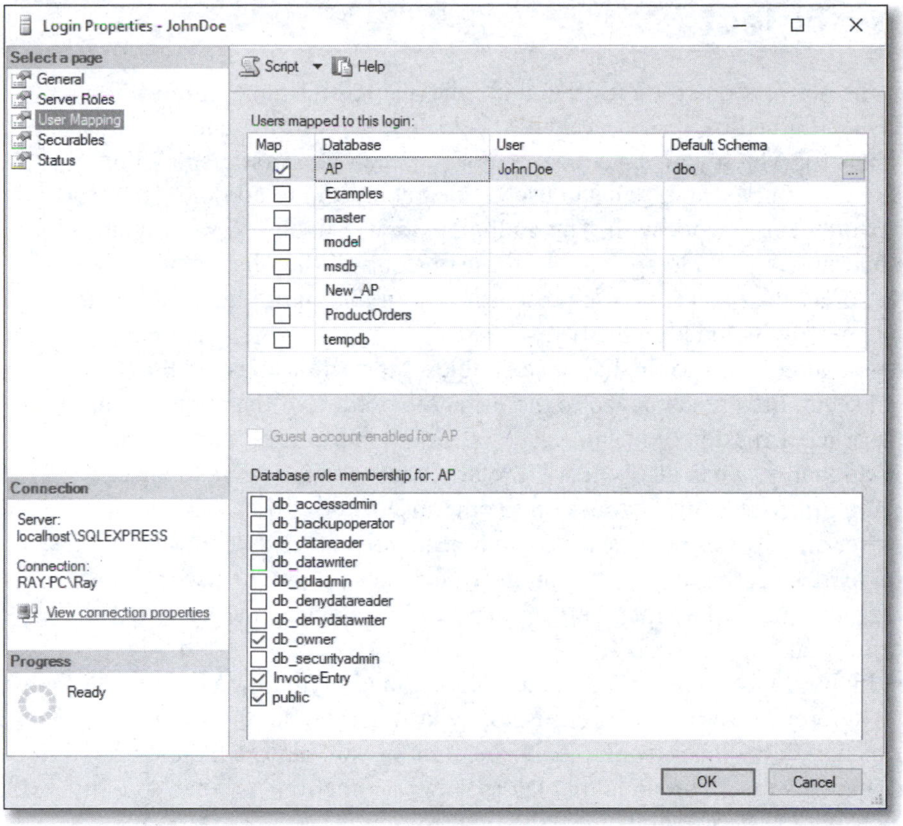

How to grant or revoke database access for a user

- To grant or revoke access to a database, display the User Mapping page of the Login Properties dialog box. Then, select or deselect the Map check box for that database.

- If you grant access to a login ID that's not associated with a database user, a user is created automatically when you complete the dialog box. By default, the user name is set to the login ID, but you can change this name in the User column.

- By default, the default schema for a new user is set to dbo. If you want to specify a different schema, click the button with the ellipsis on it in the Default Schema column and select the schema from the dialog box that's displayed.

How to add or remove a user from a database role

- If the user has access to a database, you can add or remove the user from the database roles for that database. To do that, highlight the database to display the database roles in the lower portion of the dialog box. Then, select or deselect the roles.

Figure 17-22   How to assign database access and roles by login ID

How to assign user permissions to database objects

To set the permissions for a user, you use the Securables page of the Database User dialog box shown in figure 17-23. The top of this dialog box lists the securables for which you can set permissions. When you first display this page, this list is empty. Then, you can use the Search button to add the securables you want to work with. The dialog box that's displayed when you click this button lets you add specific database objects, all the objects of one or more types, or all the objects in a selected schema. In this figure, three tables in the dbo schema are included in the list.

Once you add objects to the list of securables, the permissions for the highlighted securable are displayed in the list at the bottom of the page. Then, to grant the user a permission, you can select the Grant option for that permission. When you do that, you can also select the With Grant option to give the user permission to grant the same permission to other users.

If the user already has permission to an object, you can revoke that permission by deselecting the Grant option. You can also deny the user a permission that's granted by membership in a role by selecting the Deny option for the permission.

If you highlight a table, view, or table-valued function and then highlight the Select, References, or Update permission, you'll notice that the Column Permissions button becomes available. If you click on this button, a dialog box is displayed that lists the columns in that table, view, or function. You can use this dialog box to set the permissions for individual columns.

After you set the explicit permissions for a user from this dialog box, you might want to know what the user permissions are when the explicit permissions are combined with any permissions granted by role membership. To do that, you can highlight a securable and then display the Effective tab. This tab lists the permissions the user has for the securable, including column permissions for a table, view, or table-valued function.

The Securables page of the Database User dialog box

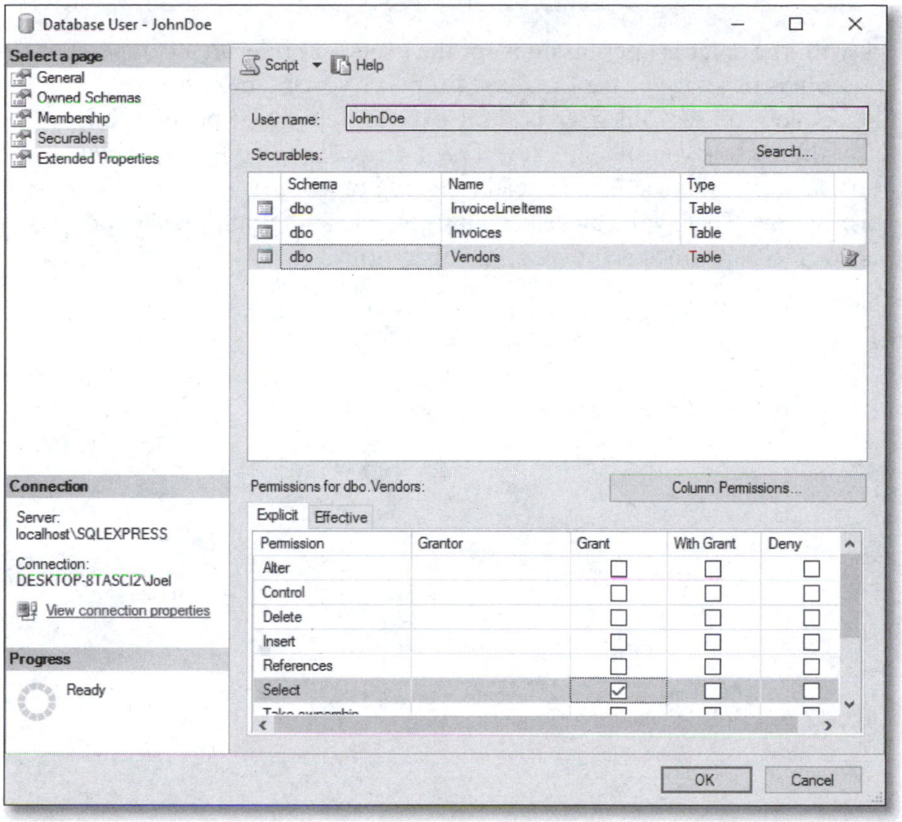

Description

- To display the Database User dialog box, expand the database in the Object Explorer, expand the Security and Users folders, right-click the user name, and select Properties.

- To work with the permissions for a user, display the Securables page. Then, click the Search button and use it to select the securables you want to work with.

- To grant the user permission to a securable, select the securable and then select the Grant option for the permission. You can also select the With Grant option.

- To revoke the user permission to a securable, deselect the Grant option.

- To deny the user permission to a securable, select the Deny option.

- To set the permissions for the columns in a table, view, or table-valued function, highlight the securable and permission. Then, click the Column Permissions button.

- The permissions that are available change depending on the type of securable that's selected.

- To display the combination of the permissions granted with this dialog box and the permissions granted through roles to a securable, display the Effective tab.

Figure 17-23   How to assign user permissions to database objects

How to work with database permissions

To work with the database permissions for the users and roles in a database, you use the Permissions page of the Database Properties dialog box shown in figure 17-24. As you can see, this page is similar to the Securables page of the Database User dialog box you saw in figure 17-23. Instead of listing securables, however, it lists users and roles. And instead of listing object permissions, it lists database permissions. Then, you can select a user or role and grant, revoke, or deny permissions to perform specific database operations.

The Permissions page of the Database Properties dialog box

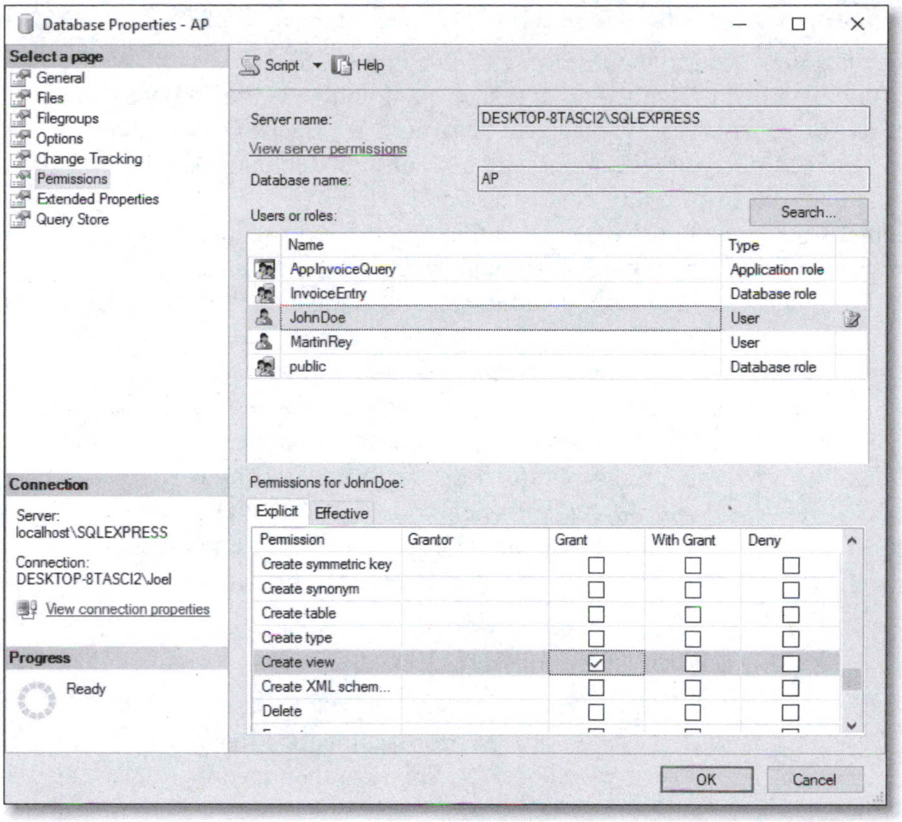

Description

- To display the permissions for a database, right-click the database in the Object Explorer, select Properties to display the Database Properties dialog box, and display the Permissions page.

- By default, all database users except for guest are included in the Users or roles list. To add the guest user or any system or user-defined roles, click the Search button and select the users and roles from the dialog box that's displayed.

- To grant a user or role permission to perform a database operation, select the user or role and then select the Grant option for the permission. You can also select the With Grant option to allow the user or role to grant the permission to other users and roles.

- To revoke a user or role permission to perform a database operation, deselect the Grant option.

- To deny the user permission to a database operation, select the Deny option.

Figure 17-24 How to work with database permissions

Perspective

Although managing security on a server can be complex, SQL Server provides useful tools to simplify the job. In this chapter, you've learned how to manage security for your server and database using both Transact-SQL and the Management Studio. Once you're familiar with both of these techniques, you can use the one that's easiest for the security task at hand.

Unfortunately, the techniques presented in this chapter don't secure your data if a thief is able to steal a hard drive or backup tape that contains the data files for the database. In that case, the thief can attach the data files to a different server and gain access to the data. To close this security hole, you can encrypt the data files and store the encryption key in a different location. That way, even if the data files are stolen, the thief won't be able to open them without the key. In the past, implementing encryption was a complicated process that involved modifying the structure of the database. Starting with SQL Server 2008, however, *transparent data encryption* (*TDE*) makes it easy to encrypt the entire database without affecting existing applications. For more information about TDE, you can refer to the SQL Server documentation.

Terms

login ID
permissions
object permissions
schema permissions
database permissions
server permissions
role
group
principal
securable
authentication mode

Windows authentication
SQL Server authentication
strong password
scope qualifier
fixed role
fixed server role
user-defined server role
fixed database role
user-defined database role
application role

Exercises

1. Write a script that creates a user-defined database role named PaymentEntry in the AP database. Give UPDATE permission to the new role for the Invoices table, UPDATE and INSERT permission for the InvoiceLineItems table, and SELECT permission for all user tables.

2. Write a script that (1) creates a login ID named "AAaron" with the password "aaar9999"; (2) sets the default database for the login to the AP database; (3) creates a user named "Aaron" for the login; and (4) assigns the user to the PaymentEntry role you created in exercise 1.

3. Write a script that creates four login IDs based on the contents of a new table called NewLogins:

    ```
    CREATE TABLE NewLogins
    (LoginName varchar(128));
    INSERT NewLogins
    VALUES ('BBrown'), ('CChaplin'), ('DDyer'), ('EEbbers');
    ```

    Use dynamic SQL and a cursor to perform four actions for each row in this table: (1) create a login with a temporary password based on the first four letters of the login name followed by "9999"; (2) set the default database to the AP database; (3) create a user for the login with the same name as the login; and (4) assign the user to the PaymentEntry role you created in exercise 1.

4. Using the Management Studio, create a login ID named "FFalk" with the password "ffal9999," and set the default database to the AP database. Then, grant the login ID access to the AP database, create a user for the login ID named "FFalk", and assign the user to the PaymentEntry role you created in exercise 1.

    Note: If you get an error that says "The MUST_CHANGE option is not supported", you can deselect the "Enforce password policy" option for the login ID.

5. Write a script that removes the user-defined database role named PaymentEntry. (Hint: This script should begin by removing all users from this role.)

6. Write a script that (1) creates a schema named Admin, (2) transfers the table named ContactUpdates from the dbo schema to the Admin schema, (3) assigns the Admin schema as the default schema for the user named Aaron that you created in exercise 2, and (4) grants all standard privileges except for REFERENCES and ALTER to AAaron for the Admin schema.

18

How to work with XML

In this chapter, you'll learn how to use SQL Server to work with XML data.
That includes using the xml data type, using an XML schema to validate the
data that's stored in an xml type, and converting relational data to XML and
XML to relational data. Many of the features presented in this chapter were
introduced with SQL Server 2005, and they make it easier to work with XML.

An introduction to XML

Before you learn how to use SQL Server to work with XML, you need to understand some basic XML concepts. In particular, you need to understand how XML can be used to structure data, and you need to understand how an XML schema can be used to validate XML data.

An XML document

XML (*Extensible Markup Language)* can be used to create an *XML document* that contains data that has been structured with *XML tags*. For example, figure 18-1 shows an XML document that contains data about an event that caused a DDL trigger to fire. You learned how to return an XML document like this one in chapter 15 using the EVENTDATA function within a DDL trigger.

Within an XML document, an *element* begins with a *start tag* and ends with an *end tag*. In this figure, for example, the <EventType> tag marks the start of the EventType element, and the </EventType> tag marks the end of this element.

Within a start tag, one or more *attributes* can be coded. In this figure, for example, the start tag for the SetOptions element contains five attributes: ANSI_NULLS, ANSI_NULL_DEFAULT, ANSI_PADDING, QUOTED_IDENTIFIER, and ENCRYPTED. Here, each attribute consists of an attribute name, an equal sign, and a string value in quotes.

Although values can be assigned to attributes, a value can also be coded between the start and end tags for an element. That's the case with most of the elements in this figure. The EventType element, for example, contains the string value "CREATE_TABLE."

Elements can also contain other elements. An element that's contained within another element is known as a *child element*. Conversely, the element that contains a child element is known as the child's *parent element*. In this figure, for example, the SetOptions element is a child element of the TSQLCommand element, and the TSQLCommand element is the parent element of the SetOptions element. Although it's not shown here, a child element can also repeat within a parent element.

The highest-level element in an XML document is known as the *root element*. In this figure, the EVENT_INSTANCE element is the root element. A well-formed XML document can have only one root element.

An XML document

```
<EVENT_INSTANCE>
  <EventType>CREATE_TABLE</EventType>
  <PostTime>2016-01-05T12:38:23.147</PostTime>
  <SPID>54</SPID>
  <ServerName>RAY-PC\SQLEXPRESS</ServerName>
  <LoginName>MicrosoftAccount\rhalliday@murach.com</LoginName>
  <UserName>dbo</UserName>
  <DatabaseName>AP</DatabaseName>
  <SchemaName>dbo</SchemaName>
  <ObjectName>VendorsTest</ObjectName>
  <ObjectType>TABLE</ObjectType>
  <TSQLCommand>
      <SetOptions ANSI_NULLS="ON" ANSI_NULL_DEFAULT="ON" ANSI_PADDING="ON"
          QUOTED_IDENTIFIER="ON" ENCRYPTED="FALSE" />
      <CommandText>
          CREATE TABLE VendorsTest
          (VendorID int, VendorName varchar(50));
      </CommandText>
  </TSQLCommand>
</EVENT_INSTANCE>
```

Description

- *XML (Extensible Markup Language)* is used to structure data using *XML tags*. An XML tag begins with < and ends with >.

- An *XML document* contains data that has been structured with XML tags.

- An *element* begins with a *start tag* and ends with an *end tag*. The start tag provides the name of the element and can contain one or more *attributes*. An attribute consists of an attribute name, an equal sign, and a string value in quotes. The end tag repeats the name, prefixed with a slash (/).

- Text can also be coded between an element's start and end tags. This text is referred to as the element's *content*.

- Elements can contain other elements. An element that's contained within another element is known as a *child element*. The element that contains a child element is known as the child's *parent element*. Child elements can also repeat within a parent element.

- The highest-level element in an XML document is known as the *root element*. An XML document can have only one root element.

- The EVENTDATA function described in chapter 15 returns an xml data type that contains an XML document like the one shown in this figure.

Figure 18-1   An XML document

An XML schema

The *XML Schema Definition (XSD)* language can be used to define an *XML schema*, which is a set of rules that an XML document must follow to be valid. Although there are several languages for defining XML schemas, the XSD language is the only one that you can use with SQL Server. Figure 18-2 shows an XML schema that can be used to validate the XML document shown in figure 18-1. In addition, you may notice that the schema itself is an XML document.

To start, this XML schema uses the schema element to specify some attributes that apply to the entire schema. That includes the xmlns attribute that defines the prefix for the XML namespace that's used throughout the rest of the schema to qualify the name of each element. Then, this schema defines each of the elements and attributes that are used by the XML document shown in figure 18-1. This definition specifies whether an element can contain other elements, the sequence of the elements, and the name and data type of each element.

Unfortunately, the details of the XSD language are beyond the scope of this book. As a result, the examples in this chapter only use the XML schema presented in this figure. Fortunately, if you're working with an industry standard XML document, an XSD has probably already been created for it. As a result, you may be able to get the XSD from a colleague, or you may be able to find the XSD by searching the Internet.

If you need to create an XML schema for an XML document, you can use the Management Studio's XML Editor to generate one as described in figure 18-4. Then, if necessary, you can edit the generated XML schema so it's appropriate for your XML document. To do that, however, you may need to learn more about the XSD language by searching the Internet or by getting a book about working with XML.

An XML Schema Definition (XSD)

```
<?xml version="1.0" encoding="utf-8"?>
<xs:schema attributeFormDefault="unqualified"
elementFormDefault="qualified"
xmlns:xs="http://www.w3.org/2001/XMLSchema">
  <xs:element name="EVENT_INSTANCE">
    <xs:complexType>
      <xs:sequence>
        <xs:element name="EventType" type="xs:string" />
        <xs:element name="PostTime" type="xs:dateTime" />
        <xs:element name="SPID" type="xs:unsignedByte" />
        <xs:element name="ServerName" type="xs:string" />
        <xs:element name="LoginName" type="xs:string" />
        <xs:element name="UserName" type="xs:string" />
        <xs:element name="DatabaseName" type="xs:string" />
        <xs:element name="SchemaName" type="xs:string" />
        <xs:element name="ObjectName" type="xs:string" />
        <xs:element name="ObjectType" type="xs:string" />
        <xs:element name="TSQLCommand">
          <xs:complexType>
            <xs:sequence>
              <xs:element name="SetOptions">
                <xs:complexType>
                  <xs:attribute name="ANSI_NULLS"
                      type="xs:string" use="required" />
                  <xs:attribute name="ANSI_NULL_DEFAULT"
                      type="xs:string" use="required" />
                  <xs:attribute name="ANSI_PADDING"
                      type="xs:string" use="required" />
                  <xs:attribute name="QUOTED_IDENTIFIER"
                      type="xs:string" use="required" />
                  <xs:attribute name="ENCRYPTED"
                      type="xs:string" use="required" />
                </xs:complexType>
              </xs:element>
              <xs:element name="CommandText" type="xs:string" />
            </xs:sequence>
          </xs:complexType>
        </xs:element>
      </xs:sequence>
    </xs:complexType>
  </xs:element>
</xs:schema>
```

Description

- The *XML Schema Definition (XSD)* language can be used to define an *XML schema*, which is a set of rules that an XML document must follow to be valid.

- You may be able to find an XSD for some types of XML documents by searching the Internet. If not, you can use the Management Studio's XML Editor to generate an XSD for an XML document as described in figure 18-4. The details for working with the XSD language are beyond the scope of this book.

- SQL Server can use the XML schema shown in this figure to validate the XML document shown in figure 18-1.

Figure 18-2   An XML schema

How to work with the xml data type

Now that you understand how XML works, you're ready to learn how to work with the xml data type. To get started quickly, the following topics show how to use the xml type without an XML schema. Since that means that the data that's stored in the xml type isn't validated, this data is known as *untyped XML*.

How to store data in the xml data type

Figure 18-3 shows how to store XML data in the xml type. For the most part, these examples show that you can use the xml data type just as you use most other SQL Server data types. In particular, you can use it as the type for a column in a table or a variable in a script, procedure, function, or trigger.

The first example shows how you can use the xml type to specify the data type for a column in a table. Here, the CREATE TABLE statement is used to create a table named DDLActivityLog that has two columns. The first column, named EventID, is an identity column that stores an int value. The second column, named EventData, stores XML data.

The second example shows a DDL trigger that inserts XML data into the second column of the DDLActivityLog table. Since a trigger like this one was described in chapter 15, you should understand that this trigger fires any time a CREATE TABLE or DROP TABLE statement is executed on the current database. After the AS keyword, the first statement declares a variable named @EventData with the xml type. Then, the second statement uses the EVENTDATA function to store an XML document like the one shown in figure 18-1 in the @EventData variable. Finally, the third statement uses an INSERT statement to insert a row with the data in the @EventData variable into the DDLActivityLog table.

The third example shows a CREATE TABLE statement that fires the trigger in the second example. This statement creates a table named VendorsTest that has two columns.

The fourth example shows a SELECT statement that retrieves all rows and columns from the DDLActivityLog table. The result set contains a single row that was inserted when the VendorsTest table was created. The first column is the identity value that's automatically generated, and the second column is the XML document that was returned by the EVENTDATA function.

The fifth and sixth examples show two INSERT statements that can be used to insert a row into the DDLActivityLog table. These statements show that SQL Server can implicitly cast a string to the xml type. As a result, when you're working with untyped XML, it's possible to insert any string into the xml type, regardless of whether the string contains well-formed XML. If you want SQL Server to enforce a specified schema for an xml type, you can use the techniques that are described later in this chapter.

A log table with a column of the xml data type

```
CREATE TABLE DDLActivityLog
(EventID int NOT NULL IDENTITY PRIMARY KEY,
EventData xml NOT NULL);
```

A trigger that inserts an XML document into the xml column

```
CREATE TRIGGER Database_CreateTable_DropTable
    ON DATABASE
    AFTER CREATE_TABLE, DROP_TABLE
AS
    DECLARE @EventData xml;
    SELECT @EventData = EVENTDATA();
    INSERT INTO DDLActivityLog VALUES (@EventData);
```

A CREATE TABLE statement that fires the trigger

```
CREATE TABLE VendorsTest
(VendorID int, VendorName varchar(50));
```

A SELECT statement that retrieves data from the table

```
SELECT * FROM DDLActivityLog;
```

The result set

	EventID	EventData
1	1	<EVENT_INSTANCE><EventType>CREATE_TABLE</EventType><PostTime>2016-02-08T13...

An INSERT statement that inserts a row into the table

```
INSERT INTO DDLActivityLog VALUES ('<root><element1>test</element1></root>');
```

Another INSERT statement that inserts a row into the table

```
INSERT INTO DDLActivityLog VALUES ('this is not xml');
```

Description

- You can use the xml data type just as you use most other SQL Server data types. In particular, you can use it as the type for a column in a table or a variable in a script, procedure, function, or trigger.

- Within a DDL trigger, the EVENTDATA function returns an XML document like the one shown in figure 18-1.

- The xml type is implicitly cast to a string when necessary and a string is implicitly cast to the xml type.

Figure 18-3   How to store data in the xml data type

How to work with the XML Editor

When you use the Query Editor to run a query that returns an xml type, the Management Studio displays the result set as it normally does. However, the XML data is displayed in blue with underlining to indicate that it is a link. If you want to view the complete XML data, you can click on this link. Then, the XML data will be displayed in the Management Studio's *XML Editor* as shown in figure 18-4.

Although the XML Editor works much like the Query Editor, its IntelliSense and color coding are designed to work with XML, and it has an XML menu instead of a Query menu. In addition, you can use the tree that's displayed to the left of the XML to collapse or expand parent elements. As a result, it's easy to edit the XML whenever that's necessary.

Once you display an XML document in the XML Editor, you can generate an XML schema for the document by selecting the Create Schema command from the XML menu. When you do, the XML Editor will generate the XSD for the current XML document and display it in a new window. Then, you can add this schema to the database so you can use it to validate other instances of the current XML document. You'll learn how to add an XML schema to a database later in this chapter.

You can also use the XML Editor to work with existing XML files and related files such as XSD files. To do that, just use the Management Studio to open these files. When you do, the Management Studio will automatically display the file in the XML Editor.

A result set that returns XML data

	EventID	EventData
1	1	<EVENT_INSTANCE><EventType>CREATE_TABLE</EventType><PostTime>2016-02-08T13...

An xml data type displayed in the Management Studio's XML Editor

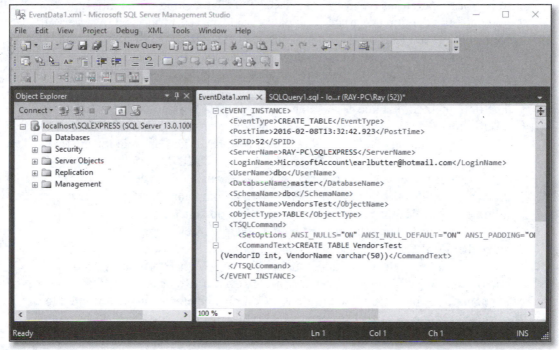

Description

- To view XML in the *XML Editor*, run a query that returns the XML that you want to view and then click on the cell that contains the XML. When you do, the XML will be displayed in the XML Editor, and the XML menu will replace the Query menu.

- To create an XML Schema Definition for an XML document, display the XML document in the XML Editor and then select the Create Schema command from the XML menu.

Figure 18-4   How to work with the XML Editor

How to use the methods of the xml data type

After you store data in the xml type, you can use the five *methods* shown in figure 18-5 to work with that data. In case you're not familiar with methods, you can use them to perform operations on objects. In this case, you can use them to perform operations on an xml data type. To call a method for an xml type, you code the column or variable name that holds the type, followed by a period, followed by the name of the method, followed by a set of parentheses. Within the parentheses, you code the arguments that are required for the method.

Of the five methods shown here, four take a string argument that specifies an *XQuery*. XQuery is a language that's designed to query an XML document. The only method that doesn't take an XQuery string as an argument is the modify method. This method takes a string argument that specifies an *XML Data Manipulation Language* (*XML DML*) statement. XML DML is a language that's designed to insert, update, or delete nodes from an XML document.

The first example shows how to use the query method to return an xml type that contains the SetOptions element. To accomplish this, the XQuery argument specifies the root element of the XML document, followed by the TSQLCommand element, followed by the SetOptions element. Note that since the TSQLCommand element contains a single SetOptions element, it's not necessary to code an attribute number. Because of that, you don't need to enclose the XQuery path in parentheses. However, if two or more SetOptions elements were included within the TSQLCommand element and you wanted to retrieve only the first element, you could do that by enclosing the XQuery path in parentheses and using square brackets to specify the element number like this:

```
'(/EVENT_INSTANCE/TSQLCommand/SetOptions)[1]'
```

You can use the same coding technique with attributes, although a well-formed XML document shouldn't have more than one attribute with the same name.

The second example shows how to use the exist method to return an int value that indicates whether the element or attribute specified by the XQuery exists and contains data. To start, this example declares a variable of the xml type and uses a SELECT statement to store an XML document in this variable. Then, it uses an IF statement to check if the variable has an EventType element that contains data. To accomplish this, the IF statement checks if the int value returned by the exist method is equal to 1. If so, it prints a message that indicates that the EventType element exists and contains data.

If you want to check an attribute instead of an element, you can use the same skills. However, you must prefix the name of the attribute with an at sign (@) like this:

```
IF @EventData.exist(
    '/EVENT_INSTANCE/TSQLCommand/SetOptions/@ANSI_NULLS') = 1
```

The methods of the xml type

Method	Description
query(XQuery)	Performs an XQuery and returns an xml type that contains the XML fragment specified by the XQuery.
exist(XQuery)	Returns a value of 1 if the XQuery returns a result set. Otherwise, returns a value of 0.
value(XQuery, SqlType)	Performs an XQuery and returns a scalar value of the specified SQL data type.
modify(XML_DML)	Uses an XML DML statement to insert, update, or delete nodes from the current xml type.
nodes(XQuery) **AS** Table(Column)	Splits the nodes of the current xml data type into rows. You can often use the OPENXML statement described in figure 18-12 to achieve similar results.

The simplified XQuery syntax

```
(/rootElement/element1/element2/@attribute)[elementOrAttributeNumber]
```

A SELECT statement that uses the query method

```
SELECT EventData.query('/EVENT_INSTANCE/TSQLCommand/SetOptions')
    AS SetOptions
FROM DDLActivityLog
WHERE EventID = 1;
```

The XML data that's returned

```
<SetOptions ANSI_NULLS="ON" ANSI_NULL_DEFAULT="ON" ANSI_PADDING="ON"
    QUOTED_IDENTIFIER="ON" ENCRYPTED="FALSE" />
```

A script that uses the exist method

```
DECLARE @EventData xml;
SELECT @EventData = EventData
FROM DDLActivityLog
WHERE EventID = 1;

IF @EventData.exist('/EVENT_INSTANCE/EventType') = 1
    PRINT 'The EventType element exists and contains data.';
```

The response from the system

```
The EventType element exists and contains data.
```

Rules for coding an XQuery

- Start each XQuery with a front slash (/).
- Use a front slash (/) to separate elements and attributes.
- Use an at symbol (@) to identify attributes.
- When necessary, use square brackets ([]) to specify an element or attribute instance.
- If you specify an element or attribute instance, you must code parentheses around the path specification for the element or attribute. Otherwise the parentheses are optional.

Figure 18-5   How to use the methods of the xml data type (part 1 of 2)

The third example shows how to use the value method to return the value of the specified element or attribute. To do that, you use the first argument of the value method to specify the XQuery string for the element or attribute. Then, you use the second argument to specify the SQL Server data type that you want to return. In this figure, for example, the varchar data type is used to store the data for the EventType element and for the ANSI_NULLS attribute of the SetOptions element. Since the value method returns a single value, this method requires its XQuery argument to specify the element or attribute number within square brackets, even if the xml type contains only one attribute or element with the specified name. As a result, the XQuery path must be enclosed in parentheses whenever you use the value method.

The fourth example shows how to use the modify method to update the data that's stored in an xml type. To start, this example declares a variable of the xml type and uses a SELECT statement to store an XML document in this variable. Then, it uses a SET statement to replace the value that's stored in the EventType element of the xml variable with a string value of "TEST". To do that, it uses the modify method with an XML DML "replace value of" statement. In addition, it uses the text() function to retrieve the string value that's stored in the EventType element. Finally, a SELECT statement is used to retrieve the modified value of the xml variable. Although you don't typically use a SELECT statement like this, you shouldn't have any trouble understanding how it works.

In addition to the "replace value of" statement, you can use the XML DML insert and delete statements to insert nodes into and delete nodes from an xml type. To learn more about these statements, you can begin by looking up "modify() Method (xml data type)" in the SQL Server documentation. Then, you can follow the links to learn more about the XML DML statements.

Although you can use the modify method to modify the data that's stored in an xml data type, you should avoid extensive use of this method whenever possible. Instead, you should consider storing the data in one or more tables. Then, you can use the DML statements that are available from SQL to insert, update, and delete the data in those tables.

A SELECT statement that uses the value method

```
SELECT
    EventData.value(
        '(/EVENT_INSTANCE/EventType)[1]',
        'varchar(40)') AS EventType,
    EventData.value(
        '(/EVENT_INSTANCE/TSQLCommand/SetOptions/@ANSI_NULLS)[1]',
        'varchar(40)') AS ANSI_NULLS_SETTING
FROM DDLActivityLog
WHERE EventID = 1;
```

The result set

	Event Type	ANSI_NULLS_SETTING
1	CREATE_TABLE	ON

A SET statement that uses the modify method

```
DECLARE @EventData xml;
SELECT @EventData = EventData
FROM DDLActivityLog
WHERE EventID = 1;

SET @EventData.modify
('replace value of (/EVENT_INSTANCE/EventType/text())[1] with "TEST"');

SELECT @EventData AS ModifiedEventData;
```

The result set

	Modified EventData
1	<EVENT_INSTANCE><EventType>TEST</EventType><Post...

Description

- *XQuery* is a language that's designed to query an XML document.
- *XML Data Manipulation Language* (*XML DML*) is a language that's designed to insert, update, or delete nodes from an XML document.

Figure 18-5   How to use the methods of the xml data type (part 2 of 2)

An example that parses the xml data type

If you use an xml type to define a column, you may occasionally need to use the value method to parse the xml type into a relational result set as shown in figure 18-6. The code in this figure starts by using a SELECT statement to retrieve the EventID column of the DDLActivityLog table. Then, this code uses the value method to retrieve the values of four elements from the EventData column. Here, the value method specifies the smalldatetime type for the PostTime element, and it specifies the varchar type for the EventType, LoginName, and ObjectName elements.

In addition, the WHERE clause uses the value method to specify that the SELECT statement should only return rows where the value stored in the EventType element is equal to "DROP_TABLE". In this figure, for example, the result set shows three rows that meet that condition. However, the result set that's displayed by your system may be different, depending on how many tables you have dropped since creating the trigger described in figure 18-3.

An example that parses an xml column into a relational result set

```
SELECT
    EventID,
    EventData.value('(/EVENT_INSTANCE/EventType)[1]', 'varchar(40)')
        AS EventType,
    EventData.value('(/EVENT_INSTANCE/PostTime)[1]', 'smalldatetime')
        AS PostTime,
    EventData.value('(/EVENT_INSTANCE/LoginName)[1]', 'varchar(40)')
        AS LoginName,
    EventData.value('(/EVENT_INSTANCE/ObjectName)[1]', 'varchar(40)')
        AS ObjectName
FROM DDLActivityLog
WHERE
    EventData.value('(/EVENT_INSTANCE/EventType)[1]', 'varchar(40)')
        = 'DROP_TABLE';
```

The result set

	EventID	Event Type	Post Time	LoginName	ObjectName
1	1	DROP_TABLE	2016-03-01 09:51:00	MicrosoftAccount\rhalliday@murach.com	VendorsTest
2	3	DROP_TABLE	2016-03-01 09:51:00	MicrosoftAccount\rhalliday@murach.com	VendorsTest

Description

- You can use the value method to parse an xml data type that has been stored in a database into multiple columns.

Figure 18-6   An example that parses the xml data type

Another example that parses the xml data type

If you find that you often need to write code like the code shown in figure 18-6, you might want to consider parsing the XML data before you store it in the database. Then, you can store the data in the database as relational data, and you can use SQL to query the database as shown in figure 18-7. Before you do that, though, you must determine the structure of the table or tables that will store the XML data, and you must create those tables.

The examples in this figure illustrate how this works. To start, the code in the first example creates a table named DDLActivityLog2 that contains five columns. Of these five columns, the last four get their data from the XML document that's returned by the EVENTDATA function.

Then, the code in the second example creates a trigger named Database_CreateTable_DropTable2. This trigger starts by using the EVENTDATA function to return an XML document that describes the event that caused the trigger to fire. Then, it uses the value method to insert the values for the EventType, PostTime, LoginName, and ObjectName elements into the DDLActivityLog2 table.

Finally, the last example uses a SELECT statement to return all rows where the EventType column contains a value of "DROP_TABLE." If you compare this SELECT statement with the one in figure 18-6, you'll see that it's shorter and easier to write. If necessary, it would also be efficient and easy to create a join between this table and another table on any of the columns in this table. In contrast, it would require more complex code to join the DDLActivityLog table shown in figure 18-3 to another table, and the join wouldn't run as efficiently. As a result, if you frequently need to query an xml type, and you need to join the xml type with other tables, you should probably parse the XML data before you store it in the database as shown in this figure.

A log table that doesn't use the xml data type

```
CREATE TABLE DDLActivityLog2
(
    EventID int NOT NULL IDENTITY PRIMARY KEY,
    EventType varchar(40) NOT NULL,
    PostTime smalldatetime NOT NULL,
    LoginName varchar(40) NOT NULL,
    ObjectName varchar(40) NOT NULL
);
```

A trigger that parses XML data and inserts it into the table

```
CREATE TRIGGER Database_CreateTable_DropTable2
    ON DATABASE
    AFTER CREATE_TABLE, DROP_TABLE
AS
    DECLARE @EventData xml;
    SELECT @EventData = EVENTDATA();
    INSERT INTO DDLActivityLog2 VALUES
    (
        @EventData.value('(/EVENT_INSTANCE/EventType)[1]', 'varchar(40)'),
        @EventData.value('(/EVENT_INSTANCE/PostTime)[1]', 'varchar(40)'),
        @EventData.value('(/EVENT_INSTANCE/LoginName)[1]', 'varchar(40)'),
        @EventData.value('(/EVENT_INSTANCE/ObjectName)[1]', 'varchar(40)')
    );
```

A SELECT statement that retrieves data from the table

```
SELECT * FROM DDLActivityLog2
WHERE EventType = 'DROP_TABLE';
```

The result set

	EventID	EventType	PostTime	LoginName	ObjectName
1	2	DROP_TABLE	2016-03-01 11:13:00	MicrosoftAccount\rhalliday@murach.com	VendorsTest
2	4	DROP_TABLE	2016-03-01 11:14:00	MicrosoftAccount\rhalliday@murach.com	VendorsTest
3	6	DROP_TABLE	2016-03-01 11:14:00	MicrosoftAccount\rhalliday@murach.com	VendorsTest

Description

- You can use the value method to parse an xml data type into multiple columns before you store it in the database.

Figure 18-7   Another example that parses the xml data type

How to work with XML schemas

Now that you understand the basics for working with the xml data type, you're ready to learn how to use an XML schema with this data type. Since an XML schema validates the data that's stored in an xml type, this data is known as *typed XML*.

How to add an XML schema to a database

Before you can use an XML schema with the xml data type, you must add the XML Schema Definition to the database. To do that, you can use the CREATE XML SCHEMA COLLECTION statement. In figure 18-8, for example, this statement is used to add the XML schema presented in figure 18-2 to the database. Although this looks like a lot of code at first glance, most of it is the string that defines the XML schema. As I've already mentioned, you may be able to get this information from a colleague or from the Internet. Or, if you have a document that the schema will be based on, you can use the XML Editor to generate the XML schema.

The first two lines of code contain the CREATE XML SCHEMA COLLECTION statement. The first line specifies EventDataSchema as the name of the schema. Since the optional database schema name isn't specified, the XML schema will be stored in the default database schema (dbo). Then, the second line contains the AS clause that indicates that the expression that follows will specify the XML schema. This expression can be coded as a string literal as shown in this figure or as a variable of the varchar, nvarchar, or xml types.

When you use the CREATE XML SCHEMA COLLECTION statement, you're actually adding the XML schema to a collection of XML schemas. In other words, you can add multiple XML schemas to the same collection. However, for this to work correctly, you must add a targetNamespace attribute to the XML schema that uniquely identifies each schema. Since this is more complicated than using one XML schema per collection, it's a common practice to only store one XML schema per collection as shown in this figure. In that case, you can think of the collection and the XML schema as being the same database object.

After you add a schema to a database, you can see it in the Object Explorer of the Management Studio. To do that, just expand the Programmability, Types, and XML Schema Collections folders. Then, you can use the menu that's displayed when you right-click on a schema to create scripts for creating and dropping the schema, to display the dependencies for the schema, and to delete the schema. This works just like it does for other database objects.

The syntax for the CREATE XML SCHEMA COLLECTION statement

```
CREATE XML SCHEMA COLLECTION [database_schema_name.]xml_schema_name
AS xml_schema_expression
```

An example that creates a schema

```
CREATE XML SCHEMA COLLECTION EventDataSchema
AS
'
<xs:schema attributeFormDefault="unqualified"
elementFormDefault="qualified"
xmlns:xs="http://www.w3.org/2001/XMLSchema">
  <xs:element name="EVENT_INSTANCE">
    <xs:complexType>
      <xs:sequence>
        <xs:element name="EventType" type="xs:string" />
        <xs:element name="PostTime" type="xs:dateTime" />
        <xs:element name="SPID" type="xs:unsignedByte" />
        <xs:element name="ServerName" type="xs:string" />
        <xs:element name="LoginName" type="xs:string" />
        <xs:element name="UserName" type="xs:string" />
        <xs:element name="DatabaseName" type="xs:string" />
        <xs:element name="SchemaName" type="xs:string" />
        <xs:element name="ObjectName" type="xs:string" />
        <xs:element name="ObjectType" type="xs:string" />
        <xs:element name="TSQLCommand">
          <xs:complexType>
            <xs:sequence>
              <xs:element name="SetOptions">
                <xs:complexType>
                  <xs:attribute name="ANSI_NULLS"
                      type="xs:string" use="required" />
                  <xs:attribute name="ANSI_NULL_DEFAULT"
                      type="xs:string" use="required" />
                  <xs:attribute name="ANSI_PADDING"
                      type="xs:string" use="required" />
                  <xs:attribute name="QUOTED_IDENTIFIER"
                      type="xs:string" use="required" />
                  <xs:attribute name="ENCRYPTED"
                      type="xs:string" use="required" />
                </xs:complexType>
              </xs:element>
              <xs:element name="CommandText" type="xs:string" />
            </xs:sequence>
          </xs:complexType>
        </xs:element>
      </xs:sequence>
    </xs:complexType>
  </xs:element>
</xs:schema>
';
```

Description

- Before you can use an XML Schema Definition with the xml data type, you must add the XSD to the database. To do that, you can use the CREATE XML SCHEMA COLLECTION statement.

Figure 18-8   How to add an XML schema to a database

How to use an XML schema
to validate the xml data type

Figure 18-9 shows how to use an XML schema to validate the xml type. To do that, you code the name of the XML schema in parentheses immediately after you specify the xml type for a column or a variable. In this figure, for example, the CREATE TABLE statement specifies the EventDataSchema XML schema that was added to the database in figure 18-8 as the schema for the EventData column. As a result, any time an INSERT statement attempts to insert data into this column, SQL Server will use this XML schema to validate the data. Since this provides a standard way to validate XML data, it is known as *XML validation*.

If the data doesn't conform to the XML schema, SQL Server will raise an appropriate error. This is illustrated by the three INSERT statements in this figure. For example, the first INSERT statement contains a string that doesn't use XML tags. As a result, SQL Server raises an error that indicates that this isn't allowed by the XML schema.

Although the second INSERT statement specifies a well-formed XML document, the tags for this document don't match the tags specified by the XML schema. As a result, SQL Server raises an error that indicates that no declaration was found for the MyRoot element, which is the first element of the XML document that raised an error.

The third INSERT statement also specifies a well-formed XML document. However, this document only contains the first two elements specified by the XML schema. As a result, SQL Server raises an error that indicates that it expected the third element in the XML document, the PostTime element.

Although all of the examples in this figure work with a column in a table, you can also use an XML schema to validate a variable. In the last example in this figure, for instance, you could declare the @CreateTableEvent variable like this:

```
DECLARE @CreateTableEvent xml (EventDataSchema)
```

Then, SQL Server would raise an error like the one shown here when the SET statement in this figure attempted to store the invalid XML data in the variable. In other words, the XML data would be validated before you even attempted to store it in the table.

The syntax for declaring XML schema validation

```
column_or_variable_name XML ([database_schema_name.]xml_schema_name)
```

A log table with a column that specifies an XML schema

```
CREATE TABLE DDLActivityLog3
(EventID int NOT NULL IDENTITY PRIMARY KEY,
EventData xml (EventDataSchema) NOT NULL);
```

An INSERT statement that attempts to insert non-XML data

```
INSERT INTO DDLActivityLog3 VALUES ('this is not xml');
```

The response from the system

```
Msg 6909, Level 16, State 1, Line 1
XML Validation: Text node is not allowed at this location, the type was defined
with element only content or with simple content.
Location: /
```

An INSERT statement that attempts to insert XML data whose tags don't match the tags in the schema

```
INSERT INTO DDLActivityLog3
VALUES ('<MyRoot><MyElement>test</MyElement></MyRoot>');
```

The response from the system

```
Msg 6913, Level 16, State 1, Line 1
XML Validation: Declaration not found for element 'MyRoot'.
Location: /*:MyRoot[1]
```

An INSERT statement that attempts to insert XML data that doesn't contain all the elements specified by the schema

```
DECLARE @CreateTableEvent xml;
SET @CreateTableEvent = '
<EVENT_INSTANCE>
  <EventType>CREATE_TABLE</EventType>
</EVENT_INSTANCE>
';
INSERT INTO DDLActivityLog3
VALUES (@CreateTableEvent);
```

The response from the system

```
Msg 6908, Level 16, State 1, Line 2
XML Validation: Invalid content. Expected element(s): PostTime.
Location: /*:EVENT_INSTANCE[1]
```

Description

- To provide *XML validation*, you can specify an XSD for the xml data type when you use it to define a column or a variable. Then, when you attempt to store data in the xml data type, SQL Server will use the XSD to make sure the data is valid. If the data isn't valid, SQL Server will display an appropriate error message.

Figure 18-9   How to use an XML schema to validate the xml data type

How to view an XML schema

Figure 18-10 shows how to view the XML schemas that have been added to the database. If you know the name of the XML schema, you can use the XML_SCHEMA_NAMESPACE function to return an xml type that contains the XML schema. In this figure, for instance, the first example uses a SELECT statement to return an xml type that contains the EventDataSchema that was added to the database in figure 18-8. Then, you can view this schema in the XML Editor by clicking on the link for the XML schema.

You can also use the sys.xml_schema_collections catalog view to get information about an XML schema. If you don't know the name of an XML schema, for example you can code a query like this:

```
SELECT name FROM sys.xml_schema_collections;
```

Then, you can find the name of the XML schema you want to view and then use the XML_SCHEMA_NAMESPACE function to view it.

How to drop an XML schema

Figure 18-10 also shows how to drop an XML schema from the database. To do that, you can use the DROP XML SCHEMA COLLECTION statement. In this figure, for instance, the last example drops the EventDataSchema collection. But first, it queries the sys.xml_schema_collections catalog view to make sure that the EventDataSchema collection exists.

Note that you can't drop an XML schema if it's being used by another object. For example, you can't drop a schema if it's being used to validate a column in a table. To do that, you must first alter the table so the column doesn't name the schema.

The syntax for the XML_SCHEMA_NAMESPACE function

```
XML_SCHEMA_NAMESPACE('database_schema_name', 'xml_schema_name')
```

A statement that returns the XML schema

```
SELECT XML_SCHEMA_NAMESPACE('dbo', 'EventDataSchema');
```

The result set

	EventDataSchema
1	<xsd:schema xmlns:xsd="http://www.w3.org/2001/XML...

The syntax for the DROP XML SCHEMA COLLECTION statement

```
DROP XML SCHEMA COLLECTION [database_schema_name.]xml_schema_name
```

An example that drops a schema

```
IF  EXISTS
    (SELECT * FROM sys.xml_schema_collections
    WHERE name = 'EventDataSchema')
BEGIN
    DROP XML SCHEMA COLLECTION EventDataSchema;
END;
```

Description

- To view an XML schema that has been added to the database, you can use the XML_SCHEMA_NAMESPACE function.

- To get information about XML schemas that have been added to the database, you can query the sys.xml_schema_collections catalog view.

- To drop an XML schema from the database, you can use the DROP XML SCHEMA COLLECTION statement. You can't drop an XML schema if it's being used by another object.

Figure 18-10   How to view or drop an XML schema

Two more skills for working with XML

When you work with XML, you may occasionally need to convert it to relational data. Conversely, you may occasionally need to convert relational data to XML. To do that, you use the skills that follow.

How to use the FOR XML clause of the SELECT statement

If you need to convert relational data that's stored in your database to XML, you can usually accomplish this by using the FOR XML clause of the SELECT statement as shown in figure 18-11. To use this clause, you use the SELECT statement to retrieve the data that you want to convert to XML. Then, you add a FOR XML clause after the SELECT statement to specify how the relational data should be converted to XML.

The first example shows how to use the FOR XML clause with the RAW and ROOT keywords. To start, the SELECT statement uses a join to select the VendorName column from the Vendors table and the InvoiceNumber and InvoiceTotal columns from the Invoices table. In addition, this SELECT statement uses the TOP 5 clause so it only returns 5 rows. Then, the FOR XML clause uses the RAW keyword, which returns one element named row for each row in the result set. In addition, the ROOT keyword is used to specify the name of the root element for the XML document. In this example, the root element is named VendorInvoices. Although the ROOT keyword isn't required, all valid XML documents must have a root element. As a result, if you want to return a complete XML document, you'll need to specify a root element.

The second example is similar, but it uses the AUTO keyword instead of the RAW keyword. The AUTO keyword causes the relationships between the Vendors and Invoices tables to be maintained in the XML document. As a result, one Vendor element is returned for each vendor, one Invoice element is returned for each invoice, and each Invoice element is stored within its related Vendor element. That means that the vendor name isn't repeated for each invoice as in the first example. Notice that to make this work more elegantly, the SELECT statement in this example uses correlation names for the Vendors and Invoices tables to make them singular instead of plural. That way, the data for a vendor is stored in an element named Vendor instead of an element named Vendors, and the data for an invoice is stored in an element named Invoice instead of an element named Invoices.

The simplified syntax of the FOR XML clause

```
select_statement
FOR XML {RAW|AUTO} [, ROOT ('RootName')] [, ELEMENTS ]
```

A SELECT statement that uses the RAW keyword

```
SELECT TOP 5 VendorName, InvoiceNumber, InvoiceTotal
FROM Vendors JOIN Invoices
    ON Vendors.VendorID = Invoices.VendorID
ORDER BY VendorName
FOR XML RAW, ROOT ('VendorInvoices');
```

The XML document that's returned

```
<VendorInvoices>
  <row VendorName="Abbey Office Furnishings"
      InvoiceNumber="203339-13" InvoiceTotal="17.5000" />
  <row VendorName="Bertelsmann Industry Svcs. Inc"
      InvoiceNumber="509786" InvoiceTotal="6940.2500" />
  <row VendorName="Blue Cross"
      InvoiceNumber="547481328" InvoiceTotal="224.0000" />
  <row VendorName="Blue Cross"
      InvoiceNumber="547479217" InvoiceTotal="116.0000" />
  <row VendorName="Blue Cross"
      InvoiceNumber="547480102" InvoiceTotal="224.0000" />
</VendorInvoices>
```

A SELECT statement that uses the AUTO keyword

```
SELECT TOP 5 VendorName, InvoiceNumber, InvoiceTotal
FROM Vendors AS Vendor JOIN Invoices AS Invoice
    ON Vendor.VendorID = Invoice.VendorID
ORDER BY VendorName
FOR XML AUTO, ROOT ('VendorInvoices');
```

The XML document that's returned

```
<VendorInvoices>
  <Vendor VendorName="Abbey Office Furnishings">
    <Invoice InvoiceNumber="203339-13" InvoiceTotal="17.5000" />
  </Vendor>
  <Vendor VendorName="Bertelsmann Industry Svcs. Inc">
    <Invoice InvoiceNumber="509786" InvoiceTotal="6940.2500" />
  </Vendor>
  <Vendor VendorName="Blue Cross">
    <Invoice InvoiceNumber="547481328" InvoiceTotal="224.0000" />
    <Invoice InvoiceNumber="547479217" InvoiceTotal="116.0000" />
    <Invoice InvoiceNumber="547480102" InvoiceTotal="224.0000" />
  </Vendor>
</VendorInvoices>
```

Description

- To specify the name of the root element for the XML document, use the ROOT keyword.
- To return one XML element for each row, use the RAW keyword.
- To automatically parse the rows of the result set so the elements reflect the structure of the tables in the database, use the AUTO keyword.

Figure 18-11   How to use the FOR XML clause of the SELECT statement (part 1 of 2)

As you saw in the first two examples in figure 18-11, the data for each column that's returned by a SELECT statement that includes the FOR XML clause is stored in attributes. However, if you want to store the data for each column in XML elements instead, you can add the ELEMENTS keyword to the FOR XML clause. The third example in this figure, for instance, is identical to the second example except that it includes the ELEMENTS keyword. Although the XML document that's returned by this example is longer than in the previous example, it's also easier to read because it uses elements instead of attributes. In some cases, you may prefer to use this type of XML document.

Most of the time, the skills presented in this figure are all you need to use the FOR XML clause to create XML documents from the relational data in a database. However, several other options are available from this clause that give you even more control over the format of the XML document that's returned by the SELECT statement. For more information, look up the SELECT statement in the SQL Server documentation and then click on the "FOR Clause" link.

A SELECT statement that uses the AUTO and ELEMENTS keywords

```
SELECT TOP 5 VendorName, InvoiceNumber, InvoiceTotal
FROM Vendors AS Vendor JOIN Invoices AS Invoice
    ON Vendor.VendorID = Invoice.VendorID
ORDER BY VendorName
FOR XML AUTO, ROOT ('VendorInvoices'), ELEMENTS;
```

The XML document that's returned

```
<VendorInvoices>
  <Vendor>
    <VendorName>Abbey Office Furnishings</VendorName>
    <Invoice>
      <InvoiceNumber>203339-13</InvoiceNumber>
      <InvoiceTotal>17.5000</InvoiceTotal>
    </Invoice>
  </Vendor>
  <Vendor>
    <VendorName>Bertelsmann Industry Svcs. Inc</VendorName>
    <Invoice>
      <InvoiceNumber>509786</InvoiceNumber>
      <InvoiceTotal>6940.2500</InvoiceTotal>
    </Invoice>
  </Vendor>
  <Vendor>
    <VendorName>Blue Cross</VendorName>
    <Invoice>
      <InvoiceNumber>547481328</InvoiceNumber>
      <InvoiceTotal>224.0000</InvoiceTotal>
    </Invoice>
    <Invoice>
      <InvoiceNumber>547479217</InvoiceNumber>
      <InvoiceTotal>116.0000</InvoiceTotal>
    </Invoice>
    <Invoice>
      <InvoiceNumber>547480102</InvoiceNumber>
      <InvoiceTotal>224.0000</InvoiceTotal>
    </Invoice>
  </Vendor>
</VendorInvoices>
```

Description

- By default, the data that's stored in a database column is stored in an XML attribute. To store data in XML elements instead, use the ELEMENTS keyword.

- The names that are used for elements and attributes correspond to the names of the tables and columns that are used in the query. However, you can specify correlation names for the tables and columns in your query to modify these names whenever that's necessary.

Figure 18-11   How to use the FOR XML clause of the SELECT statement (part 2 of 2)

How to use the OPENXML statement

If you need to convert XML data into relational data, you can usually accomplish this by using the OPENXML statement to open the XML data as a result set as shown in figure 18-12. Before you can use the OPENXML statement, you must use the sp_Xml_PrepareDocument procedure to read the XML document into memory and to return a handle to this document. This handle is a unique integer value that SQL Server can use to refer to the XML document that's stored in memory.

Once you execute the sp_Xml_PrepareDocument procedure, you can use the OPENXML statement to open an xml data type as a result set. In this figure, for example, the OPENXML statement opens the XML document shown in part 2 of figure 18-11. Since this statement returns a result set, it's coded in the FROM clause of a SELECT statement.

The OPENXML statement begins by accepting an integer argument that specifies the handle to the XML document that was prepared by the sp_Xml_PrepareDocument procedure. Then, the second argument uses an *XPath* string to identify the XML elements to be processed. XPath is an XML query language similar to XQuery. As a result, you should be able to understand how it works. In this figure, for example, the XPath argument specifies that the table should have one row for each Invoice element in the XML document.

The WITH clause of the OPENXML statement allows you to specify a definition for the table. To start, you specify the name and data type for each column in the table just as you would with a CREATE TABLE statement. Then, you specify an XPath string that identifies the element or attribute in the XML document that contains the data for the column. If necessary, this XPath string can use two dots (..) to navigate back one level in the XML hierarchy. In this figure, for example, the XPath string for the VendorName column uses two dots to navigate from the Invoice element to the Vendor element.

After you use the OPENXML statement, you should use the sp_Xml_RemoveDocument procedure to remove the XML document from memory. This frees system resources and allows SQL Server to run more efficiently.

Although this figure should get you started quickly with the OPENXML statement, it's only intended to be an introduction to this feature. For more information, look up "OPENXML statement" in the SQL Server documentation.

The simplified syntax for the OPENXML statement

```
OPENXML (xml_document_handle_int, x_path)
WITH ( table_definition )
```

The simplified syntax for the sp_Xml_PrepareDocument procedure

```
EXEC sp_Xml_PrepareDocument xml_document_handle_int OUTPUT, xml_document
```

The simplified syntax for the sp_Xml_RemoveDocument procedure

```
EXEC sp_Xml_RemoveDocument xml_document_handle_int
```

Code that uses the OPENXML statement to parse XML

```
-- Declare an int variable that's a handle for the internal XML document
DECLARE @VendorInvoicesHandle int;

-- Create an xml variable that stores the XML document
DECLARE @VendorInvoices xml;
SET @VendorInvoices = ' xml from part 2 of 18-11 goes here ';

-- Prepare the internal XML document
EXEC sp_Xml_PrepareDocument @VendorInvoicesHandle OUTPUT, @VendorInvoices;

-- SELECT the data from the table returned by the OPENXML statement
SELECT *
FROM OPENXML (@VendorInvoicesHandle, '/VendorInvoices/Vendor/Invoice')
WITH
(
    VendorName    varchar(50) '../VendorName',
    InvoiceNumber varchar(50) 'InvoiceNumber',
    InvoiceTotal  money       'InvoiceTotal'
);

-- Remove the internal XML document
EXEC sp_Xml_RemoveDocument @VendorInvoicesHandle;
```

The result set

	VendorName	InvoiceNumber	InvoiceTotal
1	Abbey Office Furnishings	203339-13	17.50
2	Bertelsmann Industry Svcs. Inc	509786	6940.25
3	Blue Cross	547479217	116.00
4	Blue Cross	547480102	224.00
5	Blue Cross	547481328	224.00

Description

- Before you can use the OPENXML statement, you must use the sp_Xml_PrepareDocument procedure to read the XML document into memory and return a handle to this document.

- You can use the OPENXML statement to open an xml data type as a result set. In the WITH clause, you can use two dots (..) to navigate back one level in the XML hierarchy.

- After you use the OPENXML statement, you should use the sp_Xml_RemoveDocument procedure to remove the XML document from memory.

Figure 18-12   How to use the OPENXML statement

Perspective

XML is a useful technology for storing and transferring data, and the features that were introduced with SQL Server 2005 make it easy to work with XML. Of course, SQL Server is a relational database that is primarily designed to work with relational data. As a result, you should think twice before using the xml data type to store XML data in a table.

Instead, whenever possible, you should parse the XML data and store it in one or more tables. That way, you can still use SQL to easily retrieve and update the data. However, if the data is structured in a way that makes it difficult to store in tables, or if you won't need to retrieve or update the data very often, you can use the skills presented in this chapter to store and work with that data.

Terms

Extensible Markup Language (XML)
XML document
tag
element
start tag
end tag
attribute
content
child element
parent element
root element

XML Schema Definition (XSD)
XML schema
untyped XML
XML Editor
method
XQuery
XML Data Manipulation Language
   (XML DML)
typed XML
XML validation
XPath

Exercises

1. Write a SELECT statement that returns an XML document that contains all of the invoices in the Invoices table that have more than one line item. This document should include one element for each of these columns: InvoiceNumber, InvoiceDate, InvoiceTotal, InvoiceLineItemDescription, and InvoiceLineItemAmount. Then, save the XML document that's returned in a file named MultipleLineItems.xml. Finally, generate an XML schema for the file and save it in a file named MultipleLineItems.xsd.

2. Write a script that uses the XML document shown below to update the contact information in the Vendors table.

    ```xml
    <ContactUpdates>
      <Contact VendorID="4">
        <LastName>McCrystle</LastName>
        <FirstName>Timothy</FirstName>
      </Contact>
      <Contact VendorID="10">
        <LastName>Flynn</LastName>
        <FirstName>Erin</FirstName>
      </Contact>
    </ContactUpdates>
    ```

    To accomplish this, begin by storing this XML document in a variable of the XML type. Then, you can use two UPDATE statements to update the Vendors table.

3. Write a script that returns a result set that contains all of the data stored in the XML document in exercise 2.

4. Write a script that (1) creates a table named Instructions, (2) inserts the XML document shown below into the table, and (3) selects all records from this table. The Instructions table should have two columns. The first column should be an identity column named InstructionsID, and the second column should be an xml column named Instructions.

    ```xml
    <Instructions>
        <Step>
          <Description>This is the first step.</Description>
          <SubStep>This is the first substep.<SubStep>
          <SubStep>This is the second substep.<SubStep>
        </Step>
        <Step>
          <Description>This is the second step.</Description>
        </Step>
        <Step>
          <Description>This is the third step.</Description>
        </Step>
    </Instructions>
    ```

How to work with BLOBs

In chapter 8, you were introduced to the data types for working with large values, including the varbinary(max) data type that's used to work with large binary values such as images, sound, and video. In this chapter, you'll learn how to use SQL and a .NET application to work with large binary values, which are often referred to as binary large objects (BLOBs). Then, you'll learn how to use a feature known as FILESTREAM storage that was introduced with SQL Server 2008. This feature provides some enhancements that you can use to efficiently work with BLOBs that are larger than 1 megabyte.

An introduction to BLOBs

Figure 19-1 describes the pros and cons of three approaches that you can use for working with large binary values, which are often referred to as *binary large objects* (*BLOBs*).

Pros and cons of storing BLOBs in files

The first approach is the oldest approach and was commonly used prior to SQL Server 2005. This approach stores a string value in a database column that points to a binary file that's stored on the file system. For an image, for example, you can include a column that includes a string value such as "8601_cover.jpg" that points to a JPG image file. If necessary, you can also store a relative path or absolute path to the file within the database.

There are two advantages to this approach. First, there is no limit on the size of the BLOB unless the file system begins to run out of disk space. Second, the file system provides fast access to the BLOB.

There are also a couple of disadvantages to this approach. First, the BLOB is not backed up as part of the database backup. Second, access to the BLOB is controlled by network permissions, not by database permissions. This can create additional work for the network administrator, and it can lead to data consistency and security issues.

Pros and cons of storing BLOBs in a column

The second approach was introduced with SQL Server 2005, and it solves the problems of storing a pointer to a file by storing the binary data in a varbinary(max) column within the database. As a result, the binary data is backed up when the database is backed up, and access to this data is controlled by database permissions.

However, this approach has two limitations. First, the binary data must be less than 2 gigabytes (GB). Second, database access is not as fast as file system access. As a result, you can't use this approach if you need to store a BLOB that's larger than 2GB, and you won't want to use it if fast access to your BLOBs is critical to your application.

When to use FILESTREAM storage for BLOBs

The third approach, which is known as *FILESTREAM storage*, was introduced with SQL Server 2008. This approach overcomes all of the limitations of the first two approaches. However, it also requires more work to set up and to use. As a result, you'll only want to use this approach when most of the BLOBs that you need to store are larger than 1 megabyte (MB) and when fast read access is critical. Otherwise, the second approach usually provides adequate performance without requiring any additional work.

Three approaches to storing binary data

- Use a varchar column in the database to store a string that points to a file in the file system that contains the binary data.
- Use a varbinary(max) column to store the binary data in the database.
- Use a varbinary(max) column with the FILESTREAM attribute to store the binary data.

Pros and cons of using a pointer to a binary file

Pros

- There is no limit on the size of the BLOB.
- The file system provides fast access to the BLOB.

Cons

- The BLOB is not backed up with the database.
- Access to the BLOB is controlled by network security, not database security.

Pros and cons of using the varbinary(max) data type

Pros

- The BLOB is backed up with the database.
- Database security can be used to control access to the BLOB.

Cons

- The BLOB must be smaller than 2GB.
- Database access is not as fast as a file system access.

Pros and cons of using FILESTREAM storage (SQL Server 2008 and later)

Pros

- The BLOB can be larger than 2GB.
- The BLOB access is as fast as file system access.
- The BLOB is backed up with the database.
- Database security can be used to control access to the BLOB.

When to use FILESTREAM storage

- When most of the BLOBs in the column are larger than 1MB.
- When fast read access is critical to the application.

Description

- With SQL Server 2008 and later, you can use a feature known as *FILESTREAM storage* to overcome several limitations for working with *binary large objects* (*BLOBs*) that existed in previous versions of SQL Server.
- To be able to use FILESTREAM storage, the drive that stores the files must be in NTFS format.

Figure 19-1   An introduction to working with BLOBs

How to use SQL to work with a varbinary(max) column

Since using a varbinary(max) column is adequate for storing binary data in many situations, this topic shows how to use this approach. To start, figure 19-2 shows how to use SQL to work with a varbinary(max) column of a table.

How to create a table with a varbinary(max) column

To create a table that has a varbinary(max) column, you can specify varbinary(max) as the data type for a column within a CREATE TABLE statement as shown in this figure. Here, the first column is the primary key for the table. This column stores an ID value for an image, and this value is automatically generated by the database. Then, the second column stores an ID value for a product. This value can be used as a foreign key to relate an image to a product. Finally, the third column uses the varbinary(max) data type to store the binary data for the image.

To keep this example simple, I only included three columns. However, a table like this might include additional columns such as a name for the image.

How to insert, update, and delete binary data

To work with binary data, you can use INSERT, UPDATE, and DELETE statements just as you would for other types of data. In this figure, for example, the three INSERT statements insert three rows into the ProductImages table. Here, the first statement uses the NULL keyword to insert a NULL value into the ProductImage column. Then, the second statement inserts an integer value of zero. Finally, the third statement uses the CAST function to convert a hexadecimal string to a varbinary(max) value.

Although these statements show how the INSERT statement works, the data that's stored in the ProductImage column is not valid data for an image. To insert valid data, you can use a .NET application like the one shown in the next figure to upload data from the file system to the database.

How to retrieve binary data

To retrieve binary data, you can use a SELECT statement just as you would for other types of data. In this figure, for example, the SELECT statement selects all columns and rows from the ProductImages table. This shows the data that was inserted by the three INSERT statements. Here, the first row in the ProductImage column stores a NULL value and the next two rows store binary data.

How to create a table with a varbinary(max) column

```
CREATE TABLE ProductImages
(
    ImageID int PRIMARY KEY IDENTITY,
    ProductID int NOT NULL,
    ProductImage varbinary(max)
);
```

Three INSERT statements that insert rows into the table

```
INSERT INTO ProductImages VALUES (1, NULL);

INSERT INTO ProductImages VALUES (2, 0);

INSERT INTO ProductImages
VALUES (3, CAST('0123456789ABCDEF' AS varbinary(max)));
```

A statement that displays the values in the table

```
SELECT * FROM ProductImages;
```

The result set

	ImageID	ProductID	ProductImage
1	1	1	NULL
2	2	2	0x00000000
3	3	3	0x303132333435363738394142434445

Description

- You can use the varbinary(max) data type for a column that stores binary data.

Figure 19-2   How to create a table and insert binary data

A .NET application
that uses a varbinary(max) column

Once you understand how to use SQL to work with binary data that's stored in a varbinary(max) column, you can use a .NET application to write binary data that's in a file to a column in a database. Then, you can use a .NET application to present binary data in a way that's meaningful to the user. In this chapter, for example, you'll learn how to read binary data for an image from a column in the database and display it in a picture box control on a Windows form.

This topic presents a simple application that uses C# to work with BLOBs. All of the principles in this application apply to Visual Basic and the other .NET languages. The differences mainly have to do with the syntax of each language. If you prefer to use Visual Basic, you can download the Visual Basic code for this application from our web site (see appendix A).

If you have some C# programming experience, you shouldn't have much trouble understanding this code. If you don't have C# experience, that's fine too. In that case, you can focus on how this code uses the .NET framework to execute SQL statements against a database. Then, if you want to learn more about writing C# applications, we recommend our current book on C#. And if you want to learn more about using C# to work with a database, we recommend our current book on ADO.NET with C#. For a current list of books, please see www.murach.com.

The user interface for the application

Figure 19-3 shows the user interface for the Product Image Manager application that's presented in this topic. You can use this application to view the images that have been stored in the database. To do that, you select the ID for the image from the combo box that's displayed at the top of the form. Then, the application displays the image in a picture box control to the right of the combo box.

You can also use this application to upload images from the file system to the database. To do that, you enter a filename for the image, and an ID for the product. In this figure, for example, an image file named "pf02_cover.jpg" with a product ID of 4 has just been added to the database. Note that this only works if the image is stored in the directory that's listed at the bottom of the form.

The user interface

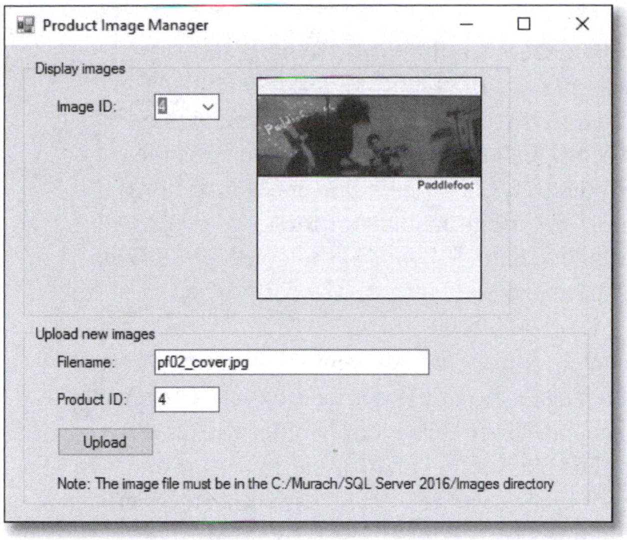

Description

- To view an image, select the ID for the image from the combo box.
- To upload an image, enter a filename and a product ID for the image, and click on the Upload button.

Figure 19-3   The user interface for the Product Image Manager application

The event handlers for the form

Figure 19-4 presents the event handlers for the form. To start, the event handler for the Load event of the form calls the LoadImageIDComboBox method. This method reads all image IDs from the database and adds them to the Image ID combo box. To accomplish this task, this method calls the GetImageIDList method of the ProductDB class that's presented in the next figure. After loading the combo box, the event handler for the Load event calls the event handler for the SelectedIndexChanged event of the combo box. This causes the first image in the database to be displayed on the form when the form is loaded.

The event handler for the SelectedIndexChanged event of the combo box begins by getting the image ID that's selected in the combo box and converting this ID from a string type to an int type. Then, this event handler uses the ReadImage method of the ProductDB class to get an array of bytes for the image. Next, it converts the array of bytes to a MemoryStream object. Finally, it sets the Image property of the picture box on the form to the image that's returned by the static FromStream method of the System.Drawing.Image class. If this event handler encounters an error, it uses a dialog box to display an error message.

The event handler for the Click event of the Upload button begins by getting the product ID that's entered into the Product ID text box on the form and converting this ID from a string type to an int type. Then, it gets the filename from the Filename text box on the form. After that, it uses the WriteImage method of the ProductDB class to write the image from the specified file to the database, and it displays a dialog box to confirm that the image has been successfully uploaded. Finally, this event handler clears all image ID values from the Image ID combo box and calls the private LoadImageIDComboBox method to load this combo box with fresh values that include the ID for the new image that was uploaded. Like the previous event handler, this event handler displays a dialog box that displays an error message if it encounters an error.

Although you can't see it here, you should know that the program.cs file for this application contains code that writes three rows to the ProductImages table if the table doesn't contain any rows. This code is executed before the Load event for the form. That way, the combo box on the form will contain at least three rows when it's first displayed.

The event handlers for the form

```csharp
private void ImageManagerForm_Load(object sender, EventArgs e)
{
    this.LoadImageIDComboBox();
    imageIDComboBox_SelectedIndexChanged(sender, e);
}

private void LoadImageIDComboBox()
{
    // load the combo box
    List<int> imageIDList = ProductDB.GetImageIDList();
    foreach (int i in imageIDList)
        imageIDComboBox.Items.Add(i);
}

private void imageIDComboBox_SelectedIndexChanged(
    object sender, EventArgs e)
{
    try
    {
        int imageID = Convert.ToInt32(imageIDComboBox.Text);

        // read image bytes from the database and display in picture box
        Byte[] imageByteArray = ProductDB.ReadImage(imageID);
        MemoryStream ms = new MemoryStream(imageByteArray);
        imagePictureBox.Image = System.Drawing.Image.FromStream(ms);
        ms.Close();
    }
    catch (Exception ex)
    {
        MessageBox.Show(this, ex.Message, "Error");
    }
}


private void uploadButton_Click(object sender, EventArgs e)
{
    try
    {
        int productID = Convert.ToInt32(productIDTextBox.Text);
        string filename = filenameTextBox.Text;
        ProductDB.WriteImage(productID, filename);
        MessageBox.Show(this, "Image upload was successful!",
            "Upload Confirmation");

        // refresh combo box
        imageIDComboBox.Items.Clear();
        this.LoadImageIDComboBox();

    }
    catch (Exception ex)
    {
        MessageBox.Show(this, ex.Message, "Error");
    }
}
```

Figure 19-4   The event handlers for the Product Image Manager form

A data access class
that reads and writes binary data

Figure 19-5 shows the ProductDB class that's used to read and write binary data from the ProductImage column of the ProductImages table. To start, this class defines a string that points to the directory for the image files that are going to be uploaded into the database. As a result, this class only allows you to upload image files that are stored in this directory. Of course, this class could be enhanced to allow the user to specify the directory for the file that he or she wants to upload.

The static WriteImage method writes the specified image file to the database. To start, this method accepts two parameters. The first parameter is an int value for the product ID that's stored in the same row as the image. The second parameter is a string value that specifies the name of the file.

The body of the WriteImage method begins by reading the specified file into an array of bytes. To start, this code creates a variable named filepath that contains an absolute path that points to the file for the image. Then, the static Exists method of the File class is used to check whether the specified file exists. If it doesn't exist, this code throws an exception and skips directly to the catch block. If the file does exist, this code continues by creating a FileStream object named sourceStream that's used to read the file from the file system into an array of bytes. To do that, this code uses the Read method of the sourceStream object to read an array of bytes from the specified file into a variable named productImage.

After reading the image from the file into an array of bytes, the WriteImage method continues by writing the product ID and image to the database. To do that, this method calls the GetConnection method to get a connection to the database. You'll see the code for this method in just a minute. Next, this method creates a SqlCommand object that contains an INSERT statement like the one shown in figure 19-2. However, instead of hard-coding values, this INSERT statement accepts two parameters: @ProductID and @ProductImage. These parameters are then added to the Parameters collection of the SqlCommand object. The @ProductID parameter is given the value of the productID parameter that was passed to the method, and the @ProductImage parameter is given the value of the image that was retrieved from the file. Finally, this method calls the Open method to open the connection, and it calls the ExecuteNonQuery method to execute the INSERT statement that's stored in the SqlCommand object.

If the method causes an exception to be thrown, the catch block throws the exception again. In most cases, this causes the exception to be caught by one of the catch blocks in the event handlers for the form.

Whether or not this method executes cleanly or throws an exception, the finally block attempts to close the Connection object that was opened. To do that, this code first checks to make sure that the connection object is not null. If it isn't, it closes the open connection.

The ProductDB class   **Part 1**

```csharp
using System;
using System.Collections.Generic;
using System.Data.SqlClient;
using System.IO;

namespace MusicStoreImageManager
{
    class ProductDB
    {
        // The directory for the images
        static string imagesPath = "C:/Murach/SQL Server 2016/Images/";

        public static void WriteImage(int productID, string imageName)
        {
            SqlConnection connection = null;
            try
            {
                // 1. Read image from file
                string filepath = imagesPath + imageName;
                if (File.Exists(filepath) == false)
                    throw new Exception("File Not Found: " + filepath);
                FileStream sourceStream = new FileStream(
                    filepath,
                    FileMode.OpenOrCreate,
                    FileAccess.Read);

                int streamLength = (int) sourceStream.Length;
                Byte[] productImage = new Byte[streamLength];
                sourceStream.Read(productImage, 0, streamLength);
                sourceStream.Close();

                // 2. Write image to database
                connection = GetConnection();

                SqlCommand command = new SqlCommand();
                command.Connection = connection;
                command.CommandText =
                    "INSERT INTO ProductImages " +
                    "VALUES (@ProductID, @ProductImage)";
                command.Parameters.AddWithValue("@ProductID", productID);
                command.Parameters.AddWithValue("@ProductImage", productImage);

                connection.Open();
                command.ExecuteNonQuery();
            }
            catch (Exception e)
            {
                throw e;
            }
            finally
            {
                if (connection != null)
                    connection.Close();
            }
        }
    }
```

Figure 19-5   The ProductDB class for varbinary(max) storage (part 1 of 3)

The ReadImage method of the ProductDB class returns an array of bytes for the specified image. To start, this method accepts a single parameter named imageID that's used to specify the image to be read. Then, the body of this method begins by getting a connection to the database. Next, it creates a SqlCommand object that contains a SELECT statement that retrieves the ProductImage column for the specified imageID value. This SELECT statement accepts a single parameter named @ImageID. After creating the SqlCommand object, this method adds a parameter to that object with the value that was passed to the method. Finally, this method opens the connection and calls the ExecuteReader method to execute the SELECT statement that's stored in the SqlCommand object and return a SqlDataReader object.

Once this method has returned the SqlDataReader object, it reads the image that's stored within this object. This is easy because the SqlDataReader object only contains a single row and a single column. In other words the SqlDataReader object only contains the binary data for the specified image. To start, the Read method of the SqlDataReader object is called to move the cursor onto the first and only row in the result set. If the Read method isn't able to move to this row, an exception is thrown and execution skips into the catch block. Otherwise, the SqlDataReader object is used to return the first column in the result set and to convert it to an array of bytes. Finally, this code closes the SqlDataReader object and returns the array of bytes for the image.

The ProductDB class   **Part 2**

```csharp
public static Byte[] ReadImage(int imageID)
{
    SqlConnection connection = null;
    try
    {
        connection = GetConnection();

        SqlCommand command = new SqlCommand();
        command.Connection = connection;
        command.CommandText =
            "SELECT ProductImage " +
            "FROM ProductImages " +
            "WHERE ImageID = @ImageID";
        command.Parameters.AddWithValue("@ImageID", imageID);

        connection.Open();
        SqlDataReader reader = command.ExecuteReader();

        Byte[] imageByteArray = null;
        if (reader.Read() == false)
            throw new Exception("Unable to read image.");
        imageByteArray = (Byte[]) reader[0];
        reader.Close();

        return imageByteArray;
    }
    catch (Exception e)
    {
        throw e;
    }
    finally
    {
        if (connection != null)
            connection.Close();
    }
}
```

Figure 19-5   The ProductDB class for varbinary(max) storage (part 2 of 3)

The GetImageIDList method of the ProductDB class reads all image ID values from the database and returns them as a List<int> object. Although this method doesn't contain any code that's used to work with binary values, it is needed by the form for this application.

To start, the body of this method gets a connection. Then, it creates a SqlCommand object that contains a SELECT statement that returns a list of all image IDs that are stored in the database. Since this SELECT statement doesn't contain any parameters, this SqlCommand object is easy to create. Next, it opens the connection and uses the ExecuteReader method of the SqlCommand object to return a SqlDataReader object for the result set.

After the SqlDataReader object has been created, the code uses a while loop to read each image ID value that's stored in the reader object and store it in a List<int> object named imageIDList. Finally, this code closes the reader object and returns the List<int> object.

The static GetConnection method that's used by all three of the other methods in this class returns a SqlConnection object for a SQL Server instance named SqlExpress that's running on the same computer as the ProductDB class. In addition, the code within this method uses the Examples database that's running on the server, and it uses integrated security to connect to this database.

The ProductDB class   **Part 3**

```
public static List<int> GetImageIDList()
{
    SqlConnection connection = null;
    try
    {
        connection = GetConnection();

        SqlCommand command = new SqlCommand();
        command.Connection = connection;
        command.CommandText =
            "SELECT ImageID FROM ProductImages " +
            "ORDER BY ImageID";

        connection.Open();
        SqlDataReader reader = command.ExecuteReader();

        List<int> imageIDList = new List<int>();
        while (reader.Read())
        {
            int imageID = (int)reader[0];
            imageIDList.Add(imageID);
        }
        reader.Close();

        return imageIDList;
    }
    catch (Exception e)
    {
        throw e;
    }
    finally
    {
        if (connection != null)
            connection.Close();
    }
}

public static SqlConnection GetConnection()
{
    SqlConnection connection = new SqlConnection();
    connection.ConnectionString =
        "Data Source=localhost\\SqlExpress;" +
        "Initial Catalog=Examples;Integrated Security=True";
    return connection;
}
    }
}
```

Figure 19-5   The ProductDB class for varbinary(max) storage (part 3 of 3)

How to use FILESTREAM storage

Now that you know how to use a varbinary(max) column to store binary data, you're ready to learn how to add FILESTREAM support to a varbinary(max) column. Although adding FILESTREAM support adds complexity to the database and to the applications that work with the binary data in the database, remember that this provides two benefits. First, it lets you store BLOBs that are larger than 2GB. Second, it improves performance, especially for BLOBs that are larger than 1MB.

How to enable FILESTREAM storage on the server

By default, FILESTREAM storage is disabled for the server. As a result, if you want to use FILESTREAM storage, you must enable it for the server as shown in figure 19-6. Here, I enabled all three levels of FILESTREAM access for the only instance of SQL Server that's running on my computer, which is named SQLEXPRESS.

If you want to allow a .NET application to work with the database, you need to allow at least the first two levels. In other words, you need to select the "Enable FILESTREAM for Transact-SQL access" check box, and you need to select the "Enable FILESTREAM for file I/O access" check box. For some applications, that's all you need to do. However, if you want to allow remote clients to access the FILESTREAM data, you'll also need to select the "Allow remote clients access to FILESTREAM data" check box.

After you set the server properties for enabling FILESTREAM storage, you have to set the filestream_access_level server configuration option before you can access FILESTREAM data. To do that, you execute the sp_configure stored procedure as shown in this figure. Here, the access level is set to 2 so FILESTREAM storage can be used from both Transact-SQL and Windows applications. Then, the RECONFIGURE statement applies the new setting to the server instance.

The FILESTREAM tab of the SQL Server Properties dialog box

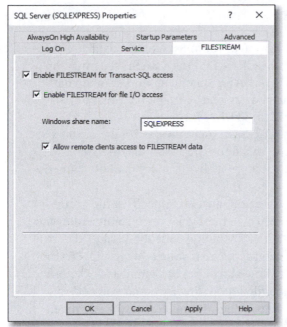

How to enable FILESTREAM storage

1. Start the SQL Server Configuration Manager tool, and select the SQL Server Services node to display the services that are available to your computer.
2. Right-click on the instance of SQL Server that you want to use and select the Properties command to display the Properties dialog box.
3. Select the FILESTREAM tab.
4. Select the "Enable FILESTREAM for Transact-SQL access" check box.
    -   If you want to read and write FILESTREAM data from Windows, select the "Enable FILESTREAM for file I/O access" check box and enter the name of the Windows share in the Windows Share Name box.
    -   If you want to allow remote clients to access the FILESTREAM data, select the "Allow remote clients access to FILESTREAM data" check box.
5. Select OK.
6. Execute these statements in the Management Studio:
    ```
    EXEC sp_configure filestream_access_level, 2;
    RECONFIGURE;
    ```
7. Use the Configuration Manager to stop and then restart the SQL Server service.
8. Close and reopen the Management Studio.

Description

-   By default, FILESTREAM storage is disabled for the server.

Figure 19-6   How to enable FILESTREAM storage on the server

How to create a database with FILESTREAM storage

Before you can use FILESTREAM storage, you must create a database that provides for it. To do that, you can use the CREATE DATABASE statement as shown in figure 19-7. This CREATE DATABASE statement works somewhat like the CREATE DATABASE statements described in chapter 11, but it also specifies a file group that provides for FILESTREAM storage.

To start, you specify a name for the database, and you specify the primary data file (an mdf file) for the database. In this figure, for example, the statement creates a database named MusicStore with a primary data file named MusicStore.mdf.

To provide for FILESTREAM storage, you must also specify a file group for the files that have FILESTREAM access. To do that, you type a comma after the closing parenthesis for the primary data file. Then, you code the FILEGROUP keyword, followed by a name for the file group. Next, you code the CONTAINS FILESTREAM DEFAULT keywords, followed by a set of parentheses. Within the parentheses, you code a name for the file group directory, and you code a path to the directory that will store the binary files. In this figure, for example, the binary files will be stored in the MusicStore_images directory.

If you prefer using the Management Studio to create a database as described in chapter 12, you can also use that tool to create a database that provides for FILESTREAM storage. In that case, you can use the New Database dialog box to add a FILESTREAM file group. Once you understand the code in this figure, you shouldn't have any trouble doing that.

How to create a database with FILESTREAM storage

```
CREATE DATABASE MusicStore
ON PRIMARY
(
    NAME = MusicStore,
    FILENAME = 'C:\Murach\SQL Server 2016\Databases\MusicStore.mdf'
),
FILEGROUP FileStreamImages CONTAINS FILESTREAM DEFAULT
(
    NAME = MusicStoreImages,
    FILENAME = 'C:\Murach\SQL Server 2016\Databases\MusicStore_images'
);
```

Description

- If you want to use the FILESTREAM feature, you must create a database that includes a file group that provides for FILESTREAM storage.

Figure 19-7   How to create a database with FILESTREAM storage

How to create a table with a FILESTREAM column

Once you've created a database that provides for FILESTREAM storage, you must create a table that provides for FILESTREAM storage as shown in figure 19-8. If you compare this table with the table shown in figure 19-2, you'll see that they're similar. However, the ProductImage column includes the FILESTREAM attribute that enables FILESTREAM storage for this column.

In addition, this table includes a column named RowID. This column stores a *globally unique identifier* (*GUID*), which is a value that's unique within the current database and other networked versions of the database around the globe. This column is required for FILESTREAM storage, and SQL Server uses it to locate the file that stores the data for the ProductImage column. Note that this column uses the uniqueidentifier data type and the ROWGUIDCOL property. In addition, this column uses the NEWID function to return a globally unique value for the column. As a result, if you don't specify a value for this column, the NEWID function will automatically return a value.

How to insert, update, and delete FILESTREAM data

Once you create a table that provides for FILESTREAM storage, you can use INSERT, UPDATE, and DELETE statements just as you would for other types of data. However, you may need to use the NEWID function to return a globally unique value for the GUID column. In this figure, for example, the three INSERT statements insert three rows into the ProductImages table. Here, the first statement doesn't specify a value for the GUID column. As a result, the table uses the NEWID function to generate this value. In contrast, the second and third statements use the NEWID function explicitly.

How to retrieve FILESTREAM data

To retrieve FILESTREAM data, you can use a SELECT statement just as you would for other types of data. In this figure, for example, the first SELECT statement selects all columns and rows from the ProductImages table. This shows the data that was inserted by the three INSERT statements. Here, the first two rows in the ProductImage column store a binary value of zero and the third row stores a longer binary value.

When you use FILESTREAM storage, you can use the PathName function to return the path to the binary file stream. Unlike most functions, this function is case sensitive. As a result, you must use the capitalization shown in the second SELECT statement. Here, the SELECT statement displays the ImageID value and the path to the binary file stream. In the next figure, you'll learn how to use this function in a .NET data access class to read and write binary data to the file stream that's returned by this method.

When you use an INSERT statement to insert a row that contains FILESTREAM data, it's important to insert a zero value instead of a NULL value to initialize the FILESTREAM column. Otherwise, the FilePath function

How to create a table with FILESTREAM storage

```
CREATE TABLE ProductImages
(
    ImageID int PRIMARY KEY IDENTITY,
    ProductID int NOT NULL,
    RowID uniqueidentifier ROWGUIDCOL NOT NULL UNIQUE DEFAULT NEWID(),
    ProductImage varbinary(max) FILESTREAM NOT NULL
);
```

Three INSERT statements that insert rows into the table

```
INSERT INTO ProductImages (ProductID, ProductImage)
VALUES (1, 0);

INSERT INTO ProductImages
VALUES (2, NEWID(), 0);

INSERT INTO ProductImages
VALUES (3, NEWID(), CAST('0123456789ABC' AS varbinary(max)));
```

A statement that displays the values in the table

```
SELECT * FROM ProductImages;
```

The result set

	ImageID	ProductID	RowID	ProductImage
1	1	1	404A4995-B1C9-400A-BD78-1572B4759105	0x00000000
2	2	2	648424AA-96C9-4D59-BAE6-AA5B37A451CC	0x00000000
3	3	3	BAF430F4-ED61-4020-8FFB-B652D0DB7509	0x303132333435363738393414243

A SELECT statement that displays the filepath

```
SELECT ImageID, ProductImage.PathName() AS FileStreamPath
FROM ProductImages;
```

The result set

	ImageID	FileStreamPath
1	1	\\RAY-PC\SQLEXPRESS\v02-A60EC2F8-2B24-11DF-9CC3-AF2E56D89593\MusicStore\dbo\ProductI...
2	2	\\RAY-PC\SQLEXPRESS\v02-A60EC2F8-2B24-11DF-9CC3-AF2E56D89593\MusicStore\dbo\ProductI...
3	3	\\RAY-PC\SQLEXPRESS\v02-A60EC2F8-2B24-11DF-9CC3-AF2E56D89593\MusicStore\dbo\ProductI...

Description

- To create a table that provides for FILESTREAM storage, you include a column definition that contains the FILESTREAM keyword. In addition, you create a column with a *globally unique identifier* (*GUID*) that's used to locate the file that stores the FILESTREAM data.

- A GUID is a value that's unique within the current database and other networked versions of the database around the globe. To define a column that contains a GUID, you specify the uniqueidentifier data type for the column, and you specify the ROWGUIDCOL property for the column.

- You can use the NEWID function to generate a globally unique value.

- You can use the PathName function to return the path to the binary file stream. This function is case sensitive, so you must use exact capitalization.

Figure 19-8 How to create a table and insert FILESTREAM data

won't return a path to the file stream, and the application won't be able to write data to the file stream.

A data access class
that uses FILESTREAM storage

Figure 19-9 shows a data access class named ProductDB that uses FILESTREAM storage. If you compare this class with the ProductDB class presented in figure 19-5, you'll see that it contains the same methods and performs the same tasks. As a result, you can use the ProductDB class shown in this figure with an application like the Product Image Manager application that was presented earlier in this chapter.

Within the ProductDB class, the code begins by defining a string for the directory for the images. Then, the GetConnection method returns a SqlConnection object. Since this works like the GetConnection method presented earlier in this chapter, you shouldn't have much trouble understanding how it works. However, the method shown in this figure uses the MusicStore database that was created by the SQL statement presented in figure 19-7.

The WriteImage method works much like the WriteImage method presented earlier in this chapter. However, since this method uses FILESTREAM storage, it's more complex. For instance, you must use the NewGuid method of the Guid class to return a globally unique identifier for the row. This has the same effect as using the NEWID function in SQL, but it allows you to use the globally unique identifier again later in this method.

The ProductDB class

Part 1

```
using System;
using System.Collections.Generic;
using System.Data.SqlClient;
using System.Data.SqlTypes;
using System.IO;

namespace MusicStoreImageManager
{
    class ProductDB
    {
        // define the directory for the images
        static string imagesPath = "C:/Murach/SQL Server 2016/Images/";

        public static SqlConnection GetConnection() {
            SqlConnection connection = new SqlConnection();
            connection.ConnectionString =
                "Data Source=localhost\\SqlExpress;" +
                "Initial Catalog=MusicStore;Integrated Security=True";
            return connection;
        }

        public static void WriteImage(int productID, string imageName) {
            SqlConnection connection = null;
            SqlTransaction transaction = null;
            try {
                // 1. Set up the input stream from the image file
                string filepath = imagesPath + imageName;
                if (File.Exists(filepath) == false)
                    throw new Exception("File Not Found: " + filepath);

                FileStream sourceStream = new FileStream(
                    filepath,
                    FileMode.Open,
                    FileAccess.Read);

                // 2. Initialize the row in the table
                connection = GetConnection();

                SqlCommand command = new SqlCommand();
                command.Connection = connection;
                command.CommandText =
                    "INSERT INTO ProductImages " +
                    "VALUES (@ProductID, " +
                    "        CAST(@RowID AS uniqueidentifier), 0)";

                Guid rowID = Guid.NewGuid();
                command.Parameters.AddWithValue("@ProductID", productID);
                command.Parameters.AddWithValue("@RowID", rowID);

                connection.Open();
                command.ExecuteNonQuery();
```

Figure 19-9   The ProductDB class for FILESTREAM storage (part 1 of 3)

After executing the query that inserts the row into the database, you must get a reference to the file stream for the BLOB. To do that, you begin by defining a SELECT statement that returns two columns. The first column uses the PathName function to return the path to the file stream. The second column uses the GET_FILESTREAM_TRANSACTION_CONTEXT function to get the context for the transaction. Note that the GUID value that was created earlier in this method is used in the WHERE clause of this SELECT statement to specify the row that was inserted by the INSERT statement earlier in the same method.

After the SELECT statement is defined, this code executes this statement. Then, it uses the reader object that's returned to check whether the result set contains data. If so, the first column is stored in a variable named path, and the second column is stored in a variable named context. Finally, this code closes the reader object.

At this point, the WriteImage method has all the data it needs to set up an output stream to the database. To do that, it creates a FileStream object with write access.

Now that the WriteImage method has an input stream and an output stream, it's ready to read data from the input stream (the image file) and write data to the output stream (the BLOB in the database). To do that, this code defines a block size of half a megabyte (524,288 bytes), a size that's usually efficient for working with streams. Then, this code defines a buffer variable that stores this array of bytes. Finally, it uses a loop to read from the input stream and write to the output stream.

Note that this allows this class to read half of a megabyte into memory at a time. For example, let's assume that you have an image file that's 4 megabytes. In that case, it would take eight trips through the loop to write the file to the database. On the other hand, the WriteImage method presented earlier in this chapter reads the entire file into memory before it begins to write the file. As a result, it can use a lot of memory if you use it with images that are larger than 1 megabyte.

Note also that this method uses a transaction. If the method completes successfully, the last statement in the try block commits the transaction, and the image is written to the database. However, if the method encounters an error, the catch block rolls back the transaction, and the image is not written to the database.

The ProductDB class   **Part 2**

```
            // 3. Get a reference to the BLOB
            transaction = connection.BeginTransaction();
            command.Transaction = transaction;
            command.CommandText =
                "SELECT ProductImage.PathName(), " +
                "       GET_FILESTREAM_TRANSACTION_CONTEXT() " +
                "FROM ProductImages " +
                "WHERE RowID = CAST(@RowID AS uniqueidentifier)";
            command.Parameters.Clear();
            command.Parameters.AddWithValue("@RowID", rowID);

            SqlDataReader reader = command.ExecuteReader();
            if (reader.Read() == false)
                throw new Exception(
                    "Unable to get path and context for BLOB.");
            string path = (string)reader[0];
            byte[] context = (byte[])reader[1];
            reader.Close();

            // 4. Set up the output stream to the database
            SqlFileStream targetStream =
                new SqlFileStream(path, context, FileAccess.Write);

            // 5. Read from file and write to database
            int blockSize = 1024 * 512;
            byte[] buffer = new byte[blockSize];
            int bytesRead = sourceStream.Read(buffer, 0, buffer.Length);
            while (bytesRead > 0) {
                targetStream.Write(buffer, 0, bytesRead);
                bytesRead = sourceStream.Read(buffer, 0, buffer.Length);
            }

            targetStream.Close();
            sourceStream.Close();
            transaction.Commit();
        }
        catch (Exception e) {
            if (transaction != null)
                transaction.Rollback();
            throw e;
        }
        finally {
            if (connection != null)
                connection.Close();
        }
    }
```

Figure 19-9   The ProductDB class for FILESTREAM storage (part 2 of 3)

The ReadImage method works much like the ReadImage method presented earlier in this chapter. However, since this method uses FILESTREAM storage, it's more complex. To start, this method executes a SELECT statement to get a path to the file stream and the transaction context. Then, it sets up a file stream for the BLOB by creating a FileStream object with read access. Since this works much like the SELECT statement of the WriteImage method that's presented in part 2 of this figure, you shouldn't have much trouble understanding how it works.

After setting up the input file stream, this code uses a loop to read the binary data from the database and stores this data in a List<byte> object named imageBytes. Then, it converts the List<byte> object to an array of byte values and returns it.

This loop works similarly to the loop in the WriteImage method that reads from one stream and writes to another. However, instead of writing to a stream, this code stores the entire stream in the List<byte> object. The advantage to this approach is that it allows you to separate the data access layer (the ProductDB class) from the presentation layer (the form). The disadvantage of this approach is that the entire image is stored in memory. If this isn't satisfactory for your application, you can add a PictureBox control as a second argument of the ReadImage method. Then, this method can stream the data from the BLOB in the database to the PictureBox control that displays the image.

For this ProductDB class to work with the Product Image Manager application presented earlier in this chapter, it must include a GetImageIDList method. However, the code for this method is the same as the code presented in part 3 of figure 19-5. To save space, it isn't presented here.

The ProductDB class

Part 3

```csharp
public static Byte[] ReadImage(int imageID) {
    SqlConnection connection = null;
    SqlTransaction transaction = null;
    try {
        connection = GetConnection();
        connection.Open();
        transaction = connection.BeginTransaction();

        SqlCommand command = new SqlCommand();
        command.Connection = connection;
        command.Transaction = transaction;
        command.CommandText =
            "SELECT ProductImage.PathName(), " +
            "       GET_FILESTREAM_TRANSACTION_CONTEXT() " +
            "FROM ProductImages " +
            "WHERE ImageID = @ImageID";
        command.Parameters.AddWithValue("@ImageID", imageID);

        SqlDataReader reader = command.ExecuteReader();
        if (reader.Read() == false)
            throw new Exception(
                "Unable to get path and context for BLOB.");
        string path = (string)reader[0];
        byte[] context = (byte[])reader[1];
        reader.Close();

        SqlFileStream sourceStream =
            new SqlFileStream(path, context, FileAccess.Read);

        int blockSize = 1024 * 512;
        byte[] buffer = new byte[blockSize];
        List<byte> imageBytes = new List<byte>();
        int bytesRead = sourceStream.Read(buffer, 0, buffer.Length);
        while (bytesRead > 0) {
            bytesRead = sourceStream.Read(buffer, 0, buffer.Length);
            foreach(byte b in buffer)
                imageBytes.Add(b);
        }
        sourceStream.Close();
        return imageBytes.ToArray();
    }
    catch (Exception e) {
        throw e;
    }
    finally {
        if (connection != null)
            connection.Close();
    }
}
public static List<int> GetImageIDList() {
    // same as part 3 of figure 19-5
}
}
```

Figure 19-9   The ProductDB class for FILESTREAM storage (part 3 of 3)

Perspective

In this chapter, you learned how to write BLOBs to a database table and to read BLOBs from a database table. In addition, you learned how to use the FILESTREAM storage feature that was introduced with SQL Server 2008. At this point, you have the core concepts and skills for working with BLOBs.

Now, if you want to develop a more sophisticated application for working with BLOBs, you should be able to do that. For example, you may want to enhance the application presented in this chapter so it can be used to update or delete an existing image. Or, you may want to enhance this application so it works more efficiently.

Terms

binary large object (BLOB)
FILESTREAM storage
globally unique identifier (GUID)

Exercises

1. Modify the first ProductDB class presented in this chapter so the ReadImage method accepts a PictureBox control as a second argument like this:

   ```
   public static void ReadImage(int imageID, PictureBox pictureBox)
   ```

   Then, modify the ReadImage method so it streams data from the database to the PictureBox control, and modify the code for the form so it works with this new method. To do this, you can begin by copying code from the form into the ProductDB class.

2. Modify the second ProductDB class so it works as described in exercise 1.

20

An introduction to CLR integration

SQL Server 2005 introduced the ability to host the .NET Framework's Common Language Runtime (CLR). This allows .NET developers to use C# or Visual Basic to create database objects such as stored procedures, functions, and triggers. In addition, it allows developers to create new types of database objects that aren't available from T-SQL such as aggregate functions and user-defined data types that have properties and methods.

This chapter shows how CLR integration works, when you might want to use it, and how to enable it. Then, it shows how to work with the SQL DDL statements that you can use to deploy a CLR object.

However, this chapter doesn't show how to use the Visual Studio IDE to code, compile, deploy, and debug a CLR object. That's because this type of work is typically done by a .NET developer who has experience using the Visual Studio IDE with C# or Visual Basic to work with ADO.NET. In addition, it requires a non-Express version of Visual Studio that's not available for free. To learn how to develop CLR objects, you can refer to a previous edition of this book such as *Murach's SQL Server 2012*.

An introduction to CLR integration

This topic introduces you to some of the concepts that you should be aware of before you enable CLR objects on a database server. Then, it shows how to enable CLR integration for a database server. This is necessary to be able to deploy any CLR objects to a database running on that server.

How CLR integration works

If you have used a .NET programming language such as C# or Visual Basic to develop applications, you are probably already familiar with some of the concepts presented in figure 20-1. In particular, you should already know that the *Common Language Runtime* (*CLR*) for the .NET Framework executes compiled code that's written in any .NET language. In addition, you should already know that compiled .NET code is stored in files known as *assemblies*. Since the CLR automatically manages the memory usage and security operations for the code that it runs, compiled .NET code is known as *managed code*.

What you may not know is that SQL Server 2005 and later can be configured to host the CLR. This is known as *CLR integration*, and it allows you to run .NET assemblies within a SQL Server instance.

When you use CLR integration, you can use C# or Visual Basic to create database objects such as the stored procedures, functions, and triggers you learned about in chapter 15. You can also create aggregate functions and user-defined types, which can't be done using SQL. Then, you can store these objects within the database. This means that these objects are stored in a secure and central location where they can be reused by other developers.

How SQL Server hosts the .NET CLR

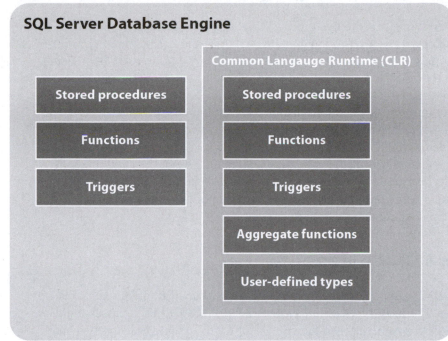

SQL Server Database Engine

Description

- The *Common Language Runtime* (*CLR*) for the .NET Framework executes compiled code that's written in the C#.NET or Visual Basic.NET programming language.

- Compiled .NET code is stored in files known as *assemblies*. Since the CLR automatically manages the memory usage and security for the code that it runs, compiled .NET code is known as *managed code*.

- SQL Server 2005 and later can be configured to host the CLR. This is known as *CLR integration*, and it lets you run .NET assemblies within a SQL Server instance.

- CLR integration lets you use C# or Visual Basic to create database objects such as stored procedures, functions, triggers, aggregate functions, and user-defined types.

Figure 20-1   How CLR integration works

The five types of CLR objects

Figure 20-2 presents the five types of CLR objects: stored procedures, functions, triggers, user-defined aggregates (UDAs), and user-defined types (UDTs). Of these five CLR objects, the first three allow you to use C# or Visual Basic instead of T-SQL to code stored procedures, functions, and triggers.

However, the last two CLR objects listed in this figure provide for functionality that isn't available from T-SQL. To start, a *user-defined aggregate* (*UDA*) is an aggregate function that works similarly to the built-in aggregate functions such as the SUM function. In addition, a *user-defined type* (*UDT*) is a data type that can perform data validation and include properties and methods. For example, you could use a UDT to define a data type for a phone number. Then, this data type could include a property or method that returns the area code for the phone number.

When to use CLR objects

Figure 20-2 also presents some guidelines for when you might want to use CLR objects. For most types of database objects, using T-SQL yields code that's shorter and performs better than the equivalent C# or Visual Basic code, which has more overhead than T-SQL. This is particularly true if the C# or Visual Basic code uses ADO.NET to retrieve or modify data in the database. As a result, whenever possible, you should avoid using CLR objects. So in what situations does it make sense to use a CLR object?

First, it makes sense to use a CLR object if you need to use elements of the .NET Framework to perform tasks that aren't available from T-SQL. For example, the .NET Framework provides for certain types of encryption and compression that aren't provided by T-SQL.

It also makes sense to use a CLR object if you need to perform complex procedural tasks that would be difficult to implement with T-SQL. That's because C# and Visual Basic are designed to use conditional statements and loops to perform procedural processing, while T-SQL's strength lies in its ability to process result sets.

If you need to create user-defined aggregates (UDAs) or user-defined types (UDTs), you have to use CLR objects since these types of objects aren't available from T-SQL.

And finally, if you are an experienced .NET developer, you may know how to solve a problem using C# or Visual Basic, but you can't figure out how to do it using T-SQL. In that case, it may make sense to use a CLR object just to get the job done, even though a T-SQL solution might perform better.

The five types of CLR objects

CLR object	SQL equivalent?
Stored procedures	Yes
Functions	Yes
Triggers	Yes
Aggregate functions	No
User-defined types	No

Description

- CLR integration lets you use C# or Visual Basic to create stored procedures, functions, and triggers instead of using T-SQL to create these database objects as described in chapter 15.

- A *user-defined aggregate* (*UDA*) is an aggregate function that works similarly to built-in aggregate functions such as the SUM function described in chapter 5.

- A *user-defined type* (*UDT*) is a data type that can include data validation, properties, and methods.

- If necessary, CLR objects can use the ADO.NET class libraries to retrieve and modify the data that's in the database.

- Most database objects will perform better when they are written in T-SQL instead of C# or Visual Basic.

When to use CLR objects

- When you need to use elements of the .NET Framework to perform tasks that aren't available from T-SQL.

- When you need to perform complex procedural tasks that would be difficult to implement with T-SQL.

- To create user-defined aggregates (UDAs) or user-defined types (UDTs), which aren't available from T-SQL.

- To solve a problem that you don't know how to solve using T-SQL.

Figure 20-2   The five types of CLR objects and when to use them

How to enable CLR integration

For security and performance reasons, CLR integration is disabled by default for newly installed instances of SQL Server. As a result, before anyone can use CLR integration on the server, you must enable it as shown in figure 20-3. To start, in the Management Studio's Object Explorer, you can right-click on the server node. Then, you can select the Facets command from the resulting menu. This displays the View Facets dialog box shown in this figure. From this dialog box, you can select the Surface Area Configuration option from the Facet combo box and set the ClrIntegrationEnabled property to True.

If it turns out that you don't need to use CLR integration, it's generally considered a best practice to disable CLR integration. This should improve performance and security.

The View Facets dialog box for the database server

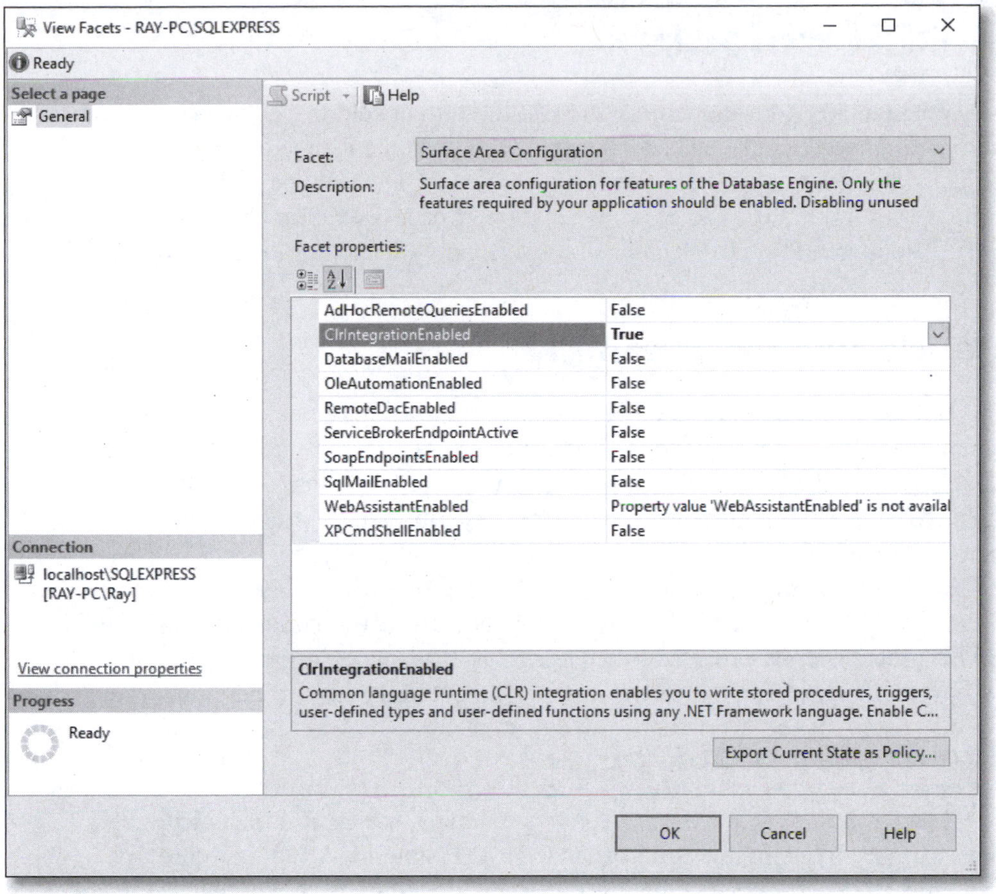

Description

- To enable CLR integration, start the Management Studio, right-click on the server node, and select the Facets command to display the View Facets dialog box. Then, select the Surface Area Configuration option from the Facet drop-down list, and set the ClrIntegrationEnabled property to True.

Figure 20-3   How to enable CLR integration

How to use SQL to work with CLR objects

When a .NET developer uses Visual Studio to develop CLR objects, it automatically generates and executes the DDL statements needed to deploy CLR objects. However, if you ever need to write these DDL statements yourself, you can refer to figure 20-11 to get started. Then, if necessary, you can consult SQL Server documentation for details about working with each of the types of CLR objects.

How to deploy an assembly

Before you can deploy a CLR object, you must deploy the assembly that contains the compiled code for the object to the database. To do that, you use the CREATE ASSEMBLY statement. In this figure, for example, the CREATE ASSEMBLY statement shown deploys the assembly that's stored in the dll file named ApClrObjects.dll.

Note that when you deploy an assembly, the PERMISSION_SET property is set to SAFE by default, which is what Microsoft recommends in most cases. SAFE prevents code executed by an assembly from accessing external system resources such as files, the network, environment variables, or the registry.

How to deploy a CLR object

After you deploy an assembly, you can deploy any CLR objects within the assembly by using the appropriate CREATE statement. In this figure, for example, the CREATE statement for a stored procedure is shown. All of the code up to the AS keyword works as described in chapter 15. Here, you must make sure that the data types for the parameters match the data types specified by the CLR object. Then, after the AS keyword, you must use the EXTERNAL NAME clause to specify the assembly, class, and method name for the procedure.

How to drop an assembly

If you want to drop an assembly from a database, you must first drop all CLR objects within the assembly that have been deployed. To do that, you can use DROP statements like the ones presented in chapter 15. For example, you can use the DROP PROC statement to drop any stored procedures that have been deployed. Then, you can use the DROP ASSEMBLY statement shown in this figure to drop the assembly. This deletes the dll file for the assembly from the database.

But first, you might want to check if the assembly exists in the database. To do that, you can use the ASSEMBLYPROPERTY function to return the SimpleName property of the specified assembly. If this property returns a value, the assembly exists and will be dropped. Otherwise, the DROP ASSEMBLY statement won't be executed.

How to deploy an assembly

The syntax of the CREATE ASSEMBLY statement

```
CREATE ASSEMBLY assembly_name
    [AUTHORIZATION owner_name]
     FROM client_assembly_specifier
    [WITH PERMISSION_SET = {SAFE|EXTERNAL_ACCESS|UNSAFE}]
```

Code that deploys an assembly

```
CREATE ASSEMBLY ApClrObjects
FROM 'C:\Murach\SQL Server 2016\Scripts\Chapter 20\ApClrObjects.dll';
```

How to create a CLR stored procedure

The syntax of the CREATE PROCEDURE statement

```
CREATE {PROC|PROCEDURE} procedure_name
    [parameter_declarations]
    [WITH [RECOMPILE] [, ENCRYPTION] [, EXECUTE_AS_clause]]
AS
    EXTERNAL NAME AssemblyName.ClassName.MethodName
```

Code that creates a CLR stored procedure

```
CREATE PROC GetInvoiceReport
AS
EXTERNAL NAME ApClrObjects.StoredProcedures.GetInvoiceReport;
```

Code that creates a CLR stored procedure that has parameters

```
CREATE PROC GetInvoiceTotalSum
    @InvoiceTotalSum money OUTPUT,
    @StartDate smalldatetime = NULL,
    @VendorName nvarchar(40) = '%'
AS
EXTERNAL NAME ApClrObjects.StoredProcedures.GetInvoiceTotalSum;
```

How to drop an assembly

The syntax of the DROP ASSEMBLY statement

```
DROP ASSEMBLY assembly_name
```

The syntax of the ASSEMBLYPROPERTY function

```
ASSEMBLYPROPERTY('AssemblyName', 'PropertyName')
```

Code that drops an assembly

```
IF ASSEMBLYPROPERTY('ApClrObjects', 'SimpleName') IS NOT NULL
    DROP ASSEMBLY ApClrObjects;
```

Description

- To deploy a CLR object, you start by deploying the assembly that contains the compiled code for the object using the CREATE ASSEMBLY statement.

- After you deploy the assembly, you can create the object in the database. To create a stored procedure, for example, you use the CREATE PROCEDURE statement.

- You can use the DROP ASSEMBLY statement to drop an assembly from the database. But first, you must drop all the CLR objects it contains. You can also use the ASSEMBLYPROPERTY function to check that an assembly exists before you drop it.

Figure 20-4   How to use SQL to deploy and drop CLR objects

Perspective

This chapter introduces CLR objects. In addition, this chapter shows how to enable CLR integration on a database server and how to use SQL DDL to deploy CLR objects. However, since CLR objects are typically developed by .NET developers, this chapter doesn't present the details that you need to be able to develop these types of objects. If you want to learn how to do that, we recommend using a previous edition of this book, such as *Murach's SQL Server 2012*.

Terms

Common Language Runtime (CLR)
assembly
managed code
CLR integration
user-defined aggregate (UDA)
user-defined type (UDT)

Exercises

1. Use the Management Studio to enable CLR integration for your instance of SQL Server.

2. Write a script that deploys the ApExClrObjects assembly to the AP database. You can find the dll file for this assembly in this directory:

   `C:\Murach\SQL Server 2016\Exercises\Chapter 20`

3. Write a script that deploys the GetTop10Vendors stored procedure in the ApExClrObjects assembly.

4. Write a script that calls the GetTop10Vendors stored procedure. This should return the top 10 vendors in the AP database. Note: This stored procedure doesn't require any parameters.

5. Write a script that deletes the GetTop10Vendors procedure and the ApExClrObjects assembly. This script should check that the procedure and assembly exist before deleting them.

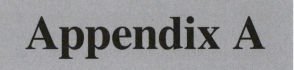

Appendix A

How to set up your computer for this book

To run the SQL statements described in chapters 1 through 18 of this book, you only need to have two software products installed: the SQL Server 2016 database engine and the SQL Server Management Studio (SSMS). Both of these products are available from Microsoft's website for free, and you can download and install them both on your computer as described in this appendix.

Once you install these software products, you can install the files for this book. To do that, you can download these files from www.murach.com. Then, you can use the Management Studio to create the databases for this book. After that, you can start experimenting with the SQL scripts for this book.

To use a .NET language such as C# or VB to work with BLOBs as described in chapter 19, you can use Visual Studio. If you don't already have Visual Studio installed on your system, you can install Visual Studio Express as described in this appendix. This product is also available from Microsoft's website for free.

Three editions of SQL Server 2016 Express

Figure A-1 describes three editions of SQL Server 2016 Express. Of the three editions listed in this figure, we recommend that you install SQL Server 2016 Express. This edition includes the database engine that provides for all of the features covered in this book.

The Express with Advanced Services edition includes all of the features of the Express edition, plus two additional features that aren't covered in this book. If you eventually want to learn about these features, you can install this edition and use it with this book. However, it requires more system resources than the Express edition.

The LocalDB edition also has the same features as the Express edition, but it's designed to be embedded within an application. As a result, you should be aware of this edition in case you ever need to embed a database into an application. It has the same features as the Express edition, but it doesn't accept remote connections and can't be administered remotely.

The tool for working with all editions of SQL Server

This figure also describes a tool named SQL Server Management Studio (SSMS). You can use this tool to work with any edition of SQL Server, including non-Express editions of SQL Server such as the Enterprise edition.

Three editions of SQL Server 2016 Express

Edition	Description
LocalDB	A lightweight version of Express that can be embedded into an application. Doesn't accept remote connections and can't be administered remotely.
Express	The core Express database server. Contains only the database engine. Accepts remote connections and can be administered remotely.
Express with Advanced Services	Contains the Full Text Search and Reporting Services features in addition to the database engine. These features aren't covered in this book.

The tool for working with all editions of SQL Server

Tool	Description
SQL Server Management Studio (SSMS)	You can use the Management Studio to connect to SQL Server and work with its databases.

Description

- For this book, we recommend that you install the Express edition of SQL Server 2016, but you can install the Express with Advanced Services edition if you want to install the advanced features and don't mind a larger download and install.

Figure A-1   Three editions of SQL Server 2016 Express

How to install SQL Server 2016 Express

Figure A-2 shows how to install SQL Server 2016 Express. Before you get started, you should know that SQL Server 2016 only runs on Windows 8 and later. As a result, if you're still using an older version of Windows, such as Windows 7, you need to upgrade to a later version of Windows, such as Windows 10.

If you don't already have SQL Server Express installed on your system, the procedure in this figure installs SQL Server 2016 Express with an instance name of SQLEXPRESS, which is what you want for this book. However, it's possible that you may have an older instance of SQL Server Express, such as SQL Server 2012 Express, on your computer. If you do, the older instance of SQL Server is probably named SQLEXPRESS. As a result, the 2016 instance can't use this name.

In that case, the procedure in this figure leaves the old instance of SQL Server on your computer and installs the 2016 instance of the database engine with a new name such as SQLEXPRESS01. That's what the Basic installation does automatically. However, the examples in this book assume that SQL Server 2016 Express has an instance name of SQLEXPRESS. As a result, if you choose this approach, you may have to modify some of the examples in this book to get them to run successfully on your computer.

If an older instance of SQL Server is installed on your computer, you also have two other options. First, you may be able to upgrade the database server by selecting the Custom installation in step 4, instead of selecting the Basic installation. Then, you can select the "Upgrade" option. This will upgrade the old instance to 2016, but it will run the existing databases as if they are running on the earlier version. In that case, if you want to update a database so it can use the features of SQL Server 2016, you can change its compatibility level. For information on how to do that, see chapter 2.

Second, if you can't upgrade the old instance of SQL Server Express, you can uninstall it. Then, you can install a 2016 instance. That way, you can use the default name of SQLEXPRESS for the 2016 instance. To do that, you should start by backing up any databases that are running on the older SQL Server instance. One way to do that is to detach them from the server and copy the data (mdf) and log (ldf) files for the databases to a safe location. Then, you can uninstall all components of SQL Server Express, including the Management Studio components. Next, you can install SQL Server 2016 Express as described in this figure. Finally, you can attach the databases that you backed up to this server. For more information about detaching and attaching databases, see chapter 2.

How to install SQL Server Management Studio

This figure also shows how to install SQL Server Management Studio (SSMS), the main tool for working with databases. If you already have SQL Server 2016 Express installed on your computer, you only need to install Management Studio. To do that, you can skip the steps for installing SQL Server and just follow the steps for installing the Management Studio.

Chapter 2 presents the basic techniques for using the Management Studio. You can use it to develop and run all of the SQL statements in this book.

How to install SQL Server 2016 Express

1. Search the Internet for "SQL Server 2016 Express download".

2. Follow the links to the official download page for SQL Server 2016 Express at Microsoft's website (www.microsoft.com).

3. Download the setup program for SQL Server 2016 Express. This program should be stored in a file named SQLServer2016-SSEI-Expr.exe.

4. Start the setup program and select the Basic installation. Then, respond to the resulting prompts and dialogs.

5. At the last dialog (the "Installation has completed successfully" dialog), make a note of the instance name for the server.

    -   If SQL Server Express wasn't already installed on your computer, the instance name should be SQLEXPRESS.

    -   If SQL Server Express was already installed on your computer, the instance name might be slightly different such as SQLEXPRESS01.

6. At the last dialog, click the Install Tools button to go to the web page for downloading SQL Server Management Studio (SSMS).

How to install the Management Studio

7. At the web page for downloading the Management Studio, follow the links to download the setup program. This program should be stored in a file named SSMS-Setup-ENU.exe.

8. Start the setup program and respond to the resulting prompts and dialogs.

Notes

-   This book assumes that an instance of SQL Server 2016 Express is installed with a name of SQLEXPRESS. If it's installed on your system with a different name, you may have to modify some of the examples to get them to run successfully on your computer.

-   SQL Server 2016 supports Windows 8 and later. Support for Windows 7 has been dropped.

Figure A-2   How to install SQL Server 2016 Express

How to install the files for this book

Figure A-3 begins by describing the files for this book that are contained in the self-extracting zip file (an exe file) that you can download from www.murach.com. When you download and execute this zip file, it will unzip the five directories described in this figure into this directory:

```
C:\Murach\SQL Server 2016
```

The Databases directory contains the SQL scripts used to create the three databases that are used throughout the book. To do that, you can use the Management Studio to open and execute these scripts as described in the next figure.

The Scripts directory contains the SQL code that's described throughout this book. You can use the Management Studio to open these scripts. Then, you can run them to view the results. Or, you can experiment with these scripts by modifying them before you run them.

The Exercises directory contains the solutions to the exercises that are presented at the end of each chapter. You can use these solutions to check that the solutions you develop are correct. You can also use these solutions to find out how to solve an exercise if you're unable to do it on your own. Keep in mind, though, that you'll get more out of the exercises if you try to solve them on your own first.

The Projects directory contains two subdirectories that contain the Visual Studio projects for chapters 1 and 19. These projects are available in two versions: a C# version and a Visual Basic version. You can use the Windows Desktop edition of Visual Studio Express to open these projects.

The files for this book

Directory	Description
Databases	The SQL scripts that create the databases for this book.
Scripts	The SQL scripts for the examples shown throughout this book.
Exercises	The solutions to the exercises at the end of each chapter.
Projects	The Visual Studio projects for chapters 1 and 19. These projects use C# and Visual Basic code to work with SQL Server.
Images	The image files that are used by the application presented in chapter 19.

The databases for this book

Database	Description
AP	The Accounts Payable (AP) database that's used in the examples throughout this book. This database only includes tables so you can add other objects such as views and stored procedures yourself.
ProductOrders	The Product Orders database that's used in some of the examples in this book.
Examples	A database that contains several small tables that are used in some of the examples for which the AP database couldn't be used.

How to install the files for this book

1. Go to www.murach.com.
2. Find the page for *Murach's SQL Server 2016 for Developers*.
3. If necessary, scroll down. Then, click the "FREE Downloads" tab.
4. Click the link to download the exe file for the book examples and exercises. Then, respond to the resulting pages and dialog boxes. This should download an installer file named sq16_allfiles.exe.
5. Double-click this file and respond to the dialog boxes that follow. If you accept the defaults, this installs the files into the directory shown below.

The default installation directory

```
C:\Murach\SQL Server 2016
```

Description

- All of the files for the databases and code described in this book are contained in a self-extracting zip file (an exe file) that can be downloaded from www.murach.com.

Figure A-3   How to install the files for this book

How to create the databases for this book

Before you can run the SQL statements presented in this book, you need to create the three databases described in the previous figure. The easiest way to do that is to use the SQL Server Management Studio to run the SQL scripts that create the databases. For example, the create_ap.sql script creates the AP database. The procedure for running these scripts is described in figure A-4.

To determine if a script ran successfully, you can review the results in the Messages tab. In this figure, for example, the Messages tab shows a series of statements that have executed successfully. In addition, the Object Explorer window shows the three databases.

If the script encounters problems, the SQL Server Management Studio displays one or more errors in the Messages tab. Then, you can read these errors to figure out why the script didn't execute correctly.

Before you can run the SQL scripts that create the databases, the database server must be running. By default, the database server is automatically started when you start your computer, so this usually isn't a problem. However, if it isn't running on your system, you can start it as described in chapter 2.

How to restore the databases for this book

As you work with the examples in this book, you may make changes to the databases or tables that you don't intend to make. In that case, you may want to restore a database to its original state. To do that, you can run the script that creates the database again. This will drop the database and recreate it.

The directory that contains the scripts for creating the databases

`C:\Murach\SQL Server 2016\Databases`

The Management Studio after executing the three database scripts

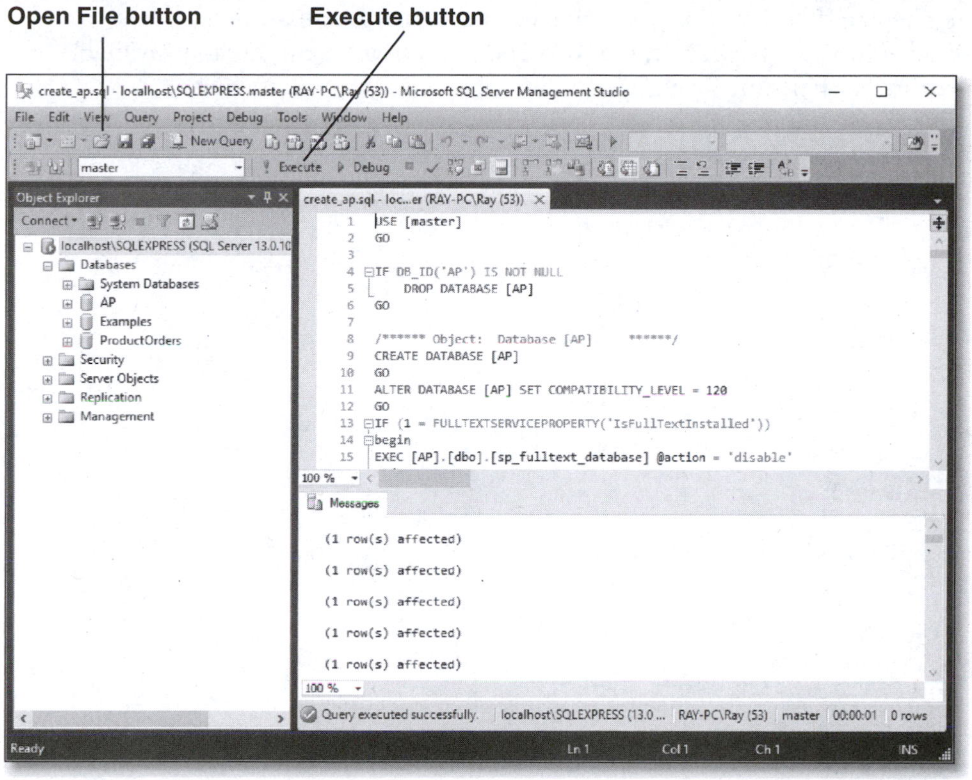

Open File button   **Execute button**

How to create the databases

1. Start the SQL Server Management Studio.

2. Connect to the database server as shown in chapter 2.

3. Open a script file by clicking the Open File button and then using the resulting dialog box to locate the script that creates the database. To create the AP database, for example, open the create_ap.sql file. When you do, the Management Studio displays this script in a Query window.

4. Execute the script by clicking the Execute button. When you do, the Messages tab indicates whether the script executed successfully.

5. Repeat steps 3 and 4 until you have created all three databases.

How to restore a database

• Run the create database script again to drop the database and recreate it.

Description

• For these scripts to work, the database server must be running. By default, the database server is automatically started when you start your system. If it isn't running on your system, you can start it as described in chapter 2.

Figure A-4   How to create and restore the databases for this book

How to install Visual Studio Express

You only need Visual Studio for chapter 19 of this book. As a result, if Visual Studio isn't already installed on your computer, you can wait until you get to chapter 19 to install it. Then, you can install the Express for Windows Desktop edition as shown in figure A-5. This edition of Visual Studio is available for free from Microsoft's website.

How to install Visual Studio Express

1. Search the Internet for "Visual Studio Express".

2. Follow the links to the download page for Express for Windows Desktop.

3. Follow the directions to download the setup program for the Express for Windows Desktop edition.

4. Run the setup program and respond to its dialogs.

Description

*   You only need to install Visual Studio for chapter 19 of this book. If you don't already have Visual Studio installed on your system, you can install Visual Studio Express for Windows Desktop, which is available for free from Microsoft.

Figure A-5   How to install Visual Studio Express

Index

U

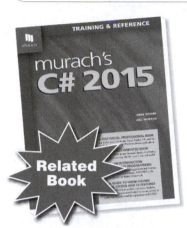

Related Book

Books for .NET developers

Murach's C# 2015	$57.50
Murach's ASP.NET 4.6 Web Programming with C# 2015	59.50
Murach's Visual Basic 2015	57.50

Books for database developers

Murach's SQL Server 2016 for Developers	$57.50
Murach's MySQL (2nd Ed.)	54.50
Murach's Oracle SQL and PL/SQL for Developers (2nd Ed.)	54.50

Books for developers

Murach's Python Programming	$57.50
Murach's Beginning Java with NetBeans	57.50
Murach's Beginning Java with Eclipse	57.50
Murach's Java Programming (5th Ed.)	59.50

Books for web developers

Murach's HTML5 and CSS3 (3rd Ed.)	$54.50
Murach's JavaScript and jQuery (3rd Ed.)	57.50
Murach's Java Servlets and JSP (3rd Ed.)	57.50
Murach's PHP and MySQL (2nd Ed.)	54.50

Prices and availability are subject to change. Please visit our website or call for current information.

Become a .NET programmer

This book gives you the core language, .NET, and Visual Studio skills you need to create any C# application. You'll soon see how knowing SQL lets you code database applications more easily.

We want to hear from you

Do you have any comments, questions, or compliments to pass on to us? It would be great to hear from you! Please share your feedback in whatever way works best.

 www.murach.com

 1-800-221-5528
(Weekdays, 8 am to 4 pm Pacific Time)

 murachbooks@murach.com

 twitter.com/MurachBooks

facebook.com/murachbooks

linkedin.com/company/
mike-murach-&-associates

The software for this book

- SQL Server 2016 Express (a free download)
- SQL Server Management Studio (a free download)
- Visual Studio Express (a free download)

  SQL Server 2016 only runs on Windows 8 and later. As a result, if you're using Windows 7 or earlier, you'll need to upgrade your operating system before you can install SQL Server 2016 Express.

  For information about downloading and installing these products, please see appendix A.

The source code for this book

- Scripts that create the databases for this book
- Scripts for the SQL statements presented throughout this book
- Solutions to the exercises that are at the end of each chapter
- C# and Visual Basic projects for the application presented in chapter 19

How to download and install the source code

1. Go to www.murach.com.
2. Navigate to the page for *Murach's SQL Server 2016 for Developers*.
3. Follow the instructions to download the exe file.
4. Double-click on the exe file to run it.

   For details, please see appendix A.

How to create the databases

1. Start the SQL Server Management Studio and connect to the database server.
2. Use the Management Studio to run the three scripts in this directory:

   `C:\Murach\SQL Server 2016\Databases`

   For details, please see appendix A.

www.murach.com